ATLAS
OF THE
WORLD

Published in 2003 by Borders Press in
association with HarperCollins

Borders Press is a division of Borders Group, Inc.
100 Phoenix Drive, Ann Arbor, Michigan, 48108.
All rights reserved.

Borders Press is a trademark of Borders Properties, Inc.

First published 1996
Reprinted with revisions 1997, reprinted 1998, 1999, 2000, 2003

© HarperCollins*Publishers* Ltd 1998
Maps © Bartholomew Ltd 1997

Collins ® is a registered trademark of
HarperCollins*Publishers* Ltd

The contents of this edition of the Collins Atlas of the World
are believed correct at the time of printing. Nevertheless
the publisher can accept no responsibility for errors or
omissions, changes in the detail given or for any expense
or loss thereby caused.

Printed and bound in Slovenia

ISBN 0-681-50289-4

Globe images: data ©1995 The Living Earth, Inc.
Cover photograph: Zefa Pictures

www.fireandwater.com
Visit the book lover's website

ATLAS
OF THE WORLD

CONTENTS

THE WORLD
MAPS 6–24

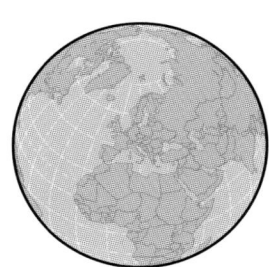

EUROPE
MAPS 2–29

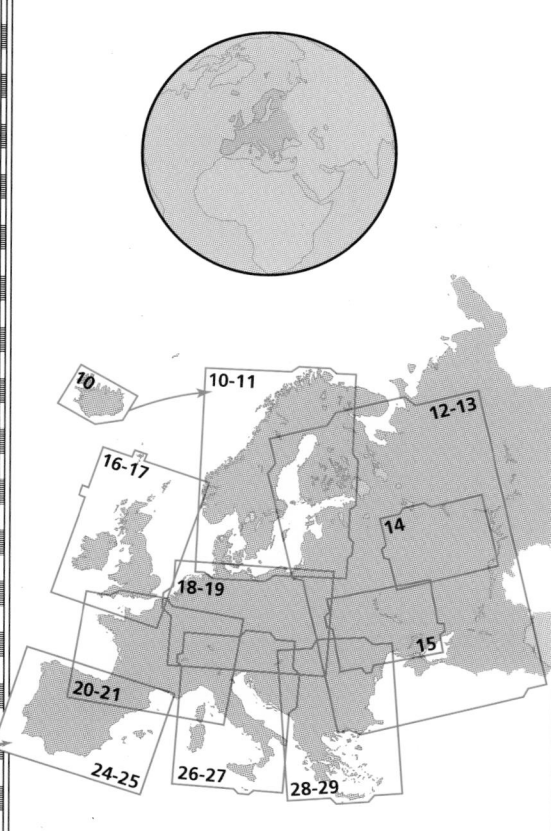

ASIA
MAPS 30–65

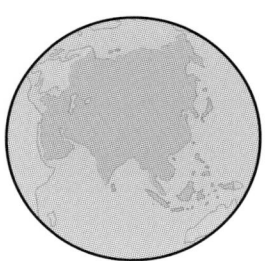

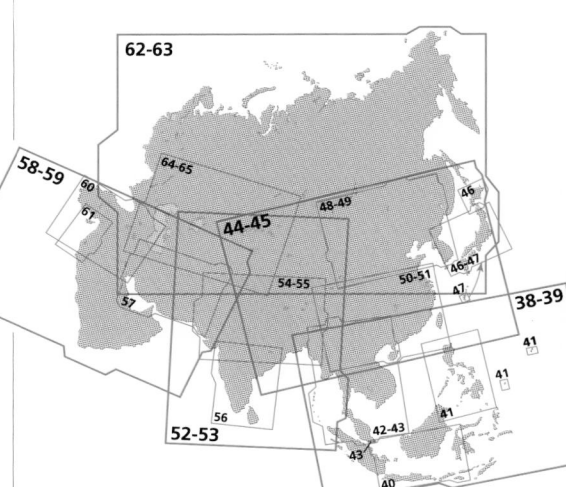

AFRICA
MAPS 66–83

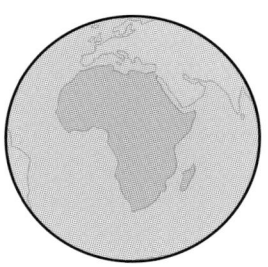

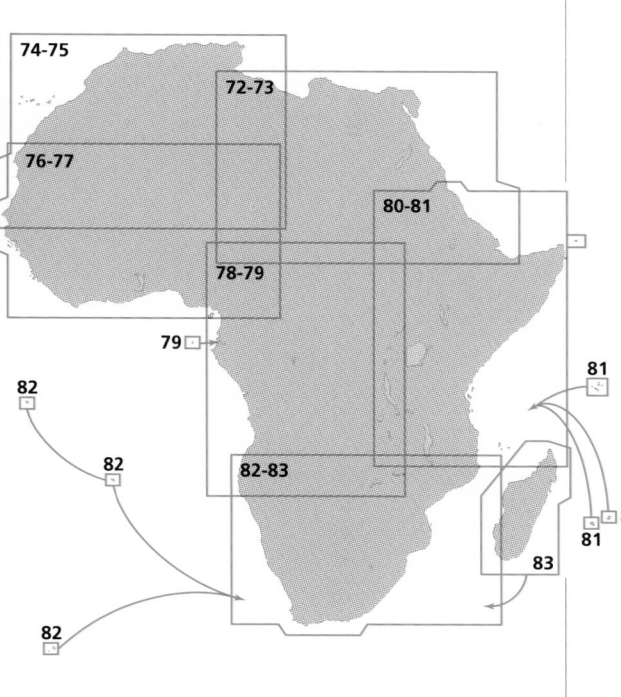

74-75
72-73
76-77
80-81
78-79
79
82
82
82-83
83
82

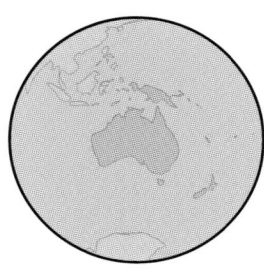
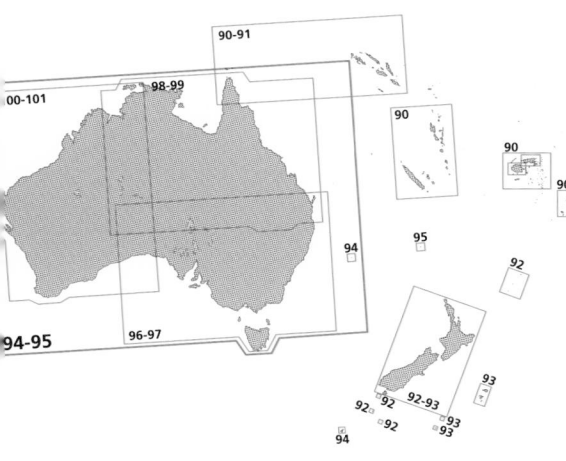

90-91
98-99
00-101
90
91
90
90
94
95
92
94-95
96-97
92 92-93 93
92 92 93
94

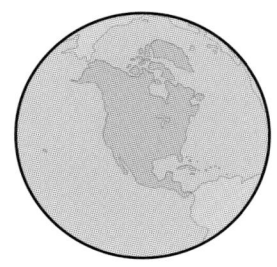
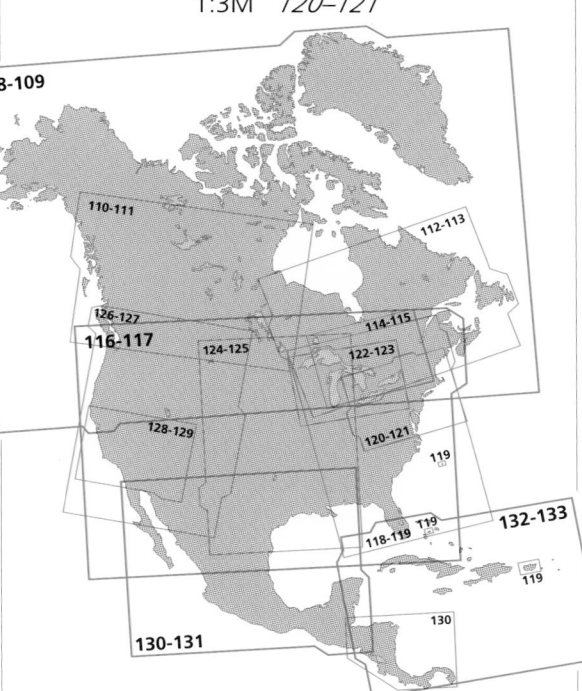

108-109
110-111
112-113
126-127
114-115
116-117
124-125
122-123
128-129
120-121
119
118-119 119 132-133
119
130
130-131

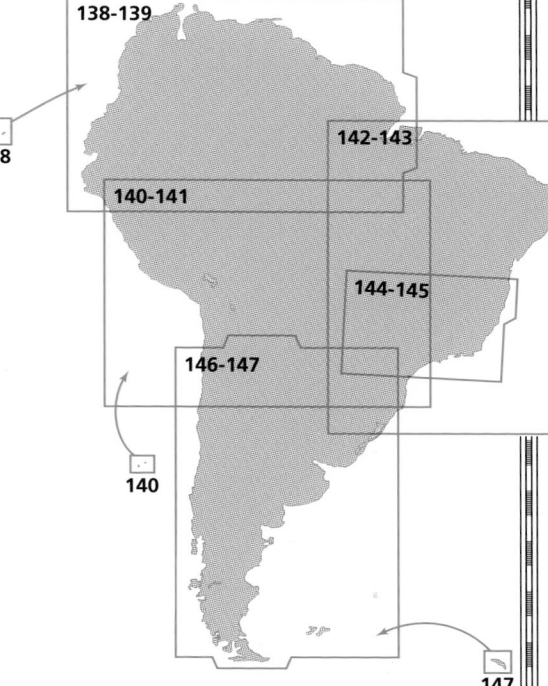

138-139
142-143
138
140-141
144-145
146-147
140
147

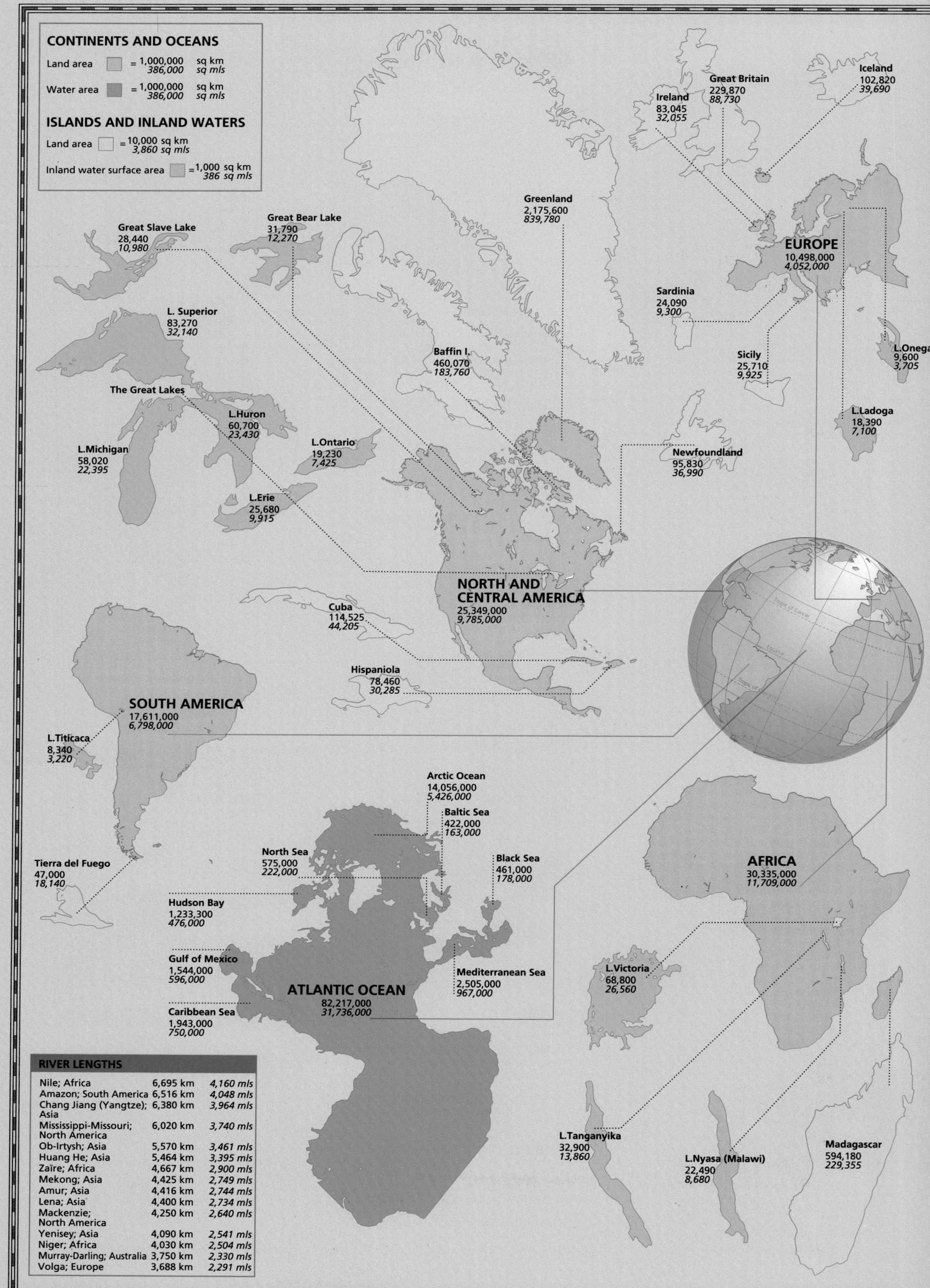

CONTINENTS AND OCEANS

Land area ☐ = 1,000,000 sq km
386,000 sq mls

Water area ■ = 1,000,000 sq km
386,000 sq mls

ISLANDS AND INLAND WATERS

Land area ☐ = 10,000 sq km
3,860 sq mls

Inland water surface area ☐ = 1,000 sq km
386 sq mls

Iceland
102,820
39,690

Great Britain
229,870
88,730

Ireland
83,045
32,055

Greenland
2,175,600
839,780

EUROPE
10,498,000
4,052,000

Sardinia
24,090
9,300

Great Slave Lake
28,440
10,980

Great Bear Lake
31,790
12,270

Sicily
25,710
9,925

L.Onega
9,600
3,705

L. Superior
83,270
32,140

Baffin I.
460,070
183,760

L.Ladoga
18,390
7,100

The Great Lakes

L.Huron
60,700
23,430

L.Ontario
19,230
7,425

Newfoundland
95,830
36,990

L.Michigan
58,020
22,395

L.Erie
25,680
9,915

NORTH AND
CENTRAL AMERICA
25,349,000
9,785,000

Cuba
114,525
44,205

SOUTH AMERICA
17,611,000
6,798,000

Hispaniola
78,460
30,285

L.Titicaca
8,340
3,220

Arctic Ocean
14,056,000
5,426,000

Baltic Sea
422,000
163,000

North Sea
575,000
222,000

Black Sea
461,000
178,000

AFRICA
30,335,000
11,709,000

Tierra del Fuego
47,000
18,140

Hudson Bay
1,233,300
476,000

Gulf of Mexico
1,544,000
596,000

ATLANTIC OCEAN
82,217,000
31,736,000

Mediterranean Sea
2,505,000
967,000

L.Victoria
68,800
26,560

Caribbean Sea
1,943,000
750,000

L.Tanganyika
32,900
13,860

L.Nyasa (Malawi)
22,490
8,680

Madagascar
594,180
229,355

RIVER LENGTHS

Nile; Africa	6,695 km	4,160 mls
Amazon; South America	6,516 km	4,048 mls
Chang Jiang (Yangtze); Asia	6,380 km	3,964 mls
Mississippi-Missouri; North America	6,020 km	3,740 mls
Ob-Irtysh; Asia	5,570 km	3,461 mls
Huang He; Asia	5,464 km	3,395 mls
Zaïre; Africa	4,667 km	2,900 mls
Mekong; Asia	4,425 km	2,749 mls
Amur; Asia	4,416 km	2,744 mls
Lena; Asia	4,400 km	2,734 mls
Mackenzie; North America	4,250 km	2,640 mls
Yenisey; Asia	4,090 km	2,541 mls
Niger; Africa	4,030 km	2,504 mls
Murray-Darling; Australia	3,750 km	2,330 mls
Volga; Europe	3,688 km	2,291 mls

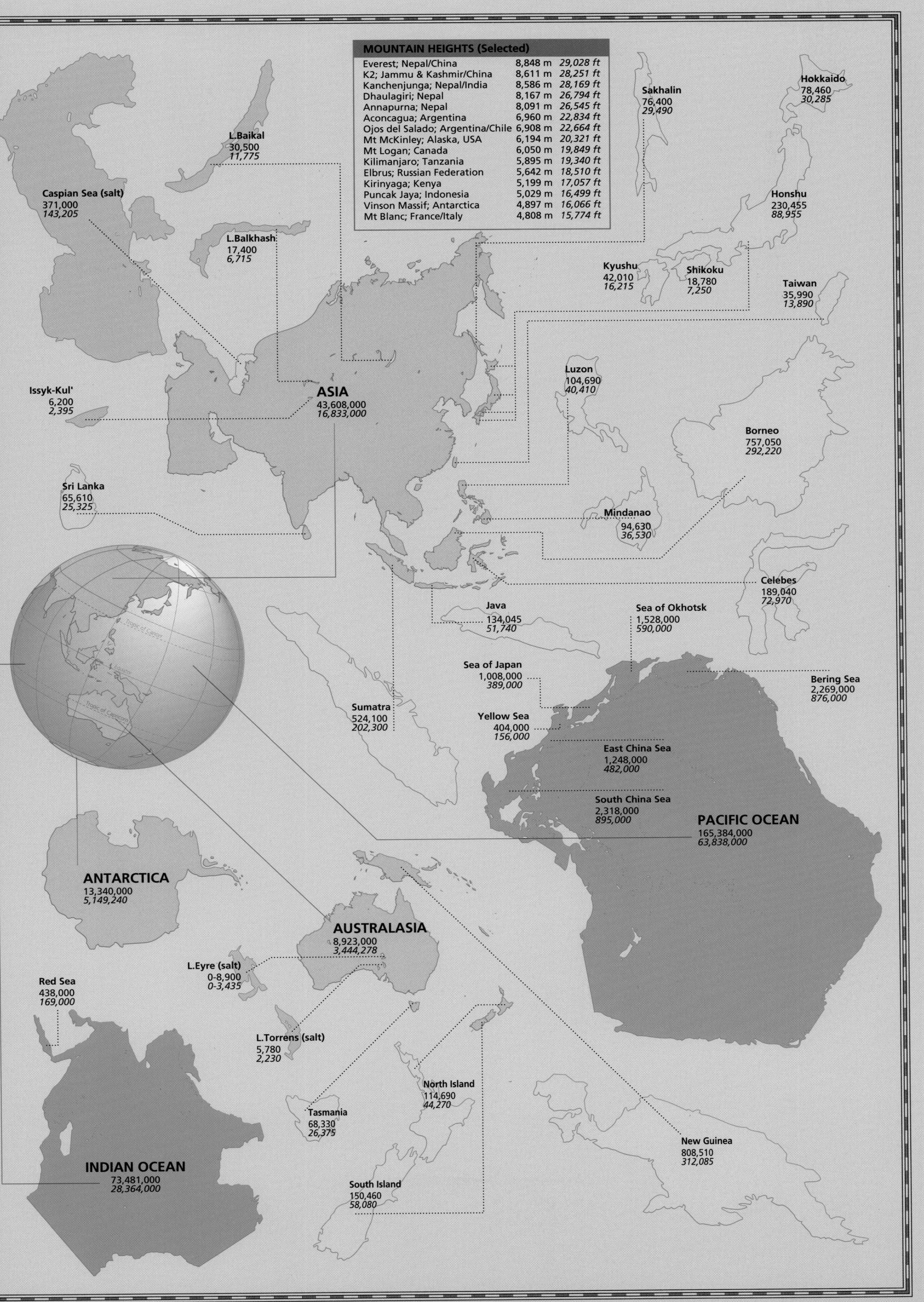

MOUNTAIN HEIGHTS (Selected)

Everest; Nepal/China	8,848 m	*29,028 ft*
K2; Jammu & Kashmir/China	8,611 m	*28,251 ft*
Kanchenjunga; Nepal/India	8,586 m	*28,169 ft*
Dhaulagiri; Nepal	8,167 m	*26,794 ft*
Annapurna; Nepal	8,091 m	*26,545 ft*
Aconcagua; Argentina	6,960 m	*22,834 ft*
Ojos del Salado; Argentina/Chile	6,908 m	*22,664 ft*
Mt McKinley; Alaska, USA	6,194 m	*20,321 ft*
Mt Logan; Canada	6,050 m	*19,849 ft*
Kilimanjaro; Tanzania	5,895 m	*19,340 ft*
Elbrus; Russian Federation	5,642 m	*18,510 ft*
Kirinyaga; Kenya	5,199 m	*17,057 ft*
Puncak Jaya; Indonesia	5,029 m	*16,499 ft*
Vinson Massif; Antarctica	4,897 m	*16,066 ft*
Mt Blanc; France/Italy	4,808 m	*15,774 ft*

Sakhalin
76,400
29,490

Hokkaido
78,460
30,285

L.Baikal
30,500
11,775

Caspian Sea (salt)
371,000
143,205

L.Balkhash
17,400
6,715

Honshu
230,455
88,955

Kyushu
42,010
16,215

Shikoku
18,780
7,250

Taiwan
35,990
13,890

Issyk-Kul'
6,200
2,395

ASIA
43,608,000
16,833,000

Luzon
104,690
40,410

Borneo
757,050
292,220

Sri Lanka
65,610
25,325

Mindanao
94,630
36,530

Celebes
189,040
72,970

Java
134,045
51,740

Sea of Okhotsk
1,528,000
590,000

Sea of Japan
1,008,000
389,000

Bering Sea
2,269,000
876,000

Sumatra
524,100
202,300

Yellow Sea
404,000
156,000

East China Sea
1,248,000
482,000

South China Sea
2,318,000
895,000

PACIFIC OCEAN
165,384,000
63,838,000

ANTARCTICA
13,340,000
5,149,240

AUSTRALASIA
8,923,000
3,444,278

L.Eyre (salt)
0-8,900
0-3,435

Red Sea
438,000
169,000

L.Torrens (salt)
5,780
2,230

North Island
114,690
44,270

Tasmania
68,330
26,375

New Guinea
808,510
312,085

INDIAN OCEAN
73,481,000
28,364,000

South Island
150,460
58,080

Arctic Circle

Tropic of Cancer

Equator

Tropic of Capricorn

CLIMATIC REGIONS

1	Ice cap
2	Tundra climate, warmest month below 10°C
3	Sub-arctic, rainy climate with severe cold winters and less than 4 months over 10°C
4	Continental climate, rainy with warmest month below 22°c
5	Continental climate, rainy with warmest month above 20°C
6	Temperate, rainy climate with mild winter, coolest month above 0°C
7	Wet subtropical, coolest month above 0°C, warmest month above 22°C
8	Mediterranean, rainy with mild wet winter, dry summer
9	Semi-arid, dry climate
10	Desert climate
11	Rainy tropical climate, constantly wet throughout the year
12	Rainy tropical climate, constantly wet throughout the year

Equatorial Scale 1:66 000 00

OCEAN CURRENTS

Arctic Circle

Alaska

Californian

Tropic of Cancer

Gulf Stream North Atlantic Drift

Canaries

North Equatorial

Equatorial Counter

South Equatorial

Equator

North Equatorial

Equatorial Counter

South Equatorial

Peru (Humbolt)

Brazil

Benguela

Agulhas

Falkland

West Wind Drift

SW Monsoon

Oya Shio Kamchatka

Kuro Shio

North Equatorial

Equatorial Counter

South Equatorial

East Australia Coast

West Wind Drift

Tropic of Capricorn

Antarctic Circle

Ocean Currents

Cold Ocean Currents →
Warm Ocean Currents →
Seasonal Ocean Currents →

Robinson Projection

© HarperCollinsPublishers

TROPICAL STORMS

Tropical Storm Tracks
(winds over 62km per hour)

→ Cyclone track
→ Typhoon track
(China Sea and adjoining area)
→ Willy-willies
(Australian tropical storm)
→ Hurricanes

Source area for tropical storms

Area of regular tornado activity

• Major tropical storms

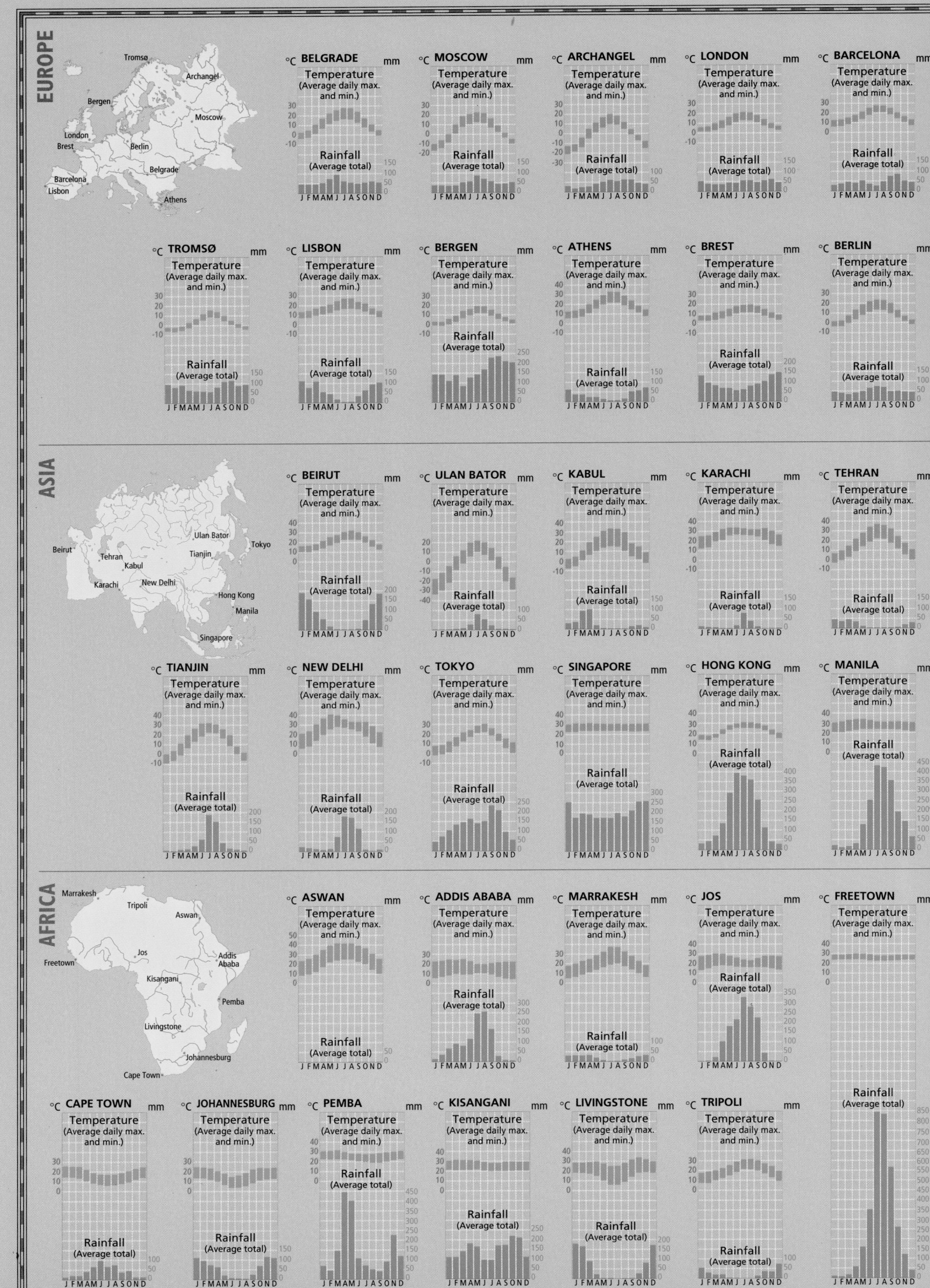

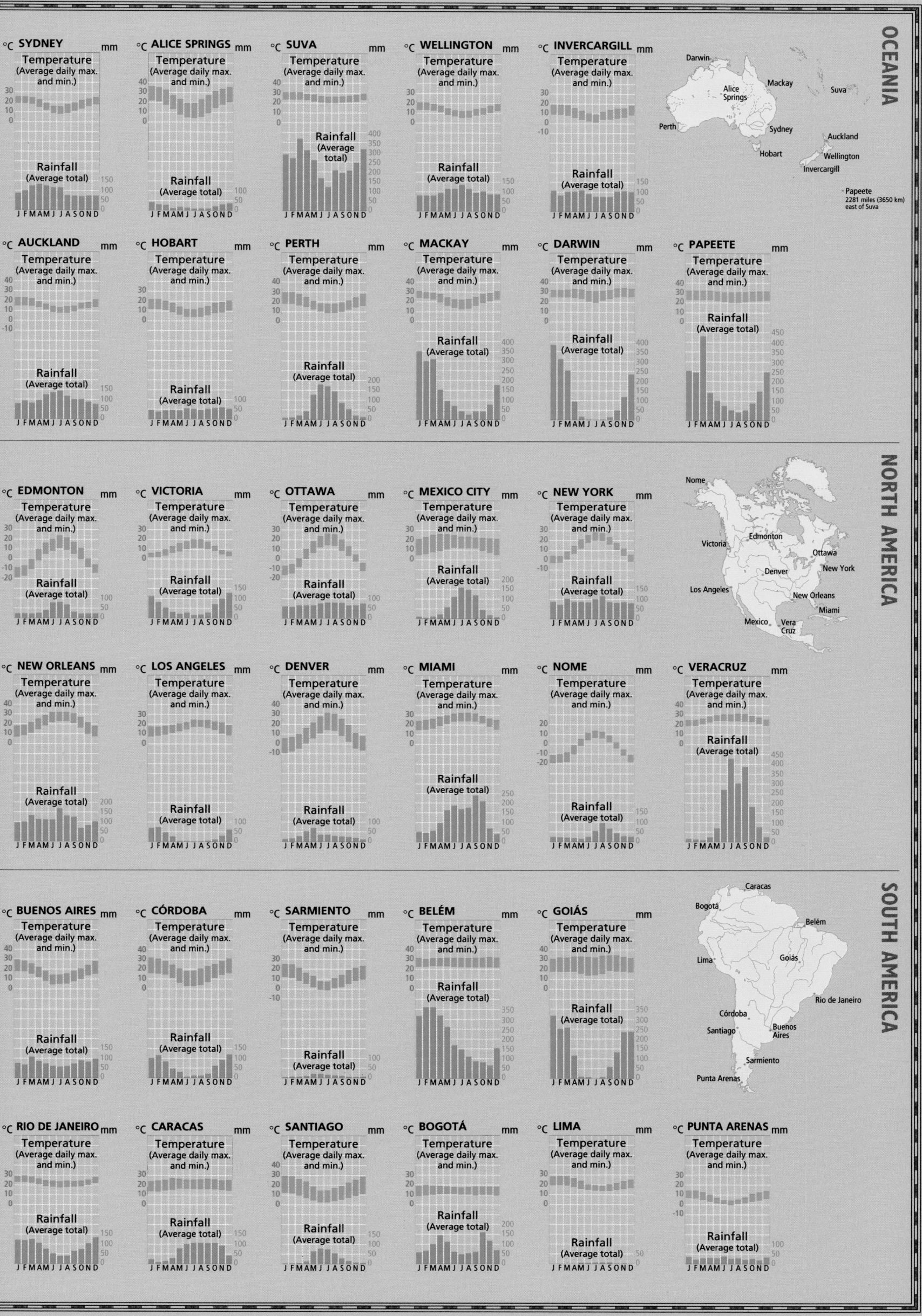

OCEANIA

NORTH AMERICA

SOUTH AMERICA

Arctic Circle

Tropic of Cancer

Equator

Tropic of Capricorn

Antarctic Circle

Equatorial Scale 1:66 000 0

Ice cap and ice shelf

Mountain vegetation
Stunted vegetation growth found on mountains of mid- and high altitudes and at very high altitudes in tropical latitudes. Absence of trees apart from low growing forms of birch and willow. Mosses and lichens are abundant.

Tundra
Region of restricted plant growth confined mostly between latitudes north of 60° N and south of the polar ice cap. Vegetation is characterised by mosses, lichens, rushes, grasses and flowering herbs.

Boreal forest (Taiga)
Continuous zone in northern hemisphere found between latitudes 50° N and 70° N. Characteristic form of vegetation is the coniferous tree with the dominant species being pine, larch, spruce and fir.

Conifer forest
Different formations of coniferous forest to that of the boreal forest, found in western North America, southeastern USA and southern Brazil. Pine, spruce and larch are dominant.

Mixed forest, mid-latitudes
Transition zone in north-central Europe, east-central North America and eastern Asia with a mixture of areas of broadleaf trees and areas of conifer trees in almost equal numbers.

Broadleaf forest
Deciduous forest found mainly in the mid-latitudes of the northern hemisphere. Before 1500 a wide variety of species existed eg. oak, ash, beech, elm, maple, hickory, alder, and birch, but due to exploitation little original forest remains.

Mediterranean scrub
Areas of shrub dominated vegetation located in the Mediterranean basin and similar bio-climatic regions in coastal parts of California, Chile, South Africa and southern Australia. A variety of aromatic herbaceous plants grow beneath low shrub thickets, pines, oaks or gorse.

Prairie
Areas of grassland where long grasses are dominant, found in central North America, the Veld of eastern South Africa and the Pampas of Argentina. Sward grasses and bunch grasses grow up to 1 metre high.

Robinson Projection

Steppe
Areas of grassland where short grasses are dominant, traditionally the wild grasslands of Euroasia but also found extensively in central North America, central and southern Africa and Australia. Drought resistant grasses grow with colourful flowering herbs.

Savannah
Grassland found in the tropics to the north and south of the tropical rain forests of South America and Africa and around the desert fringes of Australia. Grasses are interspersed with scattered thorn bushes or deciduous trees such as acacia in Africa and eucalypts in Australia.

Tropical rain forest (Selva)
Dense forest located in tropical areas of high rainfall and continuous high temperature, particularly Central America, northern South America, west-central Africa and southeast Asia. Up to three tree layers grow above a variable shrub layer.

Monsoon forest
Deciduous forest mostly occuring in eastern India, parts of Southeast Asia and northern and northeastern Australia, growing in association with the monsoon climate.

Dry tropical forest
Semi-deciduous forest growing in semi-desert areas of South America and the Indian sub-continent where rainfall is usually less than 250mm per annum. Thorny scrub and low to medium sized trees with thick bark and deep roots characterise the vegetation.

Sub-tropical forest
Hardleaf evergreen forests growing between the latitudes of 15° to 40° north and south of the equator in China, Japan, Australia, New Zealand and South Africa.

Dry tropical scrub and thorn forest
Low-growing widely spaced shrubs, bushes and succulents are characteristic of this vegetation growing in extensive areas of Central and South America, Africa, the Indian sub-continent and Australia.

Desert vegetation
Limited vegetation growth in the harsh, dry conditions of desert areas. Xerophytic shrubs, grasses and cacti adapt themselves by relying on the chance occurence of rain, storing water when it is available in short bursts and limiting water loss.

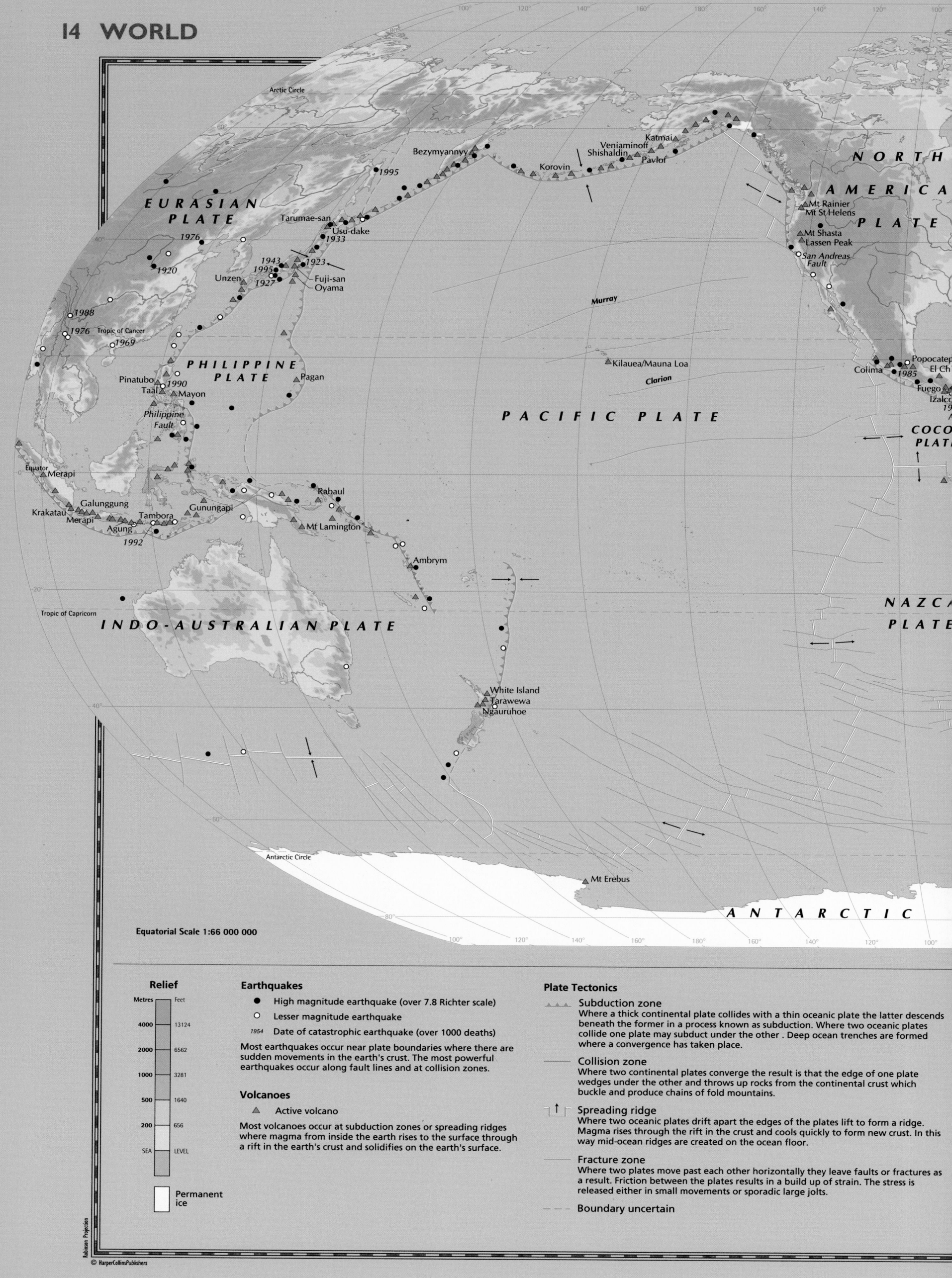

Arctic Circle

EURASIAN PLATE

Bezymyannyy
1995

Korovin
Veniaminoff
Shishaldin
Katmai
Pavlof

Tarumae-san
Usu-dake
1933
1976
1920

1943 *1923*
1995
Unzen *1927*
Fuji-san
Oyama

1988
1976 Tropic of Cancer
1969

PHILIPPINE PLATE

Pinatubo *1990*
Taal Mayon
Philippine Fault
Pagan

Equator Merapi
Galunggung
Krakatau
Merapi
Tambora
Agung
1992
Gunungapi

Rabaul

Mt Lamington

PACIFIC PLATE

Murray

Kilauea/Mauna Loa
Clarion

NORTH AMERICA PLATE

Mt Rainier
Mt St Helens
Mt Shasta
Lassen Peak
San Andreas Fault

Popocatep
El Ch
Colima *1985*
Fuego
Izalco

COCO PLAT

Ambrym

NAZCA PLATE

Tropic of Capricorn

INDO-AUSTRALIAN PLATE

White Island
Tarawewa
Ngauruhoe

Antarctic Circle

Mt Erebus

ANTARCTIC

Equatorial Scale 1:66 000 000

Robinson Projection

© HarperCollinsPublishers

Relief

Metres	Feet
4000	13124
2000	6562
1000	3281
500	1640
200	656
SEA	LEVEL

Permanent ice

Earthquakes

● High magnitude earthquake (over 7.8 Richter scale)

○ Lesser magnitude earthquake

1954 Date of catastrophic earthquake (over 1000 deaths)

Most earthquakes occur near plate boundaries where there are sudden movements in the earth's crust. The most powerful earthquakes occur along fault lines and at collision zones.

Volcanoes

▲ Active volcano

Most volcanoes occur at subduction zones or spreading ridges where magma from inside the earth rises to the surface through a rift in the earth's crust and solidifies on the earth's surface.

Plate Tectonics

▲▲▲ Subduction zone
Where a thick continental plate collides with a thin oceanic plate the latter descends beneath the former in a process known as subduction. Where two oceanic plates collide one plate may subduct under the other . Deep ocean trenches are formed where a convergence has taken place.

—— Collision zone
Where two continental plates converge the result is that the edge of one plate wedges under the other and throws up rocks from the continental crust which buckle and produce chains of fold mountains.

⊥ Spreading ridge
Where two oceanic plates drift apart the edges of the plates lift to form a ridge. Magma rises through the rift in the crust and cools quickly to form new crust. In this way mid-ocean ridges are created on the ocean floor.

—— Fracture zone
Where two plates move past each other horizontally they leave faults or fractures as a result. Friction between the plates results in a build up of strain. The stress is released either in small movements or sporadic large jolts.

- - - Boundary uncertain

EURASIAN PLATE

Arctic Circle

Beerenberg
Hekla
Surtsey

Gibbs

Oceanographer

1976
1940 *1977*
1915 *1980* *1963*
Vesuvius
1976
1988
1908 Etna *1970* *1983*
1954 *1980* *1966* *1975*
1960
Pico de Teide

1990
1962 *1968*
1972 *1978* *1981*
1935

1974
1905
1991
1988 *1950*

Tropic of Cancer

ARABIAN PLATE

Owen

1993
1967

RIBBEAN PLATE

Soufrière
Mt Pelée

as
Nevado del Ruiz
1967
1987
Cotopaxi
Sangay

AFRICAN PLATE

Lake Nyos
Mt Cameroon

1982

African Rift System

SOMALI PLATE

Romanche Chain

Ascension

Nyiragongo
Ol Doinyo Lengai
Kilimanjaro

Equator

SOUTH AMERICAN PLATE

1946

El Misti

Karthala

INDO-AUSTRALIAN PLATE

Mauritius
Piton de la Fournaise

Tropic of Capricorn

allenger
1944
Tupungato
Azul
1960 El Llaima
Villarrica

Tristan da Cunha

Agulhas

Falkland

Big Ben

Deception I

Antarctic Circle

PLATE

Plate Tectonics

NORTH AMERICA EURASIA
SOUTH AMERICA AFRICA
ANTARCTICA AUSTRALIA

LAURASIA

LAURASIA
GONDWANALAND

PANGAEA
TETHYS

50 MILLION YEARS AGO **100 MILLION YEARS AGO** **150 MILLION YEARS AGO** **200 MILLION YEARS AGO**

Norilsk
Yamburg
Vorkuta
Urengoy
Messoyakh
Medvezhye
Ukhta
Berezovo
Selizharovo
Cheboksary
Punga
Surgut
St Petersburg
Ural
Perm
Samotlor
Bol'Salym
Tallinn
Volga-Ural
Votkinsk
Tarak
Boguchany
Zyryanka
Kaishadory
Zagorsk
Moscow
Lower Kama
Kazachinskoye
Vilyuy
Yakutsk
Minsk
Tula
Samara
Arlan
Druzhbin
Tomsk
Kuznetsk
Krasnoyarsk
Ust-Ilim
Silesia
Kiev
Kanev
Volga VI
Lenin
Saratov
Sayand
Shushensk
Bratsk
Okha
Halle-Cottbus
Dnieper Basin
Donetsk
Volgograd
Emba
Karaganda
Chingshihsia
Kyzyl
Cheremkhovo
Zeya
Bureya
Komsomol'sk
Sakhalin
Matzen
Icelje
Rostov
Stavropol
Kalmyk
Karamay
Urumqi
Slyudyanka
Harbin
Khabarovsk
Valley
 Plofesti
Dmitrovgrad
Zonguldak
Astrakhan
Dagestan
Nalayh
Daqing
Hegang
Vostochno-Lugovo
Pernik
Maykop
Tangshan
Baotou
Fushun
Fuxin
Baishan
Yubari
Gela-Ragusa
Kutahya
Keban
Chirkey
Baku
Nebit Dag
Bishkek
Alma Ata
Toktogul
Fergana
Yumen
Laojunmiao
Datong
Shanxi
Beijing
Bozhong
Dalian
Zhongyuan
Pyongyang
Niigata
Chiba
Soma
Karakaya
Ataturk
Jerribe
Central Asia
Gazli
Rogun
Nurek
Qaidam
Liujiaxia
Lanzhou
Luoyang
Chungju
Chikugo
Ada Zalah
Tehran
Dushanbe
Longyangxia
Liujiaxia
Sanmenxia
Huainan
Um Barka
Zelten
Kirkuk
Karun
Bayram Ali
Dauletabad-Donmez
Tarbela
Manglal
Lahore
Welyuan
Chongqing
Gezhouba
Geheyan
Wuqiangdu
Pingxiang
Alexandria
Cairo
Suez
Rumaila
Safaniya
Bhakri
Tehri
Manwan
Ertan
Low
Yantan
Minghu
Mingtan
Ahra
Abu Sennen
Kuwait
SW Iranian Fields
Mathura
Assam
Dhaka
Tianshengqiao
Hong Kong
tine
Sarir
Ras Kharib
al'Bahr
Kangan
North
Zakum
Sui
Hyderabad
Udaipur
Baruni
Chittagong
Hoa Binh
Hon Gai
Yacheng
Gialo
Aswan High
Ghawar
Abu Dhabi
Muscat
Oman
Karachi
Sadar Sarowar
Bombay South
South Bassein
Bombay
Karnapura-Jaduguda
Chauk
Arakan
Yangon
Vientiane
Bangkok
White Tiger
Mounana
Bongkot
Tapis
Brunei
raude
nga II
te
uanda
Arun
Perlak
Kuala Lumpur
Minas
Beruk
Djambi
Talang Akar
Balikpapan
TBC-1X
Wasian
Juha
Agogo
Pascal
Port Moresby
Jakarta
Ardjuna
Jabiru
Sunrise
Darwin
South Alligator River
Rum Jungle
Cahora Bassa
Kariba
Hwange
Goodwin Rankin
Mary Kathleen
Alice Springs
Gladstone
Rossing
Morupule
Yeelirrie
Mereenie
Palm Valley
Roma
Brisbane
Witwatersrand
Transvaal
Moomba-Gidgealpa
Jackson-Naccowlah
Ipswich
Orange Free State
Natal
Drakensberg
Perth
Pinjarra
Lithgow
Newcastle
Wagga Wagga
Sydney
Canberra
Tumut 3 intake
Auckland
Adelaide
Melbourne
Yallourn
Snapper
Westport
Wellington
Barracuda
Bream
Marlin
Mackeral
Kingfish

nergy consumption in kilogram equivalents
f all types of energy used per capita,
er year, by country.

kg per capita

25000 - 50000

10000 - 24999

5000 - 9999

1400 - 4999

World average

1000 - 1400

500 - 999

0 - 499

No data available

OIL CONSUMPTION

1995

ENERGY CONSUMPTION

Percentage of world consumption

Africa
Middle East
South and Central America
former Soviet Union
Europe
Asia and Australasia
North America

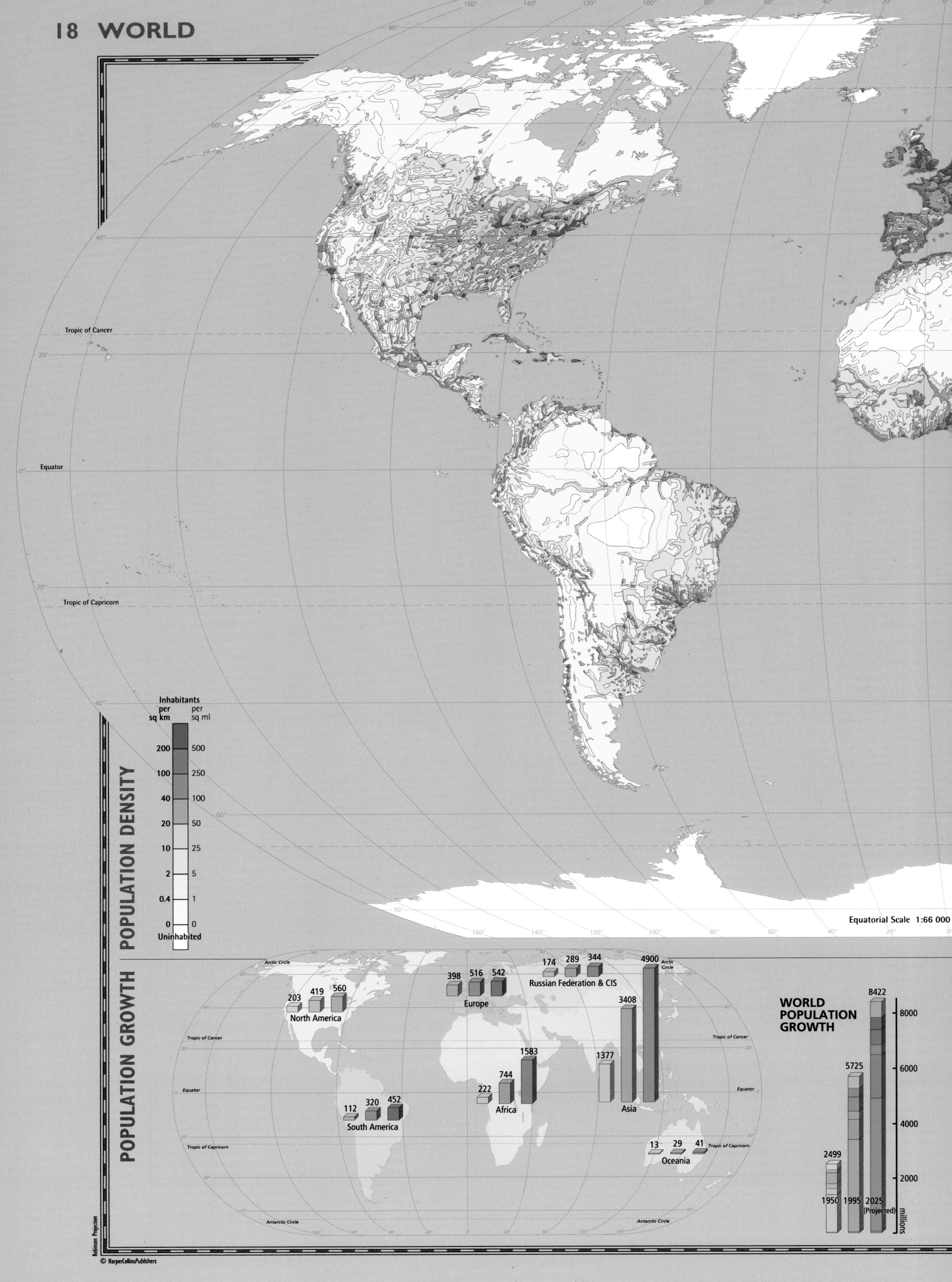

Tropic of Cancer

Equator

Tropic of Capricorn

POPULATION DENSITY

Inhabitants

per sq km	per sq ml
200	500
100	250
40	100
20	50
10	25
2	5
0.4	1
0	0
Uninhabited	

Equatorial Scale 1:66 000

POPULATION GROWTH

North America
203 419 560

Europe
398 516 542

Russian Federation & CIS
174 289 344

Asia
4900
3408
1377

Africa
222 744 1583

South America
112 320 452

Oceania
13 29 41

WORLD POPULATION GROWTH

8422
5725
2499

8000
6000
4000
2000

1950 1995 2025 (Projected)

millions

Robinson Projection

© HarperCollinsPublishers

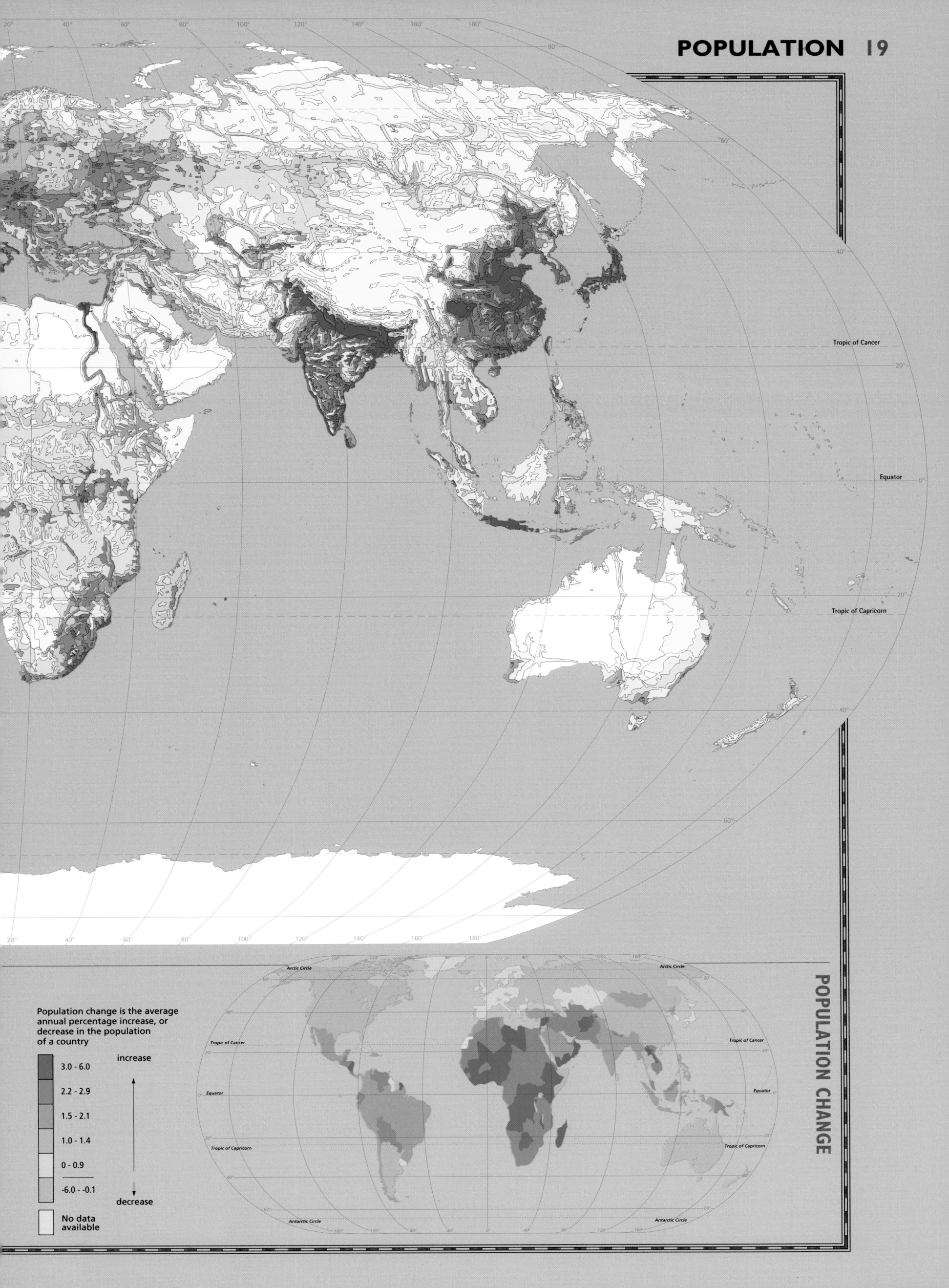

Population change is the average
annual percentage increase, or
decrease in the population
of a country

increase

3.0 - 6.0

2.2 - 2.9

1.5 - 2.1

1.0 - 1.4

0 - 0.9

-6.0 - -0.1

decrease

No data
available

GROWTH IN CITY POPULATIONS

Urban (city) population as a percentage of the total population.

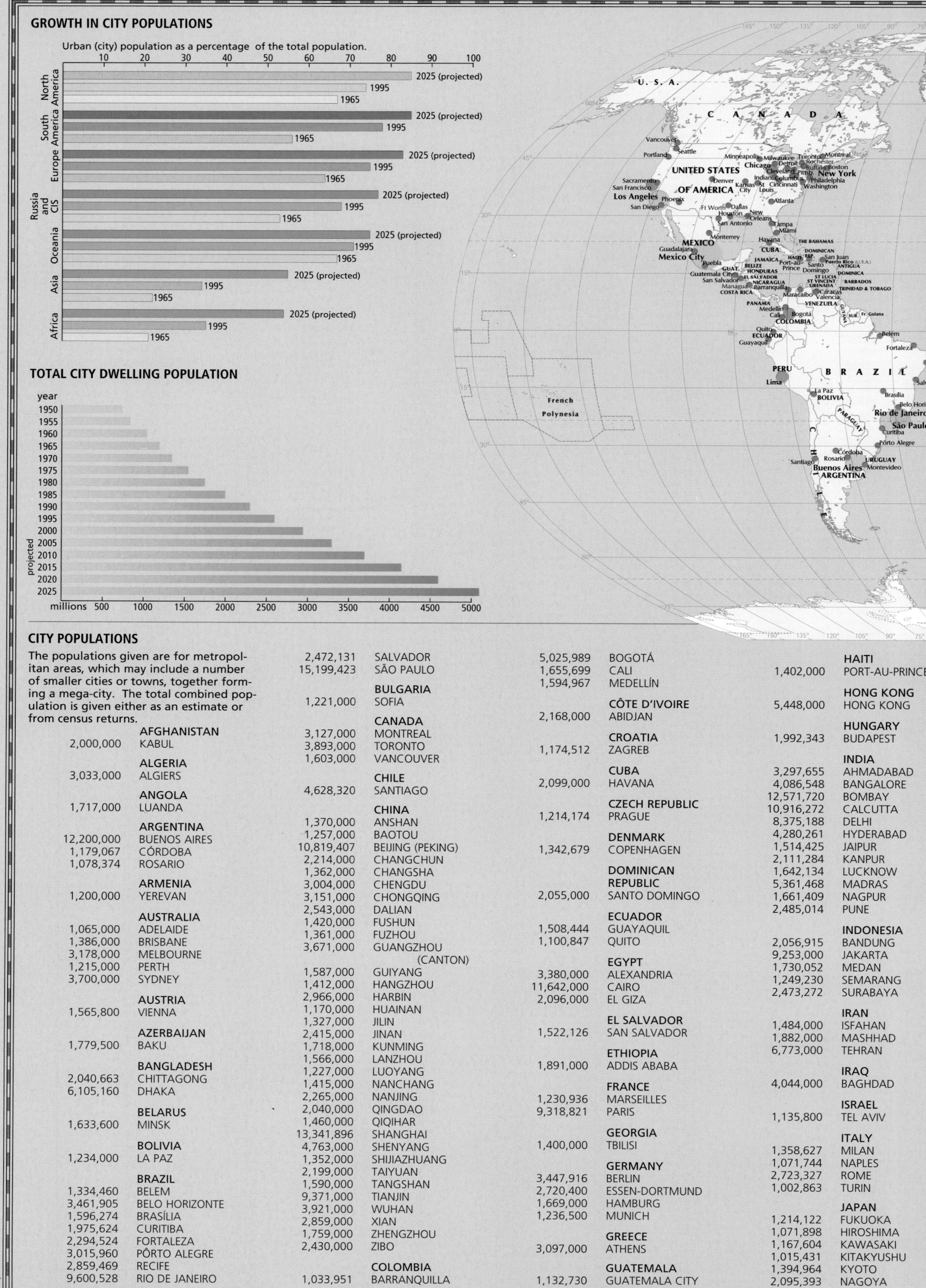

North America	2025 (projected) / 1995 / 1965	
South America	2025 (projected) / 1995 / 1965	
Europe	2025 (projected) / 1995 / 1965	
Russia and CIS	2025 (projected) / 1995 / 1965	
Oceania	2025 (projected) / 1995 / 1965	
Asia	2025 (projected) / 1995 / 1965	
Africa	2025 (projected) / 1995 / 1965	

TOTAL CITY DWELLING POPULATION

year: 1950, 1955, 1960, 1965, 1970, 1975, 1980, 1985, 1990, 1995, 2000, 2005, 2010, 2015, 2020, 2025 (projected)

millions 500 1000 1500 2000 2500 3000 3500 4000 4500 5000

CITY POPULATIONS

The populations given are for metropolitan areas, which may include a number of smaller cities or towns, together forming a mega-city. The total combined population is given either as an estimate or from census returns.

		2,472,131	SALVADOR	5,025,989	BOGOTÁ		**HAITI**
	AFGHANISTAN	15,199,423	SÃO PAULO	1,655,699	CALI	1,402,000	PORT-AU-PRINCE
2,000,000	KABUL		**BULGARIA**	1,594,967	MEDELLÍN		**HONG KONG**
	ALGERIA	1,221,000	SOFIA		**CÔTE D'IVOIRE**	5,448,000	HONG KONG
3,033,000	ALGIERS		**CANADA**	2,168,000	ABIDJAN		**HUNGARY**
	ANGOLA	3,127,000	MONTREAL		**CROATIA**	1,992,343	BUDAPEST
1,717,000	LUANDA	3,893,000	TORONTO	1,174,512	ZAGREB		**INDIA**
	ARGENTINA	1,603,000	VANCOUVER		**CUBA**	3,297,655	AHMADABAD
12,200,000	BUENOS AIRES		**CHILE**	2,099,000	HAVANA	4,086,548	BANGALORE
1,179,067	CÓRDOBA	4,628,320	SANTIAGO		**CZECH REPUBLIC**	12,571,720	BOMBAY
1,078,374	ROSARIO		**CHINA**	1,214,174	PRAGUE	10,916,272	CALCUTTA
	ARMENIA	1,370,000	ANSHAN		**DENMARK**	8,375,188	DELHI
1,200,000	YEREVAN	1,257,000	BAOTOU	1,342,679	COPENHAGEN	4,280,261	HYDERABAD
	AUSTRALIA	10,819,407	BEIJING (PEKING)		**DOMINICAN**	1,514,425	JAIPUR
1,065,000	ADELAIDE	2,214,000	CHANGCHUN		**REPUBLIC**	2,111,284	KANPUR
1,386,000	BRISBANE	1,362,000	CHANGSHA	2,055,000	SANTO DOMINGO	1,642,134	LUCKNOW
3,178,000	MELBOURNE	3,004,000	CHENGDU		**ECUADOR**	5,361,468	MADRAS
1,215,000	PERTH	3,151,000	CHONGQING	1,508,444	GUAYAQUIL	1,661,409	NAGPUR
3,700,000	SYDNEY	2,543,000	DALIAN	1,100,847	QUITO	2,485,014	PUNE
	AUSTRIA	1,420,000	FUSHUN		**EGYPT**		**INDONESIA**
1,565,800	VIENNA	1,361,000	FUZHOU	3,380,000	ALEXANDRIA	2,056,915	BANDUNG
	AZERBAIJAN	3,671,000	GUANGZHOU (CANTON)	11,642,000	CAIRO	9,253,000	JAKARTA
1,779,500	BAKU	1,587,000	GUIYANG	2,096,000	EL GIZA	1,730,052	MEDAN
	BANGLADESH	1,412,000	HANGZHOU		**EL SALVADOR**	1,249,230	SEMARANG
2,040,663	CHITTAGONG	2,966,000	HARBIN	1,522,126	SAN SALVADOR	2,473,272	SURABAYA
6,105,160	DHAKA	1,170,000	HUAINAN		**ETHIOPIA**		**IRAN**
	BELARUS	1,327,000	JILIN	1,891,000	ADDIS ABABA	1,484,000	ISFAHAN
1,633,600	MINSK	2,415,000	JINAN		**FRANCE**	1,882,000	MASHHAD
	BOLIVIA	1,718,000	KUNMING	1,230,936	MARSEILLES	6,773,000	TEHRAN
1,234,000	LA PAZ	1,566,000	LANZHOU	9,318,821	PARIS		**IRAQ**
	BRAZIL	1,227,000	LUOYANG		**GEORGIA**	4,044,000	BAGHDAD
1,334,460	BELEM	1,415,000	NANCHANG	1,400,000	TBILISI		**ISRAEL**
3,461,905	BELO HORIZONTE	2,265,000	NANJING		**GERMANY**	1,135,800	TEL AVIV
1,596,274	BRASÍLIA	2,040,000	QINGDAO	3,447,916	BERLIN		**ITALY**
1,975,624	CURITIBA	1,460,000	QIQIHAR	2,720,400	ESSEN-DORTMUND	1,358,627	MILAN
2,294,524	FORTALEZA	13,341,896	SHANGHAI	1,669,000	HAMBURG	1,071,744	NAPLES
3,015,960	PÔRTO ALEGRE	4,763,000	SHENYANG	1,236,500	MUNICH	2,723,327	ROME
2,859,469	RECIFE	1,352,000	SHIJIAZHUANG		**GREECE**	1,002,863	TURIN
9,600,528	RIO DE JANEIRO	2,199,000	TAIYUAN	3,097,000	ATHENS		**JAPAN**
		1,590,000	TANGSHAN		**GUATEMALA**	1,214,122	FUKUOKA
	COLOMBIA	9,371,000	TIANJIN	1,132,730	GUATEMALA CITY	1,071,898	HIROSHIMA
1,033,951	BARRANQUILLA	3,921,000	WUHAN			1,167,604	KAWASAKI
		2,859,000	XIAN			1,015,431	KITAKYUSHU
		1,759,000	ZHENGZHOU			1,394,964	KYOTO
		2,430,000	ZIBO			2,095,393	NAGOYA

Robinson Projection

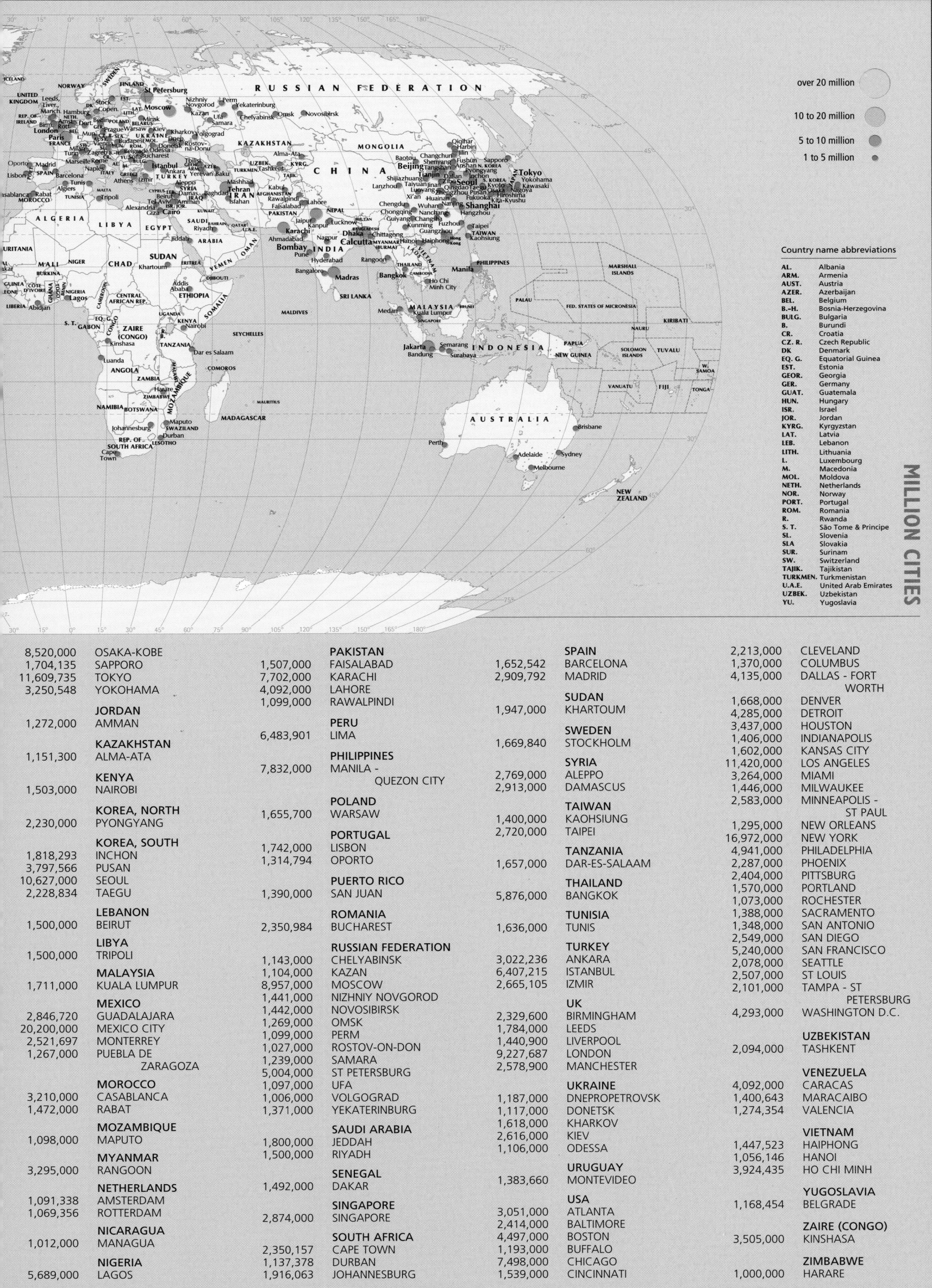

Legend:
- over 20 million
- 10 to 20 million
- 5 to 10 million
- 1 to 5 million

Country name abbreviations

AL.	Albania
ARM.	Armenia
AUST.	Austria
AZER.	Azerbaijan
BEL.	Belgium
B.-H.	Bosnia-Herzegovina
BULG.	Bulgaria
B.	Burundi
CR.	Croatia
CZ. R.	Czech Republic
DK	Denmark
EQ. G.	Equatorial Guinea
EST.	Estonia
GEOR.	Georgia
GER.	Germany
GUAT.	Guatemala
HUN.	Hungary
ISR.	Israel
JOR.	Jordan
KYRG.	Kyrgyzstan
LAT.	Latvia
LEB.	Lebanon
LITH.	Lithuania
L.	Luxembourg
M.	Macedonia
MOL.	Moldova
NETH.	Netherlands
NOR.	Norway
PORT.	Portugal
ROM.	Romania
R.	Rwanda
S. T.	São Tome & Principe
SL.	Slovenia
SLA	Slovakia
SUR.	Surinam
SW.	Switzerland
TAJIK.	Tajikistan
TURKMEN.	Turkmenistan
U.A.E.	United Arab Emirates
UZBEK.	Uzbekistan
YU.	Yugoslavia

MILLION CITIES

8,520,000	OSAKA-KOBE
1,704,135	SAPPORO
11,609,735	TOKYO
3,250,548	YOKOHAMA
JORDAN	
1,272,000	AMMAN
KAZAKHSTAN	
1,151,300	ALMA-ATA
KENYA	
1,503,000	NAIROBI
KOREA, NORTH	
2,230,000	PYONGYANG
KOREA, SOUTH	
1,818,293	INCHON
3,797,566	PUSAN
10,627,000	SEOUL
2,228,834	TAEGU
LEBANON	
1,500,000	BEIRUT
LIBYA	
1,500,000	TRIPOLI
MALAYSIA	
1,711,000	KUALA LUMPUR
MEXICO	
2,846,720	GUADALAJARA
20,200,000	MEXICO CITY
2,521,697	MONTERREY
1,267,000	PUEBLA DE ZARAGOZA
MOROCCO	
3,210,000	CASABLANCA
1,472,000	RABAT
MOZAMBIQUE	
1,098,000	MAPUTO
MYANMAR	
3,295,000	RANGOON
NETHERLANDS	
1,091,338	AMSTERDAM
1,069,356	ROTTERDAM
NICARAGUA	
1,012,000	MANAGUA
NIGERIA	
5,689,000	LAGOS
PAKISTAN	
1,507,000	FAISALABAD
7,702,000	KARACHI
4,092,000	LAHORE
1,099,000	RAWALPINDI
PERU	
6,483,901	LIMA
PHILIPPINES	
7,832,000	MANILA - QUEZON CITY
POLAND	
1,655,700	WARSAW
PORTUGAL	
1,742,000	LISBON
1,314,794	OPORTO
PUERTO RICO	
1,390,000	SAN JUAN
ROMANIA	
2,350,984	BUCHAREST
RUSSIAN FEDERATION	
1,143,000	CHELYABINSK
1,104,000	KAZAN
8,957,000	MOSCOW
1,441,000	NIZHNIY NOVGOROD
1,442,000	NOVOSIBIRSK
1,269,000	OMSK
1,099,000	PERM
1,027,000	ROSTOV-ON-DON
1,239,000	SAMARA
5,004,000	ST PETERSBURG
1,097,000	UFA
1,006,000	VOLGOGRAD
1,371,000	YEKATERINBURG
SAUDI ARABIA	
1,800,000	JEDDAH
1,500,000	RIYADH
SENEGAL	
1,492,000	DAKAR
SINGAPORE	
2,874,000	SINGAPORE
SOUTH AFRICA	
2,350,157	CAPE TOWN
1,137,378	DURBAN
1,916,063	JOHANNESBURG
SPAIN	
1,652,542	BARCELONA
2,909,792	MADRID
SUDAN	
1,947,000	KHARTOUM
SWEDEN	
1,669,840	STOCKHOLM
SYRIA	
2,769,000	ALEPPO
2,913,000	DAMASCUS
TAIWAN	
1,400,000	KAOHSIUNG
2,720,000	TAIPEI
TANZANIA	
1,657,000	DAR-ES-SALAAM
THAILAND	
5,876,000	BANGKOK
TUNISIA	
1,636,000	TUNIS
TURKEY	
3,022,236	ANKARA
6,407,215	ISTANBUL
2,665,105	IZMIR
UK	
2,329,600	BIRMINGHAM
1,784,000	LEEDS
1,440,900	LIVERPOOL
9,227,687	LONDON
2,578,900	MANCHESTER
UKRAINE	
1,187,000	DNEPROPETROVSK
1,117,000	DONETSK
1,618,000	KHARKOV
2,616,000	KIEV
1,106,000	ODESSA
URUGUAY	
1,383,660	MONTEVIDEO
USA	
3,051,000	ATLANTA
2,414,000	BALTIMORE
4,497,000	BOSTON
1,193,000	BUFFALO
7,498,000	CHICAGO
1,539,000	CINCINNATI
2,213,000	CLEVELAND
1,370,000	COLUMBUS
4,135,000	DALLAS - FORT WORTH
1,668,000	DENVER
4,285,000	DETROIT
3,437,000	HOUSTON
1,406,000	INDIANAPOLIS
1,602,000	KANSAS CITY
11,420,000	LOS ANGELES
3,264,000	MIAMI
1,446,000	MILWAUKEE
2,583,000	MINNEAPOLIS - ST PAUL
1,295,000	NEW ORLEANS
16,972,000	NEW YORK
4,941,000	PHILADELPHIA
2,287,000	PHOENIX
2,404,000	PITTSBURG
1,570,000	PORTLAND
1,073,000	ROCHESTER
1,388,000	SACRAMENTO
1,348,000	SAN ANTONIO
2,549,000	SAN DIEGO
5,240,000	SAN FRANCISCO
2,078,000	SEATTLE
2,507,000	ST LOUIS
2,101,000	TAMPA - ST PETERSBURG
4,293,000	WASHINGTON D.C.
UZBEKISTAN	
2,094,000	TASHKENT
VENEZUELA	
4,092,000	CARACAS
1,400,643	MARACAIBO
1,274,354	VALENCIA
VIETNAM	
1,447,523	HAIPHONG
1,056,146	HANOI
3,924,435	HO CHI MINH
YUGOSLAVIA	
1,168,454	BELGRADE
ZAIRE (CONGO)	
3,505,000	KINSHASA
ZIMBABWE	
1,000,000	HARARE

ARCTIC OCEAN

Parry Islands · Ellesmere Island

Greenland (Den.)

Beaufort Sea · Banks I. · Melville I. · Devon I. · Dundas · Jan Mayen (Nor.)

Barrow · Point Hope · Victoria Island · Baffin Bay · Scoresbysund · Arctic Circle

Bering Strait · Nome · Inuvik · Coppermine · Baffin Island · Tasilaq · Denmark Str.

U.S.A. · Fairbanks · Mackenzie · Great Bear L. · Godthåb · **ICELAND** · Faeroes (Den.) · NORW

Anchorage · Yukon · Whitehorse · Great Slave L. · Hay River · Hudson Bay · Frederikshåb · Reykjavik · **UNITED** · Berge

Seward · Juneau · **C A N A D A** · Churchill · Ivujivik · **KINGDOM** · North · Edinb

Aleutian Is · Prince Rupert · Edmonton · Saskatoon · Regina · Winnipeg · Fort Rupert · Goose Bay · Newfoundland · Dublin · Glasgow · Sea · NET

Vancouver · Calgary · L. Superior · Ottawa · Quebec · Sept-Îles · St John's · REP. OF · London · Birm.

Victoria · Seattle · Duluth · Montreal · Halifax · **IRELAND** · Paris · **FRANCE** · Brus

Portland · Minneapolis · Lake Michigan · Detroit · Toronto · Buffalo · Boston · **NORTH ATLANTIC** · Bay of · Bordeaux · Marseille

Sacramento · Salt Lake City · Omaha · **Chicago** · Indian. · Pittsb. · Philadelphia · New York · Biscay · Bilbao · **SPAIN** · Barce

San Francisco · Denver · Colorado · **UNITED STATES** · St. Louis · Cincinnati · Washington · Oporto · Madrid · Valen

Los Angeles · Phoenix · Oklahoma City · Kansas City · Memphis · Atlanta · Norfolk · Azores (Port.) · Lisbon · PORT. · Gibraltar · Algier

San Diego · El Paso · **OF AMERICA** · Memphis · Birmingham · Jacksonville · Bermuda (U.K.) · Tangier · Casablanca · Rabat · **MOROCCO**

NORTH PACIFIC · Guadalupe I. (Mex.) · Dallas · Ft Worth · Houston · New · Tampa · Madeira (Port.) · Marrakesh

OCEAN · Torreón · Rio Grande · San Antonio · Orleans · Miami · Canary Is (Sp.) · Laâyoune · Western Sahara · **ALGER**

Revillagigedo Is (Mex) · **MEXICO** · Tampico · Gulf of Mexico · Havana · **THE BAHAMAS** · Nassau · Tamar

Hawaiian Is · Guadalajara · **CUBA** · Nouakchott · **MAURITANIA**

Honolulu · **U.S.A.** · **Mexico City** · Veracruz · **JAMAICA** · **HAITI** · DOMINICAN REP. · San Juan · Puerto Rico (U.S.A.) · **CAPE VERDE** · **SENEGAL** · **MALI**

Hawaii · Hilo · Acapulco · Puebla · Belmopan · **BELIZE** · Kingston · Santo Domingo · **ANTIGUA** · Dakar · Bamako · Mopti · **BURKINA** · Nia

Guatemala City · **GUAT.** · **HONDURAS** · Caribbean Sea · **ST LUCIA** · **DOMINICA** · **THE GAMBIA** · Bissau · Ouagadougou · **CÔTE**

EL SALVADOR · Tegucigalpa · **ST VINCENT** · **BARBADOS** · **GUINEA-BISSAU** · **GUINEA** · **D'IVOIRE** · **GHANA** · BENIN

Clipperton I. (Fr.) · Managua · **NICARAGUA** · Barranquilla · Caracas · **GRENADA** · **TRINIDAD & TOBAGO** · Conakry · Yamoussoukro · Lom

COSTA RICA · San José · **PANAMA** · Port of Spain · **SIERRA LEONE** · Freetown · LIBERIA · Abidjan · Accra

Panama City · **VENEZUELA** · Georgetown · **SUR.** · **Fr. Guiana** · Monrovia · Libre

Medellín · Bucaramanga · Paramaribo · **GUYANA** · S.

Cali · Bogotá · **COLOMBIA** · Port C · **GA**

Quito · **ECUADOR** · Macapá · Belém

Galapagos Is (Ecuador) · Guayaquil · Manaus · Amazon · São Luís · Fernando de Noronha (Braz.)

Equator · Fortaleza

Marquesas Is (Fr.) · **PERU** · Pôrto Velho · **B R A Z I L** · Recife

Samoa (U.S.A.) · Tuamotu Islands (Fr.) · Callao · Cusco · São Francisco · Salvador

Cook Islands (N.Z.) · Tahiti · **French** · Lima · Arequipa · La Paz · **BOLIVIA** · Brasília · St Helena (U.K.) · **SOUTH ATLANTI**

Society Islands (Fr.) · **Polynesia** · Sucre · Belo Horizonte · Martin Vaz Is (Braz.) · **OCEAN**

Rarotonga · Iquique · **Rio de Janeiro** · Trindade (Braz.)

Pitcairn I. (U.K.) · I. Sala y Gómez (Chile) · San Félix (Chile) · Antofagasta · Asunción · **PARAGUAY** · **São Paulo** · Curitiba

Easter I. (Chile) · Tucumán · Paraná · Pôrto Alegre

SOUTH PACIFIC · Coquimbo · **C** · Córdoba · **URUGUAY**

OCEAN · Juan Fernandez Is (Chile) · Valparaíso · Santiago · **H** · Rosario · Montevideo · Tristan da Cunha (U.K.)

Buenos Aires · **L** · Concepción · **I** · **ARGENTINA** · Gough I. (U.K.)

Puerto Montt · **E** · Bahia Blanca

Country name abbreviations

AL.	Albania	LITH.	Lithuania
A.	Andorra	L.	Luxembourg
ARM.	Armenia	M.	Macedonia
AUST.	Austria	MOL.	Moldova
AZER.	Azerbaijan	NETH.	Netherlands
BEL.	Belgium	NOR.	Norway
B.-H.	Bosnia-Herzegovina	PORT.	Portugal
BULG.	Bulgaria	ROM.	Romania
B.	Burundi	R. F.	Russian Federation
CR.	Croatia	R.	Rwanda
CZ. R.	Czech Republic	S. T.	São Tome & Principe
DK	Denmark	SL.	Slovenia
EQ. G.	Equatorial Guinea	SLA	Slovakia
EST.	Estonia	SP.	Spain
GEOR.	Georgia	SUR.	Surinam
GER.	Germany	SW.	Switzerland
GUAT.	Guatemala	TAJIK.	Tajikistan
HUN.	Hungary	TURKMEN.	Turkmenistan
ISR.	Israel	U.A.E.	United Arab Emirates
JOR.	Jordan	U.S.A.	United States of America
KYRG.	Kyrgyzstan	UZBEK.	Uzbekistan
LAT.	Latvia	YU.	Yugoslavia
LEB.	Lebanon		

Falkland Islands (U.K.) · Stanley · Shag Rocks (U.K.) · South Georgia (U.K.)

Punta Arenas · Ushuaia · Cape Horn · Scotia Sea · South Sandwich Is (U.K.) · Bouvet I. (Nor.)

Drake Passage · South Shetland Is (U.K.) · South Orkney Is (U.K.)

Antarctic Peninsula

Amundsen Sea · Thurston I. · Bellingshausen Sea · Alexander I.

Marie Byrd Land · Ellsworth Land · Weddell Sea · Q · L

Queen · L

Equatorial Scale 1:66 000 0

LANGUAGES

Samoyede · Tungusi · Arctic Circle

Kirghiz · Mongol

Turkoman · Turki

Tropic of Cancer · Tropic of Cancer

Tuareg · A · b · i · c

Hausa · Nilotic · Kru

Equator · Somali

Swahili · Malay

Javanese

The map shows the distribution of the world's main language groups

Indo-European		
Germanic	Semitic	Uralian Group
Romance	Hamitic	Altaic Group
Slavic	Sudanese	Korean Japanese
Irano Armenian	Bantu	Tibeto Burman
Indo-Aryan	Bushman Hottentot	Sinitic
	Austronesian	Tai
	Melanesian	Amerindian
Papuan Australian	Polynesian	Other Groups or isolated Languages

Ural-Altaic · Sino-Tibetan

Robinson Projection

ARCTIC OCEAN

Barents

Bear I.
(Nor.)

Sea

Franz Josef Land

Severnaya Zemlya

New Siberia Islands   East Siberian

Sea

Nordvik

Norilsk

Wrangel I.

Murmansk

Archangel

Khatanga

St Lawrence I.
(U.S.A.)

Ust-Penzhina

FINLAND
Helsinki
St Petersburg
L. Ladoga
L. Onega
Kirov   Perm
Salekhard   Urengoy
Yenisey   Yakutsk

RUSSIAN FEDERATION

Magadan

EST.   Moscow
LAT.   Nizhniy   Yekaterinburg   Tomsk
R.F.   Novgorod   Ufa   Chelyabinsk   Omsk   Novosibirsk   Irkutsk
LITH.   Minsk   Samara   Karaganda   Barnaul   Ulaangom   Ulan-Ude
Vilnius
Warsaw   Kiev   Kharkov   Volgograd   KAZAKHSTAN   Ulan Bator
POLAND   BELARUS   Rostov-   Astrakhan   L. Balkhash   MONGOLIA
Budapest   UKRAINE   na-Donu   Aral   Alma-Ata
HUN.   MOL.   Sea   Bishkek
Belgrade   ROM.   Black Sea   UZBEK.   KYRG.
Bucharest   Tbilisi   Ashkhabad   Tashkent   Kashi
BULG.   Istanbul   Ankara   ARM.   AZER.   TURKMEN.   Ürümqi
GREECE   TURKEY   Yerevan   Baku   Dushanbe   TAJIK.
Athens   Izmir   Aleppo   Tabriz   Mashhad   Kabul   Kashi

Sea of
Okhotsk

Blagoveshchensk
Komsomolsk-
na-Amure

Khabarovsk
Sakhalin
Harbin   Vladivostok   Petropavlovsk-
Changchun   Sapporo   Kamchatskiy
Shenyang   N.KOREA   Hokkaido   Aleutian Is
Beijing   Pyongyang   Hakodate
Tianjin   Jinan   Seoul   S.KOREA   Japan   BERING
Taiyuan   Qingdao   Pusan   Kobe   Tokyo   Sea
Lanzhou   Xi'an   Yellow   Kyoto   Yokohama
CHINA   Nanjing   Sea   Fukuoka   Kita-Kyushu
Chengdu   Wuhan   Shanghai   Osaka
Lhasa   Chongqing   East
China   NORTH
NEPAL   BHUTAN   Kunming   Fuzhou   Sea   PACIFIC
Kathmandu   Guangzhou   Taipei   Okinawa   OCEAN
Delhi   Patna   BANGLADESH   Hong   TAIWAN
Agra   Lucknow   Dhaka   Kong   Kaohsiung
Jaipur   Kanpur   Calcutta   Chittagong   Hainan I.
Karachi   MYANMAR   Hanoi   Midway I.
INDIA   Nagpur   (BURMA)   Haiphong   (U.S.A.)
Ahmadabad   Luzon   Wake I.
Bombay   Hyderabad   Rangoon   LAOS   (U.S.A.)
Pune   Bay of   VIETNAM   Manila   Northern
Bengal   THAILAND   PHILIPPINES   Mariana Is
Bangalore   Bangkok   CAMBODIA   (U.S.A.)
Madras   Ho Chi   South   Guam   MARSHALL
Calicut   Madurai   Phnom   China   (U.S.A.)   ISLANDS
Penh   Minh City   Sea   Mindanao
Colombo   SRI LANKA   Bandar   Davao   Chuuk   Pohnpei
Seri Begawan   PALAU   Caroline Islands
MALDIVES   Medan   BRUNEI   Celebes   FED. STATES OF MICRONESIA   KIRIBATI
MALAYSIA   Sea
Kuala Lumpur   NAURU   Banaba   Phoenix Islands
SINGAPORE   Borneo   Halmahera
Padang   Balikpapan   Sulawesi   Moluccas   New Ireland
Palembang   Ujung Pandang   New   New   SOLOMON   TUVALU
Jakarta   Java Sea   INDONESIA   Guinea   Britain   ISLANDS   W.
Bandung   Surabaya   PAPUA   SAMOA
Java   Port   NEW GUINEA   Guadalcanal   Iles Wallis
Moresby   (Fr.)
Timor   Arafura Sea   VANUATU   FIJI   TONGA
Darwin   Coral   Suva
Timor Sea   New
Wyndham   Sea   Caledonia   Tropic of Capricorn
(Fr.)   Nouméa

CYPRUS   LEB.   Mosul   ISR.   Baghdad   Rawalpindi   Lahore
Beirut   Damas.   Tehran   Multan
SYRIA   ISK.   JOR.   Amman   IRAN   Isfahan   PAKISTAN
Jerusalem   Basra   AFGHANISTAN   Islamabad
Alexandria   IRAQ   The Gulf   Shiraz
Giza   Cairo   KUWAIT   Bandar Abbas
BYA   Kuwait   BAHRAIN
EGYPT   Riyadh   QATAR
L. Nasser   SAUDI   Abu   Muscat
Aswan   Dhabi   U.A.E.
Jiddah   ARABIA   OMAN
Wadi Halfa   Madinah
Port Sudan   Makkah
CHAD   Omdurman   SUDAN   YEMEN   OMAN   Arabian
Khartoum   ERITREA   Sana   Sea
Abéché   El Obeid   Asmara   Aden
Ndjamena   DJIBOUTI   Salalah
Addis   Djibouti   Socotra
Ababa   (Yemen)

CENTRAL   ETHIOPIA
AFRICAN REP.
Bangui   UGANDA   SOMALIA
Kisangani   Kampala   KENYA   Mogadishu   SEYCHELLES
CONGO   L. Victoria   Nairobi   Chagos
(ZAIRE)   Kigali   Mombasa   Archipelago   Cocos Is
Bujumbura   R.   B.   TANZANIA   Zanzibar   British Indian   (Aust.)
Kinshasa   Kigoma   Dodoma   Ocean Terr.
Mbala   Dar es Salaam
ANGOLA   Lubumbashi   INDIAN
Huambo   MALAWI   COMOROS
ZAMBIA   Mahajanga   OCEAN   AUSTRALIA
Lilongwe   Mozambique   Antananarivo   MAURITIUS   Alice
Lusaka   Toamasina   Réunion   Springs
Livingstone   Harare   MADAGASCAR   (Fr.)
Bulawayo   ZIMBABWE   Beira   Brisbane
MIBIA   Windhoek   BOTSWANA   Gaborone   Norfolk I.
Pretoria   Maputo   Perth   (Aust.)   Kermadec Is
Johannesburg   SWAZILAND   (N.Z.)
Kimberley   Maseru   Newcastle
REP. OF   LESOTHO   Adelaide   Sydney
SOUTH AFRICA   Canberra   Auckland
East London   Melbourne   Tasman   Wellington
Cape of   Port Elizabeth   Tasmania   Sea   Christchurch   Chatham Is
Good Hope   Hobart   NEW   (N.Z.)
ZEALAND   Dunedin

Amsterdam I.
(Fr.)

St Paul I.
(Fr.)

Prince Edward Is   Crozet Is   Stewart I.   Bounty Is
(S.A.)   (Fr.)   (N.Z.)
Marion I.   Kerguelen Is   Auckland Is   Antipodes Is
(Fr.)   (N.Z.)   (N.Z.)
Heard I.   Campbell I.
(Aust.)   (N.Z.)
SOUTHERN OCEAN   Macquarie I.
(Aust.)

C. Poinsett   Antarctic Circle
C.Darnley   Balleny Is   Scott I.
Enderby   Queen Mary   C. North
Land   Land   C. Adare
Princess   Wilkes Land   George V Land
Elizabeth   Ross Sea
u   d   Land

30°   45°   60°   75°   90°   105°   120°   135°   150°   165°   180°   60°

RELIGIONS

Roman
Catholic

Traditional
beliefs

Eastern
Orthodox

Buddhist

Christian

Protestant

Buddhist-
Taoist-Confucian

Other
Sects

Buddhist
and Shintoist

Sunni Muslim

Shiah Muslim

Hindu

Judaic

Arctic Circle   Arctic Circle

Tropic of Cancer   Tropic of Cancer

Equator   Equator

Tropic of Capricorn   Tropic of Capricorn

Antarctic Circle   Antarctic Circle

The map shows the distribution of the world's main religions

Zone Times are the Standard Times kept on land and sea compared with 12 hours (noon) Greenwich Mean Time. Daylight Saving Time (normally one hour in advance of local Standard Time), which is observed by certain countries for part of the year, is not shown on the map.

ABBREVIATIONS AND GLOSSARY

A. Alp Alpen Alpi *alp*
Alt *upper*
Abbe Abbaye *abbey*
Afr: Africa African
Ag. Agia Agioi Agion
Agios *saint*
Aig. Aiguille *peak*
Akr. Ákra Akrotírion
Akrotirion
cape, point
Anch. Anchorage
Appno Appennino *mountains*
Aqued. Aqueduct
Ar. Arroyo *water course*
Arch. Archipel
Archipelago
Archipiélago
archipelago
Arr. Arrecife *reef*
Ay. Áyioi Áyion Áyios
saint

B. Baai Bahía Baía
Baie Baja Bay
Bucht Bukhta
Bukt *bay*
Bad *spa*
Ban *village*
Bayou *inlet*
Bir *well*
Bc Banc (sand) bank
Bca Boca *mouth*
Bg Berg *mountain*
Bge Barrage
Bge. Barragem *reservoir*
Bgt Bight Bugt *bay*
Bi Bani Beni *tribe*
(sons of)
Bj Burj *hills*
Bk Bank
Bn Basin
Bol. Bol'shoy Bol'shoye
Bol'shaya Bol'shiye *big*
Bos. Bosanski *town*
Br. Bredning *bay*
Brüke *bridge*
Burun Burnu *point,*
cape
Bt Bukit *bay*
Bü. Büyük *big*

C. Cabo Cap *cape,*
headland
Cape
Col *high pass*
Ç. Çay *river*
Cabo Cabeço *summit*
Cach. Cachoeira Cachoeiro
waterfall
Can. Canal Canale *canal,*
channel
Cañon Canyon *canyon*
Cat. Cataract
Catena *mountains*
Cd Ciudad *town city*
Ch. Cataract *stream*
Chott *salt lake, marsh*
Chan. Channel
Che Chaîne *mountain*
chain
Cma Cima *summit*

Cno Corno *peak*
Co Cerro *hill, peak*
Cor. Coronel *colonel*
Cord. Cordillera *mountain*
chain
Cr. Creek
Cuch. Cuchilla *chain of*
mountains
Czo Cozzo *mountain*

D. Da *big, river*
Dag Dagh Daği
mountain
Dağları *mountains*
Danau *lake*
Darreh *valley*
Daryácheh *lake*
Diavlos *hill*
-d. -dake *peak*
Dj. Djebel *mountain*
Dr Doctor
Dz. Dzong *castle, fort*

Eil. Eiland *island*
Eilanden *islands*
Emb. Embalse *reservoir*
Equat. Equatorial
Escarp. Escarpment
Est. Estuary
Etg Etang *lake, lagoon*

F. Firth
Fj. Fjell *mountain*
Fjord Fjördur *fjord*
Fk Fork
Fl. Fleuve *river*
Fte Fonte *well*

G. Gebel *mountain*
Göl Gölö Göl *lake*
G. Golfe Golfo Gulf
gulf, bay
Góra *mountain*
Guba *bay*
Gunung *mountain*
-g. -gawa *river*
Gd Grand *big*
Gde Grande *big*
Geb. Gebergte *mountain*
range
Gebirge *mountains*
Gen. General
Gez. Gezira *island*
Ghub. Ghubbat *bay*
Gl. Glacier
Gob. Gobernador *governor*
Grp Group
Gr. Graben *trench, ditch*
Gross Grosse
Grande *big*
Gt Great Groot Groote
big
Gy Góry Gory *mountains*

H. Hawr *lake*
Hill
Hoch *high*
Hora *mountain*
Hory *mountains*
Halv. Halvøy *peninsula*
Harb. Harbour
Hd Head
Hg. Hegység *mountains*
Hgts Heights

Hist. Historic
Ht Haut *high*
Hte Haute *high*

I. Île Ilha Insel Isla
Island Isle
island, isle
Isola Isole *island*
im imeni *in the name of*
In. Inder Indre Inner
Inre *inner*
Inlet *inlet*
Inf. Inferior Infrieure *lower*
Is Islas Îles Ilhas
Islands Isles
islands, isles
Isr. Israel
Isth. Isthmus

J. Jabal Jebel *mountain*
Jibãl *mountains*
Jrvi Jaure Jezero
Jezioro *lake*
Jökull *glacier*

K. Kaap Kap Kapp *cape*
Kaikyö *strait*
Kato Káto *lower*
Kiang *river or stream*
Ko *island, lake, inlet*
Koh Küh Kühha
island
Kolpos *gulf*
Kopf *hill*
Kuala *estuary*
Kyst *coast*
Kan. Kanal Kanaal *canal*
Kep. Kepulauan
archipelago, islands
Kg Kampong *village*
Kompong *landing*
place
Kong *king*
Kh. Khawr *inlet*
Khirbet *ruins*
Khr Khrebet *mountain*
range
Kl. Klein Kleine *small*
Kör. Körfez Körfezi *bay,*
gulf
K. Küçük *small*

L. Lac Lago Lake
Liman Limni
Liqen Loch Lough
lake, loch
Lag. Lagoon Laguna
Lagôa *lagoon*
Ldg Landing
Lit. Little

M. Mae *river*
Me *great, chief,*
mother
Meer *lake, sea*
Muang *kingdom,*
province, town
Muong *town*
Mys *cape*
Maloye *small*
Mf Massif *mountains,*
upland
Mgna Montagna *mountain*

Mgne Montagne *mountain*
Mgnes Montagnes *mountains*
Mon. Monasterio Monastery
monastery
Monument *monument*
Mt Mont Mount
mountain
Mt. Mountain
Mte Monte *mountain*
Mtes Montes *mountains*
Mti Monti Munţi
mountains
Mtii Munţii *mountains*
Mtn Mountain
Mth Mouth
Mths Mouths
Mts Monts Mountains

N. Nam *south(ern),*
river
Neu Ny *new*
Nevado *peak*
Nudo *peak*
Noord Nord Nörre
Nos *spit, point*
Nac. Nacional *national*
Nat. National
Nic. Nicaragua
Nizh. Nizhneye Nizhniy
Nizhnyaya *lower*
Nizm. Nizmennost' *lowland*
N.O. Noord Oost Nord Ost
northeast
Nov. Novyy Novaya
Noviye
Novoye *new*
Nr Nether
Nva Nueva *new*

O. Oost Ost *east*
Ostrov *island*
Ø Østre *east*
Ob. Ober *upper, higher*
Oc. Ocean
Ode Oude *old*
Ogl. Oglat *well*
Or. Óri Óros Ori
mountains
Oros *mountain*
Orm. Ormos *bay*
O-va Ostrova *islands*
Ot Olet *mountain*
Öv. Över Övre *upper*
Oz. Ozero *lake*
Ozera *lakes*

P. Pass
Pic Pico Piz *peak,*
summit
Pulau *island*
Pou *mountain*
P.P. Pulau-pulau *islands*
Pass. Passage
Peg. Pegunungan
mountain range
Pen. Peninsula Penisola
peninsula
Per. Pereval *pass*
Phn. Phnom *hill, mountain*
Pgio Poggio *hill*
Pl. Planina Planinski
mountain(s)
Pla Playa *beach*

Plat. Plateau
Plosk. Ploskogor'ye *plateau*
Pno Pantano *reservoir,*
swamp
Por. Porog *rapids*
P-ov Poluostrov *peninsula*
Pr. Proliv *strait*
Przylądek *cape*
Pres. Presidente *president*
Presq. Presqu'île *peninsula*
Prom. Promontory
Prov. Province Provincial
Psa Presa *dam*
Pso Passo *pass*
Pt Point
Pont *bridge*
Petit *small*
Pta Ponta Punta *cape,*
point
Puerta *narrow pass*
Pte Pointe *cape, point*
Ponte Puente *bridge*
Pto Porto Puerto *harbour,*
port
Pzo Pizzo *mountain*
peak, mountain

Q Qala *castle, fort*

R. Reshteh *mountain*
range
Rüd *river*
Ra. Range
Rca Rocca *rock, fortress*
Reg. Region
Rep. Republic
Res. Reserve
Reservoir
Resp. Respublika *republic*
Rf Reef
Rge Ridge
Riba Ribeira *coast, bottom*
of the river valley
Rte Route

S. Salar Salina *salt pan*
San São *saint*
See *lake*
Seto *strait, channel*
Sjö *lake*
Sör Süd Sud Syd *south*
sur *on*
Sa Serra Sierra
mountain range
Sab. Sabkhat *salt flat*
Sc. Scoglio *rock, reef*
Sd Sound Sund *sound*
Seb. Sebjet Sebkhat Sebkra
salt flat
Serr. Serranía *mountain*
range
Sev. Severnaya Severnyy
north(ern)
Sh. Shã'ib *watercourse*
Shatt *river (-mouth)*
Shima *island*
Shankou *pass*
Si Sidi *lord, master*
Sk. Shuiku *reservoir*
Skt Sankt *saint*
Smt Seamount
Snra Senhora *Mrs, lady*
Snro Senhoro *Mr, gentle-*
man

Sp. Spain Spanish
Spitze *peak*
Sr Sönder Sønder
southern
Sr. Sredniy Srednyaya
middle
St Saint Sint
Staryy *old*
St. Stor Store *big*
Stung *river*
Sta Santa *saint*
Ste Sainte *saint*
Store *big*
Sto Santo *saint*
Str. Strait Stretta *strait*
Sv. Sväty Sveti *holy,*
saint

T. Tal *valley*
Tall Tell *hill*
Tepe Tepesi *hill, peak*
Terr. Territory
Tg Tanjung Tanjong
cape, point
Tk Teluk *bay*
Tmt Tablemount
Tr. Trench Trough
Tre Torre *tower, fortress*
Tte Teniente *lieutenant*

Ug Ujung *point, cape*
Unt. Unter *lower*
Upr Upper

V. Val Valle Valley *valley*
Väster Vest Vester
west(ern)
Vatn *lake*
Ville *town*
Va Vila *small town*
Vorder *near*
Vel. Velikiy Velikaya
Velikiye *big*
Verkh. Verkhniy Verkhneye
Verkhne *upper*
Verkhnyaya *upper*
Vost. Vostochnyy *eastern*
Vozv. Vozvyshennost'
hills, upland

W. Wadi *watercourse*
Wald *forest*
Wan *bay*
Water *water*
Wr Wester

-y -yama *mountain*
Yt. Ytre Ytter Ytri *outer*
Yuzh. Yuzhnaya Yuzhno
Yuzhnyy *southern*

Zal. Zaliv *bay*
Zap. Zapadnyy Zapadnaya
Zapadno Zapadnoye
western
Zem. Zemlya *land*

RELIEF

METRES	FEET
6000	19686
5000	16409
4000	13124
3000	9843
2000	6562
1000	3281
500	1640
200	656
SEA	LEVEL
200	656
2000	6562
4000	13124
6000	19686

Contour intervals used in layer colouring in the insets

METRES	FEET
4000	13124
3000	9843
2000	6562
1500	4921
1000	3281
500	1640
200	656
100	328
SEA	LEVEL
100	328
200	656
1000	3281
3000	9843

213 △ Summit *height in metres*

PHYSICAL FEATURES

Freshwater lake

Seasonal freshwater lake

Saltwater lake *or* Lagoon

Seasonal saltwater lake

Dry salt lake *or* Salt pan

Marsh

River

Waterfall

Dam *or* Barrage

Seasonal river or Wadi

Canal

Flood dyke

Reef

▲ Volcano

Lava field

Sandy desert

Rocky desert

Oasis

Escarpment

≍ Mountain pass

Ice cap *or* Glacier

COMMUNICATIONS

Motorway

Motorway tunnel

Motorways are classified separately at scales greater than 1:4 million, at smaller scales motorways are classified with main roads.

Main road

Main road *under construction*

Main road tunnel

Other road

Other road *under construction*

Other road tunnel

Track

Car ferry

Main railway

Main railway *under construction*

Main railway tunnel

Other railway

Other railway *under construction*

Other railway tunnel

Train ferry

✈ Main airport

✈ Other airport

BOUNDARIES

Reference maps

International

International *through water*

International *disputed*

Ceasefire line

main administrative (U.K.)

main administrative (U.K.) *through water*

main administrative

main administrative *through water*

Continent maps

International

International *disputed*

Ceasefire line

main administrative

OTHER FEATURES

National park

Reserve

Ancient wall

∴ Historic *or* Tourist site

SETTLEMENTS

POPULATION	NATIONAL CAPITAL	ADMINISTRATIVE CAPITAL	CITY OR TOWN
Over 5 million	▣ **Beijing**	◉ **Tianjin**	◉ **New York**
1 to 5 million	▣ **Soul**	◉ **Lagos**	◉ **Barranquilla**
500000 to 1 million	▣ **Bangui**	◎ **Douala**	◎ **Memphis**
100000 to 500000	▢ Wellington	○ Mansa	○ Mara
50000 to 100000	▫ Port of Spain	○ Lubango	○ Arecibo
10000 to 50000	▫ Malabo	○ Chinhoyi	○ El Tigre
Less than 10000	▫ Roseau	○ Áti	○ Soledad

Urban area

STYLES OF LETTERING

Country name	**FRANCE**	BARBADOS
Main administrative name	PORTO	
Area name	*ARTOIS*	

Physical feature	ISLAND	LAKE	MOUNTAIN	RIVER
	Gran Canaria	*LAKE ERIE*	*SOUTHERN ALPS*	*Zambezi*

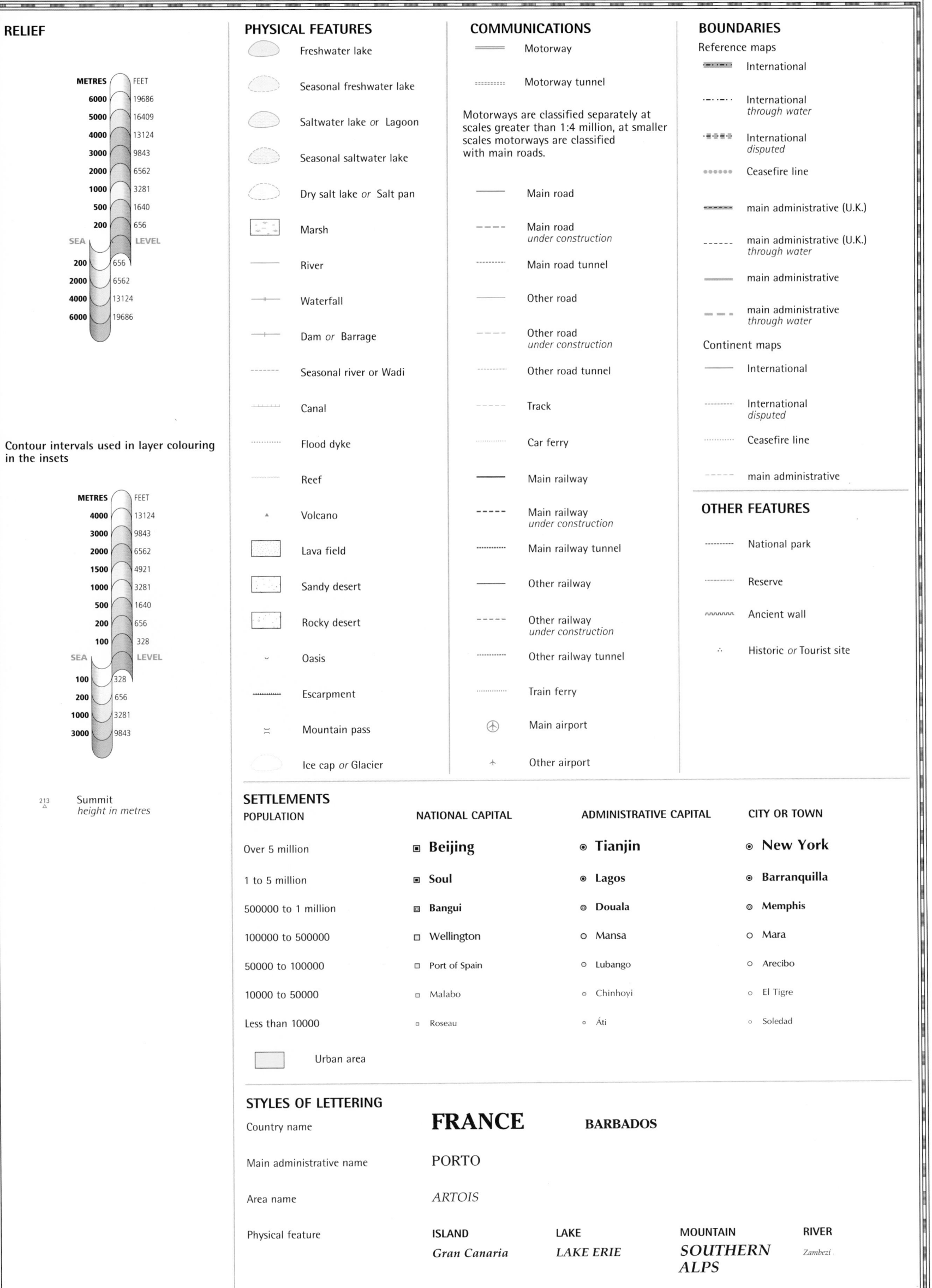

2

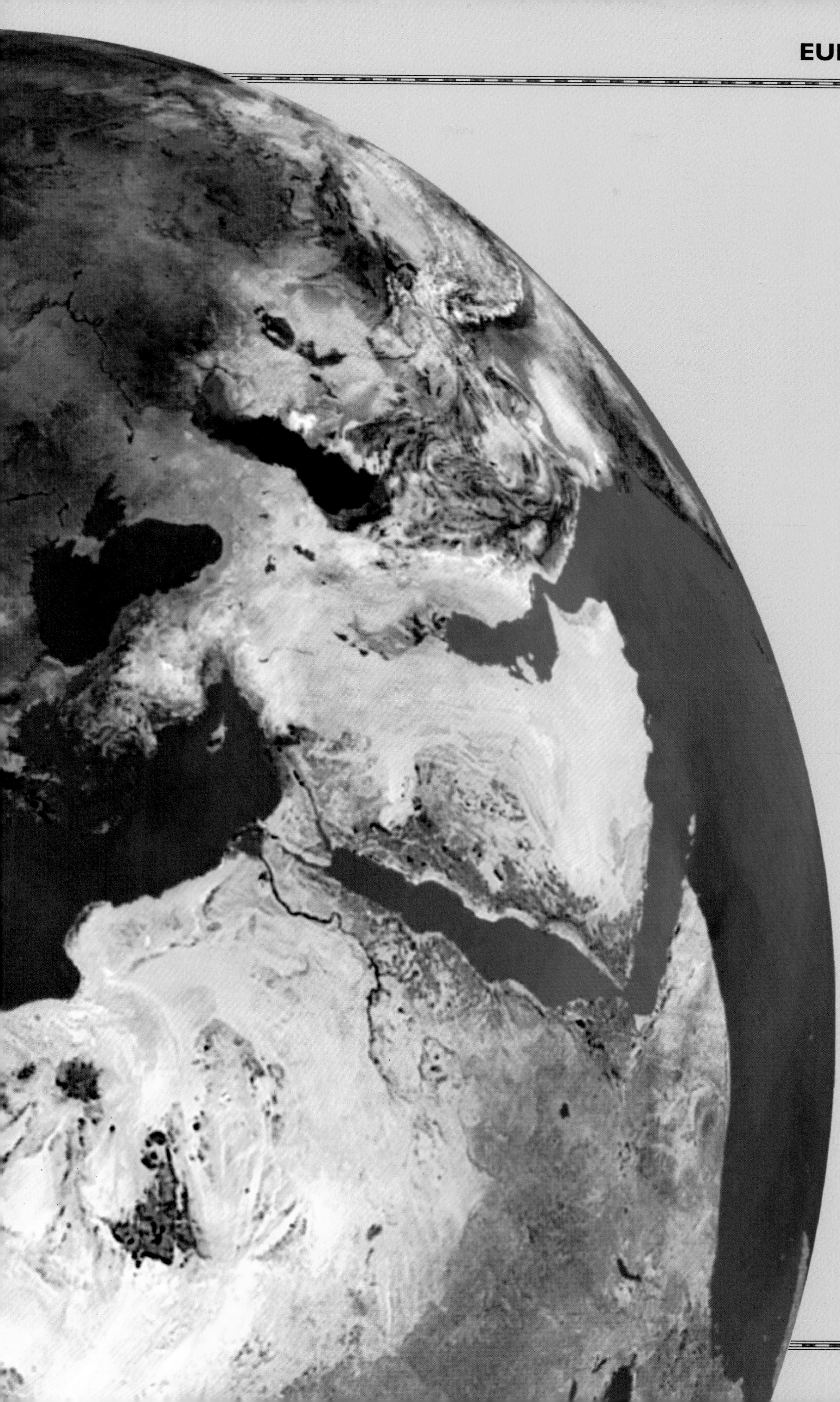

2 A 1
B
Greenland
(Den.)

Labrador Sea
Frederikshåb
King Christian X Land
King Christian IX Land
C
King Frederick VI Coast
C. Farewell

Spitsb
Longyearbyen
Svalbard
(Nor.)
Be

10
Greenland Sea
Shannon I.
Traill I.
Scoresbysund
D

Denmark Strait
Ísafjörður
Húnaflói
Siglufjörður
Keflavík
Reykjavík
Vatnajökull
ICELAND
Höfn

Jan Mayen
(Nor.)
E

F
G
Tro

NORWEGIAN SEA
Vesterålen
Lofoten
Mo i Rana

3

40°
60°
50°

Faeroes
(Den.)
Tórshavn

Shetland
Trondheim
Kristiansund
Ålesund
NORWAY
Östersund
Harnösand
Pi

SWEDE

Outer Hebrides
Orkney
Bergen
Voss
Lillehammer
Falun

Inverness
SCOTLAND
Aberdeen
Stavanger
Egersund
Arendal
Drammen
Oslo
Uppsala

UNITED
KINGDOM
Glasgow
Dundee
Edinburgh
Kristiansand
Skagerrak
Skagen
Karlstad
Örebro
Stockholm

Londonderry
N. Belfast
IRELAND
I. of
Man
Newcastle
NORTH
SEA
Ålborg
Århus
Göteborg
Borås
Jönköping
Vättern

REP. OF
IRELAND
Manchester
Irish
Sea
York
Leeds
DENMARK
Copenhagen
Helsingborg
Malmö
Kalmar
Öland

Tralee
Limerick
Dublin
Liverpool
Esbjerg
Odense
Bornholm
Balt

Cork
Swansea
WALES
ENGLAND
Norwich
Kiel
Rostock
Lübeck
Gdańsk
Szczecin

Birmingham
London
Cardiff
Bristol
NETHERLANDS
Groningen
Amsterdam
Hamburg
Bremen
Hannover
Berlin
Bydgoszcz
POL

Plymouth
Southampton
Dover
The Hague
Rotterdam
Elbe
Frankfurt
Poznań
Kalisz
Łó

Isles of
Scilly
Calais
Brussels
Essen
GERMANY
Leipzig
Dresden
Legnica
Wrocł

English Channel
BELGIUM
Düsseldorf
Cologne

Channel
Is.
Cherbourg
Amiens
Lille
Bonn
Koblenz
Prague
Katowice
Ostr

Brest
Caen
Rouen
Reims
LUXEMBOURG
Luxembourg
Frankfurt
CZECH REP.
Plzeň
Brno
SI

Rennes
Le Mans
Paris
Nancy
Saarbrücken
Mannheim
Nürnberg
České
Budějovice
Vienna
Bratisl

St-Nazaire
Angers
Orléans
Seine
Strasbourg
Stuttgart
Munich
Salzburg
Budapest

Nantes
Tours
Loire
Dijon
Mulhouse
Freiburg
Bolzano
Innsbruck
AUSTRIA
HUN

La Rochelle
Bay of
Biscay
FRANCE
Bern
SWITZERLAND
LIECHTEN-
STEIN
Graz
L. Balaton
Kecs
Sz

A Coruña
C. Finisterre
Gijón
Oviedo
Santander
Bilbao
Limoges
Clermont-
Ferrand
Lyon
Geneva
Mt Blanc
4808
Milan
Brescia
Trieste
Maribor
Ljubljana
SLOV
Zagreb

Vigo
Ourense
León
Burgos
Donostia-
San Sebastián
St-Étienne
Grenoble
Turin
Genoa
Parma
Venice
Rijeka
CROATIA

Oporto
Braga
Douro
Logroño
Pamplona
Pyrenees
Nîmes
Toulon
Nice
MONACO
La Spezia
Pisa
Bologna
SAN
MARINO
Pula
BOSNIA-
HERZ.
Zadar

Coimbra
Valladolid
Zaragoza
Ebro
Andorra
ANDORRA
Marseille
Perpignan
Livorno
Florence
Ancona
Split

PORTUGAL
Salamanca
SPAIN
Madrid
Castelló
de la Plana
Corsica
ITALY
Perugia
VATICAN CITY
Rome
Adriatic
Sea
Dubrovnik
Podgoric

Lisbon
Setúbal
Tajo
Toledo
Ciudad
Real
Tarragona
Balearic Islands
Valencia
Palma
Mallorca
Menorca
Sardinia
Ajaccio
Civitavecchia
Foggia
Bari
ALB.

Badajoz
C. St Vincent
Huelva
Sevilla
Córdoba
Granada
Málaga
Murcia
Cartagena
Alicante
Ibiza
Naples
Salerno
Taranto
Ti

Madeira
(Port.)
Funchal
Cádiz
Algeciras
Gibraltar (U.K.)
Almería
Cagliari
Cosenza

Str. of
Gibraltar
Tangier
Ceuta
(Sp.)
Tétouan
Melilla
(Sp.)
Oran
MEDITERR
Palermo
Messina
Reggio
di Calabria
Ioni
Se

La Palma
Canary Islands
(Spain)
Santa Cruz
Tenerife
Lanzarote
Fuerteventura
Casablanca
Rabat
Fez
Meknès
Sidi Bel Abbès
Algiers
Sétif
Annaba
Tunis
I Sicilian Channel
Sicily
Mount Etna
3323
Catania
Siracusa
Se

Gran
Canaria
Las Palmas
Marrakesh
MOROCCO
Sousse
MALTA
Valletta

Béchar
ALGERIA
Gabès
TUNISIA

Chamberlin Trimetric Projection
D
E
F
Tripoli
LIBYA
G

5

4

20°

30°

10°

© HarperCollins Publishers

ATLANTIC OCEAN

São
Jorge
Terceira
Pico
Azores
(Port.)
São Miguel
Santa Maria

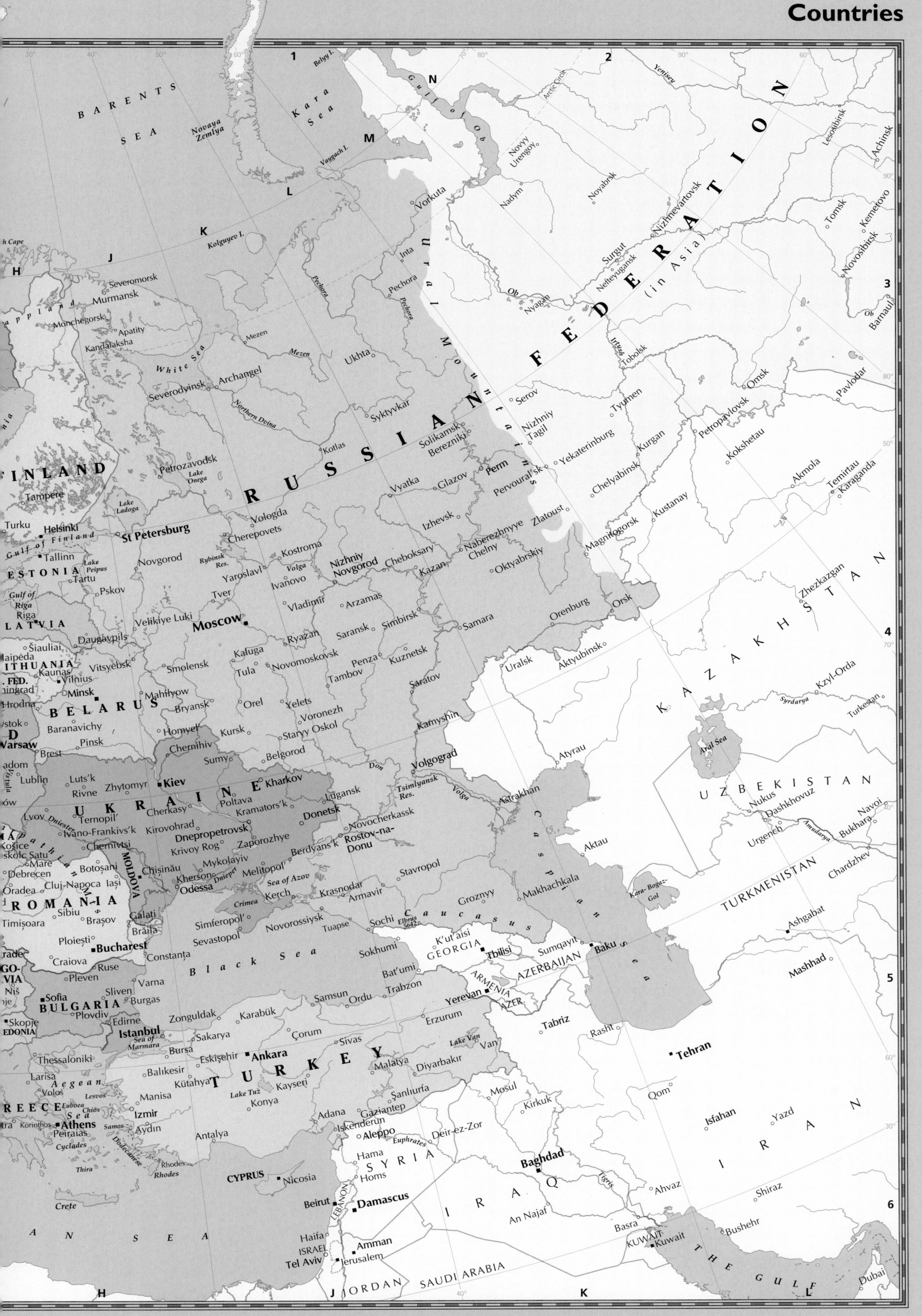

1:15 500 000

0   100   200   300   400   500 MILES
0   100   200   300   400   500   600   700   800 KM

COUNTRY	AREA sqml	AREA sqkm	POPULATION total	density per sqml	density per sqkm	Form of Government	Capital City	MAIN LANGUAGES	MAIN RELIGIONS	CURRENCY
ALBANIA	11 100	28 748	3 414 000	308	119	republic	Tirana	Albanian (Gheg, Tosk dialects), Greek,	Muslim, Greek Orthodox, Roman Catholic	Lek
ANDORRA	180	465	65 000	362	140	principality	Andorra la Vella	Catalan, Spanish, French	Roman Catholic	French franc, Spanish peseta
AUSTRIA	32 377	83 855	8 031 000	248	96	republic	Vienna	German, Serbo-Croat,	Roman Catholic, Protestant	Schilling
AZORES	868	2 247	237 800	274	106	Portuguese territory	Ponta Delgada	Turkish Portuguese	Roman Catholic, Protestant	Port. escudo
BELARUS	80 155	207 600	10 355 000	129	50	republic	Minsk	Belorussian, Russian, Ukrainian	Belorussian Orthodox, Roman Catholic	Rouble
BELGIUM	11 784	30 520	10 080 000	855	330	monarchy	Brussels	Dutch (Flemish), French, German (all official), Italian	Roman Catholic, Protestant	Franc
BOSNIA-HERZEGOVINA	19 741	51 130	4 459 000	226	87	republic	Sarajevo	Serbo-Croat	Sunni Muslim, Serbian Orthodox, Roman Catholic, Protestant	Dinar
BULGARIA	42 855	110 994	8 443 000	197	76	republic	Sofia	Bulgarian, Turkish, Romany, Macedonian	Bulgarian Orthodox, Sunni Muslim	Lev
CHANNEL ISLANDS	75	195	147 000	1952	754	UK territory	St Helier, St Peter Port	English, French	Protestant, Roman Catholic	Pound
CROATIA	21 829	56 538	4 777 000	219	84	republic	Zagreb	Serbo-Croat	Roman Catholic, Orthodox, Sunni Muslim	Kuna
CZECH REPUBLIC	30 450	78 864	10 336 000	339	131	republic	Prague	Czech, Moravian, Slovak	Roman Catholic, Protestant	Koruna
DENMARK	16 631	43 075	5 205 000	313	121	monarchy	Copenhagen	Danish	Protestant, Roman Catholic	Krone
ESTONIA	17 452	45 200	1 499 000	86	33	republic	Tallinn	Estonian, Russian	Protestant, Russian Orthodox	Kroon
FAROE ISLANDS	540	1 399	47 000	87	34	Danish territory	Tórshavn	Danish, Faeroese	Protestant	Danish krone
FINLAND	130 559	338 145	5 088 000	39	15	republic	Helsinki	Finnish, Swedish	Protestant, Finnish (Greek) Orthodox	Markka
FRANCE	210 026	543 965	57 903 000	276	106	republic	Paris	French, French dialects, Arabic, German (Alsatian), Breton	Roman Catholic, Protestant, Sunni Muslim	Franc
GERMANY	138 174	357 868	81 410 000	589	227	republic	Berlin	German, Turkish	Protestant, Roman Catholic, Sunni Muslim	Mark
GIBRALTAR	3	7	28 000	11157	4308	UK territory	Gibraltar	English, Spanish	Roman Catholic, Protestant, Sunni Muslim	Pound
GREECE	50 949	131 957	10 426 000	205	79	republic	Athens	Greek, Macedonian	Greek Orthodox, Sunni Muslim	Drachma
HUNGARY	35 919	93 030	10 261 000	286	110	republic	Budapest	Hungarian, Romany, German, Slovak	Roman Catholic, Protestant	Forint
ICELAND	39 699	102 820	266 000	7	3	republic	Reykjavik	Icelandic	Protestant, Roman Catholic	Króna
ISLE OF MAN	221	572	73 000	331	128	UK territory	Douglas	English	Protestant, Roman Catholic	Pound
ITALY	116 311	301 245	57 193 000	492	190	republic	Rome	Italian, Italian dialects	Roman Catholic	Lira
LATVIA	24 595	63 700	2 548 000	104	40	republic	Riga	Latvian, Russian	Protestant, Roman Catholic, Russian Orthodox	Lat
LIECHTENSTEIN	62	160	31 000	502	194	monarchy	Vaduz	German	Roman Catholic, Protestant	Swiss franc
LITHUANIA	25 174	65 200	3 721 000	148	57	republic	Vilnius	Lithuanian, Russian, Polish	Roman Catholic, Protestant, Russian Orthodox	Litas
LUXEMBOURG	998	2 586	404 000	405	156	monarchy	Luxembourg	Letzeburgish (Luxembourgian), German, French, Portuguese	Roman Catholic, Protestant	Franc
MACEDONIA, Former Yugoslavian Republic of	9 928	25 713	2 142 000	216	83	republic	Skopje	Macedonian, Albanian, Serbo-Croat, Turkish, Romany	Macedonian Orthodox, Sunni Muslim, Roman Catholic	Denar
MADEIRA	307	794	253 000	825	319	Port territory	Funchal	Portuguese	Roman Catholic, Protestant	Port. escudo
MALTA	122	316	368 000	3016	1165	republic	Valletta	Maltese, English	Roman Catholic	Lira
MOLDOVA	13 012	33 700	4 350 000	334	129	republic	Chişinău	Romanian, Russian, Ukrainian, Gagauz	Moldovan Orthodox, Russian Orthodox	Leu
MONACO	1	2	31 000	41174	15897	monarchy	Monaco	French, Monegasque, Italian	Roman Catholic	French franc
NETHERLANDS	16 033	41 526	15 380 000	959	370	monarchy	Amsterdam	Dutch, Frisian, Turkish, Indonesian languages	Roman Catholic, Protestant, Sunni Muslim	Guilder
NORWAY	125 050	323 878	4 325 000	35	13	monarchy	Oslo	Norwegian	Protestant, Roman Catholic	Krone
POLAND	120 728	312 683	38 544 000	319	123	republic	Warsaw	Polish, German	Roman Catholic, Polish Orthodox	Złoty
PORTUGAL	34 340	88 940	9 902 000	288	111	republic	Lisbon	Portuguese	Roman Catholic, Protestant	Escudo
REPUBLIC OF IRELAND	27 136	70 282	3 571 000	132	51	republic	Dublin	English, Irish	Roman Catholic, Protestant	Punt
ROMANIA	91 699	237 500	22 731 000	248	96	republic	Bucharest	Romanian, Hungarian	Romanian Orthodox, Roman Catholic, Protestant	Leu
RUSSIAN FEDERATION	6 592 849	17 075 400	148 673 000	23	9	republic	Moscow	Russian, Tatar, Ukrainian, many local languages	Russian Orthodox, Sunni, Muslim, other Christian, Jewish	Rouble
RUSSIAN FEDERATION IN EUROPE	1 527 343	3 955 800	106 918 000	70	27					
SAN MARINO	24	61	25 000	1061	410	republic	San Marino	Italian	Roman Catholic	Ital. lira
SLOVAKIA	18 933	49 035	5 347 000	282	109	republic	Bratislava	Slovak, Hungarian, Czech	Roman Catholic, Protestant, Orthodox	Koruna
SLOVENIA	7 819	20 251	1 989 000	254	98	republic	Ljubljana	Slovene, Serbo-Croat	Roman Catholic, Protestant	Tólar
SPAIN	194 897	504 782	39 143 000	201	78	monarchy	Madrid	Spanish, Catalan, Galician, Basque	Roman Catholic	Peseta
SWEDEN	173 732	449 964	8 781 000	51	20	monarchy	Stockholm	Swedish	Protestant, Roman Catholic	Krona
SWITZERLAND	15 943	41 293	6 995 000	439	169	federation	Bern	German, French, Italian, Romansch	Roman Catholic, Protestant	Franc
UNITED KINGDOM	94 241	244 082	58 395 000	620	239	monarchy	London	English, South Indian languages, Chinese, Welsh, Gaelic	Protestant, Roman Catholic, Muslim, Sikh, Hindu, Jewish	Pound
UKRAINE	233 090	603 700	51 910 000	223	86	republic	Kiev	Ukrainian, Russian, regional languages	Ukrainian Orthodox, Roman Catholic	Karbovanets
VATICAN CITY		0.44	1 000	5886	2273	ecclesiastical state		Italian	Roman Catholic	Ital. lira
YUGOSLAVIA	39 449	102 173	10 516 000	267	103	republic	Belgrade	Serbo-Croat, Albanian,	Serbian Orthodox, Montenegrin	Dinar

Greenland
(Den.)

Denmark Strait

Reykjavík **ICELAND**

| NETHERLANDS |
| LUXEMBOURG |
| LIECHTENSTEIN |
| BELGIUM |

Faeroes •Tórshavn
(Den.)

Shetland

Orkney

**UNITED
KINGDOM**

REP. OF
IRELAND
••Dublin

London•

English Channel

Channel Is

I. of Man

Bay of
Biscay

FRANCE

PORTUGAL

•Lisbon

•Madrid

SPAIN

Str. of Gibraltar

Balearic Islands
Menorca
Ibiza Mallorca

Andorra •ANDORRA

MONACO

Pyrenees

Corsica

Sardinia

ITALY

•Rome

Greenland
Sea

Svalbard
(Nor.)

Spitsbergen

Jan Mayen
(Nor.)

**NORWEGIAN
SEA**

Lappland

NORWAY

SWEDEN

Oslo•

•Stockholm

Gulf of Bothnia

White Sea

FINLAND

Helsinki•

Gulf of Finland

Lake
Onega

**BARENTS
SEA**

Novaya
Zemlya

Kara
Sea

Gulf of Ob

**RUSSIAN
FEDERATION**

NORTH
SEA

Skagerrak

DENMARK

Copenhagen•

Kattegat

Vänern

Vättern

Gotland

Öland

Bornholm

Baltic Sea

•Tallinn

Lake
Ladoga

ESTONIA

Riga•

LATVIA

LITHUANIA

Rybinsk
Res.

•Moscow

•Vilnius

RUS. FED.

•Minsk

BELARUS

KAZAKHSTAN

NETHERLANDS
•Amsterdam
•The Hague

Brussels•
BELGIUM •Bonn
LUXEMBOURG
•Luxembourg

•Paris

Berlin•

GERMANY

POLAND

•Warsaw

•Kiev

UKRAINE

•Prague

CZECH REP.

LIECHTEN-
STEIN
Bern•
SWITZERLAND
ALPS
Ljubljana•
SLOVENIA

•Vienna

•Bratislava
SLOVAKIA

AUSTRIA

HUNGARY

•Budapest

Zagreb•
CROATIA
BOSNIA–
HERZ.
Sarajevo•

YUGO-
SLAVIA

•Belgrade

MOLDOVA

•Chisinău

Carpathian Mts

ROMANIA

•Bucharest

Crimea

Sea of
Azov

Caucasus

Black Sea

GEORGIA

AZERBAIJAN
ARMENIA
AZER.

Caspian Sea

SAN
MARINO

Adriatic Sea

Tirana•

BULGARIA

•Sofia

Skopje•

MACEDONIA

ALBANIA

Istanbul•

Sea of
Marmara

•Ankara

T U R K E Y

Aegean
Sea

Ionian
Sea

Sicily

GREECE
•
Athens

Valletta •
MALTA

Corfu

Sea

Crete

Rhodes

CYPRUS •Nicosia

M E D I T E R R A N E A N   S E A

© HarperCollins Publishers

■ EUROPEAN FREE TRADE ASSOCIATION (EFTA)

Founded in 1960 by the Stockholm Convention, the original members were Austria, Denmark, Norway, Portugal, Sweden, Switzerland and the United Kingdom. Denmark and the United Kingdom left in 1972 to join the EU, as did Portugal in 1985. The original objectives were to eliminate tariffs and other trade restrictions between members, and to create a free-trade area throughout Western Europe. The formation of the EEA virtually achieves this.

Headquarters : Geneva, Switzerland

EUROPEAN ECONOMIC AREA (EEA)

On 1 January 1994 the EU nations and the EFTA nations (except Liechtenstein, who later joined in April 1995), formed the European Economic Area, the World's largest multi-lateral trading area.

■ EUROPEAN UNION (EU)

Originally the European Economic Community, founded by the Treaty of Rome in 1957, which was signed by Belgium, France, West Germany, Italy, Luxembourg and the Netherlands. Denmark, the Republic of Ireland and the United Kingdom joined in 1973; Greece joined in 1981 and Spain and Portugal in 1986, the former East Germany became a part of the EU following the reunification of Germany in October 1990. The objectives, under the Treaty of Rome, are to lay the foundations of an ever closer union among the peoples of Europe, and to ensure economic and social progress.

Headquarters : Brussels, Belgium

■ COMMONWEALTH OF INDEPENDENT STATES (CIS)

Established by the Minsk Agreement signed by Belarus, the Russian Federation and Ukraine on 8 December 1991 following the collapse of the U.S.S.R. The Alma-Ata Declaration was signed on 21 December 1991 by these countries and Armenia, Kazakhstan, Kyrgyzstan, Moldova, Tajikistan, Turkmenistan and Uzbekistan; Azerbaijan also signed the declaration but did not formally join until September 1993; Georgia was admitted in December 1993.

Headquarters : Minsk, Belarus

see
map
above

BELARUS
UKRAINE
MOLDOVA
GEORGIA
AZERBAIJAN
ARMENIA

RUSSIAN FEDERATION

KAZAKHSTAN
UZBEKISTAN

KYRGYZSTAN
TAJIKISTAN
TURKMENISTAN

■ ORGANIZATION FOR ECONOMIC CO-OPERATION AND DEVELOPMENT (OECD)

Established in 1961 as the successor to the Organization for European Economic Co-operation (OEEC) which was set up in 1948 to administer the Marshall Plan for the post-World War II reconstruction of Europe, the OECD's objective is to promote economic and social welfare throughout the OECD area. It does this by assisting member governments in the formulation and co-ordination to policies to meet this objective; it also aims to stimulate and harmonise members' efforts in favour of developing countries.

Headquarters : Paris, France

CANADA

ICELAND

U.S.A.

MEXICO

IRELAND
FRANCE
PORTUGAL

NORWAY
U.K.
NETH.
BELG.
LUX.
SPAIN

FINLAND
SWEDEN
DENMARK
GERMANY
AUSTRIA
SWITZ.
ITALY
GREECE

TURKEY

JAPAN

AUSTRALIA

NEW ZEALAND

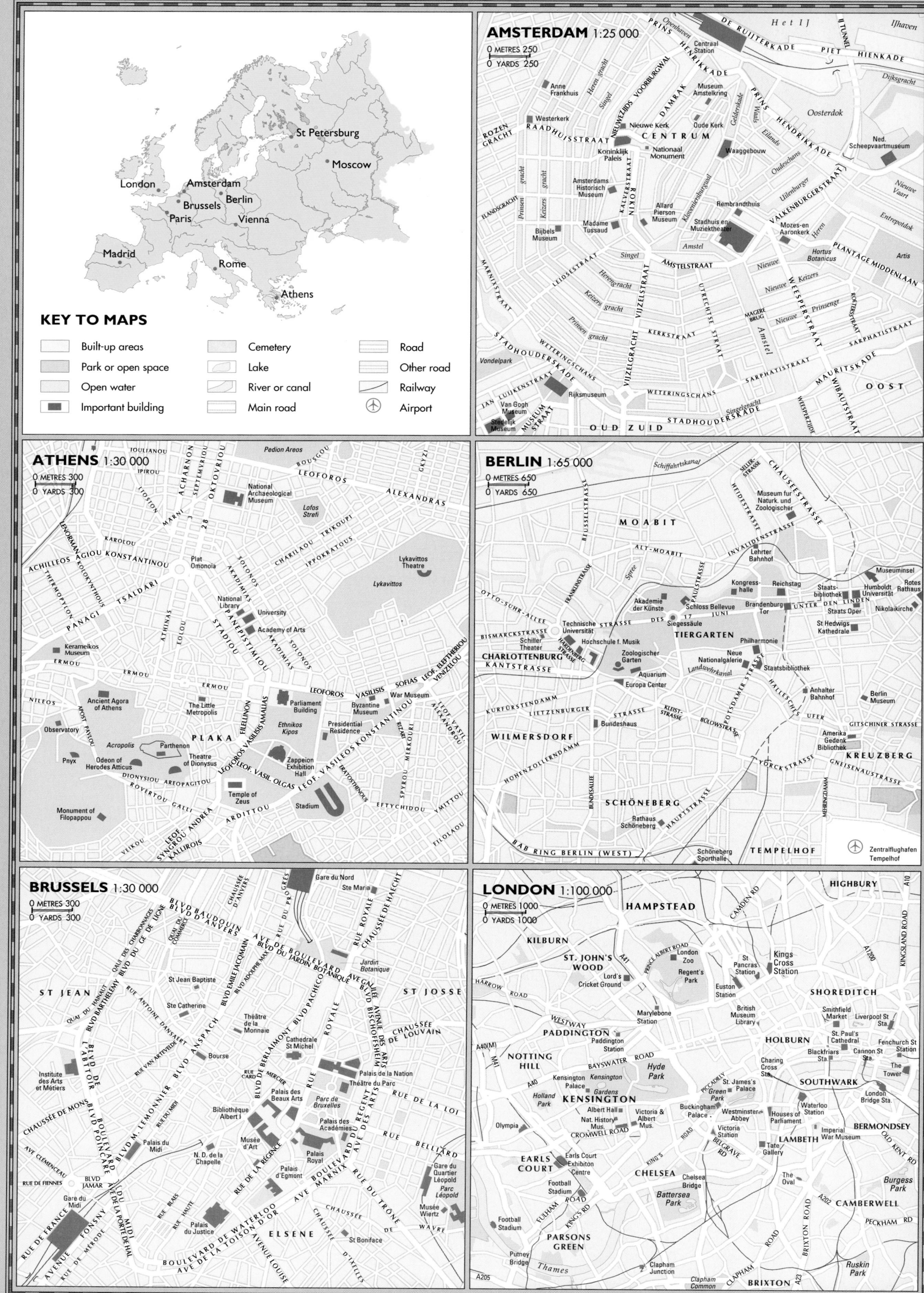

AMSTERDAM 1:25 000

0 METRES 250
0 YARDS 250

ATHENS 1:30 000

0 METRES 300
0 YARDS 300

BERLIN 1:65 000

0 METRES 650
0 YARDS 650

BRUSSELS 1:30 000

0 METRES 300
0 YARDS 300

LONDON 1:100 000

0 METRES 1000
0 YARDS 1000

KEY TO MAPS

	Built-up areas		Cemetery		Road
	Park or open space		Lake		Other road
	Open water		River or canal		Railway
	Important building		Main road		Airport

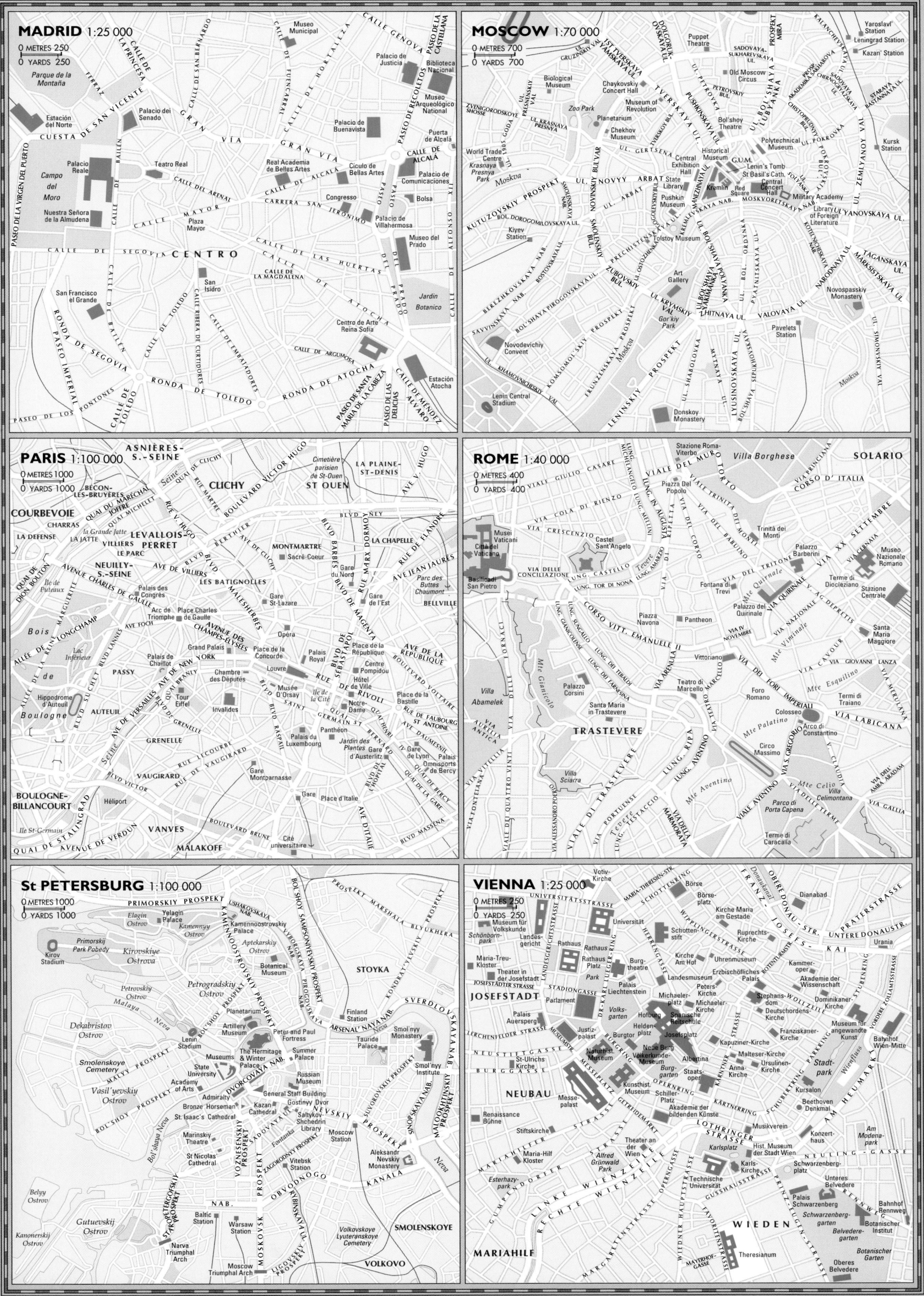

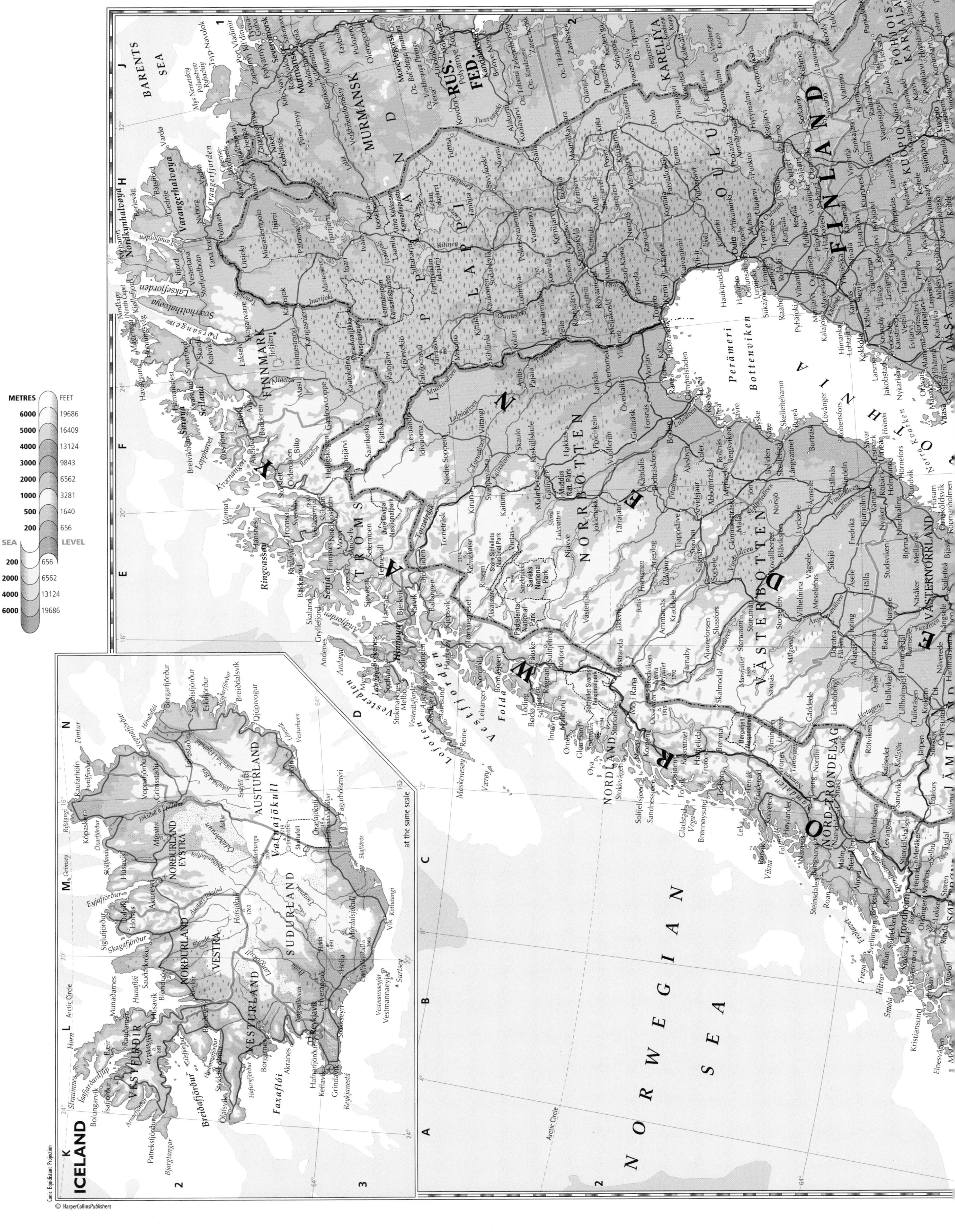

METRES	FEET
6000	19686
5000	16409
4000	13124
3000	9843
2000	6562
1000	3281
500	1640
200	656
SEA	LEVEL
200	656
2000	6562
4000	13124
6000	19686

BARENTS SEA

MURMANSK

RUS. FED.

FINLAND

LAPPI

OULU

KARELIYA

POHJOIS-KARJALA

KUOPIO

FINNMARK

NORRBOTTEN

VÄSTERBOTTEN

VÄSTERNORRLAND

TROMS

NORWEGIAN SEA

NORD-TRØNDELAG

NORDLAND

Perämeri

Bottenviken

Conic Equidistant Projection

ICELAND

VESTFIRÐIR

VESTURLAND

NORÐURLAND VESTRA

NORÐURLAND EYSTRA

AUSTURLAND

SUÐURLAND

Vatnajökull

Reykjavík

Arctic Circle

at the same scale

© HarperCollinsPublishers

1:4 000 000

METRES | FEET
6000 | 19686
5000 | 16409
4000 | 13124
3000 | 9843
2000 | 6562
1000 | 3281
500 | 1640
200 | 656

SEA | LEVEL

200 | 656
2000 | 6562
4000 | 13124
6000 | 19686

Transverse Mercator Projection

© HarperCollins Publishers

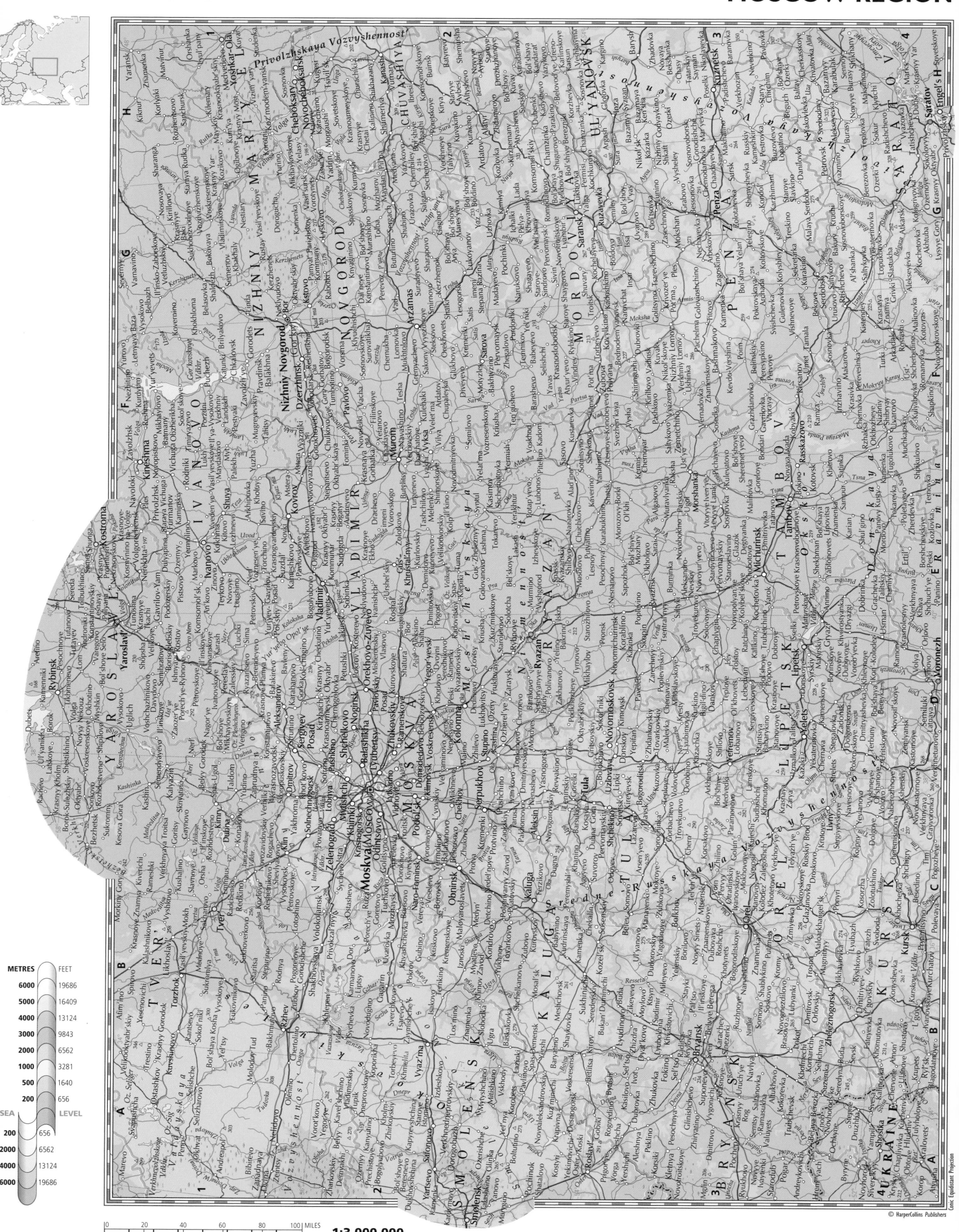

METRES / FEET

METRES		FEET
6000		19686
5000		16409
4000		13124
3000		9843
2000		6562
1000		3281
500		1640
200		656
SEA		LEVEL
200		656
2000		6562
4000		13124
6000		19686

0 20 40 60 80 100 MILES
0 20 40 60 80 100 120 140 160 KM

1:3 000 000

© HarperCollins Publishers

Lambert Conformal Conic Projection

RUSSIAN FEDERATION

BELARUS

BREST

HOMYEL'

KURS'K

BELGOROD

KHARKIV

DONETS'K

Sea of Azov

SUMY

CHERNIHIV

POLTAVA

DNIPROPETROVS'K

ZAPORIZHZHYA

RIVNE

KYIV

CHERKASY

KIROVOHRAD

HERSON

MYKOLAYIV

ODESA

Odesa (Odessa)

BLACK SEA

ZHYTOMYR

VINNYTSYA

MOLDOVA (MOLDAVIA)

Chişinău

Tiraspol

Tighina

KHMEL'NYTS'KYY

CHERNIVTSI

TERNOPIL'

IVANO-FRANKIVS'K

L'VIV

VOLYN'

CARPATHIAN MTS

ROMANIA

Kyiv (Kiev)

Kharkiv

Donets'k

Mariupol'

Kherson

Mykolayiv

Dnipropetrovs'k

Zaporizhzhya

Kremenchuk

Kirovohrad

Kursk

Belgorod

Sumy

Conic Equidistant Projection

© HarperCollins Publishers

METRES	FEET
6000	19686
5000	16409
4000	13124
3000	9843
2000	6562
1000	3281
500	1640
200	656
SEA LEVEL	
200	656
2000	6562
4000	13124
6000	19686

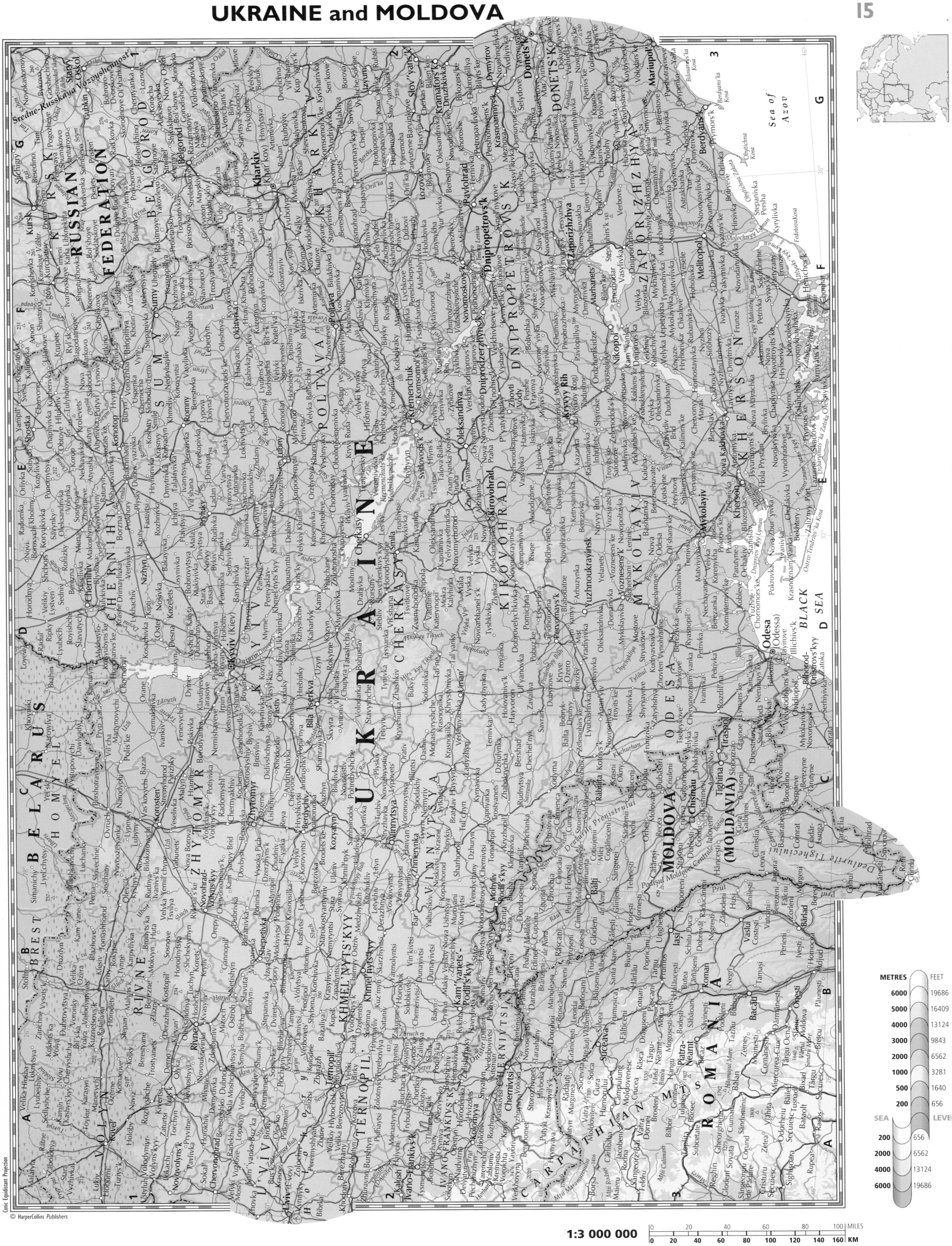

1:3 000 000

0   20   40   60   80   100 MILES
0 20 40 60 80 100 120 140 160 KM

NORWAY

SOGN OG FJORDANE

HORDALAND

Bergen

Florø, Naustdal, Førde, Stongfjorden, Askvoll, Sande, Hoyanger, Vadheim, Lavik, Masfjorden, Vik, Modalen, Fedje, Rysjedal, Eivindvik, Oppedal, Tjeldstø, Lindás, Dale, Hyllestad, Sula, Hardbakke, Steinsland, Stamnes, Storø, Store Sotra, Husøy, Kleppestø, Fitjar, Usken, Brennes, Bømla, Langevág, Sveio, Stord, Sunde, Grindafjord, Leirvik, Kopervik, Karmøy, Haugesund, Utsira, Akrehamn, Skudeneshavn, Kvitsøy

NORTH SEA

ATLANTIC OCEAN

Shetland Is
Hermla Ness, Unst, Fetlar, Yell, Whalsay, Out Skerries, Yell Sd., Lerwick, Isle of Noss, Bressay, Scalloway, Mainland, Sumburgh Head, Isbister, The Faither, Hillswick, Papa Stour, Sumburgh, Fair Isle, Foula

Orkney Is
North Ronaldsay, Sanday, Stronsay, Papa Westray, Eday, Rousay, Shapinsay, Kirkwall, Westray, Birsay, Stromness, Ronaldsay Firth, South Ronaldsay, St Margaret's Hope, Burwick, Duncansby, Hoy, Stroma, Head, South Walls

FAEROES (FØROYAR) (Denmark)
Eiði, Mikladalur, Fuglafjørður, Klaksvík, Strøymoy, Vestmanna, Borðoy, Skopunarfjørður, Sandoy, Eysturoy, Tvøroyri, Tórshavn, Vágar, Skúvoy, Dimunarfjørður, Hvalbø, Húsavik, Mykines, Suðuroy, Sumba

Rona, Sule Sgeir, Sula Sgeir, Sule Skerry, Roma

SCOTLAND

GRAMPIAN MOUNTAINS

Aberdeen, Fraserburgh, Rattray Head, Peterhead, Rosehearty, Macduff, Banff, Turriff, Mintlaw, Ellon, Newburgh, Lossiemouth, Buckie, Keith, Huntly, Inverurie, Dyce, Elgin, Dufftown, Oldmeldrum, Westhill, Forres, Grantown-on-Spey, Nairn, Ballater, Banchory, Stonehaven, Inverbervie, Kirriemuir, Braemar, Brechin, Montrose, Aviemore, Kingussie, Blair Atholl, Kirkcaldy Firth of Forth, Pitlochry, Arbroath, Forfar, Broughty Ferry, Dundee, St Andrews, Dunkeld, Blairgowrie, Crieff, Perth, Glenrothes, Crail, Anstruther, Callander, Leven, North Berwick, Dunfermline, Haddington, Stirling, Falkirk, Edinburgh, Dunbar, Eyemouth, Glasgow, Paisley, Greenock, Helensburgh, Dumbarton, Rothesay

Cape Wrath, Durness, Tongue, Kinbrace, Helmsdale, Brora, Scourie, Lochinver, Lairg, Golspie, Tain, Dornoch, Wick, Thurso, John o' Groats, Dunnet Head, Pentland Firth

Loch Ness, Inverness, Beauly, Loch Maree, Gairloch, Applecross, Stromeferry, Kyle of Lochalsh, Fort Augustus, Fort William, Mallaig, Arisaig, Ben Nevis

Skye, Portree, Raasay, Broadford, Cuillin Hills, Rum (Rhum), Eigg, Muck, Canna, Coll, Tiree, Mull, Tobermory, Oban, Iona, Colonsay, Jura, Islay, Campbeltown

Outer Hebrides, Lewis, Stornoway, Butt of Lewis, Tarbert (An Tairbeart), Harris, North Uist (Uibhist a Tuath), Benbecula (Beinn na Faoghla), South Uist (Uibhist a Deas), Barra (Eilean Bharraigh), Sound of Barra, Flannan Is, St Kilda

Little Minch, The Minch

at the same scale
Rockall

METRES FEET
6000 19686
5000 16409
4000 13124
3000 9843
2000 6562
1000 3281
500 1640
200 656
SEA LEVEL
200 656
2000 6562
4000 13124
6000 19686

Conic Equidistant Projection

© HarperCollinsPublishers

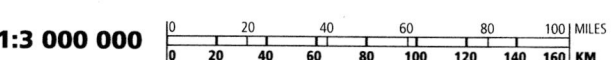

NORTH SEA

DENMARK

NETHERLANDS

BELGIUM

GERMANY

FRANCE

LUXEMBOURG

SWITZERLAND

ITALY

NORDRHEIN-WESTFALEN

NIEDERSACHSEN

SCHLESWIG-HOLSTEIN

MECKLENBURG-VORPOMMERN

BRANDENBURG

SACHSEN-ANHALT

THÜRINGEN

HESSEN

RHEINLAND-PFALZ

SAARLAND

BAYERN

BADEN-WÜRTTEMBERG

LORRAINE

ALSACE

CHAMPAGNE-ARDENNE

FRANCHE-COMTÉ

BOURGOGNE

RHÔNE-ALPES

VLAANDEREN

ZEELAND

NOORD-BRABANT

LIMBURG

NOORD-HOLLAND

ZUID-HOLLAND

UTRECHT

GELDERLAND

OVERIJSSEL

FLEVOLAND

DRENTHE

GRONINGEN

FRIESLAND

Amsterdam, Rotterdam, 's-Gravenhage (Den Haag) (The Hague), Haarlem, Utrecht, Eindhoven, Tilburg, Groningen, Leeuwarden, Arnhem, Nijmegen, Breda, Dordrecht, Leiden, Delft

Bruxelles, Antwerpen, Gent, Brugge, Oostende (Ostende), Namur, Liège, Charleroi, Mons, Hasselt, Maastricht, Aachen

Hamburg, Bremen, Hannover, Bremerhaven, Oldenburg, Osnabrück, Münster, Bielefeld, Dortmund, Essen, Duisburg, Düsseldorf, Köln, Bonn, Wuppertal, Kassel, Göttingen, Frankfurt am Main, Mainz, Wiesbaden, Mannheim, Heidelberg, Karlsruhe, Stuttgart, München (Munich), Nürnberg, Würzburg, Regensburg, Augsburg, Freiburg im Breisgau, Ulm, Kiel, Lübeck, Rostock, Schwerin, Magdeburg, Leipzig, Erfurt

Strasbourg, Metz, Nancy, Reims, Dijon, Besançon, Mulhouse, Colmar

LUXEMBOURG

Zürich, Bern, Basel, Genève (Geneva), Lausanne, Luzern (Lucerne), St Gallen, LIECHTENSTEIN

AUSTRIA (AUS), TIROL, VORARLBERG, Innsbruck

Bolzano, TRENTINO-ALTO ADIGE, FRIULI-VENEZIA GIULIA, VENETO, LOMBARDIA

Ostfriesische Inseln, Nordfriesische Inseln, Helgoland, Sylt, Amrum, Föhr, Borkum, Norderney, Juist, Terschelling, Vlieland, Texel, Ameland, Schiermonnikoog, Waddenzee, IJsselmeer

METRES	FEET
6000	19686
5000	16409
4000	13124
3000	9843
2000	6562
1000	3281
500	1640
200	656
SEA LEVEL	
200	656
2000	6562
4000	13124
6000	19686

Conic Equidistant Projection

© HarperCollins Publishers

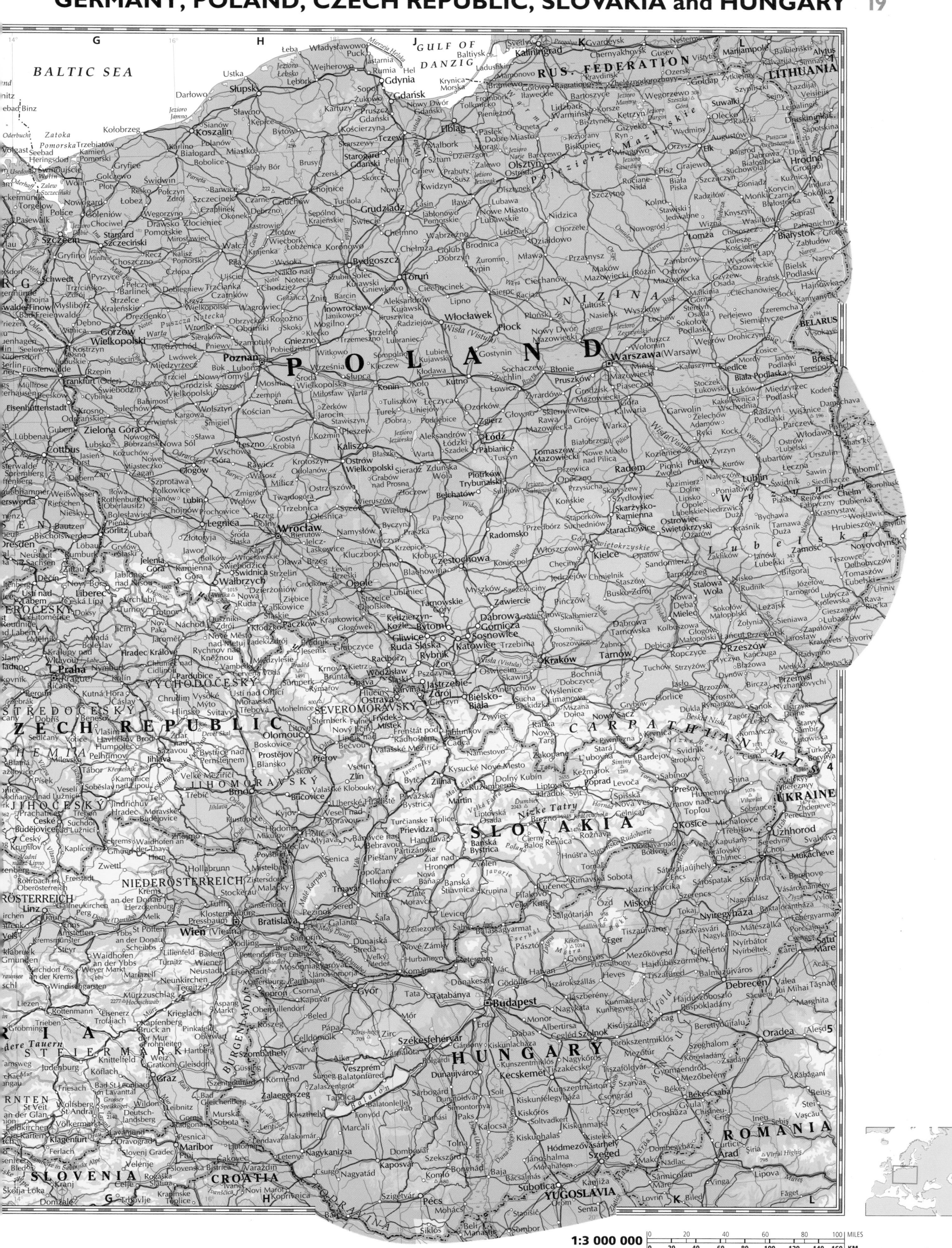

1:3 000 000

0   20   40   60   80   100 MILES
0 20 40 60 80 100 120 140 160 KM

1:3 000 000

METRES | FEET
6000 | 19686
5000 | 16409
4000 | 13124
3000 | 9843
2000 | 6562
1000 | 3281
500 | 1640
200 | 656

SEA | LEVEL

200 | 656
2000 | 6562
4000 | 13124
6000 | 19686

Lambert Conformal Conic Projection

© HarperCollinsPublishers

CANARY ISLANDS
(Spain)

1:3 000 000

| 0 | 20 | 40 | 60 | 80 | 100 MILES |
| 0 | 20 40 60 80 100 120 140 160 KM |

at the same scale

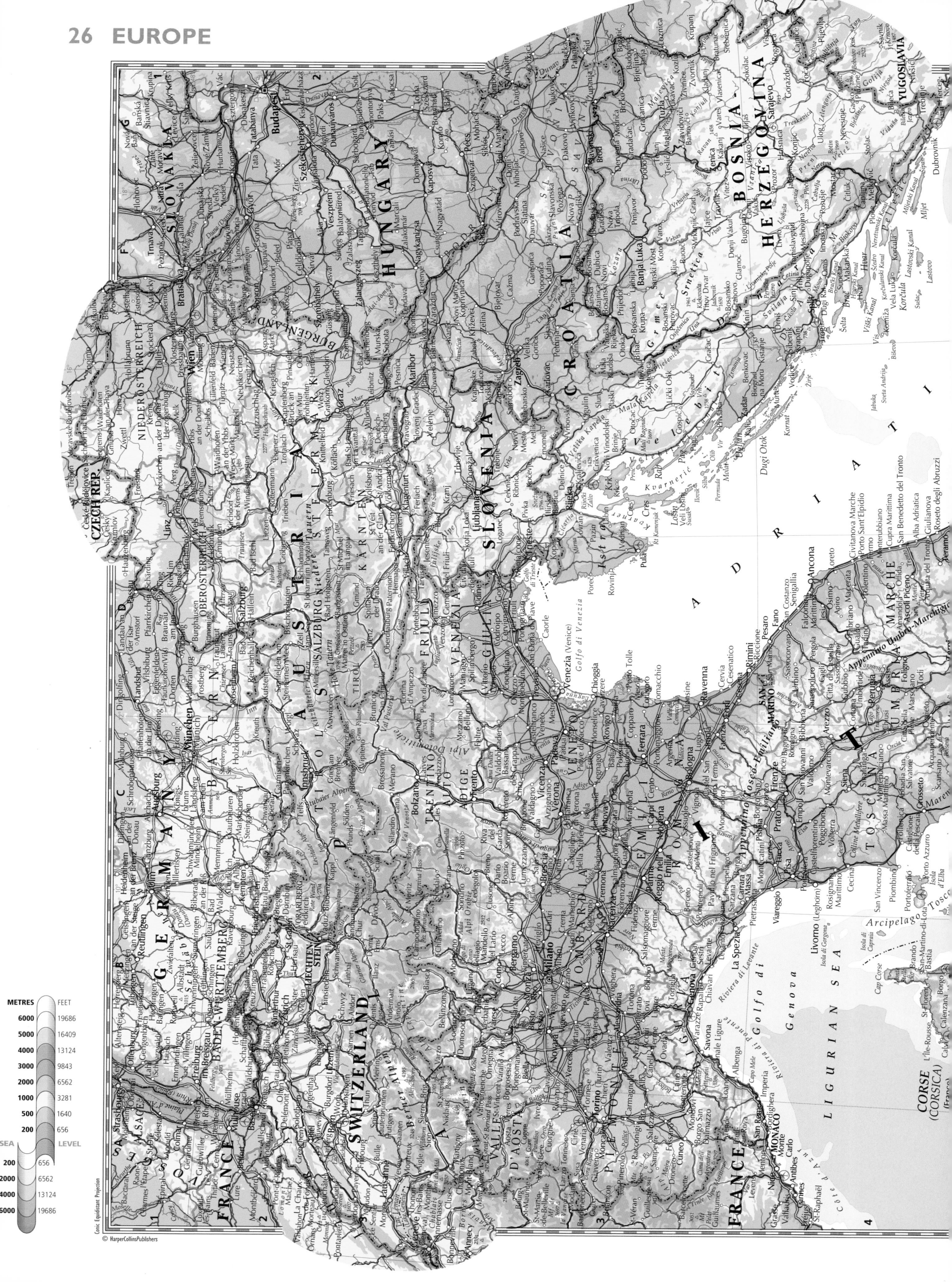

METRES   FEET
6000   19686
5000   16409
4000   13124
3000   9843
2000   6562
1000   3281
500   1640
200   656

SEA   LEVEL

200   656
2000   6562
4000   13124
6000   19686

Conic Equidistant Projection

© HarperCollinsPublishers

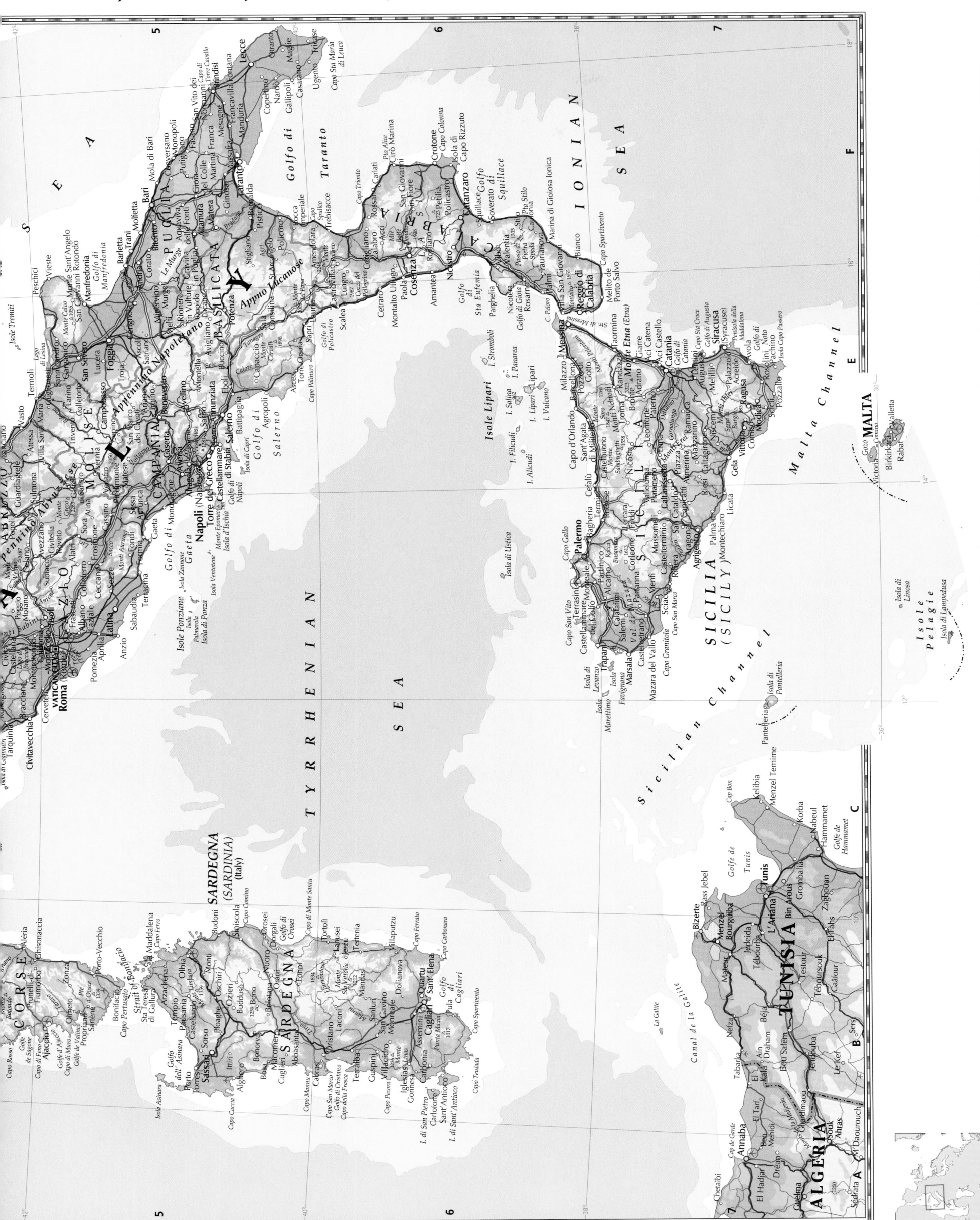

ADRIATIC SEA

Lecce
Otranto
Capo di Leuca
Maglie
Santa Maria di Leuca
Brindisi
Mesagne
Francavilla Fontana
Manduria
Gallipoli
Nardò
Copertino
Ugento
Taranto
Golfo di Taranto

Bari
Mola di Bari
Monopoli
Conversano
Putignano
Barletta
Trani
Molfetta
Corato
Andria
Gravina in Puglia
Altamura
Matera
Le Murge
PUGLIA

Crotone
Capo Colonna
Ciro Marina
Rossano
Cariati
Isola di Capo Rizzuto
San Giovanni in Fiore
Catanzaro
Squillace
Golfo di Squillace
Soverato
CALABRIA

IONIAN SEA

Policoro
Pisticci
Policoro
Stigliano
Rotondella
BASILICATA
Appno Lucanese
Potenza
Tricarico

Cosenza
Paola
Amantea
Montalto Uffugo
Golfo di Sta Eufemia
Pizzo
Nicotera
Golfo di Gioia
Rosarno
Palmi
Villa San Giovanni
Reggio di Calabria
Melito de Porto Salvo
Capo Spartivento
Marina di Gioiosa Ionica
Stilo
Monte Etna
Taurianova
Bianco

Messina
Milazzo
Barcellona
Patti
Sant'Agata di Militello
Capo d'Orlando
Isole Lipari
I. Salina
I. Lipari
Lipari
I. Vulcano
I. Panarea
I. Stromboli
I. Filicudi
I. Alicudi

Taormina
Giarre
Acireale
Aci Castello
Catania
Golfo di Catania
Augusta
Siracusa (Syracuse)
Avola
Noto
Capo Passero
Pachino
Pozzallo
Modica
Ragusa
Scicli
Vittoria
Comiso
Gela
Licata

Troina
Adrano
Bronte
Randazzo
Paternò
Caltagirone
Piazza Armerina
Enna
Caltanissetta
Mazzarino
Niscemi

SICILIA (SICILY)

Palermo
Monreale
Bagheria
Termini Imerese
Cefalù
Castelbuono
Petralia

Trapani
Erice
Marsala
Mazara del Vallo
Castelvetrano
Campobello
Sciacca
Menfi
Ribera
Agrigento
Canicattì
Palma di Montechiaro
Val di Mazara
Castellammare del Golfo
Alcamo
Salemi
Calatafimi
Partanna
Capo San Marco
Capo Granitola

Isola di Levanzo
Isola di Marettimo
Favignana
Isola di Pantelleria
Pantelleria

Malta Channel
Sicilian Channel

MALTA
Birkirkara
Valletta
Victoria
Rabat
Gozo
Comino

Isola di Linosa
Isola di Lampedusa
Isole Pelagie

TYRRHENIAN SEA

Isole Ponziane
Isola Ponza
Palmarola
Isola di Ventotene
Isola di Ponza
Isola di Ustica

Napoli (Naples)
Torre del Greco
Castellammare di Stabia
Salerno
Golfo di Salerno
Agropoli
Battipaglia
Capri
Isola di Capri
Ischia
Isola d'Ischia
Golfo di Gaeta
Gaeta
Formia
CAMPANIA
Caserta
Avellino
Benevento
Sapri
Scalea
Cetraro
Cirella
Capo Palinuro

MOLISE
Campobasso
Termoli
Vasto
Isole Tremiti
Isole di Lesina
San Severo
Foggia
Lucera
Manfredonia
Monte Sant'Angelo
San Giovanni Rotondo
Peschici
Vieste

ABRUZZO
Appennino Abruzzese
Atessa
Guardiagrele
Sulmona
Avezzano

LAZIO
VATICANO
Roma
Civitavecchia
Tarquinia
Anzio
Latina
Frosinone
Sabaudia
Terracina
Cervéteri
Pomezia

SARDEGNA (SARDINIA) (Italy)
Sassari
Alghero
Oristano
Nuoro
Olbia
Cagliari
Golfo di Cagliari
Carbonia
Iglesias
Sant'Antioco
Capo Spartivento
Budoni
Siniscola
Orosei
Dorgali
Tortolì
Lanusei
Tertenia
Villaputzu
Muravera
Maddalena
La Maddalena
Santa Teresa di Gallura
Stretto di Bonifacio
Palau

CORSE
Aléria
Ajaccio
Bonifacio
Porto-Vecchio
Propriano
Sartène

TUNISIA
Tunis
Bizerte
L'Ariana
Nabeul
Hammamet
Golfe de Tunis
Golfe de Hammamet
Menzel Temime
Korba
Korba
Nabeul
Grombalia
Menzel Bourguiba
Béja
Cap Bon
Kelibia
Téboursouk
Testour
Medjez el Bab
Zaghouan

ALGERIA
Annaba
El Tarf
Souk Ahras

Canal de la Galite
La Galite

1:3 000 000

| 0 | 20 | 40 | 60 | 80 | 100 | MILES |
| 0 | 20 | 40 | 60 | 80 | 100 | 120 | 140 | 160 | KM |

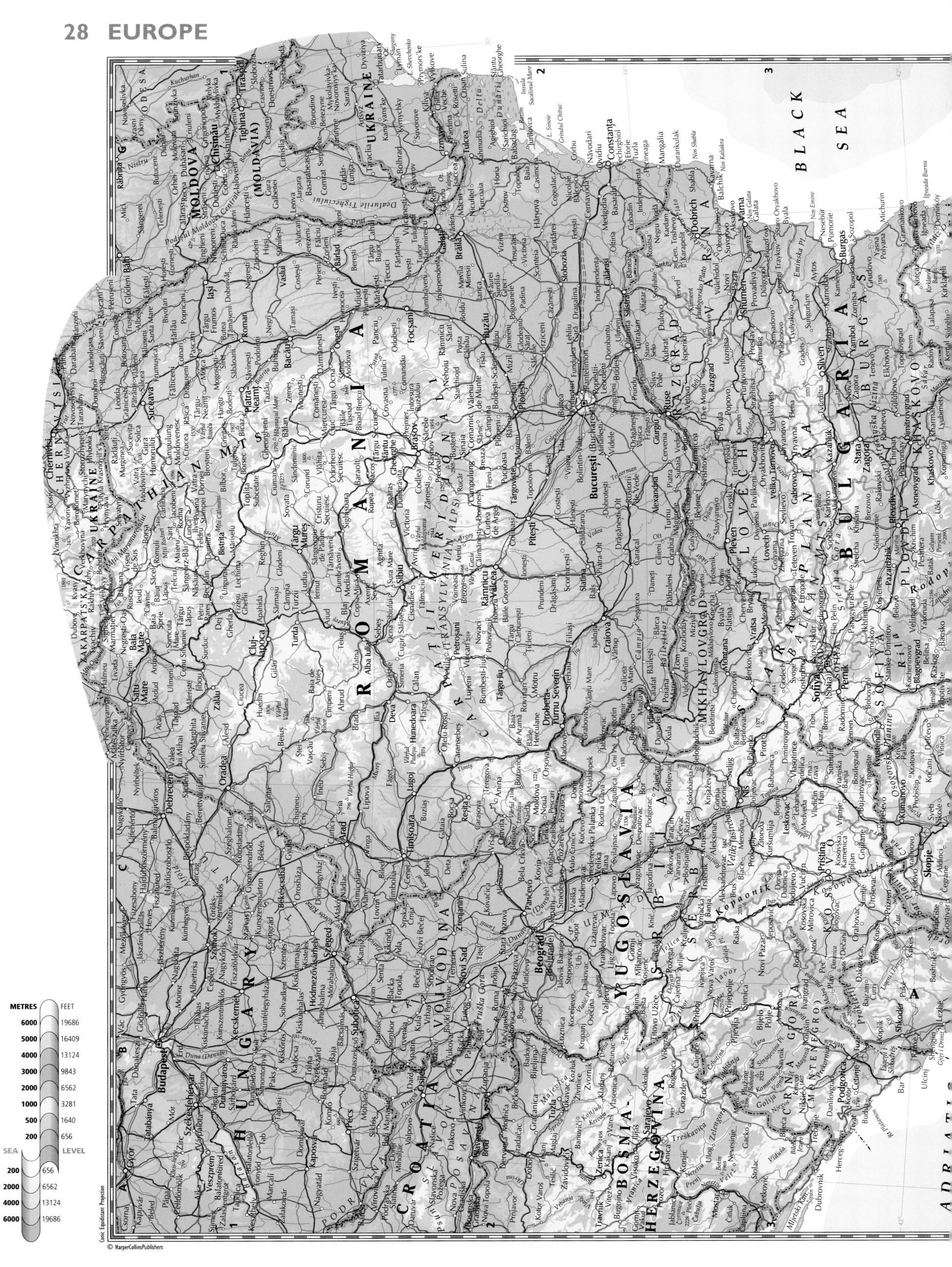

METRES FEET
6000 19686
5000 16409
4000 13124
3000 9843
2000 6562
1000 3281
500 1640
200 656

SEA LEVEL

200 656
2000 6562
4000 13124
6000 19686

Conic Equidistant Projection

© HarperCollins Publishers

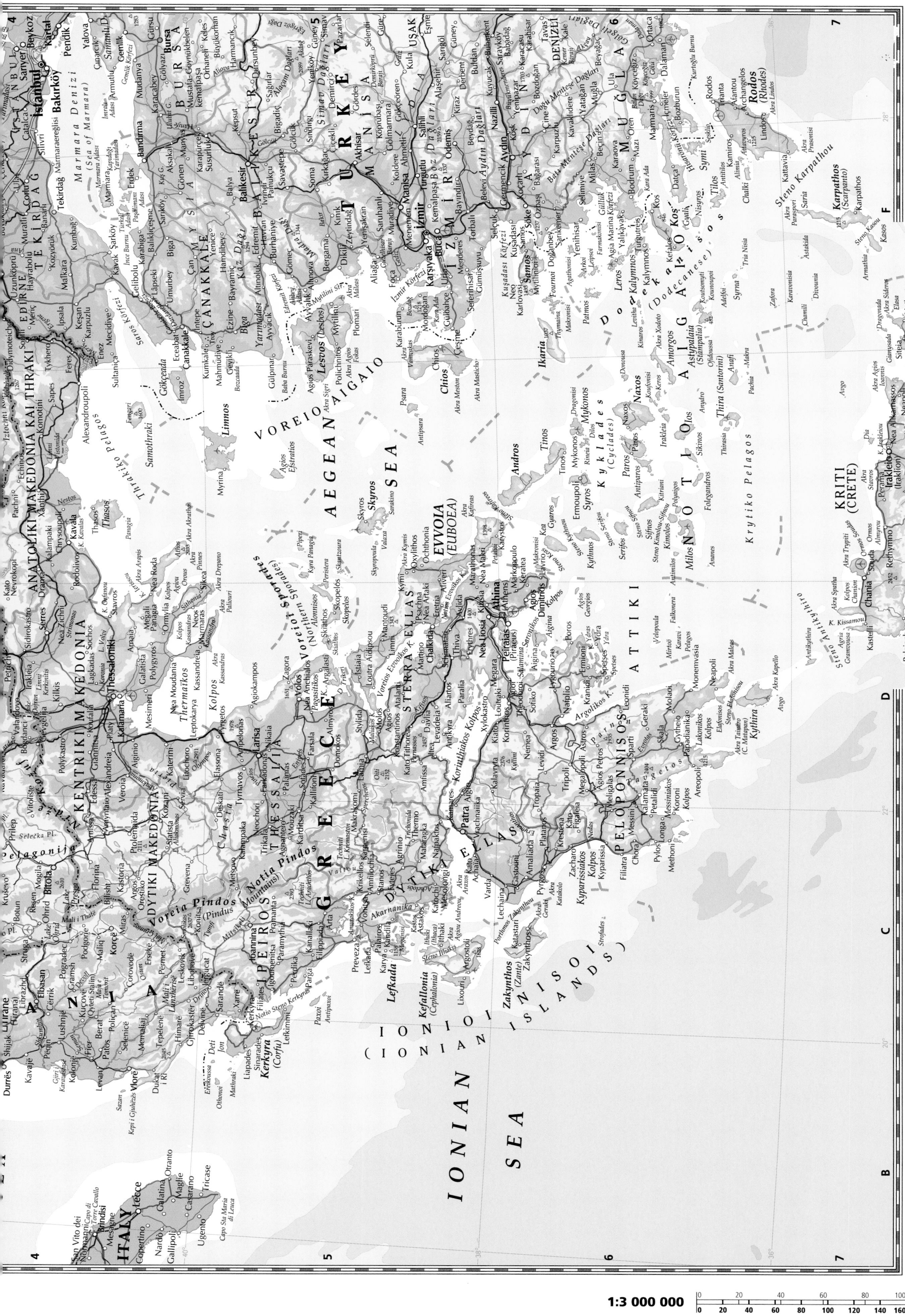

1:3 000 000

MILES
0 20 40 60 80 100

KM
0 20 40 60 80 100 120 140 160

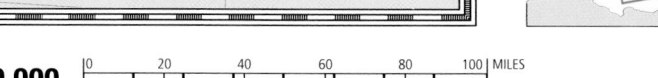

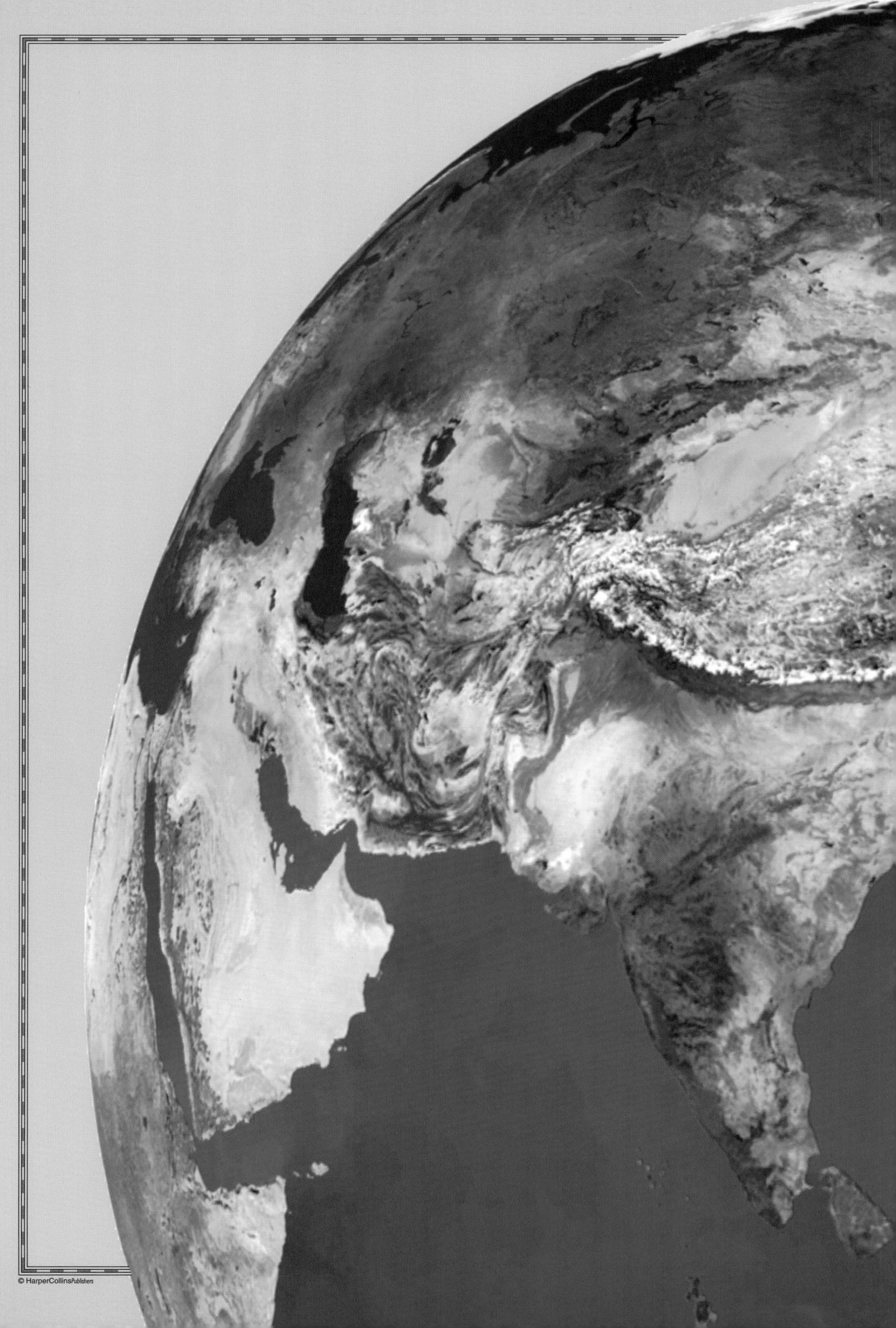

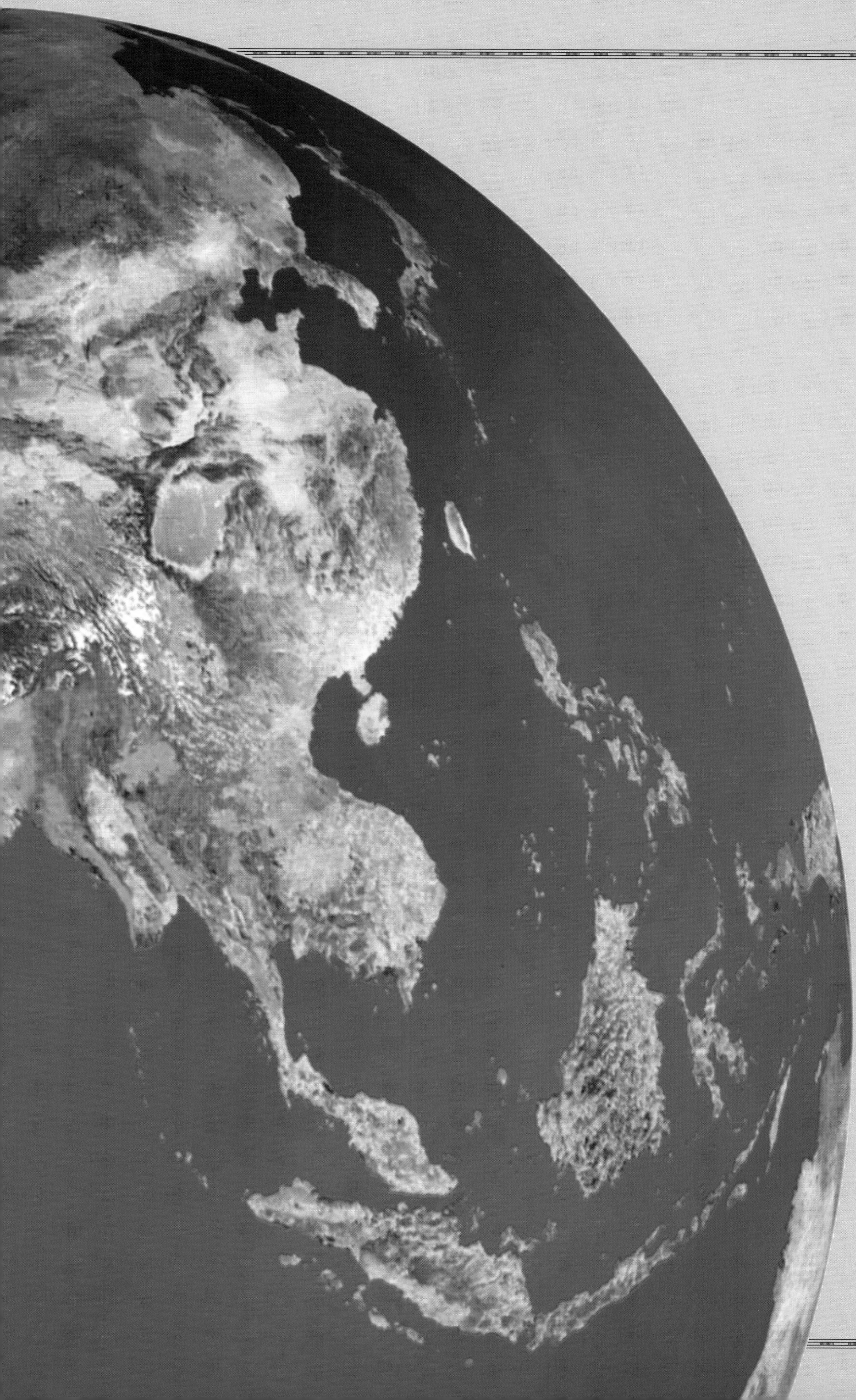

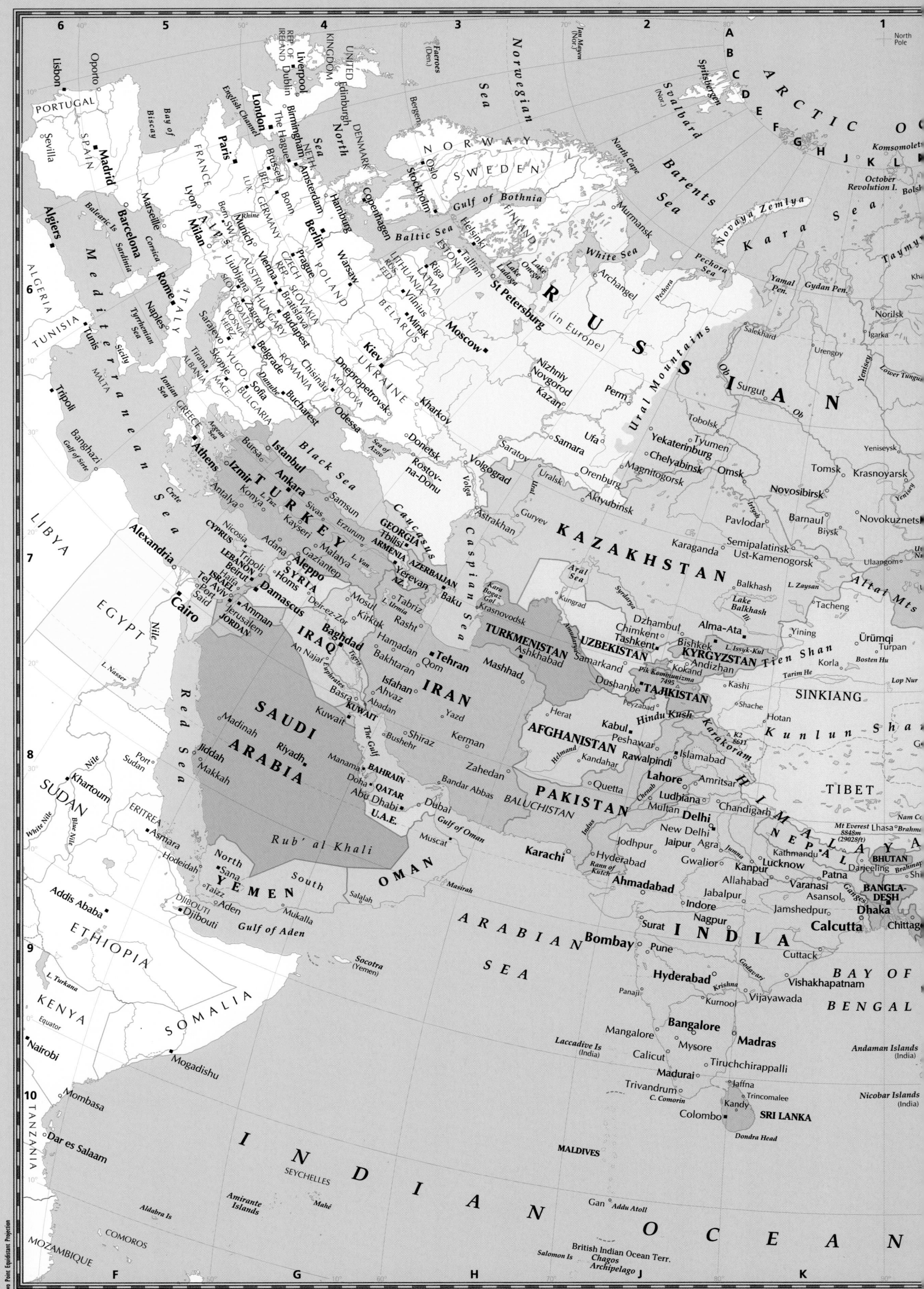

U
T
S
R
Q
P

2　**3**　**4**　**5**　**6**

Wrangel I.
De Long Str.
East Siberian Sea
Chukchi Sea
New Siberia Islands
Kotelnyy I.
Bolshoy Lyakhov I.
New Siberia I.
Medvezhi Is
Arctic Circle
St Lawrence I. (U.S.A.)
St Matthew I. (U.S.A.)
Pribilof Is (U.S.A.)
Unalaska I.
Aleutian Islands
Andreanof Is
Atka I.
Midway Is (U.S.A.)

Zemlya
Laptev Sea
Tiksi
Olenek
Indigirka
Kazachye
Druzhina
Egvekinot
Gulf of Anadyr
Anadyr
Ust-Penzhina
Egvekinot

7

BERING SEA

dvik
Verkhoyansk Ra.
Lena
Zhigansk
Yakutsk
Ust-Kut
Nizhneangarsk
Bratsk
Lena
Kazachye
Ola
Kolyma Range
Ust-Penzhina
Korf
Ola
Magadan
Orotukan
Susuman
Kamchatka
BERING SEA
Petropavlovsk-Kamchatskiy

F
E
D
E
R
A
T
I
O
N

Mirnyy
Olekminsk
Stanovoy Range
Tynda
Magdagachi
Belogorsk
Komsomolsk-na-Amure
Khabarovsk
Ayan
Okhotsk
Sea of Okhotsk
Okhyabrskiy
Paramushir
Kuril Islands
Simushir

BERIA
Bodaybo
Lake Baykal
Chita
Borzya
Blagoveshchensk
Heihe
Nenjiang
Amur
Lssuri
La Pérouse Str.
Korsakov
Sovetskaya Gavan
Sakhalin
Urup
Iturup
Kunashir

Ulan-Ude
Darhan
Erdenet
Ulan Bator
Hovsgol Nuur
Hailar
Hulun Nur
Choybalsan
Tamsagbulag
Jargalant
Qiqihar
Harbin
MANCHURIA
Jilin
Changchun
Vladivostok
Nakhodka
Sapporo
Hokkaido
Hakodate
Akita
Sendai
Niigata

NGOLIA
MONGOLIA
Gobi Desert
Saynshand
Saikhand
INNER MONGOLIA
Shenyang
Fushun
Anshan
NORTH KOREA
Pyongyang
Sea of Japan
Honshu
Kanazawa
Tokyo
Yokohama
Kyoto
Nagoya
Osaka
Hachijo-jima

Dalandzadgad
Baotou
Jining
Zhangjiakou
Jinzhou
Dalian
Tianjin
Korea Bay
Yantai
Inchon
Seoul
Taegu
Pusan
Kobe
Kita-Kyushu
Shikoku
Tori-shima (Japan)

Yinchuan
Beijing
Huang He
Zibo
Qingdao
SOUTH KOREA
Mokpo
Hiroshima
Fukuoka
Kyushu
Nagasaki
Kagoshima
Ogasawara-shoto (Japan)

Xining
Taiyuan
Jinan
Yellow Sea
Lianyungang
Kazan-retto (Japan)

hu
Lanzhou
Zhengzhou
Xuzhou
Shanghai
East China Sea
Amami O-shima

ai Hu
Xi'an
Nanjing
Ningbo
Ryukyu Islands
Daito-jima (Japan)
Pagan
Northern Mariana Is (U.S.A.)

CHINA
Wuhan
Nanchong
Hangzhou
Wenzhou
Okinawa (Japan)
Rota
Saipan
Tinian

Chengdu
Chang Jiang
Poyang Hu
Nanchang
Fuzhou
Guam (U.S.A.)

Chongqing
Dongting Hu
Changsha
Hengyang
Taipei
TAIWAN
Gaferut

Guiyang
Xiamen
Taiwan Strait
Kaohsiung
Pikelot
Hall Is

Guangzhou
Liuzhou
Macau (Port.)
Hong Kong
Batan Is
Luzon Strait
C. Engaño
Caroline Islands
Chuuk
Nomoi Is

Kunming
Nanning
Zhanjiang
Laoag
Luzon
FED. STATES OF MICRONESIA

ndalay
Hanoi
Haiphong
Hainan I.
Gulf of Tongking
PHILIPPINES
Quezon City
Yap

AR A)
Chiang Mai
Hue
Da Nang
South China Sea
Manila
Naga
Samar
PALAU
Equator

goon
Vientiane
LAOS
VIETNAM
Mindoro
Panay
Cebu
Leyte
Masbate
New Ireland

THAILAND
Nakhon Ratchasima
Mekong
Iloilo
Negros
Dipolog
Surigao
Admiralty Is

Thon Buri
Bangkok
CAMBODIA
Nha Trang
Palawan
Mindanao
Davao
New Britain
Bismarck Sea
Papua

ergui Arch
Mergui
Phnom Penh
Ho Chi Minh City
Sulu Sea
Zamboanga
Talaud Is
Jayapura
NEW GUINEA
Solomon Sea

Isthmus of Kra
Nakhon Thammarat
Gulf of Thailand
Mui Bai Bung
Kinabalu 4094
Sulu Sea
Sandakan
Celebes Sea
Sangir
Halmahera
Biak
IRIAN JAYA
New Guinea
G. of Papua
Port Moresby

George Town
Kota Baharu
MALAYSIA
Kota Kinabalu
Bandar Seri Begawan
SABAH
Manado
Molucca Sea
Manokwari
Yapen
Puncak Jaya 5029
Coral Sea

Ipoh
PEN. MALAYSIA
BRUNEI
SARAWAK
Simanggang
Celebes Sea
Moluccas
Obi
Seram Sea
Misoöl
Fakfak
Seram
Aru Is
Torres Strait
C. York
Cairns
Great Barrier Reef

Medan
Kuala Lumpur
SINGAPORE
Kuching
Borneo
Peleng
Palu
Sula Is
Buru
Trangan
Dolak I.

Str. of Malacca
Pekanbaru
Pontianak
KALIMANTAN
Balikpapan
Sulawesi
Parepare
Banjarmasin
Macassar Strait
Buton
Banda Sea
Kai Is
Tanimbar Is
Yamdena

Batu Is
Padang
Lingga
Bangka
Belitung
Jakarta
Ujung Pandang
G. of Boni
Damar
Babar
Arafura Sea

Siberut
Sipura
Selatan
Java Sea
Semarang
Madura
Wetar
Leti Is
Dili
Melville I.
Darwin
C. Arnhem
Gulf of Carpentaria
Coral Sea

entawai Islands
Bengkulu
Telukbetung
Palembang
Sumatra
INDONESIA
Flores Sea
Flores
Endeh
Timor
Kupang

Enggano
Sunda Strait
Bandung
Mt Slamet 3428
Surabaya
Surakarta
Bali
Lombok
Sumba
Sawu Sea
Roti
P　**AUSTRALIA**　**Q**

Yogyakarta
Java
Sumbawa
Raba
Sawu

1:30 000 000

0	250	500	750	1000	MILES
0	250	500	750	1000	1250	1500	KM

NORTH PACIFIC OCEAN

Woke I. (U.S.A.)

Tropic of Cancer

8

9

COUNTRY	AREA		POPULATION			Form of Government	Capital City	MAIN LANGUAGES	MAIN RELIGIONS	CURRENCY
	sq ml	sq km	total	density per sq ml	sq km					
AFGHANISTAN	251 825	652 225	18 879 000	75	29	republic	Kabul	Dari, Pushtu, Uzbek, Turkmen	Sunni & Shi'a Muslim	Afghani
ARMENIA	11 506	29 800	3 548 000	308	119	republic	Yerevan	Armenian, Azeri, Russian	Arm. Orthodox, RC, Muslim	Dram
AZERBAIJAN	33 436	86 600	7 472 000	223	86	republic	Baku	Azeri, Armenian, Russian, Lezgian	Shi'a & Sunni Muslim, Russ. and Arm. Orthodox	Manat
BAHRAIN	267	691	9 568 000	35863	13847	monarchy	Manama	Arabic, English	Shi'a & Sunni Muslim, Christian	Dinar
BANGLADESH	55 598	143 998	117 787 000	2119	818	republic	Dhaka	Bengali, Bihari, Hindi, English, local lang.	Muslim, Hindu, Buddhist, Christian	Taka
BHUTAN	18 000	46 620	1 614 000	90	35	monarchy	Thimphu	Dzongkha, Nepali, Assamese, English	Buddhist, Hindu, Muslim	Ngultrum
BRUNEI	2 226	5 765	280 000	126	49	monarchy	Bandar Seri Begawan	Malay, English, Chinese	Muslim, Buddhist, Christian	Dollar (ringgit)
CAMBODIA	69 884	181 000	9 568 000	137	53	monarchy	Phnom Penh	Khmer, Vietnamese	Buddhist, RC, Sunni Muslim	Riel
CHINA	3 691 484	9 560 900	1 208 842 000	327	126	republic	Beijing	Chinese, regional lang.	Confucian, Taoist, Buddhist, Muslim, RC	Yuan
CYPRUS	3 572	9 251	726 000	203	78	republic	Nicosia	Greek, Turkish, English	Greek Orthodox, Muslim	Pound
GEORGIA	26 911	69 700	5 450 000	203	78	republic	Tbilisi	Georgian, Russian, Armenian, Azeri, Ossetian, Abkhaz	Orthodox, Muslim	Lari
Hong Kong	415	1 075	6 061 000	14603	5638	Special Administrative Region of China		Chinese, English	Buddhist, Taoist, Protestant	Dollar
INDIA	1 269 219	3 287 263	918 570 000	724	279	republic	New Delhi	Hindi, English, regional lang.	Hindu, Muslim, Sikh, Christian, Buddhist, Jain	Rupee
INDONESIA	741 102	1 919 445	190 676 000	257	99	republic	Jakarta	Indonesian, local lang.	Muslim, Protestant, RC Hindu, Buddhist	Rupiah
IRAN	636 296	1 648 000	59 778 000	94	36	republic	Tehran	Farsi, Azeri, Kurdish, regional lang.	Shi'a & Sunni Muslim, Baha'i, Christian, Zoroastrian	Rial
IRAQ	169 235	438 317	19 925 000	118	45	republic	Baghdad	Arabic, Kurdish, Turkmen	Shi'a & Sunni Muslim, RC	Dinar
ISRAEL	8 019	20 770	5 399 000	673	260	republic	Jerusalem	Hebrew, Arabic, Yiddish, English	Jewish, Muslim, Christian, Druze	Shekel
JAPAN	145 841	377 727	124 961 000	857	331	monarchy	Tokyo	Japanese	Shintoist, Buddhist, Christian	Yen
JORDAN	34 443	89 206	5 198 000	151	58	monarchy	Amman	Arabic	Sunni & Shi'a Muslim, Christian	Dinar
KAZAKHSTAN	1 049 155	2 717 300	17 027 000	16	6	republic	Alma-Ata	Kazakh, Russian, German, Ukrainian, Uzbek, Tatar	Muslim, Russ. Orthodox, Protestant	Tanga
KUWAIT	6 880	17 818	1 620 000	235	91	monarchy	Kuwait	Arabic	Sunni & Shi'a Muslim, Christian, Hindu	Dinar
KYRGYZSTAN	76 641	198 500	4 473 000	58	23	republic	Bishkek	Kirghiz, Russian, Uzbek	Muslim, Russian Orthodox	Som
LAOS	91 429	236 800	4 742 000	52	20	republic	Vientiane	Lao, local languages	Buddhist, trad. beliefs, RC, Sunni Muslim	Kip
LEBANON	4 036	10 452	2 915 000	722	279	republic	Beirut	Arabic, French, Armenian	Shi'a & Sunni Muslim, Protestant, RC	Pound
MACAU	7	17	403 000	61398	23706	Portuguese terr.	Macau	Chinese, Portuguese	Buddhist, RC, Protestant	Pataca
MALAYSIA	128 559	332 965	20 097 000	156	60	federation	Kuala Lumpur	Malay, English, Chinese, Tamil, local lang.	Muslim, Buddhist, Hindu, Christian, trad. beliefs	Dollar (ringgit)
MALDIVES	115	298	246 000	2138	826	republic	Male	Divehi (Maldivian)	Sunni Muslim	Rufiyaa
MONGOLIA	604 250	1 565 000	2 363 000	4	2	republic	Ulan Bator	Khalka (Mongolian), Kazakh, local lang.	Buddhist, Muslim, trad. beliefs	Tugrik
MYANMAR	261 228	676 577	43 922 000	168	65	republic	Rangoon	Burmese, Shan, Karen, local lang.	Buddhist, Muslim, Protestant, RC	Kyat
NEPAL	56 827	147 181	21 360 000	376	145	monarchy	Kathmandu	Nepali, Maithili, Bhojpuri, English, local lang.	Hindu, Buddhist, Muslim	Rupee
NORTH KOREA	46 540	120 538	23 483 000	505	195	republic	Pyongyang	Korean	Trad. beliefs, Chondoist, Buddhist, Confucian, Taoist	Won
OMAN	105 000	271 950	2 096 000	20	8	monarchy	Muscat	Arabic, Baluchi, Farsi, Swahili, Indian lang.	Muslim,	Rial
PAKISTAN	310 403	803 940	126 467 000	407	157	republic	Islamabad	Urdu, Punjabi, Sindhi, Pushtu, English	Muslim, Christian, Hindu	Rupee
PALAU	192	497	17 000	89	34	republic	Koror	Palauan, English	RC, Protestant, trad.beliefs	US dollar
PHILIPPINES	115 831	300 000	68 624 000	592	229	republic	Manila	English, Filipino, Cebuano, local lang.	RC, Aglipayan, Muslim, Protestant	Peso
QATAR	4 416	11 437	593 000	134	52	monarchy	Doha	Arabic, Indian lang.	Muslim, Christian, Hindu	Riyal
RUSSIAN FEDERATION	6 592 849	17 075 400	148 673 000	23	9	republic	Moscow	Russian, Tatar, Ukrainian, local lang.	Russ. Orthodox, Muslim, other Christian, Jewish	Rouble
RUSSIAN FEDERATION (IN ASIA)	5 065 506	13 119 600	41 755 000	8	3					
SAUDI ARABIA	849 425	2 200 000	17 451 000	21	8	monarchy	Riyadh	Arabic	Sunni & Shi'a Muslim	Riyal
SINGAPORE	247	639	2 930 000	11876	4585	republic	Singapore	Chinese, English, Malay, Tamil	Buddhist, Taoist, Muslim, Christian, Hindu	Dollar
SOUTH KOREA	38 330	99 274	44 453 000	1160	448	republic	Seoul	Korean	Buddhist, Protestant, RC, Confucian, trad. beliefs	Won
SRI LANKA	25 332	65 610	17 865 000	705	272	republic	Colombo	Sinhalese, Tamil, English	Buddhist, Hindu, Muslim, RC	Rupee
SYRIA	71 498	185 180	13 844 000	194	75	republic	Damascus	Arabic, Kurdish, Armenian	Muslim, Christian	Pound
TAIWAN	13 969	36 179	21 074 000	1509	582	republic	Taipei	Chinese, local lang.	Buddhist, Taoist, Confucian, Christian	Dollar
TAJIKISTAN	55 251	143 100	5 933 000	107	41	republic	Dushanbe	Tajik, Uzbek, Russian	Muslim	Rouble
THAILAND	198 115	513 115	59 396 000	300	116	monarchy	Bangkok	Thai, Lao, Chinese, Malay, Mon-Khmer lang.	Buddhist, Muslim	Baht
TURKEY	300 948	779 452	60 576 000	201	78	republic	Ankara	Turkish, Kurdish	Sunni & Shi'a Muslim	Lira
TURKMENISTAN	188 456	488 100	4 010 000	21	8	republic	Ashkhabad	Turkmen, Russian	Muslim	Manat
UNITED ARAB EMIRATES	30 000	77 700	1 861 000	62	24	federation	Abu Dhabi	Arabic, English, Hindi, Urdu, Farsi	Sunni & Shi'a Muslim, Christian	Dirham
UZBEKISTAN	172 742	447 400	22 633 000	131	51	republic	Tashkent	Uzbek, Russian, Tajik, Kazakh	Muslim, Russ.Orthodox	Som
VIETNAM	127 246	329 565	72 510 000	570	220	republic	Hanoi	Vietnamese, Thai, Khmer, Chinese, local lang.	Buddhist, Taoist, RC, Cao Dai, Hoa Hao	Dong
YEMEN	203 850	527 968	12 672 000	62	24	republic	Sana	Arabic	Sunni & Shi'a Muslim	Dinar, rial

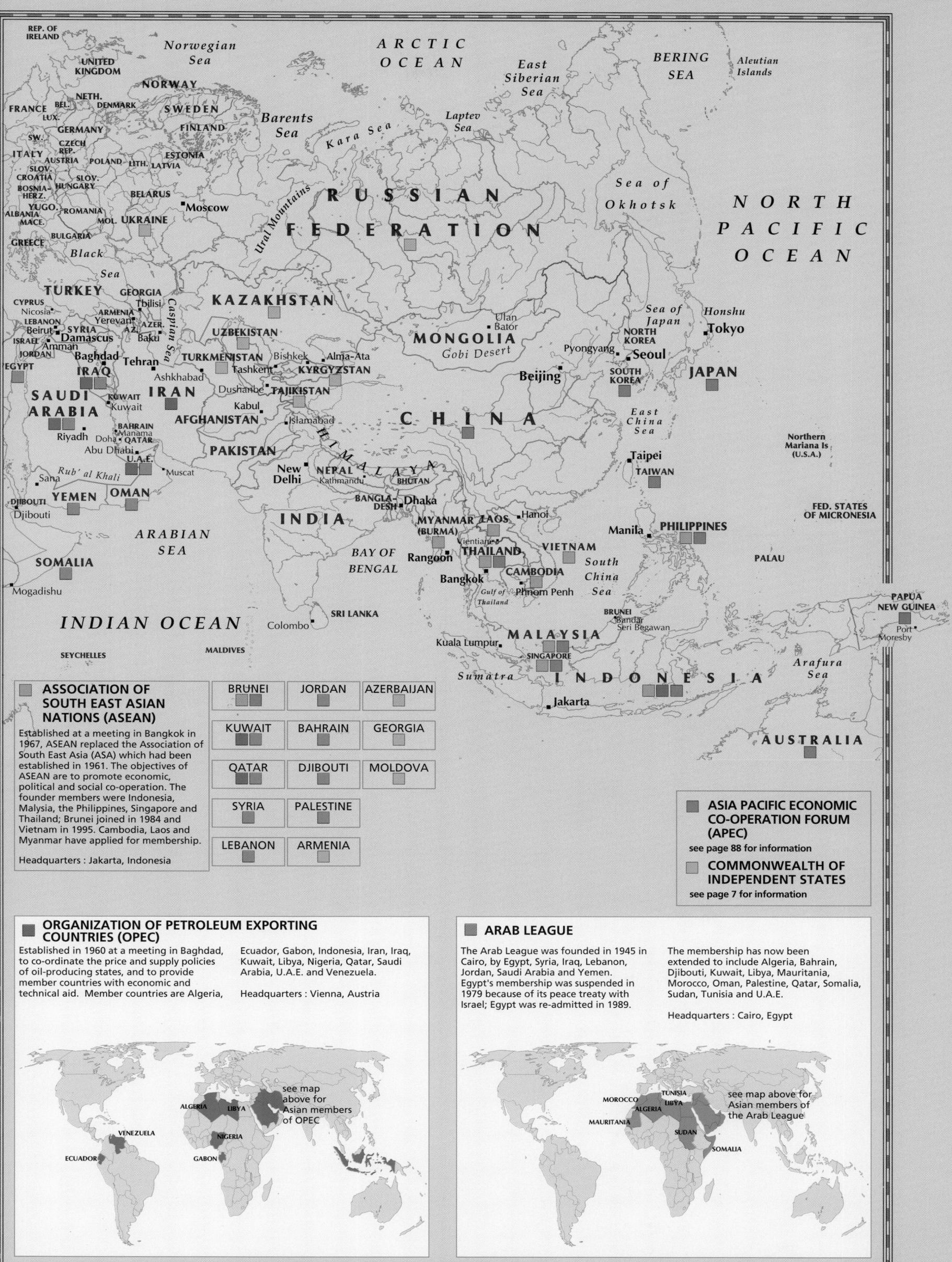

ASSOCIATION OF SOUTH EAST ASIAN NATIONS (ASEAN)

Established at a meeting in Bangkok in 1967, ASEAN replaced the Association of South East Asia (ASA) which had been established in 1961. The objectives of ASEAN are to promote economic, political and social co-operation. The founder members were Indonesia, Malysia, the Philippines, Singapore and Thailand; Brunei joined in 1984 and Vietnam in 1995. Cambodia, Laos and Myanmar have applied for membership.

Headquarters : Jakarta, Indonesia

BRUNEI	JORDAN	AZERBAIJAN
KUWAIT	BAHRAIN	GEORGIA
QATAR	DJIBOUTI	MOLDOVA
SYRIA	PALESTINE	
LEBANON	ARMENIA	

ASIA PACIFIC ECONOMIC CO-OPERATION FORUM (APEC)

see page 88 for information

COMMONWEALTH OF INDEPENDENT STATES

see page 7 for information

ORGANIZATION OF PETROLEUM EXPORTING COUNTRIES (OPEC)

Established in 1960 at a meeting in Baghdad, to co-ordinate the price and supply policies of oil-producing states, and to provide member countries with economic and technical aid. Member countries are Algeria, Ecuador, Gabon, Indonesia, Iran, Iraq, Kuwait, Libya, Nigeria, Qatar, Saudi Arabia, U.A.E. and Venezuela.

Headquarters : Vienna, Austria

ALGERIA LIBYA see map above for Asian members of OPEC
VENEZUELA
NIGERIA
ECUADOR GABON

ARAB LEAGUE

The Arab League was founded in 1945 in Cairo, by Egypt, Syria, Iraq, Lebanon, Jordan, Saudi Arabia and Yemen. Egypt's membership was suspended in 1979 because of its peace treaty with Israel; Egypt was re-admitted in 1989.

The membership has now been extended to include Algeria, Bahrain, Djibouti, Kuwait, Libya, Mauritania, Morocco, Oman, Palestine, Qatar, Somalia, Sudan, Tunisia and U.A.E.

Headquarters : Cairo, Egypt

MOROCCO TUNISIA see map above for Asian members of the Arab League
ALGERIA LIBYA
MAURITANIA
SUDAN
SOMALIA

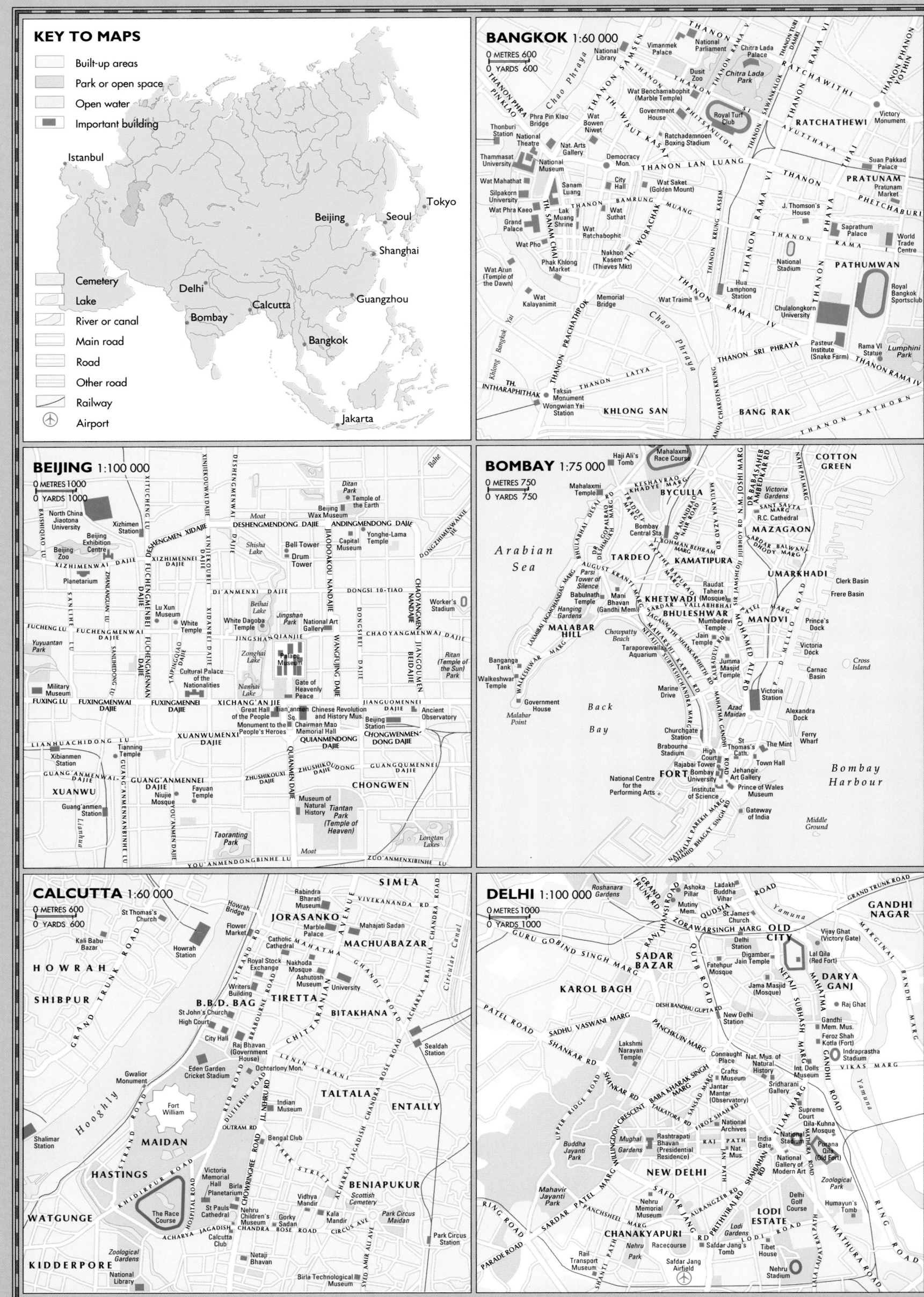

GUANGZHOU 1:30 000

0 METRES 300
0 YARDS 300

Luhu Lake

Guangzhou Station
HUANSHI XILU
Youyi (Friendship) Theatre
Abu Waqqas Grave
Orchid Garden
HUANSHI ZHONGLU
HUANSHI DONGLU
TIANSHENGCUN
West Station
HUANSHI
RENMIN BEILU
JIEFANG BEILU
Yuexiu Park
Zhenhai Tower–Guangzhou Museum
XIAO BEILU
YUEXIU BEILU
Tomb of the Nan Yue King
Xiyuan (Bonsai Garden)
Liuhua Park
LIUHUA
Calligraphy Museum
Court of the Five Celestial Rams
San Yung Tong Taoist Temple
Guangdong Sciences Hall
DONGFENG
Guangzhou Childrens Palace
JIEFANG XILU
Guangxiao Temple
Sun Yat-Sen Memorial Hall
DONGFENG
ZHONGLU
DONGFENG ZHONGLU
BAIYUN LU
Chen Family Temple (Guangdong Folk Arts and Crafts Hall)
Liurong Temple (Temple of the Six Banyans)
ZHONGLU
Peasant Movement Institute
Revolutionary Museum of Guangdong
Tomb Memorial Garden to the Martyrs
LIWAN
Children's Park
People's Park
Hongqi Theatre
Zhongshan Theatre
SANLU
World Trade Centre
RENMIN NANLU
JIEFANG NANLU
Huaisheng Mosque
Nanfang Theatre
WENMING LU
ZHONGSHAN LILU
ZHONGSHAN WULU
Lu Xun Museum
Guangdong Provincial Museum
Guangdong People's Stadium
BANTANG
Five Immortals Taoist Temple
ZHONGSHAN QILU
TAIKANG LU
DONGHUA XILU
East Station
LONGJIN ZHONGLU
LONGJIN DONGLU
BEIJING LU
WENDE LU
WANFU LU
Hualin Temple
HUIFU XILU
DADE LU
Jade Market
SHANGXIA JIU
YANJIANG ZHONGLU
Haizhu Square
YUEXIU NANLU
DISHIFU
Catholic Church of the Holy Heart
Haizhu Bridge
Dongshanhu Park
Qingping Market
YANJIANG XILU
BINJIANG ZHONGLU
Zhujiang (Pearl)
YANJIANG ZHONGLU

ISTANBUL 1:50 000

0 METRES 250
0 YARDS 250

Ferikoy Cemetery
HARBIYE
Military Museum
Yıldız Palace
BEŞİKTAŞ
Yıldız Park
Open Air Theatre
CUMHURIYET CAD.
Harbiye Cemetery
Democracy Park
PIYALEPAŞA BULVARI
DOLPADERE
CADDESI
DOLMABAHÇE
ÇIRAĞAN CADDESI
KULAKSIZ
Istanbul Technical University
İnönü Stadium
Dolmabahçe Palace
Aynalıkavak Palace (Museum)
Kulaksız Cemetery
BAHRIYE CAD.
TARLABAŞI BULVARI
Taksim Park
Atatürk Cultural Centre
Dolmabahçe Mosque
MECLIS MBUSAN CAD.
HALİÇ (Golden Horn)
E. ÇELEBI CAD.
Exhibition Centre
Republic Memorial Taksim
Galatasaray Baths
BEYOĞLU
Boğazi (Bosphorus)
ABDÜLEZEL PAŞA CAD.
RAGIP GÜMÜŞPALA CAD.
Galata Tower
KEMER ALTI CAD.
Nusretiye Mosque
Atatürk Br.
TERSANE CAD.
Galata Br.
KARAKÖY
Mihrimah Mosque
ÜSKÜDAR
İhlamur Pavilion
Aqueduct of Valens
Botanical Institute
Rüstem Paşa Mosque
KENNEDY CAD.
Kız Kulesi (Maiden's Tower)
Şemsi Paşa Mosque
ATATÜRK BULVARI
Süleymaniye Mosque
EMİNÖNÜ
Yeni Mosque
Mısır Çarşısı (Egyptian Bazaar)
Sirkeci Station
Atatürk Heykeli
Gülhane Park
SAHIL YOLU
ŞIZADEBAŞI CAD.
HATBAŞI CAD.
Istanbul University
Beyazit Tower
Kapalı Çarşı (Grand Bazaar)
Govt House
Archaeological Museum
St Irene Museum
Topkapı Palace
ORDU CAD.
YENI CERILER CAD.
Ahmet III Fountain
Ayasofya Museum (St Sophia)
KUMKAPI
Museum of Turkish and Islamic Art
Dikilitaş
SULTANAHMET
Sultan Ahmet Mosque (Blue Mosque)
SELIMIYE Barracks
HAREM SAHIL BULVARI
TUNUS BAĞI CAD.
ANKARA DEVLET YOLU
KENNEDY CADDESI
(FLORYA)

JAKARTA 1:45 000

0 METRES 450
0 YARDS 450

TAMAN SARI
Kali Krukut
IL. TAMAN SARI RAYA
IL. ANGKASA
JALAN K.H. MOH MANSYUR
JALAN GAJAH MADA
IL. GUNUNG SAHARI
Kemayoran Station
Gajah Mada Plaza
IL. SUKARJO WIRYOPRANOTO
JALAN HAYAM WURUK
Chinese Temple
JALAN K.H. HASYIM ASYHARI
IL. KH. SAMANHUDI
GAMBIR
IL. IR. HAJI JUANDA
State Palace
IL. VETERAN
Catholic Cathedral
IL. DR. SUTOMO RAYA
IL. K. CARINGIN
Bina Graha
Istana Merdeka (Presidential Palace)
Lapangan Banteng
IL. S. PRANOTO
IL. M. MERDEKA UTARA
Istiqlal Mosque
Irian Jaya Liberation Mon.
PASAR SENEN
Senen Station
IL. TOMANG RAYA
Medan Merdeka (Merdeka Square)
Baharata Theatre
STASIUN SENEN
SENEN RAYA
KRAMAT BUNDER
National Museum
Fountain Park
IL. M. MERDEKA BARAT
Monas (National Monument)
Gereja Immanuel Church
IL. PRAPATAN
JALAN KRAMAT RAYA
Cideng
Gambir Station
IL. M. MERDEKA TIMUR
IL. ABDUL MUIS
IL. M. MERDEKA SELATAN
Arjuna Wijaya
IL. KEBON SIRIH RAYA
IL. KWITANG
SENEN
Ciliwung
IL. TANAH ABANG TIMUR
IL. KH. WAHID HASYIM
IL. TEUKU CIK DITIRO
JALAN K.H. MAS MANSYUR
Tanah Abang Station
IL. HUSNI THAMRIN
Jakarta Theatre
IL. TEUKU UMAR
IL. CIKINI RAYA
Textile Museum
IL. A.K. SASUIT TUBUN RAYA
IL. K. KEBON SIRIH RAYA
HOS. COKROAMINOTO
IL. DR. SA. RATULANGI
IL. TEUKU CIK DITIRO
MENTENG
IL. JEND SUDIRMAN
IL. IMAM BONJOL
Suropati Park
Adam Malik Museum
Selamat Datang Statue
Taman Ismail Marzuki Culture Centre
Christian Cemetery
Kartini Statue
IL. DIPONEGORO

SEOUL 1:30 000

0 METRES 300
0 YARDS 300

CHONGNO-GU
Ch'angdökkung (Palace)
Seoul National University Medical College
SAMCHONGDONGGIL
Tonhwamun (Gate)
Ch'anggyonggung (Palace)
Konch'unmun (Gate)
TAEHAKNO
SAJIKNO
Kwanghwamun (Gate)
Hyundai Art Gallery
YULGOKNO
YULGOKNO
Chogye-Square Temple
SAMILLO (ELEVATED ROAD)
Chongmyo (Royal Shrine)
CHANGGYONGGONGNO
Sejong Cultural Centre
Yechong Art Gallery
Pagoda Park
Piccadilly Theatre
Danseongsa Theatre
CHONGNO
Kyönghüigung Park
CHONGGYECH'ONNO
Seoul Theatre
Asia Theatre
Tongdaemun Market
SAEMUNAN - GIL
National Museum of Modern Art
Toksugung Palace
City Hall
OLCHIRO
Gugdo Theatre
Myöngbo Theatre
OLCHIRO
Chöngdong Church
Jungang Theatre
Yönknak Church
Scala Theatre
T'AEPYONGNO
Supreme Court
SÖSUMUNNO
Myongdong Catholic Cathedral
Hoam Art Hall & Gallery
NAMDAEMUNNO
Namdaemun (South Gate)
NAMSANNO
Daehan Theatre
Korea House
Dongkook University
ÜLJIRO
Namdaemun Market
SOWOLGIL
National Central Library
CHUNG - GU
Changch'ung Baseball Field
Seoul Station
1ST NAMSAN TUNNEL
2ND NAMSAN TUNNEL
3RD NAMSAN TUNNEL
Namsan Park
Namsan Botanical Garden
Seoul Tower
National Theatre
CHANGCH'UNGDAN-GIL

SHANGHAI 1:60 000

0 METRES 600
0 YARDS 600

TIANMU LU
Shanghai Station
HENGFENG LU
Wusong Jiang
JINGAN
XIZANG BEILU
HENAN BEILU
SICHUAN BEILU
DA MING LU
JIANGNING BEILU
Friendship Store
Shanghai People's Hero Memorial Pagoda
WANHANGDU LU
BEIJING XILU
BEIJING DONGLU
ZHONGSHAN DONG-LU
Jing'an Temple
Art Museum
No. 1 Department Store
NANJING XILU
NANJING DONGLU
Huangpu Jiang
HUANGPU
Pudong Park
Shanghai Exhibition Centre
Library
Renmin (People's) Park
Muen Church
Natural History Museum
Yan'an Tunnel
Pudong
Children's Palace
Jing'an Park
Lyceum Theatre
YAN'AN ZHONGLU
People's Square
Workers' Cultural Palace
Shanghai Museum
YAN'AN DONGLU
Theatre Academy
Xiang Yang Park
Dazhong Theatre
Great World Entertainment Centre
Yuyuan Garden
HUAIHAI
Huaihai Park
ZHONGSHAN DONG 2-LU
NANSHI
Conservatory of Music
Former Residence of Sun Yat-Sen
Fuxing Park
Site of the First National Congress of the Chinese Communist Party
HENGSHAN LU
FUXING
Former Residence of Zhou En-Lai
Cultural Square
Tuofen Museum
Confucian Temple
XILU
Hunan Stadium
Penglai Park
LUWAN
XUJIAHUI LU
LUJIABANG LU
ZHAOJIABANG LU
ZHONGSHAN NAN-LU
Napu Bridge
ZHONGSHAN NAN 2-LU
Huangpu Jiang
PUDONG NANLU

TOKYO 1:100 000

0 METRES 1000
0 YARDS 1000

Toshimagaoka Cemetery
Kishimojin Shrine
Daimyo Clock Museum
Asakusa-Chosokan Gallery
Koishikawa Botanical Garden
SHINOBAZU-DORI
KASUGA-DORI
Kisshoji Temple
Metropolitan Art Gallery
National Museum
National Science Museum
MEJIRO-DORI
St Mary's Cathedral
BUNKYO-KU
Ueno Zoo
Sensoji Temple
SHIN-MEJIRO-DORI
EXPRESSWAY
Tokyo University
Ueno Royal Museum
TAITO-KU
Asakusa Station
SHINJUKU-KU
Science University of Tokyo
Kanda Myojin Shrine
Torigoe-jinja Shrine
OKUBO-DORI
Transportation Museum
NO.5
Hôsenji Temple
ÔME-KAIDO
Yasukuni-Jinja Shrine
Science and Technology Museum
National Museum of Modern Art
CHUO-KU
Shinjuku Station
YASUKUNI-DORI
Historical Museum
Communications Museum
Suitengu Shrine
Japanese Sword Museum
National Theatre
New Imperial Palace
Tokyo Station
Fukagawa Edo Museum
Shinjuku Gyoen Garden
Geinin-Kan (State Guesthouse)
CHIYODA-KU
Kabukiza Theatre
Tokyo Stock Exchange
Meiji Jingu Shrine
National Noh Theatre
National Stadium
Suntory Museum of Art
National Diet Building
Mullion
Riccar Art Museum
Fukagawa-Fudoson Temple
Yoyogi Park
Ota Mem Museum of Art
Aoyama Cemetery
Okura Shukokan Museum
Tokyo University of Mercantile Marine
Nezu Art Museum
NHK Broadcasting Museum
Riccar Art Gallery
Tsukiji-Honhanji Temple
Shoto Museum of Art
EXPRESSWAY NO.3
Zojoji Temple
Tokyo Tower
World Trade Centre
Hamarikyu Garden
KIYOSUMI-DORI
HARUMI-DORI
The Furniture Museum
Meguro Art Gallery
National Park for Nature Study
Sengakuji Temple
MINATO-KU
KOMAZAWA-DORI
Daienji Temple
Hatakeyama Collection
Rainbow Bridge
EXPRESSWAY NO.1
Tokyo International Trade Centre

© HarperCollins Publishers

INDIA
BHUTAN
BANGLADESH
MYANMAR (BURMA)
CHINA
YUNNAN
GUIZHOU
GUANGXI
GUANGDONG
HUNAN
LAOS
VIETNAM
THAILAND
CAMBODIA
MALAYSIA
PENINSULAR MALAYSIA
MALAYA
BRUNEI
SUMATERA (SUMATRA)
BORNEO
KALIMANTAN
SARAWAK
JAWA (JAVA)
INDONESIA

BAY OF BENGAL
INDIAN OCEAN
ANDAMAN SEA
Andaman Islands (India)
North Andaman
Middle Andaman
South Andaman
Little Andaman
Nicobar Islands (India)
Car Nicobar
Great Nicobar
Ten Degree Channel
Preparis North Channel
Preparis South Channel
Preparis I.

Gulf of Martaban
Mouths of the Irrawaddy
Mouths of the Ganga
Gulf of Thailand
Gulf of Tongking
HAINAN
SOUTH CHINA SEA
Paracel Is
Spratly Is
Leizhou Bandao
Java Sea
Strait of Malacca
Selat Karimata
Selat Sunda

Koch Bihar, Bongaigaon, Tezpur, Sibsagar, Jorhat, Nagaon, Dimapur, Kohima, Dibrugarh, North Lakhimpur, Makum, Kathau, Putao, Zayü, Dêdên, Zhongdian
Rangpur, Guwahati, Shillong, Silchar, Imphal (Manipur), Myitkyina, Baoshan, Chuxiong, Dali, Liupanshui, Dukou, Dongchuan, Guiyang, Duyun, Anshun, Guilin
Mymensingh, Sylhet, Agartala, Aizawl, Bhamo, Namtu, Kunming, Yuxi, Quijing, Hechi
BANGLADESH, Pabna, Dhaka, Comilla, Faridpur, Longlei, Yeu, Mawlaik (Upr Chindwin), Wuntho, Mogok, Lashio, Kehsi Mahsam, Shuangjiang, Gejiu, Kaiyuan, Bose, Liuzhou, Wuzhou, Zhaoqing, Guangzhou
Jessore, Khulna, Barisal, Chittagong, Cox's Bazar, Monywa, Pakokku, Maymyo, Mandalay, Myingyan, Rengtung, Taung-gyi, Louang Namtha, Ha Giang, Cao Bang, Nanning, Yulin, Qinzhou, Behai, Kowloon, Macau (Port.), HONG KONG
Sittwe (Akyab), Meiktila, Magwe (Magway), Taunggyi, Loikaw, M. Chiang Rai, Muang Phayao, Phôngsali, Son La, Thai Nguyen, Lao Cai, Pingxiang, Zhanjiang, Haikou, Wenchang
Kyaukpyu, Thayetmyo, Pyè (Prome), Toungoo, Pyinmana, Chiang Mai, Muang Lamphun, Muang Nan, Muang Phrae, Louangphrabang, Xiangkhoang, Vangieng, Vinh, Ha Tinh, Dongfang, Qionghai, Wanning
Sandoway, Myanaung, Papun, Uttaradit, Sawankhalok, Vientiane, Muang Khammouan, Savannakhét, Dông Ha, Huê, Da Nang, Quang Ngai
Tharrawaddy, Shwegyin, M. Phitsanulok, M. Sakon Nakhon, Muang Khon Kaen, Saravan, Pakxé
Henzada, Pegu, Bago, Kyaikto, Bhumiphol Dam, Thaton, Tak, Maha Sarakham, Ubon Ratchathani
Bassein (Pathein), Moulmein (Mawlamyine), M. Nakhon Sawan, Lop Buri, Sara Buri, Nakhon Ratchasima (Korat), Surin, Stoeng Trêng, Qui Nhon
Pyapon, Yangon (Rangoon), M. Nakhon Sawan, Ayutthaya, Bangkok (Krung Thep), Sisophon, CAMBODIA, Kampong Thum, Buon Mê Thuôt, Nha Trang, Da Lat
Tavoy (Dawei), Nam Tok, Rat Buri, Chon Buri, Phet Buri, Batdâmbâng, Pouthisat, Tonlé Sab, Kampong Cham, Kampong Thum
Mergui, Tenasserim, Prachuap Khiri Khan, Chanthaburi, Kampong Spoe, Phnum Penh (Phnom Penh), Tây Ninh, Phan Thiet
Chumphon, Sihanoukville (Kampong Saom), Kampot, Châu Dôc, Hô Chi Minh (Saigon)
Ranong, Surat Thani, Long Xuyên, My Tho, Vung Tau
B. Takua Pa, Nakhon Si Thammarat, Can Tho, Bac Liêu, Ca Mau, Mui Ca Mau, Côn Son
Phàngnga, Krabi, Phatthalung, Phuket, Songkhla (Singora)
Ban Hat Yai, Yala, Kota Bharu, Pasir Puteh, Kota Kinabalu
Alor Setar, Sungei Petani, Kuala Terengganu
George Town, Dungun, Bandar Labuan, BRUNEI, Bandar Seri Begawan, Miri, Seria
Banda Aceh, Lhokseumawe, Ipoh, Taiping, MALAYA, PENINSULAR MALAYSIA, Kuantan, Igan, Bintulu
Bireun, Langsa, Temerloh, Kepulauan Anambas, Kuching, Sibu, SARAWAK
Pangkalansusu, Kepulauan Natuna, Natuna Besar, Debak
Medan, Tebingtinggi, Kuala Lumpur, Seremban, Melaka, Keluang, Sambas, Pemangkat, Singkawang, Mempawah
Prapat, Baligé, Rantauprapat, Muar, Johor Bahru, SINGAPORE, Singapore, Tanjungpinang, Kepulauan Riau, Kepulauan Tambelan, BORNEO, Pontianak
Sibolga, Dumai, Minas, Kepulauan Lingga, Sukadana, Kapuas, KALIMANTAN
Nias, Gunungsitoli, Payakumbuh, Bukittinggi, SUMATERA (SUMATRA), Pekanbaru, Ketapang, Peg. Schwaner
Padang, Muarasiberut, Padangpanjang, Sijunjung, Muarabungo, Jambi, Belinyu, P.P. Karimata, Kendawangan, Sampit, Amuntai
Pesisir, Pegunungan Barisan, Sungaipenuh, Sarolangun, Mentok, Pangkalpinang, Bangka, Tanjungpandan, Pangkalanbuun, Banjarmasin, Martapura
Sekayu, Lubuklinggau, Palembang, Toboali, Belitung, Tg Sambar, Tg Puting, Tg Selatan
Bengkulu, Lahat, Prabumulih, Manggar
Muaradua, Martapura, Menggala
Bintuhan, Kotabumi, Metro, Tanjungkarang Telukbetung, Java Sea, Kepulauan Laut
Krui, Kotaagung, JAKARTA, Serang, Purwakarta, Cirebon, Pekalongan, Tuban, Bangkalan, Kep. Kangean, Sumenep
Bogor, Bandung, Semarang, Temanggung, Surabaya, Madura
Sukabumi, Tasikmalaya, Cilacap, Surakarta, Probolinggo, Jember
Yogyakarta, Kediri, Malang, Denpasar

Mt Victoria 3053
Arakan Yoma
Irrawaddy
Salween
Mekong

METRES / FEET
6000 / 19686
5000 / 16409
4000 / 13124
3000 / 9843
2000 / 6562
1000 / 3281
500 / 1640
200 / 656
SEA LEVEL
200 / 656
2000 / 6562
4000 / 13124
6000 / 19686

Mercator Projection
© HarperCollins Publishers

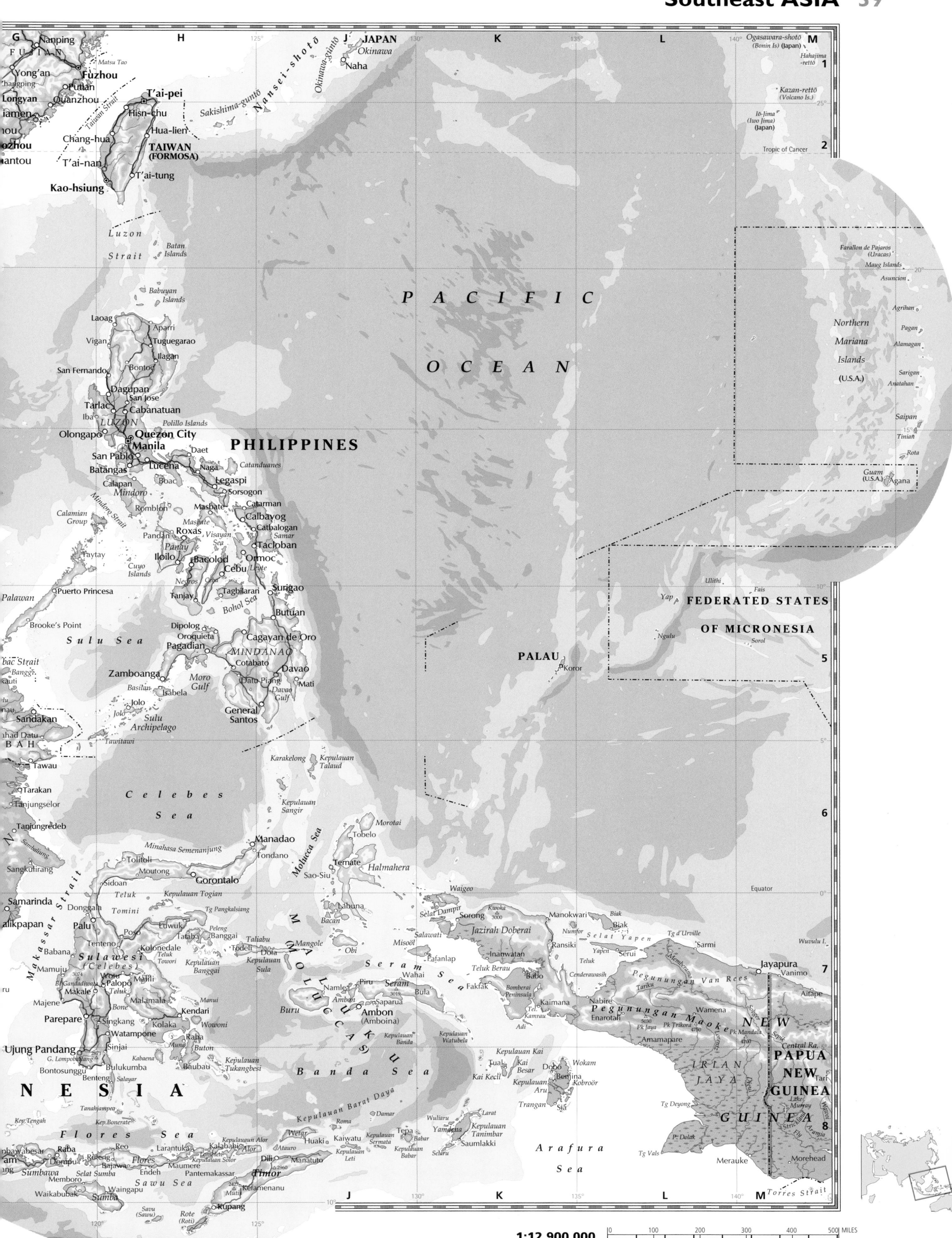

G　H　125°　J　JAPAN　130°　K　135°　L　140°　M

Nanping
FUJIAN
Yong'an
Changping
Longyan
iamen
hou
ozhou
antou

Fuzhou
Putian
Quanzhou

T'ai-pei
Hisn-chu
Hua-lien
Chang-hua
T'ai-nan
T'ai-tung
TAIWAN
(FORMOSA)

Kao-hsiung

Matsu Tao
Taiwan Strait

Okinawa
Naha

Nansei-shotō
Okinawa-guntō
Sakishima-guntō

Ogasawara-shotō
(Bonin Is.) (Japan)

Hahajima-
rettō

1

Kazan-rettō
(Volcano Is.)

Iō-Jima
(Iwo Jima)
(Japan)

25°

2

Tropic of Cancer

Luzon
Strait

Batan
Islands

PACIFIC

OCEAN

Farallon de Pajaros
(Uracas)

Maug Islands
Asuncion

20°

Northern
Mariana
Islands
(U.S.A.)

Agrihan
Pagan
Alamagan

Sarigan
Anatahan

Saipan
Tinian

Rota

Guam
(U.S.A.)

Agana

15°

Babuyan
Islands

Laoag
Vigan
Tuguegarao
Aparri
Ilagan
Bontoc

San Fernando
Dagupan
Tarlac
Iba
Olongapo

San Jose
Cabanatuan
LUZON
Quezon City
Manila
San Pablo
Lucena
Batangas
Calapan
Mindoro

Daet
Naga
Boac

Polillo Islands

PHILIPPINES

Legaspi
Sorsogon
Catarman
Calbayog
Catbalogan
Tacloban
Samar

Catanduanes

Calamian
Group

Taytay

Pandan
Roxas
Panay
Iloilo
Bacolod
Cebu
Tanjay
Tagbilaran

Masbate
Masbate
Visayan
Sea
Negros
Cebu
Leyte
Bohol Sea

Ormoc

Surigao
Butuan

FEDERATED STATES
OF MICRONESIA

Ulithi
Yap
Ngulu

Fais
Sorol

10°

Palawan

Puerto Princesa

Cuyo
Islands

Romblon

Dipolog
Oroquieta
Pagadian
MINDANAO
Cotabato
Davao
Datu Piang
Mati
Davao
Gulf

Cagayan de Oro

PALAU
Koror

5

Brooke's Point

Sulu Sea

bac Strait
Banggi
auti

Zamboanga
Basilan
Isabela
Jolo
Jolo
Sulu
Archipelago
Tawitawi

Moro
Gulf

General
Santos

5°

Sandakan
BAH
had Datu

Tawau

Tarakan
Tanjungselor

Karakelong
Kepulauan
Talaud

Kepulauan
Sangir

6

lu
nau

N

Celebes
Sea

Tanjungredeb

Samarinda
alikpapan

Sumbailang

Sangkulirang

Tolitoli
Moutong

Sidoan

Manadao
Tondano

Morotai

Tobelo

Equator

0°

Minahasa Semenanjung

Gorontalo

Molucca
Sea

Ternate
Sao-Siu
Halmahera

Waigeo

Selat Dampir
Sorong

Kwoka
3000

Manokwari

Biak
Biak

Tg d'Urville

Wuvulu I.

Donggala
Tomini
Teluk
Tomini
Tg Pangkalsiang

Luhuna
Bacan

Salawati
Misoöl

Jazirah Doberai

Numfor

Selat Yapen
Yapen
Serui

Sarmi

7

Samarinda

Palu
Poso
Luwuk
Peleng
Banggai

Jayapura
Vanimo

Makassar Strait

Tenteno
Tataba
Kolonedale
Teluk
Towori

Mangole
Obi

Pafanlap
Inanwatan

Ransiki

Aitape

Babana

Mamuju

Gandadiwata
3074

Majene
Parepare

Sulawesi
(Celebes)

Makale
Wotu
Palopo
Teluk

Mahili

Kolaka
Kendari

Singkang
Kolonedale
Malamala

Todeli
Dofa
Kepulauan
Sula
Mangole
Taliabu

Namlea
Piru
Buru
Wahai
Seram
Bula

Pegunungan Van Rees

Tariku

Babo

Cenderawasih

Nabire
Enarotali

Wamena

Pegunungan
Pk Trikora
5030
Pk Jaya
Pk Mandala
4700

NEW

Maoke

Mamasa

Singkang
Watampone

Wowoni
Muna
Raha

Manui

Amban
Ambon
(Amboina)
Saparua

Seram
3019

Faktak

Bomberai
Peninsula

Kaimana

Tel-

Mimika
Tarf

PAPUA

NEW

Parepare

Ujung Pandang
G. Lompobatang

Bontosunggu

Bantaeng

Sinjai
Kabaena
Buton
Benteng
Salayar

Bulukumba

Baubau

Wowoni

Kepulauan
Banda

Kepulauan
Watubela

Adi

Amamapare

Central Ra.

IRIAN
JAYA

Lake
Murray

GUINEA

8

Kep. Tengah
Kep. Bonerate

Flores
Sea

Tanahjampea

Banda Sea

Tual
Dobo
Benjina
Kobroör

Kai
Besar
Kai Kecil

Kepulauan
Aru

Wokam

Tg Deyong

Fly

Strickland

Morehead

Raba
Dompu

Dili

Reo
Ruteng
Bajawa

Larantuka

Solor
Maumere

Flores

Alor
Lomblen

Kepulauan
Alor

Wetar

Kepulauan
Solor

Damar
Roma

Kalabahi

Huaki
Kaiwatu

Larat
Tepa
Babar

Yamdena
Kepulauan
Tanimbar

Trangan
Sia

Wuliaru

Arafura
Sea

Tg Vals

M Torres Strait

Sumbawa
am
ang

Memboro
Waikabubak
Sumba

Waingapu

Savu
(Sawu)

Rote
(Roti)

Kupang
Soe
Timor

Pantemakassar
Kefamenanu
Atauro
Manatuto

Kepulauan
Leti

Saumlakki
Selaru

P. Dolak

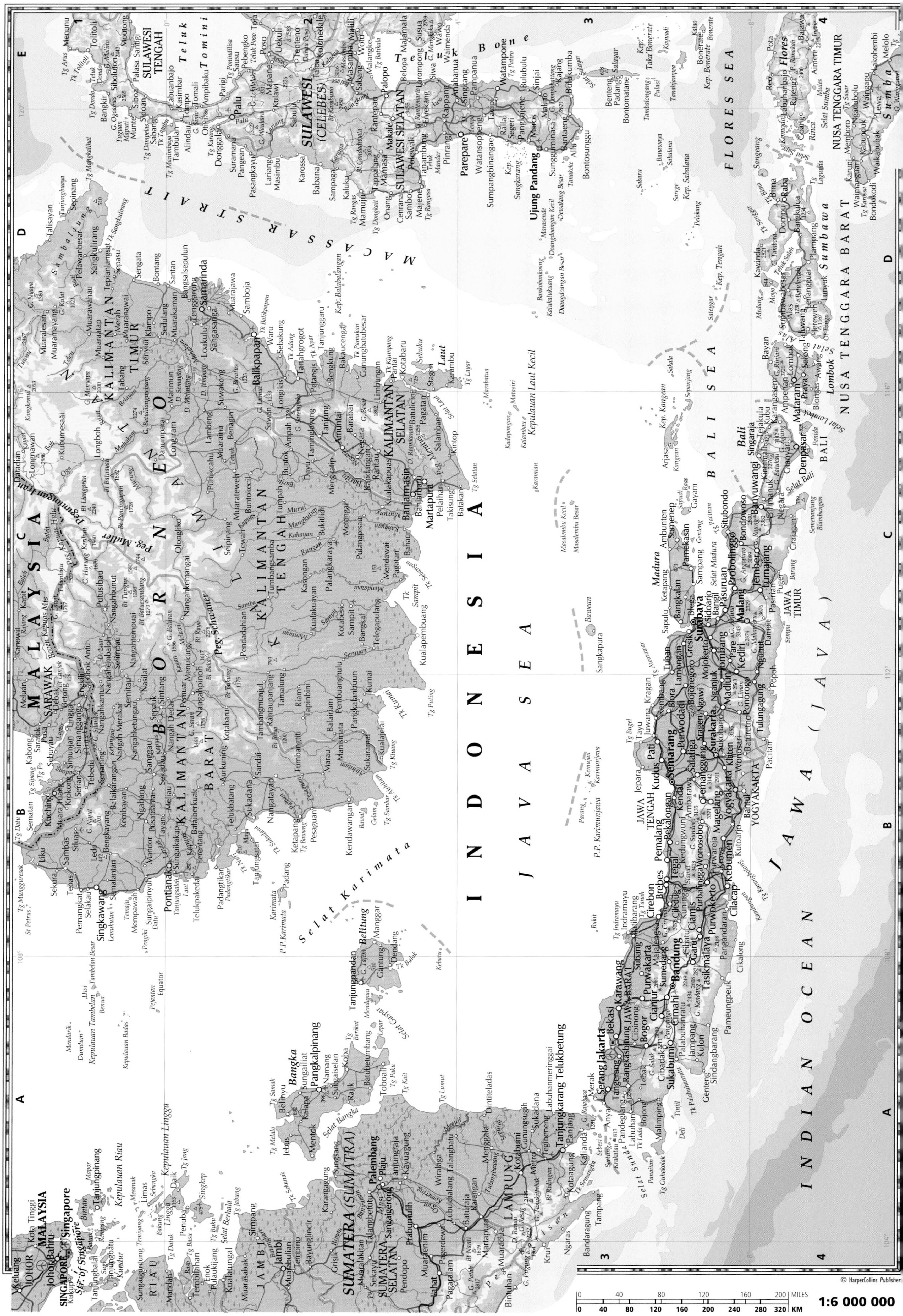

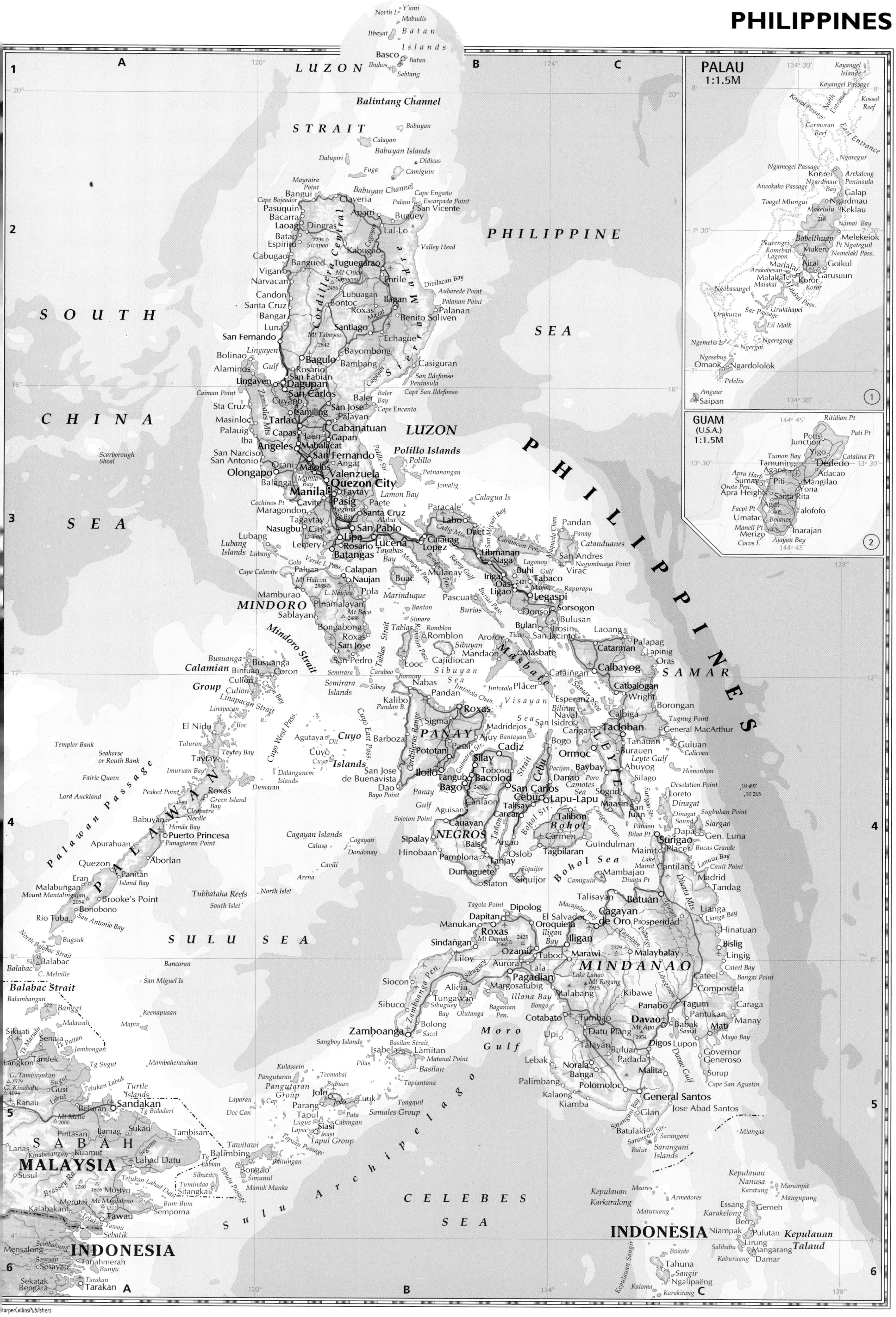

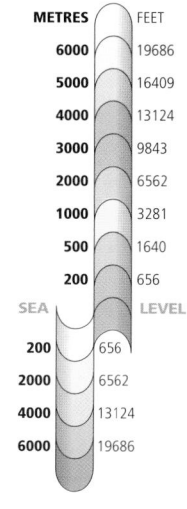

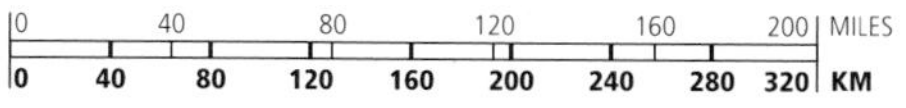

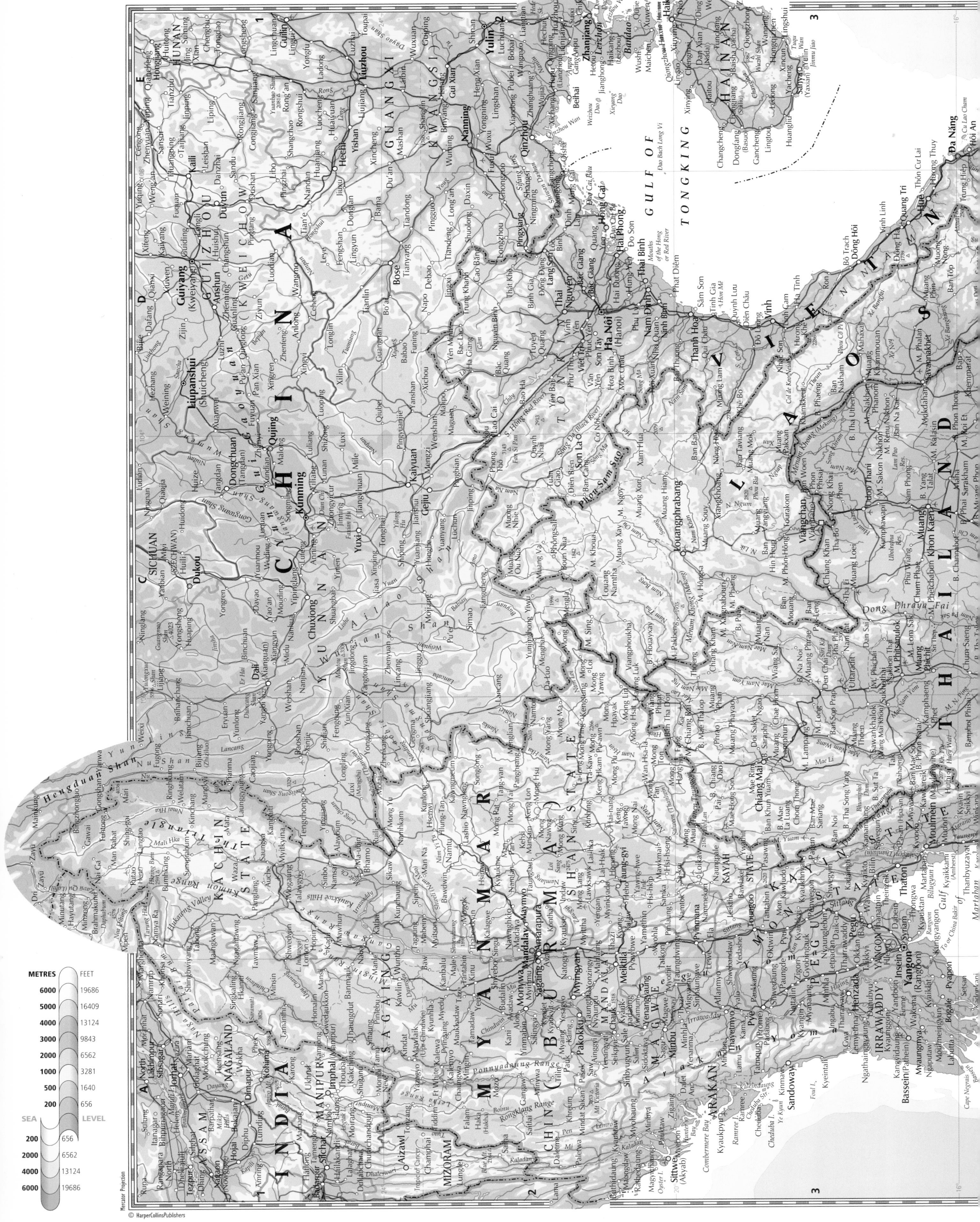

METRES | FEET
6000 — 19686
5000 — 16409
4000 — 13124
3000 — 9843
2000 — 6562
1000 — 3281
500 — 1640
200 — 656
SEA LEVEL
200 — 656
2000 — 6562
4000 — 13124
6000 — 19686

Mercator Projection

© HarperCollins Publishers

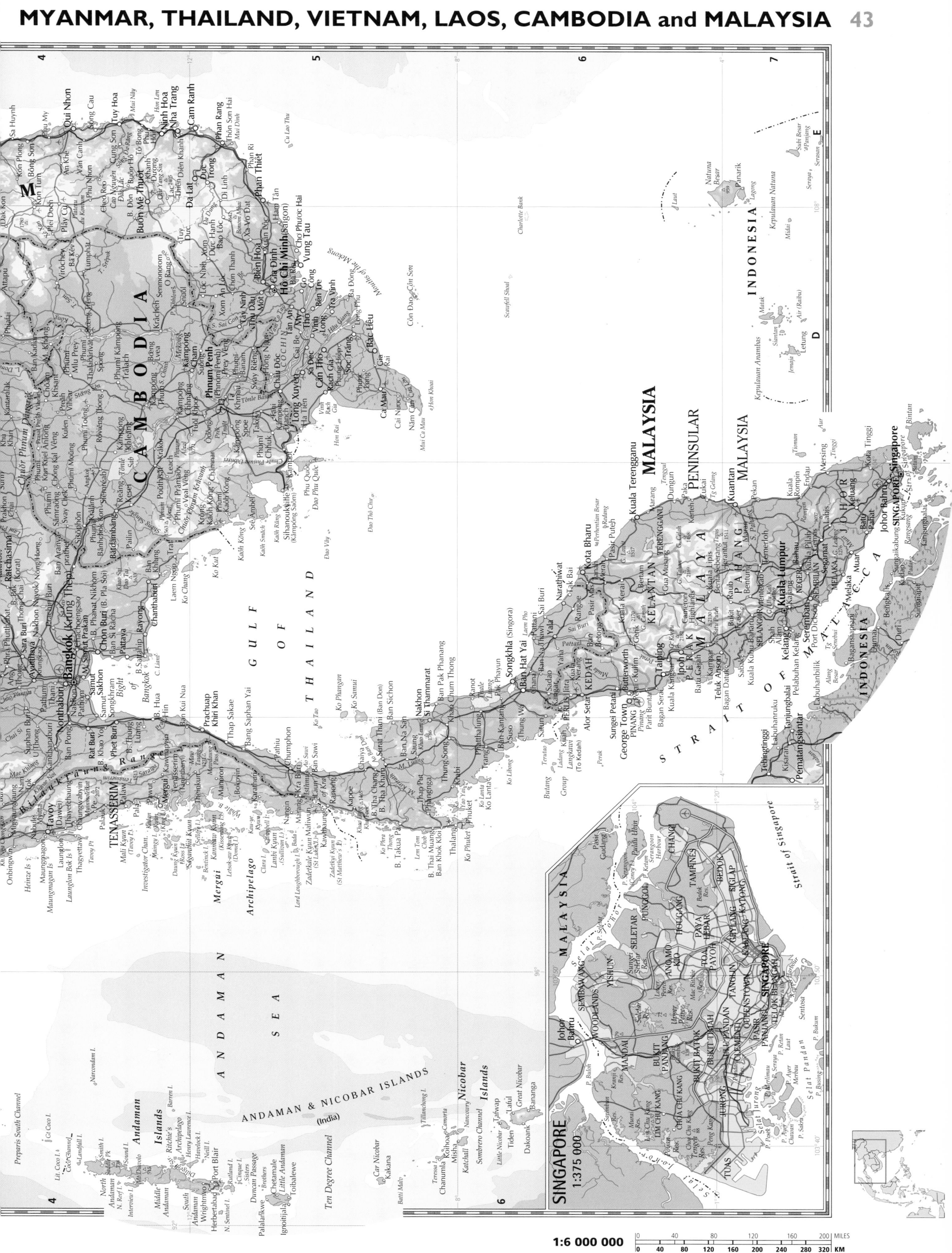

SINGAPORE
1:375 000

1:6 000 000

| | 0 | 40 | 80 | 120 | 160 | 200 MILES |
| 0 | 40 | 80 | 120 | 160 | 200 | 240 | 280 | 320 KM |

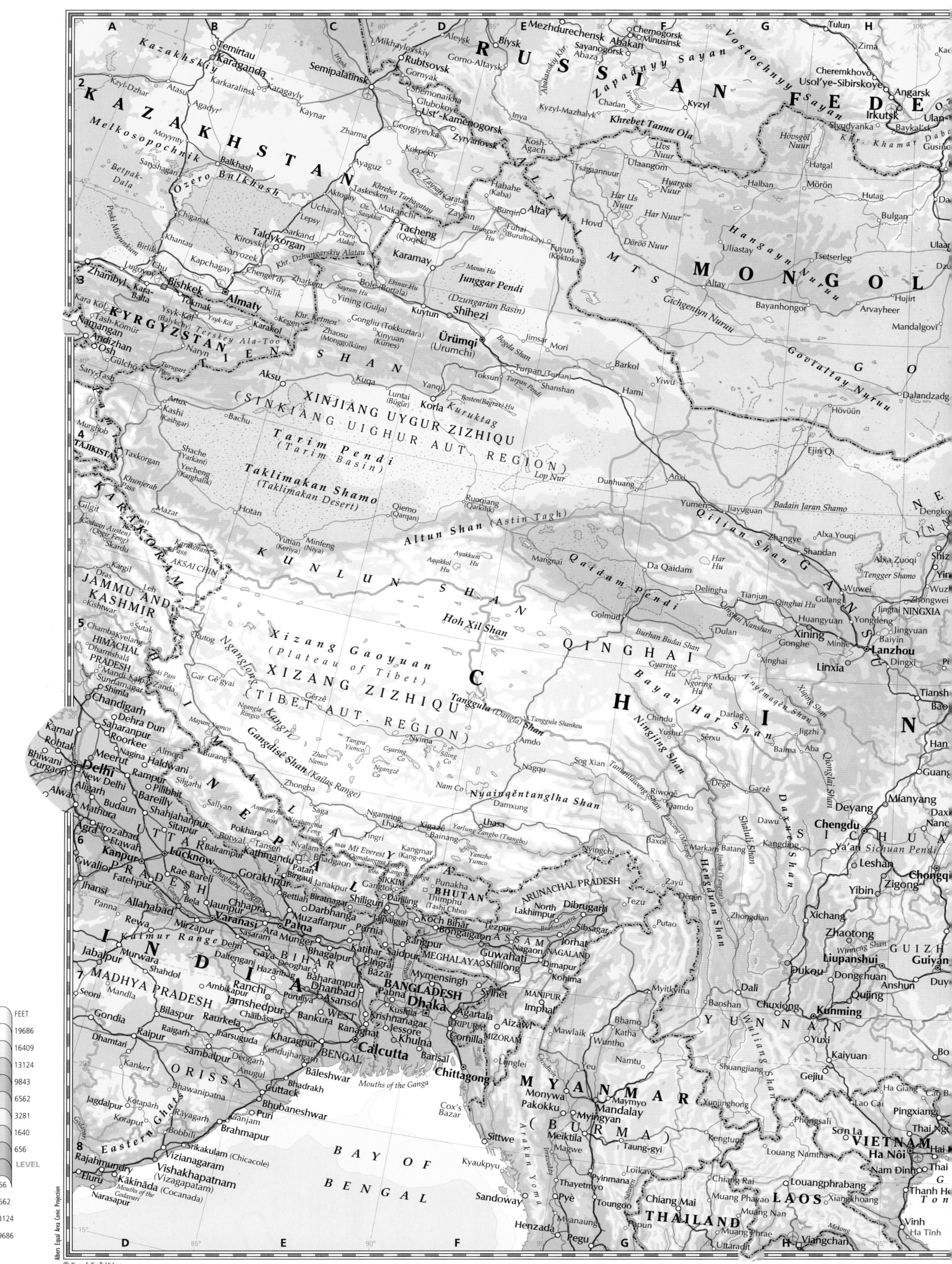

Albers Equal Area Conic Projection

METRES		FEET
6000		19686
5000		16409
4000		13124
3000		9843
2000		6562
1000		3281
500		1640
200		656
SEA		LEVEL
200		656
2000		6562
4000		13124
6000		19686

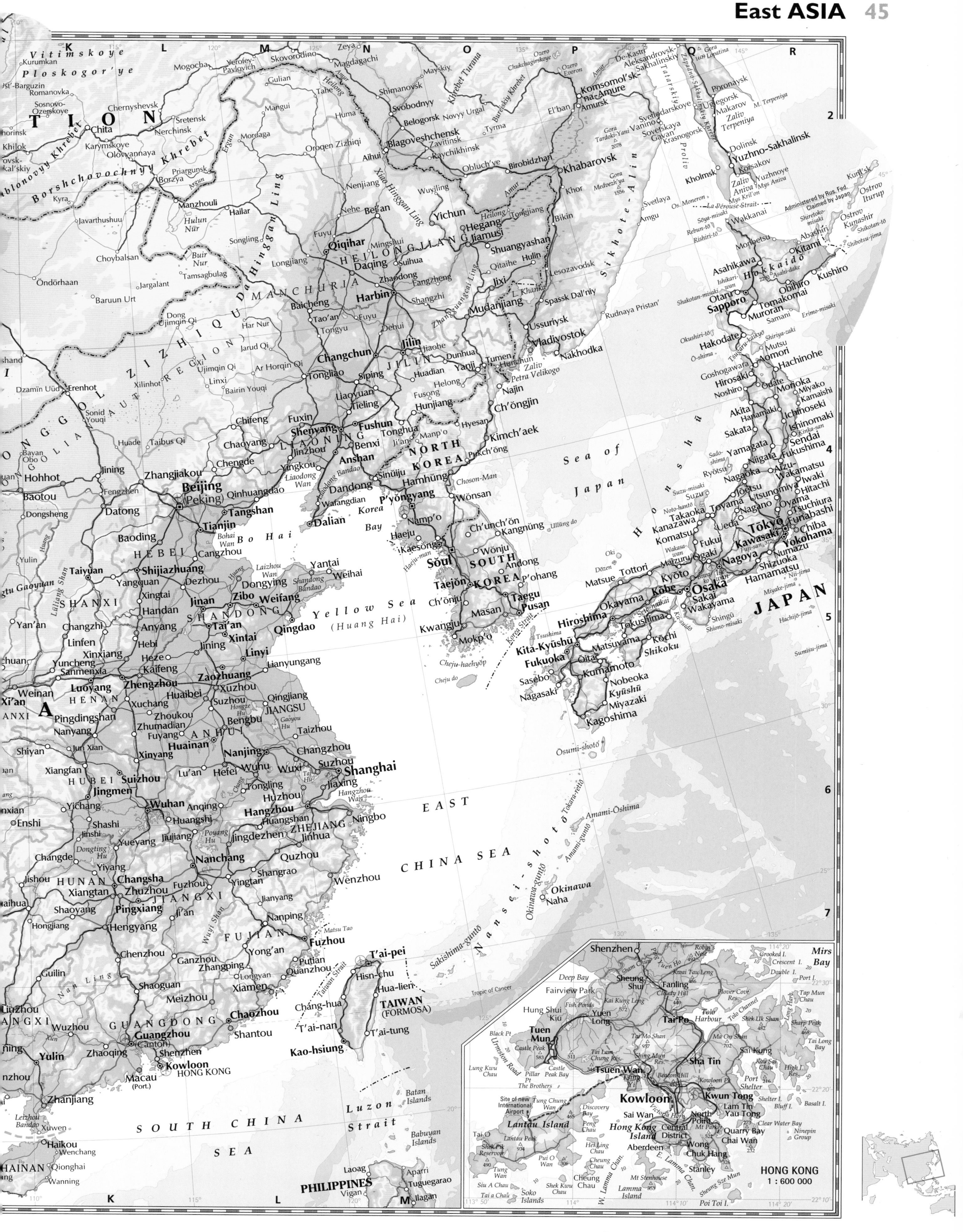

HONG KONG
1 : 600 000

1:12 600 000

| 0 | 100 | 200 | 300 | 400 | 500 MILES |

| 0 | 100 | 200 | 300 | 400 | 500 | 600 | 700 | 800 KM |

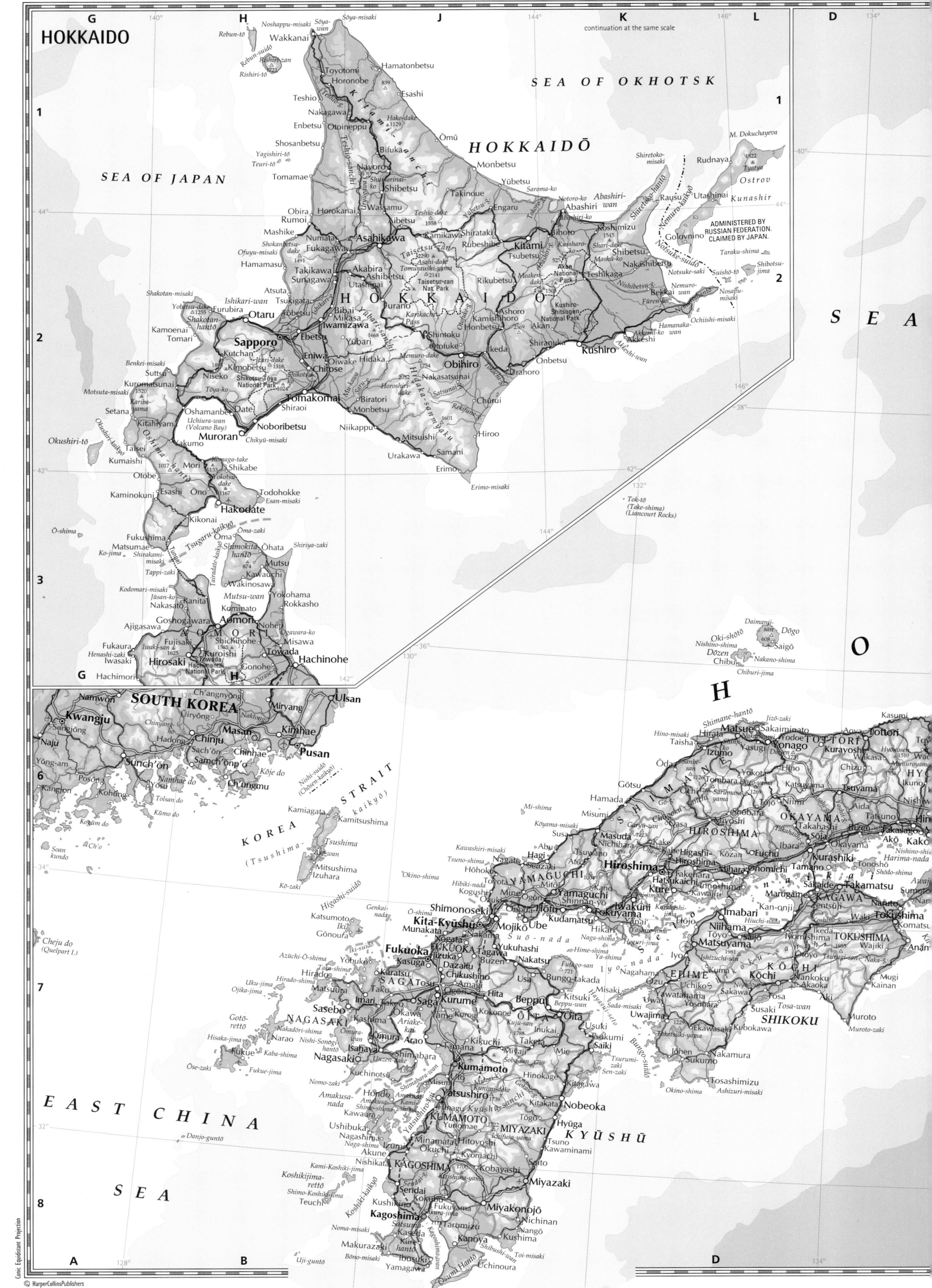

1:3 300 000

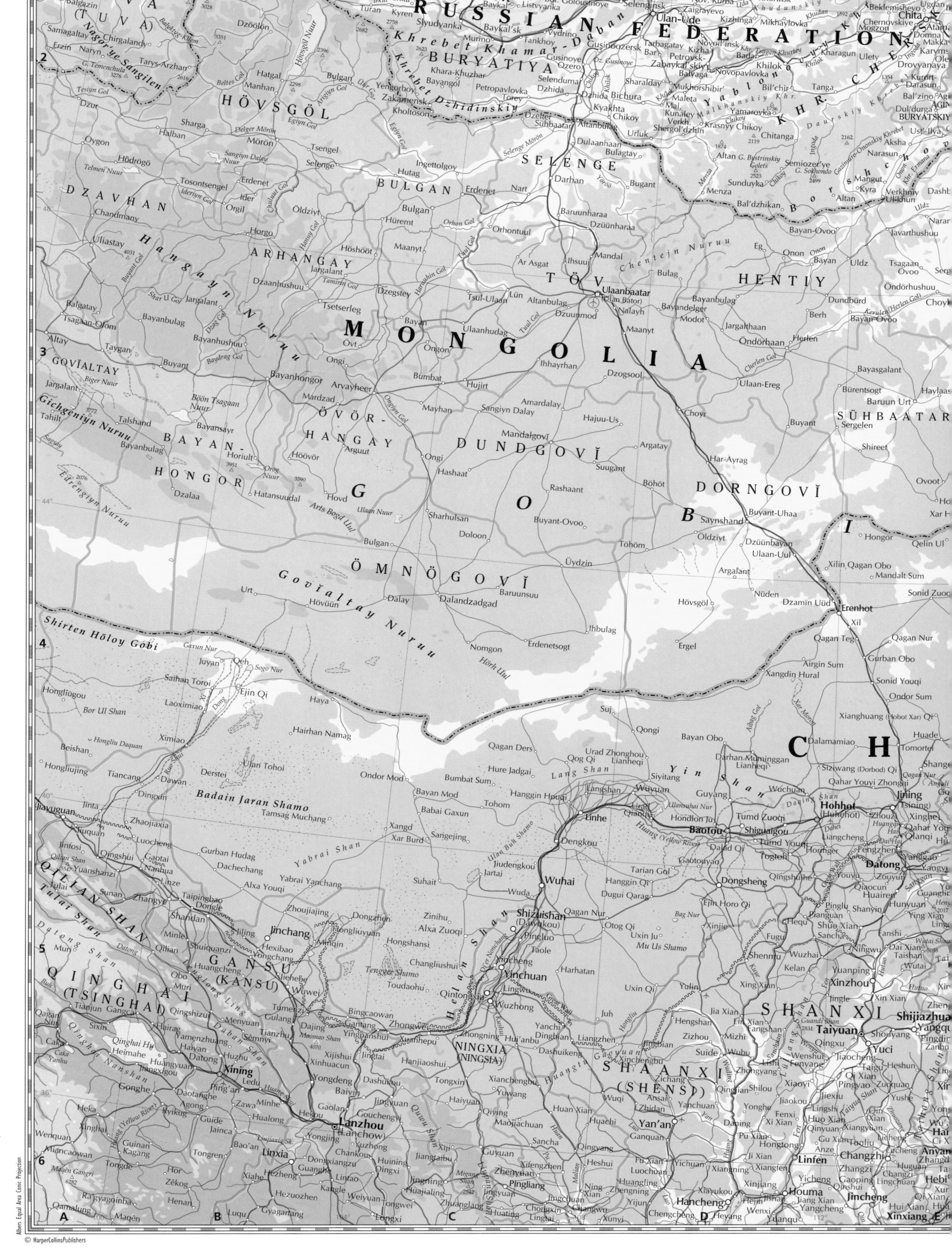

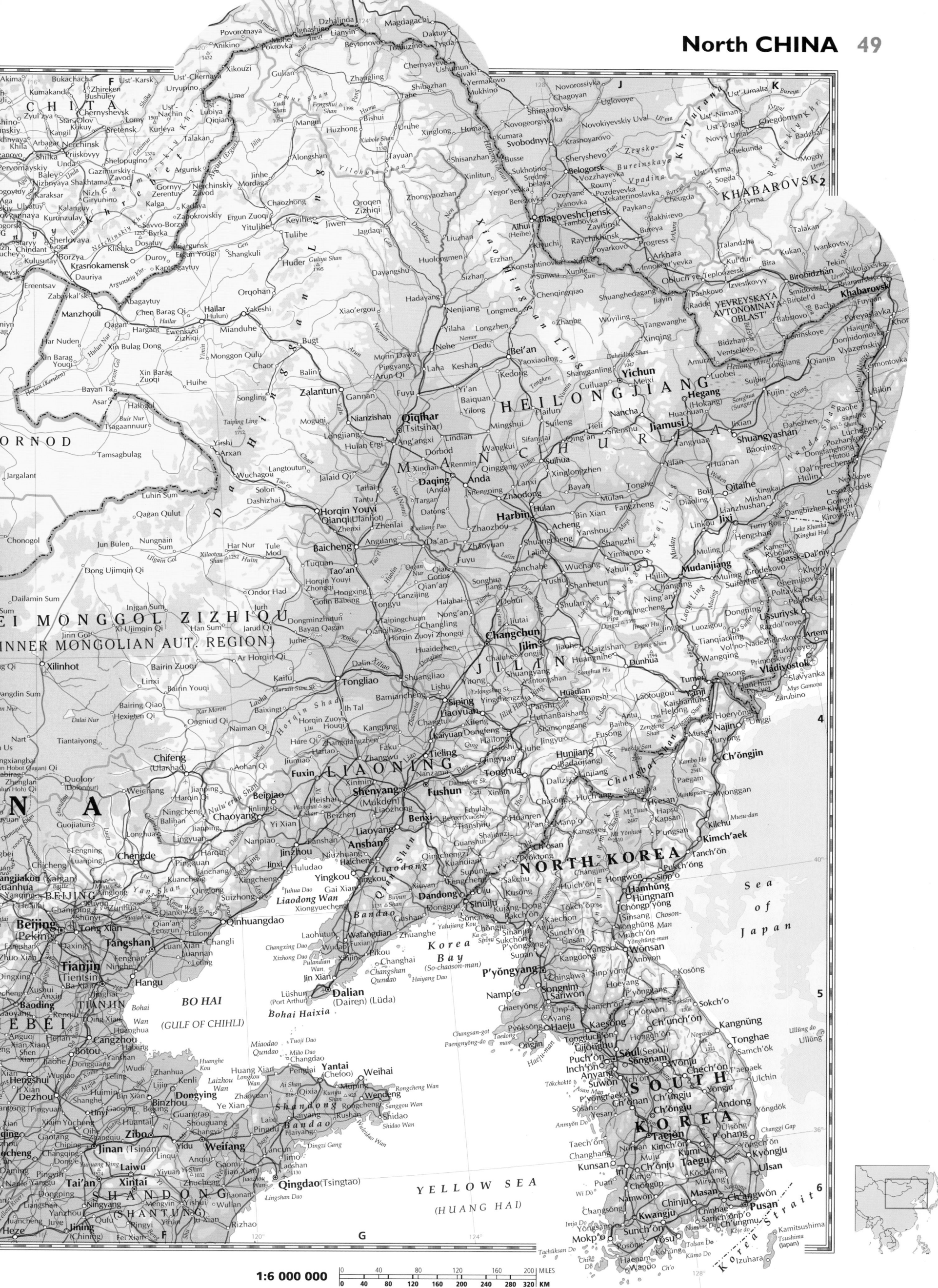

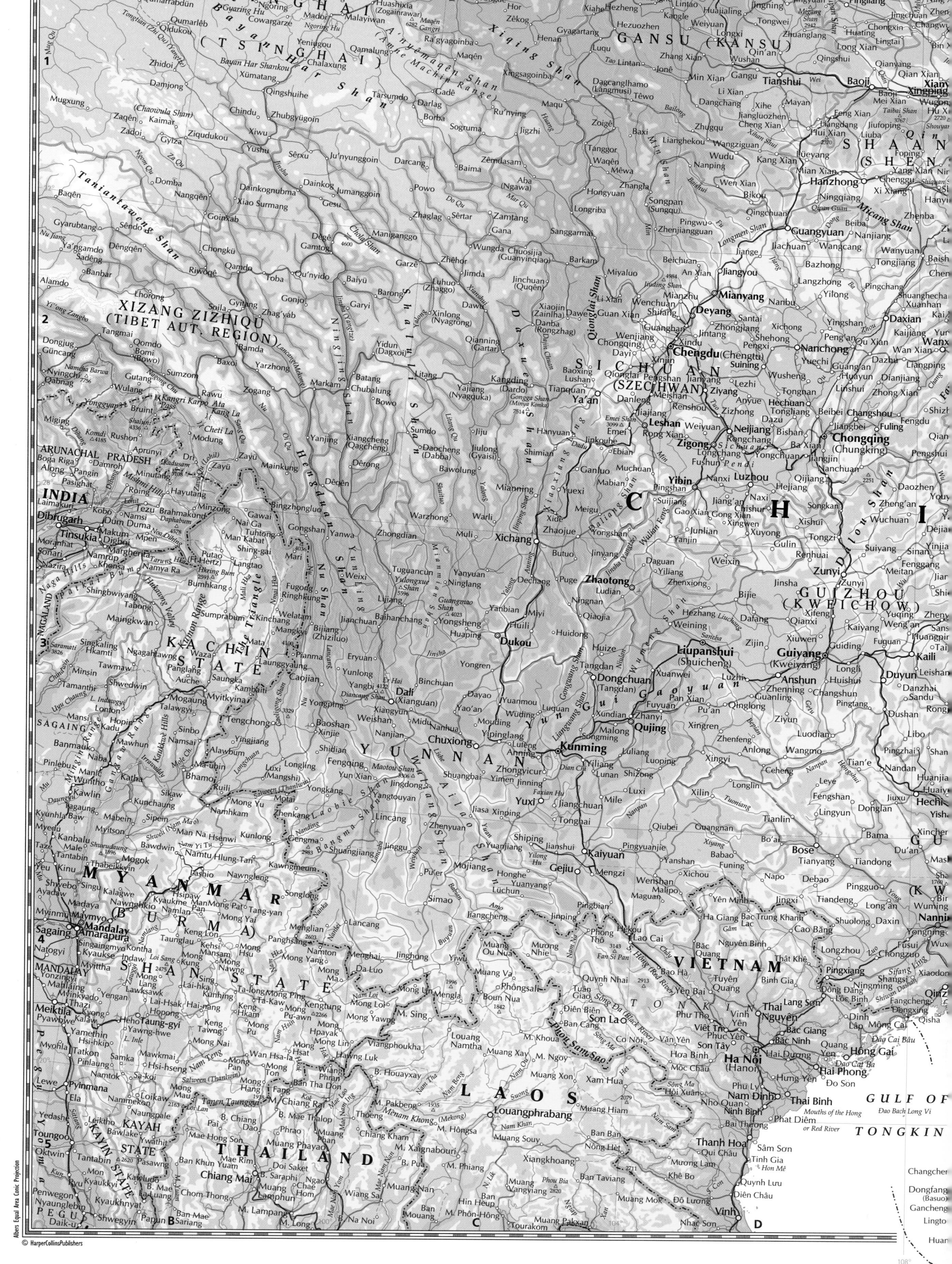

METRES	FEET
6000	19686
5000	16409
4000	13124
3000	9843
2000	6562
1000	3281
500	1640
200	656

SEA | LEVEL

200 | 656
2000 | 6562
4000 | 13124
6000 | 19686

Albers Equal Area Conic Projection

© HarperCollins Publishers

Major labels on the map (seas, provinces, and principal places):

Seas and waters: YELLOW SEA (HUANG HAI), SOUTH CHINA SEA, Taiwan Strait (Taiwan Haixia), Changjiang Kou (Mouth of the Yangtze), Balintang Channel, Babuyan Channel, Luzon Strait

Provinces / regions: SHANXI, SHANDONG (SHANTUNG), HENAN, JIANGSU (KIANGSU), ANHUI (ANHWEI), HUBEI (HUPEH), ZHEJIANG (CHEKIANG), HUNAN, JIANGXI, FUJIAN (FUKIEN), GUANGDONG (KWANGTUNG), GUANGXI (GX), HAINAN, TAIWAN (FORMOSA), PHILIPPINES, Luzon

Major cities: Shanghai, Nanjing (Nanking), Hangzhou (Hangchow), Wuhan, Changsha, Nanchang, Fuzhou (Foochow), Guangzhou (Canton), Hong Kong, Kowloon, Macau (Portugal), Shenzhen (Ba'an), Zhuhai, Xiamen (Amoy), Quanzhou, Zhangzhou, Shantou, Chaozhou, Zhanjiang, Haikou, Luoyang, Zhengzhou (Chengchow), Kaifeng, Xuzhou (Tongshan), Hefei, Wuhu, Hangzhou, Ningbo (Yin Xian), Wenzhou, Ganzhou, Guilin, Liuzhou, Wuzhou, T'ai-pei (Taibei), Kao-hsiung (Gaoxiong), T'ai-chung (Taizhong), T'ai-nan (Tainan), Chi-lung (Jilong)

Scale: 1:6 000 000 — 0 40 80 120 160 200 MILES / 0 40 80 120 160 200 240 280 320 KM

Tropic of Cancer

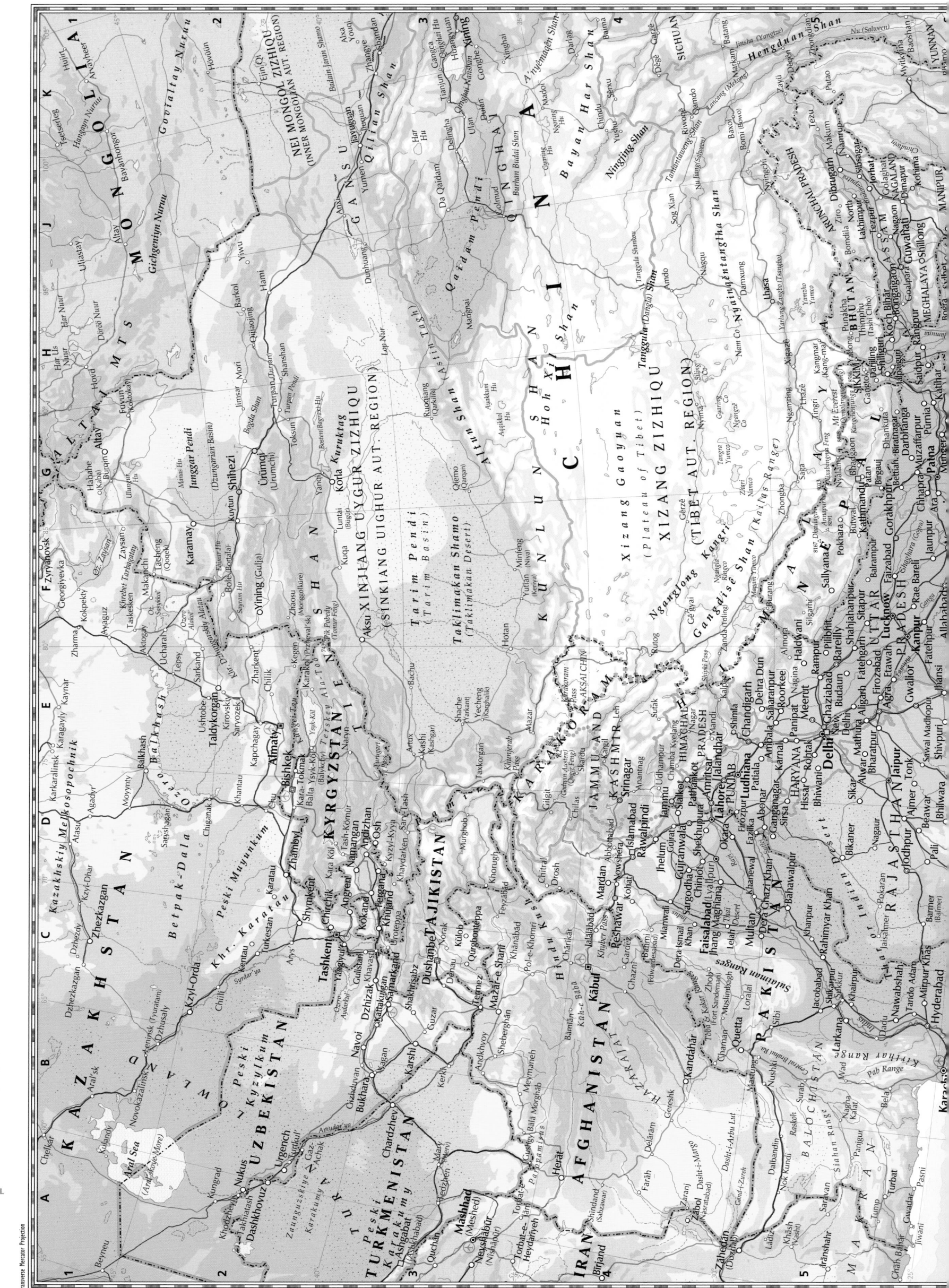

METRES	FEET
6000	19686
5000	16409
4000	13124
3000	9843
2000	6562
1000	3281
500	1640
200	656

SEA | LEVEL

200 | 656
2000 | 6562
4000 | 13124
6000 | 19686

Transverse Mercator Projection

© HarperCollinsPublishers

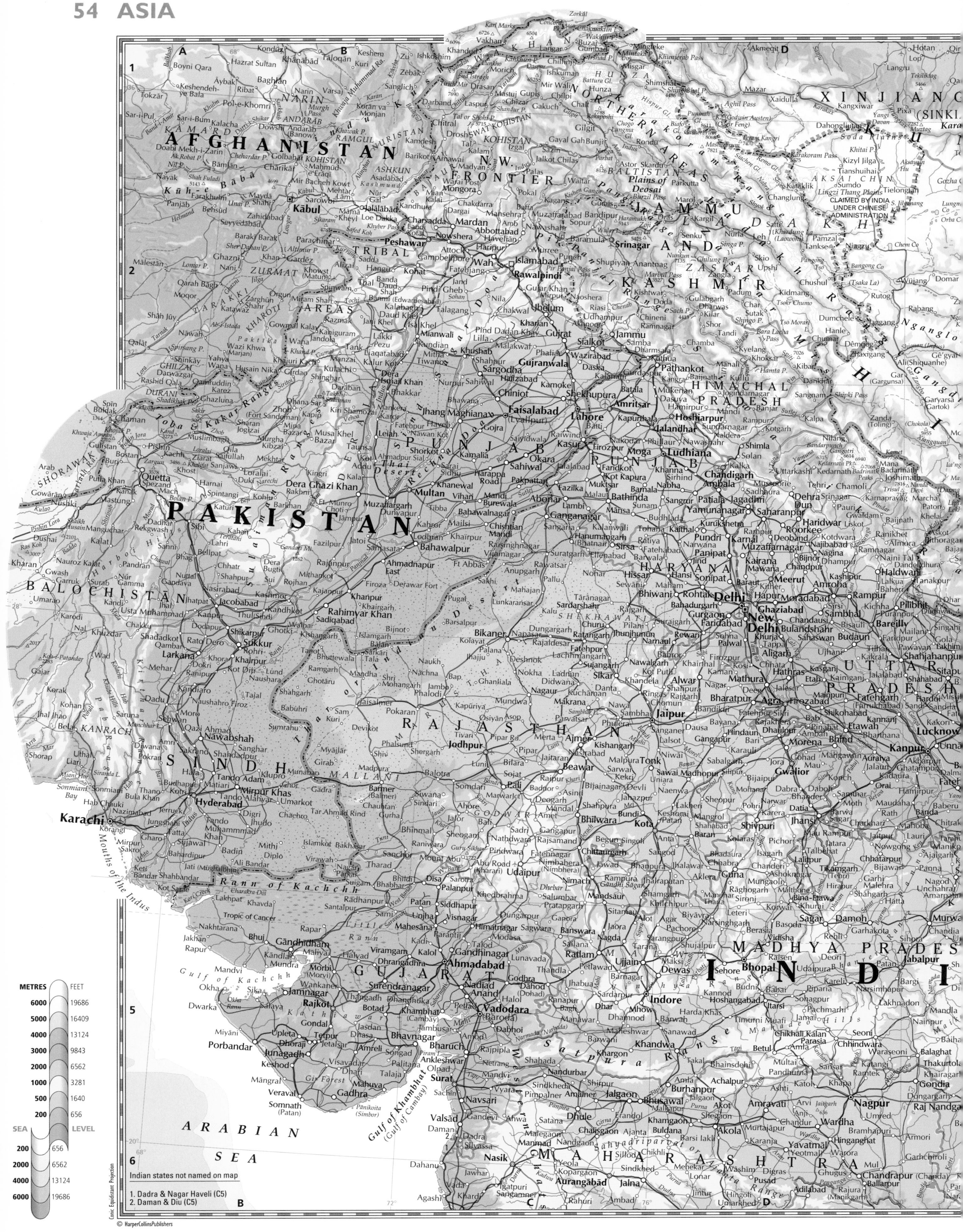

AFGHANISTAN

PAKISTAN

INDIA

BALOCHISTAN

SINDH

RAJASTHAN

PUNJAB

GUJARAT

MAHARASHTRA

MADHYA PRADESH

UTTAR PRADESH

HARYANA

HIMACHAL PRADESH

JAMMU & KASHMIR

XINJIANG (SINKIANG)

N.W. FRONTIER

TRIBAL AREAS

ARABIAN SEA

Gulf of Kachchh

Gulf of Khambhat (Gulf of Cambay)

Rann of Kachchh

Little Rann

Mouths of the Indus

Tropic of Cancer

Karachi · New Delhi · Delhi · Ahmadabad · Jaipur · Lahore · Islamabad · Rawalpindi · Kabul · Peshawar · Quetta · Hyderabad · Multan · Faisalabad · Amritsar · Ludhiana · Chandigarh · Jodhpur · Udaipur · Kota · Bhopal · Indore · Vadodara · Surat · Rajkot · Bhavnagar · Nagpur · Kanpur · Lucknow · Agra · Gwalior · Jhansi · Aurangabad · Nasik

METRES	FEET
6000	19686
5000	16409
4000	13124
3000	9843
2000	6562
1000	3281
500	1640
200	656
SEA	LEVEL
200	656
2000	6562
4000	13124
6000	19686

Conic Equidistant Projection

Indian states not named on map
1. Dadra & Nagar Haveli (C5)
2. Daman & Diu (C5)

© HarperCollinsPublishers

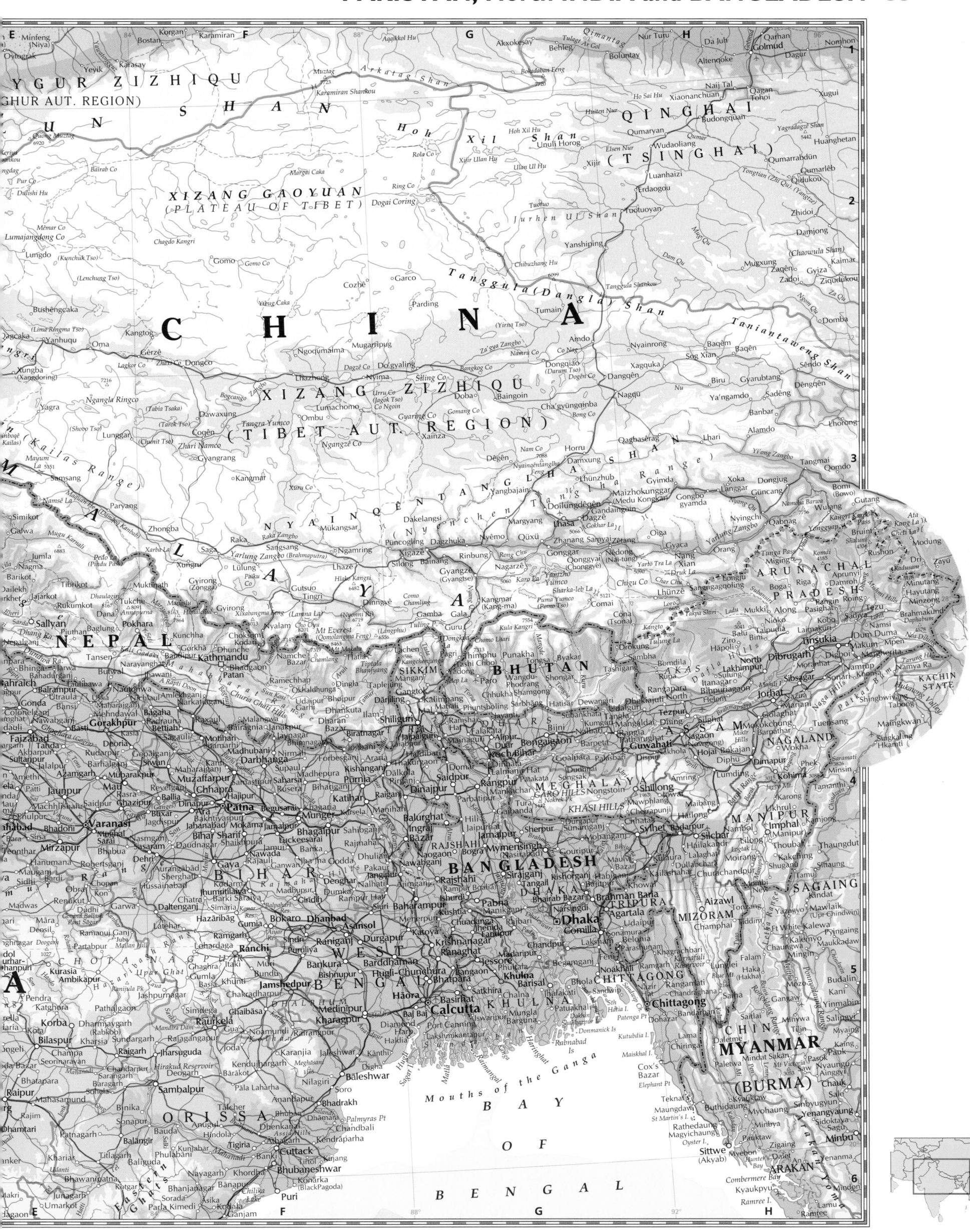

1:6 000 000

Indian states not named on map
1. Dadra & Nagar Haveli (A1)
2. Daman & Diu (A1)

© HarperCollinsPublishers

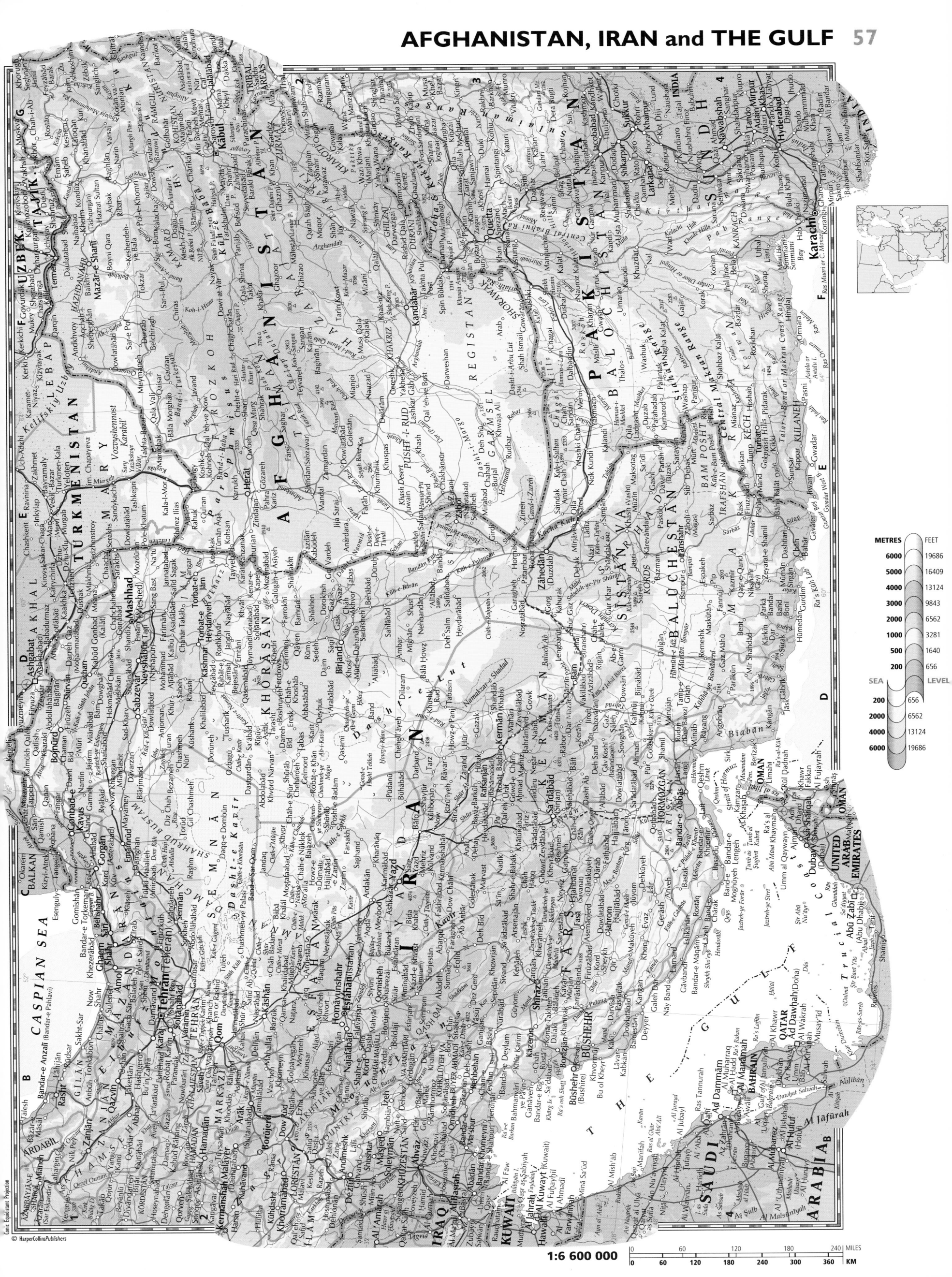

1 : 6 600 000

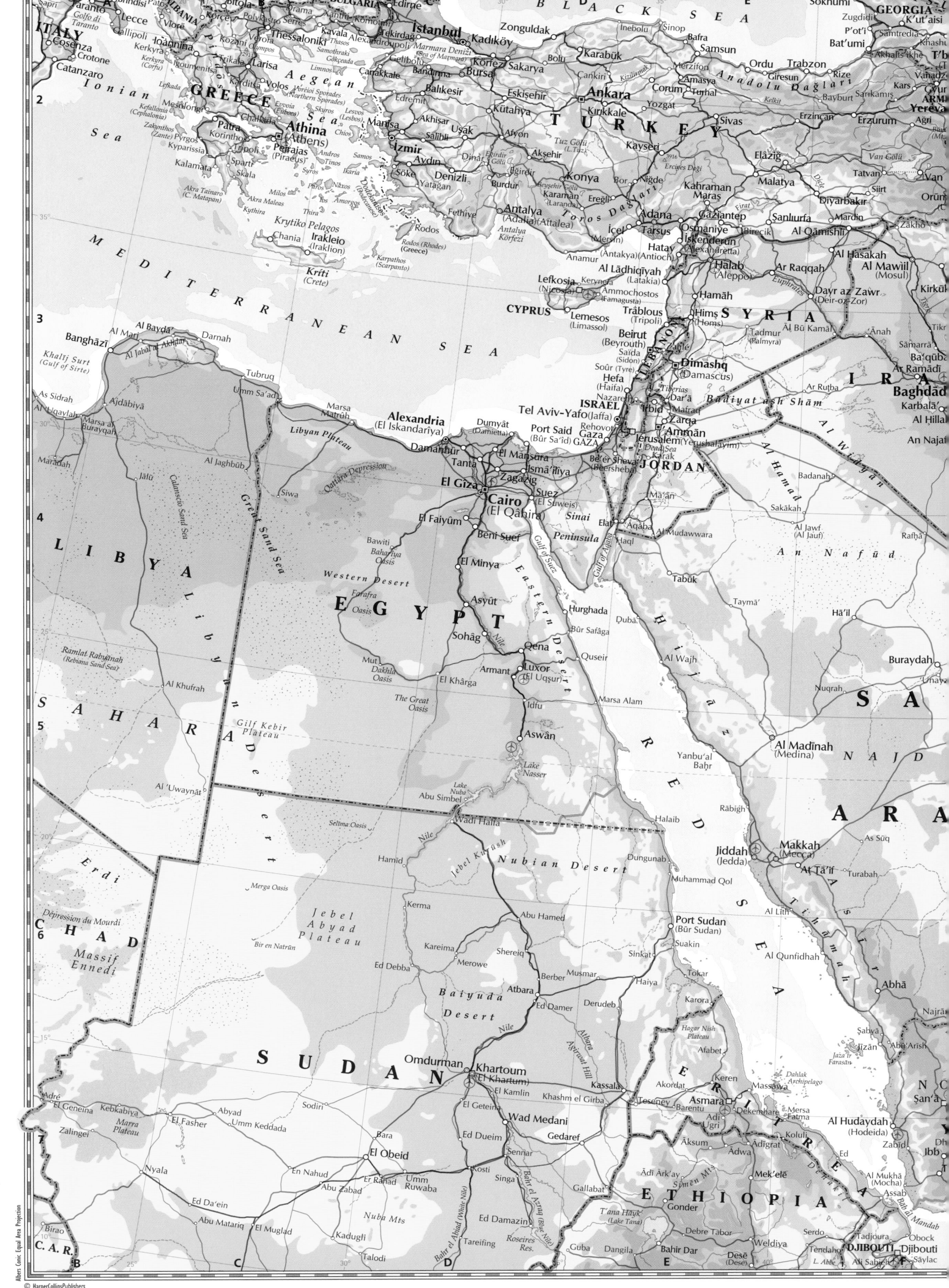

METRES | FEET
6000 | 19686
5000 | 16409
4000 | 13124
3000 | 9843
2000 | 6562
1000 | 3281
500 | 1640
200 | 656
SEA | LEVEL
200 | 656
2000 | 6562
4000 | 13124
6000 | 19686

Albers Conic Equal Area Projection

© HarperCollinsPublishers

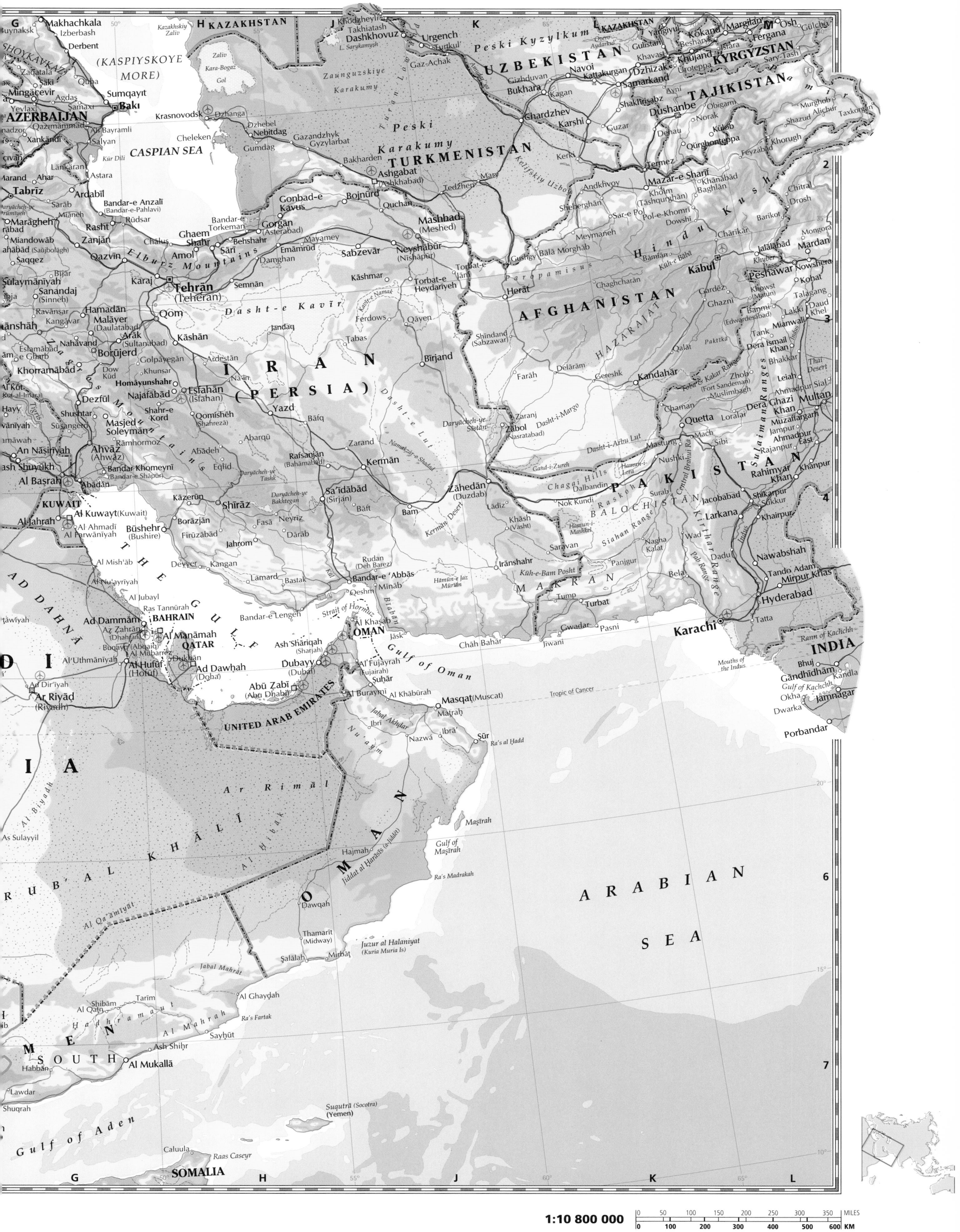

G Makhachkala Izberbash Derbent

H KAZAKHSTAN Takhiatash Khodzheyli Takhiatash Urgench Turtkul'

K Peski Kyzylkum KAZAKHSTAN Gulistan Yangiyul' Kokand Margilan Osh Gülchö

M Besharik Isfara Fergana

SHOYKHAVKAZ Zaqatala Şaki Quba Mingäçevir Ağdaş Sumqayıt Bakı

Kazakhskiy Zaliv Zaliv Kara-Bogaz-Gol Krasnovodsk Dzhanga

UZBEKISTAN Navoi Kattakurgan Samarkand Urateppa Khujand

Shakhrisabz Denau Kulob Obigarm Norak

TAJIKISTAN Murghob Shazud Alichur Taxkorgan

AZERBAIJAN Qazımämmäd Xankändi Şamaxı çivär Yevlax

Kür Dili Salyan Gizhduvan Bukhara Kagan Karshi Guzar Dushanbe

KYRGYZSTAN Sary-Tash mir

Derbent Astara Länkäran Cheleken Nebitdag Gazandzhyk Gyzylarbat

Bakharden Ashgabat (Ashkhabad) Tedzhen Mary Kerki Termez Qürghonteppa Feyzabad Khorugh

CASPIAN SEA (KASPIYSKOYE MORE) Zaunguzskiye Karakumy Gumdag

Turan Low Gaz-Achak Chardzhev Kelifskiy Uzboy Andkhvoy Mazar-e Sharif Khānābād Baghlan

Chitral Drosh Mongora

Tabrīz Marand Ahar Ardabīl Sarab Mīāneh

Bandar-e Anzalī (Bandar-e Pahlavi) Rūdsar Gonbad-e Kāvūs Bojnūrd Quchan Mashhad (Meshed)

Peski Karakumy TURKMENISTAN Bakharden

Sheberghan Sar-e Pol Pol-e Khomri Dowshi Meymaneh Bālā Morghāb Gushgy

Kholm (Tashqurghan) Bamiān Kūh-e Bābā Charikar

Jalalabad Mardan Kабul Peshawar Kohat Khyber Pass

Maragheh Miandowāb ahābād Saqqez Zanjān Qazvīn Karaj Ghaem Shahr Chalus Āmol Sārī Behshahr

Gorgan (Asterabad) Mayamey Sabzevar Neyshābūr (Nishapur) Torbat-e Jām

Herāt Chaghcharān Paropamisus HAZARAJAT

Ghazni Gordez Khowst (Matun) Bannu (Edwardesabad) Talagang Mianwali

Sulaymānīyah Sanandaj Bījar Ravānsar Hamadān Malāyer (Daulatabad) Tehrān (Teheran) Qom Semnan Dasht-e Kavīr Emāmrūd Damghan Kāshmar Torbat-e Heydarīyeh Ferdows Qāyen

AFGHANISTAN Shindand (Sabzawar) Qalat Paktīā Lakki Daud Khel

änshāh Kangāvar Nahāvand Arāk (Sultanabad) Borūjerd Golpāyegān Khunsar Dow Kūd

Kāshān Ardestān Nā'in Jandaq Tabas Birjand Delārām Gereshk Kandahār

Thal Desert Dera Ismail Khan Bhakkar Leiah

Khorramābād Eslamābād-e Gharb äm Nahāvand

Dezfūl Homāyūnshahr Najafābād Esfahān (Isfahan) Shahr-e Kord Qomīsheh (Shahreza) Yazd Bāfq

IRAN (PERSIA) Farāh Zābol (Nasratabad) Zaranj

Chaman Quetta Loralai Muslimbagh (Fort Sandeman) Zhob Fort Munro Kakar Range

Ahmadpur East Multan Muzaffargarh Jampur Ahmadpur East Rajanpur

An Nāsirīyah ash Shuyūkh Ahvāz (Ahwaz) Shushtar Süsangerd Rāmhormoz Masjed Soleymān Abādān Abadeh

Zarand Rafsanjān (Bahrāmābād) Kermān

Daryācheh-ye Sīstān Dasht-i-Margo Dasht-e Lūt Namakzar-e Shahdad

Zāhedān (Duzdab) Nok Kundi Dalbandin Chagai Hills Ladīz Khāsh (Vasht)

BALOCHISTAN PAKISTAN Surab Nushki Mastung Sibi Mach Sultaiman Ranges

Rahimyar Khan Khanpur Larkana Jacobabad Shikarpur Sukkur Khairpur

Al Başrah KUWAIT Al Jahrah Al Kuwayt (Kuwait) Al Ahmadī Al Farwānīyah

Kāzerūn Shīrāz Sa'īdābād (Sirjan) Bāft Bam Kerman Desert Saravan Panjgur Kītha Range

Nawabshah Tando Adam Mirpur Khas

Būshehr (Bushire) Borāzjān Fīrūzābād Jahrom Fasā Neyrīz Dārāb

Iranshahr Tump Turbat Gwadar Pasni Bela Pab Range

Hyderabad

Devyer Al Mish'āb Kangan Lamard Bastak Rudan (Deh Barez) Bandar-e 'Abbās Minab

Jāsk Chāh Bahar Jiwani Mouths of the Indus

Ad Dammām Az Zahrān (Dhahran) BAHRAIN Al Manāmah QATAR Bandar-e Lengeh Qeshm Strait of Hormuz Al Khaşab OMAN

Tatta INDIA Bhuj Karachi

AD DAHNA Ar Riyāḍ (Riyadh) Ad Dawḥah (Doha) Dubayy (Dubai) Ash Shāriqah (Sharjah) Al Fujayrah Şuḥār

Gulf of Oman Gulf of Kachchh Gāndhīdhām Okha Jamnagar Dwarka

THE GULF Abū Zabī (Abū Dhabi) UNITED ARAB EMIRATES Al Buraymī Al Khābūrah Masqaţ (Muscat) Maţrah

Rann of Kachchh

Porbandar

DIA As Sulayyil Al Biyādh Ar Rimāl Al Hibak Nu'ayj Ibrī Jabal Akhdar Nazwā Ibrā Sūr Ra's al Ḥadd Tropic of Cancer

RUB' AL KHĀLĪ OMAN Al Qarāmiyāt Ḥajmah Jiddat al Ḥarāsīs (al Ḥaddat) Gulf of Maṣīrah Maṣīrah Ra's Madrakah

ARABIAN SEA

Dawqah Thamarīt (Midway) Şalālah Mirbāţ Juzur al Halaniyat (Kuria Muria Is)

MEN Shibām Tarim Al Qaṭn Ḥaḍramaut Al Mahrah Al Ghaydah Ra's Fartak Jabal Mahrāt Sayhūt

SOUTH Habban Ash Shiḥr Al Mukallā

Lawdar Shuqrah Caluula Raas Caseyr

Gulf of Aden Suquţrā (Socotra) (Yemen)

G SOMALIA H J K L

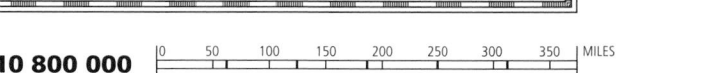

| 0 | 50 | 100 | 150 | 200 | 250 | 300 | 350 | MILES |
| 0 | 100 | 200 | 300 | 400 | 500 | 600 | KM |

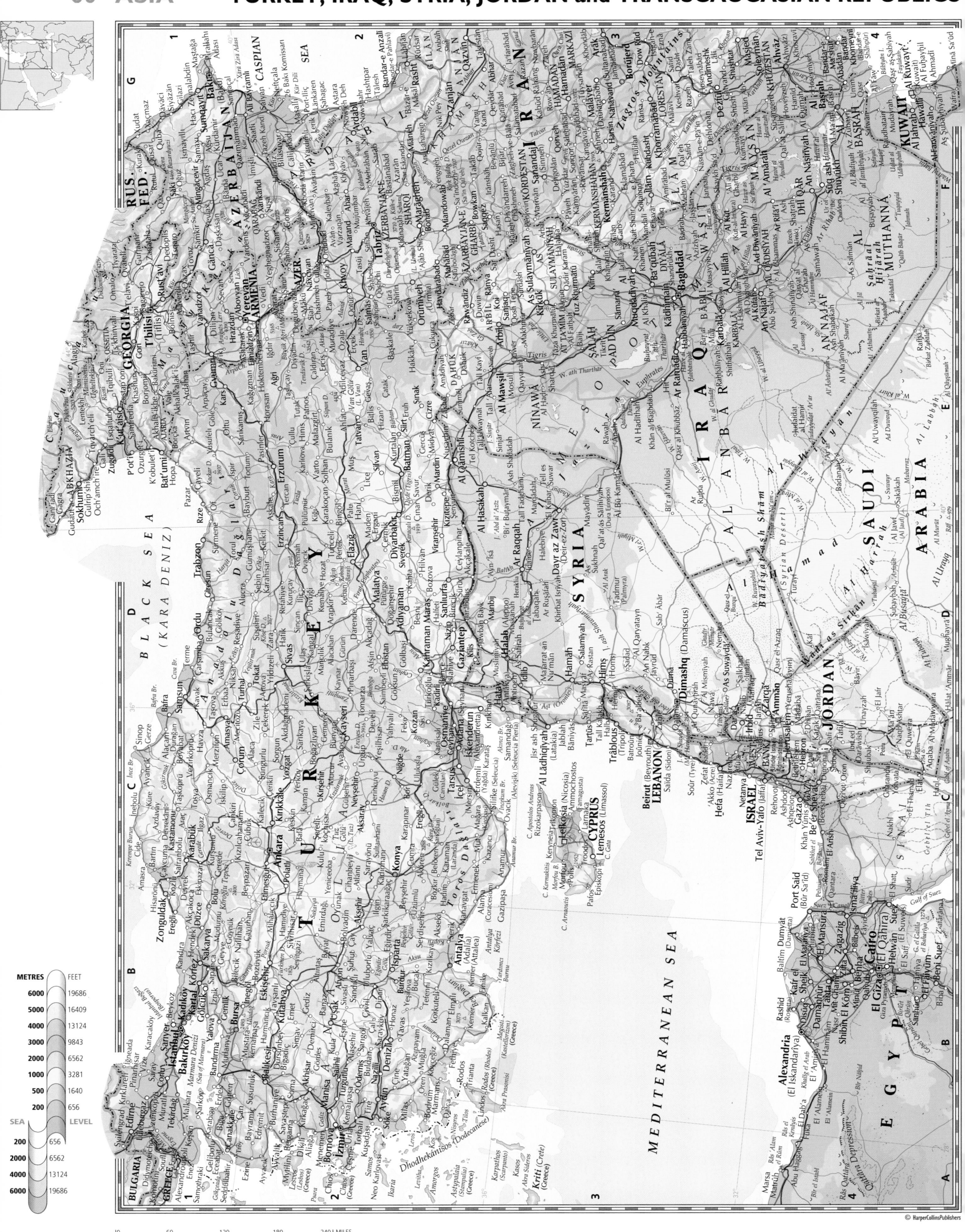

METRES | FEET
6000 | 19686
5000 | 16409
4000 | 13124
3000 | 9843
2000 | 6562
1000 | 3281
500 | 1640
200 | 656
SEA | LEVEL
200 | 656
2000 | 6562
4000 | 13124
6000 | 19686

0   60   120   180   240 MILES
0 60 120 180 240 300 360 KM

1:6 600 000

HarperCollinsPublishers

MEDITERRANEAN SEA

CYPRUS

TURKEY

SYRIA

LEBANON

ISRAEL

JORDAN

EGYPT

SAUDI ARABIA

SINAI

METRES	FEET
6000	19686
5000	16409
4000	13124
3000	9843
2000	6562
1000	3281
500	1640
200	656
SEA LEVEL	
200	656
2000	6562
4000	13124
6000	19686

© HarperCollins Publishers

1:3 300 000

	MILES
0 30 60 90	
0 30 60 90 120 150 180	KM

METRES | FEET
6000 | 19686
5000 | 16409
4000 | 13124
3000 | 9843
2000 | 6562
1000 | 3281
500 | 1640
200 | 656
SEA | LEVEL
200 | 656
2000 | 6562
4000 | 13124
6000 | 19686

Conic Equidistant Projection

© HarperCollinsPublishers

1:18 000 000

							MILES
0	120	240	360	480		600	
0	120	240	360	480	600	720	840	960 KM

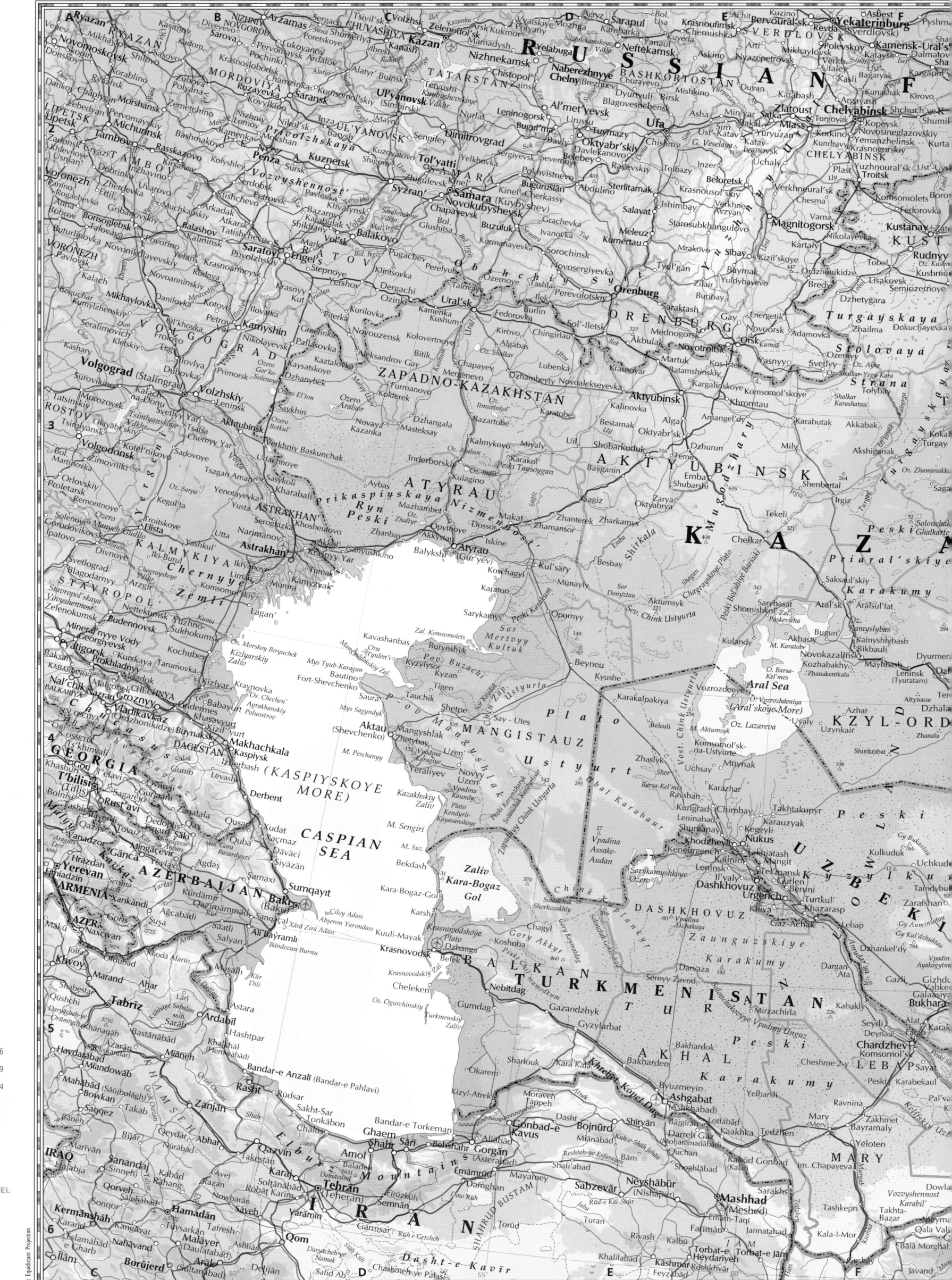

METRES | FEET
6000 | 19686
5000 | 16409
4000 | 13124
3000 | 9843
2000 | 6562
1000 | 3281
500 | 1640
200 | 656

SEA | LEVEL

200 | 656
2000 | 6562
4000 | 13124
6000 | 19686

Conic Equidistant Projection

© HarperCollins Publishers

TYUMEN'

NOVOSIBIRSK

KEMEROVO

Novosibirsk

Omsk

Barnaul

Biysk

SEVERO-KAZAKHSTAN

KOKSHETAU

Kokshetau

Petropavlovsk

PAVLODAR

Pavlodar

AKMOLA

Akmola

ALTAYSKIY KRAY

RESPUBLIKA ALTAY

Altai Mountains

Rubtsovsk

Semipalatinsk

Leninogorsk

Ust'-Kamenogorsk

VOST.-KAZAKHSTAN

MON.

KARAGANDA

Karaganda

Temirtau

SEMIPALATINSK

Altay

K A Z A K H S T A N

ZHEZKAZGAN

Zhezkazgan

Betpak-Dala

Oz. Balkhash

Balkhash

Junggar Pendi
(Dzungarian Basin)

Karamay

Shihezi

TALDYKORGAN

Taldykorgan

Yining
(Gulja)

Barohoro Shan

YUZHNO-

ZHAMBYL

ALMATY

Almaty
(Alma Ata)

XINJIANG UYGUR ZIZHIQU

Korla

Bishkek

KAZAKHSTAN

Turkestan

KYRGYZSTAN

TIEN SHAN

Naryn

Aksu

Tashkent

Chirchik

Namangan
Andizhan

Osh

Fergana

Margilan

Kokand

CHINA
(SINKIANG UIGHUR AUT. REGION)

Tarim Pendi (Tarim Basin)

Khujand

Samarkand

TAJIKISTAN

Dushanbe

Taklimakan Shamo
(Taklimakan Desert)

Kulob

KUNLUN SHAN

HUNZA

NORTHERN AREAS

Mazār-e Sharīf

Termez

AFGHANISTAN

AKSAI CHIN
CLAIMED BY INDIA
UNDER CHINESE
ADMIN.

XIZANG ZIZHIQU
(TIBET AUT. REGION)

N.W.
FRONTIER

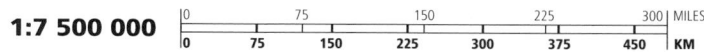

1:7 500 000

| 0 | 75 | 150 | 225 | 300 MILES |

| 0 | 75 | 150 | 225 | 300 | 375 | 450 KM |

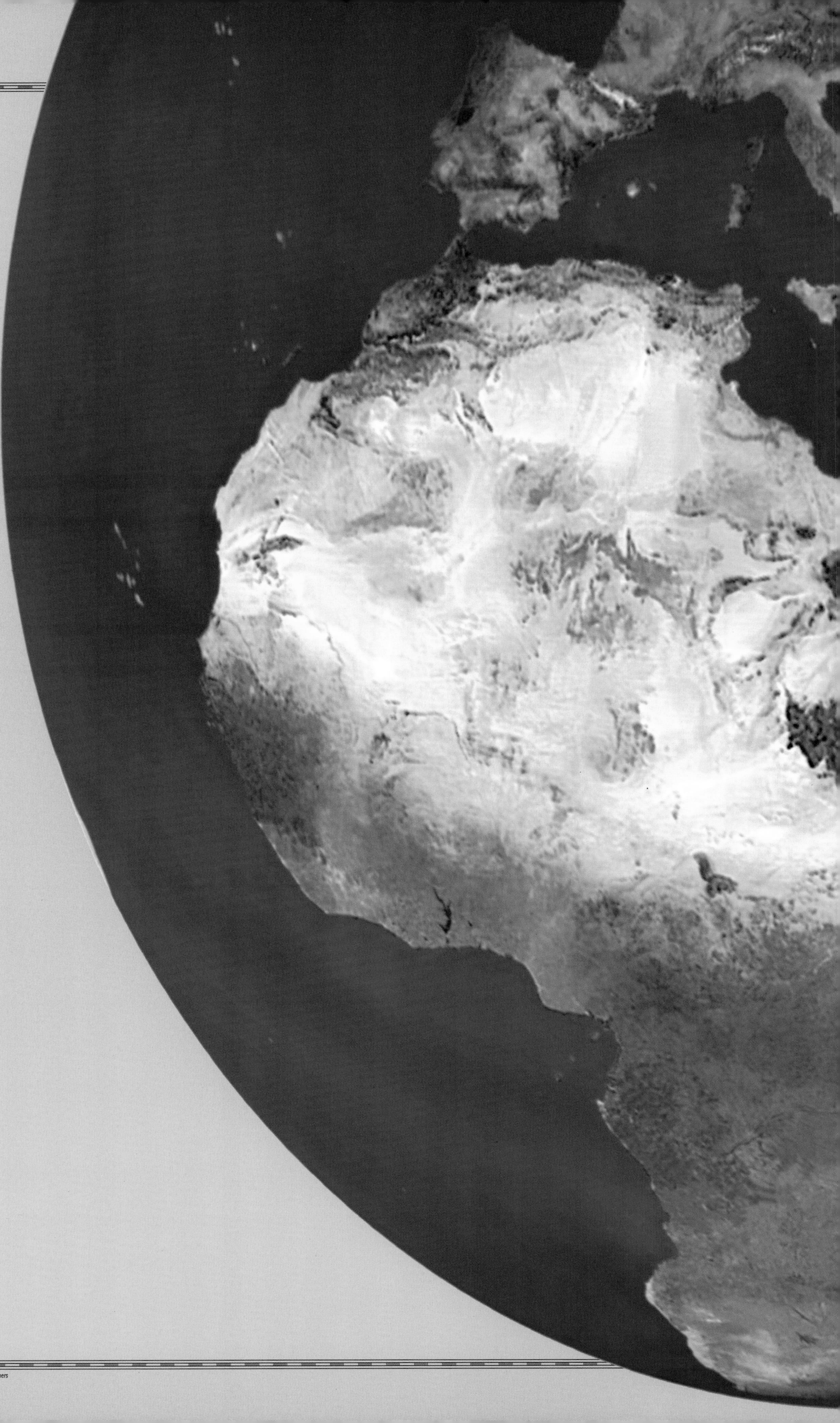

© HarperCollins Publishers

MILES 0   150   300   450   600   750
KM 0 150 300 450 600 750 900 1050 1200

1:25 000 000

Oblard Stereographic Projection

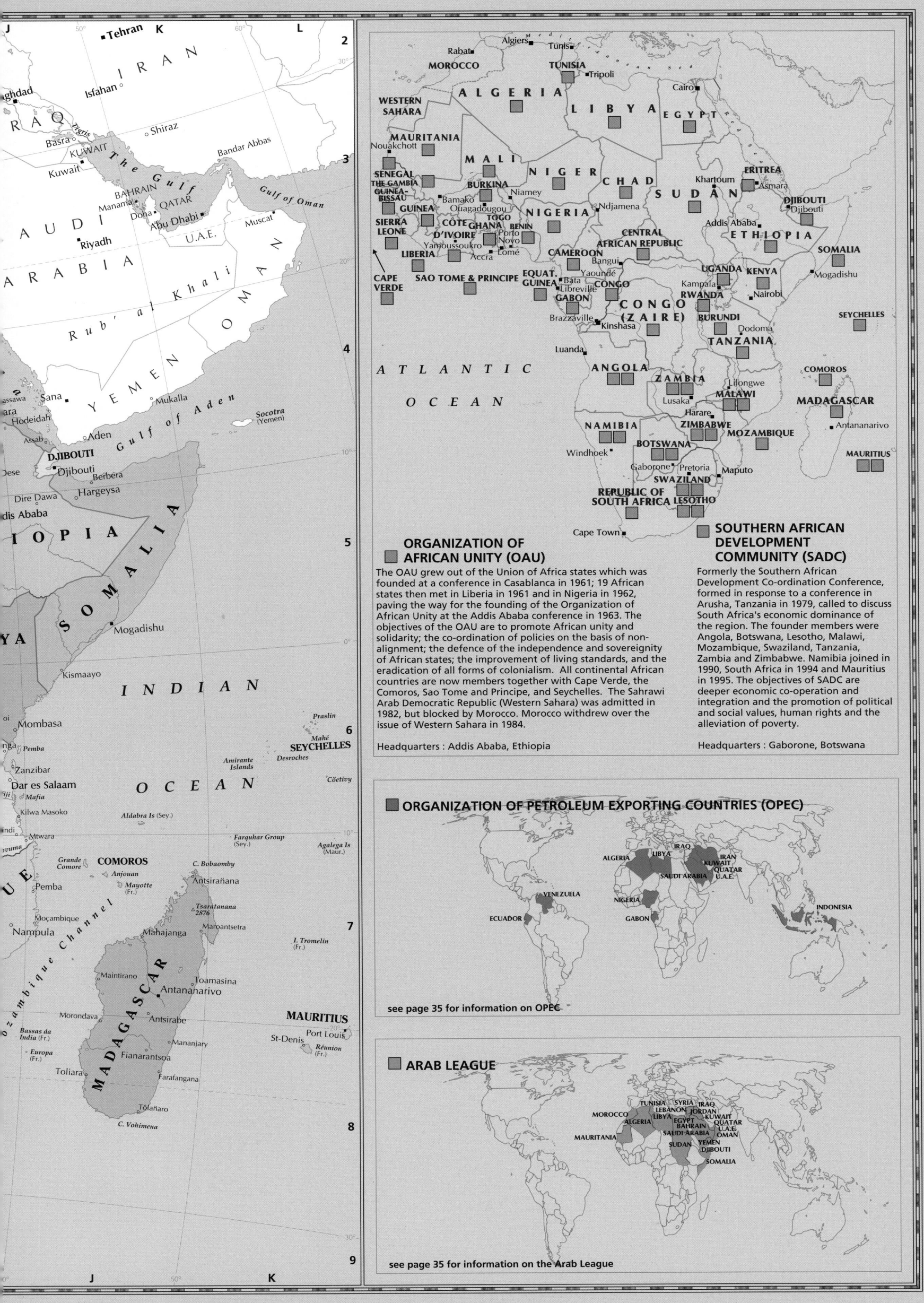

ORGANIZATION OF AFRICAN UNITY (OAU)

The OAU grew out of the Union of Africa states which was founded at a conference in Casablanca in 1961; 19 African states then met in Liberia in 1961 and in Nigeria in 1962, paving the way for the founding of the Organization of African Unity at the Addis Ababa conference in 1963. The objectives of the OAU are to promote African unity and solidarity; the co-ordination of policies on the basis of non-alignment; the defence of the independence and sovereignty of African states; the improvement of living standards, and the eradication of all forms of colonialism. All continental African countries are now members together with Cape Verde, the Comoros, Sao Tome and Principe, and Seychelles. The Sahrawi Arab Democratic Republic (Western Sahara) was admitted in 1982, but blocked by Morocco. Morocco withdrew over the issue of Western Sahara in 1984.

Headquarters : Addis Ababa, Ethiopia

SOUTHERN AFRICAN DEVELOPMENT COMMUNITY (SADC)

Formerly the Southern African Development Co-ordination Conference, formed in response to a conference in Arusha, Tanzania in 1979, called to discuss South Africa's economic dominance of the region. The founder members were Angola, Botswana, Lesotho, Malawi, Mozambique, Swaziland, Tanzania, Zambia and Zimbabwe. Namibia joined in 1990, South Africa in 1994 and Mauritius in 1995. The objectives of SADC are deeper economic co-operation and integration, and the promotion of political and social values, human rights and the alleviation of poverty.

Headquarters : Gaborone, Botswana

ORGANIZATION OF PETROLEUM EXPORTING COUNTRIES (OPEC)

see page 35 for information on OPEC

ARAB LEAGUE

see page 35 for information on the Arab League

COUNTRY	AREA sq ml	sq km	POPULATION total	density per sq ml	sq km	FORM OF GOVERNMENT	CAPITAL CITY	MAIN LANGUAGES	MAIN RELIGIONS	CURRENCY
ALGERIA	919 595	2 381 741	27 561 000	30	12	republic	Algiers	Arabic, French, Berber	Muslim, R.C.	Dinar
ANGOLA	481 354	1 246 700	10 674 000	22	9	republic	Luanda	Portuguese, local lang	R.C., Protestant, trad. beliefs	Kwanza
BENIN	43 483	112 620	5 387 000	124	48	republic	Porto Novo	French, Fon, Yoruba, Adja, local lang	Trad. beliefs, R.C., Muslim	CFA franc
BOTSWANA	224 468	581 370	1 443 000	6	2	republic	Gaborone	English (official), Setswana, Shona, local lang	Trad. beliefs, Protestant, R.C.	Pula
BURKINA	105 869	274 200	9 889 000	93	36	republic	Ouagadougou	French, More (Mossi), Fulani, local lang	Trad. beliefs, Muslim, R.C.	CFA franc
BURUNDI	10 747	27 835	6 134 000	571	220	republic	Bujumbura	Kirundi (Hutu, Tutsi), French	R.C., trad. beliefs, Protestant, Muslim	Franc
CAMEROON	183 569	475 442	12 871 000	70	27	republic	Yaoundé	French, English, Fang, Bamileke, local lang	Trad. beliefs, R.C., Muslim, Protestant	CFA franc
CAPE VERDE	1 557	4 033	381 000	245	94	republic	Praia	Portuguese, Portuguese Creole	R.C., Protestant, trad. beliefs	Escudo
C. A. R.	240 324	622 436	3 235 000	13	5	republic	Bangui	French, Sango, Banda, Baya, local lang	Protestant, R.C., trad. beliefs, Muslim	CFA franc
CHAD	495 755	1 284 000	6 214 000	13	5	republic	Ndjamena	Arabic, French, local lang	Muslim, trad. beliefs, R.C.	CFA franc
COMOROS	719	1 862	630 000	876	338	republic	Moroni	Comorian, French, Arabic	Muslim, R.C.	Franc
CONGO	132 047	342 000	2 516 000	19	7	republic	Brazzaville	French, Kongo, Monokutuba, local lang	R.C., Protestant, trad. beliefs, Muslim	CFA franc
CÔTE D'IVOIRE	124 504	322 463	13 695 000	110	42	republic	Yamoussoukro	French, Akan, Kru, Gur, local lang	Trad. beliefs, Muslim, R.C.	CFA franc
DJIBOUTI	8 958	23 200	566 000	63	24	republic	Djibouti	Somali, French, Arabic, Issa, Afar	Muslim, R.C.	Franc
EGYPT	386 199	1 000 250	57 851 000	150	58	republic	Cairo	Arabic, French	Muslim, Coptic Christian	Pound
EQUATORIAL GUINEA	10 831	28 051	389 000	36	14	republic	Malabo	Spanish, Fang	R.C., trad. beliefs	CFA franc
ERITREA	45 328	117 400	3 437 000	76	29	republic	Asmara	Tigrinya, Arabic, Tigre, English	Muslim, Coptic Christian	Ethiopian birr
ETHIOPIA	437 794	1 133 880	54 938 000	125	48	republic	Addis Ababa	Amharic, Oromo, local lang	Ethiopian Orthodox, Muslim, trad. beliefs	Birr
GABON	103 347	267 667	1 283 000	12	5	republic	Libreville	French, Fang, local lang	R.C., Protestant, trad. beliefs	CFA franc
GAMBIA	4 361	11 295	1 081 000	248	96	republic	Banjul	English, Malinke, Fulani, Wolof	Muslim, Protestant	Dalasi
GHANA	92 100	238 537	16 944 000	184	71	republic	Accra	English, Hausa, Akan, local lang	Protestant, R.C., Muslim, trad. beliefs	Cedi
GUINEA	94 926	245 857	6 501 000	68	26	republic	Conakry	French, Fulani, Malinke, local lang	Muslim, trad. beliefs, R.C.	Franc
GUINEA-BISSAU	13 948	36 125	1 050 000	75	29	republic	Bissau	Portuguese, Portuguese Creole, local lang	Trad. beliefs, Muslim, R.C.	Peso
KENYA	224 961	582 646	29 292 000	130	50	republic	Nairobi	Swahili, English, local lang	R.C., Protestant, trad. beliefs	Shilling
LESOTHO	11 720	30 355	1 996 000	170	66	monarchy	Maseru	Sesotho, English, Zulu	R.C., Protestant, trad. beliefs	Loti
LIBERIA	43 000	111 369	2 700 000	63	24	republic	Monrovia	English, Creole, local lang	Trad. beliefs, Muslim, Protestant, R.C.	Dollar
LIBYA	679 362	1 759 540	4 899 000	7	3	republic	Tripoli	Arabic, Berber	Muslim, R.C.	Dinar
MADAGASCAR	226 658	587 041	14 303 000	63	24	republic	Antananarivo	Malagasy, French	Trad. beliefs, R.C., Protestant, Muslim	Franc
MALAWI	45 747	118 484	9 461 000	207	80	republic	Lilongwe	English, Chichewa, Lomwe, local lang	Protestant, R.C., trad. beliefs, Muslim	Kwacha
MALI	478 821	1 240 140	10 462 000	22	8	republic	Bamako	French, Bambara, local lang	Muslim, trad. beliefs, R.C.	CFA franc
MAURITANIA	397 955	1 030 700	2 211 000	6	2	republic	Nouakchott	Arabic, French, local lang	Muslim	Ouguiya
MAURITIUS	788	2 040	1 113 000	1413	546	republic	Port Louis	English, French Creole, Hindi, Indian languages	Hindu, R.C., Muslim, Protestant	Rupee
MOROCCO	172 414	446 550	26 590 000	154	60	monarchy	Rabat	Arabic, Berber, French, Spanish	Muslim, R.C.	Dirham
MOZAMBIQUE	308 642	799 380	16 614 000	54	21	republic	Maputo	Portuguese, Makua, Tsonga, local lang	Trad. beliefs, R.C., Muslim	Metical
NAMIBIA	318 261	824 292	1 500 000	5	2	republic	Windhoek	English, Afrikaans, German, Ovambo, local lang	Protestant, R.C.	Dollar
NIGER	489 191	1 267 000	8 846 000	18	7	republic	Niamey	French, Hausa, Fulani, local lang	Muslim, trad. beliefs	CFA franc
NIGERIA	356 669	923 768	108 467 000	304	117	republic	Abuja	English, Creole, Hausa, Yoruba, Ibo, Fulani	Muslim, Protestant, R.C., trad. beliefs	Naira
RÉUNION	985	2 551	644 000	654	252	French territory	St-Denis	French, French Creole	R.C.	French franc
RWANDA	10 169	26 338	7 750 000	762	294	republic	Kigali	Kinyarwanda, French, English	R.C., trad. beliefs, Protestant, Muslim	Franc
SÃO TOMÉ AND PRÍNCIPE	372	964	125 000	336	130	republic	São Tomé	Portuguese, Portuguese Creole	R.C., Protestant	Dobra
SENEGAL	75 954	196 720	8 102 000	107	41	republic	Dakar	French, Wolof, Fulani, local lang	Muslim, R.C., trad. beliefs	CFA franc
SEYCHELLES	176	455	74 000	421	163	republic	Victoria	Seychellois, English	R.C., Protestant	Rupee
SIERRA LEONE	27 699	71 740	4 402 000	159	61	republic	Freetown	English, Creole, Mende, Temne, local lang	Trad. beliefs, Muslim, Protestant, R.C.	Leone
SOMALIA	246 201	637 657	9 077 000	37	14	republic	Mogadishu	Somali, Arabic	Muslim	Shilling
SOUTH AFRICA	470 689	1 219 080	40 436 000	86	33	republic	Pretoria/Cape Town	Afrikaans, English, local lang	Protestant, R.C., Muslim, Hindu	Rand
SUDAN	967 500	2 505 813	28 947 000	30	12	republic	Khartoum	Arabic, Dinka, Nubian, Beja, Nuer, local lang	Muslim, trad. beliefs, R.C., Protestant	Dinar
SWAZILAND	6 704	17 364	879 000	131	51	monarchy	Mbabane	Swazi, English	Protestant, R.C., trad. beliefs	Emalangeni
TANZANIA	364 900	945 087	28 846 000	79	31	republic	Dodoma	Swahili, English, Nyamwezi, local lang	R.C., Muslim, trad. beliefs, Protestant	Shilling
TOGO	21 925	56 785	3 928 000	179	69	republic	Lomé	French, Ewe, Kabre, local lang	Trad. beliefs, R.C., Muslim, Protestant	CFA franc
TUNISIA	63 379	164 150	8 814 000	139	54	republic	Tunis	Arabic, French	Muslim	Dinar
UGANDA	93 065	241 038	20 621 000	222	86	republic	Kampala	English, Swahili, Luganda, local lang	R.C., Protestant, Muslim, trad. beliefs	Shilling
ZAIRE (CONGO)	905 568	2 345 410	42 552 000	47	18	republic	Kinshasa	French, Lingala, Swahili, Kongo, local lang	R.C., Protestant, Muslim, trad. beliefs	Zaïre
ZAMBIA	290 586	752 614	9 196 000	32	12	republic	Lusaka	English, Bemba, Nyanja, Tonga, local lang	Protestant, R.C., trad. beliefs, Muslim	Kwacha
ZIMBABWE	150 873	390 759	11 150 000	74	29	republic	Harare	English, Shona, Ndebele	Protestant, R.C., trad. beliefs	Dollar

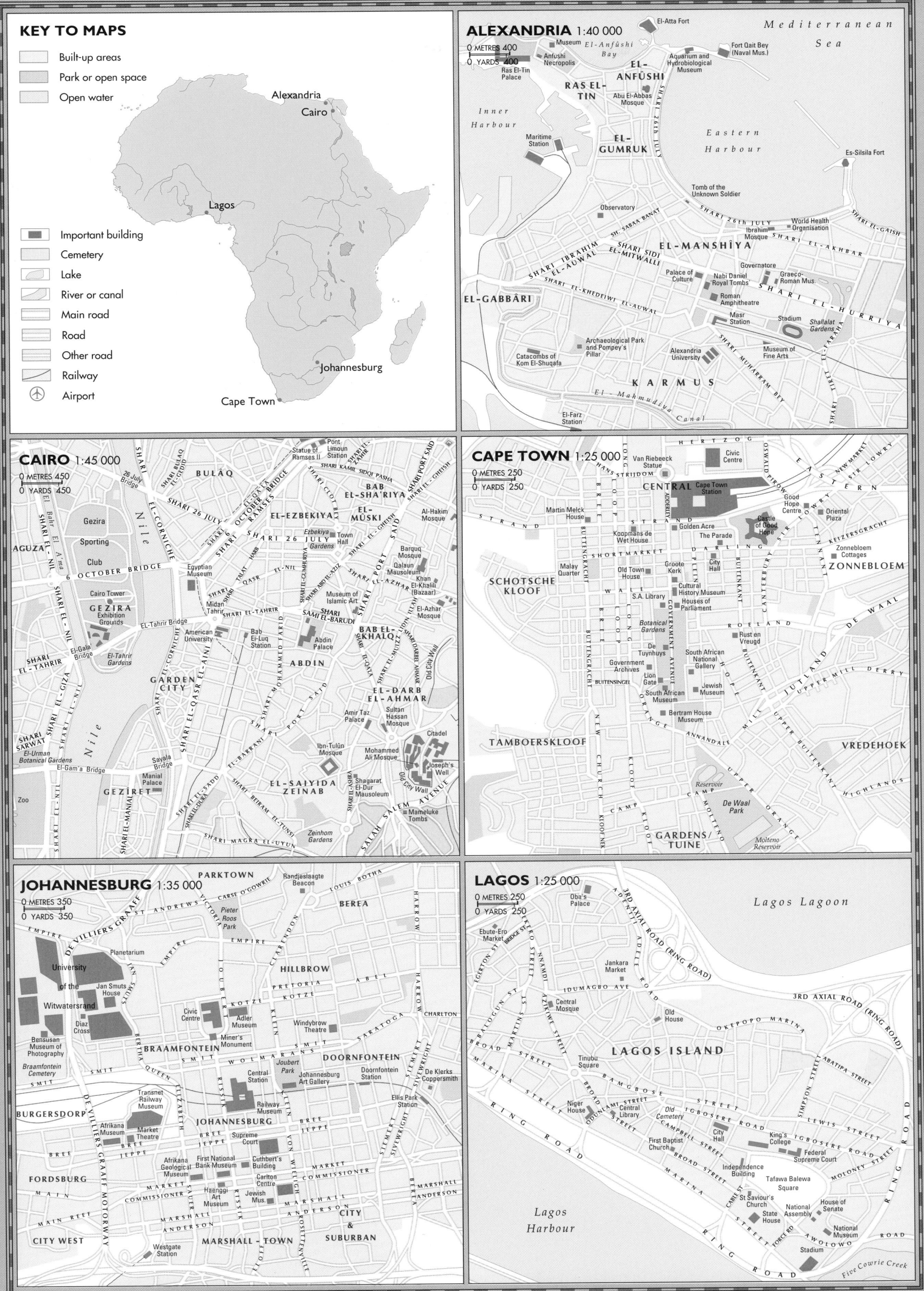

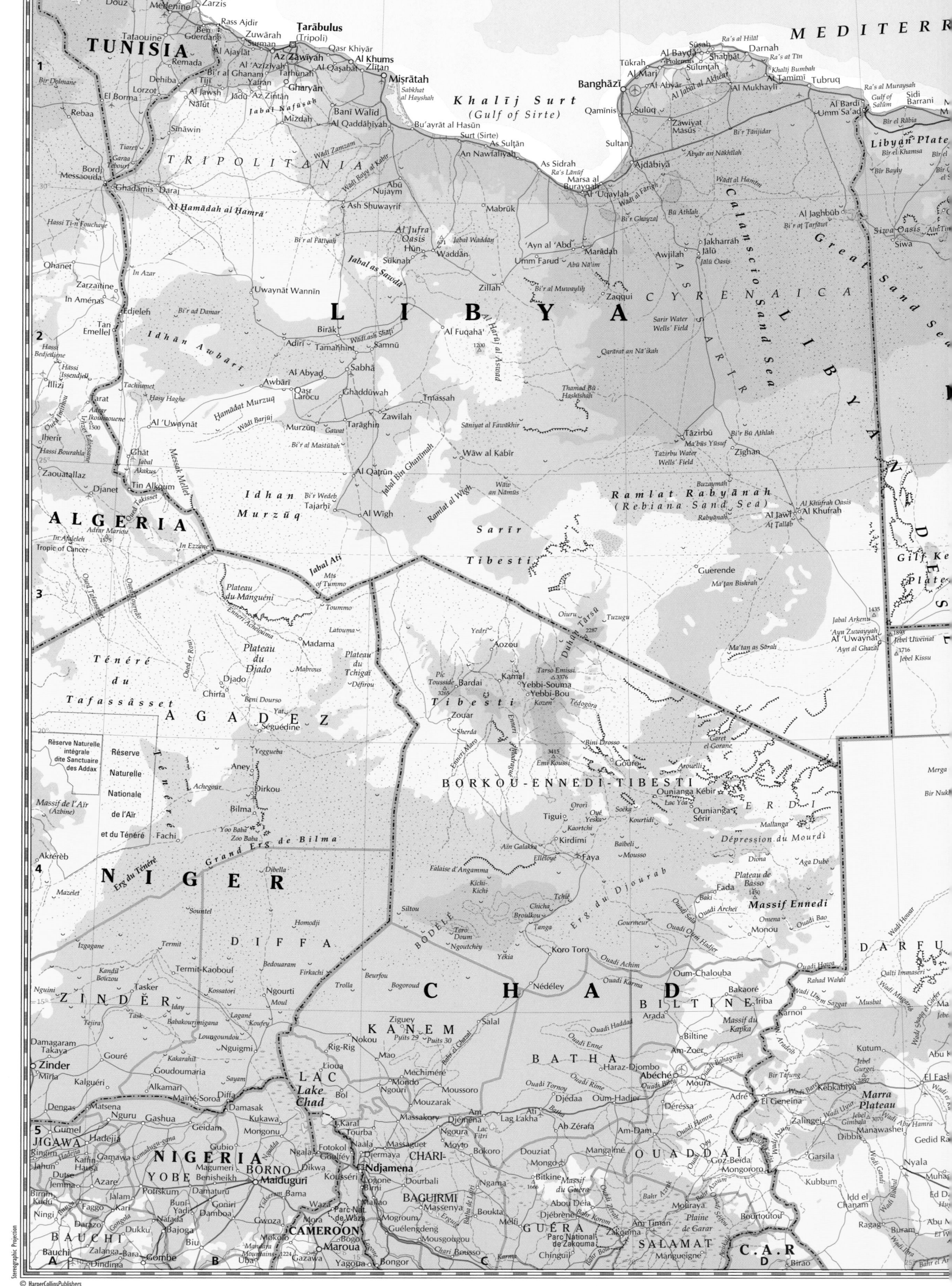

METRES | **FEET**
6000 | 19686
5000 | 16409
4000 | 13124
3000 | 9843
2000 | 6562
1000 | 3281
500 | 1640
200 | 656

SEA | **LEVEL**

200 | 656
2000 | 6562
4000 | 13124
6000 | 19686

Stereographic Projection

© HarperCollinsPublishers

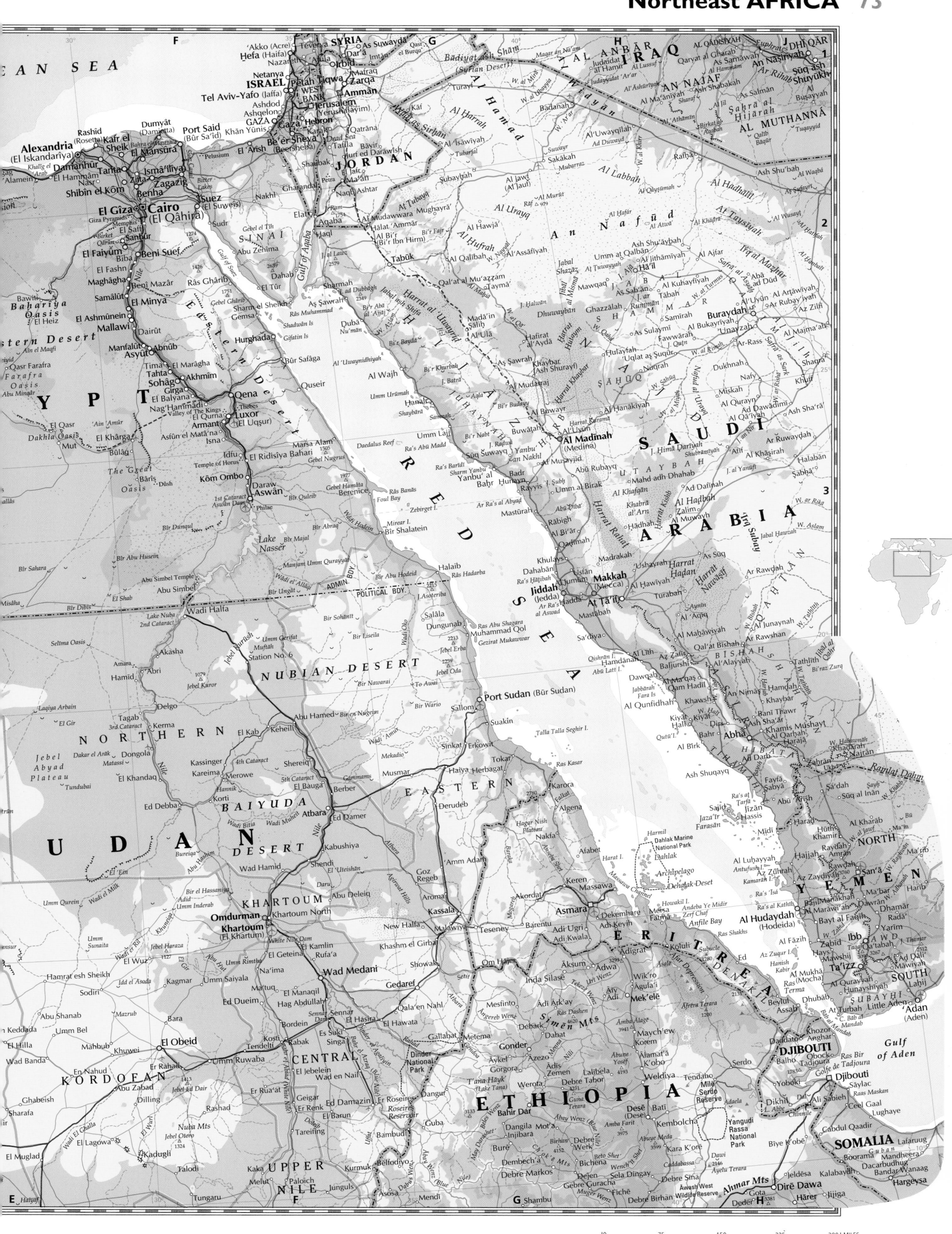

A   15   B   10   C

ATLANTIC

OCEAN

MADEIRA
(Portugal)
Ilha da Madeira
Funchal
Ilhas Desertas

Ilhas Selvagens

ISLAS CANARIAS
(CANARY ISLANDS)
(Spain)

La Palma
Sta Cruz
de la Palma
Tenerife
La Gomera
Santa Cruz
de Tenerife
El Hierro
Fuerteventura
Gran Canaria
Las Palmas
de Gran Canaria
Lanzarote
Arrecife
Puerto
del Rosario

Cap Juby
Tarfaya

MOROCCO

Cádiz
Jerez de la
Frontera
San Fernando
Málaga
Algeciras
Gibraltar (U.K.)
Tanger (Tangier)
Ceuta (Sp.)
Asilah
Larache
Tétouan (Tetua)
Al Hoceima
Ksar el Kebir
Souk el Arbaâ
du Rharb
Chaouen
Quezzane
Kénitra
Sidi
Kacem
Fès
Taza
Casablanca
Rabat
Azemmour
El Jadida
Ben Slimane
Khemisset
Meknès
Settat
Berrechid
Benahmed
Safi
Sidi
Bennour
Khouribga
Oued
Zem
Kasba
Tadla
Boulemane
Youssoufia
Fkih Ben
Salah
Beni Mellal
Chemaïa
Essaouira
Marrakech
(Marrakesh)
El Kelaâ des
Srarhna
Azilal
HAUT
ATLAS
(HIGH ATLAS)
Amizmiz
Cap Rhir
Agadir
Jbel Toubkal
Ouarzazate
Taroudannt
Oulad
Teima
Tiznit
Sidi Ifni
Tafraoute
Guelmine
Bou Izakarn
Tan-Tan
Akka
Anti Atlas
Tata
Foum
Zguid
Zagora
Er Rachidia
Erfoud
Jbel Sarhro
Hammada du Drâa

Laâyoune
Al Haggounia
As Saguia al Hamra
Es Semara
Boujdour
WESTERN
SAHARA
Amsine
Boukra
Hassi
Ardal
Sabkhat
Aridal
Imlidiy Labyad
Galtat Zemmour
Bir Mogrein
Bir Lahmar
Tfaritiy
Al Mahbas
Al Hamra
Aïn Ben Tili
TIRIS
ZEMMOUR
Ti-n-Bessaïs
El Hammâmi
Zouérat
Fdérik
Tichla
Imeimichât

Tropic of Cancer

Ad Dakhla
Al Argoub
B. de Rio de Oro
Bir Anzarane
EL AIÛN
Skaymat
Cap Corbeiro
Bir Gandouz
Nouâdhibou
Râs Nouâdhibou
Râs Agâtir
DAKHLET
NOUÂDHIBOU
Cansado
Bir Gâreb
Nutalfa
Âmeyim
INCHIRI
El Tidra
Râs Tìmirist
Nouâmghâr
Parc National
du Banc
d'Arguin

Choûm
Atâr
Chinguetti
Ouâdâne
ADRAR
Toueïrma
OUARÂNE
El Bêyyed
El Ghallâouîya
Maqteïr
Bir 'Amrâne
Mejaoudâ
Zoukar
MAURITANIA
Oujeft
Kseïb el Touerg
Akjoujt
Boû Rjeïmât

SAHARA
Agâraktem
Oumm el A'sel
Bir Chali
Hamâda El Haricha
Taoudenni
Telig
I-n-Dagouber
El Khnâchich
El Gçeïb
Bir Ounâne
Erg Aîouila
El Mreyyé

Jreïda
Sebkhet
Te-n-Dghâmcha
Tâtilt
Boû Nâga
El Moïnane
El Gât
I-n-Échaî

Nouakchott
TRARZA
Tiguent
Afjoujt
Mederdra
Boutilimit
Ijnaouèn
Magta'Lahjar
El Melhes
El Houeïtat
Tidjikja
TAGANT
Gâneb
Tîchît
Dhar Tîchît
Aghrîjît
Touîjinet
Oujâf
HODH ECH
Araouane
Boû Djébéha
TOMBOUCTOU
CHARGUI
Dhar Oualâta
Tombouctou
Niger
Araouane
Gôssi

Richard Toll
Rosso
St Louis
Lougâ
Dagana
Bogué
Podor
Bababé
Kaédi
Boghé
Lac Rkiz
Aleg
BRÂKNA
Guérou
Boû Blei'ine
El Méchoual
ASSABA
Kiffa
Tâmchekket
Nijerâne
Outfene
Oualâta
Nkhaîlé
Guïr
Oualâta
Lac Faguibine
Ras el Mâ
Goundam
Diré
Mboro
Mpal
Lac de
Guier
Kébémer
Mékhé
Dara
Touba
Linguère
Ranérou
Matam
Maghama
GORGOL
Kobenni
HOD
HODH EL GHARBI
Tintâne
Ayoûn El Atroûs
Néma
Kehoula
Timbédgha
Diéguéra
Djiguéni
Nioû
Dendâra
Léré
El Aghlâf
Lerneb
Lac Garou
Fintou

Cap Vert
Pikine
Dakar
Rufisque
Thiès
Bambey
Mbour
Diourbel
Mbacké
Joal-Fadiout
Fatick
Guinguinéo
Bambey
Gossas
Koki
Kaffrine
SENEGAL
Kaolack
Nioro du Rip
Kounghel
Koumpentoum
Vélingara
Tambacounda
Bakel
Sélibabi
Kidira
Kayes
Ségala
Diamou
Nioro
Yélimané
Kirane
Balle
Nara
Goumbou
Sokolo
Niono
Ténenkou
Mopti
MOPT
SÉGOU
KOULIKORO

THE GAMBIA
Banjul
Gunjur
Brikama
Zinguinchor
Sédhiou
Kolda
Vélingara
KAYES
KAARTA
Kayes
Bafoulabé
Kéniéba
Satadougou
Kita
Manantali
Diafarabé
Dioumanou
Markala
Bambouk
Casamance
Parc National du
Delta du Saloum
Parc National
du Niokolo-Koba
BAMBOUK

© HarperCollinsPublishers

Oblated Stereographic

METRES FEET
6000 19686
5000 16409
4000 13124
3000 9843
2000 6562
1000 3281
500 1640
200 656
SEA LEVEL
200 656
2000 6562
4000 13124
6000 19686

2

3

4

5

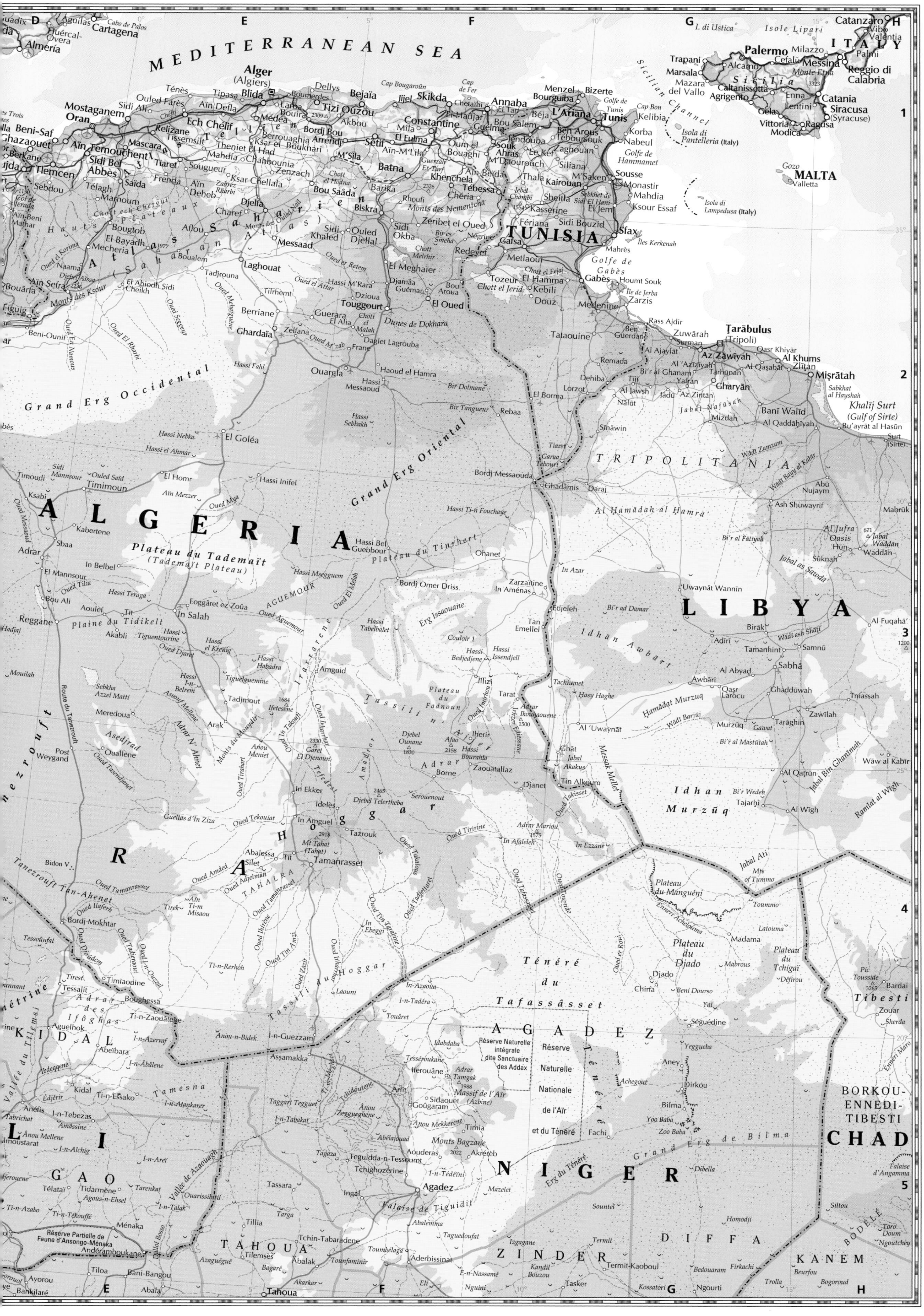

1:7 500 000

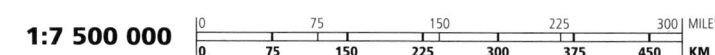

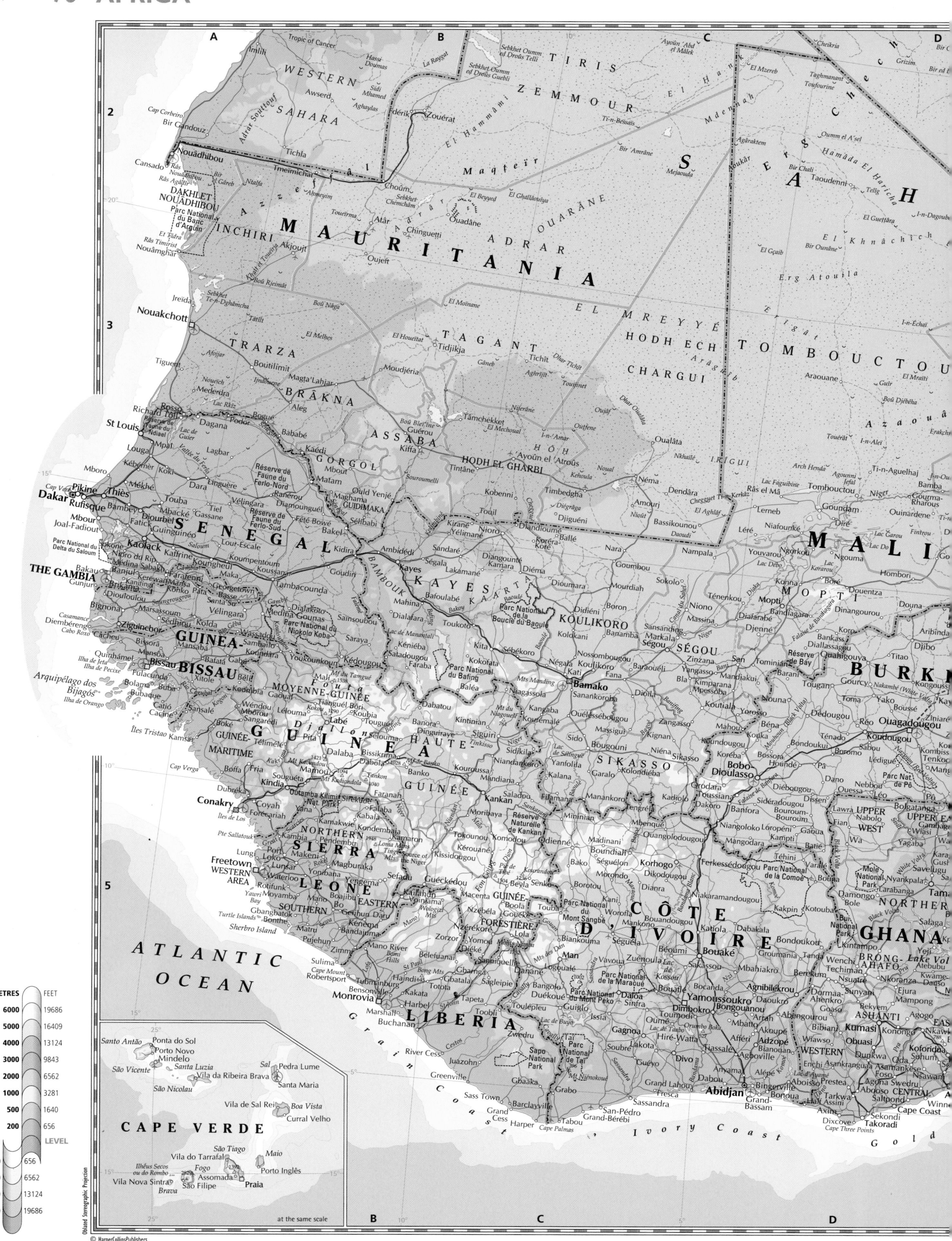

METRES	FEET
6000	19686
5000	16409
4000	13124
3000	9843
2000	6562
1000	3281
500	1640
200	656
SEA	LEVEL
200	656
2000	6562
4000	13124
6000	19686

Oblated Stereographic Projection

CAPE VERDE

at the same scale

© HarperCollinsPublishers

1:7 500 000

0	75	150	225	300 MILES
0	75	150	225	300	375	450 KM

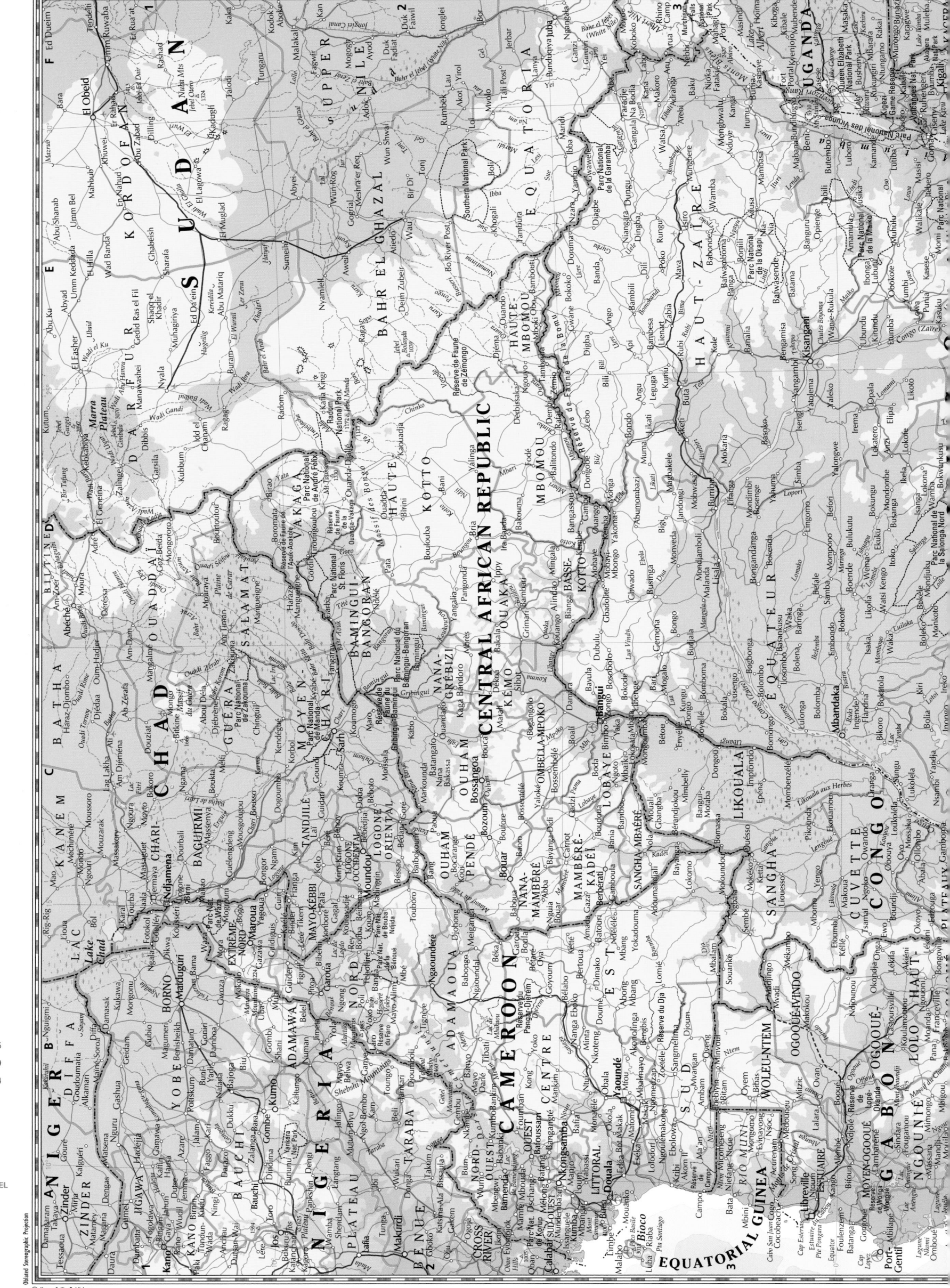

METRES	FEET
6000	19686
5000	16409
4000	13124
3000	9843
2000	6562
1000	3281
500	1640
200	656
SEA	LEVEL
200	656
2000	6562
4000	13124
6000	19686

Oblated Stereographic Projection

© HarperCollinsPublishers

SAO TOME and PRINCIPE

1:7 500 000

| 0 | 75 | 150 | 225 | 300 | MILES |
| 0 | 75 | 150 | 225 | 300 | 375 | 450 | KM |

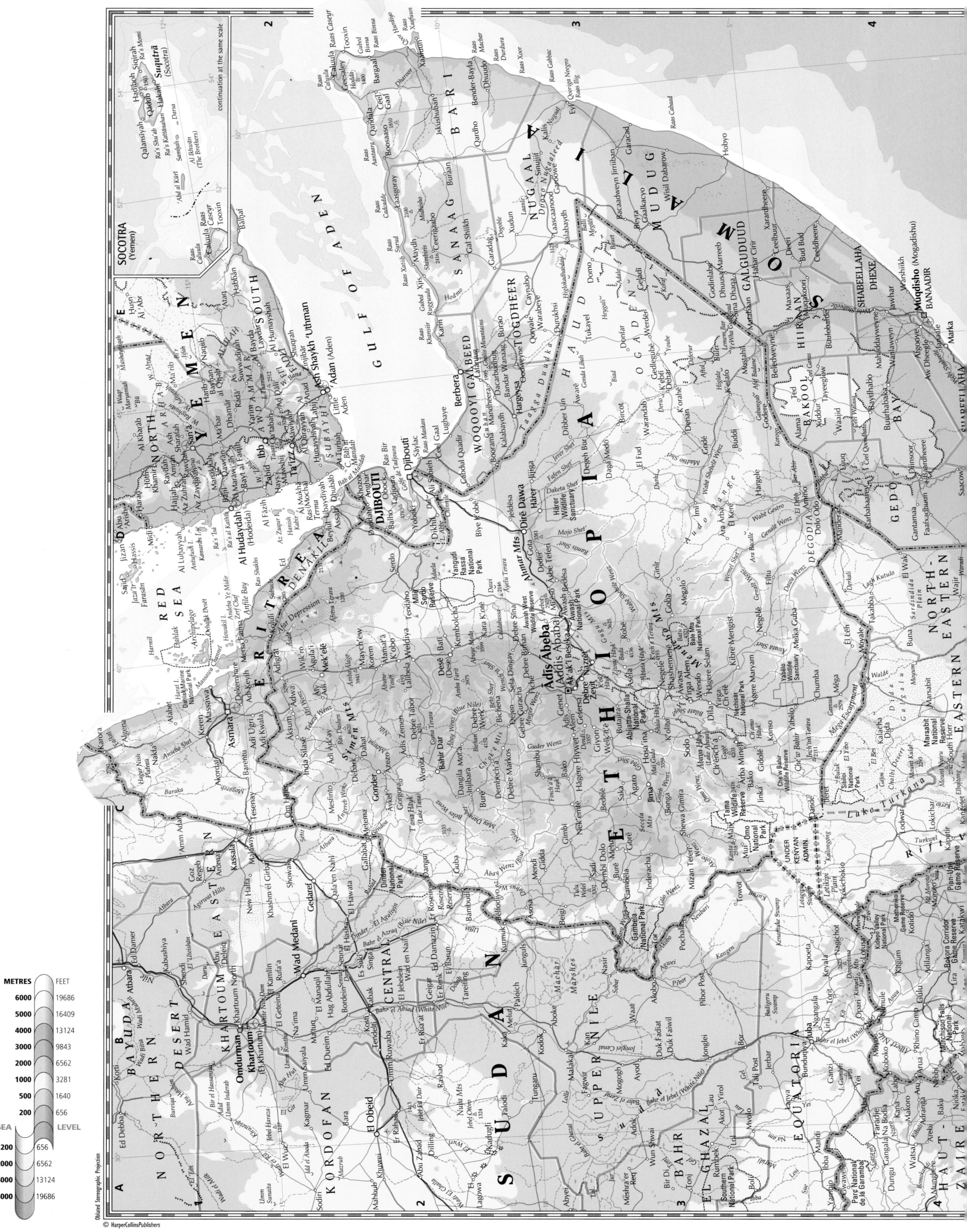

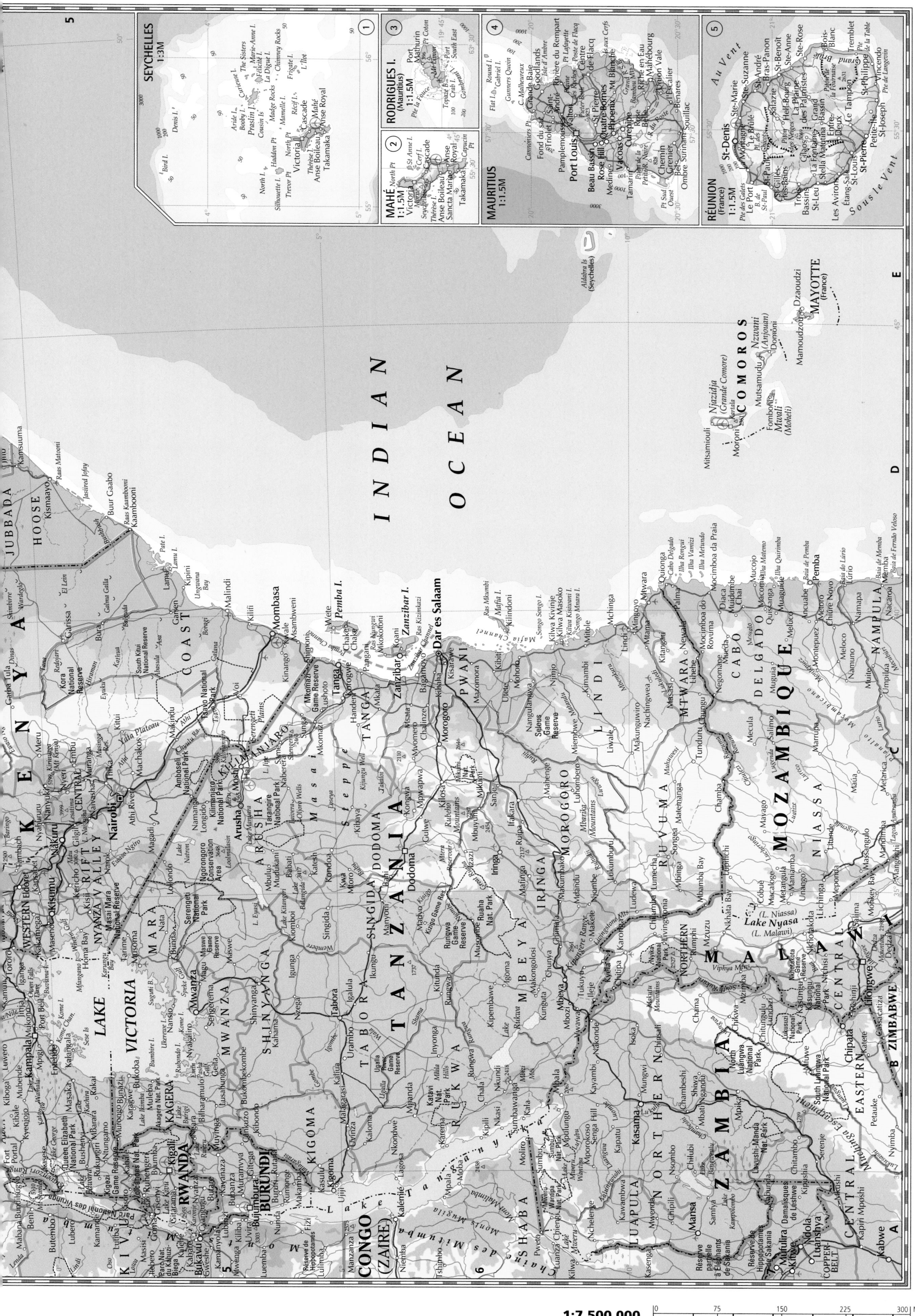

1:7 500 000

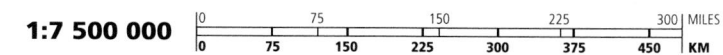

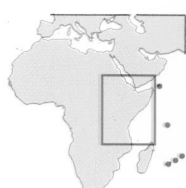

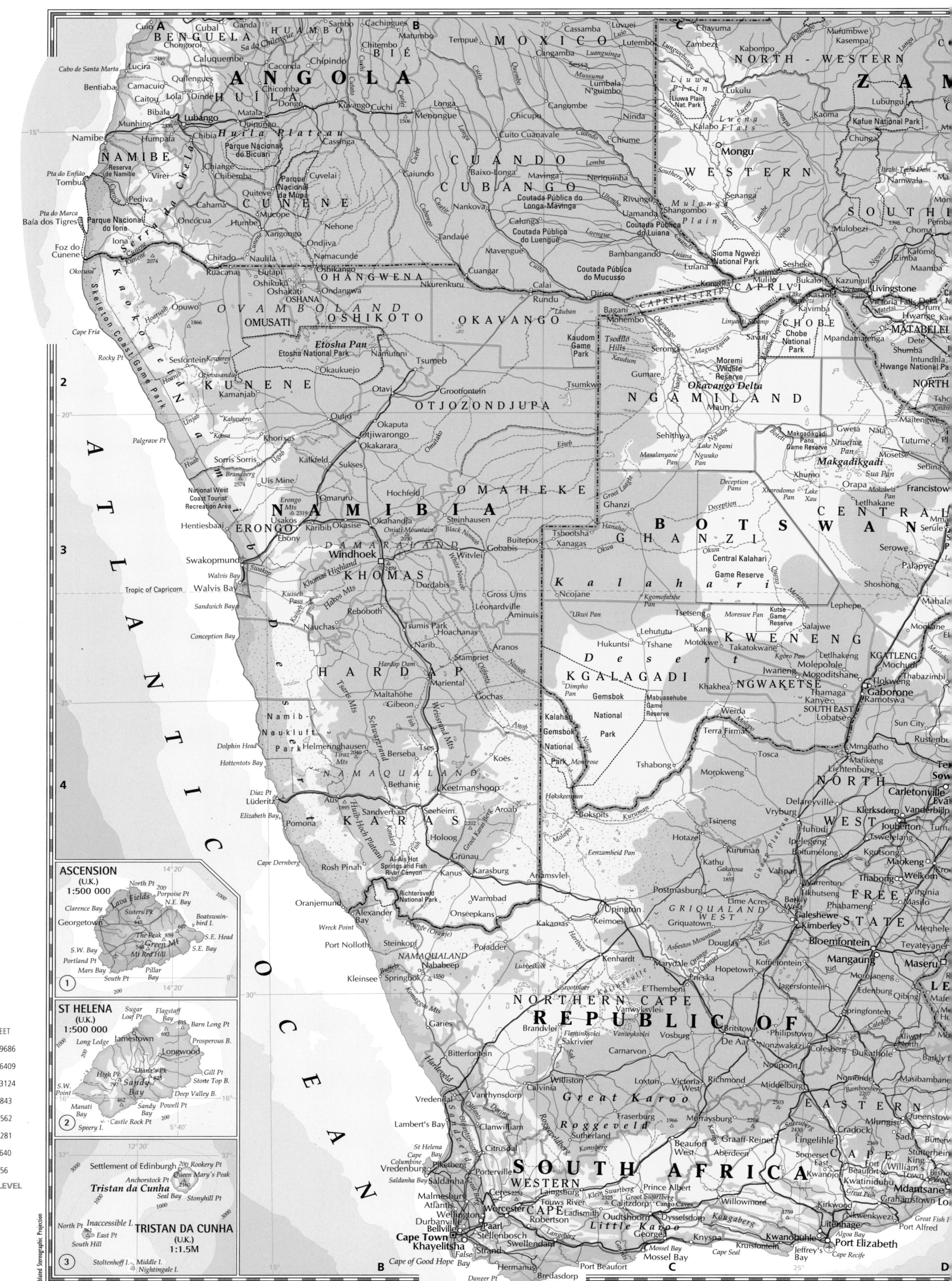

ANGOLA

BENGUELA
Cuio A Cubal Ganda
Chongoroi Sa da Chilengue HUAMBO
Caluquembe Chipindo BIÉ
Quilengues Caconda Chitembo MOXICO
Lucira 2489 Camacuio Lola Dinde Caluquembe
Bentiaba HUÍLA Dongo Cuvango
Caitou Bibala Lubango Matala Cuango Menongue
Munhino 2230 Chibia Cassinga CUANDO
Namibe Humpata Huíla Plateau CUBANGO
NAMIBE Reserva de Namibe Virei Chiange Cahama
Pta do Enfião Tombua Chibemba Parque Nacional Cuvelai
Pta do Marca Baía dos Tigres Oncócua Humbe
Parque Nacional do Iona CUNENE
Foz do Cunene Chitado Namacunde
Cape Fria Ruacaná Outapi OHANGWENA
Okotusu Oshikango Ondangwa Nkurenkuru
OVAMBOLAND Oshakati

CAPRIVI STRIP CHOBE

NAMIBIA

KUNENE
Khorixas
Kamanjab

OTJOZONDJUPA

OMAHEKE

NGAMILAND

BOTSWANA

GHANZI

KALAHARI

Windhoek
KHOMAS

HARDAP

KARAS

ATLANTIC OCEAN

REPUBLIC OF SOUTH AFRICA

NORTHERN CAPE

WESTERN CAPE

EASTERN CAPE

Cape Town
Khayelitsha
Cape of Good Hope

SOUTH AFRICA

METRES | FEET
6000 | 19686
5000 | 16409
4000 | 13124
3000 | 9843
2000 | 6562
1000 | 3281
500 | 1640
200 | 656
SEA LEVEL
200 | 656
2000 | 6562
4000 | 13124
6000 | 19686

ASCENSION (U.K.) 1:500 000
North Pt
Porpoise Pt
N.E. Bay
Clarence Bay
Lava Fields Sisters Pk
Georgetown
The Peak 859
Green Mt Mt Red Hill
S.W. Bay
Portland Pt
Mars Bay
Pillar Bay
South Pt
①

ST HELENA (U.K.) 1:500 000
Sugar Loaf Pt Flagstaff Bay
Long Ledge Jamestown Barn Long Pt
Prosperous B.
Longwood
Diana's Pk Gill Pt
High Pk 797 Stone Top B.
S.W. Point
Deep Valley B.
Manati Bay
Sandy Bay Powell Pt
Speery I.
②

Settlement of Edinburgh Rookery Pt
Queen Mary's Peak
Anchorstock Pt
Tristan da Cunha
Seal Bay Stonyhill Pt
Inaccessible I.
East Pt
South Hill
TRISTAN DA CUNHA (U.K.) 1:1.5M
Stoltenhoff I. Middle I. Nightingale I.
③

© HarperCollinsPublishers
Oblard Stereographic Projection

MOZAMBIQUE CHANNEL

NIASSA

CABO DELGADO

NAMPULA

ZAMBÉZIA

MOZAMBIQUE

TETE

SOUTHERN

SOFALA

MANICA

GAZA

INHAMBANE

MASVINGO

MASHONALAND CENTRAL

MASHONALAND EAST

MASHONALAND WEST

ZIMBABWE

MATABELELAND SOUTH

NORTHERN PROVINCE

MPUMALANGA

SWAZILAND

KWAZULU-NATAL

MALAWI

MADAGASCAR

ANTSIRAÑANA

MAHAJANGA

TOAMASINA

ANTANANARIVO

FIANARANTSOA

TOLIARA

Juan de Nova (Fr.)

Tropic of Capricorn

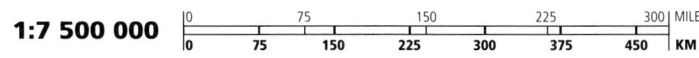

1:7 500 000

| 0 | 75 | 150 | 225 | 300 MILES |

| 0 | 75 | 150 | 225 | 300 | 375 | 450 KM |

continuation at the same scale

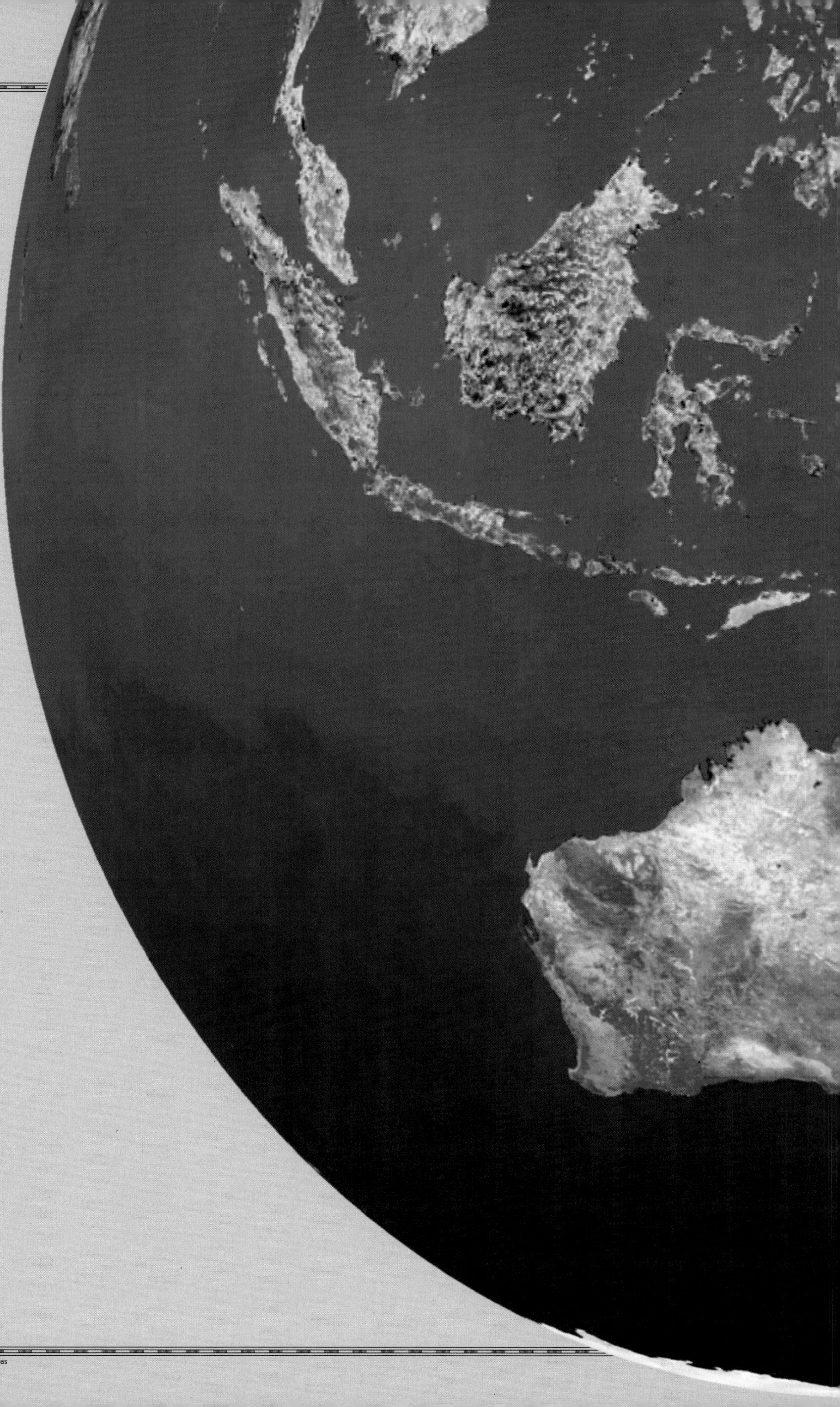

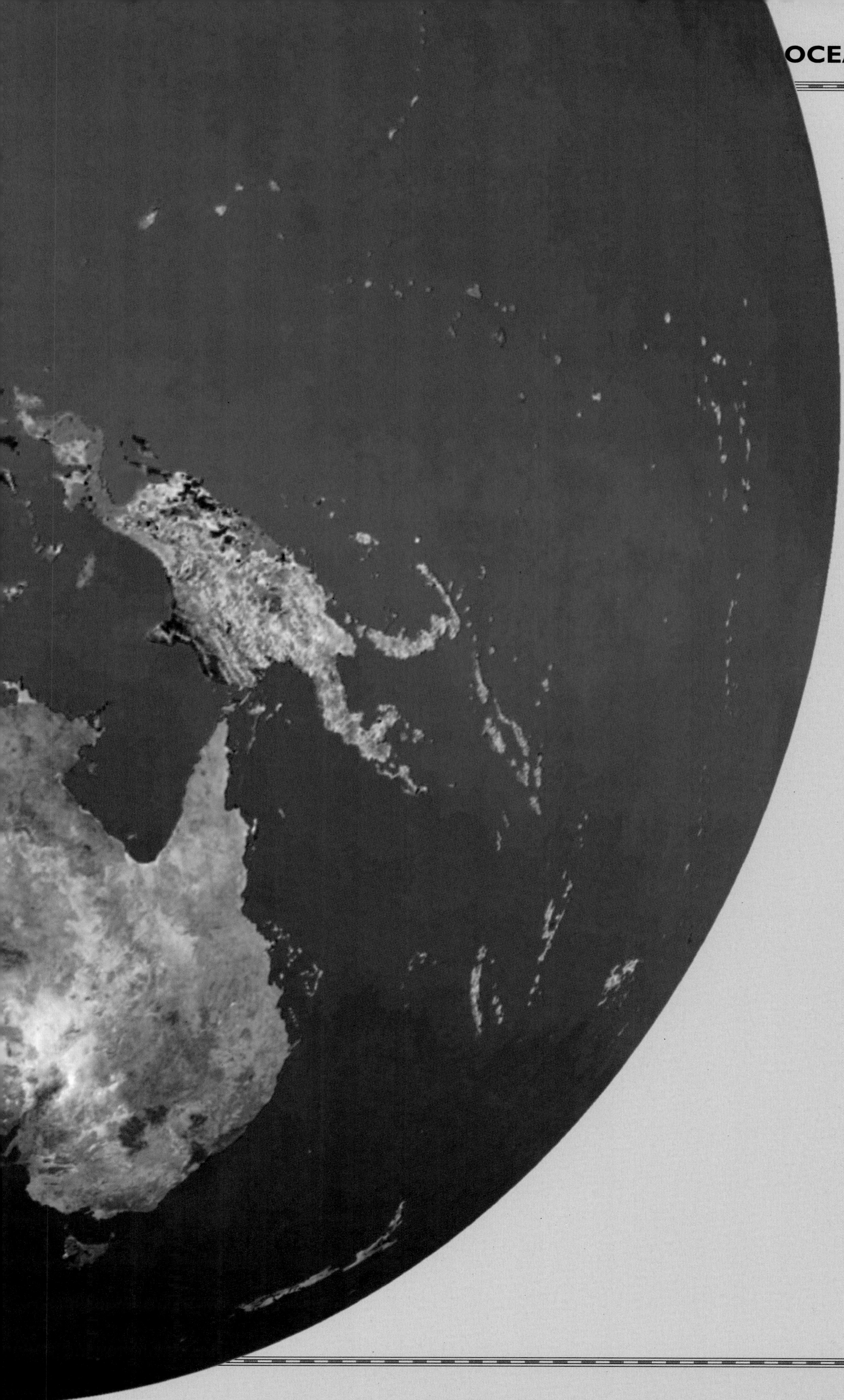

B · C · D · E · F · G · H · J

Nanchong · Chang · **Nanjing** · **Shanghai** · Fukuoka · Kita-Kyushu · Hachijo-jima (Japan) · Nagasaki

Wuhan · Hangzhou · Ningbo · *East* · Kyushu · JAPAN

CHINA · Nanchang · Wenzhou · *China* · Kagoshima

Changsha · *Sea* · Amami O-shima · Tori-shima (Japan)

Hengyang · Ryukyu Islands · Ogasawara-shoto (Japan)

Fuzhou · Okinawa (Japan) · Daito-jima (Japan)

Xiamen · **Taipei** · Kazan-retto (Japan)

Guangzhou · TAIWAN

Macau (Port.) · **Hong Kong** · Kaohsiung

Batan Is · Wake I. (U.S.A.)

Luzon Strait · Pagan

Laoag · C. Engaño · **Northern Mariana Islands** (U.S.A.)

Luzon · Saipan

PHILIPPINES · Rota · Tinian

Manila · Quezon City · Guam (U.S.A.) · **MARSHALL**

Naga · **ISLANDS**

South · Mindoro · Bikini · Ratak Chain

China · Masbate · Samar · Yap · Gaferut · Pikelot · Hall Is · Ralik Chain · Dalap-Uliga-Darrit

Sea · Panay · Cebu · Leyte · Chuuk

Iloilo · Negros · Surigao · Pohnpei · Palikir

Palawan · Dipolog · Kosrae · Tarawa

Sulu · Mindanao · PALAU · *Caroline Islands* · Nomoi Is

Kota · Zamboanga · Davao · **FED. STATES OF MICRONESIA** · Nonouti

Kinabalu · Sandakan · Banaba · Tabiteuea · Beru · Nukum

MALAYSIA · Sulu Arch. · **NAURU** · Nauru · Onotoa · *Gilbert Islands* · Arore

BRUNEI · Talaud Is · *Celebes* · Sangir · *Sea* · Manado

Halmahera · Nanumea · Nanumanga

Borneo · Molucca Sea · Manokwari · Biak · Admiralty Is · New Hanover · Nukumanu Is · Nanumea · **TUVALU**

Balikpapan · Palu · Peleng · *Moluccas* · Yapen · Jayapura · Wewak · New Ireland · Nukufetau · Funa

Macassar Strait · Sula Is · Obi · Misoöl · *Bismarck* · Rabaul · Tauu Is · Fong

Banjarmasin · Parepare · Buru · Seram · Fakfak · *Sea* · Madang · Bougainville · Ontong Java Atoll · Nui v

Padang · G. of Bone · Buton · Pk Jaya 5029 · Wokam · *New* · **PAPUA** · New · Choiseul · **SOLOMON** · Nukufetau

Java Sea · Ujung · Seram · Aru Is · *Guinea* · Lae · Britain · Santa Isabel · Malaita · **ISLANDS** · Rotuma

Surabaya · Damar · Yamdena · Kikori · **NEW GUINEA** · Solomon Sea · New Georgia · Honiara

Bali · Sumbawa · Flores · Trangan · Daru · G. of · Woodlark I. · Guadalcanal · Santa Cruz Is · Cherry I. · Niu

Madura · *Banda Sea* · Kai Is · Papua · Port · San Cristobal · Mitre I. · Tikopia

Flores Sea · Wetar · Leti Is · Dolak I. · Moresby · D'Entrecasteaux Is · Rennell · Banks Is

Lombok · Sumba · Sawu · Alor · Timor · *Arafura Sea* · Torres Strait · Louisiade Arch. · Espiritu Santo · Ambrym

Sawu Sea · Endeh · Roti · C. York · Malakula · Éfaté · **FIJI**

Kupang · Melville I. · C. Arnhem · *Coral Sea* · **VANUATU** · Vila · Viti Levu

Timor Sea · Darwin · Groote · Gulf of · *Islands* · Erromango · Suv

Bathurst I. · Eylandt · Carpentaria · Cooktown · **Territory** · Tanna · Anatom

C. Londonderry · Katherine · Wellesley Is · Cairns · *Coral* · Loyalty Is

Larrimah · Daly Waters · Normanton · *Sea* · New Caledonia (Fr.) · Nouméa · Hunter I.

Wyndham · Île des Pins

C. Lévêque · Derby · Townsville · Great Barrier Reef

Broome · **NORTHERN** · Tennant · Mount Isa · Cloncurry · Mackay · Rockhampton · Norfolk I. (Aust.)

Halls Creek · Creek · **TERRITORY** · **QUEENSLAND** · Longreach · Gladstone

Port Hedland · Great Sandy · Alice · Bundaberg · Maryborough

Barrow I. · Dampier · Desert · Springs · **A U S T R A L I A** · Charleville · Toowoomba · **Brisbane** · Lord Howe I. (Aust.)

Onslow · Paraburdoo · Newman · Oodnadatta · Cunnamulla · Ipswich · Gold Coast · Lismore

North West C. · Lismore · Grafton · C. Maria van Diemen

Carnarvon · **WESTERN** · **SOUTH** · Walgett · Armidale · Tamworth · Kaitaia · Great Bar

Meekatharra · Mt Magnet · Leonora · **AUSTRALIA** · Leigh Creek · Bourke · Dubbo · **Auckland** · Hamilton

Geraldton · Woomera · Broken · Orange · Bathurst · North Island · Roto

Moora · Coolgardie · Kalgoorlie · Ceduna · Whyalla · Port Augusta · Hill · **NEW SOUTH** · **Sydney** · New Plymouth · Gisb

Merredin · Great · Port Pirie · Wagga · **WALES** · Wollongong · Wanganui · Na

Perth · Northam · Esperance · Norseman · *Australian* · Port Lincoln · **Adelaide** · Wagga · A.C.T. · **Canberra** · Albury · **Wellington** · Palmer

Fremantle · *Bight* · Kangaroo I. · Murray · **VICTORIA** · **Melbourne** · Nelson · North

Bunbury · Mount Gambier · Ballarat · **T A S M A N** · Blenheim

Augusta · Warrnambool · Geelong · Flinders I. · *SEA* · Greymouth · Southern Alps · Christchurch

C. Leeuwin · Albany · King I. · Bass Strait · South Island

Launceston · Timaru · **NEW**

Hobart · **TASMANIA** · Kingston · Oamaru · Dunedin

South East C. · West C. · **ZEALAN**

Invercargill · Bou

Snares Is · Stewart I.

Antipode

Auckland Is

Macquarie I. (Aust.) · Campbell I. (NZ)

A · B · C · D · E · F · G · H

K 170° L 160° M 150° N 140° O 130° P Q U. S. A. R

San Diego
Mexicali
El Paso
Ciudad
Juarez
1

MEXICO

NORTH PACIFIC OCEAN

Guadalupe
(Mex.)

2

Atoll

Midway Is

Laysan I.

Gardner
Pinnacles

Necker I.

Tropic of Cancer

Hawaiian Islands

Kauai
Oahu
Honolulu
Maui
U.S.A.
Hilo
Hawaii

Is Revillagigedo
(Mex.)
I. Clarión

20°

Johnston I.
(U.S.A.)

3

10°

Palmyra I.
(U.S.A.)

Teraina

Tabuaeran

Kiritimati

Howland I.
Baker I.
(U.S.A.)

Jarvis I.
(U.S.A.)

4

Phoenix Islands

Kanton I.

McKean I.

Rawaki

Nikumaroro

Manra

Orona

Malden I.

Starbuck I.

Line Islands

KIRIBATI

Equator 0°

Tokelau
(N.Z.)
Atafu

Nukunono
Fakaofo

Rakahanga

Manihiki

Tongareva

Caroline I.

Nuku Hiva
Marquesas Islands

5

Danger Is

Nassau
(New Zealand)

Vostok I.

Flint I.

Hiva Oa

Swains I.
American

lles Wallis
Wallis & Futuna
(Fr.)
Îles de Horn

WESTERN
Savaii
Apia
Upolu

Samoa

Manua Is

Suvorov I.

SAMOA
Tutuila
Rose I.

Îles du Roi Georges

Îles de Désappointement

Ninatoputopu
Tafahi

Fenua Ura

Motu One

Rangiroa

Raroia

Pukapuka

10°

Vavau
Group

Palmerston I.
(N.Z.)

Raiatea

Huahine

Fakarava

Tuamotu Archipelago

Raiatea

Moorea
Tahiti

Society
Islands

Anaa

French

Tofua

Niue
(N.Z.)

Aitutaki
Cook Is
(N.Z.)

Hervey Is

Mêhétia

Hao

o-i-Lau
Nuku'alofa

TONGA
Tongatapu
Group
Ata

Atiu
Mauke

Héréhérétué

Rarotonga

Mangaia

Îles Maria

Îles Duc de Gloucester

Polynesia

Rurutu

Mururoa

Groupe Actéon

6

Rimatara
Tubuai

Raivavae

Tubuai Islands

Îles Gambier

20°

Raoul

Rapa

Marotiri

Oeno
Henderson I.
(U.K.)
Pitcairn I.
Ducie I.

Kermadec Is
(NZ)

Tropic of Capricorn

I. Sala y Gómez
(Chile)

7

Easter I.
(Chile)

Chatham Is
(NZ)
Pitt I.

SOUTH PACIFIC OCEAN

30°

8

K 170° L 160° M 150° N 140° O 130° P 120° Q 110° R 100° S

1:30 000 000

| 0 | 250 | 500 | 750 | 1000 | MILES |

| 0 | 250 | 500 | 750 | 1000 | 1250 | 1500 | KM |

COUNTRY	AREA		POPULATION		Form of Government	Capital City	MAIN LANGUAGES	MAIN RELIGIONS	CURRENCY
	sq ml	sq km	total	density per sq ml sq km					
AMERICAN SAMOA	76	197	55 000	723 279	US territory	Pago Pago	Samoan, English	Protestant, RC	US dollar
AUSTRALIA	2 966 153	7 682 300	17 838 000	6 2	federation	Canberra	English, Italian, Greek, Aboriginal languages	Protestant, RC, Orthodox, Aboriginal beliefs	Dollar
FIJI	7 077	18 330	784 000	111 43	republic	Suva	English, Fijian, Hindi	Protestant, Hindu, RC, Sunni Muslim	Dollar
FRENCH POLYNESIA	1 261	3 265	215 000	171 66	French territory	Papeete	French, Polynesian languages	Protestant, RC, Mormon	Pacific franc
GUAM	209	541	146 000	699 270	US territory	Agana	Chamorro, English, Tagalog	RC	US dollar
KIRIBATI	277	717	77 000	278 107	republic	Bairiki	I-Kiribati (Gilbertese), English	RC, Protestant, Baha'i, Mormon	Austr. dollar
MARSHALL ISLANDS	70	181	54 000	773 298	republic	Dalap-Uliga-Darrit	Marshallese, English	Protestant, RC	US dollar
FED. STATES OF MICRONESIA	271	701	104 000	384 148	republic	Palikir	English, Trukese, Pohnpeian, local languages	Protestant, RC	US dollar
NAURU	8	21	11 000	1357 524	republic	Yaren	Nauruan, Gilbertese, English	Protestant, RC	Austr. dollar
NEW CALEDONIA	7 358	19 058	184 000	25 10	French territory	Nouméa	French, local languages	RC, Protestant, Sunni Muslim	Pacific franc
NEW ZEALAND	104 454	270 534	3 493 000	33 13	monarchy	Wellington	English, Maori	Protestant, RC	Dollar
NIUE	100	258	2 000	20 8	NZ territory	Alofi	English, Polynesian (Niuean)	Protestant, Mormon, RC	NZ dollar
NORTH. MARIANA IS.	184	477	47 000	255 99	US territory	Saipan	English, Chamorro, Tagalog, local languages	RC, Protestant	US dollar
PAPUA NEW GUINEA	178 704	462 840	3 997 000	22 9	monarchy	Port Moresby	English, Tok Pisin, many local languages	Protestant, RC, traditional beliefs	Kina
SOLOMON ISLANDS	10 954	28 370	366 000	33 13	monarchy	Honiara	English, Pidgin, many local languages	Protestant, RC	Dollar
TOKELAU	4	10	2 000	518 200	NZ territory		English, Tokelauan	Protestant, RC	NZ dollar
TONGA	289	748	98 000	339 131	monarchy	Nuku'alofa	Tongan, English	Protestant, RC, Mormon	Pa'anga
TUVALU	10	25	9 000	932 360	monarchy	Fongafale	Tuvaluan, English (official)	Protestant	Dollar
VANUATU	4 707	12 190	165 000	35 14	republic	Port-Vila	English, Bislama, French	Protestant, RC, traditional beliefs	Vatu
WALLIS AND FUTUNA	106	274	14 000	132 51	French territory	Mata-Utu	French, Polynesian	RC	Pacific franc
WESTERN SAMOA	1 093	2 831	164 000	150 58	monarchy	Apia	Samoan, English	Protestant, RC, Mormon	Tala

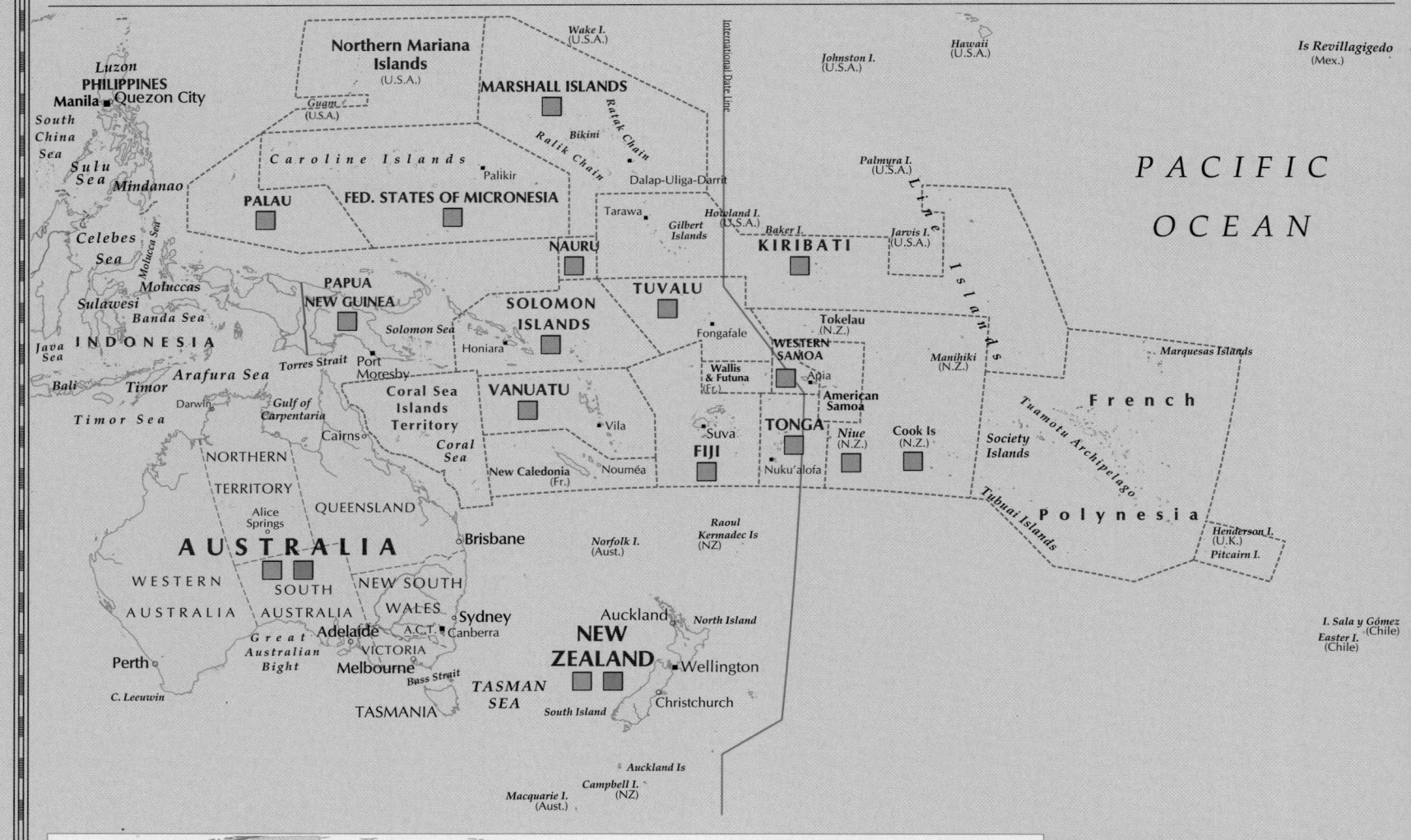

ASIA PACIFIC ECONOMIC CO-OPERATION FORUM (APEC)

Formed in 1989 to promote trade and economic co-operation, with the long term aim of the creation of a Pacific free trade area. The original members were Australia, Brunei, Canada, Indonesia, Japan, Malaysia, New Zealand, the Philippines, Singapore, South Korea, Thailand and U.S.A.. China, Hong Kong and Taiwan joined in 1991, Mexico and Papua New Guinea in 1993, and Chile in 1994.

Headquarters : Singapore

SOUTH PACIFIC FORUM

Originally established as a 'Trade Bureau' in 1972, it later became the South Pacific Bureau for Economic Co-operation (SPEC), before its current title was approved in 1988, and ratified in 1993. The objectives are to encourage and promote regional co-operation through trade and investment, and economic development including telecommunications and air transport. There are 16 members: Australia, the Cook Islands, Federated States of Micronesia, Fiji, Kiribati, Marshall Islands, Nauru, New Zealand, Niue, Palau, Papua New Guinea, Solomon Islands, Tonga, Tuvalu, Vanuatu and Western Samoa. In 1990 five of the smallest island states : Kiribati, the Cook Islands, Nauru, Niue and Tuvalu formed an economic sub-group to address their specific concerns.

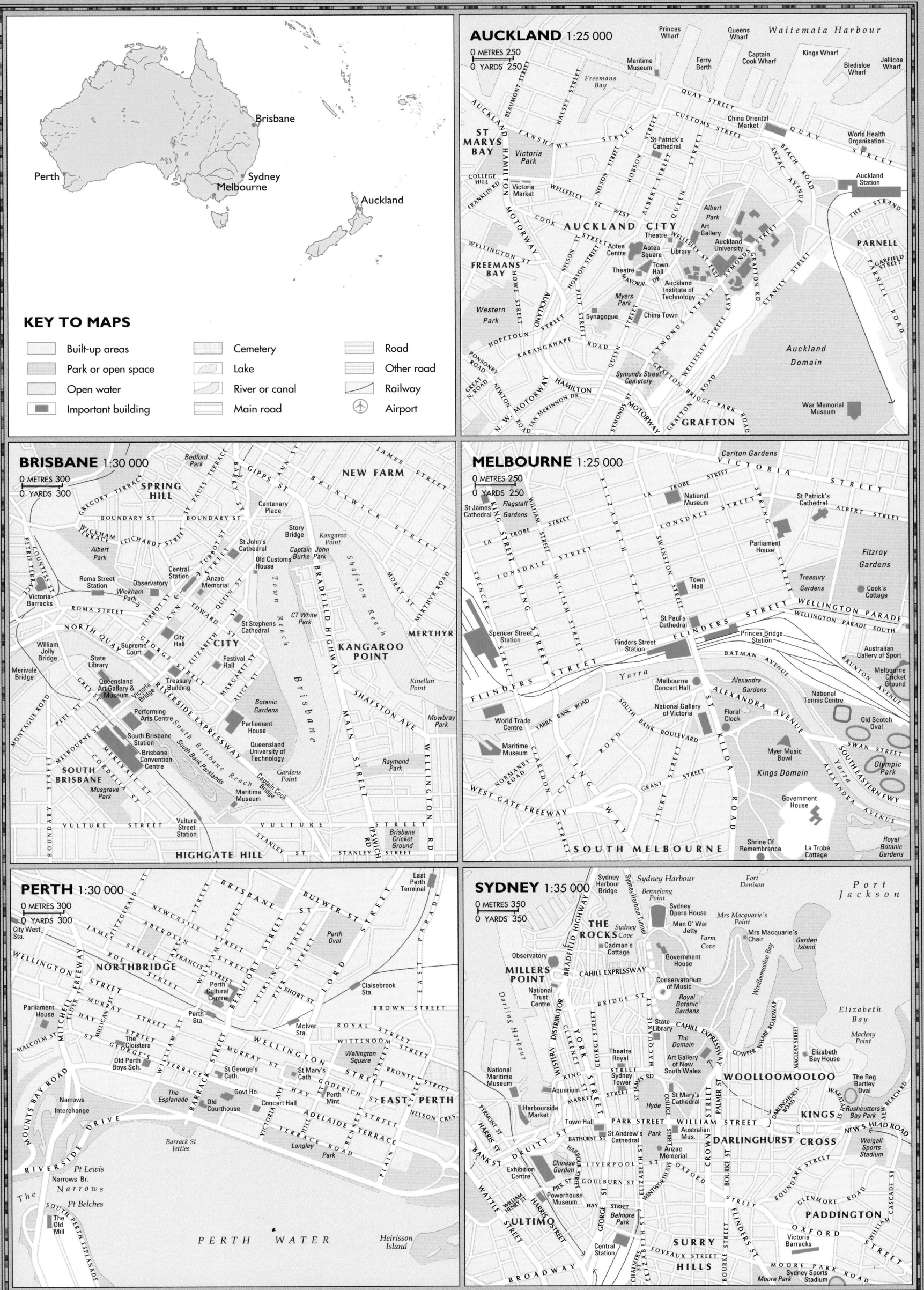

KEY TO MAPS

	Built-up areas		Cemetery		Road
	Park or open space		Lake		Other road
	Open water		River or canal		Railway
	Important building		Main road	✈	Airport

AUCKLAND 1:25 000

0 METRES 250
0 YARDS 250

BRISBANE 1:30 000

0 METRES 300
0 YARDS 300

MELBOURNE 1:25 000

0 METRES 250
0 YARDS 250

PERTH 1:30 000

0 METRES 300
0 YARDS 300

SYDNEY 1:35 000

0 METRES 350
0 YARDS 350

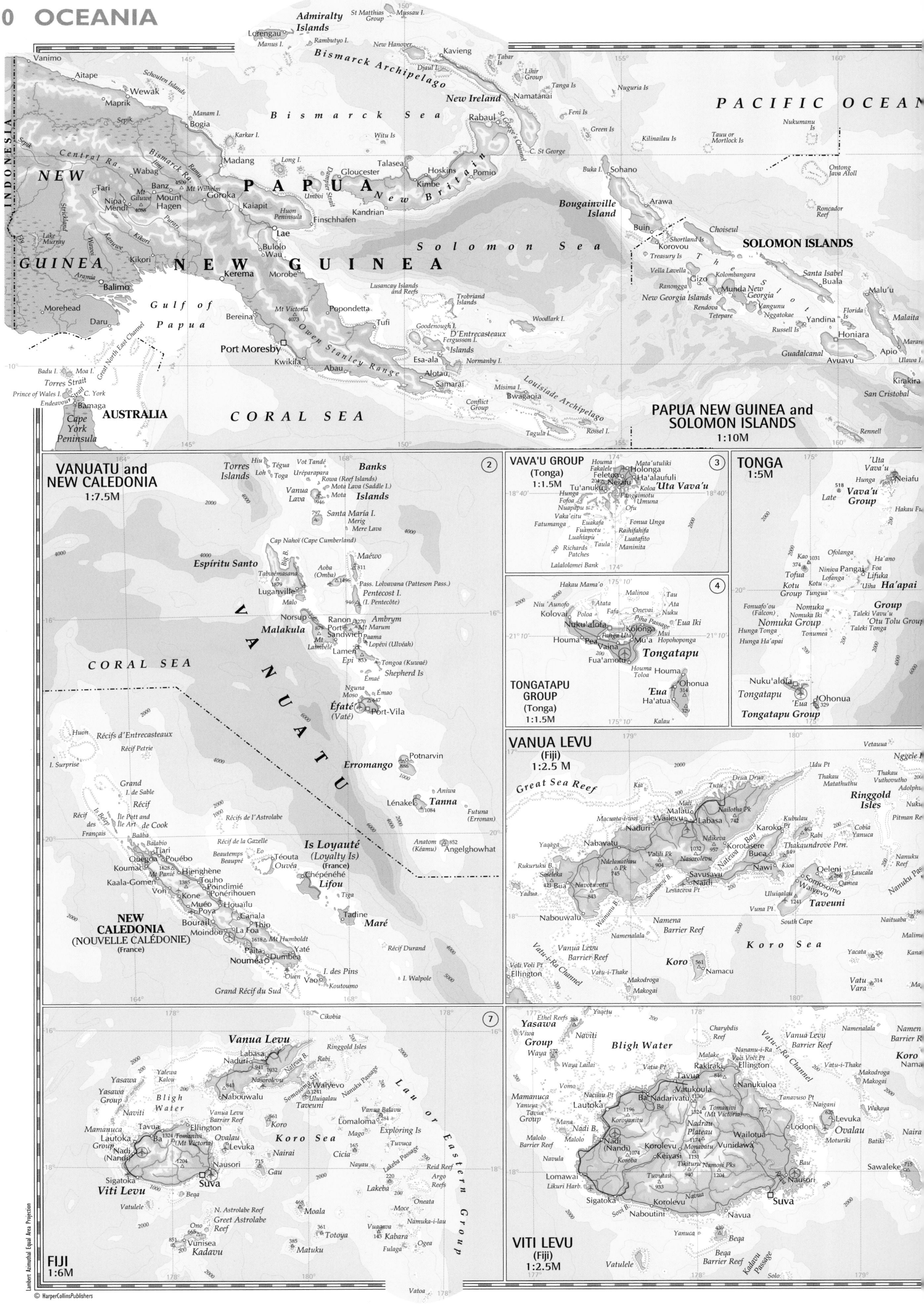

PACIFIC OCEAN

Admiralty Islands
Bismarck Archipelago
New Ireland
Bismarck Sea
Rabaul
New Britain
SOLOMON ISLANDS
Bougainville Island
Solomon Sea

INDONESIA
NEW GUINEA
PAPUA
NEW GUINEA
Central Ra.
Mt Wilhelm 4508
Mount Hagen
Lae
Port Moresby
Owen Stanley Range
Gulf of Papua

AUSTRALIA
Cape York Peninsula
Torres Strait

CORAL SEA

Louisiade Archipelago

PAPUA NEW GUINEA and SOLOMON ISLANDS
1:10M

VANUATU and NEW CALEDONIA
1:7.5M

Torres Islands
Banks Islands
Espíritu Santo
Luganville
Malakula
Norsup
Port Sandwich
Ambrym
Pentecost I.
Shepherd Is
Éfaté (Vaté)
Port-Vila

VANUATU

CORAL SEA

Erromango
Tanna
Lénakel
Futuna (Erronan)

Is Loyauté (Loyalty Is) (France)
Lifou
Maré
Ouvéa

NEW CALEDONIA (NOUVELLE CALÉDONIE) (France)
Nouméa
I. des Pins
Grand Récif du Sud

VAVA'U GROUP (Tonga)
1:1.5M
Neiafu
'Uta Vava'u

TONGA
1:5M
Vava'u Group
Ha'apai Group
Nomuka Group
Nuku'alofa
Tongatapu
'Eua
Tongatapu Group

TONGATAPU GROUP (Tonga)
1:1.5M
Nuku'alofa
Kolonga
Tongatapu
'Eua
Ha'atua
Ohonua

VANUA LEVU (Fiji)
1:2.5M
Great Sea Reef
Labasa
Savusavu
Taveuni
Ringgold Isles
Koro
Koro Sea

FIJI
1:6M
Vanua Levu
Labasa
Yasawa Group
Bligh Water
Viti Levu
Suva
Nadi (Nandi)
Sigatoka
Koro Sea
Lau or Eastern Group
Kadavu

VITI LEVU (Fiji)
1:2.5M
Yasawa Group
Bligh Water
Lautoka
Nadi (Nandi)
Nausori
Suva
Sigatoka
Ovalau
Levuka
Beqa

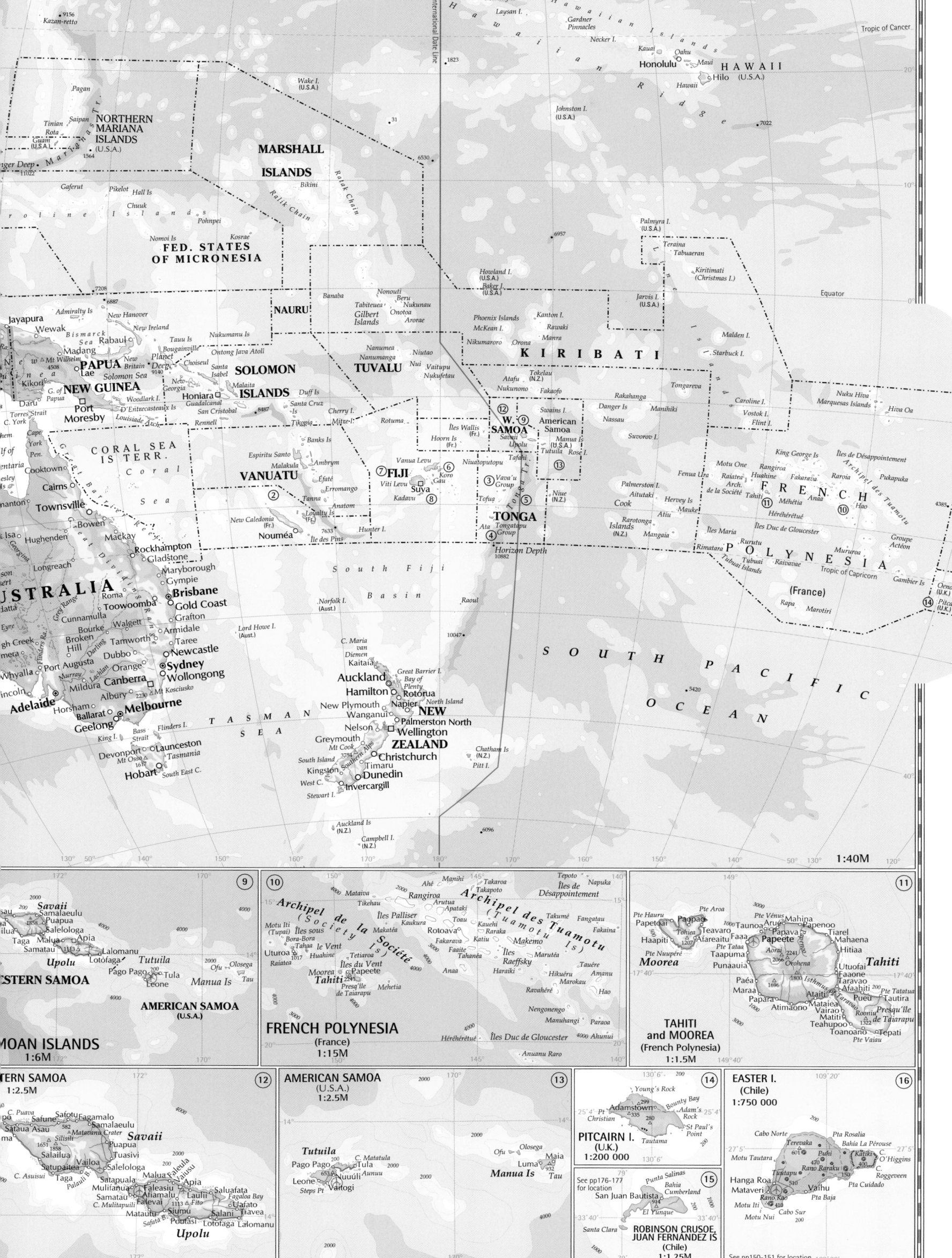

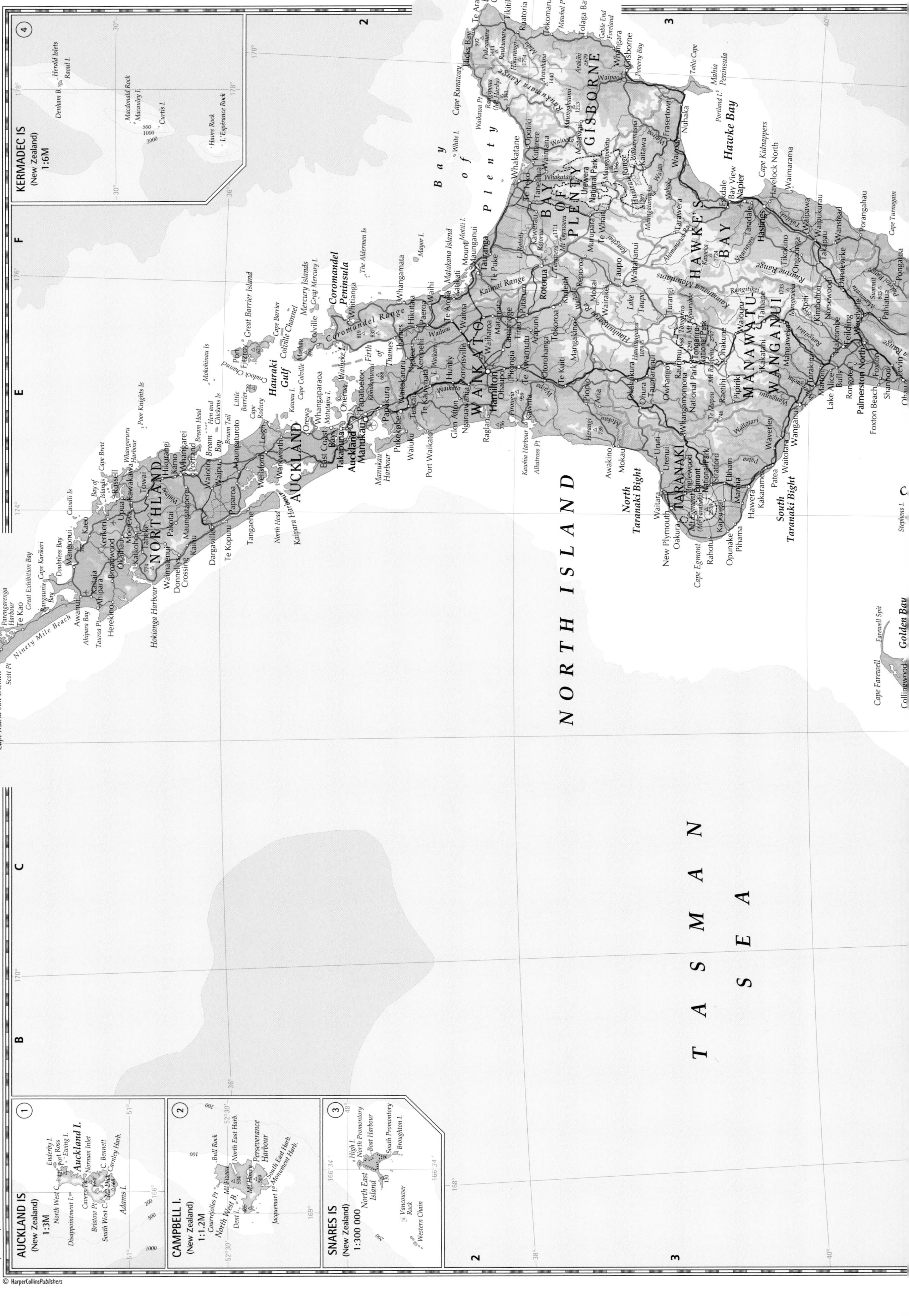

KERMADEC IS
(New Zealand) 1:6M

Herald Islets
Raoul I.
Denham B.
Macdonald Rock
Macauley I.
Curtis I.
Havre Rock
L'Esperance Rock

NORTH ISLAND

NORTHLAND

AUCKLAND

WAIKATO

BAY OF PLENTY

GISBORNE

HAWKE'S BAY

TARANAKI

MANAWATU-WANGANUI

Coromandel Peninsula

Hauraki Gulf

Bay of Plenty

North Taranaki Bight

South Taranaki Bight

Hawke Bay

TASMAN SEA

Golden Bay

Three Kings Is
North Cape
Cape Reinga
Cape Maria van Diemen
Te Kao
Te Paki
Ninety Mile Beach
North Cape
Ahipara Bay
Awanui
Kaitaia
Herekino
Taurou Pt
Broadwood
Okaihau
Opua
Russell
Cape Brett
Kaeo
Mangonui
Doubtless Bay
Cape Karikari
Rangaunu Bay
Great Exhibition Bay
Parengarenga Harbour
Kerikeri
Bay of Islands
Whangaruru Harbour
Whangarei
Kawakawa
Kaikohe
Moerewa
Kamo
Hikurangi
Hokianga Harbour
Waimamaku
Donnelly's Crossing
Dargaville
Kaihu
Maungaturoto
Te Kopuru
Paparoa
Maungatapere
Waipu
Bream Bay
Bream Head
Hen and Chickens Is
Poor Knights Is
Cape Rodney
Leigh
Warkworth
Wellsford
Tangaehe
Kaipara Harbour
North Head
Helensville
Takapuna
Auckland
Manukau
Manukau Harbour
Waiuku
Port Waikato
Pukekohe
Waikato
Glen Afton
Ngaruawahia
Raglan
Raglan Harbour
Aotea Harbour
Kawhia Harbour
Albatross Pt
Awakino
Mokau
Urenui
Waitara
New Plymouth
Oakura
Cape Egmont
Mt Egmont (Mt Taranaki)
Opunake
Pihama
Hawera
Patea
Waverley
Wanganui
Bulls
Palmerston North
Foxton
Foxton Beach

Great Barrier Island
Little Barrier I.
Mokohinau Is
Hauraki Gulf
Firth of Thames
Thames
Coromandel
Whitianga
Mercury Islands
Great Mercury I.
Mayor I.
Motiti I.
Whakatane
Opotiki
White I.
Tauranga
Te Puke
Whakatane
Te Araroa
East Cape
Tikitiki
Ruatoria
Tokomaru Bay
Tolaga Bay
Gisborne
Poverty Bay
Hicks Bay
Hawke Bay
Napier
Hastings
Waipawa
Waipukurau
Porangahau
Cape Turnagain
Cape Kidnappers
Mahia Peninsula
Table Cape
Wairoa
Hamilton
Cambridge
Te Awamutu
Otorohanga
Te Kuiti
Taumarunui
Taupo
Lake Taupo
Turangi
Rotorua
Lake Rotorua
Reporoa
Tongariro National Park
Raetihi
Ohakune
Taihape
Marton

AUCKLAND IS
(New Zealand)
1:3M

Enderby I.
Port Ross
Ewing I.
Auckland I.
Disappointment I.
Norman Inlet
Carnley Harbour
Adams I.

CAMPBELL I.
(New Zealand)
1:1.2M

Bull Rock
North East Harb.
Perseverance Harbour
Monument Harb.

SNARES IS
(New Zealand)
1:300 000

High I.
North Promontory
Boat Harbour
South Promontory
Broughton I.
North East Island
Vancouver Rock
Western Chain

METRES	FEET
6000	19686
5000	16409
4000	13124
3000	9843
2000	6562
1000	3281
500	1640
200	656
SEA	LEVEL
200	656
2000	6562
4000	13124
6000	19686

Conic Equidistant Projection

© HarperCollinsPublishers

SOUTH PACIFIC OCEAN

SOUTH ISLAND

CHATHAM IS
(New Zealand) 1:3M

The Sisters · C. Young · C. Pattisson · Pt Somes · Tupuenga Pt · Manning Pt · Okawa Pt · **Chatham I.** · Waitangi · Te One · Petre Bay · Hanson Bay · Point Gap · C. Fournier · C. L'Eveque · The Forty Fours · Star Keep · Pitt Strait · Owenga · Mangere I. · Kahuiana I. · Rangatira I. · Pitt I. · Pyramid I. · Western Reef

BOUNTY IS
(New Zealand) 1:600 000

Western Group · Eastern Group

ANTIPODES IS
(New Zealand) 1:1.2M

Remarkable Arch · North C. · Bollons I. · Antipodes I. · Leeward I. · Mt Galloway · Albatross Pt · Windward Is · South Isld

---

TASMAN · Karamea Bight · Karamea · Little Wanganui · Tasman Mountains · Tasman · Mt Kendall · Takaka · Riwaka · Motueka · Wakefield · Mt Arthur · Mt Richmond · NELSON · Nelson · Richmond · Spring Creek · Blenheim · Havelock · Picton · Waitohi · MARLBOROUGH · Seddon · Cloudy Bay · Clifford Bay · Cape Campbell

WELLINGTON · Upper Hutt · Lower Hutt · Wellington · Eastbourne · Petone · Palliser Bay · Cape Palliser · Turakirae Head · C. Terawhiti · Rimutaka Mts · Tawa · Porirua · Featherston

Kaikoura Peninsula · Kaikoura · Kekerengu · Clarence · Oaro · Hapuku · Hundalee · Cheviot · Parnassus · Waiau · Rotherham · Culverden · Hanmer Springs · Waikari · Amberley · Rangiora · Kaiapoi · Belfast · **Christchurch** · Banks Peninsula · Lyttelton · Sumner · Little River · Akaroa · Akaroa Harb. · Pegasus Bay

SOUTH PACIFIC OCEAN

Westport · Waimangaroa · Granity · Seddonville · Mokihinui · Ngakawau · Charleston · Cape Foulwind · Paparoa Range · Runanga · Greymouth · Hokitika · Ross · Ruatapu · Kowhitirangi · Lake Kaniere · Westland National Park · Franz Josef Glacier · Fox Glacier · Okarito Lagoon · Gillespies Pt · Abut Head · Haast · Jackson Head · Jackson Bay · Cascade Pt

SOUTHERN ALPS · **WESTLAND** · Mt Cook National Park · Mt Cook 3764 · Mt Tasman · Mt Sefton · Mt Aspiring National Park · Mt Aspiring · Victoria Range · Spenser Mts · Lewis Pass · Arthur's Pass · Arthur's Pass National Park

CANTERBURY · **Canterbury Plains** · Oxford · Sheffield · Springfield · Darfield · Leeston · Southbridge · Rakaia · Dunsandel · Methven · Ashburton · Mayfield · Rangitata · Hinds · Longbeach · Geraldine · Temuka · Pleasant Point · Timaru · Pareora · Makikihi · Waimate · Morven · Glenavy · Oamaru

Lake Tekapo · L. Pukaki · Lake Ohau · Twizel · Omarama · Kurow · Duntroon · Palmerston · Waikouaiti · Port Chalmers · **Dunedin** · Mosgiel · Brighton · Otago Peninsula · Otago Harbour · Cape Saunders · Shag Pt · Moeraki Pt · Hampden · Herbert · Maheno · Waianakarua

OTAGO · Cromwell · Clyde · Alexandra · Roxburgh · Lawrence · Milton · Balclutha · Kaitangata · Nugget Pt · Clutha · Lake Wanaka · Wanaka · Cardrona · Arrowtown · Queenstown · Lake Wakatipu · Kingston · Lake Hawea · Dunstan Mts · Naseby · Ranfurly · Hyde · Middlemarch · Outram · Mosgiel

SOUTHLAND · Invercargill · Bluff · Gore · Mataura · Edendale · Wyndham · Wallacetown · Winton · Otautau · Nightcaps · Ohai · Tuatapere · Riverton · Lumsden · Mossburn · Te Anau · L. Te Anau · L. Manapouri · Manapouri · Mavora · Eyre Mts · Takitimu Mts · Longwood

Fiordland National Park · Milford Sound · Milford Sd · Bligh Sd · George Sd · Caswell Sd · Thompson Sd · Doubtful Sd · Dagg Sd · Breaksea Sd · Dusky Sd · Resolution I. · Chalky Inlet · Preservation Inlet · Puysegur Pt · Five Fingers Pt · West C.

Foveaux Strait · Ruapuke I. · Oreti · Toetoes Bay · The Neck · Halfmoon Bay · Oban · Port Pegasus · Mt Anglem · Mt Allen · Codfish I. · **Stewart Island** · South West Cape · North Trap

---

1:3 000 000

| 0 | 20 | 40 | 60 | 80 | 100 MILES |

| 0 | 20 | 40 | 60 | 80 | 100 | 120 | 140 | 160 KM |

COCOS IS.
(Australia)
1:1.2M

N. Keeling I.

Horsburgh I.
(Luar)   Direction I.
Bantam
West I.
(Panjang)   Home I.
Kambling I.
South I.
(Atas)

CHRISTMAS I.
(Australia)
1:1.2M   N.E.Point
N.W. Point   Flying Fish
Cove   Northern
Murray Hill △ 357   Headridge
Hill
Point   Low Pt
Jones Pt   Ross
Hill
Phosphate Works
Stubbings Pt   Medwin Pt

INDIAN

OCEAN

Timor Sea

INDONESIA
Savu
(Sawu)   Tg Bua   Rote
(Roti)

Croker I.
Coburg
Pen.
Bathurst   Melville   Van Diemen
Island   Island   Gulf   Goulburn
Beagle Gulf
Darwin   Jabiru
Rum Jungle   Batchelor   Arnhem La
Adelaide River   Pine
Creek
Katherine   Mataranka
C. Londonderry   Joseph
Bonaparte
Gulf
Admiralty   Timber
Gulf   Creek   Daly Wa
C. Lévêque   Wyndham   Ord   Victoria
Lombardina   Kununurra   River   Larrimah
King   Lake
Sound   Argyle
Collier   Kimberley   Kalkaringi   Lake
Bay   Mt Ord   Plateau   Woods
Derby   King Leopold Ranges   Ord
Broome   Halls Creek   Lajamanu   NORTH
Roebuck Bay   Fitzroy
Liveringa   Crossing
Lagrange   Tanami
Desert   Tennant Creek
Eighty Mile Beach   Sturt Creek   TERRIT
Sandfire Roadhouse   Gregory
Lake
GREAT SANDY DESERT   Lake   Lake
Port Hedland   Shay Gap   Goldsworthy   Wills   White   Barr
Dampier   Roebourne   Warrawagine   Yuendumu   Cree
Barrow I.   Karratha   Marble Bar
Nullagine   Lake
North West C.   Onslow   Pannawonica   Fortescue   Chichester Range   Mackay   Lake   Mount   Ali
Exmouth   Hamersley   Range   Macdonald   Liebig   Spe
Exmouth Gulf   Mt Bruce   1250   Lake   1524   Macdonnell Ranges
Nanutarra   △1235   Disappointment   Lake
Roadhouse   Tom Price   Mt Meharry   AUS   Macdonald
Paraburdoo   Newman   T   R
Cardabia   Ashburton   WESTERN   Lake   Gibson Desert   Petermann Ranges   Yulara   △867   Erldunda
Hopkins   Ayers Rock (Uluru)   Kulgera
Minilya   Mt Augustus   Lake Carnegie   Warburton   Musgrave Ranges
Lake   1106   Mt Woodroffe △ 1440   Marla
Macleod   Gascoyne   Everard Range
Bernier I.   Carnarvon   Robinson Ranges   Lake Wells
Dorre I.   Gascoyne   AUSTRALIA
Junction   Murchison   Meekatharra   Wiluna
Shark Bay
Denham
Dirk Hartog I.   Overlander   GREAT VICTORIA
Roadhouse   Mount Magnet   Laverton   Lake
Houtman   Leonora   Maurice
Abrolhos   Kalbarri   DESERT   AUS
Northampton   Lake   Lake   Kookynie   Maralinga
Geraldton   Mullewa   Barlee   Ballard   Menzies   Lake Marmion
Dongara   Lake   Lake Carey   Penong
Moore   Kalgoorlie   Nullarbor Plain   Ced
Bonnie Rock   Coolgardie   Fowlers
Mooru   Mukinbudin   Southern Cross   Kambalda   Mundrabilla   Eucla   Bay
Yanchep   Merredin   Lake   Streaky Bay
Northam   Cowan   Norseman   Streaky Ba
Perth   York   Balladonia
Fremantle   Hyden   GREAT AUSTRALIAN   Anxious
Rockingham   Narrogin
Mandurah   Pinjarra   BIGHT
Harvey   Collie   Wagin   Ravensthorpe
Bunbury   Donnybrook   Katanning   Jerramungup   Esperance
Geographe Bay   Kojonup   Archipelago of
Busselton   Bridgetown   the Recherche
Margaret River   Manjimup   Mount Barker   Hood Pt
C. Leeuwin   Augusta   Flinders   Denmark
Bay   Albany
Pt d'Entrecasteaux

SOUTHERN OCEAN

MACQUARIE I.
(Australia)
1:900 000
Hasselborough Bay   Elliot Reef
Handspike Pt   North Hd
Anare Station   Buckles Bay
Langdon Pt   371
Bauer Bay   Mt Elder
Sandy Bay
Prion Lake
Mt Waite
433
Sandell Bay   Victoria Pt
Major Lake
Mt Hamilton   Lusitania
Mt Fletcher   433   Bay
Caroline Cove
South West Pt
South East Reef
158° 45'   159°

LORD HOWE I.
(Australia)
1:900 000
North I.
Sugarloaf Pass
Phillip Pt   209   Admiralty Is.
Gov. Ho.   Blinkenthorpe B.
777   Mutton Bird I.
East Pt
Mt Gower △   Lord Howe I.
875
King Pt
Ball's
Pyramid
Observatory Rock
Wheatsheaf I.
S. E. Rock

METRES	FEET
6000	19686
5000	16409
4000	13124
3000	9843
2000	6562
1000	3281
500	1640
200	656
SEA	LEVEL
200	656
2000	6562
4000	13124
6000	19686

Lambert Azimuthal Equal Area Projection

© HarperCollinsPublishers

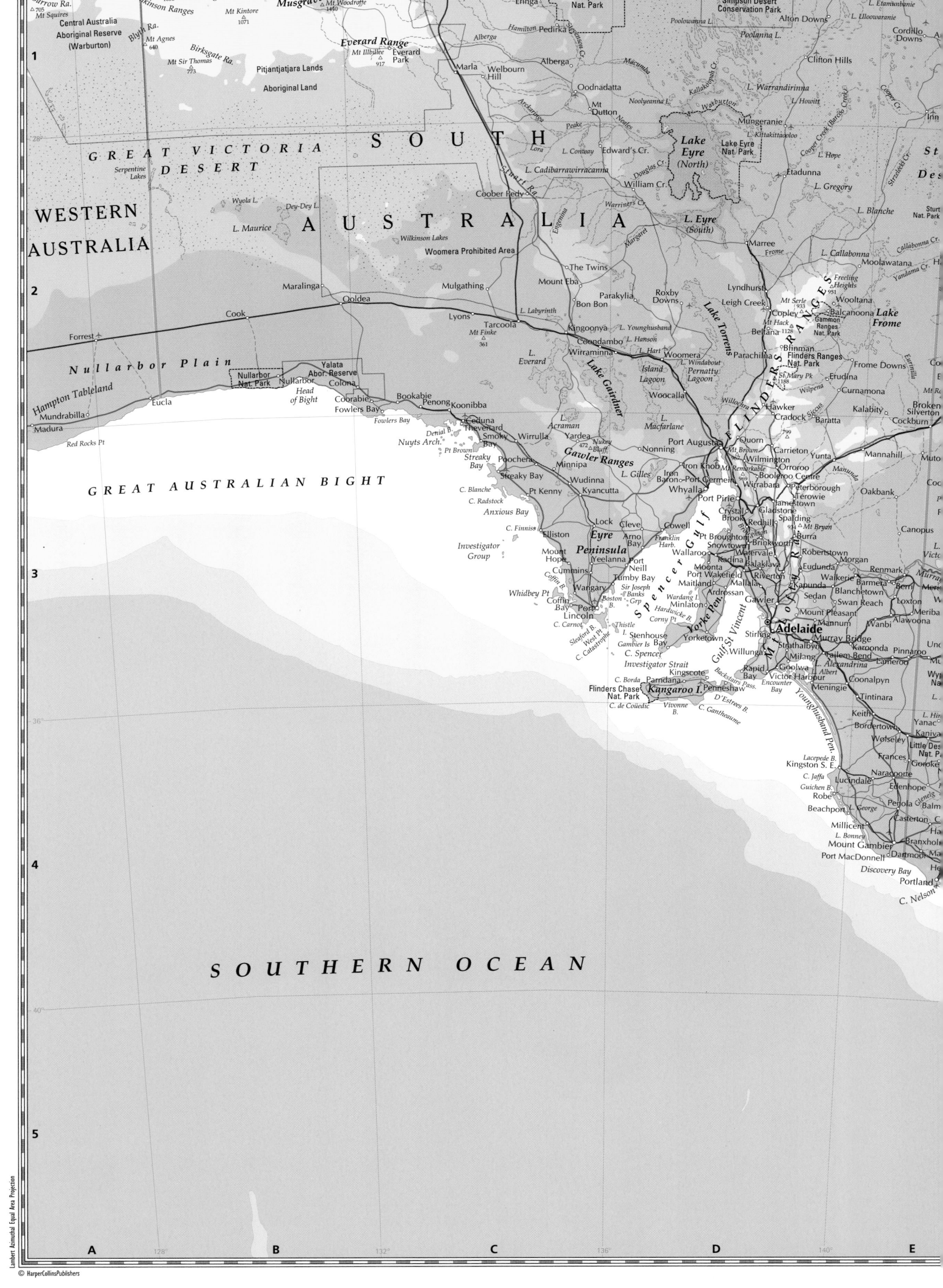

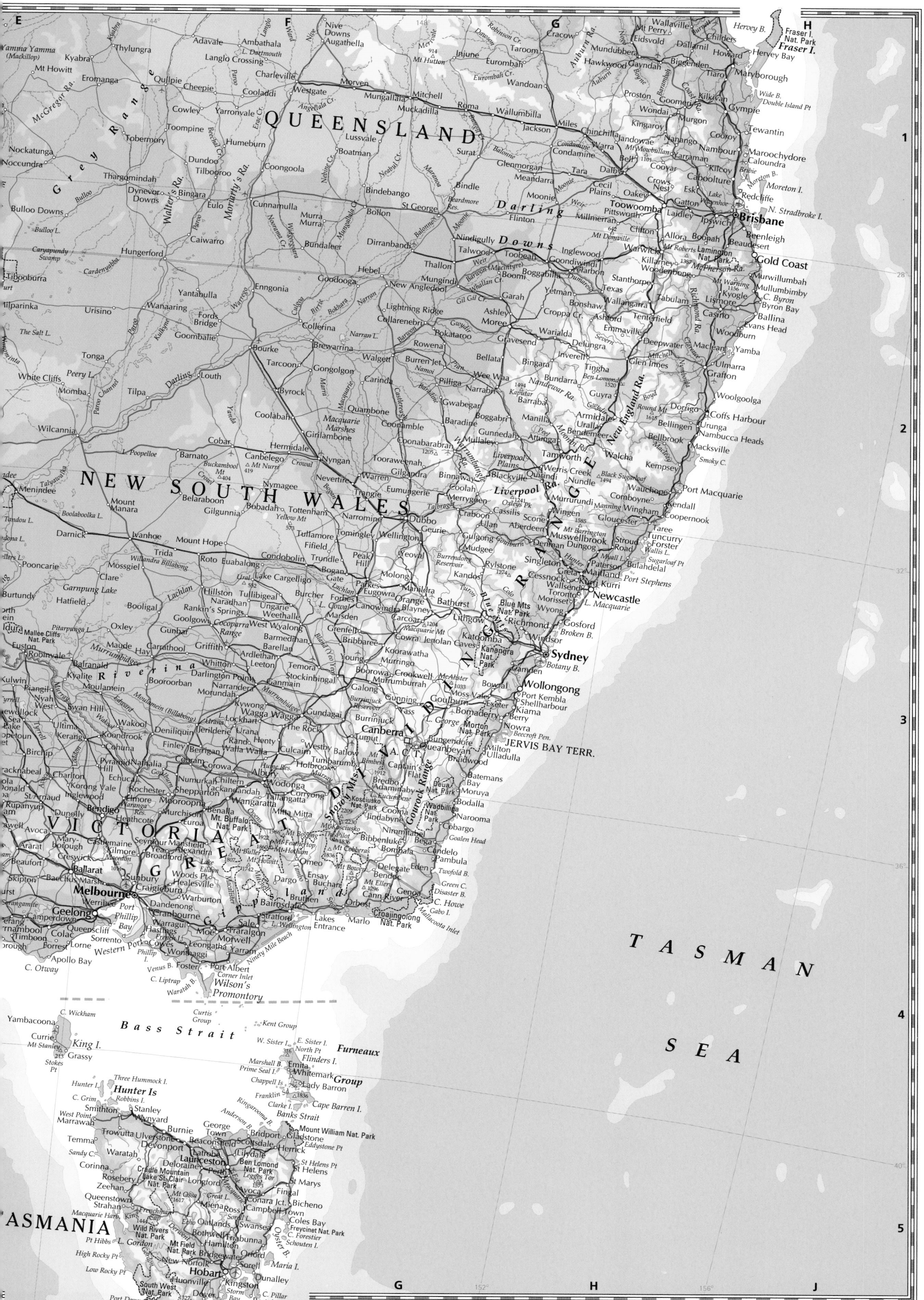

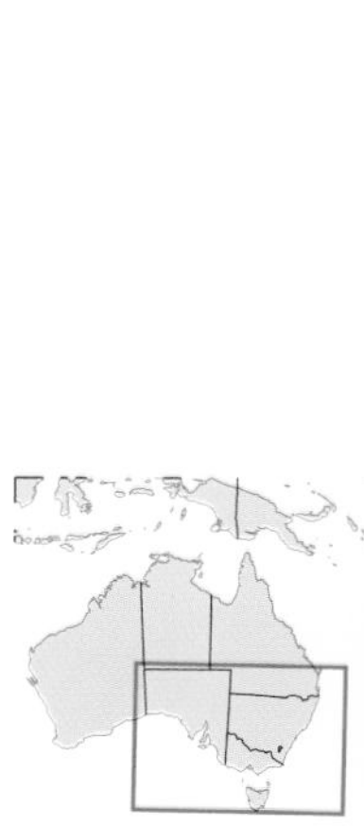

QUEENSLAND

NEW SOUTH WALES

VICTORIA

TASMANIA

GREAT DIVIDING RANGE

NEW ENGLAND RANGE

Riverina

Darling Downs

Gippsland

Brisbane
Gold Coast
Toowoomba
Newcastle
Sydney
Wollongong
Canberra
A.C.T.
Melbourne
Geelong
Ballarat
Bendigo
Hobart
Launceston
Devonport

TASMAN

SEA

Bass Strait

King I.
Furneaux Group
Flinders I.
Cape Barren I.

Fraser I.
Hervey Bay
Wilson's Promontory

JERVIS BAY TERR.

1:6 000 000

| 0 | 40 | 80 | 120 | 160 | 200 MILES |

| 0 | 40 | 80 | 120 | 160 | 200 | 240 | 280 | 320 KM |

A 128°

TIMOR SEA

Bathurst I.
Gordon B.
Bathurst I.
Abor. Land
Mitchell Pt
C. Gambier
Melville I.
Abor. Land
Melville I.
Clarence Str.
C. Hotham
Apsley Str.
Gurig
Nat. Park
**Cobourg
Pen.**
Croker I.
McCluer I.
Grant I.
C. Van Diemen
Dundas Str.
Van Diemen Gulf
Field I.
Goulburn Is
Maningrida
C. Stewart
Junction B.
Howard I.
Drysdale I.
Elcho I.
Buckingham B.
Nhulunbuy
C. Arnhem
Napier Pen.
Melville B.
Port Bradshaw
Caledon B.
Trial B.
C. Shield
Woodah I.
Bickerton I.
Alyangula
213
**Groote
Eylandt**
Groote Eylandt
Abor. Land
C. Barrow
Numbulwar
Edward I.
Maria I.
Limmen Bight
C. Beatrice
**Gulf of
Carpentaria**

Beagle Gulf
Port Darwin
Pt Blaze
Peron Is.
C. Scott
Anson Bay
Darwin
Wagait
Abor. Land
Batchelot
Adelaide
River
Rum jungle
Oenpelli
Woolwonga
Abor. Land
Jabiru
**Kakadu
National Park**
E. Alligator
Liverpool
F. Alligator
Arnhem Land
Mann
Aboriginal Land
Blyth
Goyder
Rose
Warrick Cham.
C. Barrow
C. Shield

Pt Blaze
Burrundie
Mt Saunders
305
Pine Creek
Katherine
Gorge
Nat. Park
Katherine
Beswick
Abor. Land
Roper
Roper
Numbulwar

**Joseph
Bonaparte
Gulf**
Forrest
River
Abor. Res.
Forrest
Pearce Pt
Cambridge G.
Queens Chn.
Quoin
Daly River
Aboriginal Land
Wingate Mts
Mataranka
Larrimah
Nutwood
Downs
West I.
Sir Edward Pellew
Group
Vanderlin I.
Port McArthur
Limmen Bight
Wellesley Is
Mornington I.
C. Van Di
Bountiful
Gununa
Denham I.
Bentinck I.
S. Wellesley Is

Wyndham
Legune
Timber
Creek
Victoria River
Willeroo
Daly Waters
Dunmarra
Borroloola
Manangoora
Doomadgee
Abor. Land
Burketown
Inve

Kununurra
Fitzmaurice
Angalarri
Stokes Ra.
East Baines
Gregory
Nat. Park
Victoria
River
Downs
Montejinnie
Armstrong
Daly Waters
Limmen Bight
Wearyan
Robinson
River
Calvert
Hills
Westmoreland
Nicholson
Gregory
Downs
Floraville
Leichhardt
Falls

Durack Ra.
Cockburn Ra.
Wilson
Lake
Argyle
Bow
Mt Lush
786
Turkey
Creek
Kimberley
Violet Valley
Abor. Reserve
Plateau
Mt John
Bungle Bungle
Nat. Park
Ord
Mt Wickham
424
Stirling Cr.
Giles Cr.
Kalkaringi
Wickham
Mt Maiyu
479
Inverway
Newcastle
Waters
**Sturt
Plain**
Newcastle Cr.
Beetaloo
Elliot
Eva
Downs
Cresswell
Anthony Lagoon
Brunette Downs
Corella L.
Mt Sylvester
Barkly Tableland
Clipsham
Spring Cr.
Lawn Hill
Lorraine
Riversleigh

Mt Barrett
696
Halls Creek
**Antrim
Plateau**
Gordon
Downs
Nicholson
Sturt Cr.
Hooker Creek
Abor. Reserve
Lajamanu
Winnecke Cr.
NORTHERN
L. Woods
Banka Banka
Rockhampton
Downs
Frewena
Alexandria
Playford
Avon Downs
Camooweal
Lake
Julius

McClintock
Denison
Plains
WESTERN
Billiluna
Gregory
Lake
Balgo
Mission
Balwina
Abor. Reserve
Lewis Ra.
Tanami
Central Desert
Aboriginal Land
TERRITORY
**Tanami
Desert**
Mt Woodcock
373
Tennant Creek
Mt Samuel
436
Kurundi
Soudan
Buckley
Barkly Downs
Mingera Cr.
Mount Isa
Quamby
Cloncur
Ft Constan

AUSTRALIA
Stansmore Ra.
L. Wills
L. White
L. Hazlett
**Central
Australia
Aboriginal
Reserve**
Lake Mackay
Aboriginal Land
Mt Singleton
844
Mt Davenport
817
Willowra Aboriginal
Land Trust
Wallowra
Lander
Davenport Ra.
Warrabri
Abor.
Reserve
Murray
Downs
Elkedra
Hatches Creek
Elkedra
Lake Nash
Austral Downs
Headingly
Woodroffe
Urandangi
Dajarra
Duchess
Selwyn Ra

Lake Mackay
Angas Ra.
L. MacDonald
Kintore Ra.
Mt Leister
901
Ehrenberg Ra.
Mt Liebig
1524
Mt Liebig
Yuendumu
Yuendumu
Abor. Reserve
Barrow Creek
Central Mt Stuart
844
Ti Tree
Mt Freeling
998
Ammaroo
Sandover
Sandover
Bundey
Ooratippa
Mt Hogarth
339
Tobermory
Roxborough
Downs
Herbert
Downs
Boulia
Georgina
Hamilto
Glenormiston
Marion
Downs
Spring

Barrons Ra.
Stuart Bluff Ra.
1067
Central Mt Wedge
Papunya
Mt Edward
1416
Macdonnell Ranges
Mt Ziel
1510
1249
Mt Hay
Mt Laughlen
116?
Ambalindum
Reynolds Ra.
Jervois Ra.
Marshall
Sandringham

Mt Lyell Brown
881
Haasts Bluff
Aboriginal Land
Haast Bluff
James Ranges
Hermannsburg
Mt Riddock
1105
Mt Brassey
1128
Santa Teresa
Waterhouse Ra.
George Gills Ra.
Palm
Valley
Finke Gorge
Nat. Park
Alice Springs
Finke
High
Palmer
Hale
Todd
Plenty
Hay
Pituri Cr.
Georgina
Cluny
L. Machattie
Glengyle
L. Kooltoo

L. Hopkins
L. Neale
Tempe Downs
Lake Amadeus
Angas Downs
Erldunda
Rumbalara
Andado
**Simpson
Desert**
L. Philippi
Bedourie
Monkira
L. Koolivoo

Rawlinson Ra.
Petermann Ranges
Mt
Deering
1219
Petermann Aboriginal Land
Mt Olga
1069
Yulara
Ayers Rock
(Uluru)
Uluru Nat. Park
Kulgera
Goyder
Finke
Finke
L. Muncoonie
Bilpa Morea
Claypan
Durri
Betoo

Mt
Rawlinson
689
Mt Aloysius
Mt Cockburn
1138
Mt Davies
1085
1251
Mt Whinham
Mt Morris
1254
Mann Ranges
Musgrave Ranges
Mt Everard
Mt Woodroffe
1440
Tieyon
Abminga
Eringa
Witjira
Nat. Park
**Simpson
Desert
Nat. Park**
L. Thomas
Simpson Desert
Conservation Park
Poolowanna L.
Pandie Pandie
Birdsville
Moonda L.
Alton Downs
Cordillo
Downs
Moora

Mt
Squires
705
Mt Sir Thomas
773
Tonkinson Ranges
Mt Kintore
1071
Barrow Creek Ra.
**Central Australia
Aboriginal Reserve
(Warburton)**
Bluff Ra.
Mt Agnes
640
Birksgate Ra.
Everard Range
Mt Illbillee
917
Everard
Park
Hamilton
Pedirka
Alberga
Welbourn
Hill
Alberga
Stevenson Cr.
Macumba
L. Etamunbanie
Poolanna L.
Clifton Hills
L. Uloowaranie

GREAT VICTORIA DESERT
Serpentine
Lakes
Pitjantjatjara Lands
Aboriginal Land
Marla
Macumba
Oodnadatta
Mt
Dutton
Peake
Neales
Lora
Warburton
Kallakoopah Cr.
L. Warrandirrinna
L. Howitt
Mungeranie
Innaminck

SOUTH
Wyola L.
Dey-Dey L.
Woomera Prohibited Area
Cooper Pedy
Cadibarrawirracanna
Edward's Cr.
Conway
Douglas Cr.
Warriners Cr.
Peake
**Lake
Eyre
(North)**
Lake Eyre
Nat. Park
L. Hope
L. Gregory
Etadunna
Cooper Creek
Barcoo Cr.
Strzelecki Cr.

A 128°   B   132°   **AUSTRALIA**   C   136°   **L. Eyre
(South)**   L. Blanche   D

METRES	FEET
6000	19686
5000	16409
4000	13124
3000	9843
2000	6562
1000	3281
500	1640
200	656
SEA	LEVEL
200	656
2000	6562
4000	13124
6000	19686

Lambert Azimuthal Equal Area Projection

© HarperCollinsPublishers

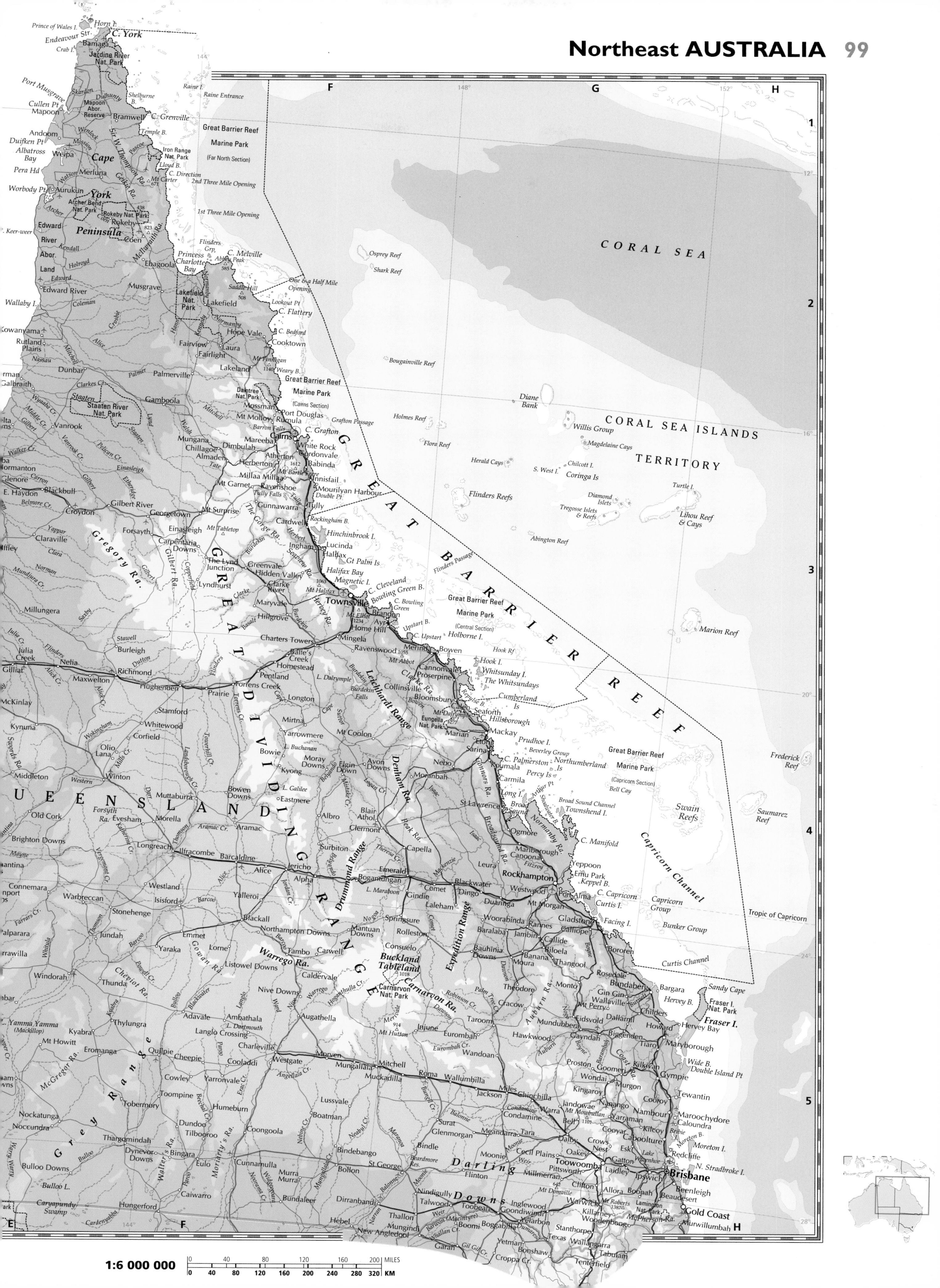

1:6 000 000

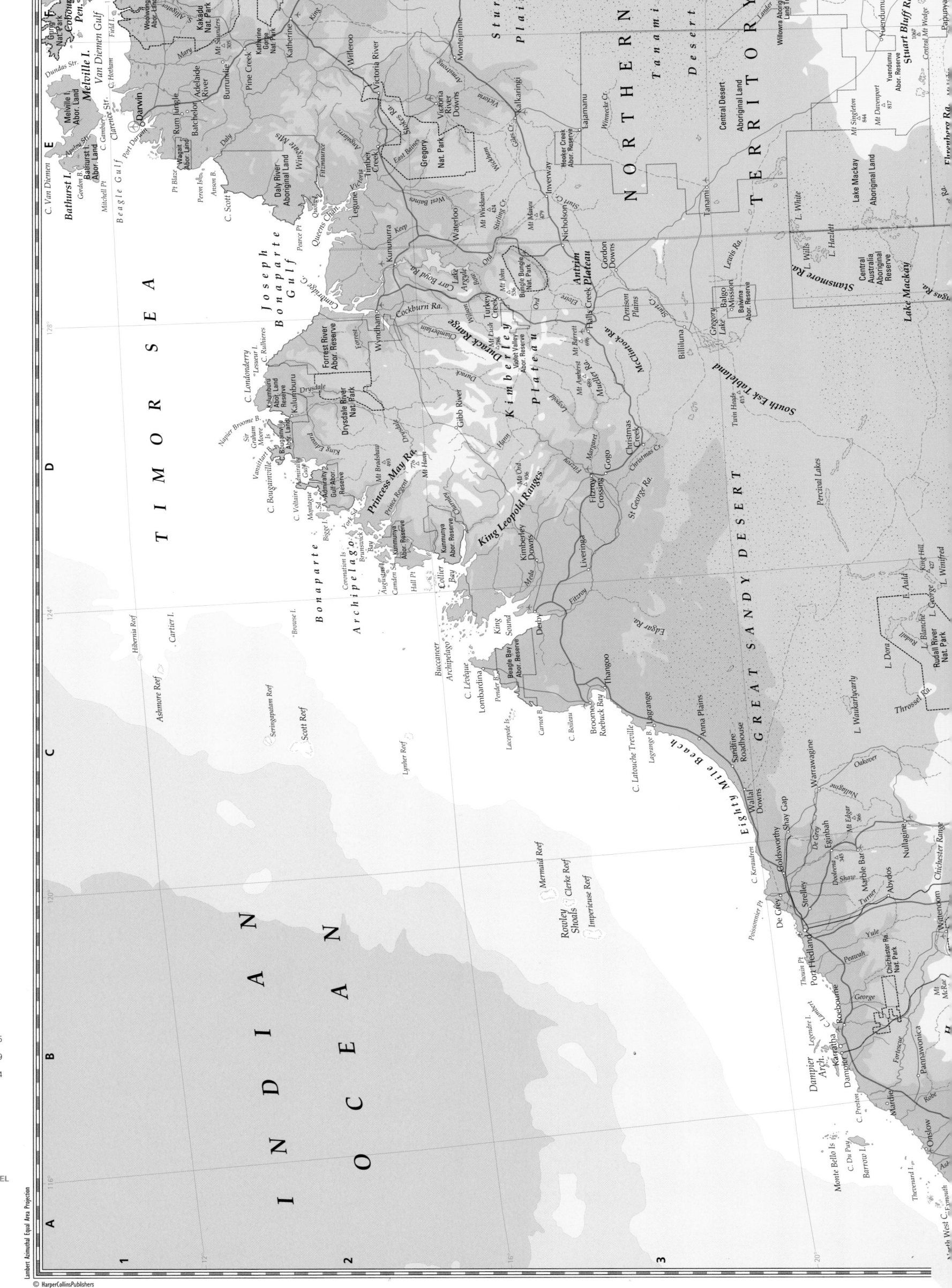

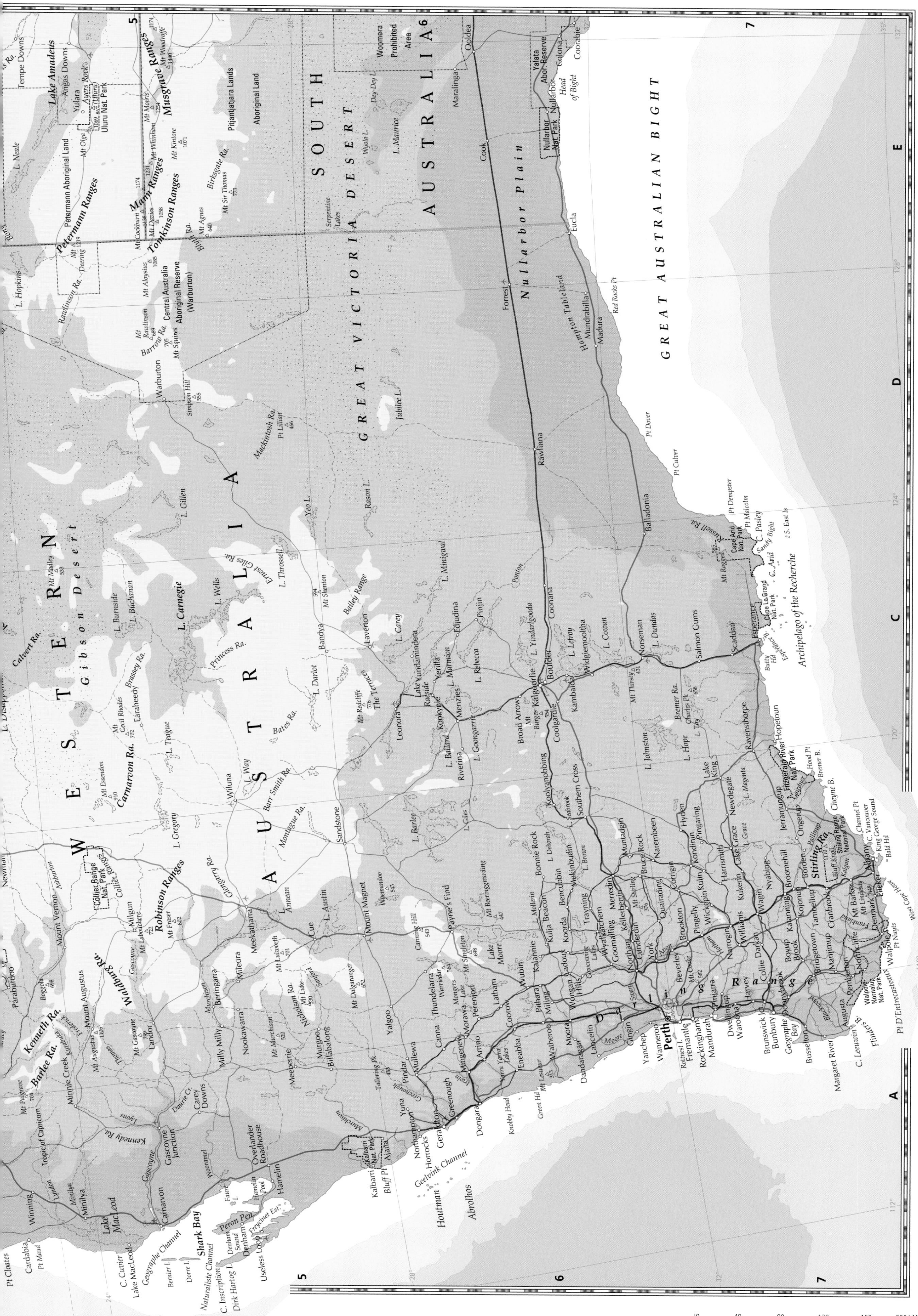

SOUTH

AUSTRALIA

WESTERN AUSTRALIA

GREAT VICTORIA DESERT

Gibson Desert

Nullarbor Plain

GREAT AUSTRALIAN BIGHT

Great Australian Bight

Musgrave Ranges
Mann Ranges
Tomkinson Ranges
Petermann Ranges
Petermann Aboriginal Land
Lake Amadeus
Tempe Downs
Angas Downs
Yulara
Ayers Rock
Uluru Nat. Park
Mt Olga
Mt Woodroffe
Mt Morris
Mt Agnes
Mt Sir Thomas
Mt Squires
Birksgate Ra.
Pitjantjatjara Lands
Aboriginal Land
Central Australia Aboriginal Reserve (Warburton)
Warburton
Simpson Hill
Mackintosh Ra.
Mt Lillian
Serpentine Lakes
Jubilee L.
L. Maurice
Wyola L.
Day-Dey L.
Woomera Prohibited Area
Maralinga
Ooldea
Yalata Abor. Reserve
Nullarbor
Nullarbor Nat. Park
Colona
Coorabie
Head of Bight
Eucla
Mundrabilla
Madura
Hampton Tableland
Cook
Forrest
Rawlinna
Red Rocks Pt
Pt Culver
Pt Dover
Balladonia
Russell Ra.
Pt Dempster
Pt Malcolm
Cape Arid Nat. Park
Israelite Bay
C. Arid
C. Pasley
Sandy Bight
S. East Is.
Archipelago of the Recherche
Cape Le Grand Nat. Park
Esperance
Scaddan
Salmon Gums
Norseman
L. Dundas
L. Cowan
L. Lefroy
Widgiemooltha
Coolgardie
Kalgoorlie
Boulder
Kambalda
Kanowna
Broad Arrow
Menzies
Mt Burges
L. Yindarlgooda
Coonana
Ponton
Kookynie
Leonora
Laverton
L. Carey
L. Minigwal
Rason L.
Yeo L.
Ernest Giles Ra.
Mt Shenton
L. Throssell
Princess Ra.
Bates Ra.
Carnarvon Ra.
L. Wells
L. Carnegie
L. Burnside
L. Gillen
L. Darlot
Bandya
Mt Maulley
Calvert Ra.
Mt Cecil Rhodes
Earaheedy
Brassey Ra.
Robinson Ranges
Mt Fraser
Collier Range Nat. Park
Kennedy Ra.
Lyons
Kenneth Ra.
Lake MacLeod
Carnarvon
Shark Bay
Dirk Hartog I.
Denham
Peron Pen.
Hamelin Pool
Overlander Roadhouse
Gascoyne Junction
Carey Downs
Wooramel
Mt Augustus
Mount Augustus
Milgun
Cobra
Kumarina
Mount Vernon
Ashburton
Newman
Paraburdoo
Mt Padbury
Meekatharra
Wiluna
Sandstone
Mount Magnet
Cue
Mt Magnet
L. Austin
L. Way
Lake Barlee
Barr Smith Ra.
Montague Ra.
Youanmi
Payne's Find
Bonnie Rock
L. Moore
Wubin
Dalwallinu
Kalannie
Mullewa
Morawa
Perenjori
Three Springs
Eneabba
Dongara
Geraldton
Greenough
Northampton
Horrocks
Kalbarri Nat. Park
Kalbarri
Ajana
Bluff Pt
Houtman Abrolhos
Geelvink Channel
Murchison
Yuna
Canna
Latham
Coorow
Carnamah
Moora
Watheroo
Dandaragan
Lancelin
Gingin
Wanneroo
Perth
Fremantle
Rockingham
Mandurah
Pinjarra
Waroona
Harvey
Brunswick
Bunbury
Busselton
Geographe Bay
Margaret River
Augusta
C. Leeuwin
Dunsborough
Nannup
Collie
Donnybrook
Bridgetown
Boyup Brook
Manjimup
Northcliffe
Pemberton
Walpole
Denmark
Albany
King George Sound
Stirling Ra.
Stirling Range Nat. Park
Mt Barker
Cranbrook
Tambellup
Kojonup
Katanning
Broomehill
Gnowangerup
Ongerup
Jerramungup
Fitzgerald River Nat. Park
Hopetoun
Ravensthorpe
Bremer Ra.
Lake King
Newdegate
Lake Grace
Lake Magenta
Hyden
Kondinin
Narembeen
Bruce Rock
Merredin
Southern Cross
Koolyanobbing
Bullfinch
Mukinbudin
Bencubbin
Trayning
Kellerberrin
Quairading
York
Beverley
Brookton
Corrigin
Kulin
Wickepin
Narrogin
Wagin
Williams
Kukerin
Dumbleyung
Bullaring
Wandering
Dwellingup

Scale 1:6 000 000

0 40 80 120 160 200 MILES
0 40 80 120 160 200 240 280 320 KM

COUNTRY	AREA		POPULATION			Form of Government	Capital City	MAIN LANGUAGES	MAIN RELIGIONS	CURRENCY
	sqml	sqkm	total	density per sqml	sqkm					
ANGUILLA	60	155	8 000	134	52	UK territory	The Valley	English	Protestant, RC	E. Carib. dollar
ANTIGUA & BARBUDA	171	442	65 000	381	147	monarchy	St John's	English, Creole	Protestant, RC	E. Carib. dollar
THE BAHAMAS	5 382	13 939	272 000	51	20	monarchy	Nassau	English, Creole, French Creole	Protestant, RC	Dollar
BARBADOS	166	430	264 000	1590	614	monarchy	Bridgetown	English, Creole (Bajan)	Protestant, RC	Dollar
BELIZE	8 867	22 965	211 000	24	9	monarchy	Belmopan	English, Creole, Spanish, Mayan	RC, Protestant, Hindu	Dollar
BERMUDA	21	54	63 000	3022	1167	UK territory	Hamilton	English	Protestant, RC	Dollar
CANADA	3 849 674	9 970 610	29 251 000	8	3	federation	Ottawa	English, French, Amerindian languages, Inuktitut (Eskimo)	RC, Protestant, Greek Orthodox, Jewish	Dollar
CAYMAN ISLANDS	100	259	31 000	310	120	UK territory	George Town	English	Protestant, RC	Dollar
COSTA RICA	19 730	51 100	3 071 000	156	60	republic	San José	Spanish	RC, Protestant	Colón
CUBA	42 803	110 860	10 960 000	256	99	republic	Havana	Spanish	RC, Protestant	Peso
DOMINICA	290	750	71 000	245	95	republic	Roseau	English, French Creole	RC, Protestant	E. Carib. dollar,
DOMINICAN REPUBLIC	18 704	48 442	7 769 000	415	160	republic	Santo Domingo	Spanish, French Creole	RC, Protestant	Peso
EL SALVADOR	8 124	21 041	5 641 000	694	268	republic	San Salvador	Spanish	RC, Protestant	Colón
GREENLAND	840 004	2 175 600	55 000			Danish territory	Nuuk	Greenlandic, Danish	Protestant	Danish krone
GRENADA	146	378	92 000	630	243	monarchy	St George's	English, Creole	RC, Protestant	E. Carib. dollar
GUADELOUPE	687	1 780	421 000	613	237	French territory	Basse-Terre	French, French Creole	RC, Hindu	French franc
GUATEMALA	42 043	108 890	10 322 000	246	95	republic	Guatemala City	Spanish, Mayan languages	RC, Protestant	Quetzal
HAITI	10 714	27 750	7 041 000	657	254	republic	Port-au-Prince	French, French Creole	RC, Protestant, Voodoo	Gourde
HONDURAS	43 277	112 088	5 770 000	133	51	republic	Tegucigalpa	Spanish, Amerindian languages	RC, Protestant	Lempira
JAMAICA	4 244	10 991	2 429 000	572	221	monarchy	Kingston	English, Creole	Protestant, RC, Rastafarian	Dollar
MARTINIQUE	417	1 079	375 000	900	348	French territory	Fort-de-France	French, French Creole	RC, Protestant, Hindu, traditional beliefs	French franc
MEXICO	761 604	1 972 545	93 008 000	122	47	republic	Mexico City	Spanish, many Amerindian languages	RC, Protestant	Peso
MONTSERRAT	39	100	11 000	285	110	UK territory	Plymouth	English	Protestant, RC	E. Carib. dollar
NETH. ANTILLES (North)	26	68	35 240	1342	518	Neth. territory		Dutch, Papiamento, English	RC, Protestant	Guilder
NICARAGUA	50 193	130 000	4 401 000	88	34	republic	Managua	Spanish, Amerindian languages	RC, Protestant	Córdoba
PANAMA	29 762	77 082	2 583 000	87	34	republic	Panama City	Spanish, English Creole, Amerindian languages	RC, Protestant, Sunni Muslim, Baha'i	Balboa
PUERTO RICO	3 515	9 104	3 686 000	1049	405	US territory	San Juan	Spanish, English	RC, Protestant	US dollar
ST KITTS & NEVIS	101	261	41 000	407	157	monarchy	Basseterre	English, Creole	Protestant, RC	E. Carib. dollar
ST LUCIA	238	616	141 000	593	229	monarchy	Castries	English, French Creole	RC, Protestant	E. Carib. dollar
ST PIERRE & MIQUELON	93	242	6 000	64	25	French territory	St-Pierre	French	RC	French franc
ST VINCENT & THE GRENADINES	150	389	111 000	739	285	monarchy	Kingstown	English, Creole	Protestant, RC	E. Carib. dollar
TURKS & CAICOS IS.	166	430	14 000	84	33	UK territory	Grand Turk	English	Protestant	US dollar
USA	3 787 425	9 809 386	260 660 000	69	27	republic	Washington	English, Spanish, Amerindian languages	Protestant, RC, Sunni Muslim, Jewish, Mormon	Dollar
VIRGIN ISLANDS (UK)	59	153	18 000	305	118	UK territory	Road Town	English	Protestant, RC	US dollar
VIRGIN ISLANDS (USA)	136	352	104 000	765	295	US territory	Charlotte Amalie	English, Spanish	Protestant, RC	US dollar

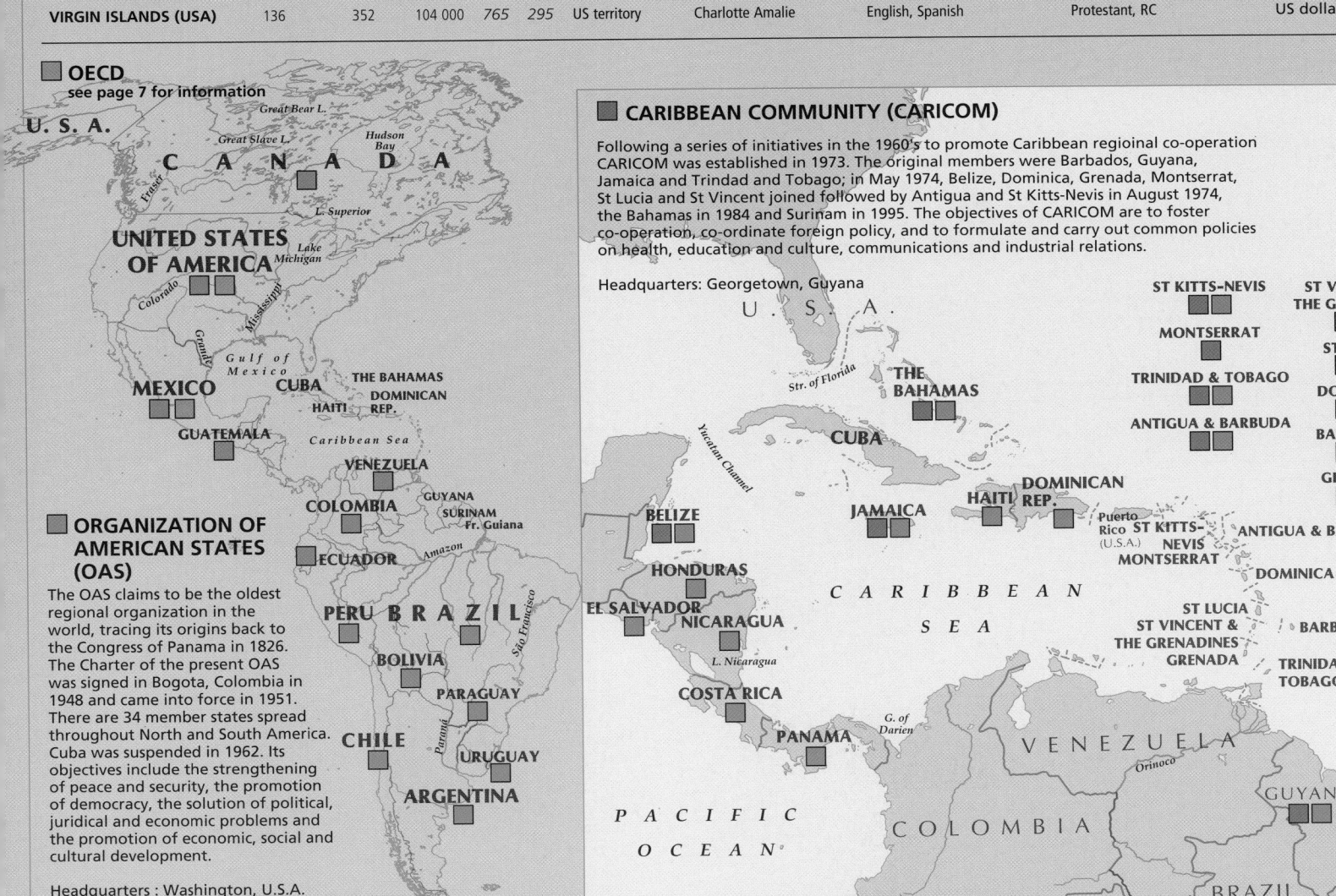

■ OECD
see page 7 for information

■ ORGANIZATION OF AMERICAN STATES (OAS)

The OAS claims to be the oldest regional organization in the world, tracing its origins back to the Congress of Panama in 1826. The Charter of the present OAS was signed in Bogota, Colombia in 1948 and came into force in 1951. There are 34 member states spread throughout North and South America. Cuba was suspended in 1962. Its objectives include the strengthening of peace and security, the promotion of democracy, the solution of political, juridical and economic problems and the promotion of economic, social and cultural development.

Headquarters : Washington, U.S.A.

■ CARIBBEAN COMMUNITY (CARICOM)

Following a series of initiatives in the 1960's to promote Caribbean regional co-operation CARICOM was established in 1973. The original members were Barbados, Guyana, Jamaica and Trinidad and Tobago; in May 1974, Belize, Dominica, Grenada, Montserrat, St Lucia and St Vincent joined followed by Antigua and St Kitts-Nevis in August 1974, the Bahamas in 1984 and Surinam in 1995. The objectives of CARICOM are to foster co-operation, co-ordinate foreign policy, and to formulate and carry out common policies on health, education and culture, communications and industrial relations.

Headquarters: Georgetown, Guyana

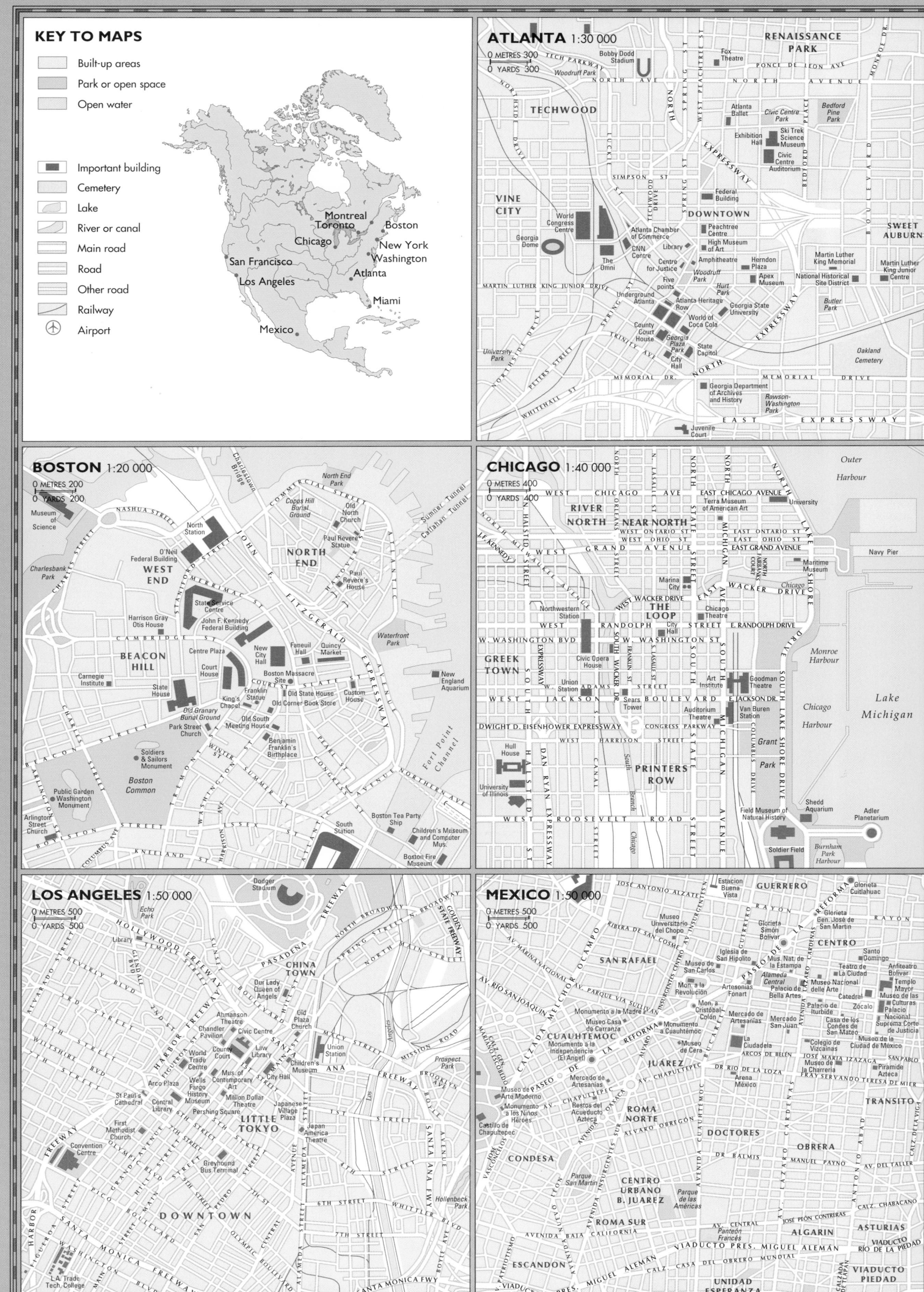

MIAMI 1:30 000

0 METRES 300
0 YARDS 300

South Florida Centre
N.W. 20TH STREET N.E. 20TH ST
Museum of Modern Art
Biscayne Park
City Cemetery
Margaret Pace Park
Williams Park
Dorsey Park
Civic Centre Area
Highland Park
International Fine Arts College
VENETIAN CAUSEWAY
DOLPHIN EXPRESSWAY
Creek
Gibson Park
McARTHUR CAUSEWAY
Bicentennial Park
City Yacht Basin
Reeves Park
Miami Arena
Freedom Tower
Bayfront Park
HMS Bounty
LITTLE
Henderson Park
Old Fort Dallas
Courthouse
Bayside Amphitheatre
Torch of Friendship
HAVANA
Lummus Park
Metro-Dade Cultural Centre
Christopher Columbus Mon.
Miami Memorial Public Library
W. FLAGLER STREET
W. FLAGLER STREET
Gusman Centre
S.W. 1ST STREET
World Trade Centre
James Knight Convention Centre
Riverside Park
José Marti Riverfront Park
Brickell Point

MONTRÉAL 1:20 000

0 METRES 200
0 YARDS 200

Musée des Hospitalières de l'Hôtel-Dieu
RUE SHERBROOKE
Université Mc Gill
Place des Arts
Cathédrale Christ Church
Musée des Beaux-Arts
Place Ville-Marie
Palais des Congrès
Hôtel de Ville
Chapelle Notre-Dame de Bonsecours
Square Dorchester
Cathédrale Marie-Reine-du-Monde
Vieux Palais de Justice
Marché Bonsecours
Gare Windsor
Gare Centrale
Basilique Notre-Dame
Quai Jacques-Cartier
Quai King-Edward
Musée Marguerita D'Youville
Bourse de Montréal
Lé Pelican
Quai Alexandra
Montréal Planétarium
RUE ST-JACQUES
Pont de la Concorde
RUE NOTRE-DAME
St Lawrence
Île Sainte-Hélène
Parc des Îles
Canal de Lachine
RUE ST-PATRICK
AUTOROUTE BONAVENTURE
RUE WELLINGTON
VICTORIA BRIDGE
Pont Victoria
Ile Notre-dame
Lac des Régates
Bassin Olympique

NEW YORK 1:100 000

0 METRES 1000
0 YARDS 1000

Hudson
UNION CITY
WEEHAWKEN
Natural History Museum
Central Park
Museum of Art
Wards Island
Hell Gate
MANHATTAN
Lincoln Centre
Lincoln Tunnel
Rockefeller Centre
Grand Central Station
LONG ISLAND CITY
Madison Square Garden
Empire State Building
Queensboro Bridge
Queens-Midtown Tunnel
HOBOKEN
GREENWICH VILLAGE
United Nations Headquarters
SUNNYSIDE
JERSEY CITY
Holland Tunnel
LONG ISLAND EXPRESSWAY
New Calvary Cemetery
CHINA TOWN
BROOKLYN - QUEENS EXPRESSWAY
World Trade Centre
Williamsburg Bridge
Station
WILLIAMSBURG
Ellis Island (N.Y.)
Castle Clinton
Manhattan Bridge
Brooklyn Battery Tunnel
BUSHWICK
Liberty Island (N.Y.)
Long Island University
Pratt Institute
BEDFORD-STUYVESANT
Statue of Liberty
Governor's Island

SAN FRANCISCO 1:100 000

0 METRES 1000
0 YARDS 1000

Golden Gate Bridge
Fisherman's Wharf
Maritime Museum
Colt Tower
San Francisco Bay
MARINA
Palace of Fine Arts
Transamerica Pyramid
World Trade Centre
PACIFIC OCEAN
PRESIDIO
PACIFIC HEIGHTS
Chinatown
Embarcadero Centre
Lincoln Park
Grace Cathedral
Oakland Bay Bridge
St Mary's Cath.
City Hall
Moscone Convention Centre
RICHMOND
GEARY BLVD
University of San Francisco
Mus. of Modern Art
Opera House
Railway Depot
De Young Museum
Golden Gate Park
Conservatory of Flowers
Golden Gate Park Stadium
Natural History Museum
Kezar Stadium
SUNSET
TWIN PEAKS
MISSION
POTRERO
NOE VALLEY
PARKSIDE
PORTOLA DRIVE
BAYVIEW
Harding Park
OUTER MISSION
INGLESIDE
EXCELSIOR
McLaren Park
Lake Merced
Stadium

TORONTO 1:40 000

0 METRES 400
0 YARDS 400

BLOOR STREET
Royal Ontario Museum
Varsity Stadium
Planetarium
HARBORD STREET
University of Toronto
Queens Park
Ontario Government Buildings
WELLESLEY STREET
Parliament Buildings
COLLEGE STREET
CARLTON ST
Art Gallery of Ontario
Ryerson Institute of Technology
DUNDAS STREET
Grange Park
Trinity Bellwoods Park
City Hall
Royal Alexandra Theatre
Osgoode Hall
Nathan Phillips Square
St Lawrence Centre for the Arts
QUEEN STREET
ADELAIDE STREET
Roy Thomson Hall
O'Keefe Centre
KING STREET
FRONT STREET
THE ESPLANADE
GARDINER EXPRESSWAY
Exhibition Park
Sky Dome
Old Fort York
CN Tower
Union Station
GARDINER EXPWY
LAKE SHORE BLVD
Marine Museum
LAKE SHORE BOULEVARD
Harbour Front
Queens Quay
Island Ferries Terminal
Lake Ontario

WASHINGTON 1:60 000

0 METRES 600
0 YARDS 600

Oak Hill Cemetery
Dupont Circle
Logan Circle
RHODE ISLAND AVE
FLORIDA AVE
Georgetown University
Washington Circle
National Geographic Society
MASSACHUSETTS AVENUE
GEORGETOWN
K STREET
Convention Centre
Watergate Complex
PENNSYLVANIA AVE
NEW YORK AVE
Theodore Roosevelt Mem.
George Washington University
National Theatre
Union Station
ROSSLYN
J.F. Kennedy Centre
The White House
National Archives
Union Station Plaza
Theodore Roosevelt I.
The Ellipse
Nat. History Museum
CONSTITUTION AVE
Theodore Roosevelt Br.
Lincoln Memorial
Constitution Gardens
Nat. Mus. of American History
Nat. Gallery of Art
Supreme Court
Library of Congress
U.S. Marine Memorial
The Mall
U.S. Capitol
INDEPENDENCE AVE
Washington Monument
Smithsonian Inst.
Nat. Air & Space Mus.
Hirshorn Museum
CLARENDON
West Potomac Park
Tidal Basin
Jefferson Memorial
SOUTHWEST FWY
Arlington
National Cemetery
Tomb of the Unknown Soldier
Arlington Memorial Br.
Potomac
Jefferson Memorial
East Potomac Park
Pentagon
COLUMBIA PIKE
Washington Navy Yard
Fredrick Douglass Br.
Waterfowl Sanctuary
Washington National Airport
Anacostia

© HarperCollins Publishers

© HarperCollinsPublishers

Chamberlin Trimetric Projection

METRES	FEET
6000	19686
5000	16409
4000	13124
3000	9843
2000	6562
1000	3281
500	1640
200	656
SEA LEVEL	
200	656
2000	6562
4000	13124
6000	19686

1:13 000 000

| 0 | 100 | 200 | 300 | 400 | 500 | MILES |
| 0 | 100 | 200 | 300 | 400 | 500 | 600 | 700 | 800 | KM |

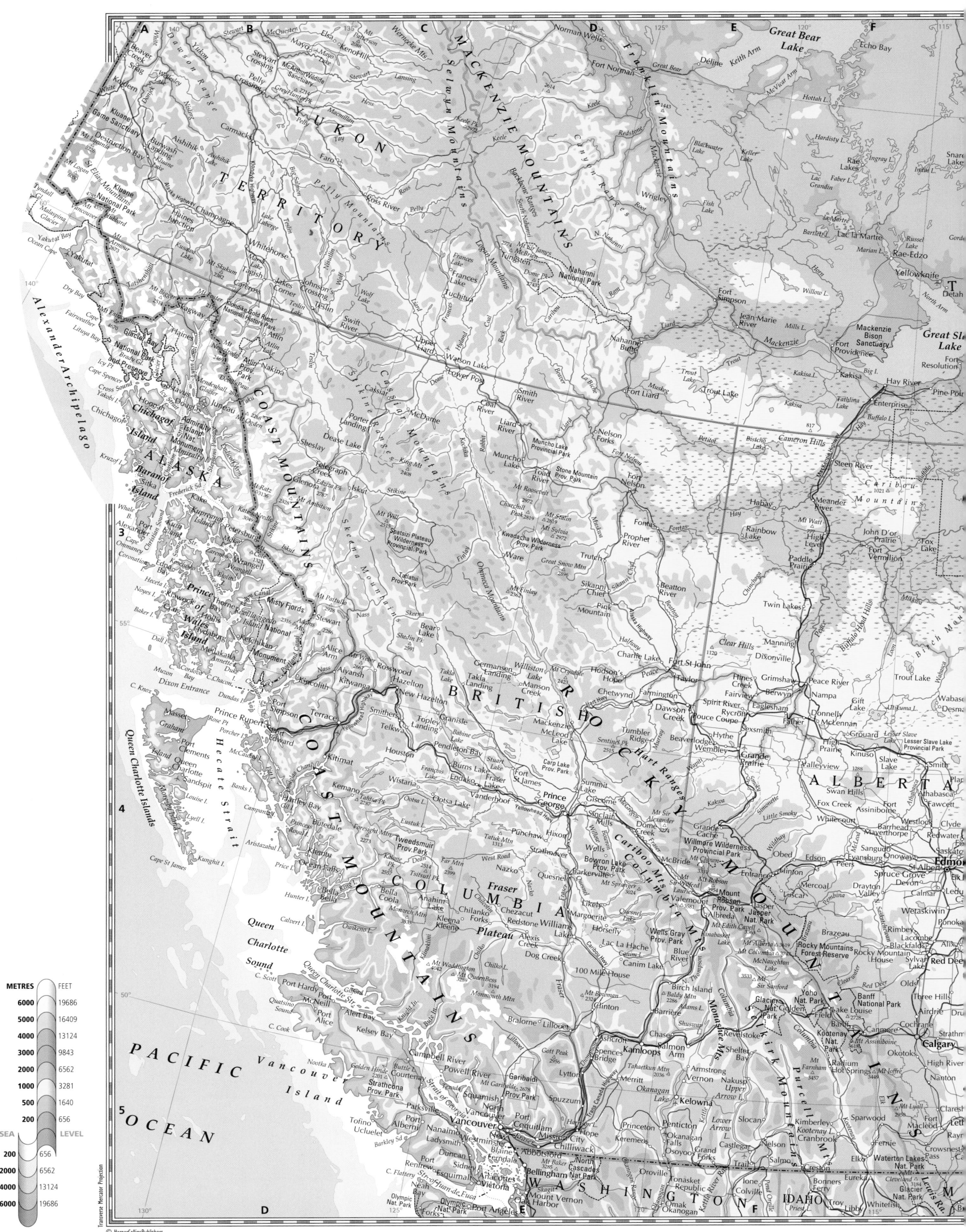

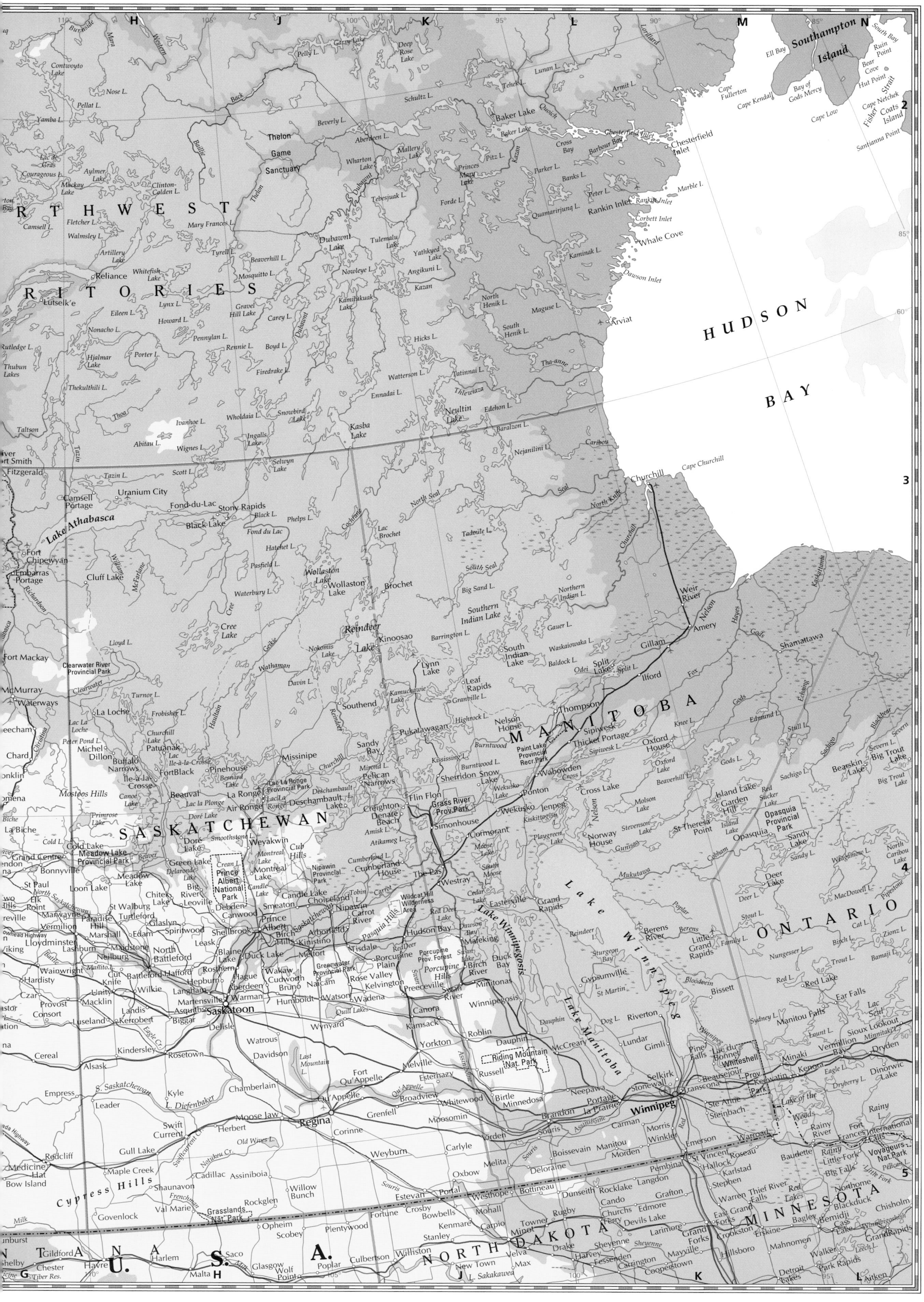

1:6 000 000

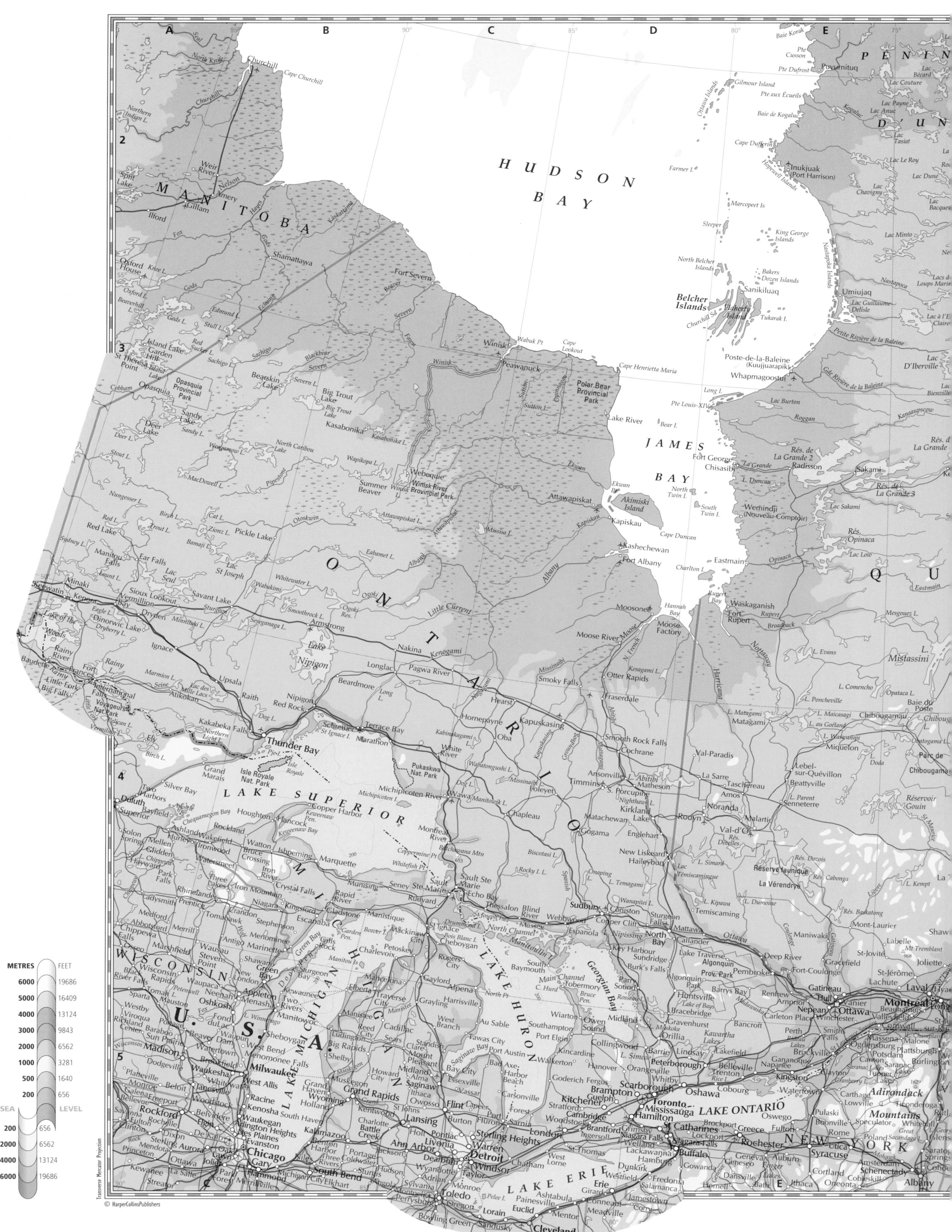

METRES	FEET
6000	19686
5000	16409
4000	13124
3000	9843
2000	6562
1000	3281
500	1640
200	656

SEA LEVEL

200 | 656
2000 | 6562
4000 | 13124
6000 | 19686

Transverse Mercator Projection

© HarperCollinsPublishers

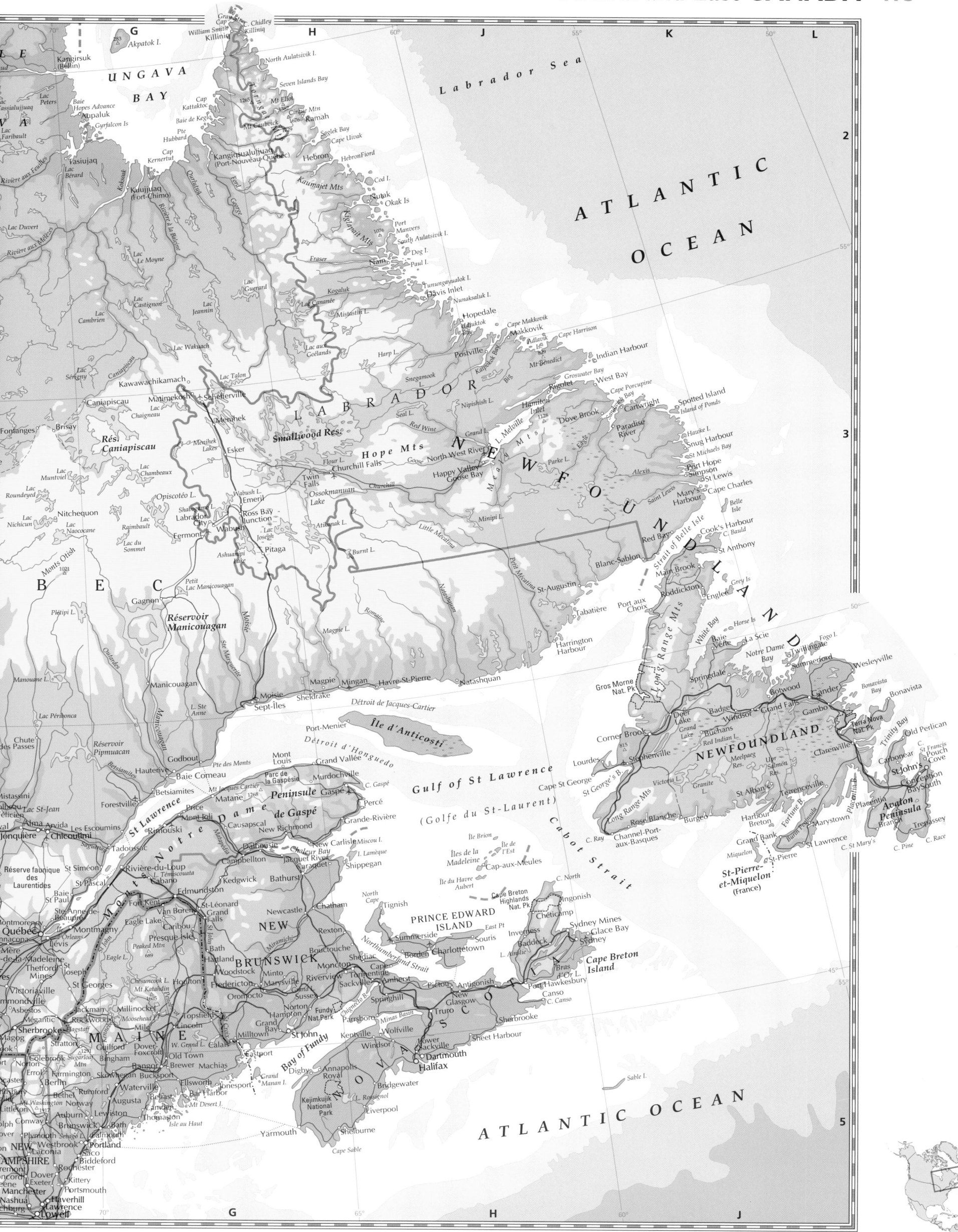

UNGAVA BAY

Labrador Sea

ATLANTIC OCEAN

LABRADOR

NEWFOUNDLAND

Hope Mts

Smallwood Res.

Rési Caniapiscau

Réservoir Manicouagan

BEC

QUÉBEC

Gulf of St Lawrence
(Golfe du St-Laurent)

Île d'Anticosti

Détroit de Jacques-Cartier

Détroit d'Honguedo

Péninsule de Gaspé

Peninsule de Gaspé

St Lawrence

Mont Notre Dame

Cabot Strait

NEWFOUNDLAND

Long Range Mts

Gros Morne Nat. Pk

Corner Brook

Terra Nova Nat. Pk

Avalon Peninsula

St John's

Conception Bay

Îles de la Madeleine

PRINCE EDWARD ISLAND

Northumberland Strait

Charlottetown

Cape Breton Island

Cape Breton Highlands Nat. Pk

NEW BRUNSWICK

NOVA SCOTIA

Fredericton

Halifax

Bay of Fundy

St-Pierre-et-Miquelon (France)

MAINE

NEW HAMPSHIRE

ATLANTIC OCEAN

1:6 000 000

0 40 80 120 160 200 MILES

0 40 80 120 160 200 240 280 320 KM

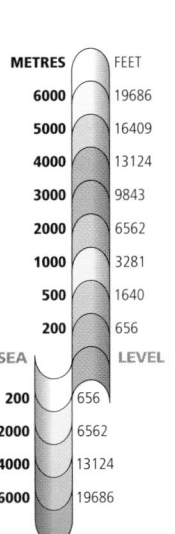

METRES	FEET
6000	19686
5000	16409
4000	13124
3000	9843
2000	6562
1000	3281
500	1640
200	656
SEA	LEVEL
200	656
2000	6562
4000	13124
6000	19686

Conic Equidistant Projection

© HarperCollinsPublishers

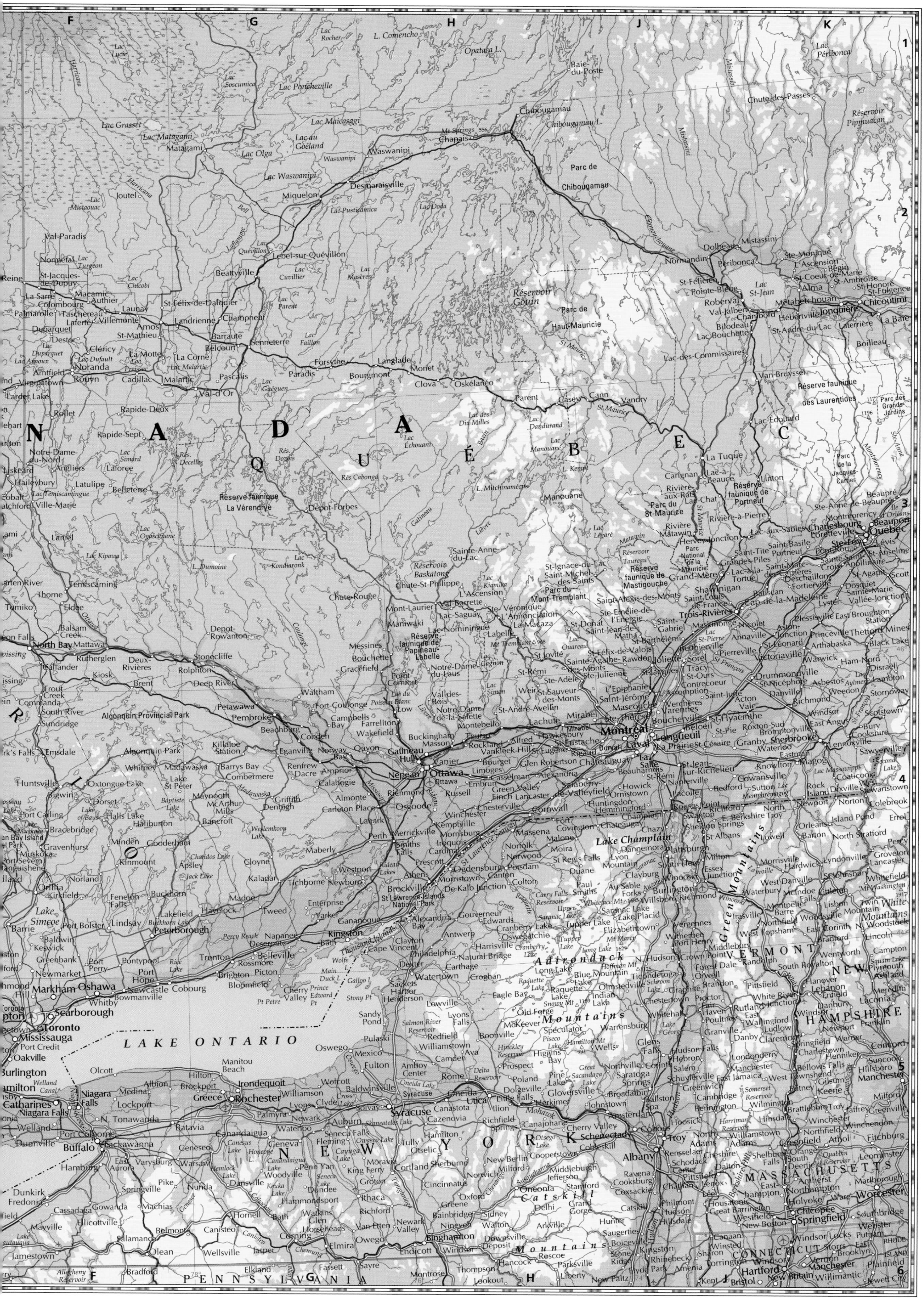

1:3 000 000

	0	20	40	60	80	100 MILES
0	20	40	60	80	100	120 140 160 KM

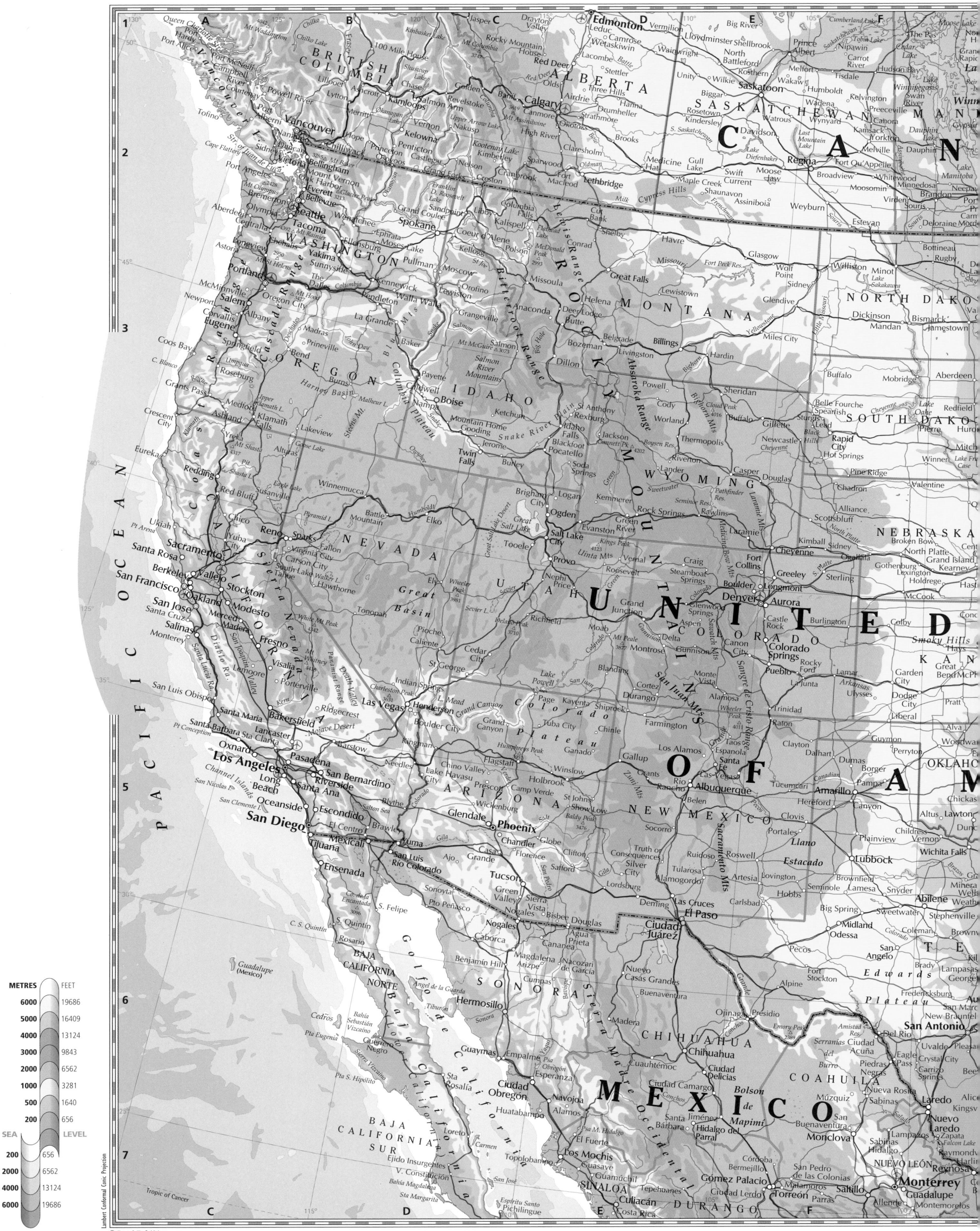

BRITISH COLUMBIA

ALBERTA

SASKATCHEWAN

CANADA

WASHINGTON

OREGON

IDAHO

MONTANA

NORTH DAKOTA

SOUTH DAKOTA

WYOMING

NEBRASKA

NEVADA

UTAH

COLORADO

KANSAS

CALIFORNIA

ARIZONA

NEW MEXICO

OKLAHOMA

UNITED OF AMERICA

PACIFIC OCEAN

BAJA CALIFORNIA NORTE

BAJA CALIFORNIA SUR

SONORA

CHIHUAHUA

COAHUILA

MEXICO

DURANGO

SINALOA

NUEVO LEÓN

TEXAS

METRES / **FEET**

6000	19686
5000	16409
4000	13124
3000	9843
2000	6562
1000	3281
500	1640
200	656

SEA LEVEL

200	656
2000	6562
4000	13124
6000	19686

Lambert Conformal Conic Projection

© HarperCollinsPublishers

Tropic of Cancer

1:10 000 000

| | 0 | 100 | 200 | 300 MILES |

| | 0 | 100 | 200 | 300 | 400 | 500 KM |

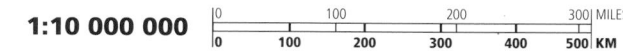

METRES	FEET
6000	19686
5000	16409
4000	13124
3000	9843
2000	6562
1000	3281
500	1640
200	656
SEA	LEVEL
200	656
2000	6562
4000	13124
6000	19686

Lambert Conformal Conic Projection

© HarperCollinsPublishers

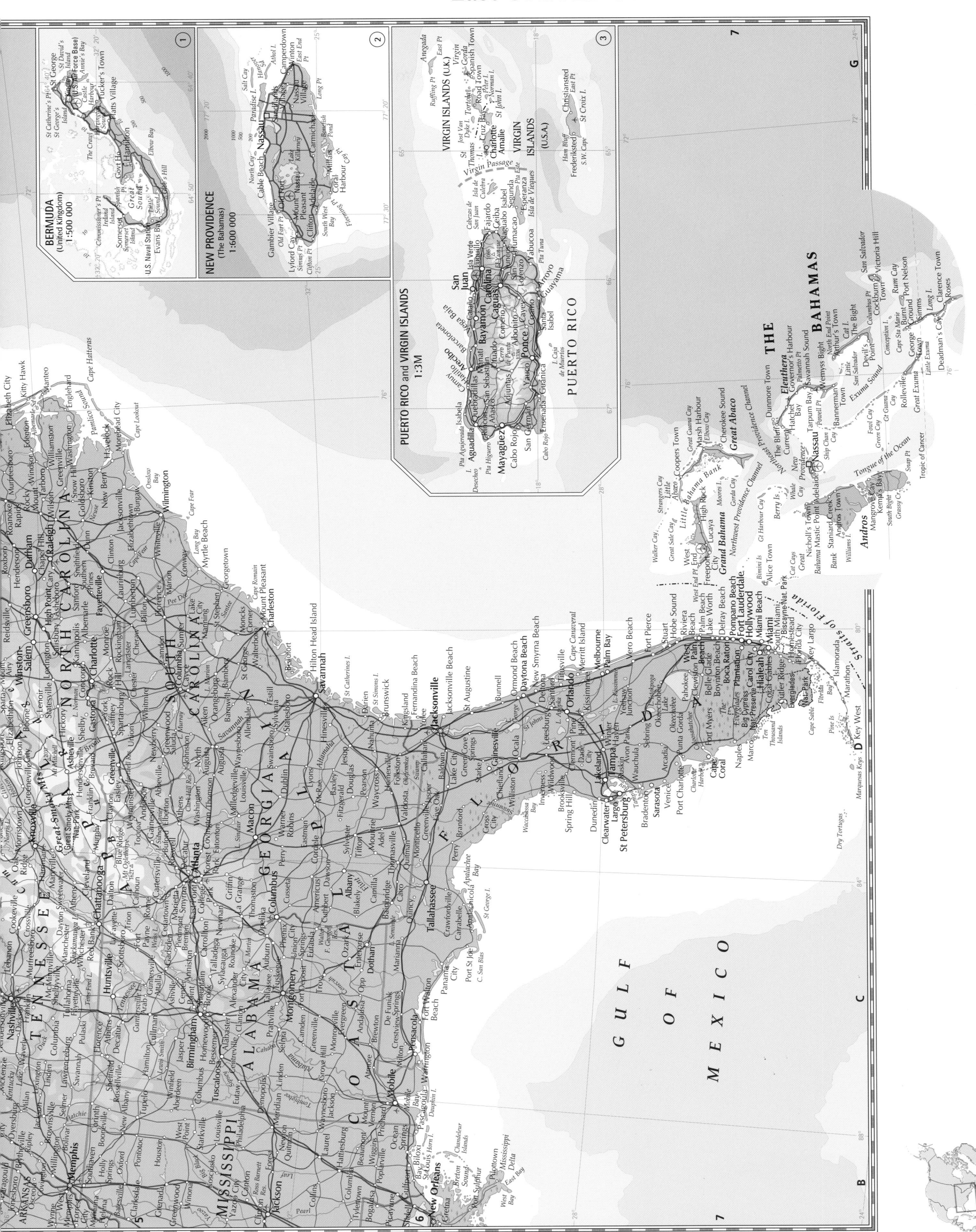

BERMUDA
(United Kingdom) 1:500 000

NEW PROVIDENCE
(The Bahamas) 1:600 000

PUERTO RICO and VIRGIN ISLANDS 1:3M

1:6 000 000

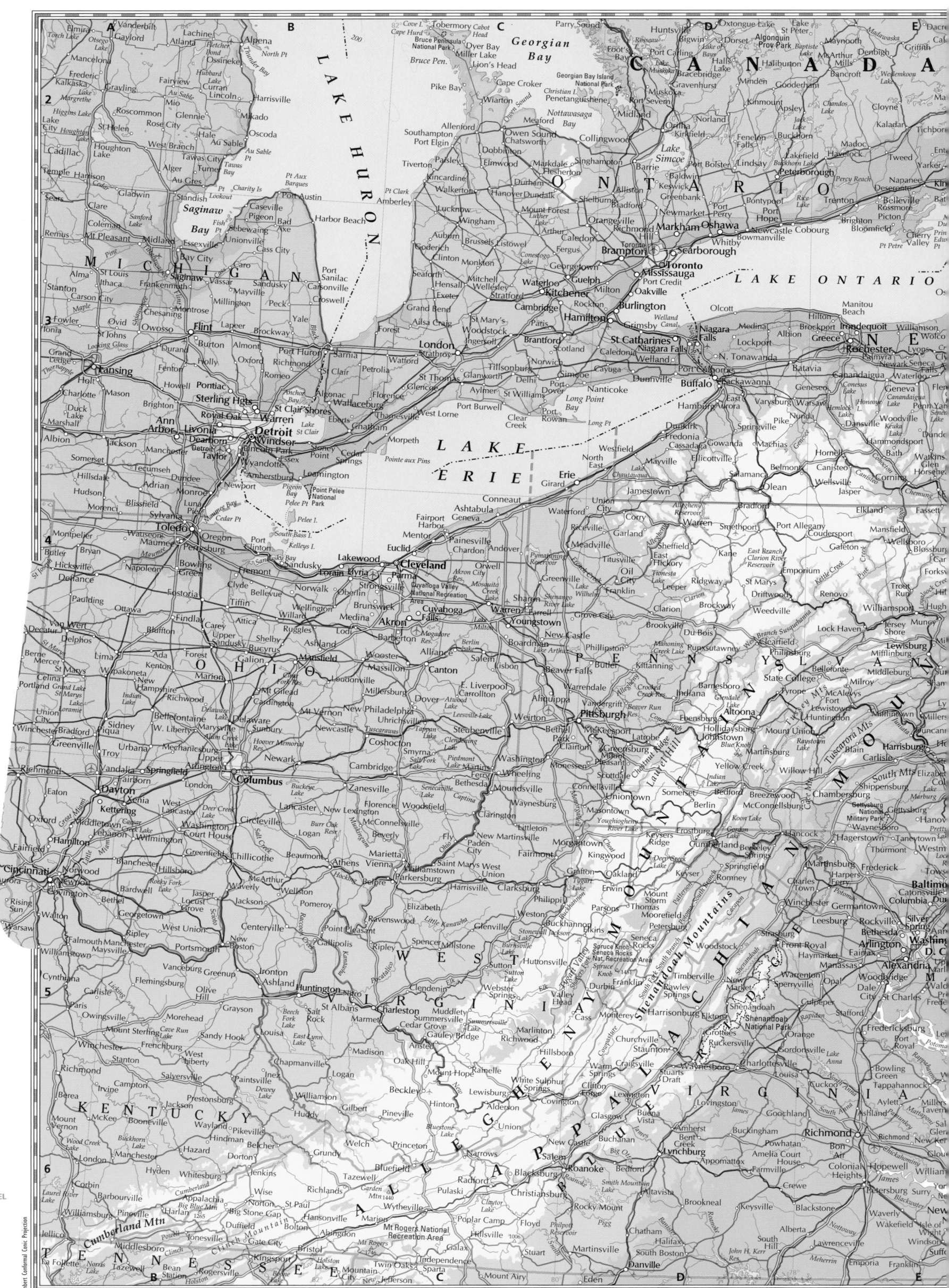

1:3 000 000

MILES

KM

LAKE SUPERIOR

LAKE MICHIGAN

MINNESOTA

WISCONSIN

MICHIGAN

IOWA

ILLINOIS

INDIANA

MISSOURI

Michipicoten Bay

Isle Royale

Isle Royale National Park

Apostle Islands National Lakeshore

Pukaskwa National Park

Pictured Rocks National Lakeshore

Keweenaw Peninsula

Keweenaw Bay

Green Bay

Door Peninsula

Mesabi Range

Gogebic Range

Sawtooth Mountains

Misquah Hills

Thunder Bay

Duluth, Superior

St Paul, Minneapolis, Bloomington

Eau Claire

La Crosse

Madison

Milwaukee

Green Bay

Appleton

Oshkosh

Rockford

Davenport, Moline, Rock Island

Cedar Rapids

Iowa City

Peoria

Bloomington

Springfield

Decatur

Champaign, Urbana

Chicago

Gary

South Bend

Fort Wayne

Grand Rapids

Kalamazoo

Muskegon

Holland

Racine

Kenosha

Waukegan

Evanston

Indianapolis

Escanaba

Marquette

Houghton, Hancock

Sault Ste Marie

Manistee

Ludington

Traverse City

Scale legend:

METRES	FEET
6000	19686
5000	16409
4000	13124
3000	9843
2000	6562
1000	3281
500	1640
200	656
SEA	LEVEL
200	656
2000	6562
4000	13124
6000	19686

Lambert Conformal Conic Projection

© HarperCollinsPublishers

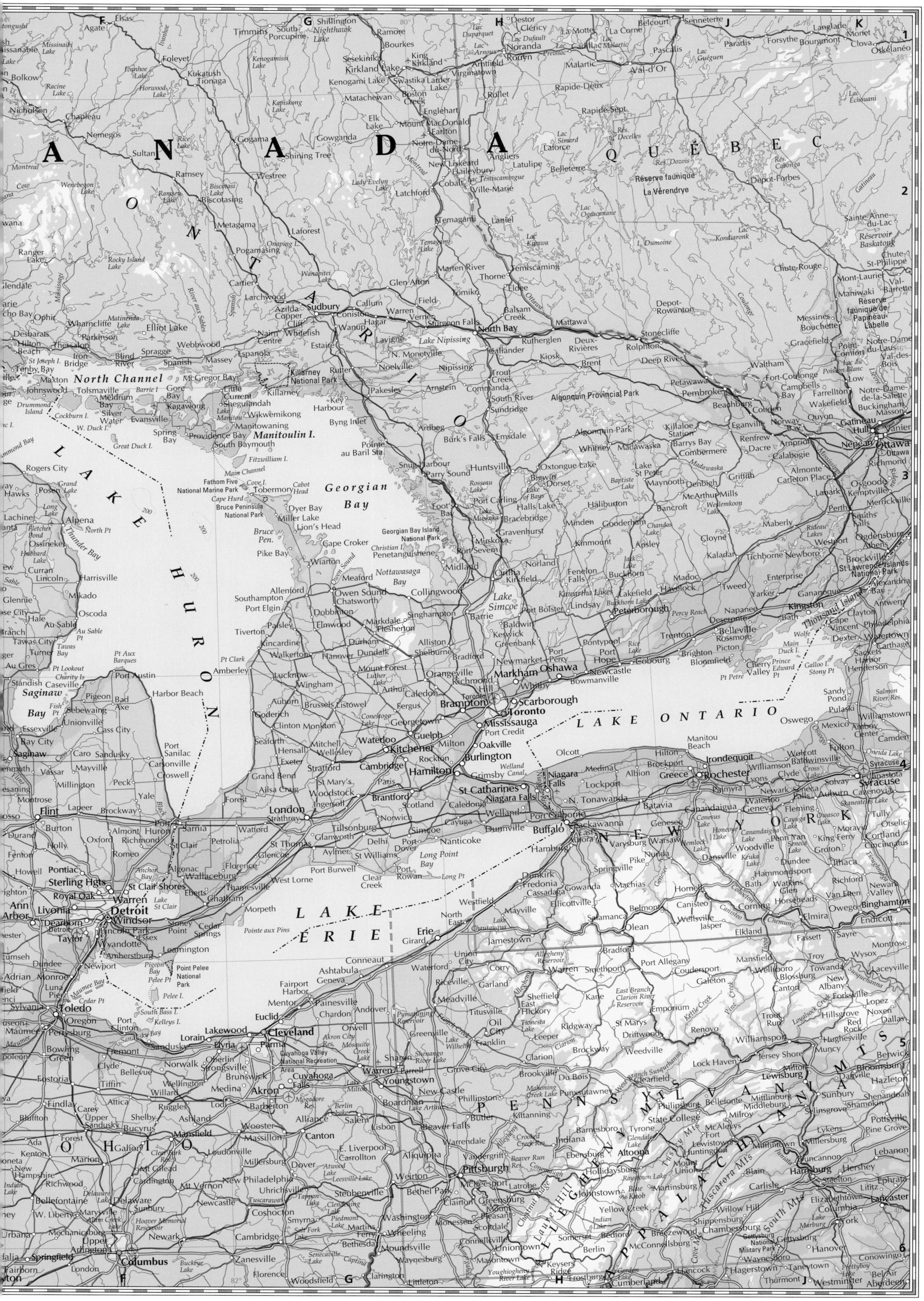

1:3 000 000

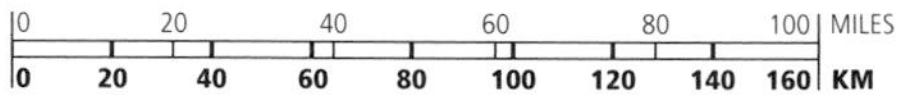

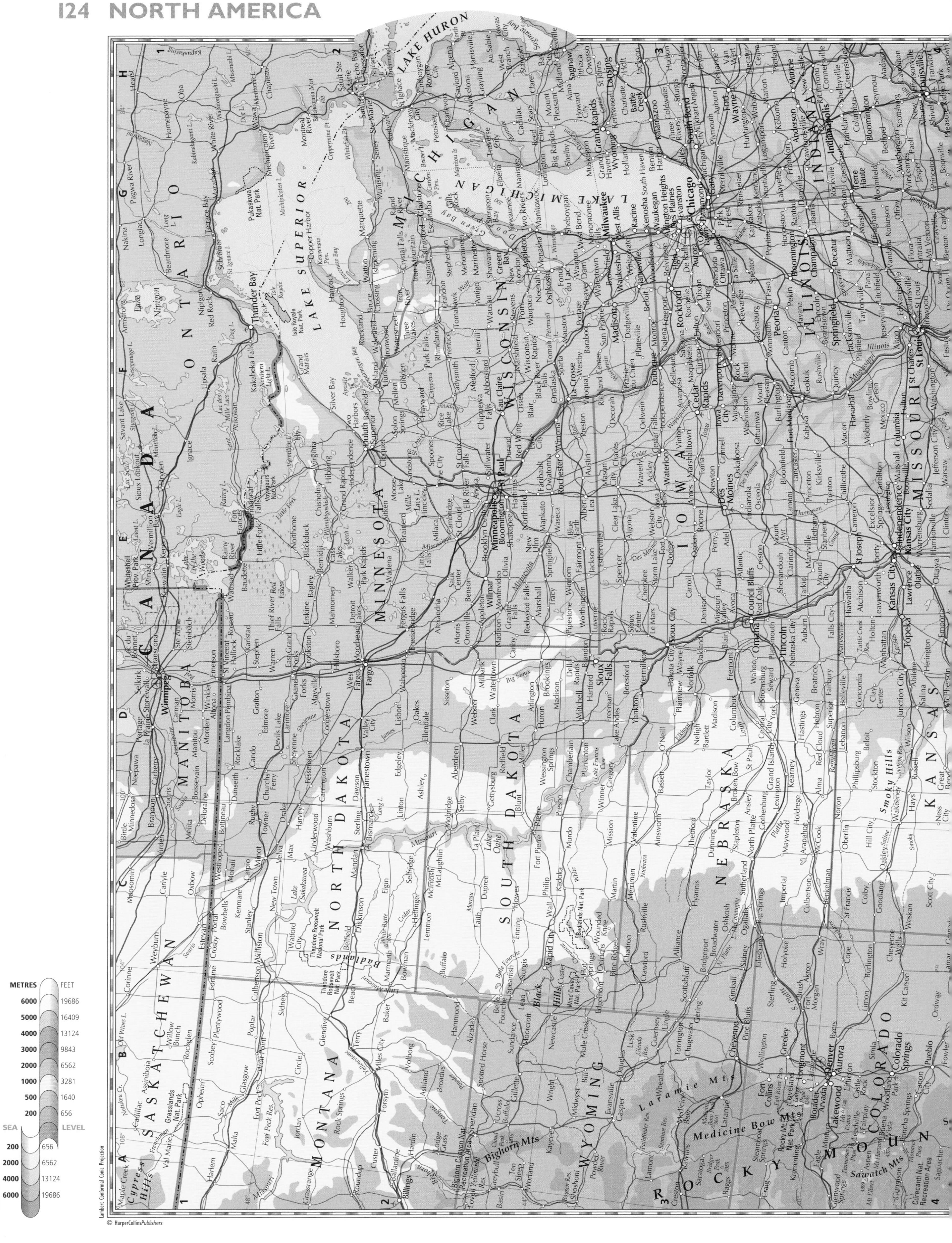

LAKE HURON

LAKE SUPERIOR

LAKE MICHIGAN

CANADA

ONTARIO

MANITOBA

SASKATCHEWAN

MONTANA

WYOMING

COLORADO

NORTH DAKOTA

SOUTH DAKOTA

NEBRASKA

KANSAS

MINNESOTA

IOWA

MISSOURI

WISCONSIN

ILLINOIS

MICHIGAN

INDIANA

ROCKY MOUNTAINS

Black Hills

Bighorn Mts

Medicine Bow

Smoky Hills

Laramie Mts

Badlands

Cypress Hills

METRES	FEET
6000	19686
5000	16409
4000	13124
3000	9843
2000	6562
1000	3281
500	1640
200	656
SEA	LEVEL
200	656
2000	6562
4000	13124
6000	19686

Lambert Conformal Conic Projection

© HarperCollins Publishers

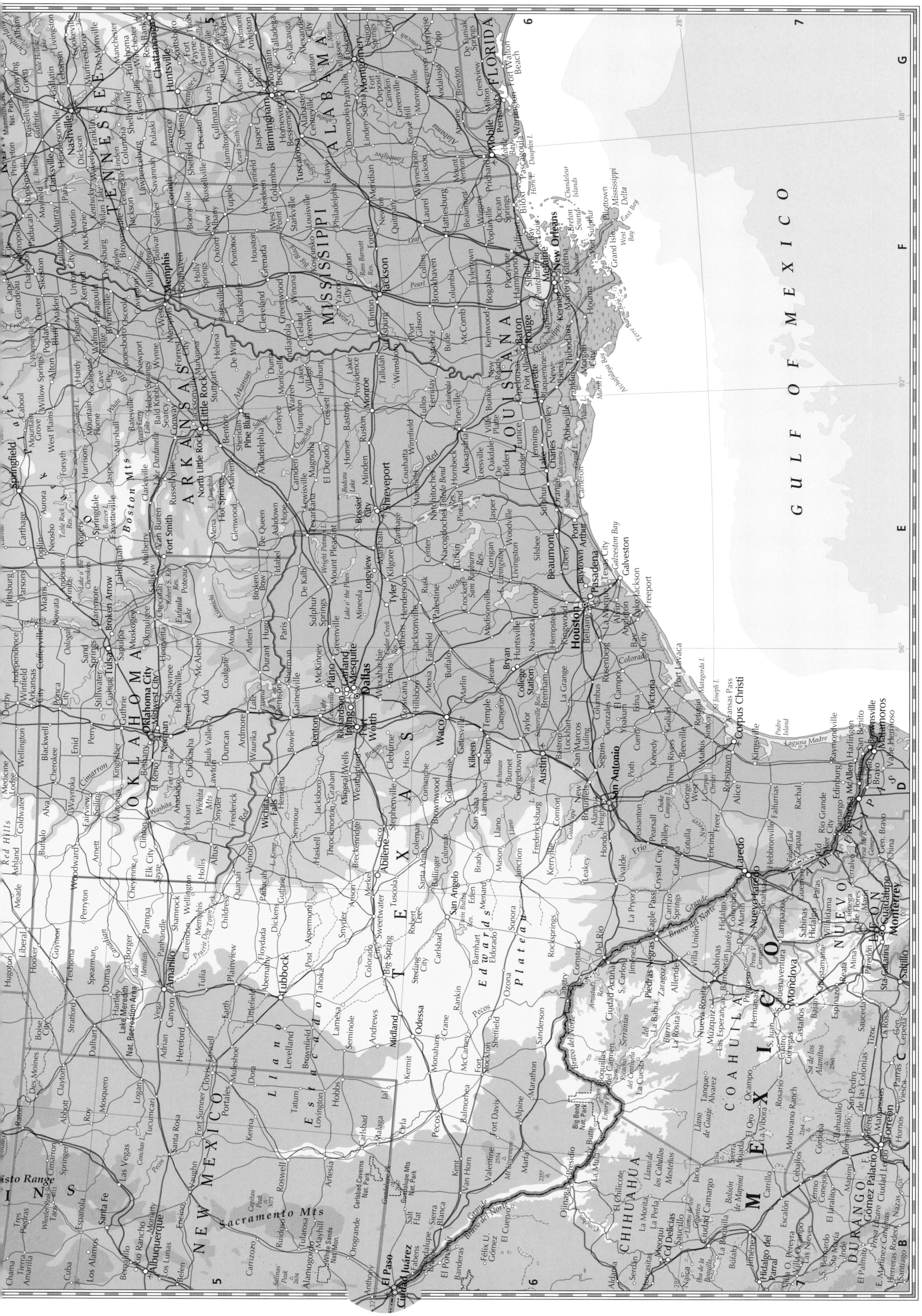

1:6 000 000

| 0 | 40 | 80 | 120 | 160 | 200 MILES |

| 0 | 40 | 80 | 120 | 160 | 200 | 240 | 280 | 320 KM |

METRES	FEET
6000	19686
5000	16409
4000	13124
3000	9843
2000	6562
1000	3281
500	1640
200	656
SEA	LEVEL
200	656
2000	6562
4000	13124
6000	19686

Lambert Conformal Conic Projection

© HarperCollins Publishers

COLORADO

NEW MEXICO

TEXAS

CHIHUAHUA

ARIZONA

SONORA

MEXICO

NEVADA

GREAT BASIN

COLORADO PLATEAU

CALIFORNIA

BAJA CALIFORNIA NORTE

Golfo de California

Sacramento Mountains

Sangre de Cristo Range

San Joaquin Valley

PACIFIC OCEAN

HAWAIIAN ISLANDS
(Main group)
(U.S.A.)

OAHU
(Hawaii) 1:1.5M

Hawaii

Hawaii Volcanoes
National Park

at the same scale

1:6 000 000

| 0 | 40 | 80 | 120 | 160 | 200 | MILES |

| 0 40 80 120 160 200 240 280 320 | KM |

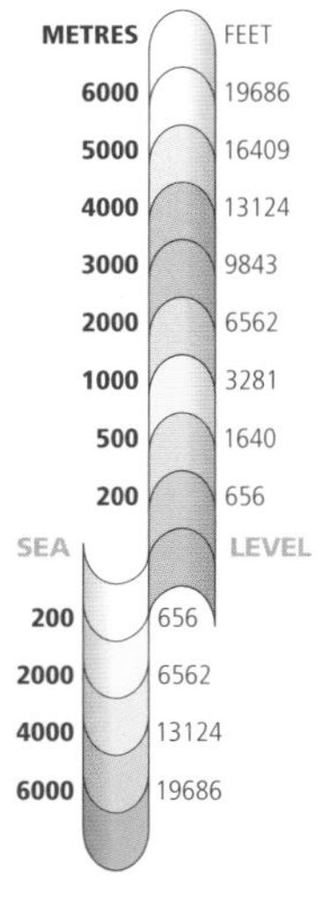

CALIFORNIA

NEVADA

SIERRA NEVADA

PACIFIC OCEAN

Channel Islands

Death Valley

Mojave Desert

Legend

METRES	FEET
6000	19686
5000	16409
4000	13124
3000	9843
2000	6562
1000	3281
500	1640
200	656
SEA LEVEL	
200	656
2000	6562
4000	13124
6000	19686

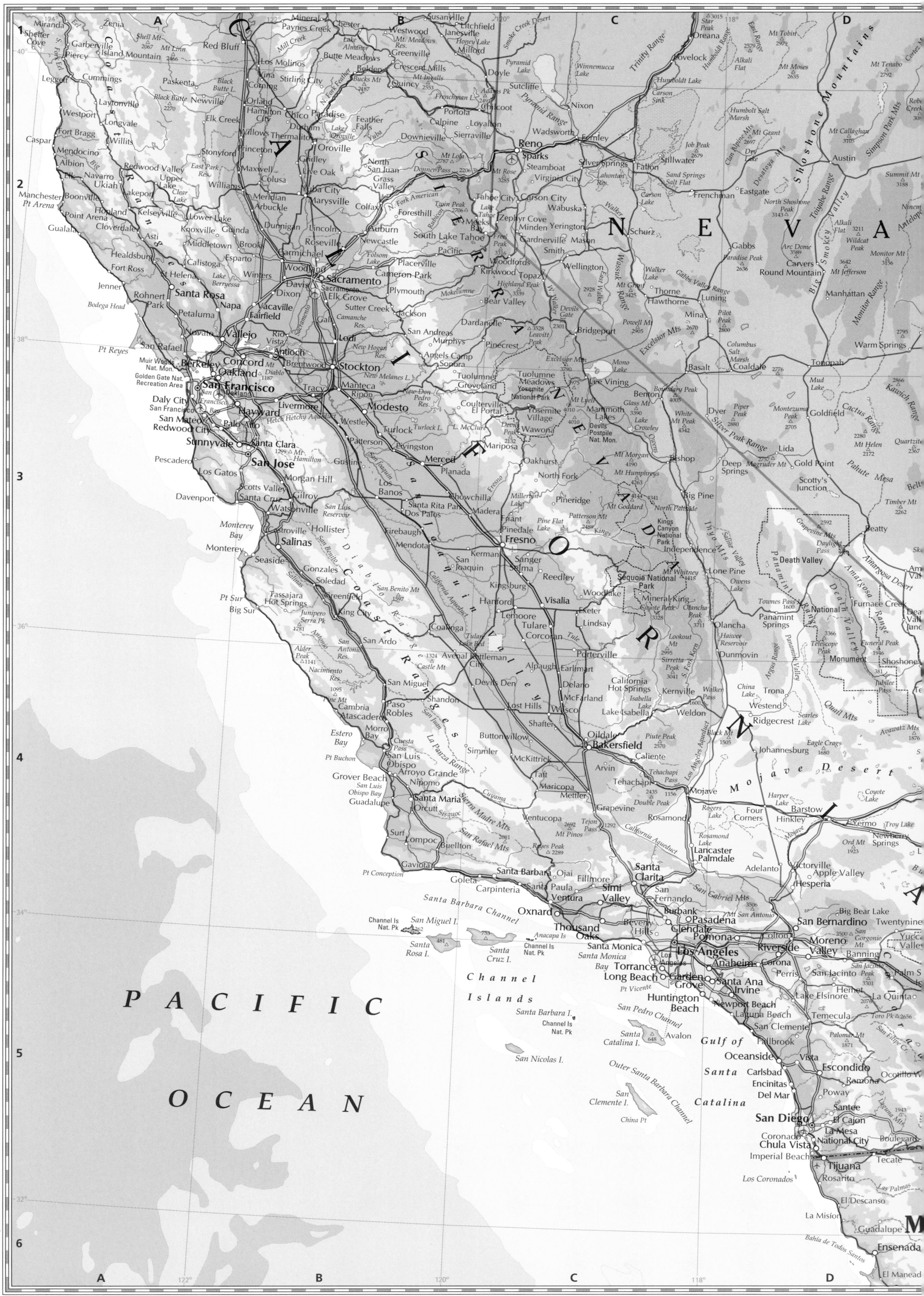

Lambert Conformal Conic Projection

© HarperCollins Publishers

Major cities and places: Reno, Sparks, Carson City, Sacramento, San Francisco, Oakland, Berkeley, San Jose, Santa Cruz, Monterey, Salinas, Fresno, Modesto, Stockton, Bakersfield, Santa Barbara, Los Angeles, Long Beach, Anaheim, Santa Ana, Pasadena, San Bernardino, Riverside, Oceanside, Escondido, San Diego, Chula Vista, Tijuana, Ensenada.

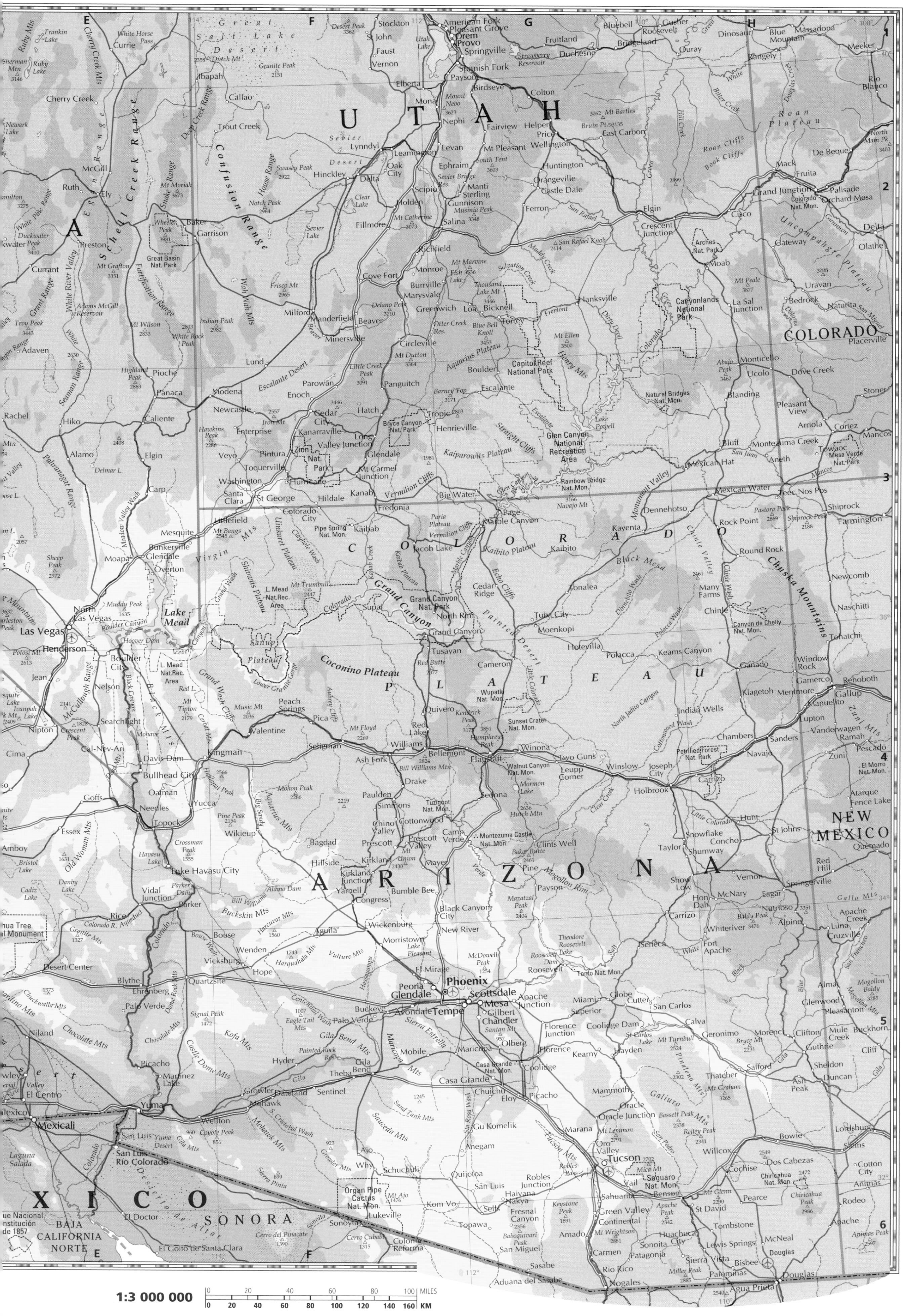

1:3 000 000

PACIFIC OCEAN

CARIBBEAN SEA

HONDURAS

NICARAGUA

COSTA RICA

EL SALVADOR

PANAMA

BAJA CALIFORNIA NORTE

BAJA CALIFORNIA SUR

ARIZONA

NEW MEXICO

SONORA

CHIHUAHUA

Islas Revillagigedo (Mexico)

at the same scale

continuation at the same scale

METRES	FEET
6000	19686
5000	16409
4000	13124
3000	9843
2000	6562
1000	3281
500	1640
200	656
SEA	LEVEL
200	656
2000	6562
4000	13124
6000	19686

Lambert Conformal Conic Projection

© HarperCollinsPublishers

GULF OF MEXICO

1:6 600 000

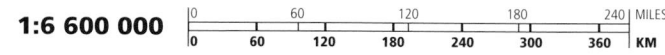

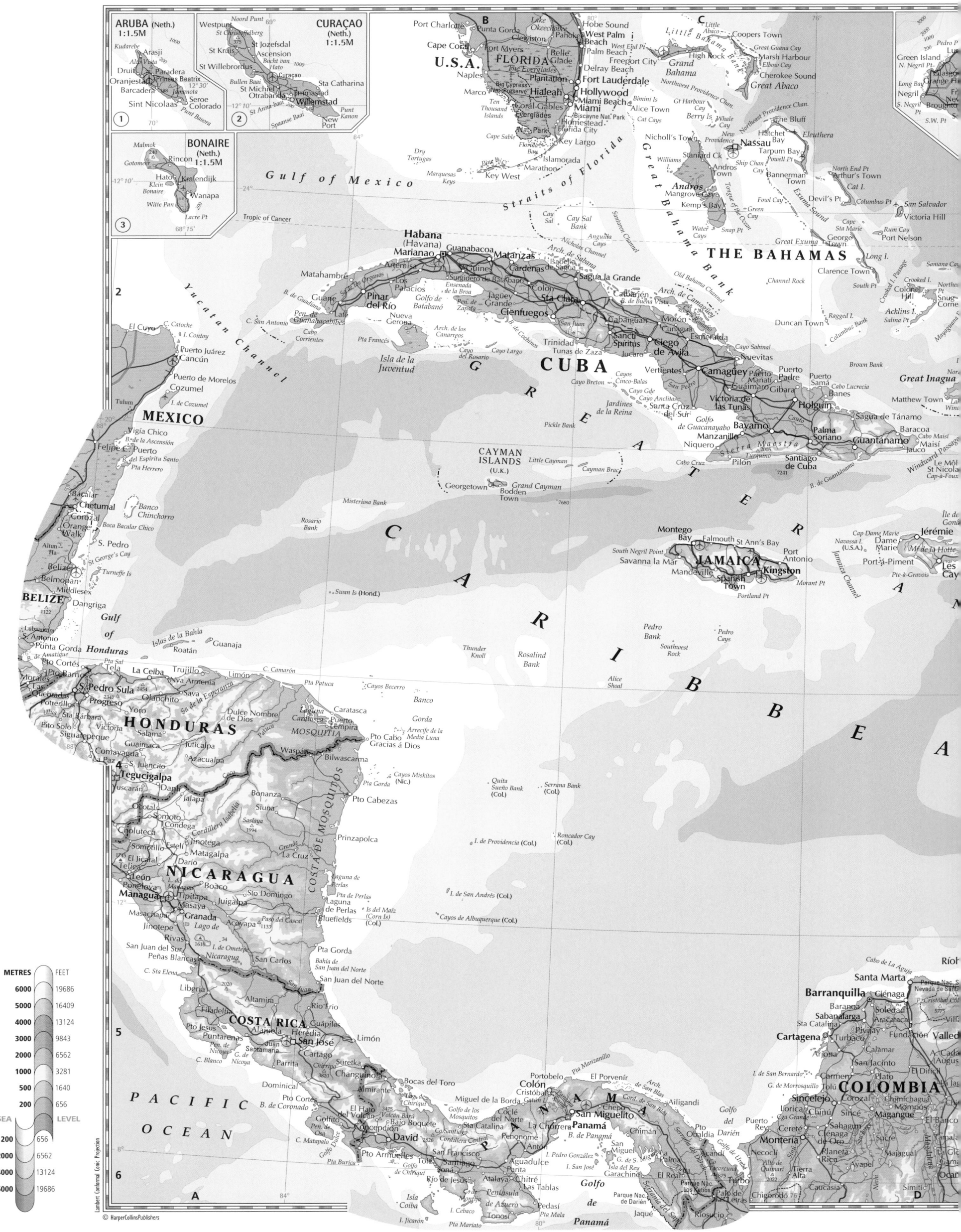

JAMAICA
1:1.5M

Montego Bay, ST JAMES, Montpelier, Reading, Falmouth, Duncans, Rio Bueno, Discovery Bay, Runaway Bay, St Ann's Bay, Ocho Rios, Oracabessa, Galina Pt, Port Maria, Annotto Bay, TRELAWNEY, Wakefield, Clark's Town, Brown's Town, Stewart Town, Claremont, Maroon Town, The Cockpit Country, Albert Town, Dry Harbour Mts, Moneague, Richmond, ST MARY, Albany, Buff Bay, St Margaret's Bay, Port Antonio, Catadupa, Cockpit, Troy, Mt Diablo 838, Ewarton, Castleton, Hope Bay, Berrydale, Fellowship, PORTLAND, ST ELIZABETH, Maggotty, Balaclava, Mile Gully, Frankfield, Chapelton, Linstead, Bog Walk, ST ANDREW, Stony Hill, Priestmans River, Long Bay, Williamsfield, Mocho Mts, Spanish Town, Kingston, Blue Mtn Pk 2256, Comfort, Manchioneal, MANCHESTER, Mandeville, Newport, Four Paths, CLARENDON, Old Harbour, Portmore, Port Royal, Norman Manley, Cedar Valley, Seaforth, Bath, ST THOMAS, Port Morant, Morant Bay, Bowden, Black River, Sta Cruz, Malvern, Bull Savannah, Alligator Pond, Lionel Town, Salt River, Hellshire Hills, White Horses, Morant Pt, Treasure Beach, Gt Pedro Bluff, Rocky Point, Portland Bight, Portland Ridge, Portland Pt

TOBAGO
1:1.5M

Man of War B., St Giles Is, Charlotteville, Parlatuvier, Castara, Moriah, Speyside, Plymouth, Scarborough, Pigeon Pt, Canaan, Columbus Point

TRINIDAD
1:1.5M

VENEZUELA, GULF OF PARIA, Port of Spain, CARONI, Chaguanas, Waterloo, California, NARIVA, Pointe-à-Pierre, San Fernando, Point Fortin, Pitch Lake, La Brea, VICTORIA, Penal, Siparia, MAYARO, ST PATRICK, Basse Terre, Moruga, Guayaguayare, Fullarton, San Francique, Erin Point, Cape Casa Cruz

GUADELOUPE (France)
1:1.5M

Pte de la Gde Vigie, Anse Bertrand, Port Louis, GRANDE TERRE, Petit Canal, Les Mangles, Vieux-Bourg, Moule, La Désirade, Deshaies, Rose, Le Baizet, Morne-à-l'Eau, Les Abymes, Gde Anse, Pointe Noire, Mahaut, Ste Marin, Ponte-à-Pitre, Le Gosier, St François, BASSE TERRE, Bouillante, Goyave, Vieux Habitants, Soufrière 1467, St Claude, Capesterre, Baillif, Gourbeyre, Trois-Rivières, St Louis, Morne Constant, Basse Terre, Pte du Vieux Fort, Vieux Fort, Terre de Haut, Marie Galante, Îles des Saintes, Terre de Bas, Grand Bourg, Capesterre

MARTINIQUE (France)
1:1.5M

Cap St Martin, Grand Rivière, Basse Pointe, Mgne Pelée 1397, Le Lorrain, Marigot, Sainte Marie, Presqu'île de la Caravelle, Le Prêcheur, Le Morne Rouge, St Pierre, GrosMorne, La Trinité, Baie du Galion, Le Carbet, Bellefontaine, St Joseph, Le Robert, Îlet Ramville, Schoelcher, Lamentin, Îlet Long, Fort-de-France, Le François, Baie de Fort de France, Ducos, Le St Esprit, Les Trois Îlets, Le Vauclin, Cap Salomon, Le Diamant, Rivière Pilote, Les Anses d'Arlets, Ste Luce, Le Marin, Rocher du Diamant, Ste Anne, Pte Baham, Îlet Cabrits

ST KITTS-NEVIS
1:1.5M

Helden's Pt, Dieppe Bay Town, Sandy Pt, Mt Misery 1156, Cayon, St Kitts (St Christopher), Old Road Town, Basseterre, Golden Rock, S. Friar's Bay, N. Friar's Bay, Horse Shoe Pt, The Narrows, Newcastle, Nevis Pk, Zion, Charlestown, Nevis, Dogwood Pt

ANTIGUA
1:1.5M

Boon Pt, Beggars Pt, V.C. Bird, Cedar Grove, St John's, Parham, Jennings, Willikie's, Boggy Pk, Freetown, Johnsons Pt, Falmouth, Old Road, English Harbour Town

GRENADA
1:1.5M

North Pt, Bedford Pt, Victoria, Sauteurs, Mt St Catherine 840, Gouyave (Charlotte Town), Telescope Pt, Woodford, Grenville, St George's, Gt Bacolet Pt, Westerhall, Pt Salines, L'Ance aux Épines

BARBADOS
1:1.5M

North Pt, Greenland, Bruce, Speightstown, Blackman's, Holetown, Bridgetown, Ragged Pt, Hastings, Marchfield, Worthing, The Crane, Oistins, Grantley Adams, South Pt

HISPANIOLA

HAITI, DOMINICAN REPUBLIC, Monte Cristi, Isabela, Puerto Plata, Santiago, Moca, La Vega, Bahía Escocesa, San Francisco de Macoris, Samaná, Bahía de Samaná, Hinche, Bonao, Cotui, Hato Mayor, El Seibo, Cabo Engaño, REPUBLIC, La Romana, Azua, Bani, San Pedro de Macoris, Santo Domingo, La Selle, Barahona, Pta Salinas, Palenque, I. Beata, Cabo Beata

TURKS & CAICOS ISLANDS (U.K.), Kew, Caicos Is, Cockburn Harbour, Turks Is, Cockburn Town, Gd Turk, Seal Cays, Mouchoir Bank, Silver Bank, Milwaukee Depth 9200, Navidad Bank

PUERTO RICO (U.S.A.)

Aguadilla, Arecibo, San Juan, Isla Verde, Charlotte Amalie, VIRGIN IS (U.K.), Tortola, Virgin Gorda, Road Town, Mayagüez, Caguas, Fajardo, St Thomas, St John, Ponce, Guayama, VIRGIN IS (U.S.A.), St Croix, Guánica, Frederiksted, Mona Passage, Cabo Rojo, Mona

ANGUILLA (U.K.), The Valley, St Maarten (Neth.), St Barthélemy (Fr.), Philipsburg, Saba (Neth. Ant.), St Eustatius (Neth. Ant.), Saba Bank, ST KITTS-NEVIS, Basseterre, ANTIGUA & BARBUDA, Barbuda, St John's, Antigua, Plymouth, MONTSERRAT (U.K.), Guadeloupe Passage, Port Louis, GUADELOUPE (Fr.), Grande Terre, Basse Terre, Pointe-à-Pitre, Marie Galante, Dominica Passage, Portsmouth, Aves (Ven.), DOMINICA, Morne Diablotin 1447, Roseau, Martinique Passage, Mgne Pelée 1397, Ste Marie, Fort-de-France, MARTINIQUE (Fr.), St Lucia Channel, Castries, ST LUCIA, Vieux Fort, St Vincent Passage, Soufrière 1234, ST VINCENT & THE GRENADINES, BARBADOS, Bridgetown, Kingstown, Bequia, Mustique, Canouan, Union, The Grenadines, Carriacou, St George's, GRENADA

CARIBBEAN SEA

GREATER ANTILLES, LESSER ANTILLES, LEEWARD ISLANDS, WINDWARD ISLANDS

NETHERLANDS ANTILLES, Kudarebe, Aruba (Neth.), Oranjestad, St Nicolaas, St Christoffelberg, Brandaris, Kralendijk, Bonaire (Neth.), Curaçao, Willemstad, Sta Catharina, Klein Curaçao, Los Roques (Ven.), Las Aves (Ven.), Cayo de Sal, Isla Orchila (Ven.), I. Blanquilla (Ven.), Los Testigos (Ven.), I. de Margarita, La Asunción, Juangriego, Porlamar, I. La Tortuga (Ven.), I. Coche, I. Cubagua, Charlotteville, Tobago, Scarborough, TRINIDAD & TOBAGO

VENEZUELA

Pta Gallinas, Pta Estrella, Península de Guajira, Golfo de Venezuela, Pto López, Uribía, Cojoro, Maracaibo, Cabimas, Lagunillas, Lago de Maracaibo, Coro, Punto Fijo, Puerto Cumarebo, Pta Zamuro, San Juan de los Cayos, Maiquetía, Caracas, Petare, La Guaira, Higuerote, Rio Chico, Cumaná, Carúpano, Río Caribe, Port of Spain, Arima, Sangre Grande, Valencia, Maracay, Los Teques, Pto La Cruz, Guanta, Barcelona, Caripe, San Fernando, Barquisimeto, El Tocuyo, Acarigua, San Carlos, El Sombrero, Maturín, Mérida, Barinas, Guanare, Zaraza, El Tigre, San Felipe, El Tocuyo, Valera, Bocono, Ospino, Valle de la Pascua, El Chaparro, Ciudad Guayana, Pto Miranda, San Fernando de Apure, Ciudad Bolívar, GUYANA, Matthews Ridge, San Cristóbal, Achaguas, Orinoco

1:6 600 000

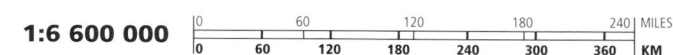

| 0 | 60 | 120 | 180 | 240 | MILES |
| 0 | 60 | 120 | 180 | 240 | 300 | 360 | KM |

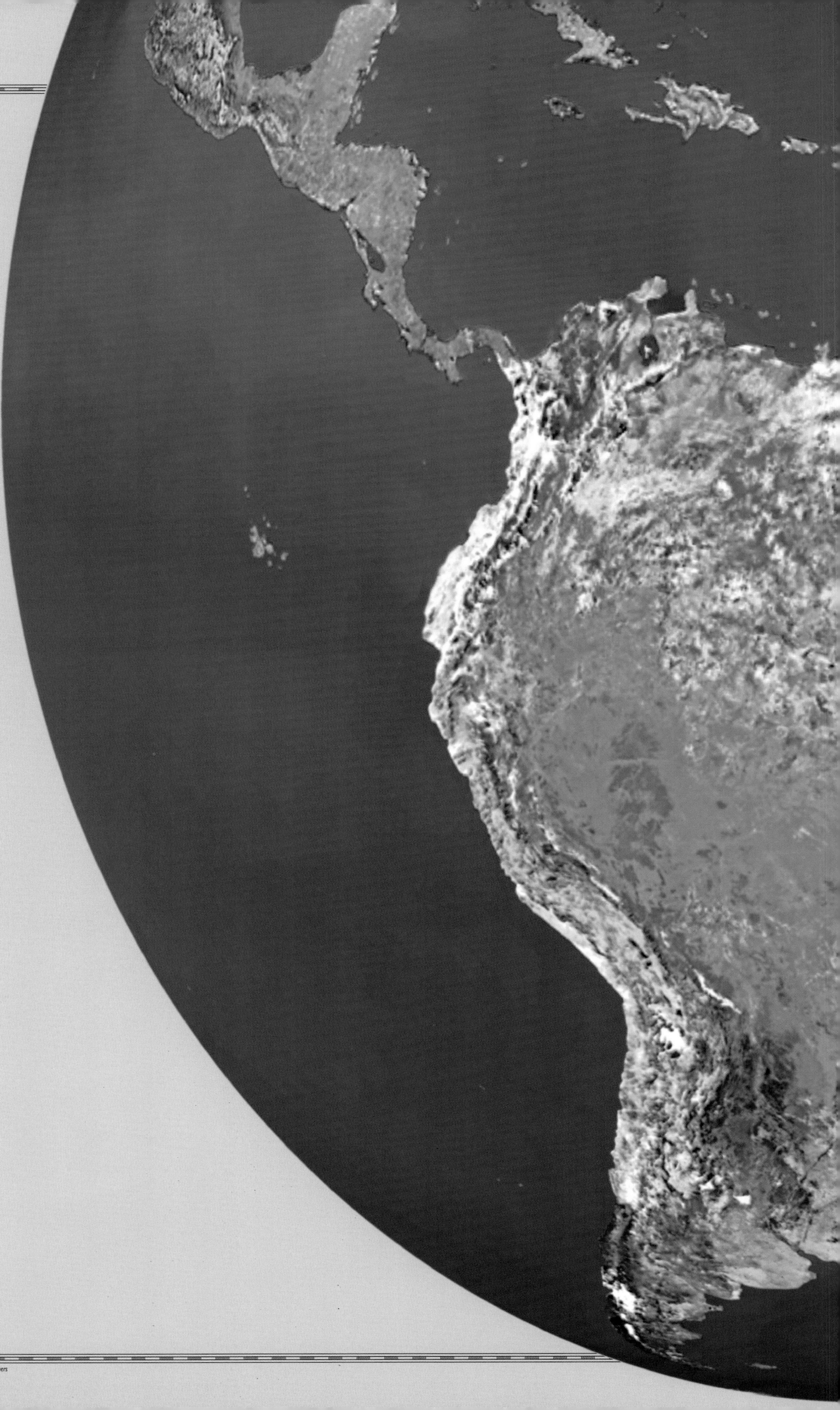

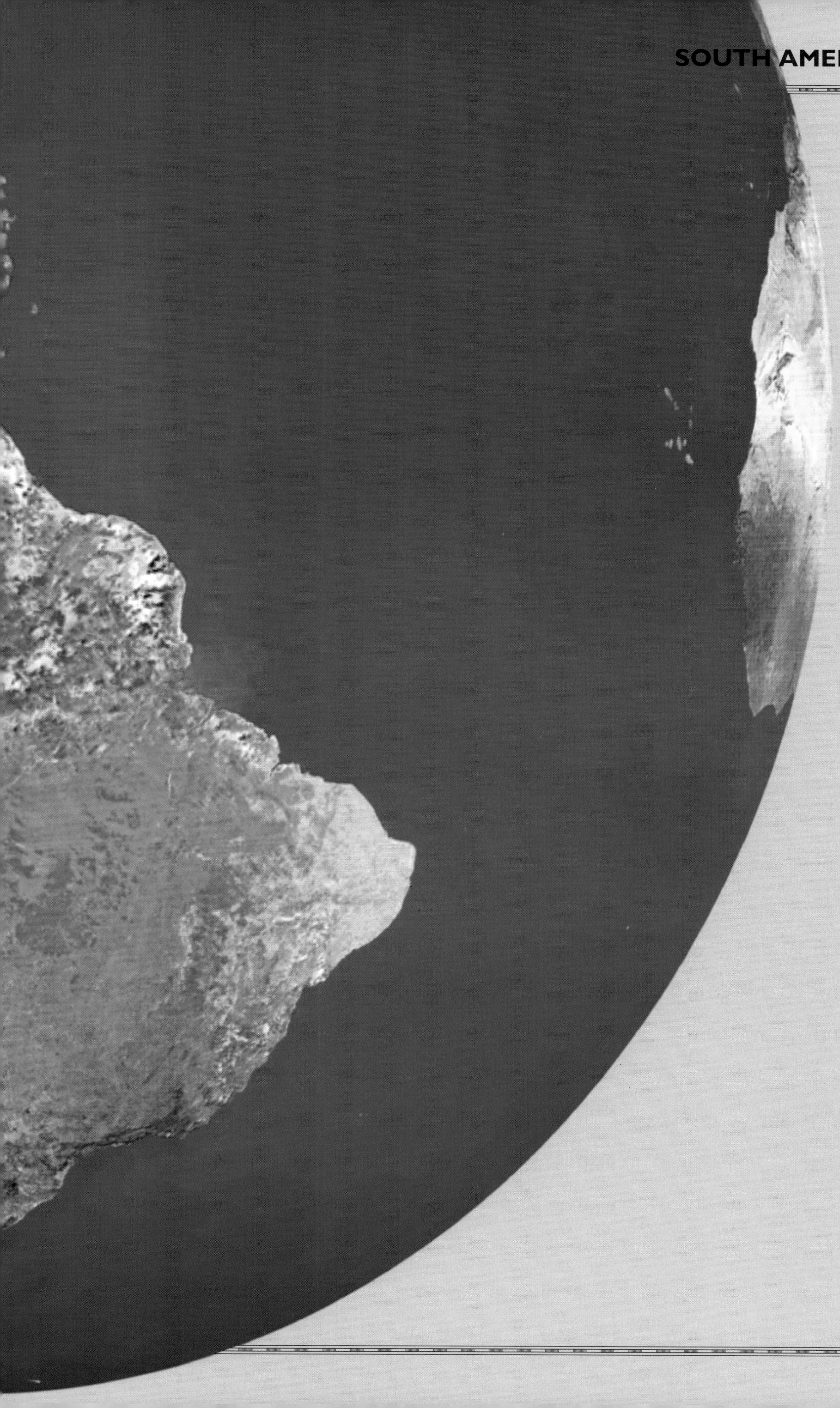

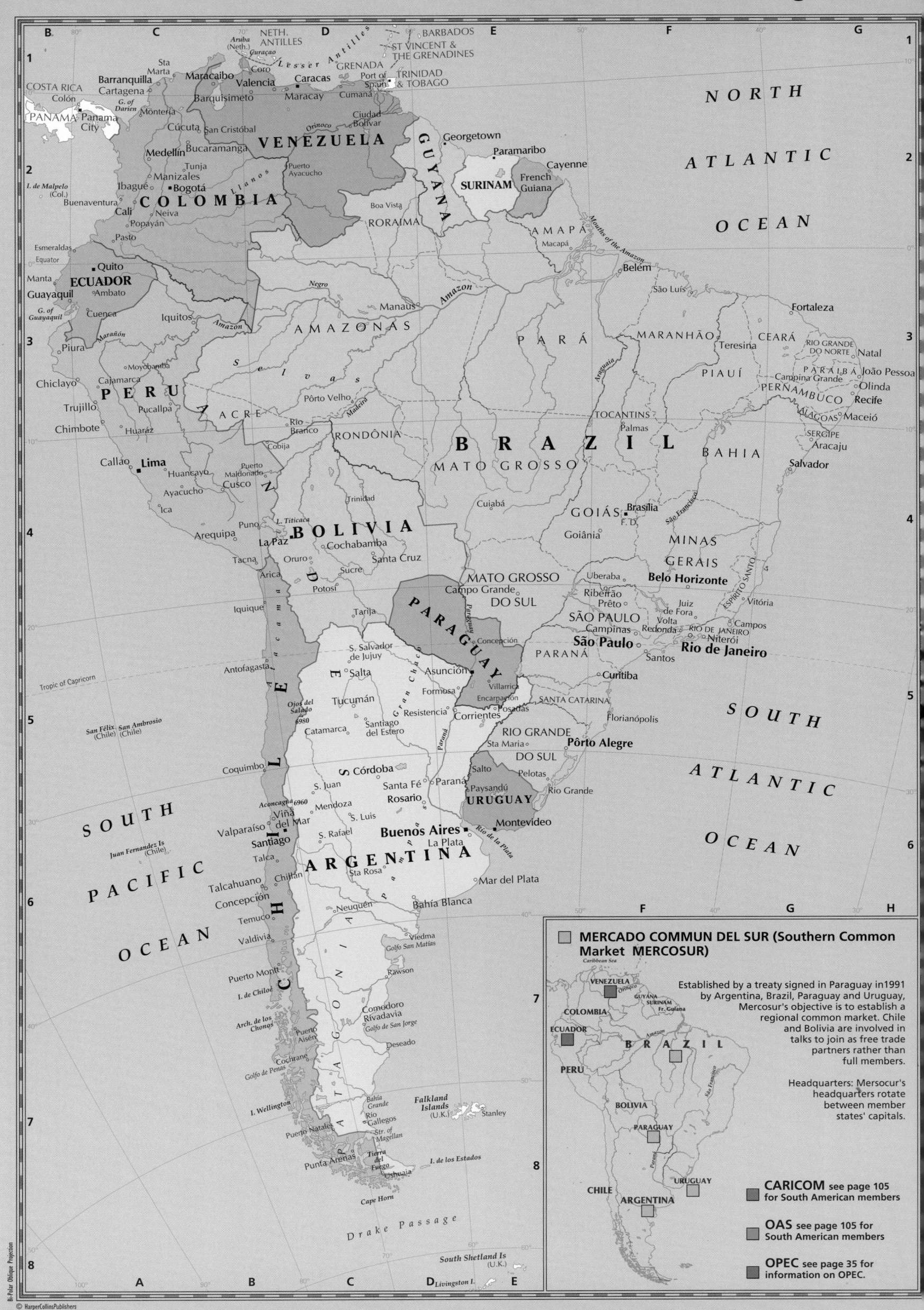

NORTH ATLANTIC OCEAN

SOUTH ATLANTIC OCEAN

SOUTH PACIFIC OCEAN

COSTA RICA
Colón
PANAMA
Panama City

Sta Marta
Barranquilla
Cartagena

Aruba (Neth.)
Curaçao
NETH. ANTILLES
Coro
Maracaibo
Valencia
Caracas
Maracay
Cumaná
Barquisimeto

Lesser Antilles
GRENADA
ST VINCENT & THE GRENADINES
BARBADOS
Port of Spain
TRINIDAD & TOBAGO

Montería
Cúcuta
San Cristóbal
VENEZUELA
Ciudad Bolívar
Orinoco

Georgetown
Paramaribo
Cayenne

I. de Malpelo (Col.)

Medellín
Bucaramanga
Tunja
Manizales
Ibagué
Bogotá

Puerto Ayacucho

GUYANA
SURINAM
French Guiana

COLOMBIA
Cali
Neiva
Popayán
Pasto

Boa Vista
RORAIMA

AMAPÁ
Macapá
Mouths of the Amazon

Esmeraldas
Equator
Quito
ECUADOR
Ambato
Negro

Amazon
Manaus

Belém
São Luís
Fortaleza

Manta
Guayaquil
G. of Guayaquil
Cuenca

Iquitos

AMAZONAS
Amazon

PARÁ
MARANHÃO
Teresina
CEARÁ
RIO GRANDE DO NORTE
Natal

Piura
Chiclayo
Cajamarca
Moyobamba
Marañón

PERU
s e l v a s
ACRE
Pôrto Velho
RONDÔNIA
Rio Branco
Madeira

PIAUÍ
PARAÍBA
João Pessoa
Campina Grande
PERNAMBUCO
Olinda
Recife

Trujillo
Pucallpa
Chimbote
Huaraz

Cobija

TOCANTINS
Palmas

ALAGOAS
Maceió
SERGIPE
Aracaju

Callao
Lima
Huancayo
Puerto Maldonado
Cusco
Ayacucho
Ica

Trinidad

BRAZIL
MATO GROSSO

BAHIA
Salvador

Arequipa
Puno
L. Titicaca
BOLIVIA
La Paz
Cochabamba

Cuiabá
Brasília
GOIÁS
F.D.
São Francisco

Tacna
Arica
Oruro
Sucre
Santa Cruz

Campo Grande
MATO GROSSO DO SUL
Goiânia
MINAS GERAIS
Uberaba
Belo Horizonte
ESPÍRITO SANTO

Iquique
Potosí
Tarija
D E S
Paraguay
Ribeirão Prêto
Juiz de Fora
Vitória

Tropic of Capricorn
Antofagasta
Ojos del Salado 6980
PARAGUAY
Concepción
SÃO PAULO
Campinas
Volta Redonda
RIO DE JANEIRO
Campos
Niterói

San Félix (Chile)
San Ambrosio (Chile)
S. Salvador de Jujuy
Salta
Gran Chaco
Asunción
Villarrica
São Paulo
Santos
Rio de Janeiro

A T A C A M A
Tucumán
Formosa
Encarnación
Posadas
PARANÁ
Curitiba
SANTA CATARINA

Catamarca
Resistencia
Corrientes
Florianópolis

Coquimbo
Santiago del Estero
Paraná
RIO GRANDE DO SUL
Sta Maria
Pôrto Alegre

Córdoba
Santa Fé
Rosario
Salto
Pelotas
Rio Grande

San Juan
Mendoza
Paraná
Paysandú
URUGUAY

Juan Fernández Is (Chile)
Aconcagua 6960
S. Luis
Montevideo

Valparaíso
Viña del Mar
S. Rafael
Buenos Aires
La Plata
Río de la Plata

Santiago
Talca
ARGENTINA
Sta Rosa
Mar del Plata

Talcahuano
Chillán
Neuquén

Concepción
Temuco
Bahía Blanca

Valdivia
P A T A G O N I A

Puerto Montt
I. de Chiloé
Viedma
Golfo de San Matías

Arch. de los Chonos
Rawson

Comodoro Rivadavia
Golfo de San Jorge

Puerto Aisén
Cochrane
Deseado

Golfo de Penas

I. Wellington
Falkland Islands (U.K.)
Stanley

Puerto Natales
Río Gallegos

Str. of Magellan
Punta Arenas
Tierra del Fuego
I. de los Estados
Ushuaia

Cape Horn

Drake Passage

South Shetland Is (U.K.)
Livingston I.

Bi-Polar Oblique Projection
© HarperCollins Publishers

MERCADO COMMUN DEL SUR (Southern Common Market MERCOSUR)

Established by a treaty signed in Paraguay in 1991 by Argentina, Brazil, Paraguay and Uruguay, Mercosur's objective is to establish a regional common market. Chile and Bolivia are involved in talks to join as free trade partners rather than full members.

Headquarters: Mersocur's headquarters rotate between member states' capitals.

Caribbean Sea
VENEZUELA
GUYANA
SURINAM
Fr. Guiana
COLOMBIA
Orinoco
ECUADOR
Amazon
BRAZIL
PERU
São Francisco
BOLIVIA
PARAGUAY
URUGUAY
CHILE
ARGENTINA

CARICOM see page 105 for South American members

OAS see page 105 for South American members

OPEC see page 35 for information on OPEC.

MILES
0 200 400 600 800
0 200 400 600 800 1000 1200 1400 KM
1:25 000 000

COUNTRY	AREA		POPULATION		FORM OF GOVERNMENT	CAPITAL CITY	MAIN LANGUAGES	MAIN RELIGIONS	CURRENCY
	sq ml	sq km	total	density per sq ml sq km					
ARGENTINA	1 068 302	2 766 889	34 180 000	32 12	republic	Buenos Aires	Spanish, Italian, Amerindian languages	RC, Protestant, Jewish	Peso
ARUBA	75	193	69 000	926 358	Netherlands terr.	Oranjestad	Dutch , Papiamento, English	RC, Protestant	Florin
BOLIVIA	424 164	1 098 581	7 237 000	17 7	republic	La Paz	Spanish, Quechua, Aymara	RC, Protestant, Baha'i	Boliviano
BRAZIL	3 286 488	8 511 965	153 725 000	47 18	republic	Brasília	Portuguese, German, Japanese, Italian, Amerindian languages	RC, Spiritist, Protestant	Real
CHILE	292 258	756 945	13 994 000	48 18	republic	Santiago	Spanish, Amerindian languages	RC, Protestant	Peso
COLOMBIA	440 831	1 141 748	34 520 000	78 30	republic	Bogotá	Spanish, Amerindian languages	RC, Protestant	Peso
ECUADOR	105 037	272 045	11 221 000	107 41	republic	Quito	Spanish, Quechua, Amerind. lang.	RC, Protestant	Sucre
FALKLAND ISLANDS	4 699	12 170	2 000		UK territory	Stanley	English	Protestant, RC	Pound
FRENCH GUIANA	34 749	90 000	141 000	4 2	French territory	Cayenne	French, French Creole	RC, Protestant	French franc
GUYANA	83 000	214 969	825 000	10 4	republic	Georgetown	English, Creole, Hindi, Amerind. lang.	Protestant, Hindu, RC, Muslim	Dollar
NETH. ANTILLES (South)	283	732	158 206	560 216	Neth terr.	Willemstad	Dutch, Papiamento, English	RC, Protestant	Guilder
PARAGUAY	157 048	406 752	4 700 000	30 12	republic	Asunción	Spanish, Guaraní	RC, Protestant	Guaraní
PERU	496 225	1 285 216	23 088 000	47 18	republic	Lima	Spanish, Quechua, Aymara	RC, Protestant	Sol
SURINAM	63 251	163 820	418 000	7 3	republic	Paramaribo	Dutch, Surinamese, English, Hindi, Javanese	Hindu, RC, Protestant, Muslim	Guilder
TRINIDAD AND TOBAGO	1 981	5 130	1 250 000	631 244	republic	Port of Spain	English, Creole, Hindi	RC, Hindu, Protestant, Muslim	Dollar
URUGUAY	68 037	176 215	3 167 000	47 18	republic	Montevideo	Spanish	RC, Protestant, Jewish	Peso
VENEZUELA	352 144	912 050	21 177 000	60 23	republic	Caracas	Spanish, Amerindian languages	RC, Protestant	Bolívar

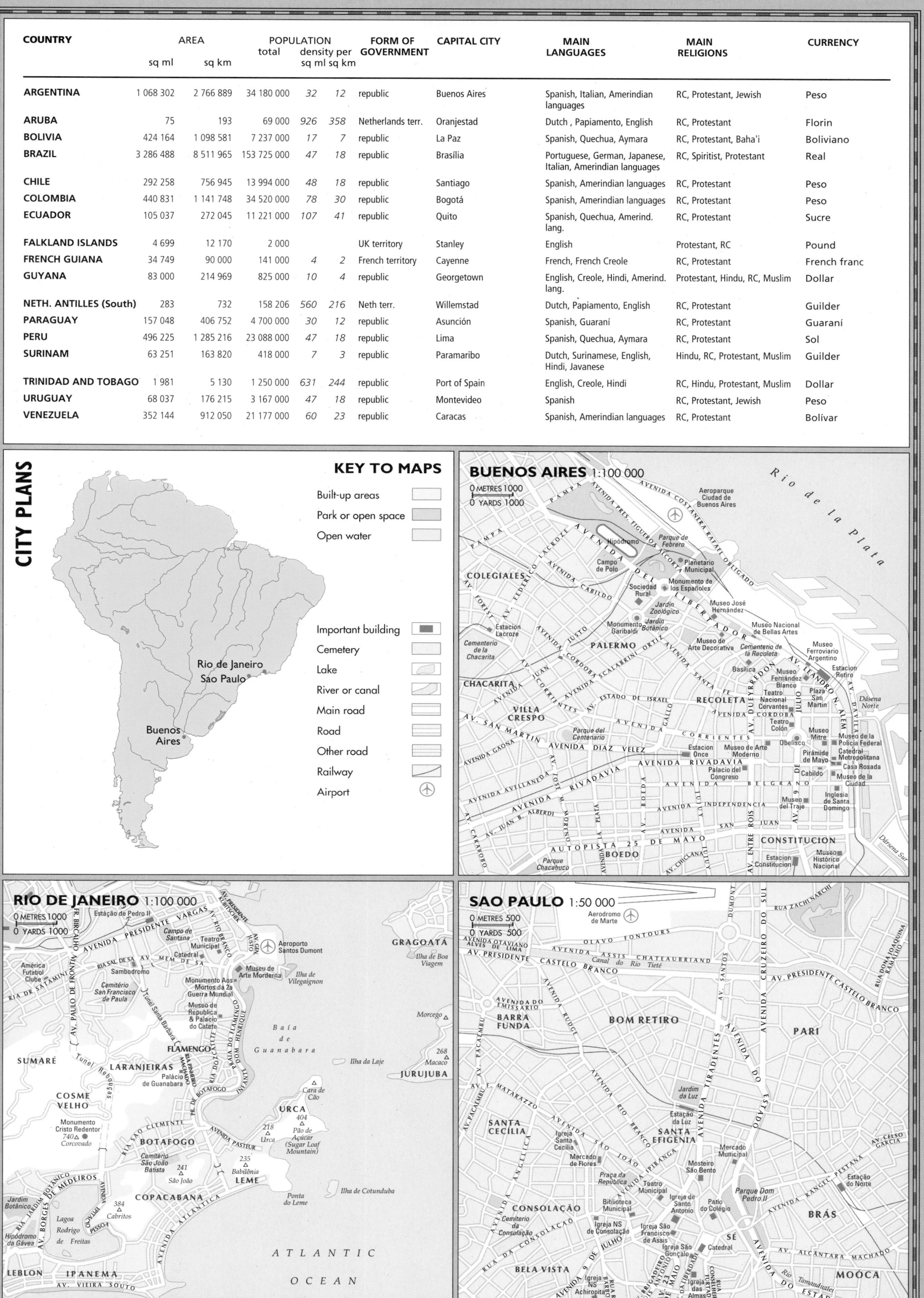

CITY PLANS

KEY TO MAPS

- Built-up areas
- Park or open space
- Open water
- Important building
- Cemetery
- Lake
- River or canal
- Main road
- Road
- Other road
- Railway
- Airport

BUENOS AIRES 1:100 000

RIO DE JANEIRO 1:100 000

SAO PAULO 1:50 000

CARIBBEAN SEA

NETHERLANDS ANTILLES

VENEZUELA

COLOMBIA

PANAMA

ECUADOR

PERU

GALAPAGOS IS
(Ecuador)
at the same scale

Golfo de Panamá

Golfo de Guayaquil

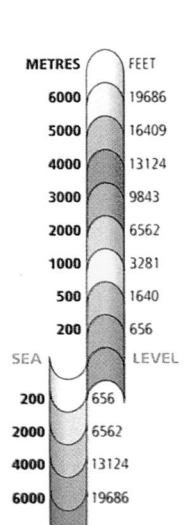

METRES	FEET
6000	19686
5000	16409
4000	13124
3000	9843
2000	6562
1000	3281
500	1640
200	656
SEA	LEVEL
200	656
2000	6562
4000	13124
6000	19686

Lambert Azimuthal Equal Area Projection

© HarperCollinsPublishers

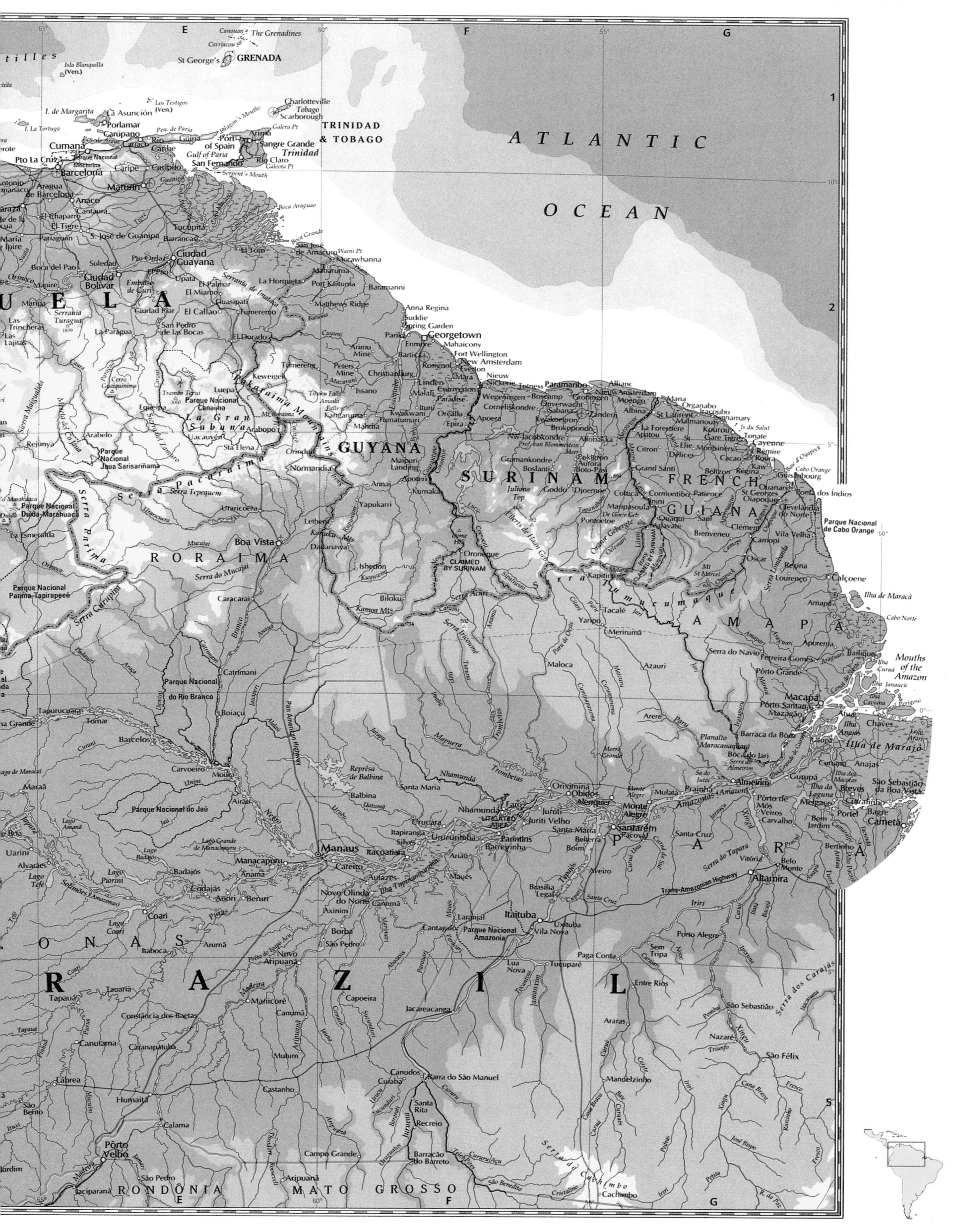

1:7 500 000

0	75	150	225	300	MILES
0	75	150	225	300	375	450	KM

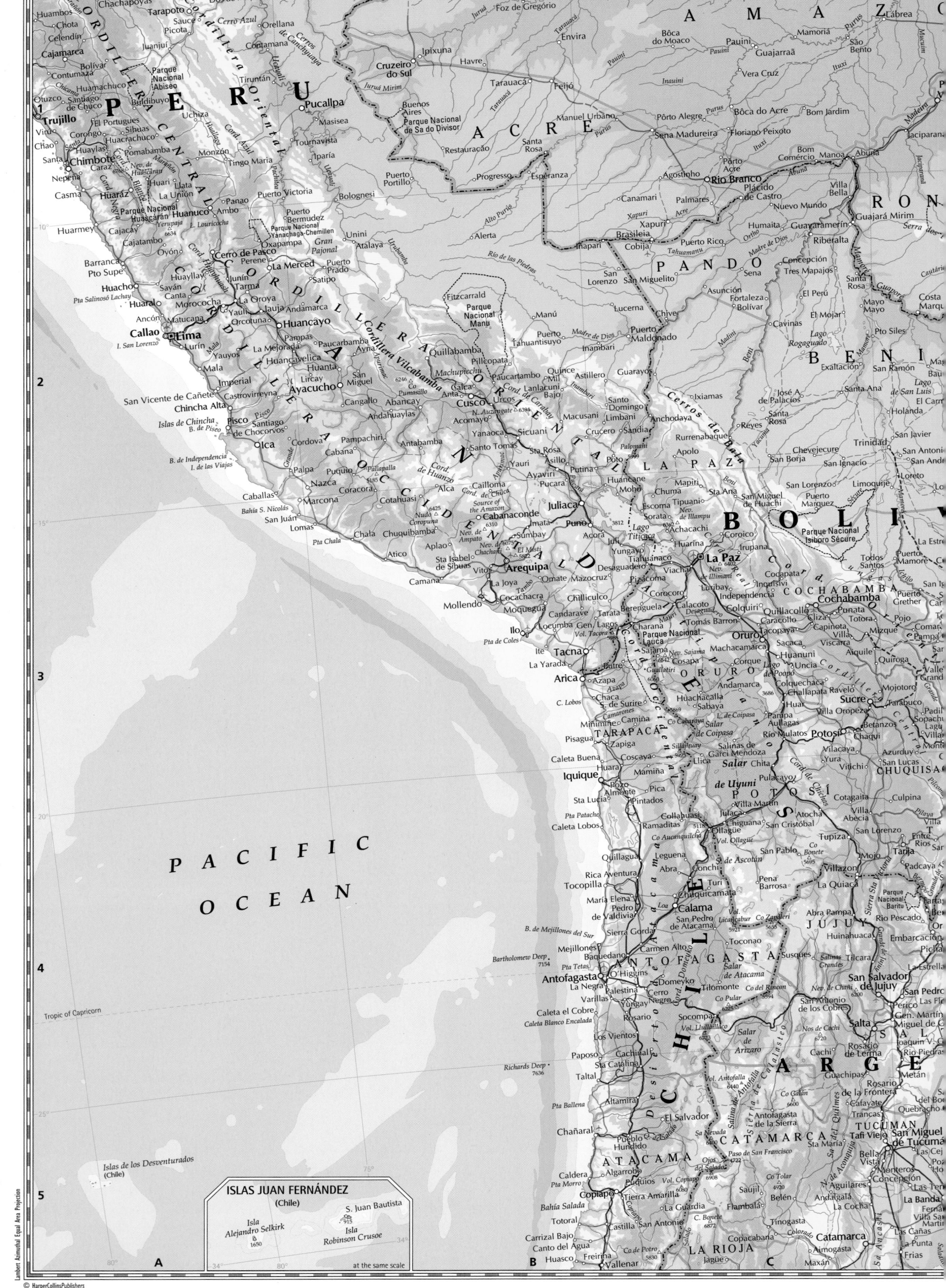

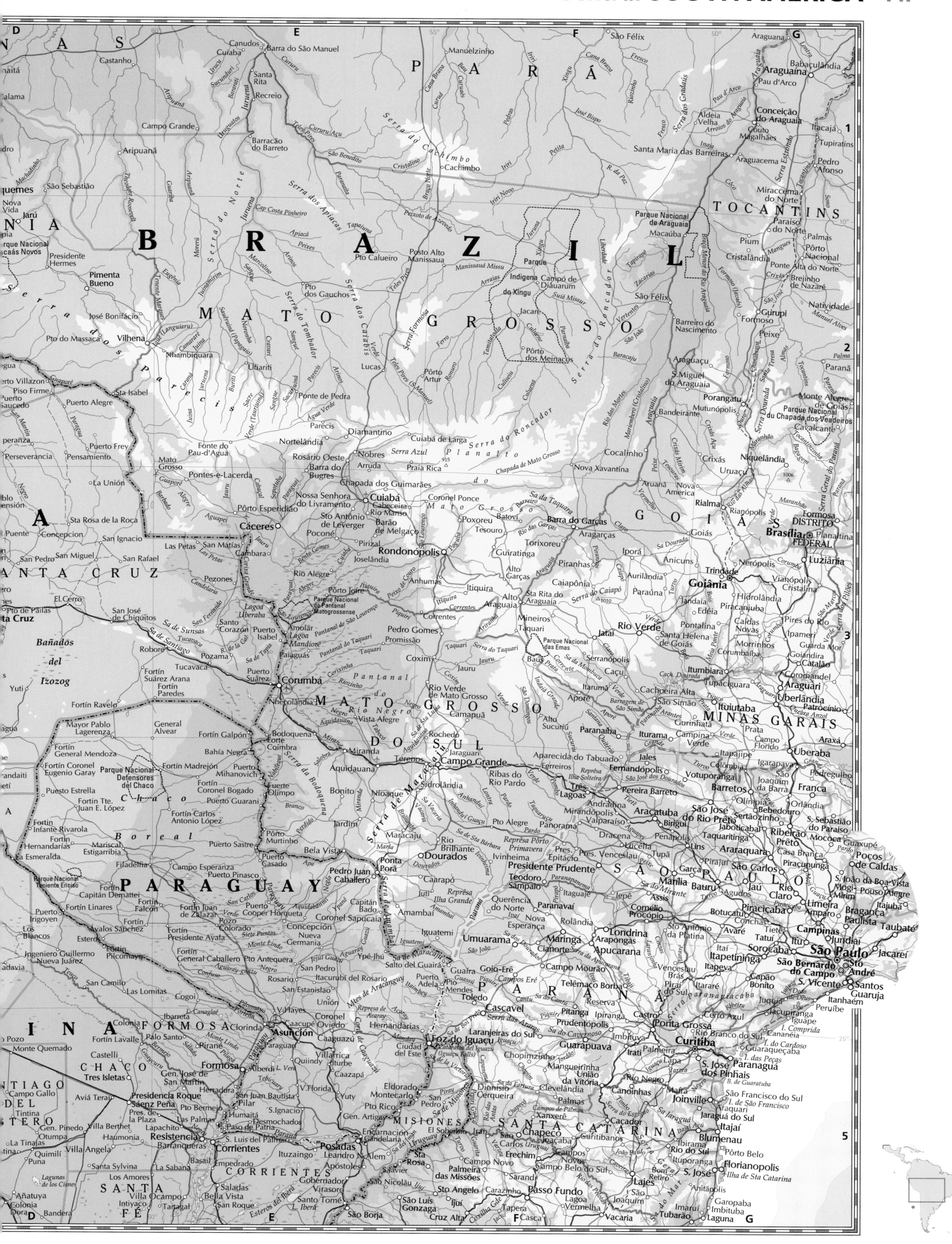

1:7 500 000

| 0 | 75 | 150 | 225 | 300 | MILES |

| 0 | 75 | 150 | 225 | 300 | 375 | 450 | KM |

METRES	FEET
6000	19686
5000	16409
4000	13124
3000	9843
2000	6562
1000	3281
500	1640
200	656
SEA	LEVEL
200	656
2000	6562
4000	13124
6000	19686

Lambert Azimuthal Equal Area Projection

© HarperCollinsPublishers

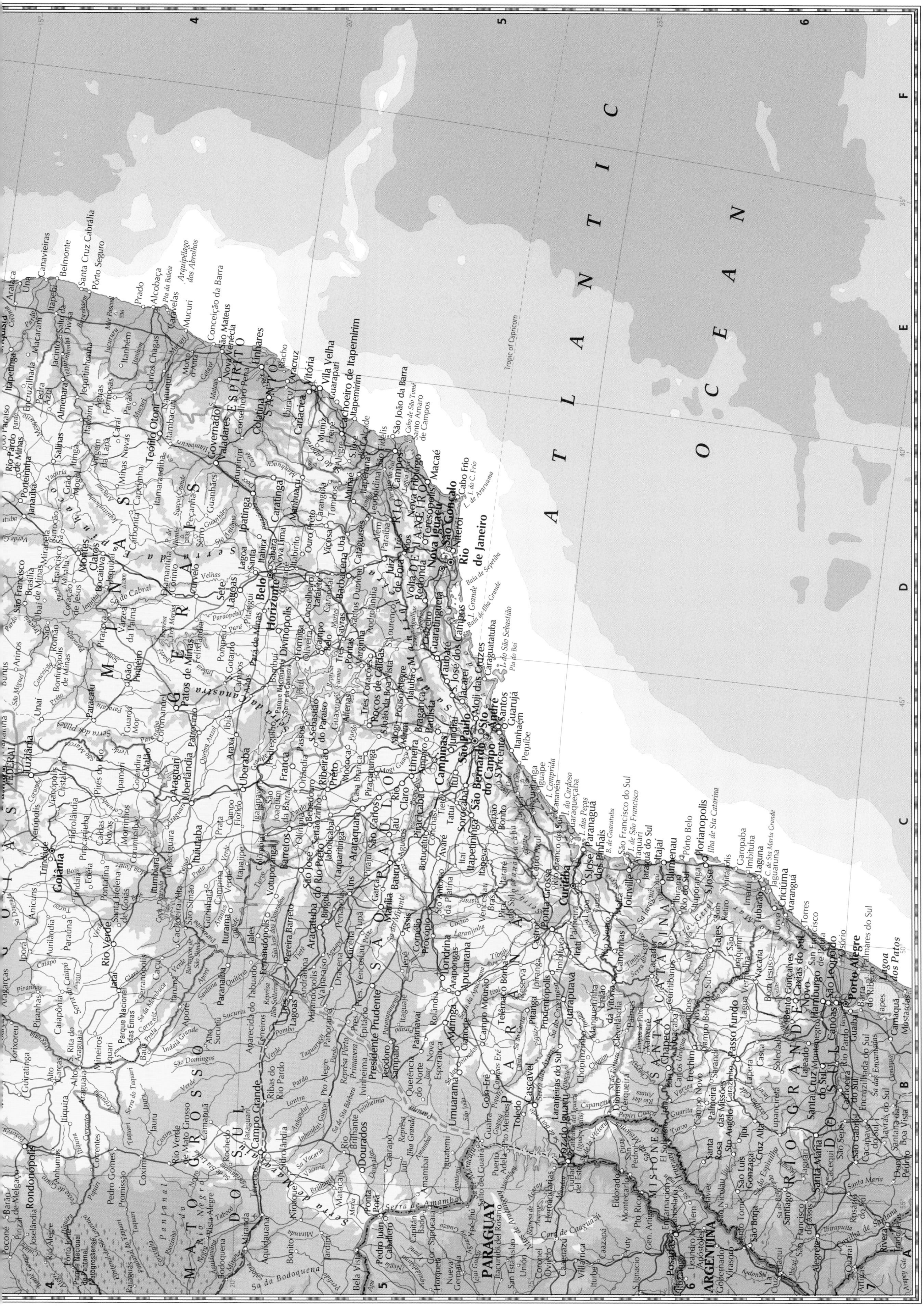

ATLANTIC OCEAN

1:7 500 000

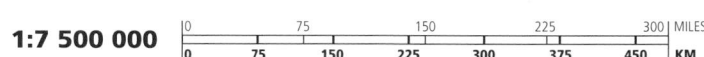

| 0 | 75 | 150 | 225 | 300 | MILES |
| 0 | 75 | 150 | 225 | 300 | 375 | 450 | KM |

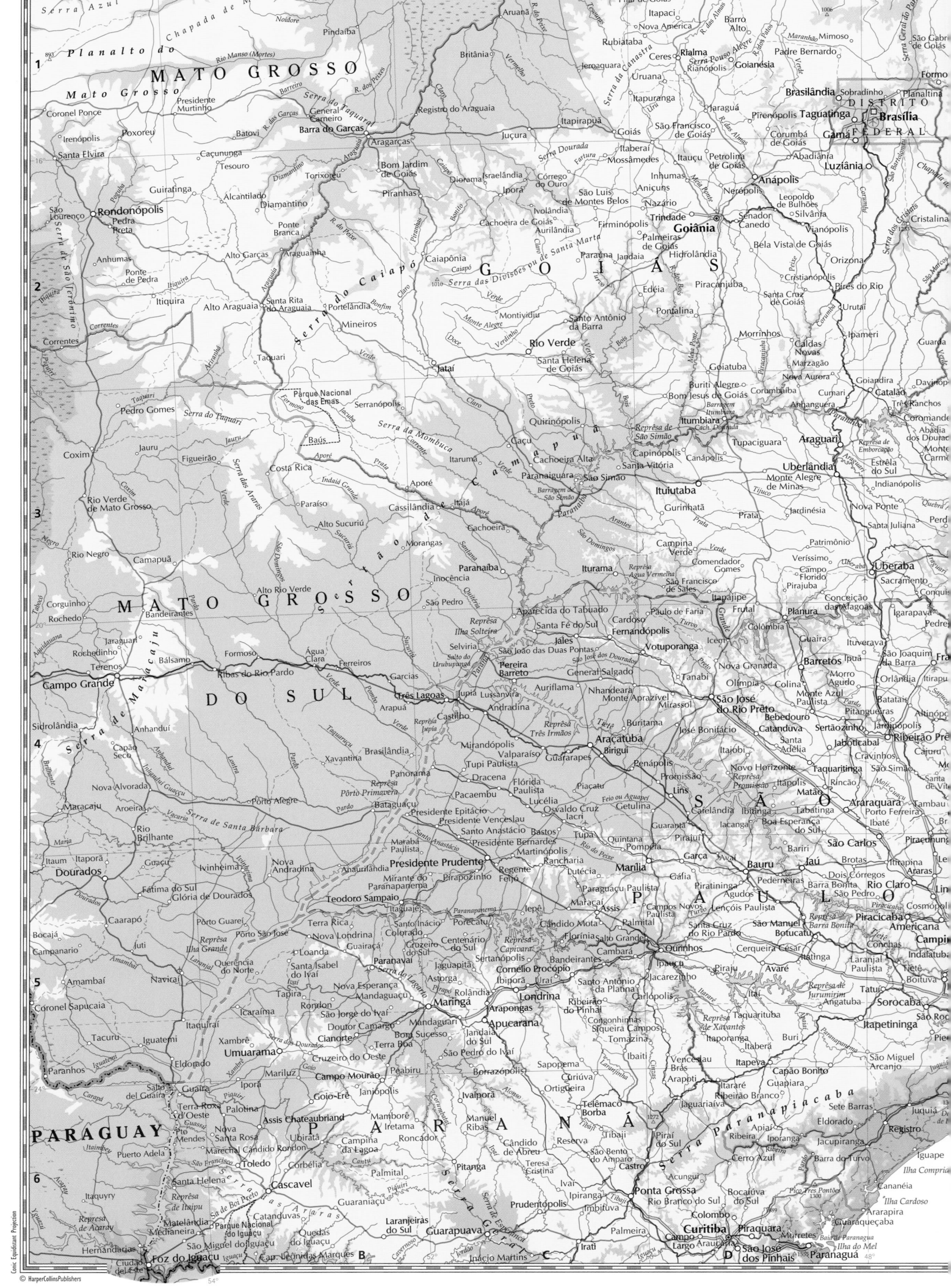

METRES / FEET

METRES	FEET
6000	19686
5000	16409
4000	13124
3000	9843
2000	6562
1000	3281
500	1640
200	656

SEA / LEVEL

SEA	LEVEL
200	656
2000	6562
4000	13124
6000	19686

Conic Equidistant Projection

© HarperCollins Publishers

ATLANTIC OCEAN

1:3 750 000

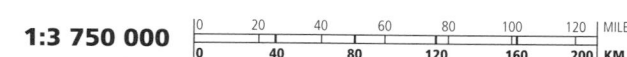

SOUTH ATLANTIC OCEAN

SOUTH GEORGIA (U.K.)
C. Alexandra
North C.
C. Disappointment
at the same scale

FALKLAND ISLANDS
(ISLAS MALVINAS) (U.K.)
West Falkland
East Falkland
Jason Is
Pebble I.
C. Dolphin
Mt. Usborne
Stanley
Choiseul Sound
Darwin
Goose Green
Lively I.
King George B.
Queen Charlotte B.
Weddell I.
Falkland Sound
B. of Harbours
Stephen's
C. Meredith
Beauchene I.

ARGENTINA
RIO NEGRO
CHUBUT
SANTA CRUZ
LOS LAGOS
AISEN
MAGALLANES & ANTARTICA CHILENA
TIERRA DEL FUEGO

Golfo San Matías
Golfo San Jorge
Península Valdés
Puerto Madryn
Trelew
Rawson
Comodoro Rivadavia
Río Gallegos
Punta Arenas
Puerto Natales
Ushuaia
Río Grande
Bahía Grande
Cabo de Hornos
Estrecho de Magallanes

Archipiélago de los Chonos
Isla de Chiloé
Golfo de Penas
Valdivia
Puerto Montt
Castro

1:7 500 000

0   75   150   225   300 MILES
0   75   150   225   300   375   450 KM

A
B
C
2
D
E
F
G
H
J
K
L
M
N
O
2

Greenland

Baffin Bay
Davis Strait
Hudson Bay
James Bay
Foxe Basin
Ungava Bay
Hudson Strait
Lancaster Sd
Nares Strait
Barents Sea
North Cape
.357
3884
Bjørnøya
26
Greenland Basin
East Jan Mayen Ridge
Jan Mayen
Norwegian Basin
3970
Norwegian Sea
Iceland
Denmark Strait
Arctic Circle

NORTH AMERICA
St Lawrence
Newfoundland
C. Race
St John's
C. Sable
Sable I.
.69
Grand Banks
Labrador Sea
Cap Farvel
Reykjanes Ridge
.550
.4685
.678
North - Eastern Atlantic Basin
Faeroes
Shetland Is
Rockall Bank
North Sea
.31
Irish Sea
London
Land's End
English Chan.
38.
Skagerrak
Rhine
Gulf of Bothnia
G. of Finland
Baltic Sea
EUROPE
Danube
.2210
Black Sea

NORTH
Newfoundland Basin
New York
C. Hatteras
Bermuda
Bermuda Rise
North American Basin
Mid Atlantic Ridge
Oceanographer Fracture
.265
Atlantis Fracture
1092
.5943
.6690
Azores
Azores - Cape St Vincent Ridge
Str. of Gibraltar
Lisbon
Bay of Biscay
Marseille
Corse
Sardegna
Baleares
2875
Palas
Tyrrhenian Sea
Mediterranean Sea
Ionian Sea
5121
Aegean Sea
Kriti
Sea
Cyp

ATLANTIC
OCEAN
Canary Basin
Canary Is
Tropic of Cancer
4

Gulf of Mexico
New Orleans
Mississippi
Bahía de Campeche
Yucatán Channel
Str. of Florida
The Bahamas
Greater Antilles
Cayman Tr.
7535
G. of Honduras
Middle America Trench
6662
Caribbean Sea
Colombian Basin
Venezuelan Basin
Puerto Rico Tr.
871
Lesser Antilles
Sargasso Sea
Cape Verde Fracture
Cape Verde Plateau
Cape Verde Islands
Cape Verde Basin
Dakar
AFRICA
Niger
15

Panama City
I. de Coco
Cocos Ridge
I. de Malpelo
3901
Caracas
Orinoco
Guiana Basin
Vema Fracture
.1627
São Pedro e São Paulo
Sierra Leone Rise
Sierra Leone Basin
Guinea Basin
5212
Gulf of Guinea
Bioco
Príncipe
São Tomé
Lagos
Bight of Benin
Equator

Mouths of the Amazon
Amazon
SOUTH AMERICA
Fernando de Noronha
Recife
.6697
Romanche Gap
7856
Annobón
Congo
Luanda
6

Lima
.6601
Peru or Nazca Ridge
S.W. Peru or Nazca Ridge
8066
Brazil Basin
Ascension
St Helena Fracture
St Helena
SOUTH
Angola Basin
15

San Félix
San Ambrosio
Chile Trench
Rio de Janeiro
Trindade
Martin Vaz Is
Rio Grande Rise
.550
ATLANTIC
Mid Atlantic Ridge
.1670
St Helena
Walvis Ridge
Cape Basin
Tropic of Capricorn
.24
Orange
7

Chile Basin
Islas Juan Fernández
Paraná
Buenos Aires
Río de la Plata
Golfo San Matías
Golfo de San Jorge
Argentine Basin
.6681
OCEAN
.11
Cape Town
Cape of Good Hope
.5520
Tristan da Cunha
Gough I.
30

Falkland Islands
.45
Scotia Ridge
Shag Rocks
South Georgia
Meteor Depth
8325
South Sandwich Is
.5870
Scotia Sea
South Orkney Is
Scotia Ridge
South Sandwich Trench
Atlantic - Indian Ridge
.1330
Bouvetøya
Agulhas Plateau
Agulhas Basin
.6195
Crozet Plateau
Prince Edward Is
8

Cabo de Hornos
Drake Passage
South Shetland Is
Antarctic Peninsula
South - East Pacific Basin
D
C
E
F
G
H
J
Atlantic - Indian Antarctic Basin
.5750
.6972
Maud Seamount
.1200
Antarctic Circle
M
9

METRES
SEA LEVEL
FEET
200 | 656
3000 | 9842
5000 | 16404
6000 | 19686

0 300 600 900 1200 1500 1800 MILES
0 500 1000 1500 2000 2500 3000 KM
1:48 000 000

1:48 000 000

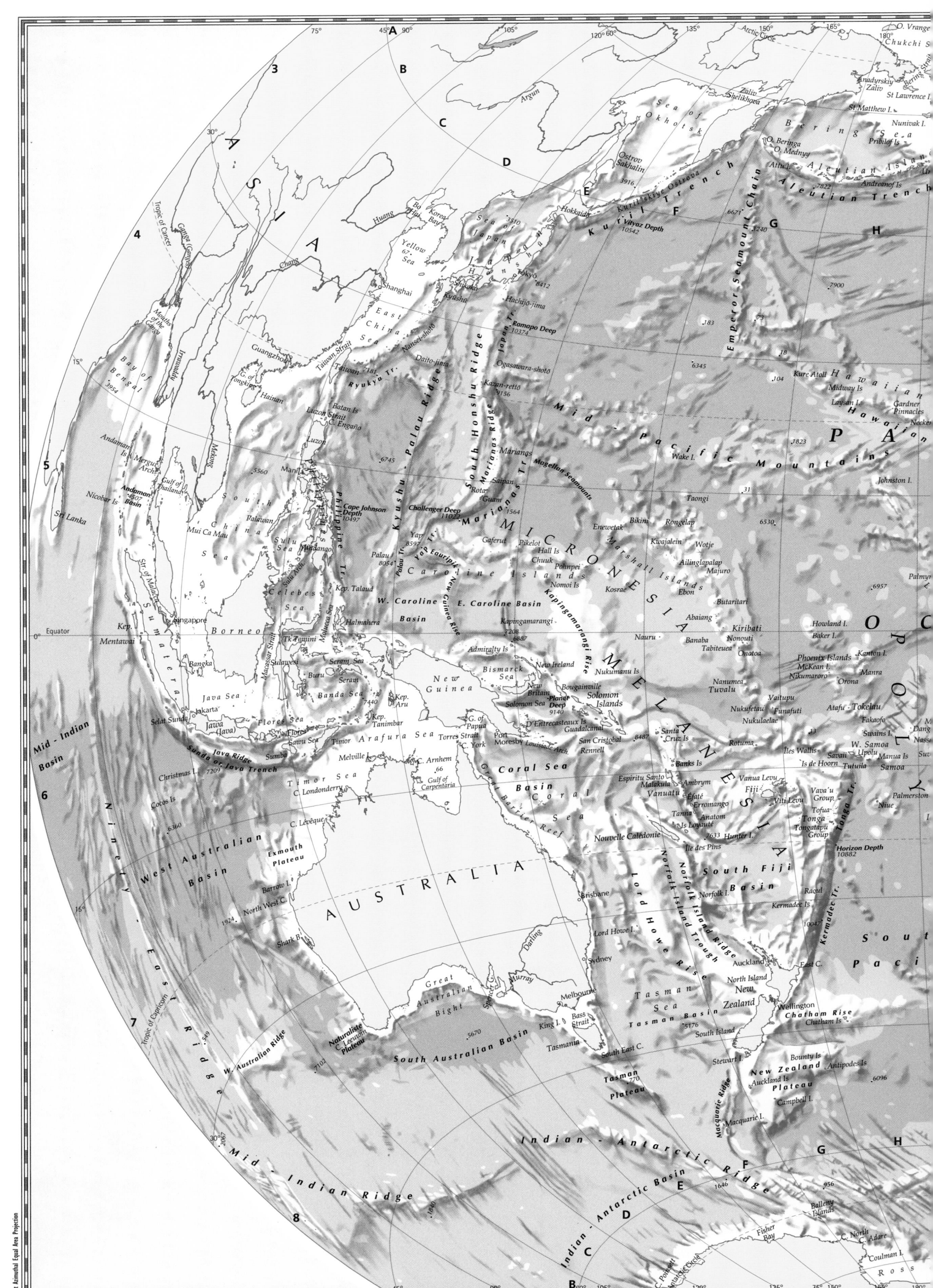

ASIA

O. Vrange
Chukchi S.
Arctic Circle
O. Beringa
O. Mednyy
Attu I.
Andreanof Is
Aleutian Islands
Aleutian Trench
Emperor Seamount Chain

Bering Sea
Pribilof Is
St Matthew I.
St Lawrence I.
Nunivak I.
Chanadyrskiy
Zaliv
Bering St.

Sea of
Okhotsk
Ostrov
Sakhalin
3916
Hokkaido
Kurilskiye Ostrova
Kuril'skiy Trench
Vityaz Depth
10542
7822
7240
6671

Huang
Korea
Bay
Yellow
Sea
67
Japan
Tokyo
8412
Hachijō-jima
Ramapo Deep
10374

Shanghai
East
China
Sea
Kyūshū
Nansei-shotō
Daitō-jima
Ogasawara-shotō
Kazan-rettō
156

Mid - Pacific Mountains
7900
.183
6345
18
.104
Kure Atoll
Hawaiian
Midway Is
Laysan I.
Gardner
Pinnacles
Necker
.1823
Johnston I.
31
Taongi
Wake I.
Enewetak
Bikini
Rongelap
6530
Marshall Islands
Kwajalein
Wotje
Ailinglapalap
Majuro
Kosrae
Ebon
Butaritari
6957

PACIFIC

Bay of
Bengal
3954
Andaman
Is
Mergui
Arch.
Tongking
Hainan
Taiwan Strait
Batan Is
Engaño
Luzon Strait
Luzon
Manila
Palawan
6745
Challenger Deep
11022
Cape Johnson
Depth
10497
Ryukyu Tr.
Kyūshū - Palau Ridge
South Honshu Ridge
Japan Tr.
Mariana Tr.
Marianas
Saipan
Rota
Guam
1564
Magellan Seamounts
Marianas Tr.
W. Caroline
Basin
E. Caroline Basin
Yap
8597
Yap Tr.
Palau
8054
Palau Tr.
Philippine Tr.
Gaferut
Pikelot
Hall I.
Chuuk
Pohnpei
Nomoi Is
Caroline Islands
Eauripik
New Guinea Rise
Kapingamarangi Rise
7208
Kapingamarangi
6687
MICRONESIA
Abaiang
Nauru
Banaba
Tabiteuea
Nonouti
Onotoa
Kiribati
Howland I.
Baker I.
Phoenix Islands
McKean I.
Nikumaroro
Kanton I.
Orona
Manra
Nanumea
Tuvalu
Nukufetau
Funafuti
Nukulaelae
Vaitupu
Atafu
Fakaofo
Tokelau

Sri Lanka
Andaman
Basin
7207
Nicobar Is
Mui Ca Mau
Str. of Malacca
Mentawai
Singapore
Kep.
Mentawai
Sumatera
Jakarta
Selat Sunda
Jawa
(Java)
Java Sea
Flores Sea
Flores
Sumba
Sunda or Java Trench
7209
Christmas I.
South
China
Sea
Sulu
Sea
Mindanao
Celebes
Sea
Borneo
Sulawesi
Tk. Tomini
Makassar Strait
Buru
Seram Sea
Seram
Banda Sea
Kep. Tanimbar
7440
Kep. Aru
Molucca Sea
Halmahera
Kep. Talaud
Admiralty Is
New
Guinea
Bismarck
Sea
New Ireland
New
Britain
Bougainville
Solomon Sea
Planet
Deep
9140
Solomon
Islands
Equator
Nukumanu Is
MELANESIA
D'Entrecasteaux Is
Guadalcanal
San Cristobal
8487
Rennell
Santa
Cruz Is
Banks Is
Rotuma
Iles Wallis
Is de Hoorn
Savaii
Upolu
W. Samoa
Manua Is
Samoa
Tutuila

Mid - Indian
Basin
Ninetyeast Ridge
6360
West Australian
Basin
Exmouth
Plateau
Barrow I.
North West C.
1924
Shark B.
Timor
Sea
Arafura Sea
Melville I.
C. Londonderry
C. Arnhem
66
Gulf of
Carpentaria
Torres Strait
C. York
Port
Moresby
G. of
Papua
Louisiade Arch.
Coral Sea
Basin
Coral
Sea
Great Barrier Reef
Espiritu Santo
Malakula
Ambrym
Efaté
Vanuatu
Tanna
Erromango
Anatom
Iles Loyauté
Nouvelle Calédonie
Ile des Pins
Hunter I.
2633
Norfolk Ridge
Lord Howe Rise
Norfolk Island Ridge
Vanua Levu
Fiji
Viti Levu
Vava'u
Group
Tofua
Tongatapu
Group
Tonga
Niue
Tonga Tr.
Horizon Depth
10882
South Fiji
Basin
Norfolk I.
Raoul
Kermadec Is
1047
Kermadec Tr.
South
Pacific
AUSTRALIA
Brisbane
Darling
Lord Howe I.
Sydney
Auckland
North Island
Tasman
Sea
New
Zealand
Wellington
Chatham Rise
Chatham Is
Melbourne
Murray
King I.
Bass Strait
Tasman Basin
5176
South Island
Great
Australian
Bight
5670
Spencer Gulf
Naturaliste
Plateau
C. Leeuwin
7102
South Australian Basin
Tasmania
South East C.
Tasman
Plateau
770
Stewart I.
New Zealand
Plateau
Auckland Is
Bounty Is
Antipodes Is
6096
Campbell I.
West Australian Ridge
Macquarie Ridge
Macquarie I.
Indian - Antarctic Ridge
G
H
F
E
Indian - Antarctic Basin
1646
956
D
Fisher
Bay
C
North
Adare
Coulman I.
Ross
Mid - Indian Ridge
1080
8
Tropic of Capricorn
Mid - Indian Ridge

B
90°
60°
105°
120°
75°
150°
165°
180°
Antarctic Circle

R
Q
P
O
N
M
L
K

NORTH AMERICA

Gulf of Alaska
Kodiak I.
Alexander Archipelago
Queen Charlotte Islands
Vancouver Island
Vancouver

Hudson Bay
James Bay
Mackenzie
Columbia
Missouri
Colorado
Grande
Mississippi

Newfoundland
C. Sable
Sable I.
New York
Hatteras
Bermuda
Bermuda Rise

Mid-Atlantic Ridge
North American Basin
Atlantis Fracture

Mendocino Seascarp 2733
C. Mendocino
San Francisco
Erben Tablemount 412
Los Angeles
Murray Seascarp
,6217
Guadalupe
Golfo de California
New Orleans
Gulf of Mexico
Bahía de Campeche
The Bahamas
Str. of Florida
Greater Antilles
Yucatán Channel
Puerto Rico Tr. 8742
Cayman Tr. 7535
Venezuelan Basin
Cape Verde Fracture
Vema Fracture

Molokai Fracture Zone
IFIC
Maui
Hawaii
7022
Clarion Fracture Zone
Is Revillagigedo
I. Clarión
I. Socorro
G. de Tehuantepec
Tehuantepec Ridge
Middle America Trench
6662
G. of Honduras
Caribbean Sea
Colombian Basin
Lesser Antilles
Caracas
Orinoco
Guiana Basin

nds
aeran
Kiritimati
AN
I.
lands
Malden I.
Starbuck I.

Clipperton Fracture Zone
Clipperton I.
,20
,10
I. de Coco
Cocos Ridge
I. de Malpelo 3901
Islas Galápagos
Carnegie Ridge
G. de Guayaquil
Mouths of the Amazon
0°

East Pacific Rise

SOUTH AMERICA
Amazon

Tongareva
Caroline I.
Flint I.
Is du Roi Georges
ua Ura
Raiatea
Is de la Société
vey Is
Tahiti
Anaa
Hao
Héréhérétué
Iles Maria
Iles Du. de Gloucester
tonga
agaia
Tubuai
Raivavae
Rapa
SIA
West Basin
,5420

Is Marquises
Nuku Hiva
Hiva Oa
Iles de Désappointement
Is Tuamotu
Raroia
4385
Groupe Actéon
Is Gambier
Henderson I.
Ducie I.
Pitcairn I.
1929
Peru Basin
Lima
Peru or Nazca Ridge
S.W. Peru or Nazca Ridge
6601
5470

East Pacific Ridge
Easter Island Fracture Zone
3314
Easter I.
I. Sala y Gómez
371
San Félix San Ambrosio
6060
Chile Trench
Peru - Chile Trench

East Pacific Ridge
Antarctic Ridge
K L M N O P
Eltanin Fracture Zone
Pacific
South - East Pacific Basin
5230
Amundsen Sea
Peter I. Øy
Drake Passage
Scotia Sea
Scotia Ridge
5870

Challenger Fracture Zone
Is Juan Fernández
Robinson Crusoe
Basin
2743
Santiago
Río de Janeiro
Paraná
Buenos Aires
Río de la Plata
Golfo San Matías
Golfo de San Jorge
Falkland Islands
Argentine Basin
6091

8

0 300 600 900 1200 1500 1800 MILES
0 500 1000 1500 2000 2500 3000 KM

METRES   FEET
SEA   LEVEL
200   656
3000   9842
5000   16404
6000   19686

0	200	400	600	800	MILES
0	200	400	600	800	1000	1200	KM

1:24 000 000

ANTARCTIC RESEARCH STATIONS
1 Teniente Rodolfo Marsh (Chile)
2 Comandante Ferraz (Brazil)
3 Capitán Arturo Prat (Chile)
4 Bellingshausen (Rus. Fed.)
5 Teniente Jubany (Arg.)
6 Arctowski (Poland)
7 General Bernardo O'Higgins (Chile)
8 Esperanza (Arg.)
9 Vicecomodoro Marambio (Arg.)
10 Chang Cheng (Great Wall) (China)
11 Palmer (U.S.A.)
12 Faraday (Ukraine)
13 Rothera (U.K.)
14 Artigas (Ury.)
15 General San Martín (Arg.)

KERGUELEN
(France)
1:3M

Note: Under the Antarctic Treaty of 1959 all territorial claims are held in abeyance in the interest of international co-operation for scientific purposes.

THE INDEX INCLUDES the names on the maps in the ATLAS of the WORLD section. Names are indexed to the largest scale map on which they appear, and can be located using the grid reference letters and numbers around the map frame. Names on insets have a symbol: □, followed by the inset number. Although the maps have been revised to account for the change in name from Zaire to Congo and the reversion of Hong Kong to Chinese rule, this index reflects the prior situation.
Abbreviations used to describe features in the index are explained on the right. Abbreviations used in feature names on the maps and in the index, are explained on page 24. A glossary of alternative name forms is included on page 199.

A.C.T.	Australian Capital Territory
b.	bay
B.C.	British Columbia
Bos.-Herz.	Bosnia-Herzegovina
c.	cape
chan.	channel
div.	division
est.	estuary
g.	gulf
gl.	glacier
h.	hill, hills
i., I.	island
is, Is	islands
l.	lake
lag.	lagoon
mt.	mountain
mts	mountains
N.	North
nat. park	national park
N.W.T.	Northwest Territories
pen.	peninsula
plat.	plateau
P.N.G.	Papua New Guinea
pt	point
r.	river
reg.	region
Rep.	Republic
res.	reserve
resr	reservoir
Rus. Fed.	Russian Federation
S.	South
Str.	Strait
Terr.	Territory
U.A.E.	United Arab Emirates
U.K.	United Kingdom
U.S.A.	United States of America
v.	valley

A

18 C3 **Aachen** Germany
18 E4 **Aalen** Germany
18 B3 **Aalst** Belgium
21 J3 **Aarau** Switz.
21 H3 **Aarberg** Switz.
18 B3 **Aarschot** Belgium
50 C1 **Aba** China
77 F5 **Aba** Nigeria
78 F3 **Aba** Zaire
73 H2 **Abā ad Dūd** Saudi Arabia
139 F5 **Abacaxis r.** Brazil
57 B3 **Abādān** Iran
57 C3 **Abādeh** Iran
144 E3 **Abadia dos Dourados** Brazil
144 D2 **Abadiânia** Brazil
74 D2 **Abadla** Algeria
145 F3 **Abaeté** Brazil
145 F3 **Abaeté r.** Brazil
142 C1 **Abaetetuba** Brazil
49 F2 **Abagaytuy** Rus. Fed.
49 E4 **Abag Qi** China
24 B1 **A Baiuca** Spain
77 F5 **Abaji** Nigeria
127 E4 **Abajo Pk summit** U.S.A.
77 F5 **Abakaliki** Nigeria
65 M2 **Abakan** Rus. Fed.
65 L2 **Abakan r.** Rus. Fed.
65 L2 **Abakanskiy Khrebet mt. ra.** Rus. Fed.
78 C4 **Abala** Congo
77 E4 **Abala** Niger
77 F3 **Abalak** Niger
77 F3 **Abalemma well** Niger
75 E4 **Abalessa** Algeria
57 C3 **Āb Anbār** Iran
140 B2 **Abancay** Peru
78 B3 **Abanga r.** Gabon
25 F3 **Abanilla** Spain
57 C3 **Abarqū** Iran
46 K1 **Abashiri** Japan
46 K2 **Abashiri-gawa r.** Japan
46 K2 **Abashiri-ko l.** Japan
46 K1 **Abashiri-wan b.** Japan
81 C5 **Abasula waterhole** Kenya
65 H1 **Abatskiy** Rus. Fed.
90 □1 **Abau** P.N.G.
65 H3 **Abay** Kazak.
80 C3 **Ābaya Hāyk' l.** Ethiopia
65 M2 **Abaza** Rus. Fed.
78 C2 **Abba** C.A.R.
26 C4 **Abbadia San Salvatore** Italy
57 D2 **Abbāsābād** Iran
27 B5 **Abbasanta** Italy
122 C2 **Abbaye, Pt pt** U.S.A.
80 D2 **Abbe, L. l.** Ethiopia
20 E1 **Abbeville** France
125 E6 **Abbeville** U.S.A.
119 D5 **Abbeville** U.S.A.
99 F2 **Abbey Peak h.** Aust.
10 E2 **Abborrträsk** Sweden
152 A3 **Abbot Ice Shelf ice feature** Ant.
99 F4 **Abbot, Mt mt.** Aust.
110 E5 **Abbotsford** Can.
122 B3 **Abbotsford** U.S.A.
127 F4 **Abbott** U.S.A.
54 C2 **Abbottabad** Pakistan
60 D2 **'Abd al 'Azīz, J. h.** Syria
80 □ **'Abd al Kūrī i.** *Socotra* Yemen
12 J4 **Abdi** Rus. Fed.
57 D2 **Abdolabād** Iran
57 D1 **Abdollāhābād** Iran
57 C2 **Abdollāhābād** Iran
64 D2 **Abdulino** Rus. Fed.
72 D5 **Abéché** Chad
57 D3 **Āb-e Garm** Iran
77 E3 **Abeïbara well** Mali
77 F5 **Abejukolo** Nigeria
77 F3 **Abélajouad well** Niger
93 D4 **Abel Tasman National Park nat. park** N.Z.
76 D5 **Abengourou** Côte d'Ivoire
24 D3 **Abenójar** Spain
11 C5 **Åbenrå** Denmark
18 E4 **Abensberg** Germany
77 E5 **Abeokuta** Nigeria
17 E5 **Aberaeron** U.K.
17 F6 **Aberdare** U.K.
97 G3 **Aberdeen** Aust.
111 H4 **Aberdeen** Can.
45 □ **Aberdeen** Hong Kong
82 C5 **Aberdeen** R.S.A.
16 F3 **Aberdeen** U.K.
121 E5 **Aberdeen** U.S.A.
125 F5 **Aberdeen** U.S.A.
124 D2 **Aberdeen** U.S.A.
126 B2 **Aberdeen** U.S.A.
111 J2 **Aberdeen Lake l.** Can.
16 E3 **Aberfoyle** U.K.
17 F6 **Abergavenny** U.K.
125 C5 **Abernathy** U.S.A.
17 E5 **Aberystwyth** U.K.
73 H4 **Abhā** Saudi Arabia
57 B1 **Abhar r.** Iran
57 B1 **Abhar** Iran
77 F5 **Abia div.** Nigeria
80 C3 **Ābīata Hāyk' l.** Ethiopia
57 B2 **Ab-i Bazuft r.** Iran
76 D5 **Abidjan** Côte d'Ivoire
57 G2 **Ab-i-Istada l.** Afghanistan
80 C3 **Abijatta-Shalla National Park nat. park** Ethiopia
57 D2 **Ab-i-Kavir salt flat** Iran
47 H6 **Abiko** Japan
124 D4 **Abilene** U.S.A.
125 D5 **Abilene** U.S.A.
17 G6 **Abingdon** U.K.
122 B5 **Abingdon** U.S.A.
120 C6 **Abingdon** U.S.A.
99 G3 **Abington Reef reef** *Coral Sea Islands Terr.* Pac. Oc.
13 F6 **Abinsk** Rus. Fed.
57 E2 **Ab-i-Rahuk** Afghanistan
57 F1 **Ab-i-Safed r.** Afghanistan
140 A1 **Abiseo, Parque Nacional nat. park** Peru
111 H2 **Abitau Lake l.** Can.
114 E2 **Abitibi r.** Can.
114 E2 **Abitibi Canyon Dam dam** Can.
114 E2 **Abitibi, Lake l.** Can.
13 G7 **Abkhazia div.** Georgia
96 C1 **Abminga** Aust.
73 F2 **Abnûb** Egypt
76 D5 **Aboisso** Côte d'Ivoire
80 B3 **Aboke** Sudan
77 E5 **Abomey** Benin
54 C3 **Abonar** India
78 B3 **Abong Mbang** Cameroon
76 D5 **Abooso** Ghana
41 A4 **Aborlan** Phil.
78 C1 **Abou Déia** Chad
60 F1 **Abovyan** Armenia
140 C4 **Abra** Chile
80 E1 **Abrād, W. w** Yemen
133 D2 **Abraham's Bay** The Bahamas
147 D5 **Abra, L. del l.** Arg.
146 C1 **Abra Pampa** Arg.
145 G4 **Abre Campo** Brazil
73 F3 **'Abri** Sudan
145 J2 **Abrolhos, Arquipélago dos is** Brazil
28 D1 **Abrud** Romania
27 D4 **Abruzzo div.** Italy
126 E2 **Absaroka Range mt. ra.** U.S.A.
59 H1 **Abşeron Yarımdası pen.** Azerbaijan
46 C6 **Abu** Japan
61 D2 **Abū aḍ Ḍuhūr** Syria
57 B4 **Abū'Alī i.** Saudi Arabia
57 C4 **Abual Jirab i.** U.A.E.
61 D5 **Abu 'Amūd, W. w** Jordan
73 H4 **Abū 'Arīsh** Saudi Arabia
61 C4 **Abu 'Aweigîla well** Egypt
73 E3 **Abu Ballûs h.** Egypt
73 F4 **Abu Deleiq** Sudan
73 G3 **Abū Ḍībā'** Saudi Arabia
61 B5 **Abu Durba** Egypt
61 B5 **Abu Hâd, W. w** Egypt
61 D3 **Abu Hafrah, W. w** Jordan
73 E1 **Abu Haggag** Egypt
61 D4 **Abū Hallūfa, J. h.** Jordan
73 F4 **Abu Hamed** Sudan
73 F4 **Abu Hashim w** Sudan
73 F5 **Abu Hut w** Sudan
77 F5 **Abuja** Nigeria
61 A4 **Abu Kebîr** Egypt
72 E5 **Abu Ku** Sudan
47 H5 **Abukuma-gawa r.** Japan
47 H5 **Abukuma-kochi plat.** Japan
73 G4 **Abū Latt I. i.** Saudi Arabia
78 E1 **Abu Matariq** Sudan
78 D3 **Abumombazi** Zaire
57 C4 **Abū Mūsá i.** U.A.E.
140 C1 **Abunã r.** Bolivia
140 C1 **Abunã** Brazil
138 D4 **Abunai** Brazil
72 C2 **Abū Nā'im well** Libya
80 C2 **Ābune Yosēf mt.** Ethiopia
72 C1 **Abū Nujaym** Libya
61 D2 **Abū Qa'ţūr** Syria
61 A6 **Abu Qurqâs** Egypt
78 F3 **Aburo mt.** Zaire
54 C4 **Abu Road** India
73 G3 **Abū Rubayq** Saudi Arabia
61 B5 **Abu Rudeis** Egypt
61 D5 **Abu Sallah w** Saudi Arabia
73 E5 **Abu Shanab** Sudan
73 F3 **Abu Simbel** Egypt
73 F3 **Abu Simbel Temple** Egypt
60 F4 **Abū Şukhayr** Iraq
93 C5 **Abut Head hd** N.Z.
61 D5 **Abū Ujayyijāt well** Saudi Arabia
80 C2 **Abuye Meda mt.** Ethiopia
41 C4 **Abuyog** Phil.
73 E5 **Abu Zabad** Sudan
57 C4 **Abū Ẓabī** U.A.E.
73 F2 **Abu Zenîma** Egypt
73 E5 **Abyad** Sudan
72 D1 **Abyār an Nākhīlah well** Libya
61 C5 **Abyār Banī Murr well** Saudi Arabia
100 B4 **Abydos** Aust.
78 E2 **Abyei** Sudan
72 C5 **Ab Zérafa** Chad
121 J2 **Acadia Nat. Park nat. park** U.S.A.
131 E4 **Acambaro** Mexico
131 H4 **Acancéh** Mexico
138 B2 **Acandí** Colombia
24 B1 **A Cañiza** Spain
130 D4 **Acaponeta** Mexico
131 F5 **Acapulco** Mexico
142 C1 **Acará r.** Brazil
142 C1 **Acará** Brazil
142 C1 **Acará Miri r.** Brazil
142 D1 **Acaraú** Brazil
142 D1 **Acaraú r.** Brazil
141 E5 **Acaray r.** Paraguay
142 E2 **Acarí** Brazil
145 F1 **Acari r.** Brazil
138 D2 **Acarigua** Venezuela
28 D1 **Acâş** Romania
131 F5 **Acatlan** Mexico
131 G5 **Acayucán** Mexico
76 D5 **Accra** Ghana
140 C3 **Achacachi** Bolivia
138 D2 **Achaguas** Venezuela
54 D5 **Achalpur** India
56 B2 **Achampet** India
63 T3 **Achayvayam** Rus. Fed.
77 G3 **Achegour well** Niger
29 C5 **Acheloös r.** Greece
49 H3 **Acheng** China
13 H6 **Achikulak** Rus. Fed.
17 B5 **Achill Island i.** Rep. of Ire.
63 L4 **Achinsk** Rus. Fed.
65 G4 **Achisay** Kazak.
64 E1 **Achit** Rus. Fed.
16 E3 **Achnasheen** U.K.
61 B2 **Achno** Cyprus
27 E7 **Aci Castello** Italy
27 E7 **Aci Catena** Italy
60 B2 **Acıpayam** Turkey
124 E3 **Ackley** U.S.A.
132 D2 **Acklins I. i.** The Bahamas
140 B2 **Acomayo** Peru
146 B3 **Aconcagua, Cerro summit** Arg.
142 E2 **Acopiara** Brazil
140 C3 **Acora** Peru
24 B1 **A Coruña** Spain
130 J7 **Acoyapa** Nicaragua
26 C4 **Acquapendente** Italy
26 B3 **Acqui Terme** Italy
96 C3 **Acraman, L. salt flat** Aust.
140 C2 **Acre r.** Brazil
140 B1 **Acre div.** Brazil
27 F6 **Acri** Italy
151 L7 **Actéon, Groupe is** *Fr. Poly.* Pac. Oc.
115 J4 **Acton Vale** Can.
142 E2 **Açu** Brazil
144 D6 **Acungui** Brazil
78 B3 **Acurenam** Equatorial Guinea
47 □2 **Ada** Japan
120 B4 **Ada** U.S.A.
125 D5 **Ada** U.S.A.
28 C2 **Ada** Yugo.
41 □2 **Adacao** *Guam* Pac. Oc.
80 D2 **Adaela well** Ethiopia
24 D2 **Adaja r.** Spain
80 E3 **Adale well** Ethiopia
78 B2 **Adamaoua div.** Cameroon
77 G5 **Adamawa div.** Nigeria
97 G4 **Adaminaby** Aust.
147 E7 **Adam, Mt h.** Falkland Is.
64 F2 **Adamovka** Rus. Fed.
19 L3 **Adamów** Poland
121 G3 **Adams** U.S.A.
122 C4 **Adams** U.S.A.
56 B4 **Adam's Bridge reef** India/Sri Lanka
92 □1 **Adams I. i.** *Auckland Is* N.Z.
110 F4 **Adams L. l.** Can.
129 E2 **Adams McGill Reservoir resr** U.S.A.
93 C5 **Adams, Mt mt.** N.Z.
93 E4 **Adams, Mt h.** N.Z.
110 C3 **Adams Mt. mt.** U.S.A.
126 B2 **Adams, Mt mt.** U.S.A.
128 B2 **Adams Peak mt.** U.S.A.
56 C5 **Adam's Pk** Sri Lanka
91 □14 **Adam's Rock rock** *Pitcairn I.* Pac. Oc.
91 □14 **Adamstown** *Pitcairn I.* Pac. Oc.
80 D2 **'Adan** Yemen
60 C2 **Adana** Turkey
61 C1 **Adana div.** Turkey
40 D2 **Adang, Tk b.** Indon.
17 C5 **Adare** Rep. of Ire.
152 A5 **Adare, C. c.** Ant.
99 F5 **Adavale** Aust.
129 E2 **Adaven** U.S.A.
78 D2 **Adda w** C.A.R./Sudan
26 B2 **Adda r.** Italy
73 H3 **Ad Dafīnah** Saudi Arabia
59 G4 **Ad Dahnā reg.** Saudi Arabia
74 A4 **Ad Dakhla** *Western Sahara*
80 D2 **Aḍ Ḍāli'** Yemen
57 B4 **Ad Dammām** Saudi Arabia
73 H4 **Ad Darb** Saudi Arabia
73 H3 **Ad Dawādimī** Saudi Arabia
57 B4 **Ad Dawḥah** Qatar
61 D2 **Ad Daww plain** Syria
77 F3 **Addax, Réserve Naturelle intégrale dite Sanctuaire des res.** Niger
59 G5 **Ad Dir'īyah** Saudi Arabia
121 K2 **Addison** U.S.A.
60 F4 **Ad Dīwānīyah** Iraq
149 J4 **Addu Atoll atoll** Maldives
61 D2 **Ad Duraykīsh** Syria
73 H1 **Ad Duwayd well** Saudi Arabia
119 D6 **Adel** U.S.A.
124 E3 **Adel** U.S.A.
96 D3 **Adelaide** Aust.
119 □2 **Adelaide** The Bahamas
152 B2 **Adelaide I i.** Ant.
98 B2 **Adelaide River** Aust.
128 D4 **Adelanto** U.S.A.
29 F6 **Adelfoi i.** Greece
59 G7 **Aden, Gulf of g.** Somalia/Yemen
77 F3 **Aderbissinat** Niger
80 D1 **Adhanah, W. w** Yemen
57 C4 **Adh Dhayd** U.A.E.
39 K7 **Adi i.** Indon.
80 C2 **Ādī Ārk'ay** Ethiopia
73 F4 **'Adid Umm Inderab well** Sudan
26 C3 **Adige r.** Italy
80 C2 **Ādīgrat** Ethiopia
80 C2 **Adi Keyih** Eritrea
80 C2 **Adi Kwala** Eritrea
56 B2 **Adilabad** India
80 B4 **Adilanga** Uganda
60 E2 **Adilcevaz** Turkey
126 B3 **Adin** U.S.A.
72 B2 **Adīrī** Libya
121 F2 **Adirondack Mountains mt. ra.** U.S.A.
80 C3 **Ādīs Ābeba** Ethiopia
80 C3 **Ādīs Alem** Ethiopia
80 C2 **Ādīs Zemen** Ethiopia
80 C2 **Adi Ugri** Eritrea
60 D2 **Adıyaman** Turkey
28 F1 **Adjud** Romania
119 □3 **Adjuntas** Puerto Rico
131 F4 **Adjuntas, Presa de las resr** Mexico
113 J3 **Adlavik Islands is** Can.
13 F7 **Adler** Rus. Fed.
100 D2 **Admiralty Gulf b.** Aust.
100 D2 **Admiralty Gulf Abor. Reserve res.** Aust.
109 K2 **Admiralty Inlet inlet** Can.
94 □4 **Admiralty Is is** *Lord Howe I.* Pac. Oc.
110 C3 **Admiralty Island i.** U.S.A.
110 C3 **Admiralty Island Nat. Monument res.** U.S.A.
90 □1 **Admiralty Islands is** P.N.G.
152 A5 **Admiralty Mts mt. ra.** Ant.
77 F5 **Ado-Ekiti** Nigeria
80 B3 **Adok** Sudan
90 □6 **Adolphus Reef reef** Fiji
56 B3 **Adoni** India
78 C3 **Adoumandjali** C.A.R.
20 D5 **Adour r.** France
24 E4 **Adra** Spain
78 F3 **Adranga** Zaire
27 E7 **Adrano** Italy
75 D3 **Adrar** Algeria
75 F4 **Adrar mts** Algeria
74 B4 **Adrar div.** Mauritania
74 B4 **Adrâr h.** Mauritania
77 E3 **Adrar des Ifôghas reg.** Mali
75 F3 **Adrar Ikouhaouene mt.** Algeria
75 F4 **Adrar Mariou mt.** Algeria
75 E3 **Adrar N'Ahnet mts** Algeria
74 A4 **Adrar Souttouf mts** *Western Sahara*
77 F3 **Adrar Tamgak mt.** Niger
61 B1 **Adras D. mt.** Turkey
57 E2 **Adraskand r.** Afghanistan
72 D5 **Adré** Chad
26 D3 **Adria** Italy
123 E5 **Adrian** U.S.A.
125 C5 **Adrian** U.S.A.
23 F3 **Adriatic Sea sea** Mediterranean Sea
129 G6 **Aduana del Sasabe** Mexico
11 G4 **Aduliena** Latvia
56 B4 **Adur** India
78 E3 **Adusa** Zaire
80 C2 **Ādwa** Ethiopia
63 P3 **Adycha r.** Rus. Fed.
13 F6 **Adygeya div.** Rus. Fed.
13 F6 **Adygeysk** Rus. Fed.
13 H6 **Adyk** Rus. Fed.
15 E2 **Adzhamka** Ukraine
76 D5 **Adzopé** Côte d'Ivoire
29 E5 **Aegean Sea sea** Greece/Turkey
18 D2 **Aerzen** Germany
24 B1 **A Estrada** Spain
91 □11 **Afaahiti** *Fr. Poly.* Pac. Oc.
80 C1 **Afabet** Eritrea
80 D3 **Afaf Badane well** Ethiopia
29 G6 **Afantou** Greece
75 F3 **Afao mt.** Algeria
80 D2 **Afar Depression depression** Eritrea/Ethiopia
91 □11 **Afareaitu** *Fr. Poly.* Pac. Oc.
76 D5 **Afféri** Côte d'Ivoire
139 F2 **Affobakka** Surinam
32 H6 **Afghanistan country** Asia
80 E4 **Afgooye** Somalia
91 □12 **Afiamalu** Western Samoa
73 H3 **'Afīf** Saudi Arabia
77 F5 **Afikpo** Nigeria
14 B1 **Afim'ino** Rus. Fed.
10 C3 **Åfjord** Norway
77 E5 **Aflao** Ghana
75 E2 **Aflou** Algeria
81 D4 **Afmadow** Somalia
108 C4 **Afognak I. i.** U.S.A.
74 A5 **Afojjar well** Mauritania
24 C1 **A Fonsagrada** Spain
145 H4 **Afonso Cláudio** Brazil
27 E5 **Afragola** Italy
142 D2 **Afrânio** Brazil
80 D2 **Āfrēra Terara mt.** Ethiopia
10 J2 **Afrikanda** Rus. Fed.
61 D1 **'Afrīn** Syria
61 D1 **'Afrīn r.** Syria/Turkey
60 D2 **Afşin** Turkey
18 B2 **Afsluitdijk dam** Netherlands
80 D3 **Aftol well** Ethiopia
126 E3 **Afton** U.S.A.
142 B1 **Afuá** Brazil
61 C3 **'Afula** Israel
60 B2 **Afyon** Turkey
61 A4 **Aga** Egypt
49 E2 **Aga r.** Rus. Fed.
49 E2 **Aga** Rus. Fed.
77 F2 **Agadez div.** Niger
77 F3 **Agadez** Niger
74 C2 **Agadir** Morocco
72 D4 **Aga Dubé well** Chad
65 H3 **Agadyr'** Kazak.
69 K7 **Agalega Islands is** Seychelles
41 □2 **Agana** *Guam* Pac. Oc.
54 D5 **Agar** India
76 C2 **Agâraktem well** Mali
80 C3 **Āgaro** Ethiopia
55 G5 **Agartala** India
56 A2 **Agashi** India
41 □2 **Agat** *Guam* Pac. Oc.
123 F2 **Agate** Can.
65 G3 **Agat, G. h.** Kazak.
29 F6 **Agathonisi i.** Greece
53 D8 **Agatti i.** India
77 F5 **Agbor Bojiboji** Nigeria
76 D5 **Agboville** Côte d'Ivoire
60 F1 **Ağcabädi** Azerbaijan
60 F1 **Agdaş** Azerbaijan
21 F5 **Agde** France
20 E4 **Agen** France
47 G5 **Ageo** Japan
80 C3 **Āgere Maryam** Ethiopia
14 C2 **Ageyevo** Rus. Fed.
74 B4 **Aghaylas well** *Western Sahara*
54 D1 **Aghil Pass pass** China
74 C5 **Aghrîjît well** Mauritania
29 F6 **Agia Marina** *Notio Aigaio* Greece
29 E7 **Agia Vervara** Greece
28 G2 **Agighiol** Romania
60 D2 **Ağin** Turkey
48 E2 **Aginskiy-Buryatskiy Avt. Okr.** Rus. Fed.
48 E2 **Aginskoye** Rus. Fed.
29 D6 **Agioi Theodoroi** *Peloponnisos* Greece
29 D5 **Agiokampos** Greece
29 D6 **Agios Dimitrios** *Attiki* Greece
29 E5 **Agios Efstratios i.** Greece
29 D6 **Agios Georgios i.** Greece
29 D5 **Agios Konstantinos** *Sterea Ellas* Greece
29 E7 **Agios Nikolaos** *Kriti* Greece
29 F5 **Agios Paraskevi** Greece
29 D6 **Agios Petros** Greece
73 G4 **Agirwat Hills h.** Sudan
29 C5 **Agnantero** Greece
96 B1 **Agnes, Mt h.** Aust.
76 D5 **Agnibilékrou** Côte d'Ivoire
28 E2 **Agnita** Romania
76 D5 **Agogo** Ghana
76 D5 **Agona Swedru** Ghana
48 B5 **Agong** China
140 C1 **Agostinho** Brazil
76 D3 **Agounni Jefal well** Mali
77 E3 **Agous-n-Ehsel well** Mali
54 D4 **Agra** India
13 H7 **Agrakhanskiy Poluostrov pen.** Rus. Fed.
25 F2 **Agreda** Spain
27 F5 **Agri r.** Italy
60 E2 **Ağri** Turkey
29 D7 **Agria Gramvousa i.** Greece
27 D7 **Agrigento** Italy
39 M3 **Agrihan i.** *Northern Mariana Is* Pac. Oc.
29 C5 **Agrinio** Greece
27 E5 **Agropoli** Italy
64 D1 **Agryz** Rus. Fed.
130 E4 **Ags div.** Mexico
60 G1 **Ağsu** Azerbaijan
145 G2 **Água Boa** Brazil
130 D4 **Agua Brava, L. lag.** Mexico
144 B4 **Água Clara** Brazil
131 H5 **Aguada** Mexico
133 E5 **Aguada Grande** Venezuela
138 B2 **Aguadas** Colombia
138 C3 **Agua de Dios** Colombia
119 □3 **Aguadilla** Puerto Rico
147 C5 **Aguado Cecilio** Arg.
130 K7 **Aguadulce** Panama
141 E3 **Aguapei r.** Brazil
146 E2 **Aguapey r.** Arg.
130 C2 **Agua Prieta** Mexico
141 E4 **Aguaray-guazu r.** Paraguay
141 E4 **Aguaray Guazú r.** Paraguay
24 B2 **A Guardia** Spain
138 D2 **Aguaro-Guariquito, Parque Nacional nat. park** Venezuela
130 E4 **Aguascalientes** Mexico
145 H2 **Águas Formosas** Brazil
145 H1 **Águas Vermelhas** Brazil
141 E2 **Água Verde r.** Brazil
144 D5 **Agudos** Brazil
24 B2 **Águeda** Portugal
77 E3 **Aguelhok** Mali
75 E3 **Aguemour reg.** Algeria
77 F4 **Aguié** Niger
129 F5 **Aguila** U.S.A.
24 D1 **Aguilar de Campóo** Spain
146 C2 **Aguilares** Arg.
25 F4 **Águilas** Spain
41 B4 **Aguisan** Phil.
119 □3 **Agujereada, Pta pt** Puerto Rico
80 C2 **Āgula'i** Ethiopia
149 F7 **Agulhas Basin** Indian Ocean
82 C5 **Agulhas, Cape c.** R.S.A.
145 F5 **Agulhas Negras, Pico das mt.** Brazil
149 F6 **Agulhas Plateau** Indian Ocean
40 C4 **Agung, G. vol** Indon.
41 C4 **Agusan r.** Phil.
41 B4 **Agutaya** Phil.
13 D7 **Ağva** Turkey
80 B3 **Agwei r.** Sudan
47 □2 **Aha** Japan
77 E5 **Ahamasu** Ghana
60 F2 **Ahar** Iran
93 C5 **Ahaura r.** N.Z.
93 C5 **Ahaura** N.Z.
18 C2 **Ahaus** Germany
91 □10 **Ahé i.** *Fr. Poly.* Pac. Oc.
92 F3 **Ahimanawa Ra. mt. ra.** N.Z.
92 D1 **Ahipara** N.Z.
92 D1 **Ahipara Bay b.** N.Z.
61 B1 **Ahırlı** Turkey
108 B4 **Ahklun Mts** U.S.A.
60 E2 **Ahlat** Turkey
18 C3 **Ahlen** Germany
54 C5 **Ahmadabad** India
57 D3 **Ahmadī** Iran
56 A2 **Ahmadnagar** India
54 B3 **Ahmadnapur East** Pakistan
54 B3 **Ahmadpur Sial** Pakistan
80 D3 **Ahmar Mountains mt. ra.** Ethiopia
29 F5 **Ahmetli** Turkey
74 B4 **Aḥmeyim well** Mauritania
54 C4 **Ahore** India
18 C3 **Ahrweiler** Germany
11 G3 **Ähtäri** Finland
11 G4 **Ahtme** Estonia
131 H6 **Ahuachapán** El Salvador
131 E4 **Ahualulco** Mexico
91 □10 **Ahunui i.** *Fr. Poly.* Pac. Oc.
93 B6 **Ahuriri r.** N.Z.
57 B3 **Ahvāz** Iran
54 C5 **Ahwa** India
82 B4 **Ai-Ais Hot Springs and Fish River Canyon res.** Namibia
48 D4 **Aibag Gol r.** China
46 J2 **Aibetsu** Japan
119 □3 **Aibonito** Puerto Rico
18 E4 **Aichach** Germany
47 F6 **Aichi div.** Japan
46 E6 **Aida** Japan
127 □1 **Aiea** U.S.A.
61 C2 **Aigialousa** Cyprus
29 D6 **Aigina i.** Greece
29 D6 **Aigina** Greece
29 D4 **Aiginio** Greece
29 D5 **Aigio** Greece
21 H3 **Aigle** Switz.
146 F3 **Aiguá** Uruguay
20 E4 **Aiguillon** France
152 □ **Aiguillon, C. d' c.** *Kerguelen* Indian Ocean
49 H2 **Aihui** China
47 G4 **Aikawa** Japan
119 D5 **Aiken** U.S.A.
50 C3 **Ailao Shan mt. ra.** China
130 L7 **Ailigandi** Panama
114 E5 **Ailsa Craig** Can.
40 E4 **Aimere** Indon.
146 C2 **Aimogasta** Arg.
145 H3 **Aimorés** Brazil
145 H3 **Aimorés, Sa dos h.** Brazil
73 F2 **'Ain 'Amûr spring** Egypt
75 F1 **Aïn Beïda** Algeria
75 D2 **Aïn Beni Mathar** Morocco
74 C3 **'Aïn Ben Tili** Mauritania
75 E1 **Aïn Defla** Algeria
75 E2 **Aïn Deheb** Algeria
61 B5 **Ain el Bâgha well** Egypt
61 C5 **'Ain el Furtâga well** Egypt
73 E2 **Aîn el Maqfi spring** Egypt
72 C4 **Aïn Galakka spring** Chad
42 A2 **Ainggyi** Myanmar
75 E3 **Aïn Mezzer well** Algeria
75 F1 **Aïn-M'Lila** Algeria
75 D2 **Aïn Sefra** Algeria
113 H4 **Ainslie, Lake l.** Can.
61 B5 **Ain Sukhna** Egypt
124 D3 **Ainsworth** U.S.A.
75 D1 **Aïn Temouchent** Algeria
72 E2 **'Aîn Timeira spring** Egypt
75 E4 **Aïn Ti-m Misaou well** Algeria
138 B3 **Aipe** Colombia
140 C3 **Aiquile** Bolivia
43 D7 **Air i.** Indon.
41 □1 **Airai** Palau
20 E2 **Airaines** France
139 E4 **Airão** Brazil
110 G4 **Airdrie** Can.
16 F4 **Airdrie** U.K.
21 G2 **Aire r.** France
20 D5 **Aire-sur-l'Adour** France
77 G3 **Aïr et du Ténéré, Rés. Naturelle Nat. de l' res.** Niger
109 L3 **Air Force I. i.** Can.
48 D4 **Airgin Sum** China
40 B2 **Airhitam r.** Indon.
40 B2 **Airhitam, Tk b.** Indon.
77 F3 **Aïr, Massif de l' mts** Niger
21 J3 **Airolo** Switz.
111 H3 **Air Ronge** Can.
20 D3 **Airvault** France
147 B6 **Aisén div.** Chile
147 B6 **Aisén, Pto** Chile
49 G5 **Ai Shan h.** China
110 B2 **Aishihik** Can.
110 B2 **Aishihik Lake l.** Can.
21 G2 **Aisne r.** France
75 D2 **Aïssa, Djebel mt.** Algeria
10 G2 **Aitamännikkö** Finland
90 □1 **Aitape** P.N.G.
124 E2 **Aitken** U.S.A.
87 L6 **Aitutaki i.** *Cook Islands* Pac. Oc.
28 D1 **Aiud** Romania
41 □1 **Aiwokako Passage chan.** Palau
21 F4 **Aix r.** France
21 F2 **Aix-en-Othe** France
21 G5 **Aix-en-Provence** France
20 E4 **Aixe-sur-Vienne** France
21 G4 **Aix-les-Bains** France
80 C2 **Āīy Ādī** Ethiopia
110 D3 **Aiyansh** Can.
55 F5 **Aiyar Res.** India
77 E5 **Aiyetoro** Nigeria
55 H5 **Aizawl** India
20 D3 **Aizenay** France
11 G4 **Aizkraukle** Latvia
11 F4 **Aizpute** Latvia
47 G5 **Aizutakada** Japan
47 G5 **Aizu-wakamatsu** Japan
60 F2 **'Ajab Shīr** Iran
21 J6 **Ajaccio** France
21 J6 **Ajaccio, Golfe d' b.** France
54 E4 **Ajaigarh** India
73 H2 **Ajā, J. mts** Saudi Arabia
131 F5 **Ajalpán** Mexico
101 A5 **Ajana** Aust.
54 C5 **Ajanta** India
77 F5 **Ajaokuta** Nigeria
13 G7 **Ajaria div.** Georgia
10 D2 **Ajaureforsen** Sweden
93 D5 **Ajax, Mt mt.** N.Z.
41 □2 **Ajayan Bay b.** *Guam* Pac. Oc.
72 D1 **Ajdābiyā** Libya
46 H3 **Ajigasawa** Japan
55 G4 **Ājimganj** India
19 H5 **Ajka** Hungary
57 C4 **Ajman** U.A.E.
54 C4 **Ajmer** India
129 F5 **Ajo** U.S.A.
129 F5 **Ajo, Mt mt.** U.S.A.
41 B4 **Ajuy** Phil.
46 J2 **Akabira** Japan
75 E3 **Akabli** Algeria
47 G5 **Akadomari** Japan
47 G4 **Aka-gawa r.** Japan
81 B5 **Akagera National Park nat. park** Rwanda
80 C3 **Āk'ak'ī Beseka** Ethiopia
72 B3 **Akakus, Jabal mts** Libya
56 B2 **Akalkot** India
46 K2 **Akan** Japan
46 K2 **Akan National Park nat. park.** Japan
61 B2 **Akanthou** Cyprus
46 D7 **Akaoka** Japan
47 □2 **Akarie-Ue** Japan
77 F3 **Akarkar well** Niger
29 C5 **Akarnanika mt. ra.** Greece
93 D5 **Akaroa** N.Z.
93 D5 **Akaroa Har inlet** N.Z.
55 H4 **Akas reg.** India
73 F3 **Akasha** Sudan
65 H3 **Akbakay** Kazak.
65 J3 **Akbalyk** Kazak.
55 E4 **Akbarpur** India
54 E4 **Akbarpur** India
64 F3 **Akbasty** Kazak.
65 H5 **Akbaytal** Tajikistan
65 H5 **Akbaytal P. pass** Tajikistan
75 E1 **Akbou** Algeria
64 E2 **Akbulak** Rus. Fed.
60 D2 **Akçadağ** Turkey
60 D2 **Akçakale** Turkey
60 B1 **Akçakoca** Turkey
61 D1 **Akçakoyunlu** Turkey
29 G6 **Akçay r.** Turkey
64 E4 **Akchakaya, Vpadina depression** Turkmenistan
65 H3 **Akchatau** Kazak.
29 G5 **Akdağ mt.** Turkey
60 C2 **Akdağmadeni** Turkey
11 E4 **Åkersberga** Sweden
11 C3 **Akershus div.** Norway
78 D3 **Aketi** Zaire
64 E5 **Akhal div.** Turkmenistan
13 G7 **Akhalk'alak'i** Georgia
13 G7 **Akhalts'ikhe** Georgia
59 J5 **Akhḍar, Jabal mt. ra.** Oman
61 D5 **Akhḍar, W. al w** Saudi Arabia
60 A2 **Akhisar** Turkey
73 F2 **Akhmîm** Egypt
54 C2 **Akhnoor** India
14 G4 **Akhtuba** Rus. Fed.
13 H5 **Akhtubinsk** Rus. Fed.
13 H7 **Akhty** Rus. Fed.
57 B2 **Ākhvoreh-ye Bālā** Iran
46 D7 **Aki** Japan
78 B4 **Akiéni** Gabon
49 E1 **Akima** Rus. Fed.
112 D3 **Akimiski Island i.** Can.
60 C2 **Akıncı Br. pt** Turkey
47 H4 **Akita div.** Japan
47 H4 **Akita** Japan
74 B5 **Akjoujt** Mauritania
74 C3 **Akka** Morocco
64 F3 **Akkabak** Kazak.
10 E2 **Akkajaure l.** Sweden
65 G3 **Akkanse** Kazak.
46 K2 **Akkeshi** Japan
46 K2 **Akkeshi-ko l.** Japan
46 K2 **Akkeshi-wan b.** Japan
61 C3 **'Akko** Israel
65 H4 **Akkol'** Kazak.
64 C3 **Akkol'** Kazak.
60 D1 **Akkuş** Turkey
64 D3 **Akkystau** Kazak.
77 E5 **Aklampa** Benin
54 D4 **Aklera** India
11 F4 **Akmenrags pt** Latvia
54 D1 **Akmeqit** China
65 H2 **Akmola** Kazak.
65 H2 **Akmola div.** Kazak.
46 E6 **Akō** Japan
80 B3 **Akobo r.** Ethiopia/Sudan
80 B3 **Akobo** Sudan
54 D5 **Akola** India
78 B3 **Akom II** Cameroon
78 B3 **Akonolinga** Cameroon
80 C1 **Akordat** Eritrea
60 C2 **Akören** Turkey
54 D5 **Akot** India
80 B3 **Akot** Sudan
76 D5 **Akoupé** Côte d'Ivoire
113 G1 **Akpatok Island i.** Can.
61 B1 **Akpınar** Turkey
65 J4 **Akqi** China
29 F5 **Akra Agios Fokas pt** Greece
29 E7 **Akra Agios Ioannis pt** Greece
29 C5 **Akra Agiou Andreou pt** Greece
29 E4 **Akra Akrathos pt** Greece
29 E4 **Akra Arapis pt** Greece
29 C5 **Akra Araxos pt** Greece
61 D1 **Akrād, Jabal al mt. ra.** Syria
29 D5 **Akra Drepano pt** Greece
29 C6 **Akra Geraki pt** Greece
61 C2 **Akra, J. mt.** Turkey
29 E5 **Akra Kafireas pt** Greece
29 D6 **Akra Kapello pt** Greece
29 D5 **Akra Kassandras pt** Greece
29 C6 **Akra Katakolo pt** Greece
29 E5 **Akra Kymis pt** Greece
29 G6 **Akra Lindos pt** Greece
29 E7 **Akra Lithino pt** Greece
29 D6 **Akra Maleas i.** Greece
29 F5 **Akra Maleas pt** Greece
29 E5 **Akra Masticho pt** Greece
29 E5 **Akra Meston pt** Greece
10 L2 **Akranes** Iceland
29 D5 **Akra Paliouri pt** Greece
29 F7 **Akra Paraspori pt** Greece
29 E4 **Akra Pinnes pt** Greece
29 F7 **Akra Prasonisi pt** Greece
29 F7 **Akra Sideros pt** Greece
29 E5 **Akra Sigri pt** Greece
29 D7 **Akra Spatha pt** Greece
29 E7 **Akra Stavros pt** *Kriti* Greece
29 D6 **Akra Tainaro pt** Greece
29 E7 **Akra Trypiti pt** *Kriti* Greece
29 F5 **Akra Vamvakas pt** Greece
29 F6 **Akra Xodoto pt** Greece
11 B4 **Åkrehamne** Norway
77 F3 **Akrérèb** Niger
57 F2 **Ak Robat P. pass** Afghanistan
126 G3 **Akron** U.S.A.
120 C4 **Akron** U.S.A.
120 C4 **Akron City Reservoir resr** U.S.A.
61 B2 **Akrotirion B. b.** Cyprus
54 D2 **Aksai Chin reg.** *Jammu and Kashmir*
29 G4 **Aksakal** Turkey
28 F3 **Aksakovo** Bulgaria
60 C2 **Aksaray** Turkey
13 F6 **Aksay** Rus. Fed.
54 D2 **Aksayqin Hu l.** China/Jammu and Kashmir
60 B2 **Akşehir** Turkey
60 B2 **Akseki** Turkey
57 C3 **Aks-e Rostam r.** Iran
48 E2 **Aksha** Rus. Fed.
64 F3 **Akshiganak** Kazak.
65 J4 **Akshiy** Kazak.
65 K4 **Aksu** China
65 K4 **Aksu r.** China
65 H2 **Aksu** Kazak.
65 J3 **Aksu** Kazak.
65 J3 **Aksu r.** Kazak.
60 B2 **Aksu r.** Turkey
64 F2 **Aksuat** *Kustanay* Kazak.
65 K3 **Aksuat** *Semipalatinsk* Kazak.
65 H3 **Aksu-Ayuly** Kazak.
65 H4 **Aksuek** Kazak.
80 C2 **Āksum** Ethiopia
65 G4 **Aksumbe** Kazak.
60 E2 **Aktas Dāgh mt.** Turkey
65 H2 **Aktau** *Karaganda* Kazak.
64 D4 **Aktau** *Mangistau* Kazak.
65 H3 **Aktau** *Zhezkazgan* Kazak.
65 J5 **Akto** China
65 J3 **Aktogay** *Semipalatinsk* Kazak.
65 H3 **Aktogay** *Zhezkazgan* Kazak.
13 D4 **Aktsyabrski** Belarus
65 G3 **Aktuma** Kazak.
64 E3 **Aktumsyk** Kazak.
64 E4 **Aktumsyk, Mys pt** Uzbekistan
64 E2 **Aktyubinsk** Kazak.
64 E3 **Aktyubinsk div.** Kazak.
109 L3 **Akulivik** Can.
46 C7 **Akune** Japan
77 F5 **Akure** Nigeria
10 M2 **Akureyri** Iceland
108 B4 **Akutan** U.S.A.
77 F6 **Akwa Ibom div.** Nigeria
77 F5 **Akwanga** Nigeria
55 G1 **Akxokesay** China
61 C1 **Akyatan Gölü l.** Turkey
65 H3 **Akzhal** Kazak.
65 G4 **Akzhaykyn, Ozero salt l.** Kazak.
11 C3 **Ål** Norway
57 B4 **Al 'Abā** Saudi Arabia
119 C6 **Alabama r.** U.S.A.
119 C5 **Alabama div.** U.S.A.
119 C5 **Alabaster** U.S.A.
41 B3 **Alabat i.** Phil.
72 B2 **Al Abyaḍ** Libya
72 D1 **Al Abyār** Libya
60 C1 **Alaca** Turkey
60 D2 **Alacahan** Turkey
60 C1 **Alaçam** Turkey
29 G5 **Alaçam Dağları mt. ra.** Turkey
131 H4 **Alacrán, Arrecife atoll** Mexico
60 C2 **Ala Dağ mts** Turkey
14 E2 **Alad'ino** Rus. Fed.
24 D2 **Alaejos** Spain
60 F1 **Alagir** Rus. Fed.
142 E2 **Alagoas div.** Brazil
142 E3 **Alagoinhas** Brazil
25 F2 **Alagón** Spain
10 F3 **Alahärmä** Finland
60 F4 **Al Ahmadī** Kuwait
25 J3 **Alaior** Spain
65 H5 **Alai Range mt. ra.** Kyrgyzstan
10 F3 **Alajärvi** Finland
72 B1 **Al Ajaylāt** Libya
73 H2 **Al Ajfar** Saudi Arabia
130 J7 **Alajuela** Costa Rica
61 D5 **Al Akhḍar** Saudi Arabia
61 A1 **Alakır r.** Turkey
65 K3 **Alakol', Oz. salt l.** Kazak.
12 D1 **Alakurtti** Rus. Fed.
139 E4 **Alalaú r.** Brazil
73 H4 **Al'Alayyah** Saudi Arabia
80 D4 **Alama** Somalia
39 M3 **Alamagan i.** *Northern Mariana Is* Pac. Oc.
60 F4 **Al 'Amārah** Iraq
80 C2 **Ālamat'ā** Ethiopia
55 H3 **Alamdo** China
41 A2 **Alaminos** Phil.
130 E3 **Alamítos, Sa de los mt.** Mexico
129 E3 **Alamo** U.S.A.
129 F4 **Alamo Dam dam** U.S.A.
127 F5 **Alamogordo** U.S.A.
125 D6 **Alamo Heights** U.S.A.
127 E6 **Alamos** *Sonora* Mexico
127 F4 **Alamosa** U.S.A.
56 B3 **Alampur** India
80 D2 **Al 'Anad** Yemen
10 D2 **Alanäs** Sweden
60 E3 **Al Anbār div.** Iraq
11 F3 **Åland div.** Finland
11 E3 **Åland is** Finland
56 B2 **Aland** India
60 F2 **Aland r.** Iran
11 E3 **Åland div.** Sweden
61 D2 **Al Andarīn** Syria
43 C7 **Alang Besar i.** Indon.
122 E3 **Alanson** U.S.A.
78 B2 **Alantika Mountains mt. ra.** Cameroon/Nigeria
60 C2 **Alanya** Turkey
73 H3 **Al 'Aqīq** Saudi Arabia
60 D3 **Al Arak oasis** Syria
25 E3 **Alarcón, Embalse de resr** Spain
74 A4 **Al Argoub** *Western Sahara*
73 J2 **Al Arţāwīyah** Saudi Arabia
40 D4 **Alas** Indon.
60 B2 **Alaşehir** Turkey
65 M2 **Alash, Plato plat.** Rus. Fed.
60 E4 **Al 'Āshūrīyah well** Iraq
108 C3 **Alaska div.** U.S.A.
108 D4 **Alaska, Gulf of g.** U.S.A.
110 E3 **Alaska Highway** Can./U.S.A.
108 B4 **Alaska Peninsula pen.** U.S.A.
108 C3 **Alaska Range mt. ra.** U.S.A.
73 G2 **Al 'Assāfīyah** Saudi Arabia
59 G2 **Älät** Azerbaijan
64 F5 **Alat** Uzbekistan
60 E4 **Al 'Athāmīn h.** Iraq
27 D5 **Alatri** Italy
73 H2 **Al Atwā' well** Saudi Arabia
14 G2 **Alatyr' r.** Rus. Fed.
14 H2 **Alatyr'** Rus. Fed.
138 B4 **Alausí** Ecuador
60 F1 **Alaverdi** Armenia
57 B2 **'Alavī** Iran
10 G2 **Alavieska** Finland
11 F3 **Alavus** Finland
42 B1 **Alawbum** Myanmar
96 E3 **Alawoona** Aust.
14 H3 **Alay r.** Rus. Fed.
65 H4 **Alaykuu** Kyrgyzstan
13 H7 **Alazani r.** Azerbaijan/Georgia
60 F3 **Al 'Azīzīyah** Iraq
72 B1 **Al 'Azīzīyah** Libya
26 B3 **Alba** Italy
26 D4 **Alba Adriatica** Italy
61 D1 **Al Bāb** Syria
25 F3 **Albacete** Spain
96 E3 **Albacutya, L. l.** Aust.
61 C5 **Al Bad'** Saudi Arabia
24 D2 **Alba de Tormes** Spain
60 F4 **Al Bādiyah al Janūbīyah h.** Iraq
65 L2 **Al'bagan, G. mt.** Rus. Fed.
61 C2 **Al Bahlūlīyah** Syria
28 D1 **Alba Iulia** Romania
25 F2 **Albalate de Arzobispo** Spain
112 F3 **Albanel, L. l.** Can.
4 G4 **Albania country** Europe
27 D5 **Albano Laziale** Italy
101 B7 **Albany** Aust.
112 C3 **Albany r.** Can.
133 □1 **Albany** Jamaica
119 C6 **Albany** U.S.A.
122 E5 **Albany** U.S.A.
118 C4 **Albany** U.S.A.
121 G3 **Albany** U.S.A.
126 B2 **Albany** U.S.A.
146 F3 **Albardão do João Maria** Brazil
72 E1 **Al Bardī** Libya
60 F4 **Al Başrah div.** Iraq
60 F4 **Al Başrah** Iraq
99 E2 **Albatross Bay b.** Aust.
93 □3 **Albatross Pt pt** *Antipodes Is* N.Z.
92 E3 **Albatross Pt pt** N.Z.
72 D1 **Al Bayḍā'** Libya
80 E2 **Al Bayda** Yemen
138 □ **Albemarle, Pta pt** *Galapagos Is* Ecuador
119 E5 **Albemarle Sd chan.** U.S.A.
26 B3 **Albenga** Italy
24 D2 **Alberche r.** Spain
141 E5 **Alberdi** Paraguay
96 C1 **Alberga** Aust.
96 C1 **Alberga w** Aust.
24 B2 **Albergaria-a-Velha** Portugal
98 D3 **Albert r.** Aust.
20 F2 **Albert** France
110 F4 **Alberta div.** Can.
120 E6 **Alberta** U.S.A.
110 F4 **Alberta, Mt mt.** Can.
19 J5 **Albertirsa** Hungary
96 D3 **Albert, L. l.** Aust.
81 B4 **Albert, Lake l.** Uganda/Zaire
124 E3 **Albert Lea** U.S.A.
80 B4 **Albert Nile r.** Sudan/Uganda
147 B7 **Alberto de Agostini, Parque Nacional nat. park** Chile
133 □1 **Albert Town** Jamaica
21 H4 **Albertville** France
28 F1 **Albeşti** Romania
20 F5 **Albi** France
73 G3 **Al Bi'ār** Saudi Arabia
139 G2 **Albina** Surinam
26 B3 **Albino** Italy
128 A2 **Albion** U.S.A.
121 J2 **Albion** U.S.A.
122 E4 **Albion** U.S.A.
120 D3 **Albion** U.S.A.
73 G2 **Al Bi'r** Saudi Arabia
73 H4 **Al Birk** Saudi Arabia
11 C4 **Ålborg** Denmark
11 C4 **Ålborg Bugt b.** Denmark
25 E4 **Albox** Spain
110 F4 **Albreda** Can.
99 F4 **Albro** Aust.
18 D4 **Albstadt** Germany
57 B4 **Al Budayyi** Bahrain
24 B4 **Albufeira** Portugal
60 E3 **Āl Bū Kamāl** Syria
73 H2 **Al Bukayrīyah** Saudi Arabia
21 J3 **Albula Alpen mt. ra.** Switz.
127 F5 **Albuquerque** U.S.A.
61 D2 **Al Burayj** Syria
59 J5 **Al Buraymī** Oman
24 C3 **Alburquerque** Spain
97 F4 **Albury** Aust.
60 D4 **Al Busayţā' plain** Saudi Arabia
60 F4 **Al Buşayyah** Iraq
73 G3 **Al Buwayr** Saudi Arabia
140 B3 **Alca** Peru
24 B3 **Alcácer do Sal** Portugal
24 B3 **Alcáçovas** Portugal
25 G2 **Alcalá de Chivert** Spain
24 D4 **Alcalá de Guadaira** Spain
24 E2 **Alcalá de Henares** Spain
24 D4 **Alcalá de los Gazules** Spain
24 E4 **Alcalá la Real** Spain
27 D7 **Alcamo** Italy
25 G2 **Alcanar** Spain
25 F2 **Alcañiz** Spain
24 C3 **Alcántara** Spain
24 C3 **Alcántara II, Embalse de resr** Spain
25 F4 **Alcantarilla** Spain
144 B2 **Alcantilado** Brazil
25 E3 **Alcaraz** Spain
25 E3 **Alcaraz, Sierra de mt. ra.** Spain
24 D4 **Alcaudete** Spain
24 E3 **Alcázar de San Juan** Spain
13 F5 **Alchevs'k** Ukraine
24 D3 **Alcoba** Spain
145 J2 **Alcobaça** Brazil
24 C3 **Alconchel** Spain
25 F2 **Alcora** Spain
146 D3 **Alcorta** Arg.
25 F3 **Alcoy** Spain
25 H3 **Alcúdia** Spain
69 J6 **Aldabra Islands is** Seychelles
60 F3 **Al Daghghārah** Iraq
130 D2 **Aldama** *Chihuahua* Mexico
131 F4 **Aldama** *Tamaulipas* Mexico
63 P3 **Aldan r.** Rus. Fed.
63 O4 **Aldan** Rus. Fed.
17 H5 **Aldeburgh** U.K.
142 B2 **Aldeia Velha** Brazil
92 F2 **Aldermen Is, The is** N.Z.
17 F7 **Alderney i.** Channel Is.
128 B4 **Alder Peak summit** U.S.A.
120 C6 **Alderson** U.S.A.
28 C4 **Aldinci** Macedonia
122 B5 **Aledo** U.S.A.
74 B5 **Aleg** Mauritania
25 □ **Alegranza i.** *Canary Is* Spain
145 H4 **Alegre** *Espirito Santo* Brazil
142 C1 **Alegre** *Pará* Brazil
141 E3 **Alegre r.** Brazil
144 C2 **Alegre, Monte r.** Brazil
142 B1 **Alegre, Monte h.** Brazil
79 □ **Alegre, Pto pt** Sao Tome and Principe
143 A6 **Alegrete** Brazil
146 E4 **Alejandro Korn** Arg.
12 E2 **Alekhovshchina** Rus. Fed.
64 D4 **Aleksandra Bekovicha-Cherkassogo, Zaliv b.** Kazak.
14 E3 **Aleksandro-Nevskiy** Rus. Fed.
14 D1 **Aleksandrov** Rus. Fed.
28 C3 **Aleksandrovac** Yugo.
13 J5 **Aleksandrov Gay** Rus. Fed.
28 E3 **Aleksandrovo** Bulgaria
13 H6 **Aleksandrovskoye** Rus. Fed.
45 Q1 **Aleksandrovsk-Sakhalinskiy** Rus. Fed.
19 J2 **Aleksandrów Kujawski** Poland
19 J3 **Aleksandrów Łódzki** Poland
65 L3 **Alekseyevka** Kazak.
65 H2 **Alekseyevka** Kazak.
65 J2 **Alekseyevka** Kazak.
65 G2 **Alekseyevka** Kazak.
13 F5 **Alekseyevka** Rus. Fed.
14 H3 **Alekseyevka** Rus. Fed.
14 F4 **Alekseyevka** Rus. Fed.
15 G1 **Alekseyevka** Rus. Fed.
14 C2 **Aleksin** Rus. Fed.
28 C3 **Aleksinac** Yugo.
14 D2 **Aleksino-Shatur** Rus. Fed.
131 F5 **Alemán, Presa, M. resr** Mexico
78 B4 **Alèmbé** Gabon
145 G4 **Além Paraíba** Brazil
10 C3 **Ålen** Norway
20 E2 **Alençon** France
142 B1 **Alenquer** Brazil
24 C3 **Alentejo reg.** Portugal
127 □2 **Alenuihaha Channel chan.** U.S.A.
76 D5 **Alépé** Côte d'Ivoire
21 J5 **Aléria** France
109 M1 **Alert** Can.
140 B2 **Alerta** Peru
110 D4 **Alert Bay** Can.
21 G4 **Alès** France
28 D1 **Aleşd** Romania
26 B3 **Alessandria** Italy
10 B3 **Ålesund** Norway
21 H3 **Aletschhorn mt.** Switz.
108 B4 **Aleutian Islands is** U.S.A.
108 C4 **Aleutian Range mt. ra.** U.S.A.
151 G2 **Aleutian Trench** Pac. Oc.
63 R4 **Alevina, Mys c.** Rus. Fed.
121 K2 **Alexander** U.S.A.
108 E4 **Alexander Archipelago is** U.S.A.

82 B4 Alexander Bay R.S.A.
119 C5 Alexander City U.S.A.
152 A2 Alexander I. i. Ant.
98 E3 Alexandra r. Aust.
97 F4 Alexandra Aust.
93 B6 Alexandra N.Z.
147 G7 Alexandra, C. c. Atlantic Ocean
29 D4 Alexandreia Greece
98 D3 Alexandria Aust.
115 H4 Alexandria N.Z.
73 E1 Alexandria Egypt
28 E3 Alexandria Romania
122 E5 Alexandria U.S.A.
125 E6 Alexandria U.S.A.
124 E2 Alexandria U.S.A.
120 E5 Alexandria U.S.A.
121 F2 Alexandria Bay U.S.A.
96 D3 Alexandrina, L. l. Aust.
29 E4 Alexandroupoli Greece
113 J3 Alexis r. Can.
122 B5 Alexis U.S.A.
110 E4 Alexis Creek Can.
61 C3 'Aley Lebanon
65 K2 Aley r. Rus. Fed.
65 K2 Aleysk Rus. Fed.
25 F2 Alfambra r. Spain
25 F1 Alfaro Spain
60 F4 Al Farwāniyah Kuwait
27 J4 Alfatar Bulgaria
25 F3 Alfatar Spain
60 E3 Al Fatḥah Iraq
60 G4 Al Fāw Iraq
80 D2 Al Fāzih Yemen
18 D3 Alfeld (Leine) Germany
145 H4 Alfenas Brazil
19 K5 Alföld plain Hungary
26 D3 Alfonsine Italy
115 H4 Alfred U.S.A.
121 H3 Alfred U.S.A.
145 H4 Alfredo Chaves Brazil
60 G4 Al Fujayl Kuwait
57 D4 Al Fujayrah U.A.E.
64 E3 Alga Kazak.
64 D2 Algabas Kazak.
11 B4 Algård Norway
146 B2 Algarrobo Atacama Chile
146 C4 Algarrobo del Aguilla Arg.
24 B4 Algarve reg. Portugal
14 E3 Algasovo Rus. Fed.
24 D4 Algeciras Spain
25 F3 Algemesí Spain
80 C1 Algena Eritrea
75 E1 Alger Algeria
23 G3 Alger U.S.A.
68 D3 Algeria country Africa
60 F4 Al Ghammas Iraq
59 H6 Al Ghaydah Yemen
27 B5 Alghero Italy
82 D5 Algoa Bay b. R.S.A.
23 G3 Algoma U.S.A.
124 E3 Algona U.S.A.
123 F4 Algonac U.S.A.
115 F4 Algonquin Park Can.
115 F4 Algonquin Provincial Park res. Can.
42 A4 Alguada Reef reef Myanmar
73 H3 Al Ḥadbah reg. Saudi Arabia
57 B4 Al Ḥadd Bahrain
73 H2 Al Ḥadhālīl plat. Saudi Arabia
61 D2 Al Hadīyah Saudi Arabia
60 E3 Al Ḥadīthah Iraq
61 D4 Al Ḥadīthah Saudi Arabia
60 E3 Al Ḥadr Iraq
73 H2 Al Ḥafar well Saudi Arabia
74 B3 Al Ḥaggounia Western Sahara
60 D3 Al Ḥamad plain Jordan/Saudi Arabia
72 B2 Al Ḥamādah al Ḥamrā' plat. Libya
24 E4 Alhama de Granada Spain
25 F4 Alhama de Murcia Spain
61 C2 Al Ḥamīdīyah Syria
60 F4 Al Ḥammām well Iraq
74 C3 Al Ḥamra r Western Sahara
61 D2 Al Ḥamrā' Syria
73 H3 Al Ḥanākīyah Saudi Arabia
73 J2 Al Ḥanbalī plain Saudi Arabia
73 G1 Al Ḥarrah h. Saudi Arabia
73 H3 Al Ḥarūj al Aswad mt. ra. Libya
60 E2 Al Ḥasakah Syria
60 F3 Al Hāshimīyah Iraq
73 J2 Al Ḥatīfah plain Saudi Arabia
73 H3 Al Ḥawiyah Saudi Arabia
73 G2 Al Ḥawjā' Saudi Arabia
60 F3 Al Ḥayy Iraq
61 D5 Al Ḥazm Saudi Arabia
60 D3 Al Ḥillah Iraq
61 D4 Al Ḥinn well Saudi Arabia
73 G2 Al Ḥisma plain Saudi Arabia
74 D1 Al Hoceima Morocco
24 E5 Al Hoceima, Baie d' b. Morocco
80 D2 Al Hudaydah Yemen
73 G2 Al Ḥufrah reg. Saudi Arabia
57 B4 Al Hufuf Saudi Arabia
61 C5 Al Ḥumayḍah Saudi Arabia
80 E2 Al Ḥumaysh Yemen
28 F3 Al Ḥunayy Saudi Arabia
61 D2 Al Ḥuwayz Syria
54 D2 'Alīābād Iran
57 D2 'Alīābād Iran
57 C1 'Alīābād Iran
80 D2 'Alīābād Iran
60 A2 Aliaga Turkey
29 D4 Aliakmonas r. Greece
60 F3 'Alī al Gharbī Iraq
29 D5 Aliartos Greece
54 B2 Ali Bayramli Azerbaijan
56 B4 Ali Bandar Pakistan
60 B2 Alibey Adası i. Turkey
77 F4 Alibori r. Benin
28 C2 Alibunar Yugo.
25 F3 Alicante Spain
59 F4 Alice r. Aust.
125 D7 Alice U.S.A.
110 D3 Alice Arm Can.
27 F6 Alice, Punta pt Italy
132 C3 Alice Shoal Caribbean
132 C1 Alice Town The Bahamas
43 H5 Alichur Tajikistan
41 B5 Alicia Phil.
99 E4 Alick Cr. r. Aust.
27 E6 Alicudi, Isola i. Italy
54 D4 Aligarh India
24 C2 Alijó Portugal
80 □1 Al Ikhwān is Socotra Yemen
14 H2 Alikovo Rus. Fed.
29 D6 Alimia i. Greece
79 F6 Alima r. Congo
40 D2 Alindao C.A.R.
40 D2 Alingar r. Afghanistan
11 D4 Alingsås Sweden
55 G4 Alipur Duar India
120 C4 Aliquippa U.S.A.
80 D2 Ali Sabieh Djibouti
127 E6 Alisos r. Mexico
82 D5 Aliveri Greece
82 D5 Aliwal North R.S.A.

110 G4 Alix Can.
54 B2 Alizai Pakistan
72 D1 Al Jabal al Akhḍar mts Libya
57 B4 Al Jafūrah desert Saudi Arabia
72 D2 Al Jaghbūb Libya
60 F4 Al Jahrah Kuwait
57 B4 Al Jamālīyah Qatar
73 G3 Al Jawf Libya
73 G2 Al Jawf Saudi Arabia
72 B1 Al Jawsh Libya
60 E3 Al Jazīrah reg. Iraq/Syria
61 D5 Al Jībān reg. Saudi Arabia
60 F4 Al Jil well Iraq
73 H2 Al Jīh escarpment Saudi Arabia
72 D1 Al Jishshah Saudi Arabia
73 H2 Al Jithāmīyah Saudi Arabia
57 B4 Al Jubayl Saudi Arabia
72 C2 Al Jufra Oasis oasis Libya
73 G3 Al Jumūm Saudi Arabia
73 H3 Al Junaynah Saudi Arabia
57 B4 Al Jurayd i. Saudi Arabia
24 B4 Aljustrel Portugal
61 D3 Al Juwayf depression Syria
61 D5 Al Kabid waterhole Jordan
57 B4 Al Kamari Niger
59 J5 Al Khābūrah Oman
73 H3 Al Khaḍrā' well Saudi Arabia
73 H3 Al Khafjah salt pan Saudi Arabia
60 F3 Al Khālis Iraq
80 D1 Al Kharāb Yemen
57 A4 Al Khaṣab Oman
73 H3 Al Khaṣrah Saudi Arabia
57 B4 Al Khawr Qatar
61 D5 Al Khiṣah well Saudi Arabia
72 D3 Al Khufrah Libya
72 D1 Al Khufrah Oasis oasis Libya
72 B1 Al Khums Libya
61 C3 Al Khushnīyah Syria
57 B4 Al Kir'ānah Qatar
61 D3 Al Kiswah Syria
18 B2 Alkmaar Netherlands
61 D2 Al Kūfah Iraq
73 H2 Al Kuhayfīyah Saudi Arabia
60 F3 Al Kumayt Iraq
60 F3 Al Kūt Iraq
60 F4 Al Kuwayt Kuwait
73 H2 Al Labbah plain Saudi Arabia
61 C2 Al Lādhiqīyah Syria
121 J1 Allagash U.S.A.
121 J1 Allagash r. U.S.A.
121 J1 Allagash Lake l. U.S.A.
55 E4 Allahabad India
61 D3 Allakh-Yun' Rus. Fed.
24 C1 Allariz Spain
83 D3 Alldays R.S.A.
122 C4 Allegan U.S.A.
120 D4 Allegheny r. U.S.A.
120 C5 Allegheny Mountains U.S.A.
120 D4 Allegheny Reservoir resr U.S.A.
133 □5 Allegre, Pte pt Guadeloupe Caribbean
119 D5 Allendale U.S.A.
131 E2 Allende Coahuila Mexico
131 D2 Allende Nuevo León Mexico
114 E4 Allenford Can.
23 C5 Allen, Lough l. Rep. of Ire.
93 H3 Allen, Mt h. N.Z.
121 F4 Allentown U.S.A.
56 B4 Alleppey India
23 E2 Allepuz Spain
61 D3 Allgäuer Alpen mt. ra. Austria/Germany
139 G2 Alliance Suriname
124 C3 Alliance U.S.A.
120 C4 Alliance U.S.A.
21 F4 Allier r. France
133 □3 Alligator Pond Jamaica
119 D5 Alliston Can.
11 E4 Alloa U.K.
16 F3 Alma r. Norway
146 D3 Alta Gracia Arg.
133 F5 Altagracia de Orituco Venezuela
24 D1 Allariz Spain
11 F4 Allston U.K.
119 D6 Altamaha r. U.S.A.
142 B1 Altamira Brazil
146 E4 Altamira Chile
131 F3 Altamira Colombia
130 J7 Altamira Costa Rica
24 D3 Altamira, Sierra de mt. ra. Spain
93 D6 Alta, Mt mt. N.Z.
27 F5 Altamura Italy
48 C3 Altan China
48 D2 Altanbulag Mongolia
48 C2 Altanbulag Mongolia
131 D2 Altar Mexico
130 D2 Altar, Desierto de desert Mexico
131 D2 Altavista Mexico
120 D6 Altavista U.S.A.
48 E2 Altay China
48 A2 Altay Mongolia
65 L4 Altay, Respublika div. Rus. Fed.
65 L2 Altayskiy Rus. Fed.
65 L2 Altayskiy Kray div. Rus. Fed.
21 H3 Altdorf Switz.
25 F3 Altea Spain
10 F1 Alteidet Norway
19 F3 Altenberg Germany
18 C2 Altenburg Germany
18 C3 Altensteig Germany
18 C2 Altentreptow Germany
24 C2 Alter do Chão Portugal
57 D2 Altīmur P. pass Afghanistan
29 F5 Altınoluk Turkey
144 E4 Altinópolis Brazil
29 F5 Altıntaş Turkey
147 C5 Altiplano de Hakeluincul plat. Arg.
140 D3 Altiplano plain Bolivia
18 E2 Altmühl r. Germany
79 B5 Altndy Turkey/Uzbekistan
140 C4 Alto Chicapa Angola
141 J6 Alto Garças Brazil
142 C2 Alto Longá Brazil
79 C4 Alto Molócuè Mozambique
115 E3 Alton Can.
124 B4 Alton U.S.A.
118 E4 Altoona U.S.A.
120 D4 Altoona U.S.A.
142 C1 Alto Parnaíba Brazil
138 C3 Alto Purús r. Peru
145 H2 Alto Rio Doce Brazil
145 G4 Alto Rio Verde Brazil
142 B2 Alto Santo Brazil
144 B3 Altotonga Mexico
18 F4 Altötting Germany
14 B2 Alto Vista h. Aruba Caribbean
14 D3 Altukhovo Rus. Fed.

115 G4 Almonte Can.
24 D3 Almonte r. Spain
54 D3 Almora India
54 D3 Almora r. Spain
25 F3 Almoradí Spain
24 D2 Almorox Spain
77 F3 Almoustarat Mali
57 B4 Al Mubarrez Saudi Arabia
60 C4 Al Mudawwara Jordan
73 H2 Al Muḍīq Saudi Arabia
61 D5 Al Muḥtaṭab depression Saudi Arabia
59 G7 Al Mukallā Yemen
80 D2 Al Mukhā Yemen
72 D1 Al Muknayf Libya
24 E4 Almuñécar Spain
73 H2 Al Muqdādīyah Iraq
73 G2 Al Murūt well Saudi Arabia
57 B4 Al 'Uthmānīyah Saudi Arabia
73 G3 Al Musayyid Saudi Arabia
60 F3 Al Musayyib Iraq
60 F4 Al Muthannā div. Iraq
73 H3 Al Muwayh Saudi Arabia
29 C5 Almyros Greece
127 □1 Alna Haina U.S.A.
17 G4 Alnwick U.K.
42 A4 Aloja Latvia
42 A2 Alon Myanmar
49 G2 Alongshan China
24 □1 Alonnisos i. Greece
39 H6 Alor i. Indon.
39 H8 Alor, Kepulauan is Indon.
18 B3 Alost Belgium
54 D4 Alot India
90 □1 Alotau P.N.G.
101 E5 Aloysius, Mt mt. Aust.
128 C4 Alpaugh U.S.A.
10 F2 Alpena U.S.A.
142 C2 Alpercatas r. Brazil
21 G4 Alpes du Dauphiné mts France
26 B2 Alpi Maritimes mt. ra. France/Italy
99 F4 Alpha Aust.
21 H4 Alpi Cozie mt. ra. France/Italy
26 B2 Alpi Lepontine mt. ra. Italy/Switz.
129 H4 Alpine U.S.A.
125 C6 Alpine U.S.A.
125 C6 Alpine U.S.A.
145 E4 Alpinópolis Brazil
26 A3 Alpi Pennine mt. ra. Italy/Switz.
22 E2 Alps Europe
38 A4 Al Qa'āmīyāt reg. Saudi Arabia
72 C1 Al Qaddāḥīyah Libya
60 F4 Al Qādisīyah div. Iraq
61 D2 Al Qā'iyah Saudi Arabia
24 D3 Al Qalībah Saudi Arabia
61 D2 Al Qāmishlī Syria
73 H3 Al Qarqar Saudi Arabia
61 D2 Al Qaryatayn Syria
72 B1 Al Qaṣabāt Libya
73 H3 Al Qaṭif Saudi Arabia
59 G6 Al Qaṭn Yemen
73 H2 Al Qayṣūmah well Saudi Arabia
73 H4 Al Qunayṭirah div. Syria
73 H4 Al Qunfidhah Saudi Arabia
73 H3 Al Qurayn Saudi Arabia
80 D2 Al Qurayyah Yemen
60 F4 Al Qurnah Iraq
61 D3 Al 'Quşayr Syria
60 D3 Al Quṭayfah Syria
98 C1 Alroy Downs Aust.
58 D4 Alsace div. France
111 H4 Alsask Can.
139 G2 Alsfeld Germany
14 D3 Alshanva Rus. Fed.
17 F4 Alston U.K.
42 A4 Alsunga Latvia
10 F1 Alta Norway
146 D3 Alta Gracia Arg.
133 F5 Altagracia de Orituco Venezuela
44 E2 Altai Mountains mt. ra. Asia
119 D6 Altamaha r. U.S.A.
142 B1 Altamira Brazil
146 E4 Altamira Chile
131 F3 Altamira Colombia
130 J7 Altamira Costa Rica
24 D3 Altamira, Sierra de mt. ra. Spain
93 D6 Alta, Mt mt. N.Z.
27 F5 Altamura Italy
48 C3 Altan China

131 H5 Altun Ha Belize
44 E4 Altun Shan mt. ra. China
126 B3 Alturas U.S.A.
125 D5 Altus U.S.A.
15 E1 Altynivka Ukraine
14 H2 Altyshevo Rus. Fed.
60 D1 Alucra Turkey
11 G4 Alūksne Latvia
61 D3 Al 'Ulā Saudi Arabia
80 E2 Al'ulah reg. Yemen
120 B4 Alum Creek Lake l. U.S.A.
13 E6 Alupka Ukraine
72 C1 Al 'Uqaylah Libya
57 B4 Al 'Uqayr Saudi Arabia
73 G2 Al Urayq desert Saudi Arabia
43 C6 Alur Setar Malaysia
13 E6 Alushta Ukraine
61 D5 Al Uthaylī Saudi Arabia
57 B4 Al 'Uthmānīyah Saudi Arabia
72 D3 Al 'Uwaynāt Libya
72 B2 Al 'Uwaynāt Libya
73 G2 Al 'Uwaynidhīyah i. Saudi Arabia
73 H1 Al 'Uwayqīlah Saudi Arabia
73 H2 Al 'Uyūn Saudi Arabia
73 G3 Al 'Uyūn Saudi Arabia
24 A2 Alva r. Portugal
125 D4 Alva U.S.A.
131 G5 Alvarado Mexico
139 E4 Alvarães Brazil
11 C3 Ålvdal Norway
11 D3 Älvdalen Sweden
24 B3 Alverca do Ribatejo Portugal
11 D4 Alvesta Sweden
11 B3 Ålvik Norway
126 C6 Alvin U.S.A.
145 □5 Alvinópolis Brazil
11 D4 Alvsborg, Lv. Sweden
10 F2 Älvsbyn Sweden
73 G2 Al Wajh Saudi Arabia
57 B4 Al Wakrah Qatar
60 C3 Al Wannān Saudi Arabia
73 J2 Al Waqbā' well Saudi Arabia
54 D4 Alwar India
56 B4 Alwaye India
60 E4 Al Widyān desert Iraq/Saudi Arabia
72 D3 Al Wigh Libya
73 H2 Al Wusayl well Saudi Arabia
48 B3 Alxa Youqi China
48 C3 Alxa Zuoqi China
98 D2 Alyangula Aust.
11 G5 Alytus Lithuania
126 F2 Alzada U.S.A.
18 D4 Alzey Germany
138 C4 Amacayacu, Parque Nacional nat. park Colombia
40 A4 Amada Gaza C.A.R.
101 E4 Amadeus, Lake salt flat Aust.
80 B5 Amaḍīn well Saudi Arabia
109 M3 Amadjuak Lake l. Can.
24 B3 Amadora Portugal
46 C7 Amagi Japan
139 F2 Amaila Falls waterfall Guyana
46 C7 Amakusa-Kami-shima i. Japan
46 B7 Amakusa-nada b. Japan
46 C7 Amakusa-Shimo-shima i. Japan
11 D4 Åmål Sweden
56 C2 Amalapuram India
29 C6 Amaliada Greece
27 F5 Amalfi Italy
136 C2 Amalfi Colombia
54 C5 Amalner India
114 C5 Amamapare Indon.
144 A5 Amambaí r. Brazil
144 A5 Amambaí Brazil
45 N6 Amami-guntō is Japan
45 N6 Amami-Ōshima i. Japan
78 E4 Amanab Zaire
124 D2 Amanã, Lago l. Brazil
24 A5 Amanave American Samoa
65 U2 Amangel'dy Aktyuibinsk Kazak.
64 D2 Amangel'dy Turgay Kazak.
65 E4 Amankol Chile
27 F6 Amantea Italy
9 □10 Amanu i. Fr. Poly. Pac. Oc.
82 D2 Amanzimtoti R.S.A.
139 G3 Amapá div. Brazil
139 G3 Amapá Brazil
74 C3 Amara r. Morocco
54 D5 Amaravati India
139 G3 Amargosa r. Brazil
128 D3 Amargosa Desert desert U.S.A.
128 D3 Amargosa Range mts U.S.A.
128 C3 Amargosa Valley U.S.A.
125 C5 Amarillo U.S.A.
54 C5 Amarkantak India
74 B3 Amasine Western Sahara
60 C1 Amasra Turkey
60 D1 Amasya Turkey
131 G6 Amatán Mexico
138 C4 Amatitlán de Cañas Mexico
130 D4 Amatitlán de Cañas Mexico
139 E3 Amazon r. S. America
142 A1 Amazonas div. Brazil
142 A1 Amazonia, Parque Nacional nat. park Brazil
139 F2 Amazon, Mouths of the river mouth Brazil
140 D2 Amazon, Source of the river source Peru
54 C2 Amb Pakistan
80 C2 Āmba Ālagē mt. Ethiopia
80 C2 Āmba Farit mt. Ethiopia
39 J7 Ambai i. Indon.
43 A6 Ambalangoda Sri Lanka
54 D4 Ambala India
83 H1 Ambalakida Madagascar
83 H1 Ambalamanasy II Madagascar
83 H3 Ambalavao Madagascar
40 A4 Ambam Cameroon
83 H1 Ambanja Madagascar
55 H4 Ambarnath India
83 H2 Ambarovavo Madagascar
65 R3 Ambarchik Rus. Fed.
56 B4 Ambasamudram India
83 H1 Ambato Ecuador
41 E5 Ambato Finandrahana Madagascar
83 H2 Ambatolampy Madagascar
83 H2 Ambatomainty Madagascar
83 H2 Ambatondrazaka Madagascar

20 E4 Ambazac France
18 E4 Amberg Germany
133 E2 Ambergris Cays is Turks and Caicos Is Caribbean
21 G4 Ambérieu-en-Bugey France
114 C4 Amberley Can.
93 D5 Amberley N.Z.
21 F4 Ambert France
76 B4 Ambidédi Mali
83 H3 Ambila Madagascar
83 H1 Ambilobe Madagascar
83 H2 Ambininony Madagascar
110 C3 Ambition, Mt mt. Can.
73 G2 Al Urayq desert Saudi Arabia
43 C6 Alur Setar Malaysia
83 H2 Ambilobe Madagascar
72 C2 Al 'Uqaylah Libya
83 H1 Ambohitra mt. Madagascar
83 H2 Ambohitralanana Madagascar
20 E3 Amboise France
39 J7 Ambon i. Indon.
39 J7 Ambon Indon.
83 H3 Amboromptsy Madagascar
81 C5 Amboseli National Park nat. park Kenya
83 H2 Ambositra Madagascar
83 H3 Ambovombe Madagascar
129 E4 Amboy U.S.A.
122 C5 Amboy U.S.A.
121 F3 Amboy Center U.S.A.
81 □1 Ambre, Isle d' i. Mauritius
79 B5 Ambriz Angola
21 H4 Ambrym i. Vanuatu
40 C3 Ambunten Indon.
84 □ Am-Dam Chad
27 D5 Amdermo Rus. Fed.
77 D3 Amdilis well Mali
72 C5 Am-Djarass Chad
55 G2 Amdo China
130 D4 Ameca Mexico
131 F5 Amecameca Mexico
46 C7 Amedi well Mali
120 E6 Amelia Court House U.S.A.
27 E6 Amendolara Italy
144 E1 Amenia U.S.A.
126 D2 American Falls U.S.A.
126 D2 American Falls Res. resr U.S.A.
129 G1 American Fork U.S.A.
24 A5 American Samoa terr. Pac. Oc.
13 F6 Amersfoort Netherlands
18 B2 Amersfoort Netherlands
111 J1 Amery Can.
152 D5 Amery Ice Shelf ice feature Ant.
124 E3 Ames U.S.A.
121 J2 Amesbury U.S.A.
29 C5 Amfilochia Greece
29 D4 Amfissa Greece
63 P3 Amga Rus. Fed.
75 E2 Amguid Algeria
65 P4 Amgun' r. Rus. Fed.
113 H4 Amherst Can.
121 G3 Amherst U.S.A.
120 D6 Amherst U.S.A.
114 E5 Amherstburg Can.
100 D3 Amherst, Mt h. Aust.
31 N. Korea
138 C5 Amico r. Peru
61 C1 Amik Ovası marsh Turkey
20 F3 Amiens France
57 D4 Amindivi Islands is India
60 C3 Amino Japan
80 C3 Amino Ethiopia
123 E5 Amir Chah Pakistan
54 E3 Amla India
54 D5 Amla Madhya Pradesh India
56 B3 Amli Norway
142 C2 Amlwch U.K.
80 C2 'Amm Adam Sudan
60 C3 'Ammān Jordan
10 G2 Ämmänsaari Finland
10 H2 Ämmänsaari Finland
125 C5 Amarillo U.S.A.
18 E5 Ammersee l. Germany
82 D2 Ammaroo Aust.
61 D2 Amioûn Lebanon
24 A4 Amora Portugal
50 C4 Amoy r. China
141 J3 Amontada Brazil

152 C5 Amundsen, Mt mt. Ant.
152 A2 Amundsen-Scott U.S.A. Base Ant.
83 H1 Andranopasy Madagascar
83 H1 An Nabk Saudi Arabia
60 D3 An Nabk Syria
74 B3 An Nafūd desert Saudi Arabia
104 A4 Andreanof Is U.S.A.
139 F3 Annai Guyana
47 G5 Annaka Japan
120 E5 Annam reg. Vietnam
17 F4 Annan U.K.
17 F4 Annan r. U.K.
14 E2 Annapolis Royal Can.
113 G5 Annapolis U.S.A.
14 F3 Annapurna mt. Nepal
123 E5 Ann Arbor U.S.A.
60 D3 An Nāşirīyah Iraq
100 D3 Annean, L. salt flat Aust.
21 G4 Annecy France
14 A2 Annemasse France
110 C4 Annette Island i. U.S.A.
50 B3 Anning China
119 C5 Anniston U.S.A.
148 K6 Annobón i. Equatorial Guinea
21 G4 Annonay France
133 □3 Annotto Bay Jamaica
57 B4 An Nu'ayrīyah Saudi Arabia
78 B4 Anzi Zaire
27 D5 Anzio Italy
90 □2 Aoba i. Vanuatu
47 H5 Aoga-shima i. Japan
43 B5 Ao Ban Don b. Thailand
49 F4 Aohan Qi China
46 H3 Aomori Japan
46 H3 Aomori Japan
91 □11 Aorai Mt. Fr. Poly. Pac. Oc.
93 C6 Aoraki mts N.Z.
92 D4 Aorere r. N.Z.
43 B5 Ao Sawi b. Thailand
26 A3 Aosta Italy
77 E4 Aoukâr reg. Mauritania
83 H2 Anosibe An'Ala Madagascar
78 A3 Aozou Chad
72 C3 Apa r. Brazil

83 G3 Andranovondrona Madagascar
83 H1 An Nabk Saudi Arabia
60 F4 An Najaf div. Iraq
40 C2 Amursk Rus. Fed.
60 F4 An Najaf Iraq
49 J3 Amurzet Rus. Fed.
47 G5 Annaka Japan
29 C5 Amvrosiyivka Ukraine
42 D3 Annam reg. Vietnam
29 C4 Amyntaio Greece
61 C5 An Na'mil well Saudi Arabia
114 C2 Amyot Can.
72 D5 Am-Zoer Chad
73 H2 An Myanmar
29 A4 Ana r. Myanmar
60 F3 Anā Iraq
29 C4 Ana r. Myanmar
61 D5 Anaa i. Fr. Poly. Pac. Oc.
144 A2 Anaba r. Rus. Fed.
63 K2 Anabarskiy Zaliv b. Rus. Fed.
128 C4 Anacapa Is is U.S.A.
139 E2 Anaco Venezuela
126 D2 Anaconda U.S.A.
126 B1 Anacortes U.S.A.
125 D5 Anadarko U.S.A.
60 D1 Anadolu Dağları mt. ra. Turkey
63 T3 Anadyr' Rus. Fed.
63 T3 Anadyr' r. Rus. Fed.
108 A3 Anadyrskiy Zaliv b. Rus. Fed.
29 E6 Anafi i. Greece
25 □ Anaga, Pta de pt Canary Is Spain
24 H3 Anah Iraq
128 D5 Anaheim U.S.A.
110 D4 Anahim Lake Can.
125 D7 Anahuac Mexico
57 B4 Anai Mudi Pk mt. India
142 B1 Anajás Brazil
142 B1 Anajás, Ilha i. Brazil
145 H4 Anajé Brazil
56 C2 Anakapalle India
83 H1 Analalava Madagascar
83 H3 Analavelona mts Madagascar
77 F5 Anambra div. Nigeria
77 F5 Anamosa U.S.A.
60 C2 Anamur Br. pt Turkey
46 C7 Anan Japan
54 C5 Anand India
25 G1 Aneto mt. Spain
80 D2 Anadolu Dağları mt. ra. Turkey
83 H3 Anantapur India
54 D2 Anantnag India
13 D6 Anan'yiv Ukraine
55 F5 Anantapur India
55 F4 Anantnag India
144 D3 Anápolis Brazil
57 D3 Anār Iran
57 D2 Anārak Iran
57 E2 Anār Darreh Afghanistan
41 B5 Anbu China
31 N. Korea
120 D4 Ancares, Serra do mt. ra. Spain
146 C2 Ancasti, Sa mt. ra. Arg.
140 D3 Ancón Peru
20 F3 Ancenis France
77 F4 Anchau Nigeria
40 Ang Mo Kio Singapore
140 C3 Anchovy Jamaica
108 D3 Anchorage U.S.A.
146 C3 Anchorstock Pt pt Tristan da Cunha Atlantic Ocean
146 E2 Ancón Peru
80 C3 Ancora Italy
81 C7 Ancuabe Mozambique
146 B6 Ancud Chile
146 B6 Ancud, G. de g. Chile
54 D2 Andado Aust.
140 C5 Andahuaylas Peru
146 C2 Andalgalá Arg.
11 C4 Åndalsnes Norway
24 D4 Andalucía div. Spain
119 C6 Andalusia U.S.A.
55 H6 Andaman and Nicobar Islands div. India
43 A5 Andaman Basin Indian Ocean
43 A5 Andaman Islands is Andaman and Nicobar Islands
41 A5 Andaman Sea sea Asia
83 H2 Andapa Madagascar
57 E1 Andarāb Afghanistan
14 H3 Andenne Belgium
11 Andenes Norway
18 B4 Andernach Germany
144 A6 Anderson r. Can.
122 C5 Anderson U.S.A.
119 D5 Anderson U.S.A.
126 B3 Anderson U.S.A.
83 H2 Andevoranto Madagascar
93 □ Andes, Cord. de los Andes S. America
141 E2 Andfjorden chan. Norway
54 B2 Andhra Pradesh div. India
83 H2 Andilanatoby Madagascar
83 H2 Andilamena Madagascar
57 G2 Andizhan Uzbekistan
83 H1 Andkhui r. Afghanistan
57 F1 Andkhvoy Afghanistan
80 C3 Andoas Peru
83 H2 Andoany Madagascar
46 D6 Andong S. Korea
49 J5 Andong China
25 H1 Andorra country Europe
25 H1 Andorra la Vella Andorra
17 F6 Andover U.K.
121 H3 Andover U.S.A.
10 E2 Andøya i. Norway
144 D3 Andradina Brazil
14 D3 Andreapol' Rus. Fed.
104 A4 Andreanof Is U.S.A.
145 H1 André Fernandes Brazil
145 G4 Andrelândia Brazil
145 F3 Andreiçé Brazil
125 C5 Andrews U.S.A.
119 D5 Andrews U.S.A.
65 M2 Andreyevka Kazak.
15 E1 Andriyika Ukraine
15 G2 Andriyivka Kharkiv Ukraine
15 E2 Andriyivka Zaporizhzhya Ukraine
83 H2 Androka Madagascar
83 H2 Androna reg. Madagascar
29 E6 Andros i. Greece
128 D5 Andros i. The Bahamas
121 H2 Androscoggin r. U.S.A.
132 C1 Andros Town The Bahamas
56 A4 Āndrott i. India
15 D1 Andrushivka Ukraine
15 C2 Andrushky Ukraine
18 C4 Andrychów Poland
148 K6 Anóbon i. Equatorial Guinea
10 E1 Andselv Norway
21 G4 Annecy France
24 D4 Andújar Spain
79 C6 Andulo Angola
82 □2 Anéchaq well Mali
80 □ Anéfis Mali

83 H1 Antsiraňana div. Madagascar
83 H1 Antsiraňana Madagascar
83 H1 Antsalova Madagascar
80 D1 Antsis Sweden
11 G3 Anttola Finland
49 J4 Antu China
146 B4 Antuco Chile
141 D2 Antuerpo Brazil
80 D1 Antufush i. i. Yemen
121 F2 Antwerp U.S.A.
18 B3 Antwerpen div. Belgium
18 B3 Antwerpen Belgium
91 □10 Anuanu Raro i. Fr. Poly. Pac. Oc.
112 E2 Anuc, Lac l. Can.
55 F5 Anugul India
54 C2 Anupgarh India
56 C4 Anuradhapura Sri Lanka
57 C4 Anveh Iran
152 B2 Anvers I. i. Ant.
51 G3 Anxi China
44 E3 Anxi China
50 D2 An Xian China
50 E3 Anxiang China
49 E5 Anxin China
76 B3 Anxious Bay b. Aust.
76 D5 Anyama Côte d'Ivoire
48 E5 Anyang China
40 A3 Anyar Indon.
29 E6 Anydro i. Greece
50 B1 A'nyêmaqên Shan mt. ra. China
51 F2 Anyi China
51 F3 Anyuan Jiangxi China
50 E3 Anyuan Jiangxi China
50 D2 Anyue China
63 S3 Anyuysk Rus. Fed.
138 B2 Anzá Colombia
48 E5 Anze China
43 H5 Anzhero-Sudzhensk Rus. Fed.
27 D5 Anzio Italy
90 □2 Aoba i. Vanuatu
43 B5 Ao Ban Don b. Thailand
46 H3 Aomori Japan
91 □11 Aorai Mt. Fr. Poly. Pac. Oc.
93 C6 Aoraki mts N.Z.
92 D4 Aorere r. N.Z.
43 B5 Ao Sawi b. Thailand
26 A3 Aosta Italy
77 E4 Aoukâr reg. Mauritania
75 E3 Aoukâr f. Mali
74 C2 Aoulime, Jbel mt. Morocco
46 E6 Aoya Japan
78 C3 Aozou Chad
129 H6 Apache Creek U.S.A.
129 G5 Apache Junction U.S.A.
129 H5 Apache Peak summit U.S.A.
28 D1 Apahida Romania
144 B5 Apaiaí r. Brazil
119 C6 Apalachee B. b. U.S.A.
131 F5 Apán Mexico
119 C6 Apalachicola U.S.A.
119 C6 Apalachicola r. U.S.A.
141 D2 Apaporis r. Colombia
138 C4 Aparados da Tabuado Brazil
93 B6 Aparima r. N.Z.
40 D2 Apari, Tk b. Indon.
41 B3 Aparri Phil.
14 J1 Apatity Rus. Fed.
139 G2 Apatou French Guiana
130 D4 Apatzingán Mexico
18 C2 Apeldoorn Netherlands
11 B4 Apen Norway
78 A3 Apere r. Bolivia
140 D2 Apía Western Samoa
142 C3 Apiacá Brazil
142 C2 Apiaú r. Brazil
146 C2 Apinó Arg.
109 Solomon Is.
74 C3 Apiro Italy
131 G6 Apízaco Mexico
77 E4 Aplao Peru
142 B1 Apodi Brazil
142 B2 Apodi r. Brazil
139 G4 Apoera Surinam
140 B4 Apolo Bolivia
140 D2 Apolobamba mt. ra. Bolivia
152 B2 Antarctic Peninsula pen. Ant.
119 D6 Apopka, L. l. U.S.A.
144 A1 Aporé r. Brazil
144 D1 Aporé Brazil
77 E5 Aposto U.S.A.
122 B2 Apostle Islands National Lakeshore rest. U.S.A.
127 E6 Anthony U.S.A.
161 E2 Apóstolos Brazil
132 A1 Apóstolos Andreas, C. hd Cyprus
139 G2 Aporé Guyana
14 C2 Apoteri Guyana
120 C6 Apoteri Guyana
133 □ Appalachian Mountains mt. ra. U.S.A.
29 E5 Antiparos i. Greece
113 G2 Antikythira i. Greece
27 D4 Appennino Napoletano mt. ra. Italy
20 E3 Appennino Abruzzese mt. ra. Italy
21 J3 Appennino Lucanese mt. ra. Italy
26 D4 Appennino Tosco-Emiliano mts Italy
29 C5 Appennino Umbro-Marchigiano mt. ra. Italy
17 F4 Appleby-in-Westmorland U.K.
28 D4 Apia r. N.Z.
11 E4 Appleton U.S.A.
128 C4 Apple Valley U.S.A.
139 G2 Appomattox r. French Guiana
41 □2 Apra Harb. inlet Guam
115 G4 Apsley Can.
95 □1 Apsley Str. chan. Aust.
14 B2 Apshur Str. Rus. Fed.
14 C2 Apua Point U.S.A.
41 □2 Apra Heights Guam Pac. Oc.
41 A4 Apucarana Brazil
40 A3 Apucarana, Serra da mt. ra. Brazil
41 A4 Apurímac r. Peru
130 K7 Antón Panama
42 B1 Antônio r. Brazil
147 21 G1 Anton Aust.
144 D2 Antônio Carlos Brazil
145 H3 Antônio Dias Brazil
127 D5 Antón Lizardo, Pta pt Mexico
61 C2 'Aqaba, Gulf of chan. Africa/Asia
61 C5 'Aqaba, W. el w Egypt
61 D5 'Aqabah, Birkat al well Iraq
61 C4 'Aqarah Iran
127 27 C2 Antrodoco Italy
55 G1 Aqqikkol Hu salt l. China
56 H2 Antsalova Madagascar
58 G3 'Aqran h. Saudi Arabia
132 D4 Antiquilla, Vol. vol Arg.
41 □1 Apra Harb. inlet Guam
43 □ Aquarius Mts mts U.S.A.
129 G3 Aquarius Plateau plat. U.S.A.

27 F5 **Aquaviva delle Fonti** Italy
141 E4 **Aquidabán mi r.** Paraguay
141 E3 **Aquidauana r.** Brazil
143 A5 **Aquidauana** Brazil
130 E5 **Aquila** Mexico
142 E1 **Aquiraz** Brazil
131 F4 **Aquismón** Mexico
20 D4 **Aquitaine div.** France
55 F4 **Ara** India
25 G1 **Ara r.** Spain
80 D3 **Āra Ārba** Ethiopia
57 F3 **Arab** Afghanistan
119 C5 **Arab** U.S.A.
57 D2 **'Arabābād** Iran
80 D3 **Ara Bacalle well** Ethiopia
139 E3 **Arabelo** Venezuela
149 J3 **Arabian Basin** Indian Ocean
149 J2 **Arabian Sea sea** Indian Ocean
139 E2 **Arabopó** Venezuela
60 C1 **Araç** Turkey
139 E3 **Araça r.** Brazil
142 E3 **Aracaju** Brazil
141 E4 **Aracanguy, Mtes de h.** Paraguay
132 D5 **Aracataca** Colombia
142 E1 **Aracati** Brazil
142 D3 **Aracatu** Brazil
144 C4 **Araçatuba** Brazil
24 C4 **Aracena** Spain
147 B7 **Aracena, I. i.** Chile
24 C4 **Aracena, Sierrra de h.** Spain
29 C5 **Arachthos, Techniti Limni resr** Greece
28 C3 **Aračinovo** Macedonia
145 H3 **Aracruz** Brazil
145 G2 **Araçuaí r.** Brazil
145 G2 **Araçuaí** Brazil
61 C4 **'Arad** Israel
28 C1 **Arad** Romania
72 D5 **Arada** Chad
39 K8 **Arafura Sea sea** Aust./Indonesia
144 B1 **Aragarças** Brazil
60 F1 **Aragats Lerr mt.** Armenia
47 G5 **Ara-gawa r.** Japan
25 F1 **Aragón r.** Spain
25 F2 **Aragón div.** Spain
27 D7 **Aragona** Italy
25 E2 **Aragoncillo mt.** Spain
142 C2 **Araguacema** Brazil
142 C3 **Araguaçu** Brazil
139 E2 **Aragua de Barcelona** Venezuela
142 C2 **Araguaia r.** Brazil
142 B3 **Araguaia, Braço Menor do r.** Brazil
142 B3 **Araguaia, Parque Nacional de nat. park** Brazil
142 C2 **Araguaína** Brazil
144 B2 **Araguainha** Brazil
142 C2 **Araguana** Brazil
133 G5 **Araguapiche, Pta pt** Venezuela
139 G3 **Araguari r.** *Amapá* Brazil
144 D3 **Araguari r.** *Minas Gerais* Brazil
144 D3 **Araguari** Brazil
142 C2 **Araguatins** Brazil
74 C5 **Arâguîb reg.** Mali/Mauritania
13 H7 **Aragvi r.** Georgia
47 G5 **Arai** Japan
61 C4 **Araif el Naga, G. h.** Egypt
142 D1 **Araiosos** Brazil
75 E3 **Arak** Algeria
57 B2 **Arāk** Iran
41 □1 **Arakabesan i.** Palau
133 G6 **Arakaka** Guyana
42 A3 **Arakan div.** Myanmar
42 A3 **Arakan Yoma mt. ra.** Myanmar
47 □2 **Arakawa** Japan
92 G3 **Arakihi h.** N.Z.
56 B3 **Arakkonam** India
64 E3 **Aral Sea salt l.** Kazak.
64 F3 **Aral'sk** Kazak.
64 D3 **Aralsor, Ozero salt l.** *Zapadno-Kazakhstan* Kazak.
64 C3 **Aralsor, Ozero l.** *Zapadno-Kazakhstan* Kazak.
64 F3 **Aralsul'fat** Kazak.
99 F4 **Aramac** Aust.
99 F4 **Aramac Cr. w** Aust.
131 F3 **Aramberri** Mexico
90 □1 **Aramia r.** P.N.G.
56 B1 **Aran r.** India
146 C3 **Arancibia** Arg.
24 E2 **Aranda de Duero** Spain
28 C2 **Aranđelovac** Yugo.
17 F5 **Aran Fawddwy h.** U.K.
56 B3 **Arani** India
17 C4 **Aran Island i.** Rep. of Ire.
17 C5 **Aran Islands is** Rep. of Ire.
24 E2 **Aranjuez** Spain
82 B3 **Aranos** Namibia
125 D7 **Aransas Pass** U.S.A.
144 C3 **Arantes r.** Brazil
46 C7 **Arao** Japan
76 D3 **Araouane** Mali
124 D3 **Arapahoe** U.S.A.
93 E4 **Arapawa Island i.** N.Z.
146 E3 **Arapey Grande r.** Uruguay
142 E2 **Arapiraca** Brazil
60 D2 **Arapkir** Turkey
144 C5 **Arapongas** Brazil
144 D6 **Arapoti** Brazil
55 F4 **A Rapti Doon r.** Nepal
144 B4 **Arapuá** Brazil
92 E3 **Arapuni** N.Z.
143 C6 **Araquari** Brazil
60 E4 **'Ar'ar** Saudi Arabia
138 C4 **Araracuara** Colombia
143 C6 **Araranguá** Brazil
144 D6 **Ararapira** Brazil
144 D4 **Araraquara** Brazil
142 B2 **Araras** *Pará* Brazil
144 E5 **Araras** *São Paulo* Brazil
60 F2 **Ararat** Armenia
97 E4 **Ararat** Aust.
142 D1 **Arari** Brazil
55 F4 **Araria** India
142 C1 **Arari, Lago l.** Brazil
142 D2 **Araripina** Brazil
145 G5 **Araruama** Brazil
145 G5 **Araruama, Lago de lag.** Brazil
143 D5 **Araruama, L. de lag.** Brazil
60 E4 **'Ar'ar, Wādī w** Iraq/Saudi Arabia
60 E2 **Aras r.** Turkey
48 C2 **Ar Asgat** Mongolia
132 □1 **Arasji** *Aruba* Caribbean
145 J1 **Arataca** Brazil
142 B1 **Arataú r.** Brazil
138 C2 **Arauca** Colombia
138 D2 **Arauca r.** Venezuela
144 D6 **Araucária** Brazil
146 B4 **Arauco** Chile
146 B4 **Arauco, Golfo de b.** Chile
138 C2 **Arauquita** Colombia
133 E5 **Araure** Venezuela
11 G4 **Aravete** Estonia
21 H4 **Aravis mts** France
90 □1 **Arawa** P.N.G.
92 F3 **Arawhana mt.** N.Z.
145 E3 **Araxá** *Minas Gerais* Brazil
143 C4 **Araxá** *Minas Gerais* Brazil
139 E1 **Araya, Pen. de pen.** Venezuela
133 F5 **Araya, Pta de pt** Venezuela
60 F2 **Araz r.** Azerbaijan/Iran
47 □2 **Ara-zaki c.** Japan
49 F2 **Arbagar** Rus. Fed.
80 C3 **Ārba Minch** Ethiopia
60 F3 **Arbat** Iraq
12 J3 **Arbazh** Rus. Fed.
14 G3 **Arbekovo** Rus. Fed.
60 F2 **Arbīl div.** Iraq
60 F2 **Arbīl** Iraq
11 D4 **Arboga** Sweden
21 G3 **Arbois** France
111 J4 **Arborfield** Can.
16 F3 **Arbroath** U.K.
128 A2 **Arbuckle** U.S.A.
15 D3 **Arbuzynka** Ukraine
20 D4 **Arcachon** France
119 D7 **Arcadia** U.S.A.
126 A3 **Arcata** U.S.A.
128 D2 **Arc Dome summit** U.S.A.
131 E5 **Arcelia** Mexico
29 G6 **Archangelos** Greece
25 F3 **Archena** Spain
99 E2 **Archer r.** Aust.
99 E2 **Archer Bend Nat. Park nat. park.** Aust.
129 H2 **Arches Nat. Park nat. park** U.S.A.
76 D3 **Arch Henda well** Mali
24 D4 **Archidona** Spain
21 G2 **Arcis-sur-Aube** France
96 C1 **Arckaringa w** Aust.
126 D3 **Arco** U.S.A.
122 C6 **Arcola** U.S.A.
145 F4 **Arcos** Brazil
25 E2 **Arcos de Jalón** Spain
24 D4 **Arcos de la Frontera** Spain
142 E2 **Arcoverde** Brazil
109 K2 **Arctic Bay** Can.
108 B2 **Arctic Ocean ocean**
108 E3 **Arctic Red r.** Can.
152 B2 **Arctowski Poland Base** Ant.
60 G2 **Ardabīl** Iran
57 B1 **Ardabīl div.** Iran
60 E1 **Ardahan** Turkey
57 C2 **Ardakān** Iran
57 B3 **Ardal** Iran
61 D3 **Arḑ al Karā' lava** Syria
11 B3 **Årdalstangen** Norway
28 F4 **Ardas r.** Greece
14 F2 **Ardatov** Rus. Fed.
14 H2 **Ardatov** Rus. Fed.
114 E4 **Ardbeg** Can.
17 D5 **Ardee** Rep. of Ire.
18 B4 **Ardenne, Plateau de l' plat.** Belgium
18 B4 **Ardennes plat.** Belgium
20 E3 **Ardentes** France
57 C2 **Ardestān** Iran
17 E4 **Ardglass** U.K.
61 D4 **Ardh es Suwwān desert** Jordan
24 C3 **Ardila r.** Portugal/Spain
29 E4 **Ardino** Bulgaria
97 F3 **Ardlethan** Aust.
125 D5 **Ardmore** U.S.A.
16 D3 **Ardnamurchan, Point of pt** U.K.
96 D3 **Ardrossan** Aust.
16 E4 **Ardrossan** U.K.
17 E4 **Ards Peninsula pen.** U.K.
28 D1 **Ardud** Romania
28 D1 **Ardusat** Romania
145 E4 **Areado** Brazil
78 E3 **Arebi** Zaire
119 □3 **Arecibo** Puerto Rico
14 D1 **Arefino** Rus. Fed.
28 E2 **Arefu** Romania
142 E1 **Areia Branca** Brazil
41 □1 **Arekalong Peninsula pen.** Palau
25 G1 **Arén** Spain
41 B4 **Arena reef** Phil.
147 B6 **Arenales, Co mt.** Chile
128 A2 **Arena, Pt pt** U.S.A.
130 C4 **Arena, Pta pt** Mexico
24 D2 **Arenas de San Pedro** Spain
11 C4 **Arendal** Norway
18 E2 **Arendsee** Germany
25 H2 **Arenys de Mar** Spain
29 D6 **Areopoli** Greece
140 B3 **Arequipa** Peru
142 B1 **Arere** Brazil
25 F2 **Ares del Maestre** Spain
24 D2 **Arévalo** Spain
26 C4 **Arezzo** Italy
60 D4 **'Arfajah well** Saudi Arabia
48 D3 **Argalant** Mongolia
29 D5 **Argalasti** Greece
24 E2 **Argana** Spain
41 B4 **Argao** Phil.
14 H3 **Argash** Rus. Fed.
48 C3 **Argatay** Mongolia
64 F1 **Argayash** Rus. Fed.
20 D5 **Argelès-Gazost** France
21 H5 **Argens r.** France
26 C3 **Argenta** Italy
20 D2 **Argentan** France
20 E4 **Argentat** France
26 A3 **Argentera, Cima dell' mt.** Italy
146 D2 **Argentina** Arg.
136 D6 **Argentina country** S. America
152 B3 **Argentina Ra. mt. ra.** Ant.
148 G8 **Argentine Basin** Atlantic Ocean
147 B7 **Argentino, Lago l.** Arg.
20 E3 **Argenton-sur-Creuse** France
28 E2 **Argeș r.** Romania
57 F3 **Arghandab r.** Afghanistan
57 F3 **Arghastan r.** Afghanistan
16 D1 **Argir** Faeroes
29 D6 **Argolikos Kolpos b.** Greece
40 C3 **Argopuro, G. vol** Indon.
90 □7 **Argo Reefs reef** Fiji
29 D6 **Argos** Greece
29 C4 **Argos Orestiko** Greece
29 C5 **Argostoli** Greece
25 F1 **Arguís** Spain
49 G2 **Argun' r.** China/Rus. Fed.
13 H7 **Argun r.** Georgia/Rus.Fed.
13 H7 **Argun** Rus. Fed.
77 E4 **Argungu** Nigeria
49 F2 **Argunsk** Rus. Fed.
49 F2 **Argunskiy Khr. mt. ra.** Rus. Fed.
152 C4 **Argus Dome ice feature** Ant.
128 D4 **Argus Range mts** U.S.A.
48 B3 **Arguut** Mongolia
122 C4 **Argyle** U.S.A.
100 E3 **Argyle, Lake l.** Aust.
80 E1 **Arḩab reg.** Yemen
48 B3 **Arhangay div.** Mongolia
49 G4 **Ar Horqin Qi** China
11 C4 **Århus** Denmark
92 E3 **Aria** N.Z.
46 C7 **Ariake- b.** Japan
82 B4 **Ariamsvlei** Namibia
27 E5 **Ariano Irpino** Italy
138 C3 **Ariari r.** Colombia
146 D3 **Arias** Arg.
53 D10 **Ari Atoll atoll** Maldives
142 A1 **Ariaú** Brazil
76 D4 **Aribinda** Burkina
140 B3 **Arica** Chile
138 B4 **Arica** Peru
46 E6 **Arida** Japan
101 C7 **Arid, C. c.** Aust.
81 □1 **Aride I. i.** Seychelles
20 E5 **Ariège r.** France
48 B2 **Arigiyn Gol r.** Mongolia
126 G4 **Arikaree r.** U.S.A.
28 C3 **Arilje** Yugo.
133 □3 **Arima** Trin. and Tobago
139 F2 **Arimu Mine** Guyana
141 E2 **Arinos r.** Brazil
145 E1 **Arinos** Brazil
131 E5 **Ario de Rosáles** Mexico
133 □3 **Aripo, Mt h.** Trin. and Tobago
139 E5 **Aripuanã r.** Brazil
141 D1 **Aripuanã** Brazil
141 D1 **Ariquemes** Brazil
144 B2 **Ariranhá r.** Brazil
16 E3 **Arisaig** U.K.
61 B4 **'Arîsh, W. el w** Egypt
133 E5 **Arismendi** Venezuela
131 G6 **Arista, Pto** Mexico
110 D4 **Aristazabal I. i.** Can.
147 C6 **Aristizábal, C. pt** Arg.
129 G4 **Arizona div.** U.S.A.
130 C2 **Arizpe** Mexico
40 C3 **Arjasa** Indon.
10 E2 **Arjeplog** Sweden
138 B1 **Arjona** Colombia
24 D4 **Arjona** Spain
40 C3 **Arjuna, G. vol** Indon.
14 F4 **Arkadak** Rus. Fed.
125 E5 **Arkadelphia** U.S.A.
16 E3 **Arkaig, Loch l.** U.K.
65 G2 **Arkalyk** Kazak.
125 F5 **Arkansas r.** U.S.A.
125 E5 **Arkansas div.** U.S.A.
125 D4 **Arkansas City** U.S.A.
55 G1 **Arkatag Shan mt. ra.** China
72 D3 **Arkenu, Jabal mt.** Libya
12 F2 **Arkhangel'sk div.** Rus. Fed.
12 G1 **Arkhangel'sk** Rus. Fed.
14 C3 **Arkhangel'skoye** Rus. Fed.
15 E3 **Arkhanhel's'ke** Ukraine
49 J2 **Arkhara** Rus. Fed.
49 J2 **Arkhara r.** Rus. Fed.
14 E1 **Arkhipovka** Rus. Fed.
17 D5 **Arklow** Rep. of Ire.
29 F6 **Arkoi i.** Greece
18 F1 **Arkona, Kap hd** Germany
62 J1 **Arkticheskogo Instituta, Ostrova is** Rus. Fed.
121 F3 **Arkville** U.S.A.
21 F4 **Arlanc** France
21 G5 **Arles** France
77 E4 **Arli** Burkina
126 B2 **Arlington** U.S.A.
124 D2 **Arlington** U.S.A.
120 E5 **Arlington** U.S.A.
122 D4 **Arlington Heights** U.S.A.
77 F3 **Arlit** Niger
18 B4 **Arlon** Belgium
21 H4 **Arly r.** France
41 C5 **Armadores i.** Indon.
17 D4 **Armagh** U.K.
63 R4 **Arman'** Rus. Fed.
21 G3 **Armançon r.** France
73 F2 **Armant** Egypt
29 F7 **Armathia i.** Greece
13 G6 **Armavir** Rus. Fed.
32 F5 **Armenia country** Asia
138 B3 **Armenia** Colombia
138 C3 **Armero** Colombia
97 G2 **Armidale** Aust.
111 L2 **Armit Lake l.** Can.
65 G1 **Armizonskoye** Rus. Fed.
54 E5 **Armori** India
110 B3 **Armour, Mt mt.** Can./U.S.A.
98 B3 **Armstrong r.** Aust.
110 F4 **Armstrong** Can.
114 A1 **Armstrong** Can.
56 B2 **Armur** India
29 G4 **Armutlu** Turkey
15 E3 **Armyans'k** Ukraine
20 E3 **Arnage** France
29 D4 **Arnaia** Greece
61 B2 **Arnaoutis, C. hd** Cyprus
10 L2 **Arnarfjörður b.** Iceland
113 F1 **Arnaud r.** Can.
54 B2 **Arnawai** Pakistan
21 G3 **Arnay-le-Duc** France
25 E1 **Arnedo** Spain
11 C3 **Årnes** Norway
125 D4 **Arnett** U.S.A.
18 B3 **Arnhem** Netherlands
98 D2 **Arnhem Bay b.** Aust.
98 D2 **Arnhem, C. c.** Aust.
98 C2 **Arnhem Land reg.** Aust.
98 C2 **Arnhem Land Abor. Land res.** Aust.
29 C4 **Arnissa** Greece
26 C4 **Arno r.** Italy
96 D3 **Arno Bay** Aust.
122 D2 **Arnold** U.S.A.
115 F2 **Arnoux, Lac l.** Can.
115 G4 **Arnprior** Can.
18 D3 **Arnsberg** Germany
18 E3 **Arnstadt** Germany
115 F4 **Arnstein** Can.
18 F4 **Arnstorf** Germany
115 F2 **Arntfield** Can.
82 B4 **Aroab** Namibia
91 □11 **Aroa, Pte pt** *Fr. Poly.* Pac. Oc.
144 A4 **Aroeira** Brazil
114 B1 **Aroland** Can.
73 G4 **Aroma** Sudan
65 G1 **Aromashevo** Rus. Fed.
26 B3 **Arona** Italy
25 □ **Arona** *Canary Is* Spain
121 K1 **Aroostook** Can.
121 J1 **Aroostook r.** Can./U.S.A.
86 J5 **Arorae i.** Kiribati
41 B3 **Aroroy** Phil.
24 B2 **Arouca** Portugal
72 D4 **Arouelli well** Chad
60 E1 **Arpa r.** Turkey
60 E1 **Arpaçay** Turkey
26 D4 **Arquata del Tronto** Italy
24 E3 **Arquillos** Spain
54 A4 **Arra r.** Pakistan
98 E5 **Arrabury** Aust.
76 D5 **Arrah** Côte d'Ivoire
142 B3 **Arraias r.** Brazil
142 C3 **Arraias, Sa da h.** Brazil
24 C3 **Arraiolos** Portugal
60 E3 **Ar Ramādī** Iraq
61 C5 **Ar Ramlah** Jordan
17 E4 **Arran i.** U.K.
60 D3 **Ar Raqqah** Syria
20 F1 **Arras** France
73 G3 **Ar Ra's al Abyaḑ pt** Saudi Arabia
73 G3 **Ar Ra's al Aswad pt** Saudi Arabia
25 E1 **Arrasate-Mondragoe** Spain
73 H2 **Ar-Rass** Saudi Arabia
60 D3 **Ar Rastan** Syria
20 E5 **Arrats r.** France
73 H3 **Ar Rawḑah** Saudi Arabia
73 H3 **Ar Rawshan** Saudi Arabia
61 D6 **Ar Rawwafah** Saudi Arabia
57 B4 **Ar Rayyān** Qatar
138 D3 **Arrecifal** Colombia
25 □ **Arrecife** *Canary Is* Spain
146 D3 **Arrecifes** Arg.
20 B2 **Arrée, Monts d'h.** France
131 G5 **Arriaga** *Chiapas* Mexico
131 E4 **Arriaga** *San Luis Potosí* Mexico
146 D3 **Arribeños** Arg.
60 F4 **Ar Rifā'ī** Iraq
60 F4 **Ar Rihāb salt flat** Iraq
59 H5 **Ar Rimāl reg.** Saudi Arabia
101 A6 **Arrino** Aust.
129 H3 **Arriola** U.S.A.
59 G5 **Ar Riyāḑ** Saudi Arabia
146 F3 **Arroio Grande** Brazil
142 B2 **Arroios do Araguaia r.** Brazil
142 C3 **Arrojado r.** Brazil
122 B1 **Arrow Lake l.** Can.
17 C4 **Arrow, Lough l.** Rep. of Ire.
126 D3 **Arrowrock Res. resr** U.S.A.
93 C5 **Arrowsmith, Mt mt.** N.Z.
93 B6 **Arrowtown** N.Z.
119 □3 **Arroyo** Puerto Rico
24 C3 **Arroyo de la Luz** Spain
131 E4 **Arroyo, Dr** Mexico
128 B4 **Arroyo Grande** U.S.A.
146 D3 **Arroyo Seco** Arg.
131 F4 **Arroyo Seco** Mexico
73 H2 **Ar Rubay'iyah** Saudi Arabia
142 A3 **Arruda** Brazil
60 D3 **Ar Ruşāfah** Syria
60 E3 **Ar Ruţba** Iraq
73 H3 **Ar Ruwayḑah** Saudi Arabia
11 C4 **Års** Denmark
57 A1 **Ars** Iran
57 C3 **Arsenajān** Iran
14 C3 **Arsen'yevo** Rus. Fed.
56 B3 **Arsikere** India
12 J3 **Arsk** Rus. Fed.
61 C1 **Arsuz** Turkey
29 C5 **Arta** Greece
130 E5 **Arteaga** Mexico
49 K4 **Artem** Rus. Fed.
132 B2 **Artemisa** Cuba
15 G2 **Artemivka** *Kharkiv* Ukraine
15 F2 **Artemivka** *Poltava* Ukraine
13 F5 **Artemivs'k** Ukraine
20 E2 **Artenay** France
127 F5 **Artesia** U.S.A.
115 K3 **Arthabaska** Can.
114 E5 **Arthur** Can.
120 C4 **Arthur, Lake l.** U.S.A.
99 G4 **Arthur Pt pt** Aust.
93 C5 **Arthur's Pass pass** N.Z.
93 C5 **Arthur's Pass National Park nat. park** N.Z.
132 D1 **Arthur's Town** The Bahamas
64 E1 **Arti** Rus. Fed.
152 B1 **Artigas Uruguay Base** Ant.
60 E1 **Art'ik** Armenia
90 □2 **Art, Île i.** Pac. Oc.
111 H2 **Artillery Lake l.** Can.
20 F1 **Artois reg.** France
60 D1 **Artova** Turkey
25 H3 **Artrutx, Cap d' pt** Spain
48 B3 **Arts Bogd Uul mts** Mongolia
28 G2 **Artsyz** Ukraine
65 J5 **Artux** China
60 E1 **Artvin** Turkey
57 D1 **Artyk** Turkmenistan
78 F3 **Aru** Zaire
80 B4 **Arua** Uganda
144 C1 **Aruanã** Brazil
133 E4 **Aruba terr.** Caribbean
25 □ **Arucas** *Canary Is* Spain
20 D5 **Arudy** France
39 K8 **Aru, Kepulauan is** Indon.
139 E4 **Arumã** Brazil
47 □2 **Arume** Japan
49 G2 **Arun r.** China
55 F4 **Arun r.** Nepal
55 H4 **Arunachal Pradesh div.** India
49 G2 **Arun Qi** China
91 □11 **Aruó** *Fr. Poly.* Pac. Oc.
142 C1 **Arurandéua r.** Brazil
81 C5 **Arusha** Tanzania
81 C5 **Arusha div.** Tanzania
40 E1 **Arus, Tg pt** Indon.
40 B2 **Arut r.** Indon.
91 □10 **Arutua i.** *Fr. Poly.* Pac. Oc.
78 E3 **Aruwimi r.** Zaire
124 B4 **Arvada** U.S.A.
48 B3 **Arvayheer** Mongolia
54 D5 **Arvi** India
111 L2 **Arviat** Can.
113 F4 **Arvida** Can.
10 E2 **Arvidsjaur** Sweden
11 D4 **Arvika** Sweden
128 C4 **Arvin** U.S.A.
49 F3 **Arxan** China
63 O2 **Ary** Rus. Fed.
65 G2 **Arykbalyk** Kazak.
65 G4 **Arys'** Kazak.
65 G4 **Arys' r.** Kazak.
65 G3 **Arys, Oz. salt l.** Kazak.
27 B5 **Arzachena** Italy
14 F2 **Arzamas** Rus. Fed.
13 H6 **Arzgir** Rus. Fed.
26 C3 **Arzignano** Italy
24 B1 **Arzúa** Spain
18 F3 **Aš** Czech Rep.
81 C5 **Asa waterhole** Kenya
139 E2 **Asa r.** Venezuela
77 F5 **Asaba** Nigeria
57 G2 **Asadābād** Afghanistan
57 B2 **Asadābād** *Hamadan* Iran
57 D2 **Asadābād** *Khorāsān* Iran
43 B7 **Asahan r.** Indon.
47 H6 **Asahi** Japan
46 J2 **Asahi-dake vol** Japan
47 G4 **Asahi-dake mt.** Japan
46 D6 **Asahi-gawa r.** Japan
46 J2 **Asahikawa** Japan
47 G6 **Asaka** Japan
65 H4 **Asake** Uzbekistan
80 D2 **Āsalē l.** Ethiopia
76 D5 **Asamankese** Ghana
47 G5 **Asama-yama vol** Japan
76 D5 **Asankranguaa** Ghana
49 H5 **Asan Man b.** S. Korea
55 F5 **Asansol** India
49 F3 **Asar** China
91 □12 **Asau** Western Samoa
64 F1 **Asbest** Rus. Fed.
115 K4 **Asbestos** Can.
82 C4 **Asbestos Mountains mts** R.S.A.
80 D3 **Āsbe Teferi** Ethiopia
121 F4 **Asbury Park** U.S.A.
27 E5 **Ascea** Italy
82 A4 **Ascension i.** Atlantic Ocean
141 D3 **Ascensión** Bolivia
130 C2 **Ascensión** Mexico
132 □2 **Ascension** *Curaçao* Netherlands Ant.
131 J5 **Ascensión, B. de la b.** Mexico
18 D4 **Aschaffenburg** Germany
18 E3 **Aschersleben** Germany
26 D4 **Ascoli Piceno** Italy
27 E5 **Ascoli Satriano** Italy
138 B5 **Ascope** Peru
140 C4 **Ascotán, S. de mt.** Chile
80 D3 **Āsebot mt.** Ethiopia
11 D4 **Åseda** Sweden
75 E4 **Asedjrad plat.** Algeria
80 C3 **Āsela** Ethiopia
10 E2 **Åsele** Sweden
57 C3 **Asemānjerd** Iran
57 D2 **Aşfāk** Iran
73 F2 **Asfûn el Matâ'na** Egypt
64 E2 **Asha** Rus. Fed.
76 D5 **Ashanti div.** Ghana
101 B5 **Ashburton r.** Aust.
93 C5 **Ashburton r.** N.Z.
93 C5 **Ashburton** N.Z.
114 B2 **Ashburton Bay b.** Can.
65 H4 **Ashchikol', Oz. salt l.** Kazak.
110 E4 **Ashcroft** Can.
61 C4 **Ashdod** Israel
125 E5 **Ashdown** U.S.A.
119 E5 **Asheboro** U.S.A.
119 D5 **Asheville** U.S.A.
97 G2 **Ashford** Aust.
17 H6 **Ashford** U.K.
129 F4 **Ash Fork** U.S.A.
64 E5 **Ashgabat** Turkmenistan
46 J2 **Ashibetsu** Japan
47 G5 **Ashikaga** Japan
17 G4 **Ashington** U.K.
47 H3 **Ashiro** Japan
12 J3 **Ashit r.** Rus. Fed.
46 D7 **Ashizuri-misaki pt** Japan
57 C3 **Ashkazar** Iran
54 B2 **Ashkun reg.** Afghanistan
125 D4 **Ashland** U.S.A.
120 B5 **Ashland** U.S.A.
121 J1 **Ashland** U.S.A.
126 F2 **Ashland** U.S.A.
121 H3 **Ashland** U.S.A.
120 B4 **Ashland** U.S.A.
126 B3 **Ashland** U.S.A.
120 E6 **Ashland** U.S.A.
122 B2 **Ashland** U.S.A.
97 G2 **Ashley** Aust.
93 D5 **Ashley r.** N.Z.
124 D2 **Ashley** U.S.A.
100 C2 **Ashmore Reef reef** Aust.
61 A4 **Ashmûn** Egypt
54 D4 **Ashoknagar** India
46 J2 **Ashoro** Japan
129 H5 **Ash Peak** U.S.A.
61 C4 **Ashqelon** Israel
73 H4 **Ash Sha'ār** Saudi Arabia
60 E4 **Ash Shabakah** Iraq
60 E2 **Ash Shadādah** Syria
73 H3 **Ash Sha'rā'** Saudi Arabia
80 D1 **Ash Sharafah** Yemen
57 C4 **Ash Shāriqah** U.A.E.
60 E3 **Ash Sharqāţ** Iraq
60 F4 **Ash Shaţrah** Iraq
80 D2 **Ash Shaykh 'Uthman** Yemen
59 G7 **Ash Shiḩr** Yemen
60 F4 **Ash Shināfīyah** Iraq
57 D4 **Ash Şhināş** Oman
73 H2 **Ash Shu'āybah** Saudi Arabia
73 H2 **Ash Shu'bah** Saudi Arabia
73 H4 **Ash Shuqayq** Saudi Arabia
72 B2 **Ash Shuwayrif** Libya
120 C4 **Ashtabula** U.S.A.
60 F1 **Ashtarak** Armenia
54 D5 **Ashti** India
56 A2 **Ashti** India
57 B2 **Ashtiān** Iran
126 E2 **Ashton** U.S.A.
109 M4 **Ashuanipi Lake l.** Can.
119 C5 **Ashville** U.S.A.
61 D2 **'Āşī r.** Lebanon/Syria
61 D1 **Asi r.** Turkey
130 E4 **Asientos** Mexico
56 B2 **Asifabad** India
56 D2 **Āsika** India
74 C1 **Asilah** Morocco
140 B2 **Asillo** Peru
27 B5 **Asinara, Golfo dell' b.** Italy
27 B5 **Asinara, Isola i.** Italy
54 C4 **Asind** India
62 K4 **Asino** Rus. Fed.
12 D4 **Asipovichy** Belarus
73 H4 **Asīr div.** Saudi Arabia
60 E2 **Aşkale** Turkey
15 E3 **Askaniya Nova** Ukraine
11 C4 **Asker** Norway
11 D4 **Askersund** Sweden
11 C4 **Askim** Norway
64 E1 **Askino** Rus. Fed.
54 E3 **Askot** India
16 K1 **Askøy i.** Norway
16 K1 **Askvoll** Norway
61 B5 **Asl** Egypt
73 H3 **Aslam, W. w** Saudi Arabia
61 C1 **Aslanköy r.** Turkey
80 C1 **Asmara** Eritrea
11 D4 **Asnen l.** Sweden
28 E3 **Asneovgrad** Bulgaria
24 B1 **As Neves** Spain
54 C4 **Asop** India
80 B2 **Āsosa** Ethiopia
73 G3 **Asoteriba, J. mt.** Sudan
46 B6 **Asō-wan b.** Japan
19 H5 **Aspang-Markt** Austria
25 F3 **Aspe** Spain
127 F4 **Aspen** U.S.A.
61 A1 **Aspendos** Turkey
125 C5 **Aspermont** U.S.A.
93 B6 **Aspiring, Mt mt.** N.Z.
24 C1 **As Pontes de García Rodríguez** Spain
111 H4 **Asquith** Can.
61 D2 **As Sa'an** Syria
80 D2 **Assab** Eritrea
74 B5 **Assaba div.** Mauritania
73 H2 **Aš Sab'ān** Saudi Arabia
57 B4 **As Sabsab well** Saudi Arabia
60 D2 **As Safīrah** Syria
57 B4 **As Saji well** Saudi Arabia
64 E4 **Assake-Audan, Vpadina basin** Uzbekistan
60 F4 **As Salmān** Iraq
42 A1 **Assam div.** India
77 F3 **Assamakka** Niger
60 F4 **As Samāwah** Iraq
74 B4 **Assaq w** *Western Sahara*
74 B3 **As Saquia al Hamra w** *Western Sahara*
72 D2 **As Sarīr reg.** Libya
121 F5 **Assateague I. i.** U.S.A.
121 F6 **Assateague Island National Seashore res.** U.S.A.
73 G2 **Aş Şawrah** Saudi Arabia
73 G2 **Aş Şawrah** Saudi Arabia
21 H5 **Asse r.** France
27 B6 **Assemini** Italy
18 C2 **Assen** Netherlands
18 B3 **Assesse** Belgium
55 F5 **Assia Hills h.** India
72 C1 **As Sidrah** Libya
111 H5 **Assiniboia** Can.
111 K5 **Assiniboine r.** Can.
110 F4 **Assiniboine, Mt mt.** Can.
144 C5 **Assis** Brazil
144 B6 **Assis Chateaubriand** Brazil
26 D4 **Assisi** Italy
76 □ **Assomada** Cape Verde
75 E3 **Assouf Mellene w** Algeria
60 F4 **Aş Şubayḩīyah** Kuwait
73 J2 **Aş Şufayrī well** Saudi Arabia
73 H3 **As Sūg** Saudi Arabia
60 D3 **As Sukhnah** Syria
60 F3 **As Sulaymānīyah div.** Iraq
60 F3 **As Sulaymānīyah** Iraq
73 H2 **As Sulaymī** Saudi Arabia
57 B4 **Aş Şulb reg.** Saudi Arabia
72 C1 **As Sulţān** Libya
73 H3 **As Sūq** Saudi Arabia
61 D3 **As Suwaydā' div.** Syria
80 E2 **As Suwwādīyah** Yemen
29 F7 **Astakida i.** Greece
29 C5 **Astakos** Greece
60 G2 **Astara** Azerbaijan
26 B3 **Asti** Italy
128 A2 **Asti** U.S.A.
26 C3 **Astico r.** Italy
140 C2 **Astillero** Peru
57 E4 **Astola I. i.** Pakistan
115 J3 **Aston-Jonction** Can.
54 C2 **Astor** Pakistan
54 C2 **Astor r.** Pakistan
65 J5 **Astor** *Jammu and Kashmir*
144 C5 **Astorga** Brazil
24 C1 **Astorga** Spain
126 B2 **Astoria** U.S.A.
11 D4 **Åstorp** Sweden
14 H2 **Astradamovka** Rus. Fed.
13 H6 **Astrakhan'** Rus. Fed.
13 J6 **Astrakhan'** Rus. Fed.
15 F3 **Astrakhanka** Ukraine
152 D3 **Astrid Ridge** Ant.
90 □2 **Astrolabe, Récifs de l' reef** Pac. Oc.
29 D6 **Astros** Greece
24 C1 **Asturias div.** Spain
29 F6 **Astypalaia i.** Greece
91 □12 **Asuisui, C. c.** Western Samoa
140 C2 **Asunción** Bolivia
39 M3 **Asuncion i.** *Northern Mariana Is* Pac. Oc.
141 E5 **Asunción** Paraguay
80 B4 **Aswa r.** Uganda
73 F3 **Aswân** Egypt
73 F3 **Aswân Dam dam** Egypt
73 F2 **Asyût** Egypt
90 □4 **Ata i.** Tonga
146 B2 **Atacama div.** Chile
146 C2 **Atacama, Desierto de desert** Chile
150 H6 **Atafu i.** *Tokelau* Pac. Oc.
61 B5 **Atairtîr el Dahami, G. mt.** Egypt
61 C4 **Atā'ita, J. el mt.** Jordan
91 □11 **Ataiti** *Fr. Poly.* Pac. Oc.
50 B2 **Ata Kang La pass** China
77 E4 **Atakora, Chaîne de l' mt. ra.** Benin
77 E5 **Atakpamé** Togo
142 E2 **Atalaia** Brazil
138 C4 **Atalaia do Norte** Brazil
29 D5 **Atalanti** Greece
130 K8 **Atalaya** Panama
140 B2 **Atalaya** Peru
145 H3 **Ataléia** Brazil
48 E2 **Atamanovka** Rus. Fed.
47 G6 **Atami** Japan
80 E2 **'Ataq** Yemen
61 B5 **'Ataqa, G. h.** Egypt
74 B4 **Atâr** Mauritania
42 B3 **Atarano r.** Myanmar
129 H4 **Atarque** U.S.A.
128 B4 **Atascadero** U.S.A.
65 H3 **Atasu** Kazak.
90 □4 **Atata i.** Tonga
39 J8 **Atauro i.** Indon.
73 F4 **Atbara** Sudan
73 G4 **Atbara r.** Sudan
65 G2 **Atbasar** Kazak.
65 J4 **At-Bashy** Kyrgyzstan
125 F6 **Atchafalaya Bay b.** U.S.A.
124 E4 **Atchison** U.S.A.
76 D5 **Atebubu** Ghana
25 F2 **Ateca** Spain
130 D4 **Atenguillo** Mexico
27 E4 **Atessa** Italy
18 A3 **Ath** Belgium
108 G4 **Athabasca r.** Can.
110 G4 **Athabasca** Can.
111 G3 **Athabasca, Lake l.** Can.
55 F5 **Āthagarh** India
17 D5 **Athboy** Rep. of Ire.
17 C5 **Athenry** Rep. of Ire.
115 H4 **Athens** Can.
119 C5 **Athens** U.S.A.
119 D5 **Athens** U.S.A.
120 B5 **Athens** U.S.A.
119 C5 **Athens** U.S.A.
125 E5 **Athens** U.S.A.
99 F3 **Atherton** Aust.
81 C5 **Athi r.** Kenya
29 D6 **Athina** Greece
81 C5 **Athi River** Kenya
17 D5 **Athlone** Rep. of Ire.
56 A2 **Athni** India
93 B6 **Athol** N.Z.
121 G3 **Athol** U.S.A.
119 □2 **Athol I. i.** The Bahamas
16 F3 **Atholl, Forest of reg.** U.K.
29 E4 **Athos mt.** Greece
61 D5 **Ath Thāyat mt.** Saudi Arabia
17 D5 **Athy** Rep. of Ire.
72 C5 **Ati** Chad
57 D2 **Aţīābād** Iran
145 E5 **Atibaia** Brazil
140 B3 **Atico** Peru
78 E2 **Atiedo** Sudan
25 E2 **Atienza** Spain
72 B3 **Ati, Jabal mt. ra.** Libya
111 J4 **Atikameg L. l.** Can.
112 B4 **Atikokan** Can.
113 H3 **Atikonak L. l.** Can.
91 □11 **Atimaono** *Fr. Poly.* Pac. Oc.
27 D5 **Atina** Italy
56 B4 **Atirampattinam** India
87 M7 **Atiu i.** *Cook Islands* Pac. Oc.
63 R3 **Atka** Rus. Fed.
14 G4 **Atkara r.** Rus. Fed.
14 G4 **Atkarsk** Rus. Fed.
131 F5 **Atlacomulco** Mexico
119 C5 **Atlanta** U.S.A.
122 C5 **Atlanta** U.S.A.
123 E3 **Atlanta** U.S.A.
122 A6 **Atlanta** U.S.A.
60 C2 **Atlantı** Turkey
124 E3 **Atlantic** U.S.A.
121 F5 **Atlantic City** U.S.A.
149 M6 **Atlantic-Indian Antarctic Basin** Atlantic Ocean
148 K9 **Atlantic-Indian Ridge** Indian Ocean
82 B5 **Atlantis** R.S.A.
148 G3 **Atlantis Fracture** Atlantic Ocean
75 E2 **Atlas Saharien mt. ra.** Algeria
75 E1 **Atlas Tellien mt. ra.** Algeria
110 C3 **Atlin** Can.
110 C3 **Atlin Lake l.** Can.
110 C3 **Atlin Prov. Park** Can.
131 F5 **Atlixco** Mexico
56 B3 **Atmakur** India
56 B3 **Atmakur** India
14 F3 **Atmis r.** Rus. Fed.
125 G6 **Atmore** U.S.A.
46 C6 **Atō** Japan
140 C4 **Atocha** Bolivia
125 D5 **Atoka** U.S.A.
42 D3 **Atouat mt.** Laos
131 E5 **Atoyac de Alvarez** Mexico
55 G4 **Atrai r.** India
57 D1 **Atrak r.** Iran
138 B2 **Atrato r.** Colombia
57 C1 **Atrek r.** Iran/Turkmenistan
26 D4 **Atri** Italy
121 F5 **Atsion** U.S.A.
47 G6 **Atsugi** Japan
47 G4 **Atsumi** Japan
46 H2 **Atsuta** Japan
73 H3 **Aţ Ţā'if** Saudi Arabia
119 C5 **Attalla** U.S.A.
72 D3 **Aţ Ţallāb oasis** Libya
60 E3 **At Ta'mīm div.** Iraq
72 D1 **At Tamīmī** Libya
43 D4 **Attapu** Laos
29 F6 **Attavyros mt.** Greece
112 C3 **Attawapiskat r.** Can.
112 D3 **Attawapiskat** Can.
112 C3 **Attawapiskat L. l.** Can.
73 H2 **At Taysīyah plat.** Saudi Arabia
18 F5 **Attersee l.** Austria
122 D5 **Attica** U.S.A.
120 B4 **Attica** U.S.A.
29 D6 **Attiki div.** Greece
121 H3 **Attleboro** U.S.A.
54 C2 **Attock** Pakistan
73 G2 **Aţ Ţubayq reg.** Saudi Arabia
150 G2 **Attu Island i.** U.S.A.
97 G2 **Attunga** Aust.
56 B4 **Attur** India
80 D2 **At Turbah** Yemen
73 H2 **Aţ Ţuwayyah well** Saudi Arabia
146 C3 **Atuel r.** Arg.
11 D4 **Åtvidaberg** Sweden
120 C4 **Atwood Lake l.** U.S.A.
14 H2 **Atyashevo** Rus. Fed.
64 D3 **Atyrau div.** Kazak.
64 D3 **Atyrau** Kazak.
14 F2 **Atyur'yevo** Rus. Fed.
15 E1 **Atyusha** Ukraine
21 G5 **Aubagne** France
41 B2 **Aubarede Point pt** Phil.
21 G2 **Aube r.** France
21 G4 **Aubenas** France
20 E2 **Aubergenville** France
152 □ **Aubert, C. c.** *Kerguelen* Indian Ocean
20 F3 **Aubigny-sur-Nère** France
21 G2 **Auboué** France
129 F4 **Aubrey Cliffs cliff** U.S.A.
108 F3 **Aubry Lake l.** Can.
99 G5 **Auburn r.** Aust.
114 E5 **Auburn** Can.
119 C5 **Auburn** U.S.A.
128 B2 **Auburn** U.S.A.
122 E5 **Auburn** U.S.A.
121 H2 **Auburn** U.S.A.
124 E3 **Auburn** U.S.A.
120 E3 **Auburn** U.S.A.
126 B2 **Auburn** U.S.A.
99 G5 **Auburn Ra. h.** Aust.
20 F4 **Aubusson** France
146 C4 **Auca Mahuida, Sa de mt.** Arg.
140 C4 **Aucanquilcha, Co mt.** Chile
20 E5 **Auch** France
42 B1 **Auche** Myanmar
77 F5 **Auchi** Nigeria
92 E2 **Auckland** N.Z.
92 E2 **Auckland div.** N.Z.
92 □1 **Auckland I. i.** *Auckland Is* N.Z.
92 □1 **Auckland Is is** N.Z.
114 B1 **Auden** Can.
121 H2 **Audet** Can.
20 B2 **Audierne** France
152 □ **Audierne, Baie d' b.** *Kerguelen* Indian Ocean
21 H3 **Audincourt** France
80 D3 **Audo Range mt. ra.** Ethiopia
20 F1 **Audruicq** France
18 F3 **Auersberg mt.** Germany
99 F5 **Augathella** Aust.
123 F3 **Au Gres** U.S.A.
18 E4 **Augsburg** Germany
101 A7 **Augusta** Aust.
27 E7 **Augusta** Italy
119 D5 **Augusta** U.S.A.
125 D4 **Augusta** U.S.A.
121 J2 **Augusta** U.S.A.
122 B3 **Augusta** U.S.A.
27 E7 **Augusta, Golfo di b.** Italy
138 C1 **Augustin Cadazzi** Colombia
145 F3 **Augusto de Lima** Brazil
19 L2 **Augustów** Poland
100 D2 **Augustus I. i.** Aust.
101 B5 **Augustus, Mt mt.** Aust.
100 C4 **Auld, L. salt flat** Aust.
21 F1 **Aulnoye-Aymeries** France
20 E1 **Ault** France
91 □13 **Aunuu i.** *American Samoa* Pac. Oc.
113 G2 **Aupaluk** Can.
43 D7 **Aur i.** Malaysia
11 F3 **Aura** Finland
54 D4 **Auraiya** India
55 F4 **Aurangābād** India
56 A2 **Aurangābād** India
20 C3 **Auray** France
18 C2 **Aurich** Germany
144 C4 **Auriflama** Brazil
144 C2 **Aurilândia** Brazil
20 F4 **Aurillac** France
40 B2 **Aurkuning** Indon.
41 B5 **Aurora** Phil.
139 F3 **Aurora** Surinam
126 F4 **Aurora** U.S.A.
122 C5 **Aurora** U.S.A.
120 A5 **Aurora** U.S.A.
121 J2 **Aurora** U.S.A.
125 E4 **Aurora** U.S.A.
99 E2 **Aurukun** Aust.
27 D5 **Aurunci, Monti mts** Italy
82 B4 **Aus** Namibia
123 F3 **Au Sable** U.S.A.
123 E3 **Au Sable r.** U.S.A.
121 G2 **Ausable r.** U.S.A.
121 G2 **Ausable Forks** U.S.A.
122 D2 **Au Sable Pt pt** U.S.A.
123 F3 **Au Sable Pt pt** U.S.A.
16 F2 **Auskerry i.** U.K.
11 B4 **Aust-Agder div.** Norway
10 M2 **Austari-Jökulsá r.** Iceland
122 A4 **Austin** U.S.A.
128 D2 **Austin** U.S.A.
125 D6 **Austin** U.S.A.
101 B5 **Austin, L. salt flat** Aust.
98 D4 **Austral Downs** Aust.
86 C7 **Australia country**
152 □ **Australia, I. i.** *Kerguelen* Indian Ocean
152 C6 **Australian Antarctic Territory reg.** Ant.
97 G3 **Australian Capital Territory div.** Aust.
4 G4 **Austria country** Europe
10 D1 **Austvågøy i.** Norway
139 F4 **Autazes** Brazil
20 E5 **Auterive** France
20 E1 **Authie r.** France
115 F2 **Authier** Can.
130 D5 **Autlán** Mexico
10 G2 **Autti** Finland
21 G3 **Autun** France
20 F4 **Auvergne reg.** France
21 F4 **Auvergne div.** France
21 F3 **Auxerre** France
21 G3 **Auxonne** France
42 A2 **Ava** Myanmar
121 F3 **Ava** U.S.A.
144 D5 **Avaí** Brazil
21 F3 **Avallon** France
128 C5 **Avalon** U.S.A.
113 K4 **Avalon Peninsula pen.** Can.
146 E2 **Avalos r.** Arg.
60 F2 **Avān** Iran
60 C2 **Avanos** Turkey
144 D5 **Avaré** Brazil
60 F2 **Āvārsīn** Iran
13 H7 **Avarskoye Koysu r.** Rus. Fed.
128 D4 **Avawatz Mts mts** U.S.A.
57 E2 **Avaz** Iran
15 G2 **Avdiyivka** Ukraine
24 B2 **Ave r.** Portugal
142 A1 **Aveiro** Brazil
24 B2 **Aveiro** Portugal
24 B2 **Aveiro div.** Portugal
57 B2 **Āvej** Iran
146 E3 **Avellaneda** *Buenos Aires* Arg.
146 E2 **Avellaneda** *Santa Fé* Arg.
27 E5 **Avellino** Italy
128 B3 **Avenal** U.S.A.
27 E5 **Aversa** Italy
133 G4 **Aves i.** Venezuela
11 E3 **Avesta** Sweden
20 F4 **Aveyron r.** France
27 D4 **Avezzano** Italy
29 E7 **Avgo i.** *Kriti* Greece
29 D6 **Avgo i.** *Peloponnisos* Greece
146 D2 **Aviá Terai** Arg.
16 F3 **Aviemore** U.K.
27 E5 **Avigliano** Italy
21 G5 **Avignon** France
24 D2 **Ávila** Spain
24 D1 **Avilés** Spain
24 B1 **Aviño** Spain
56 C5 **Avissawella** Sri Lanka
29 D5 **Avlida** Greece
12 H2 **Avnyugskiy** Rus. Fed.
97 F5 **Avoca** Aust.
97 E4 **Avoca** Aust.
97 E4 **Avoca r.** Aust.
124 E3 **Avoca** U.S.A.
27 E7 **Avola** Italy
101 B6 **Avon r.** Aust.
17 G6 **Avon r.** U.K.
17 G6 **Avon r.** U.K.
122 B5 **Avon** U.S.A.
129 F5 **Avondale** U.S.A.
98 D3 **Avon Downs** Aust.
99 F4 **Avon Downs** Aust.
119 D7 **Avon Park** U.S.A.
20 D2 **Avranches** France
28 E2 **Avrig** Romania
20 D3 **Avrillé** France
90 □1 **Avuavu** Solomon Is.
47 □2 **Awa** Japan
61 D3 **A'waj r.** Syria
46 E6 **Awaji-shima i.** Japan
92 E3 **Awakino** N.Z.
57 B4 **Awālī** Bahrain
40 D4 **Awang** Indon.
92 D1 **Awanui** N.Z.
40 C3 **Awarawar, Tg pt** Indon.
80 D3 **Āwarē** Ethiopia
93 B6 **Awarua Pt pt** N.Z.
80 C3 **Āwasa** Ethiopia
80 D3 **Āwash** Ethiopia
47 G4 **Awa-shima i.** Japan
80 D3 **Āwash National Park nat. park** Ethiopia
80 D3 **Āwash West Wildlife Reserve res.** Ethiopia
65 K4 **Awat** China
80 C3 **Āwatā Shet' w** Ethiopia
93 D4 **Awatere r.** N.Z.
72 B2 **Awbārī** Libya
80 D2 **Awd reg.** Yemen
80 D4 **Aw Dheegle** Somalia
78 E2 **Aweil** Sudan
16 E3 **Awe, Loch l.** U.K.
72 D2 **Awjilah** Libya
77 F5 **Awka** Nigeria
74 B3 **Awlitis w** *Western Sahara*
40 E2 **Awo r.** Indon.
74 B4 **Awserd** *Western Sahara*
109 J2 **Axel Heiberg Island i.** Can.
28 E1 **Axente Sever** Romania
76 D6 **Axim** Ghana
139 F4 **Axinim** Brazil
142 D1 **Axixa** Brazil
64 E1 **Ay r.** Rus. Fed.
47 E6 **Ayabe** Japan
74 D2 **Ayachi, Jbel mt.** Morocco
146 E4 **Ayacucho** Arg.
140 B2 **Ayacucho** Peru
42 A2 **Ayadaw** Myanmar
65 J3 **Ayaguz w** Kazak.
65 K3 **Ayaguz** Kazak.
64 F4 **Ayakagytma, Vpadina depression** Uzbekistan
65 G4 **Ayakkuduk** Uzbekistan
44 E4 **Ayakkum Hu salt l.** China
76 D5 **Ayamé, Lac d' l.** Côte d'Ivoire
24 C4 **Ayamonte** Spain
63 P4 **Ayan** Rus. Fed.
60 C1 **Ayancık** Turkey
49 H5 **Ayang** N. Korea
77 F5 **Ayangba** Nigeria
138 B2 **Ayapel** Colombia
140 B2 **Ayaviri** Peru
57 G1 **Āybak** Afghanistan
64 C3 **Aybas** Kazak.
13 F5 **Aydar r.** Rus. Fed.
65 G4 **Aydarkul', Ozero l.** Uzbekistan
29 F6 **Aydın div.** Turkey
60 A2 **Aydın** Turkey
61 B1 **Aydıncık** Turkey
29 F5 **Aydın Dağları mt. ra.** Turkey
61 C1 **Aydos Dağı mt.** Turkey
80 D2 **Āyelu Terara mt.** Ethiopia
43 □ **Ayer Chawan, P. i.** Singapore
43 □ **Ayer Merbau, P. i.** Singapore
98 B5 **Ayers Rock h.** Aust.
80 C2 **Āykel** Ethiopia
64 F2 **Ayke, Oz. l.** Kazak.
63 N3 **Aykhal** Rus. Fed.
12 J2 **Aykino** Rus. Fed.
93 D5 **Aylesbury** N.Z.
17 G6 **Aylesbury** U.K.
120 E6 **Aylett** U.S.A.
24 E2 **Ayllón** Spain
114 E5 **Aylmer** Can.
115 K4 **Aylmer, Lac l.** Can.
111 H2 **Aylmer Lake l.** Can.
140 B2 **Ayna** Peru
72 C2 **'Ayn al 'Abd** Libya
57 B3 **'Ayn al 'Abd well** Saudi Arabia
61 D4 **'Ayn al Baidā'** Saudi Arabia
72 D3 **'Ayn al Ghazāl spring** Libya
65 G5 **Ayní** Tajikistan
73 H3 **'Aynīn well** Saudi Arabia
60 D2 **'Ayn 'Īsá** Syria
61 C5 **'Aynūnah** Saudi Arabia
72 D3 **'Ayn Zuwayyah spring** Libya
80 B3 **Ayod** Sudan
63 S3 **Ayon, O. i.** Rus. Fed.
77 E4 **Ayorou** Niger
74 C4 **'Ayoûn 'Abd el Mâlek well** Mauritania
74 C5 **'Ayoûn El 'Atroûs** Mauritania
99 F3 **Ayr** Aust.
17 E4 **Ayr r.** U.K.
17 E4 **Ayr** U.K.
61 B1 **Ayrancı** Turkey
17 E4 **Ayre, Point of pt** Isle of Man
28 F3 **Aytos** Bulgaria
43 C4 **Ayutthaya** Thailand
138 B4 **Ayuy** Ecuador
14 G3 **Ayva r.** Rus. Fed.
60 A2 **Ayvacık** Turkey
60 A2 **Ayvalık** Turkey
130 J6 **Azacualpa** Honduras
77 E3 **Azaguégué well** Niger
47 □2 **Azama** Japan
55 E4 **Azamgarh** India
76 D3 **Azaouâd reg.** Mali
77 E3 **Azaouagh, Vallée de w** Mali/Niger
140 C3 **Azapa r.** Chile
140 B3 **Azapa** Chile
12 H1 **Azapol'ye** Rus. Fed.
57 A1 **Āzarān** Iran
60 F2 **Āzarbāyjān-e Gharbī div.** Iran
57 A1 **Āzarbāyjān-e Sharqī div.** Iran
77 G4 **Azare** Nigeria
139 G3 **Azauri** Brazil
61 D1 **A'zāz** Syria
60 C1 **Azdavay** Turkey
74 C2 **Azemmour** Morocco
32 F5 **Azerbaijan country** Asia
80 C2 **Āzezo** Ethiopia
60 F2 **Āzghān** Iran
64 F4 **Azhar** Kazak.
65 L2 **Azhu-Tayga, G. mt.** Rus. Fed.
74 C2 **Azilal** Morocco
114 E3 **Azilda** Can.
121 H2 **Aziscohos Lake l.** U.S.A.
57 D3 **'Azīzābād** Iran
73 G2 **Aẓlam, W. w** Saudi Arabia
24 C4 **Aznalcóllar** Spain
138 B4 **Azogues** Ecuador
148 H3 **Azores - Cape St Vincent Ridge** Atlantic Ocean
13 F6 **Azov** Rus. Fed.
13 E6 **Azov, Sea of sea** Asia/Europe
25 E1 **Azpeitia** Spain
74 C2 **Azrou** Morocco
127 F4 **Aztec** U.S.A.
133 E3 **Azua** Dominican Rep.
24 D3 **Azuaga** Spain
25 F2 **Azuara** Spain
46 B7 **Azūchi-Ō-shima i.** Japan
24 E3 **Azuer r.** Spain
130 K8 **Azuero, Península de pen.** Panama
146 E4 **Azul** Arg.
147 B5 **Azul, C. mt.** Arg.
138 B5 **Azul, Cerro h.** Peru
138 □ **Azul, Co vol** *Galapagos Is* Ecuador
140 A1 **Azul, Cord. mt. ra.** Peru
47 H5 **Azuma-san vol** Japan
140 D4 **Azurduy** Bolivia
61 D3 **Az Zabadānī** Syria
73 H4 **Aẓ Ẓafīr** Saudi Arabia
57 B4 **Aẓ Ẓahrān** Saudi Arabia
72 B1 **Az Zāwīyah** Libya
80 D1 **Az Zaydīyah** Yemen
74 A4 **Azzeffâl h.** Mauritania
73 H2 **Az Zilfī** Saudi Arabia
72 B1 **Az Zintān** Libya
60 F4 **Az Zubayr** Iraq
80 D1 **Az Zuhrah** Yemen
80 D2 **Az Zuqur I. i.** Yemen

B

50 D2 **Ba r.** China
90 □8 **Ba** Fiji
90 □8 **Ba r.** Fiji
90 □2 **Baâba i.** Pac. Oc.
40 D1 **Baai r.** Indon.
61 D2 **Ba'albek** Lebanon
61 C3 **Baaqline** Lebanon
80 D4 **Baardheere** Somalia
54 D4 **Bab** India
74 B5 **Bababé** Mauritania
29 F5 **Baba Burnu pt** Turkey
142 C2 **Babaçulândia** Brazil
28 G2 **Babadag** Romania
29 G6 **Babadağ** Turkey
57 D1 **Babadurmaz** Turkmenistan
29 F4 **Babaeski** Turkey
138 B4 **Babahoyo** Ecuador
54 D5 **Babai** India
55 E3 **Babai r.** Nepal
48 C4 **Babai Gaxun** China
41 C5 **Babak** Phil.
57 C2 **Bābā Khalāl** Iran
77 G4 **Babakourimigana well** Niger
57 F2 **Bābā, Kūh-e mt. ra.** Afghanistan
80 D2 **Bāb al Mandab str.** Asia
80 D2 **Bāb al Mandab, C. c.** Yemen
40 D2 **Babana** Indon.
78 B2 **Babanki** Cameroon
61 D2 **Bābannā** Syria
50 D4 **Babao** China
39 J8 **Babar i.** Indon.
39 J8 **Babar, Kepulauan is** Indon.
81 C5 **Babati** Tanzania
12 E3 **Babayevo** Rus. Fed.
13 H7 **Babayurt** Rus. Fed.
122 B2 **Babbitt** U.S.A.
41 □1 **Babelthuap i.** Palau
54 E4 **Baberu** India
14 F2 **Babeyevo** Rus. Fed.
50 C4 **Babian r.** China
130 C2 **Babicora** Mexico
130 D2 **Babícora, L. de salt l.** Mexico
60 F3 **Bābil div.** Iraq
19 G2 **Babimost** Poland
99 F3 **Babinda** Aust.
110 D4 **Babine Lake l.** Can.
39 K7 **Babo** Indon.
62 G6 **Bābol** Iran
78 E3 **Babonde** Zaire
78 B2 **Babongo** Cameroon
129 G6 **Baboquivari Peak summit** U.S.A.
78 B2 **Baboua** C.A.R.
13 D4 **Babruysk** Belarus
49 K2 **Babstovo** Rus. Fed.
54 B4 **Babuhri** India
29 C4 **Babuna Planina mt. ra.** Macedonia
28 D3 **Babušnica** Yugo.
41 B2 **Babuyan i.** Phil.
41 A4 **Babuyan** Phil.
41 B2 **Babuyan Channel chan.** Phil.
41 B2 **Babuyan Islands is** Phil.
60 F3 **Babylon** Iraq
14 B2 **Babynino** Rus. Fed.
80 E3 **Bacaadweyn** Somalia
142 D1 **Bacabal** Brazil
142 B1 **Bacajá r.** Brazil
131 H5 **Bacalar** Mexico
39 J7 **Bacan i.** Indon.
41 B2 **Bacarra** Phil.
28 F1 **Bacău** Romania
21 H2 **Baccarat** France
97 F4 **Bacchus Marsh** Aust.
42 D2 **Băc Giang** Vietnam
42 D2 **Băc Giang** Vietnam
49 K2 **Bacha** China
127 F6 **Bachiniva** Mexico
65 J5 **Bachu** China
65 J5 **Bachu Liuchang** China
111 J1 **Back r.** Can.
28 B2 **Bačka Palanka** Yugo.
28 B2 **Bačka Topola** Yugo.
110 D2 **Backbone Ranges mt. ra.** Can.
10 E3 **Backe** Sweden
28 B2 **Bački Petrovac** Yugo.
96 D3 **Backstairs Pass. chan.** Aust.
42 D2 **Bac Lac** Vietnam
43 D5 **Bac Liêu** Vietnam
130 C2 **Bacoachi** Mexico
41 B4 **Bacolod** Phil.
41 B3 **Baco, Mt mt.** Phil.
42 D2 **Băc Quang** Vietnam
112 F2 **Bacqueville, Lac l.** Can.
19 J5 **Bácsalmás** Hungary
80 C3 **Bada mt.** Ethiopia
43 B5 **Bada i.** Myanmar
48 D2 **Bada** Rus. Fed.
56 A4 **Badagara** India
48 B4 **Badain Jaran Shamo desert** China
139 E4 **Badajós** *Amazonas* Brazil
142 C1 **Badajós** *Pará* Brazil
139 E4 **Badajós, Lago l.** Brazil
24 C3 **Badajoz** Spain
56 A3 **Badami** India
73 H1 **Badanah** Saudi Arabia
54 D3 **Badarīnāth** India
55 H4 **Badarpur** India
40 A1 **Badas, Kepulauan i.** Indon.
123 F4 **Bad Axe** U.S.A.
18 D3 **Bad Berleburg** Germany
18 E2 **Bad Bevensen** Germany
113 H4 **Baddeck** Can.
10 F1 **Badderen** Norway
57 F3 **Baddo w** Pakistan
18 E1 **Bad Doberan** Germany
77 F4 **Badéguichéri** Niger
18 C3 **Bad Ems** Germany
19 H4 **Baden** Austria
21 J3 **Baden** Switz.
18 D4 **Baden-Baden** Germany
18 D4 **Baden-Württemberg div.** Germany
19 G2 **Bad Freienwalde** Germany
18 F5 **Badgastein** Austria
113 J4 **Badger** Can.
19 G5 **Bad Gleichenberg** Austria
18 E3 **Bad Harzburg** Germany
18 D3 **Bad Hersfeld** Germany
18 F5 **Bad Hofgastein** Austria
18 D3 **Bad Homburg vor der Höhe** Germany
26 C3 **Badia Polesine** Italy
80 B3 **Badigeru Swamp** Sudan
54 B4 **Badin** Pakistan
130 D3 **Badiraguato** Mexico
19 F5 **Bad Ischl** Austria
60 D3 **Bādiyat ash Shām desert** Asia
18 E3 **Bad Kissingen** Germany
18 C4 **Bad Kreuznach** Germany
124 C2 **Badlands reg.** U.S.A.
124 C3 **Badlands Nat. Park nat. park.** U.S.A.
18 E3 **Bad Langensalza** Germany
18 E3 **Bad Lauterberg im Harz** Germany
18 D4 **Bad Mergentheim** Germany
18 D3 **Bad Nauheim** Germany
18 C3 **Bad Neuenahr-Ahrweiler** Germany
18 E3 **Bad Neustadt an der Saale** Germany

133 □1 Brown's Town Jamaica
119 B5 Brownsville U.S.A.
125 D7 Brownsville U.S.A.
121 J2 Brownville U.S.A.
121 J2 Brownville Junction U.S.A.
125 D6 Brownwood U.S.A.
100 C2 Browse I. i. Aust.
24 C3 Brozas Spain
13 D4 Brozha Belarus
20 F1 Bruay-en-Artois France
133 □9 Bruce *Barbados* Caribbean
93 B5 Bruce Bay b. N.Z.
122 C2 Bruce Crossing U.S.A.
100 B4 Bruce, Mt mt. Aust.
114 E4 Bruce Pen. pen. Can.
114 E4 Bruce Peninsula National Park nat. park Can.
101 B6 Bruce Rock Aust.
18 D4 Bruchsal Germany
19 H4 Bruck an der Leitha Austria
19 G5 Bruck an der Mur Austria
18 A3 Brugge Belgium
129 G2 Bruin Pt summit U.S.A.
55 H3 Bruint India
61 B4 Brûk, W. el w Egypt
122 B2 Brule U.S.A.
145 F4 Brumadinho Brazil
142 D3 Brumado Brazil
11 C3 Brumunddal Norway
126 D3 Bruneau U.S.A.
126 D3 Bruneau r. U.S.A.
33 N9 Brunei country Asia
98 C3 Brunette Downs Aust.
10 D3 Brunflo Sweden
26 C2 Brunico Italy
93 C5 Brunner, L. l. N.Z.
111 H4 Bruno Can.
18 D2 Brunsbüttel Germany
119 D6 Brunswick U.S.A.
121 J3 Brunswick U.S.A.
120 C4 Brunswick U.S.A.
100 D2 Brunswick Bay b. Aust.
101 A7 Brunswick Jct. Aust.
114 D2 Brunswick Lake l. Can.
147 B7 Brunswick, Península de pen. Chile
19 H4 Bruntál Czech Rep.
152 C3 Brunt Ice Shelf ice feature Ant.
97 F5 Bruny I. i. Aust.
28 C3 Brus Yugo.
12 G2 Brusenets Rus. Fed.
126 G3 Brush U.S.A.
114 E5 Brussels Can.
122 D3 Brussels U.S.A.
19 H2 Brusy Poland
15 C1 Brusyliv Ukraine
97 F4 Bruthen Aust.
18 B3 Bruxelles Belgium
120 A4 Bryan U.S.A.
125 D6 Bryan U.S.A.
152 A3 Bryan Coast Ant.
96 D3 Bryan, Mt h. Aust.
14 A3 Bryansk div. Rus. Fed.
14 B3 Bryansk Rus. Fed.
13 H6 Bryanskoye Rus. Fed.
129 F3 Bryce Canyon Nat. Park nat. park U.S.A.
129 H5 Bryce Mt mt. U.S.A.
15 E3 Brylivka Ukraine
11 B4 Bryne Norway
13 F6 Bryukhovetskaya Rus. Fed.
19 H3 Brzeg Poland
19 H3 Brzeg Dolny Poland
19 L4 Brzozów *Krosno* Poland
73 J4 Bū well Yemen
90 □6 Bua Fiji
81 B7 Bua r. Malawi
80 D4 Bu'aale Somalia
90 □1 Buala Solomon Is.
94 D1 Bua, Tg pt Indon.
72 D2 Bū Athlah well Libya
72 C1 Bu'ayrāt al Hasūn Libya
76 A4 Buba Guinea-Bissau
81 A5 Bubanza Burundi
76 A4 Bubaque Guinea-Bissau
83 E3 Bubi r. Zimbabwe
60 G4 Būbīyān I. i. Kuwait
41 B5 Bubuan i. Phil.
90 □6 Buca Fiji
29 F5 Buca Turkey
60 B2 Bucak Turkey
61 B1 Bucakkışla Turkey
138 C2 Bucaramanga Colombia
41 C4 Bucas Grande i. Phil.
100 C3 Buccaneer Archipelago is Aust.
27 E5 Buccino Italy
15 A2 Buchach Ukraine
97 G4 Buchan Aust.
76 B5 Buchanan Liberia
122 D5 Buchanan U.S.A.
120 D6 Buchanan U.S.A.
99 F4 Buchanan, L. salt flat Aust.
101 C5 Buchanan, L. salt flat Aust.
125 D6 Buchanan, L. l. U.S.A.
109 L2 Buchan Gulf b. Can.
113 J4 Buchans Can.
18 D2 Bucholz in der Nordheide Germany
128 B4 Buchon, Point pt U.S.A.
97 F2 Buckambool Mt h. Aust.
129 F5 Buckeye U.S.A.
120 B5 Buckeye Lake l. U.S.A.
120 C5 Buckhannon r. U.S.A.
120 C5 Buckhannon U.S.A.
115 F4 Buckhorn Can.
129 H5 Buckhorn U.S.A.
115 F4 Buckhorn Lake l. Can.
120 B6 Buckhorn Lake l. U.S.A.
16 F3 Buckie U.K.
115 H4 Buckingham Can.
17 G5 Buckingham U.K.
120 D6 Buckingham U.S.A.
98 C2 Buckingham B. b. Aust.
99 G5 Buckland Tableland reg. Aust.
152 A6 Buckle I. i. Ant.
94 □3 Buckles Bay b. *Macquarie I.* Pac. Oc.
98 D4 Buckley w Aust.
129 F4 Buckskin Mts mts U.S.A.
128 B2 Bucks Mt mt. U.S.A.
121 J2 Bucksport U.S.A.
19 H4 Bučovice Czech Rep.
79 B4 Buco-Zau *Cabinda* Angola
28 E2 Bucureşti Romania
120 B4 Bucyrus U.S.A.
14 B3 Buda Rus. Fed.
25 G2 Buda, Illa de i. Spain
42 A2 Budalin Myanmar
19 J5 Budapest Hungary
54 D3 Budaun India
80 E4 Bud Bud Somalia
152 C6 Budd Coast Ant.
80 D3 Buddi Ethiopia
27 B5 Buddusò Italy
17 E6 Bude U.K.
125 F6 Bude U.S.A.
13 H6 Budennovsk Rus. Fed.
28 F2 Budeşti Romania
54 B4 Budhapur Pakistan
61 B5 Budhîya, G. mt. ra. Egypt
54 C3 Budhlada India
78 C3 Budjala Zaire
54 D5 Budni India
12 E3 Budogoshch' Rus. Fed.
55 H2 Budongquan China
27 B5 Budoni Italy
28 B3 Budva Yugo.
78 A3 Buea Cameroon
21 G4 Buëch r. France
128 B4 Buellton U.S.A.
146 C3 Buena Esperanza Arg.
138 B3 Buenaventura Colombia
130 D2 Buenaventura Mexico
138 B3 Buenaventure, B. de b. Colombia
127 F4 Buena Vista U.S.A.
120 D6 Buena Vista U.S.A.
132 C2 Buena Vista, B. de b. Cuba
24 D1 Buenavista de Valdavia Spain
25 E2 Buendia, Embalse de resr Spain
79 C5 Buenga r. Angola
147 B5 Bueno r. Chile
145 F2 Buenópolis Brazil
146 D4 Buenos Aires div. Arg.
146 E3 Buenos Aires Arg.
140 B1 Buenos Aires Brazil
147 B6 Buenos Aires, L. l. Arg./Chile
133 □3 Buenos Ayres Trin. & Tobago
147 C6 Buen Pasto Arg.
147 C7 Buen Tiempo, C. hd Arg.
145 J1 Buerarema Brazil
24 B1 Bueu Spain
130 D3 Búfalo Mexico
110 G3 Buffalo r. Can.
120 D3 Buffalo U.S.A.
125 D4 Buffalo U.S.A.
124 C2 Buffalo U.S.A.
125 D6 Buffalo U.S.A.
122 B3 Buffalo U.S.A.
122 B3 Buffalo r. U.S.A.
126 F2 Buffalo U.S.A.
110 F3 Buffalo Head Hills h. Can.
110 F2 Buffalo Lake l. Can.
111 H3 Buffalo Narrows Can.
133 □1 Buff Bay Jamaica
82 B4 Buffels w R.S.A.
119 D5 Buford U.S.A.
28 E2 Buftea Romania
19 K2 Bug r. Poland
138 B3 Buga Colombia
77 F5 Bugana Nigeria
48 C2 Bugant Mongolia
40 B3 Bugel, Tg pt Indon.
24 □ Bugio i. *Madeira* Portugal
26 F3 Bugojno Bos.-Herz.
62 F3 Bugrino Rus. Fed.
41 A4 Bugsuk i. Phil.
49 G2 Bugt China
41 B2 Buguey Phil.
48 C1 Bugul'deyka Rus. Fed.
64 D2 Bugul'ma Rus. Fed.
64 F3 Bugun' Kazak.
64 D2 Buguruslan Rus. Fed.
48 A5 Buh r. China
57 C3 Būhābād Iran
29 G6 Buharkent Turkey
60 C3 Buḩayrat al Asad resr Syria
61 D3 Buḩayrat al Hījānah l. Syria
60 E3 Buḩayrat ath Tharthār l. Iraq
83 E2 Buhera Zimbabwe
41 B3 Buhi Phil.
18 D4 Bühl Germany
126 D3 Buhl U.S.A.
122 A2 Buhl U.S.A.
60 E2 Bühtan r. Turkey
81 C6 Buhu r. Tanzania
28 F1 Buhuşi Romania
17 F5 Builth Wells U.K.
90 □1 Buin P.N.G.
76 D5 Bui National Park nat. park Ghana
12 J4 Buinsk Rus. Fed.
14 H2 Buinsk Rus. Fed.
57 B2 Bu'in Zahrā Iran
49 F3 Buir Nur l. Mongolia
82 B3 Buitepos Namibia
24 D4 Bujalance Spain
28 C3 Bujanovac Yugo.
28 E3 Bujoru Romania
81 A5 Bujumbura Burundi
19 H2 Buk Poland
49 F1 Bukachacha Rus. Fed.
90 □1 Buka I. i. P.N.G.
82 C2 Bukalo Namibia
79 E5 Bukama Zaire
14 B3 Bukan' Rus. Fed.
57 C3 Būkand Iran
79 E4 Bukavu Zaire
64 F5 Bukhara Uzbekistan
65 K3 Bukhtarminskoye Vdkhr. resr Kazak.
41 C6 Bukide i. Indon.
43 □ Bukit Batok Singapore
43 C7 Bukit Fraser Malaysia
40 C2 Bukitlidi Indon.
43 □ Bukit Panjang Singapore
43 □ Bukit Timah Singapore
38 D7 Bukittinggi Indon.
19 K4 Bükk mts Hungary
61 C4 Bukka, J. el mt. Jordan
81 B5 Bukoba Tanzania
81 B5 Bukombekombe Tanzania
14 D2 Bukrino Rus. Fed.
43 □ Bukum, P. i. Singapore
77 F5 Bukuru Nigeria
40 A2 Buku, Tg pt Indon.
15 D2 Buky Ukraine
39 K7 Bula Indon.
21 J3 Bülach Switz.
48 D2 Bulag Mongolia
48 C2 Bulagtay Mongolia
97 H3 Bulahdelal Aust.
41 B3 Bulan Phil.
60 D1 Bulancak Turkey
54 D3 Bulandshahr India
60 E2 Bulanık Turkey
73 F2 Bûlâq Egypt
83 D3 Bulawayo Zimbabwe
65 H2 Bulayevo Kazak.
60 B2 Buldan Turkey
54 D5 Buldana India
140 A1 Buldibuyo Peru
80 D3 Bulei well Ethiopia
48 B2 Bulgan *Bulgan* Mongolia
48 B2 Bulgan *Hövsgöl* Mongolia
48 B3 Bulgan *Ömnögovĭ* Mongolia
48 B2 Bulgan div. Mongolia
5 H4 Bulgaria country Europe
25 F3 Bullas Spain
133 □1 Bull Bay Jamaica
21 H3 Bulle Switz.
132 □2 Bullen Baai b. *Curaçao* Netherlands Ant.
93 D4 Buller r. N.Z.
97 F4 Buller, Mt mt. Aust.
129 E4 Bullhead City U.S.A.
128 D4 Bullion Mts mts U.S.A.
99 E6 Bulloo w Aust.
99 E6 Bulloo Downs Aust.
99 E6 Bulloo L. salt flat Aust.
92 □2 Bull Rock i. *Campbell I.* N.Z.
92 E4 Bulls N.Z.
133 □1 Bull Savannah Jamaica
43 □ Buloh, P. i. Singapore
90 □1 Bulolo P.N.G.
29 C4 Bulqizë Albania
41 C5 Buluan Phil.
40 E3 Bulubulu Indon.
80 C4 Buluk well Kenya
40 E3 Bulukumba Indon.
78 D4 Bulukutu Zaire
63 O2 Bulun Rus. Fed.
79 C4 Bulungu *Bandundu* Zaire
79 D5 Bulungu *Kasai-Occidental* Zaire
65 G5 Bulungur Uzbekistan
41 C3 Bulusan Phil.
78 B2 Bum Cameroon
79 C5 Bumba *Bandundu* Zaire
78 D3 Bumba *Équateur* Zaire
48 C3 Bumbat Mongolia
48 C4 Bumbat Sum China
28 D2 Bumbeşti-Jiu Romania
81 B5 Bumbire I. i. Tanzania
129 F4 Bumble Bee U.S.A.
41 A5 Bum-Bum i. Malaysia
42 B1 Bumhkang Myanmar
80 C4 Buna Kenya
79 C4 Buna Zaire
81 B5 Bunazi Tanzania
101 A7 Bunbury Aust.
17 D4 Buncrana Rep. of Ire.
81 B5 Bunda Tanzania
99 H5 Bundaberg Aust.
99 F6 Bundaleer Aust.
97 G2 Bundarra Aust.
98 C4 Bundey w Aust.
54 C4 Bundi India
81 B4 Bundibugyo Uganda
55 F5 Bundu India
80 B3 Bunduqiya Sudan
77 F4 Bunga w Nigeria
17 H5 Bungay U.K.
42 C4 Bung Boraphet l. Thailand
97 G3 Bungendore Aust.
152 C6 Bunger Hills h. Ant.
99 G5 Bungil Cr. r. Aust.
100 E3 Bungle Bungle Nat. Park nat. park Aust.
79 C5 Bungo Angola
46 D7 Bungo-suidō chan. Japan
46 C7 Bungo-takada Japan
78 F3 Bunia Zaire
79 D4 Bunianga Zaire
77 G4 Buni-Yadi Nigeria
54 C2 Bunji Pakistan
65 H5 Bunji *Jammu and Kashmir*
99 H4 Bunker Group atolls Aust.
129 E3 Bunkerville U.S.A.
79 E6 Bunkeya Zaire
125 E6 Bunkie U.S.A.
119 D6 Bunnell U.S.A.
25 F3 Buñol Spain
40 C2 Buntok Indon.
40 C2 Buntokecil Indon.
77 F5 Bununu Nigeria
60 C2 Bünyan Turkey
41 A6 Bunyu i. Indon.
77 E4 Bunza Nigeria
26 F3 Buoač Bos.-Herz.
57 B3 Bu ol Kheyr Iran
43 E4 Buôn Hô Vietnam
43 E4 Buôn Mê Thuôt Vietnam
63 P2 Buorkhaya, Guba b. Rus. Fed.
57 B4 Buqayq Saudi Arabia
81 C5 Bura Kenya
80 E2 Buraan Somalia
78 E1 Buram Sudan
65 L3 Buran Kazak.
54 E3 Burang China
145 J2 Buranhaém r. Brazil
145 H2 Buranhaém Brazil
80 E3 Burao Somalia
61 D3 Burāq Syria
14 H3 Burasy Rus. Fed.
41 C4 Burauen Phil.
73 H2 Buraydah Saudi Arabia
18 D3 Burbach Germany
128 C4 Burbank U.S.A.
97 F3 Burcher Aust.
99 F4 Burdekin r. Aust.
99 F4 Burdekin Falls waterfall Aust.
60 B2 Burdur Turkey
61 A1 Burdur div. Turkey
80 C2 Burē Ethiopia
80 B3 Burē Ethiopia
10 F2 Bureå Sweden
73 F4 Bureiqa well Sudan
49 K2 Bureiskiy Khrebet mt. ra. Rus. Fed.
48 A2 Buren-Khem Rus. Fed.
48 D3 Bürentsogt Mongolia
49 J2 Bureya Rus. Fed.
49 J2 Bureya r. Rus. Fed.
18 E1 Burg *Sachsen-Anhalt* Germany
28 F3 Burgas div. Bulgaria
28 F3 Burgas Bulgaria
119 E5 Burgaw U.S.A.
18 E2 Burg bei Magdeburg Germany
18 E4 Burgbernheim Germany
21 H3 Burgdorf Switz.
19 H5 Burgenland div. Austria
113 J4 Burgeo Can.
101 C6 Burges, Mt h. Aust.
18 A3 Burgh Netherlands
18 F4 Burghausen Germany
18 F4 Burglengenfeld Germany
24 E1 Burgos Spain
11 E4 Burgsvik Sweden
44 G4 Burhan Budai Shan mt. ra. China
60 A2 Burhaniye Turkey
54 D5 Burhanpur India
55 E5 Burhar-Dhanpuri India
55 F4 Burhi Gandak r. India
144 D5 Buri Brazil
41 B3 Burias i. Phil.
41 B3 Burias Pass. chan. Phil.
64 E2 Buribay Rus. Fed.
130 K7 Burica, Pta pt Costa Rica
81 B5 Burigi, Lake l. Tanzania
113 J4 Burin Peninsula pen. Can.
43 C4 Buriram Thailand
144 C4 Buritama Brazil
142 D1 Buriti Brazil
141 E2 Buriti r. Brazil
144 D3 Buriti Alegre Brazil
142 D2 Buriti Bravo Brazil
142 C2 Buriticupu r. Brazil
142 D1 Buriti dos Lopes Brazil
142 D3 Buritirama Brazil
145 E1 Buritis Brazil
145 F2 Buritizeiro Brazil
54 A3 Burj Pakistan
25 F3 Burjassot Spain
98 D4 Burke w Aust.
152 A3 Burke I. i. Ant.
93 C6 Burke Pass N.Z.
98 D3 Burketown Aust.
68 D4 Burkina country Africa
115 F4 Burk's Falls Can.
65 J2 Burla r. Rus. Fed.
65 J2 Burla Rus. Fed.
99 E4 Burleigh Aust.
126 D3 Burley U.S.A.
64 D2 Burlin Kazak.
115 F5 Burlington Can.
124 C4 Burlington U.S.A.
122 D5 Burlington U.S.A.
122 B5 Burlington U.S.A.
121 J2 Burlington U.S.A.
121 G2 Burlington U.S.A.
122 C4 Burlington U.S.A.
14 E3 Burminka Rus. Fed.
125 D6 Burnet U.S.A.
99 H5 Burnett r. Aust.
126 B3 Burney U.S.A.
121 J2 Burnham U.S.A.
97 F5 Burnie Aust.
65 H4 Burnoye Kazak.
126 C3 Burns U.S.A.
111 H1 Burnside r. Can.
101 C5 Burnside, L. salt flat Aust.
108 F4 Burns Lake Can.
120 C5 Burnsville Lake l. U.S.A.
119 F7 Burnt Ground The Bahamas
113 H3 Burnt Lake l. Can.
95 □1 Burnt Pine *Norfolk I.* Pac. Oc.
111 K3 Burntwood r. Can.
111 J3 Burnt Wood Lake l. Can.
65 L3 Burqin China
96 D3 Burra Aust.
28 C4 Burrel Albania
97 G3 Burrendong Reservoir resr Aust.
97 G2 Burren Jct. Aust.
25 F3 Burriana Spain
97 G3 Burrinjuck Aust.
97 G3 Burrinjuck Reservoir resr Aust.
120 B5 Burr Oak Reservoir resr U.S.A.
98 B2 Burrundie Aust.
129 G2 Burrville U.S.A.
29 G4 Bursa div. Turkey
60 B1 Bursa Turkey
73 F2 Bûr Safâga Egypt
15 A2 Burshtyn Ukraine
61 B5 Bûr Taufiq Egypt
122 E3 Burt Lake l. U.S.A.
123 F4 Burton U.S.A.
112 E3 Burton, Lac l. Can.
17 C4 Burtonport Rep. of Ire.
17 G5 Burton upon Trent U.K.
10 F2 Burträsk Sweden
121 K1 Burtts Corner Can.
97 E3 Burtundy Aust.
39 J7 Buru i. Indon.
69 G6 Burundi country Africa
81 A5 Bururi Burundi
110 B2 Burwash Landing Can.
16 F2 Burwick U.K.
115 K4 Bury Can.
48 B2 Buryatiya div. Rus. Fed.
15 E1 Buryn' Ukraine
64 D3 Burynshyk Kazak.
17 H5 Bury St Edmunds U.K.
54 C2 Burzil Pass pass *Jammu & Kashmir*
78 D4 Busanga Zaire
15 C2 Busha Ukraine
81 D5 Bushbush r. Kenya/Somalia
15 B1 Bushcha Ukraine
57 B3 Būshehr div. Iran
57 B3 Būshehr Iran
55 E2 Bushêngcaka China
81 B5 Bushenyi Uganda
122 B5 Bushnell U.S.A.
28 C4 Bushtricë Albania
49 F1 Bushuley Rus. Fed.
78 D3 Businga Zaire
43 □ Busing, P. i. Singapore
78 C4 Busira r. Zaire
15 A2 Bus'k Ukraine
11 C3 Buskerud div. Norway
19 K3 Busko-Zdrój Poland
61 D3 Buşrá ash Shām Syria
49 H2 Busse Rus. Fed.
101 A7 Busselton Aust.
78 E2 Busseri w Sudan
125 C7 Bustamante Mexico
147 C6 Bustamante, B. b. Arg.
28 E2 Buşteni Romania
130 D2 Bustillos, L. l. Mexico
26 B3 Busto Arsizio Italy
41 A3 Busuanga Phil.
41 A3 Busuanga i. Phil.
18 D1 Büsum Germany
78 D3 Buta Zaire
80 C3 Butajīra Ethiopia
43 B6 Butang Group is Thailand
81 A5 Butare Rwanda
16 E4 Bute i. U.K.
28 F1 Butea Romania
110 D4 Butedale Can.
110 D4 Bute In. inlet Can.
78 E3 Butembo Zaire
83 D4 Butha-Buthe Lesotho
42 A2 Buthidaung Myanmar
122 E5 Butler U.S.A.
120 D4 Butler U.S.A.
39 H8 Buton i. Indon.
15 G1 Butovo Rus. Fed.
126 D2 Butte U.S.A.
128 B1 Butte Meadows U.S.A.
43 C6 Butterworth Malaysia
82 D5 Butterworth R.S.A.
110 D5 Buttle L. l. Can.
16 D2 Butt of Lewis hd U.K.
109 M3 Button Is is Can.
128 C4 Buttonwillow U.S.A.
101 C7 Butty Hd pt Aust.
41 C4 Butuan Phil.
15 C3 Butuceni Moldova
50 C3 Butuo China
14 G2 Buturlino Rus. Fed.
13 G5 Buturlinovka Rus. Fed.
55 E4 Butwal Nepal
14 E2 Butylitsy Rus. Fed.
18 E2 Bützow Germany
80 E4 Buulobarde Somalia
81 D5 Buur Gaabo Somalia
80 D4 Buurhabaka Somalia
80 B4 Buvuma I. i. Uganda
61 C5 Buwārah, J. mt. Saudi Arabia
73 G3 Buwāţah Saudi Arabia
55 F4 Buxar India
18 D2 Buxtehude Germany
17 G5 Buxton U.K.
12 G3 Buy Rus. Fed.
48 D3 Buyant Mongolia
48 A3 Buyant Mongolia
48 A3 Buyant Gol r. Mongolia
48 C3 Buyant-Ovoo Mongolia
48 D3 Buyant-Uhaa Mongolia
122 A1 Buyck U.S.A.
13 H7 Buynaksk Rus. Fed.
76 C5 Buyo, Lac de l. Côte d'Ivoire
50 C4 Buyuan r. China
60 E2 Büyük Ağri mt. Turkey
61 B1 Büyük Egri D. mt. Turkey
29 F4 Büyükkarıştıran Turkey
29 G6 Büyükmenderes r. Turkey
29 G5 Büyükorhan Turkey
49 G4 Buyun Shan mt. China
64 D4 Buzachi, Pov. pen. Kazak.
20 E3 Buzançais France
28 F2 Buzău Romania
72 D3 Buzaymah oasis Libya
46 C7 Buzen Japan
14 E2 Buzha r. Rus. Fed.
83 E2 Búzi Mozambique
83 E3 Búzi r. Mozambique
28 C2 Buziaş Romania
145 H5 Buzios, Cabo dos hd Brazil
145 F5 Buzios, Ilha dos i. Brazil
14 G3 Buzovlevo Rus. Fed.
13 G5 Buzuluk r. Rus. Fed.
64 D2 Buzuluk Rus. Fed.
121 H4 Buzzards Bay b. U.S.A.
90 □1 Bwagaoia P.N.G.
55 G4 Byakar Bhutan
28 F3 Byala *Burgas* Bulgaria
28 E3 Byala *Razgrad* Bulgaria
28 D3 Byala Slatina Bulgaria
12 D4 Byalynichy Belarus
108 H2 Byam Martin I. i. Can.
13 C4 Byaroza Belarus
19 L3 Bychawa Poland
14 E3 Bychki Rus. Fed.
19 J3 Byczyna Poland
19 J2 Bydgoszcz Poland
12 D4 Byerazino Belarus
126 F4 Byers U.S.A.
12 D4 Byeshankovichy Belarus
11 B4 Bygland Norway
12 D4 Bykhaw Belarus
11 B4 Bykle Norway
13 H5 Bykovo Rus. Fed.
109 L2 Bylot Island i. Can.
114 E4 Byng Inlet Can.
152 B5 Byrd Gl. gl. Ant.
49 F2 Byrka Rus. Fed.
11 B3 Byrkjelo Norway
15 E1 Byrlivka Ukraine
97 F2 Byrock Aust.
122 C4 Byron U.S.A.
121 H2 Byron U.S.A.
97 H2 Byron Bay Aust.
97 H2 Byron, C. hd Aust.
14 A3 Byryne Ukraine
15 C1 Byshiv Ukraine
10 F2 Byske Sweden
19 H4 Bystřice nad Pernštejnem Czech Rep.
48 D2 Bystrinskiy Golets, G. mt. Rus. Fed.
63 P3 Bytantay r. Rus. Fed.
19 J4 Bytča Slovakia
19 J3 Bytom Poland
14 B3 Bytosh' Rus. Fed.
19 H1 Bytów Poland
81 B5 Byumba Rwanda
64 E5 Byuzmeyin Turkmenistan
19 K2 Bzura r. Poland

C

141 E5 Caacupé Paraguay
141 E5 Caagazú, Cordillera de h. Paraguay
141 E5 Caaguazú Paraguay
79 C6 Caála Angola
144 A5 Caarapó Brazil
145 H1 Caatiba Brazil
145 F2 Caatinga Brazil
141 E5 Caazapá Paraguay
141 E3 Cabaçal r. Brazil
132 C2 Cabaiguán Cuba
140 A2 Caballas Peru
138 C4 Caballococha Peru
130 D2 Caballos Mesteños, Llano de los plain Mexico
140 B2 Cabana Peru
140 B3 Cabanaconde Peru
24 D1 Cabañaquinta Spain
25 E4 Cabañas mt. Spain
41 B3 Cabanatuan Phil.
25 E4 Cabañas mt. Spain
41 B3 Cabanatuan Phil.
113 G4 Cabano Can.
140 C3 Cabaraya, Co mt. Bolivia
80 D2 Cabdul Qaadir Somalia
143 A4 Cabeceira Rio Manso Brazil
142 F2 Cabedelo Brazil
24 D3 Cabeza del Buey Spain
141 D3 Cabezas Bolivia
119 □3 Cabezas de San Juan pt Puerto Rico
24 C4 Cabezas Rubias Spain
146 D4 Cabildo Arg.
138 C1 Cabimas Venezuela
79 B5 Cabinda div. Angola
79 B5 Cabinda Angola
126 C1 Cabinet Mts mt. ra. U.S.A.
41 B5 Cabingan i. Phil.
119 □2 Cable Beach The Bahamas
147 C6 Cabo Blanco Arg.
81 C7 Cabo Delgado div. Mozambique
145 G5 Cabo Frio Brazil
145 H5 Cabo Frio, Ilha do c. Brazil
115 G3 Cabonga, Réservoir resr Can.
125 E4 Cabool U.S.A.
99 H5 Caboolture Aust.
139 G3 Cabo Orange, Parque Nacional de nat. park Brazil
138 B4 Cabo Pantoja Peru
147 C5 Cabo Raso Arg.
130 B2 Caborca Mexico
119 □3 Cabo Rojo Puerto Rico
114 E4 Cabot Head pt Can.
113 J4 Cabot Strait str. Can.
24 D4 Cabra Spain
27 B6 Cabras Italy
25 H3 Cabrera i. Spain
24 C1 Cabrera, Sierra de la mt. ra. Spain
25 F3 Cabriel r. Spain
133 □4 Cabrits, Îlet i. *Martinique* Caribbean
142 E2 Cabrobó Brazil
138 D2 Cabruta Venezuela
41 B2 Cabugao Phil.
26 F4 Čabulja mt. Bos.-Herz.
143 B6 Caçador Brazil
131 F5 Cacahuatepec Mexico
28 C3 Čačak Yugo.
139 G3 Cacao French Guiana
145 F5 Caçapava Brazil
143 B7 Caçapava do Sul Brazil
120 D5 Cacapon r. U.S.A.
138 B2 Cácares Colombia
27 B5 Caccia, Capo pt Italy
143 B6 Cacequi Brazil
141 E3 Cáceres Brazil
24 C3 Cáceres Spain
126 D3 Cache Peak summit U.S.A.
76 A4 Cacheu Guinea-Bissau
146 C2 Cachi Arg.
142 B2 Cachimbo Brazil
79 D5 Cachimo Angola
140 C4 Cachinal Chile
79 C6 Cachingues Angola
138 C2 Cáchira Colombia
142 E3 Cachoeira *Bahia* Brazil
144 C3 Cachoeira *Mato Grosso do Sul* Brazil
142 C2 Cachoeira r. Brazil
144 C3 Cachoeira Alta Brazil
144 C2 Cachoeira de Goiás Brazil
142 C1 Cachoeira do Arari Brazil
143 B7 Cachoeira do Sul Brazil
145 F5 Cachoeira Paulista Brazil
145 G5 Cachoeiras de Macacu Brazil
145 H4 Cachoeiro de Itapemirim Brazil
24 C4 Cachopo Portugal
76 A4 Cacine Guinea-Bissau
79 C6 Cacolo Angola
79 C6 Caconda Angola
79 B5 Cacongo *Cabinda* Angola
128 D3 Cactus Range mts U.S.A.
144 C3 Caçu Brazil
79 B5 Cacuaco Angola
142 D3 Caculé Brazil
145 J2 Cacumba, Ilha i. Brazil
144 B2 Caçununga Brazil
19 J4 Čadca Slovakia
80 D2 Caddabassa I. Ethiopia
18 D2 Cadenberge Germany
131 E3 Cadereyta Mexico
96 C2 Cadibarrawirracanna, L. salt flat Aust.
41 B3 Cadig Mts mt. ra. Phil.
115 F2 Cadillac Can.
111 H5 Cadillac Can.
20 D4 Cadillac France
122 E3 Cadillac U.S.A.
41 B4 Cadiz Phil.
24 C4 Cádiz Spain
24 C4 Cádiz, Golfo de g. Spain
129 E4 Cadiz Lake l. U.S.A.
101 B6 Cadoux Aust.
20 D2 Caen France
17 E5 Caernarfon U.K.
17 E5 Caernarfon Bay b. U.K.
120 B5 Caesar Creek Lake l. U.S.A.
61 C3 Caesarea Israel
142 D3 Caetité Brazil
146 C2 Cafayate Arg.
144 D4 Cafelândia Brazil
139 F3 Cafuini r. Brazil
41 B4 Cagayan i. Phil.
41 B2 Cagayan r. Phil.
41 C4 Cagayan de Oro Phil.
41 B4 Cagayan Islands is Phil.
26 D4 Cagli Italy
27 B6 Cagliari Italy
27 B6 Cagliari, Golfo di b. Italy
138 C3 Caguán r. Colombia
119 □3 Caguas Puerto Rico
119 C5 Cahaba r. U.S.A.
79 B7 Cahama Angola
17 C6 Caha Mts h. Rep. of Ire.
17 B6 Cahersiveen Rep. of Ire.
17 D5 Cahir Rep. of Ire.
83 E2 Cahora Bassa, Barragem de dam Mozambique
83 E2 Cahora Bassa, Lago de resr Mozambique
17 D5 Cahore Point pt Rep. of Ire.
20 E4 Cahors France
138 B5 Cahuapanas Peru
15 C3 Cahul Moldova
83 F2 Caia Mozambique
79 D6 Caianda Angola
144 C2 Caiapó r. Brazil
144 C2 Caiapônia Brazil
132 C2 Caibarién Cuba
43 D5 Cai Be Vietnam
139 D2 Caicara Venezuela
142 E2 Caicó Brazil
133 D2 Caicos Is is *Turks and Caicos Is* Caribbean
133 D2 Caicos Passage chan. *The Bahamas/Turks and Caicos Is* Caribbean
140 B3 Cailloma Peru
41 A3 Caiman Point pt Phil.
43 D5 Cai Nuoc Vietnam
16 F3 Cairngorm Mts mt. ra. U.K.
99 F3 Cairns Aust.
61 A4 Cairo Egypt
119 C6 Cairo U.S.A.
26 B3 Cairo Montenotte Italy
79 B6 Caitou Angola
79 C7 Caiundo Angola
99 F6 Caiwarro Aust.
51 G2 Caizi Hu l. China
140 A2 Cajacay Peru
119 □3 Caja de Muertos, I. i. Puerto Rico
138 B5 Cajamarca Peru
20 E4 Cajarc France
142 C1 Cajari Brazil
140 A2 Cajatambo Peru
142 E2 Cajàzeiras Brazil
28 B3 Čajetina Yugo.
41 B3 Cajidiocan Phil.
26 G4 Čajniče Bos.-Herz.
144 E4 Cajuru Brazil
48 A5 Caka China
48 A5 Caka Yanhu salt l. China
61 A1 Çakırlar Turkey
61 C1 Çakit r. Turkey
26 F2 Čakovec Croatia
60 B2 Çal Turkey
77 F6 Calabar Nigeria
115 G4 Calabogie Can.
138 D2 Calabozo Venezuela
27 F6 Calabria div. Italy
140 C3 Calacoto Bolivia
28 D3 Calafat Romania
147 B7 Calafate Arg.
25 H3 Cala Figuera, Cap de pt Spain
41 B3 Calagua Islands is Phil.
25 F1 Calahorra Spain
79 C7 Calai Angola
20 E1 Calais France
121 K2 Calais U.S.A.
146 C2 Calalasteo, Sierra de mt. ra. Arg.
141 D1 Calama Brazil
140 C4 Calama Chile
138 C1 Calamar *Bolívar* Colombia
138 C3 Calamar *Guaviare* Colombia
41 A3 Calamian Group is Phil.
25 F2 Calamocha Spain
28 D2 Călan Romania
24 C4 Calañas Spain
25 F2 Calanda Spain
79 C5 Calandula Angola
72 D2 Calanscio Sand Sea desert Libya
41 B3 Calapan Phil.
15 C3 Călăraşi Moldova
28 F2 Călăraşi Romania
25 F3 Calasparra Spain
27 D7 Calatafimi Italy
25 F2 Calatayud Spain
41 B3 Calauag Phil.
41 B3 Calavite, Cape c. Phil.
41 B2 Calayan i. Phil.
41 C3 Calbayog Phil.
41 C4 Calbiga Phil.
147 B5 Calbuco Chile
140 B2 Calca Peru
142 E1 Calcanhar, Ponta do pt Brazil
125 E6 Calcasieu L. l. U.S.A.
139 G3 Calçoene Brazil
55 G5 Calcutta India
28 E2 Căldăraru Romania
24 B3 Caldas da Rainha Portugal
144 D2 Caldas Novas Brazil
146 B2 Caldera Chile
99 F5 Caldervale Aust.
60 E2 Çaldıran Turkey
126 C3 Caldwell U.S.A.
114 E5 Caledon Can.
82 D5 Caledon r. Lesotho/R.S.A.
98 D2 Caledon B. b. Aust.
115 F5 Caledonia Can.
122 B4 Caledonia U.S.A.
99 G4 Calen Aust.
21 J5 Calenzana France
130 E4 Calera Mexico
24 D3 Calera y Chozas Spain
140 B4 Caleta Blanco Encalada b. Chile
140 B3 Caleta Buena Chile
147 B7 Caleta Clarencia Chile
147 C7 Caleta Coig inlet Arg.
140 B4 Caleta el Cobre Chile
147 C7 Caleta Josefina Chile
140 B4 Caleta Lobos Chile
147 C6 Caleta Olivia Arg.
129 E5 Calexico U.S.A.
17 E4 Calf of Man i. Isle of Man
110 G4 Calgary Can.
24 □ Calheta *Madeira* Portugal
119 C5 Calhoun U.S.A.
138 B3 Cali Colombia
41 C4 Calicoan i. Phil.
56 A4 Calicut India
128 C4 Caliente U.S.A.
129 E3 Caliente U.S.A.
133 □3 California Trin. & Tobago
128 B3 California div. U.S.A.
128 B3 California Aqueduct canal U.S.A.
130 B2 California, Golfo de g. Mexico
128 C4 California Hot Springs U.S.A.
60 G2 Cäilabad Azerbaijan
28 E2 Călimăneşti Romania
28 E1 Călimani, Munţii mt. ra. Romania
127 D5 Calipatria U.S.A.
128 A2 Calistoga U.S.A.
82 C5 Calitzdorp R.S.A.
131 H4 Calkiní Mexico
96 E2 Callabonna Cr. w Aust.
96 D2 Callabonna, L. salt flat Aust.
20 C2 Callac France
128 D2 Callaghan, Mt mt. U.S.A.
119 D6 Callahan U.S.A.
115 F3 Callander Can.
16 E3 Callander U.K.
140 A2 Callao Peru
129 F2 Callao U.S.A.
131 F4 Calles Mexico
121 F4 Callicoon U.S.A.
99 G5 Callide Aust.
99 G5 Calliope Aust.
114 E3 Callum Can.
110 G4 Calmar Can.
122 B4 Calmar U.S.A.
129 E4 Cal-Nev-Ari U.S.A.
119 D7 Caloosahatchee r. U.S.A.
27 E5 Calore r. *Campania* Italy
131 H4 Calotmul Mexico
99 H5 Caloundra Aust.
25 G3 Calpe Spain
61 A1 Çalpınar Turkey
128 B2 Calpine U.S.A.
131 F5 Calpulálpan Mexico
141 E3 Cal, R. de la r. Bolivia
114 C2 Calstock Can.
27 E7 Caltagirone Italy
27 E7 Caltanissetta div. Italy
79 C6 Calucinga Angola
79 B5 Calulo Angola
122 C2 Calumet U.S.A.
79 D6 Calunda Angola
79 C7 Calunga Angola
79 B6 Caluquembe Angola
41 B4 Calusa i. Phil.
80 F2 Caluula Somalia
129 G5 Calva U.S.A.
98 D3 Calvert r. Aust.
98 D3 Calvert Hills Aust.
110 D4 Calvert I. i. Can.
101 C4 Calvert Ra. h. Aust.
21 J5 Calvi France
25 H3 Calvià Spain
130 E4 Calvillo Mexico
82 B5 Calvina R.S.A.
27 E5 Calvo, Monte mt. Italy
24 E3 Calzada de Calatrava Spain
17 H5 Cam r. U.K.
79 C5 Camabatela Angola
145 J1 Camacã Brazil
142 E3 Camaçari Brazil
128 B2 Camache Reservoir resr U.S.A.
130 E3 Camacho Mexico
79 B6 Camacuio Angola
79 C6 Camacupa Angola
138 D2 Camaguán Venezuela
132 C2 Camagüey Cuba
132 C2 Camagüey, Arch. de is Cuba
43 C6 Camah, Gunung mt. Malaysia
139 F5 Camaiú r. Brazil
130 B2 Camalli, Sa de mt. Mexico
140 B3 Camana Peru
79 D6 Camanongue Angola
144 A3 Camapuã Brazil
143 B7 Camaquã Brazil
143 B7 Camaquã r. Brazil
24 □ Câmara de Lobos *Madeira* Portugal
142 B1 Camaraipi r. Brazil
141 E2 Camararé r. Brazil
20 B2 Camaret-sur-Mer France
131 F3 Camargo Mexico
24 B1 Camariñas Spain
132 A4 Camarón, C. c. Honduras
130 D4 Camaronero, L. del lag. Mexico
147 C5 Camarones Arg.
140 C3 Camarones r. Chile
147 C5 Camarones, Bahía b. Arg.
126 B2 Camas U.S.A.
43 D5 Ca Mau Vietnam
141 E3 Cambara Brazil
144 C5 Cambará Brazil
33 M8 Cambodia country Asia
79 B6 Cambongo r. Angola
17 E6 Camborne U.K.
21 F1 Cambrai France
24 B1 Cambre Spain
128 B4 Cambria U.S.A.
17 F5 Cambrian Mountains mt. ra. U.K.
114 E5 Cambridge Can.
92 E2 Cambridge N.Z.
17 H5 Cambridge U.K.
122 B5 Cambridge U.S.A.
121 E5 Cambridge U.S.A.
121 H3 Cambridge U.S.A.
122 A3 Cambridge U.S.A.
121 G3 Cambridge U.S.A.
120 C4 Cambridge U.S.A.
108 H3 Cambridge Bay Can.
100 E2 Cambridge Gulf b. Aust.
113 G2 Cambrien, Lac l. Can.
25 G2 Cambrils de Mar Spain
145 E5 Cambuí Brazil
79 D5 Cambulo Angola
79 C6 Cambundi-Catembo Angola
145 F4 Cambuquira Brazil
97 G3 Camden Aust.
119 C5 Camden U.S.A.
125 E5 Camden U.S.A.
121 J2 Camden U.S.A.
121 F5 Camden U.S.A.
121 F3 Camden U.S.A.
119 D5 Camden U.S.A.
147 B7 Camden, Is i. Chile
100 D2 Camden Sd chan. Aust.
79 D6 Cameia Angola
79 D6 Cameia, Parque Nacional da nat. park Angola
15 C2 Camenca Moldova
129 G4 Cameron U.S.A.
125 E6 Cameron U.S.A.
124 E4 Cameron U.S.A.
125 D6 Cameron U.S.A.
122 B3 Cameron U.S.A.
114 A2 Cameron Falls Can.
43 C6 Cameron Highlands Malaysia
110 F3 Cameron Hills h. Can.
93 A7 Cameron Mts mts N.Z.
128 B2 Cameron Park U.S.A.
69 E5 Cameroon country Africa
78 A3 Cameroun, Mont mt. Cameroon
142 C1 Cametá Brazil
41 C4 Camiguin i. Phil.
41 B2 Camiguin i. Phil.
41 B3 Camiling Phil.
119 C6 Camilla U.S.A.
140 C3 Camiña Chile
142 C1 Camiranga Brazil
140 D4 Camiri Bolivia
79 D5 Camissombo Angola
61 C1 Çamlıyayla Turkey
130 C3 Camoa Mexico
142 D1 Camocim Brazil
98 D3 Camooweal Aust.
139 G3 Camopi Brazil
139 G3 Camopi r. French Guiana
43 A5 Camorta i. *Andaman and Nicobar Is* India
41 C4 Camotes Sea g. Phil.
146 E3 Campana Arg.
147 A6 Campana, I. i. Chile
145 H3 Campanário Brazil
144 A5 Campanario Brazil
145 F4 Campanha Brazil
27 E5 Campania div. Italy
110 D4 Campania I. i. Can.
93 E4 Campbell, Cape c. N.Z.
43 B5 Campbell I. i. Myanmar
92 □2 Campbell I. i. N.Z.
54 C2 Campbellpore Pakistan
110 D4 Campbell River Can.
115 G4 Campbells Bay Can.
118 C4 Campbellsville U.S.A.
113 G4 Campbellton Can.
97 F5 Campbell Town Aust.
17 E4 Campbeltown U.K.
131 H5 Campeche div. Mexico
131 H5 Campeche Mexico
131 G5 Campeche, Bahía de g. Mexico
97 E4 Camperdown Aust.
119 □2 Camperdown The Bahamas
28 D2 Câmpia Băileştilor plain Romania
15 B3 Câmpia Moldovei de Nord plain Moldova
15 C3 Câmpia Moldovei de Sud plain Moldova
28 D1 Câmpia Turzii Romania
24 D4 Campillos Spain
28 E2 Câmpina Romania
144 B6 Campina da Lagoa Brazil
142 E2 Campina Grande Brazil
144 E5 Campinas Brazil
144 D3 Campina Verde Brazil
78 A3 Campo Cameroon
138 B3 Campoalegre Colombia
27 E5 Campobasso Italy
145 F4 Campo Belo Brazil
143 B6 Campo Belo do Sul Brazil
24 E3 Campo de Criptana Spain
142 B3 Campó de Diauarum Brazil
26 B2 Campodolcino Italy
141 E4 Campo Esperanza Paraguay
144 D3 Campo Florido Brazil
142 D3 Campo Formoso Brazil
146 D2 Campo Gallo Arg.
141 E1 Campo Grande *Amazonas* Brazil
144 A4 Campo Grande *Mato Grosso do Sul* Brazil
144 D6 Campo Largo Brazil
142 D1 Campo Maior Brazil
24 C3 Campo Maior Portugal
144 B6 Campo Mourão Brazil
143 B6 Campo Novo Brazil
78 B3 Campo, Reserva de res. Cameroon
145 H4 Campos Brazil
145 E3 Campos Altos Brazil
142 C3 Campos Belos Brazil
143 B6 Campos de Palmas reg. Brazil
145 F5 Campos do Jordão Brazil
143 B5 Campos Eré reg. Brazil
145 F4 Campos Gerais Brazil
143 B6 Campos Novos Brazil
144 D5 Campos Novos Paulista Brazil
142 D2 Campos Sales Brazil
25 H1 Camprodon Spain
120 B6 Campton U.S.A.
121 H3 Campton U.S.A.
28 E2 Câmpulung Romania
28 E1 Câmpulung Moldovenesc Romania
129 G4 Camp Verde U.S.A.
43 E5 Cam Ranh Vietnam
110 G4 Camrose Can.
111 G2 Camsell Lake l. Can.
111 H3 Camsell Portage Can.
119 □3 Camuy Puerto Rico
60 A1 Çan Turkey
145 G4 Canaã Brazil
133 □2 Canaan *Tobago* Trin. & Tobago
121 G3 Canaan U.S.A.
142 A2 Cana Brava r. *Pará* Brazil
142 B2 Cana Brava r. *Pará* Brazil
145 F2 Canabrava Brazil
104 G4 Canada country N. America
121 H2 Canada Falls Lake l. U.S.A.
125 C5 Canadian r. U.S.A.
146 E2 Canaglaé, L. l. Arg.
139 E2 Canaima, Parque Nacional nat. park Venezuela
121 F3 Canajoharie U.S.A.
60 A1 Çanakkale Turkey
29 F5 Çanakkale div. Turkey
29 F4 Çanakkale Boğazı str. Turkey
90 □2 Canala Pac. Oc.
147 C7 Canal Beagle chan. Arg.
147 A7 Canal Concepción chan. Chile
27 B7 Canal de la Galite chan. Tunisia
25 E2 Canal de Trasvase canal Spain
139 G3 Canal do Norte chan. Brazil
142 B1 Canal do Sul chan. Brazil
76 C4 Canal du Sahel canal Mali
146 C4 Canalejas Arg.
147 B5 Canal Moraleda chan. Chile
142 C1 Canal Perigoso chan. Brazil
147 B7 Canal Smyth chan. Chile
25 E2 Cañamares Spain
140 C2 Canamari Brazil
120 E3 Canandaigua U.S.A.
120 E3 Canandaigua Lake l. U.S.A.
130 C2 Cananea Mexico
113 H2 Cananée, Lac l. Can.
144 E6 Cananéia Brazil
138 D3 Canapiare, Co h. Colombia
144 D3 Canápolis Brazil
138 B4 Cañar Ecuador
25 □ Canarias, Islas is Atlantic Ocean
25 □ Canarias, Islas div. Spain
132 B2 Canarreos, Arch. de los is Cuba
148 H4 Canary Basin Atlantic Ocean
121 F3 Canastota U.S.A.
142 D2 Canastra r. Brazil
130 D3 Canatlán Mexico
119 D6 Canaveral, Cape c. U.S.A.
25 E2 Cañaveras Spain
145 J1 Canavieiras Brazil
26 C2 Canazei Italy
97 F2 Canbelego Aust.
97 G3 Canberra Aust.
126 B3 Canby U.S.A.
124 D2 Canby U.S.A.
20 D2 Cancale France
131 J4 Cancún Mexico
140 B3 Candarave Peru
20 D3 Candé France
145 F4 Candeias Brazil
146 E2 Candelaria *Misiones* Arg.
141 E3 Candelaria r. Bolivia
131 H5 Candelaria *Campeche* Mexico
127 F6 Candelaria *Chihuahua* Mexico
24 D2 Candelario, Sa de mt. ra. Spain
24 D2 Candeleda Spain
97 G4 Candelo Aust.
144 C6 Cândido de Abreu Brazil
142 C1 Cândido Mendes Brazil
144 C5 Cândido Mota Brazil
145 H1 Cândido Sales Brazil
111 H4 Candle Lake Can.
111 H4 Candle Lake l. Can.
152 C1 Candlemas I. i. *S. Sandwich Is* Atlantic Ocean
121 G4 Candlewood, Lake l. U.S.A.
124 D1 Cando U.S.A.
41 B2 Candon Phil.
100 A4 Cane r. Aust.
146 B3 Canela Alta Chile
26 B3 Canelli Italy
146 E3 Canelones Uruguay
146 B4 Cañete Chile
25 F2 Cañete Spain
140 B2 Cangallo Peru
79 C6 Cangamba Angola
79 C5 Cangandala Angola
24 B1 Cangas Spain
24 C1 Cangas del Narcea Spain
24 D1 Cangas de Onís Spain
79 D6 Cangombe Angola
51 G1 Cangshan China
142 E2 Canguaretama Brazil
146 F3 Canguçu Brazil
146 F3 Canguçu, Sa do h. Brazil
51 E4 Cangwu China
49 F5 Cangzhou China
113 G3 Caniapiscau Can.
113 G2 Caniapiscau r. Can.
113 G3 Caniapiscau, Rés. resr Can.
27 D7 Canicattì Italy
41 C4 Canigao Channel chan. Phil.
25 E4 Caniles Spain
110 E4 Canim L. l. Can.
110 E4 Canim Lake Can.
142 C1 Canindé *Pará* Brazil
142 D2 Canindé r. Brazil
142 E1 Caninde Brazil
120 E3 Canisteo r. U.S.A.
120 E3 Canisteo U.S.A.
130 E4 Cañitas de Felipe Pescador Mexico
60 C1 Çankiri Turkey
81 B5 Cankuzo Burundi
41 B4 Canlaon Phil.
110 F4 Canmore Can.
115 J3 Cann Can.
101 A6 Canna Aust.
16 D3 Canna i. U.K.
56 A4 Cannanore India
56 A4 Cannanore Islands is India
21 H5 Cannes France
101 B6 Canning Hill h. Aust.
122 A3 Cannon r. U.S.A.
81 □4 Cannoniers Pt pt Mauritius
99 G4 Cannonvale Aust.
97 G4 Cann River Aust.
139 E2 Caño Araguao r. Venezuela
143 B6 Canõas Brazil
145 F3 Canoeiros Brazil
111 H3 Canoe L. l. Can.
143 B6 Canoinhas Brazil
139 E2 Caño Macareo r. Venezuela
139 E2 Caño Manamo r. Venezuela
127 F4 Canon City U.S.A.
99 G4 Canoona Aust.
96 E3 Canopus Aust.
111 J4 Canora Can.
133 G4 Canouan i. St Vincent
97 G3 Canowindra Aust.
74 A4 Cansado *Western Sahara*
113 H4 Canso, C. hd Can.
140 A2 Canta Peru
24 D1 Cantabria div. Spain
24 C1 Cantábrica, Cordillera mt. ra. Spain
139 F4 Cantagalo Brazil
24 E2 Cantalejo Spain
24 B2 Cantanhede Portugal
146 C3 Cantantal Arg.
139 E2 Cantaura Venezuela
121 K2 Canterbury Can.
93 C5 Canterbury div. N.Z.
17 H6 Canterbury U.K.
93 C6 Canterbury Bight b. N.Z.
93 C5 Canterbury Plains plain N.Z.
43 D5 Cân Thơ Vietnam
41 C4 Cantilan Phil.
146 B2 Canto del Agua Chile
142 D2 Canto do Buriti Brazil
122 B5 Canton U.S.A.
121 H2 Canton U.S.A.
125 F5 Canton U.S.A.
122 B5 Canton U.S.A.
121 F2 Canton U.S.A.
120 C4 Canton U.S.A.
120 E4 Canton U.S.A.
144 B6 Cantu r. Brazil
143 B5 Cantú, Sa do h. Brazil
139 F5 Canudos Brazil
146 E4 Cañuelas Arg.
139 E5 Canumã *Amazonas* Brazil
139 F4 Canumã *Amazonas* Brazil
139 E5 Canutama Brazil
93 D4 Canvastown N.Z.
20 E2 Cany-Barville France
125 C5 Canyon U.S.A.
126 C2 Canyon City U.S.A.
129 H3 Canyon de Chelly National Monument res. U.S.A.
126 D2 Canyon Ferry L. l. U.S.A.
129 H2 Canyonlands National Park nat. park U.S.A.
110 D2 Canyon Ranges mt. ra. Can.
126 B3 Canyonville U.S.A.
79 D5 Canzar Angola
42 D2 Cao Băng Vietnam
65 K4 Caohu China
50 B3 Caojian China
79 C5 Caombo Angola
43 E4 Cao Nguyên Đâc Lăc plat. Vietnam
26 D3 Caorle Italy
49 H4 Caoshi China
51 F1 Cao Xian China
41 B5 Cap i. Phil.
27 E5 Capaccio Italy
132 D3 Cap-à-Foux c. Haiti
79 D5 Capaia Angola
138 D2 Capanaparo r. Venezuela
143 B6 Capanema r. Brazil
142 C1 Capanema Brazil
144 D6 Capão Bonito Brazil
144 A4 Capão Seco Brazil
143 D5 Caparaó, Sa do mt. ra. Brazil
138 C2 Caparo r. Venezuela
41 B3 Capas Phil.
133 E5 Capatárida Venezuela
113 H4 Cap-aux-Meules Can.
20 D5 Capbreton France
115 J3 Cap-de-la-Madeleine Can.
25 H3 Capdepera Spain
99 F4 Cape r. Aust.
101 C7 Cape Arid Nat. Park nat. park Aust.
97 G5 Cape Barren Island i. Aust.
148 K8 Cape Basin Atlantic Ocean
100 D2 Cape Bougainville Abor. Land res. Aust.
113 H4 Cape Breton Highlands Nat. Pk nat. park Can.
113 H4 Cape Breton Island i. Can.
113 J3 Cape Charles Can.
121 E6 Cape Charles U.S.A.
76 D5 Cape Coast Ghana
121 H4 Cape Cod Bay b. U.S.A.
121 J4 Cape Cod National Seashore res. U.S.A.
119 D7 Cape Coral U.S.A.
114 E4 Cape Croker Can.
109 L3 Cape Dorset Can.
152 B5 Cape Evans Antarctic Base Ant.
125 F4 Cape Girardeau U.S.A.
150 D5 Cape Johnson Depth depth Pac. Oc.
101 C7 Cape Le Grand Nat. Park nat. park Aust.
145 G2 Capelinha Brazil
99 G4 Capella Aust.
121 F5 Cape May U.S.A.
121 F5 Cape May Court House U.S.A.
121 F5 Cape May Pt pt U.S.A.
79 C5 Capenda-Camulemba Angola
100 A4 Cape Range Nat. Park nat. park Aust.
109 H5 Cape Sable Island i. Can.
113 J4 Cape St George Can.
133 □5 Capesterre *Guadeloupe* Caribbean
113 H4 Cape Tormentine Can.
82 B5 Cape Town R.S.A.
76 □ Cape Verde country Africa
148 G5 Cape Verde Basin Atlantic Ocean
148 F5 Cape Verde Fracture Atlantic Ocean
148 H4 Cape Verde Plateau Atlantic Ocean
121 E2 Cape Vincent U.S.A.
99 E2 Cape York pen. Aust.
133 D3 Cap-Haïtien Haiti
138 D3 Capibara Venezuela
142 E2 Capiberibe r. Brazil
142 C1 Capim Brazil
142 C1 Capim r. Brazil
144 D3 Capinópolis Brazil
140 C3 Capinota Bolivia
152 B2 Capitán Arturo Prat Chile Base Ant.
141 E4 Capitán Bado Paraguay
144 B6 Capitán Leônidas Marques Brazil
127 F5 Capitan Peak mt. U.S.A.
145 G2 Capitão Enéas Brazil
129 G2 Capitol Reef National Park nat. park U.S.A.

20 E3 Cher r. Centre France
119 E5 Cheraw U.S.A.
20 D2 Cherbourg France
12 J4 Cherdakly Rus. Fed.
14 C4 Cheremisinovo Rus. Fed.
44 H1 Cheremkhovo Rus. Fed.
65 M2 Cheremushki Rus. Fed.
65 K2 Cherepanovo Rus. Fed.
12 F3 Cherepovets Rus. Fed.
12 H2 Cherevkovo Rus. Fed.
75 F1 Chéria Algeria
15 G2 Cherkas'ke Ukraine
14 H3 Cherkasskoye Rus. Fed.
15 E2 Cherkasy Ukraine
15 D2 Cherkasy div. Ukraine
13 G6 Cherkessk Rus. Fed.
14 D1 Cherkutino Rus. Fed.
56 C2 Cherla India
65 H2 Cherlak Rus. Fed.
48 D3 Cherlen Gol r. Mongolia
15 B2 Cherlenivka Ukraine
14 C3 Chern' Rus. Fed.
65 G4 Chernak Kazak.
14 D3 Chernava Rus. Fed.
14 D3 Chernava Rus. Fed.
14 F3 Chernavka Rus. Fed.
62 K2 Chernaya Rus. Fed.
15 E1 Chernecha Sloboda Ukraine
15 F2 Cherneshchyna Ukraine
14 D2 Chernevo Rus. Fed.
49 K3 Chernigovka Rus. Fed.
15 D1 Chernihiv Ukraine
15 G3 Cherninivka Ukraine
15 A2 Chernivtsi Chernivtsi Ukraine
15 C2 Chernivtsi Vinnytsya Ukraine
15 A2 Chernivtsi div. Ukraine
14 D1 Chernogolovka Rus. Fed.
65 M2 Chernogorsk Rus. Fed.
12 K2 Chernorechenskiy Rus. Fed.
48 E2 Chernovskiye Rus. Fed.
14 F3 Chernoyar Rus. Fed.
65 G1 Chernoye, Oz. l. Rus. Fed.
14 F2 Chernukha Rus. Fed.
64 E1 Chernushka Rus. Fed.
15 C1 Chernyakhiv Ukraine
11 F5 Chernyakhovsk Rus. Fed.
15 G1 Chernyanka Rus. Fed.
49 H1 Chernyayeve Rus. Fed.
49 F1 Chernyshevsk Rus. Fed.
13 H6 Chernyye Zemli reg. Rus. Fed.
12 E2 Chernyy Porog Rus. Fed.
13 H5 Chernyy Yar Rus. Fed.
124 E3 Cherokee U.S.A.
125 D4 Cherokee U.S.A.
125 E4 Cherokees, Lake o' the l. U.S.A.
132 C1 Cherokee Sound The Bahamas
55 G4 Cherrapunji India
129 E2 Cherry Creek U.S.A.
129 E1 Cherry Creek Mts mts U.S.A.
121 K2 Cherryfield U.S.A.
86 J6 Cherry Island i. Solomon Islands
115 G5 Cherry Valley Can.
121 F3 Cherry Valley U.S.A.
63 S3 Cherskiy Rus. Fed.
63 Q3 Cherskogo, Khrebet mt. ra. Rus. Fed.
13 G5 Chertkovo Rus. Fed.
93 C5 Chertsey N.Z.
12 J2 Cherva Rus. Fed.
28 E3 Cherven Bryag Bulgaria
14 B4 Chervone Rus. Fed.
15 C2 Chervone Ukraine
15 C1 Chervonoarmiys'k Ukraine
15 A1 Chervonohrad Ukraine
15 E1 Chervonozavods'ke Ukraine
15 D3 Chervonoznam"yanka Ukraine
15 G2 Chervonyy Donets' Ukraine
15 E3 Chervonyy Mayak Ukraine
12 D4 Chervyen' Belarus
123 E4 Chesaning U.S.A.
121 E6 Chesapeake U.S.A.
121 E5 Chesapeake Bay b. U.S.A.
121 G3 Cheshire U.S.A.
64 F5 Cheshme 2-y Turkmenistan
62 F3 Cheshskaya Guba b. Rus. Fed.
57 E2 Chesht-e Sharīf Afghanistan
64 F2 Chesma Rus. Fed.
17 F5 Chester U.K.
128 B1 Chester U.S.A.
118 B4 Chester U.S.A.
121 E5 Chester r. U.S.A.
126 E1 Chester U.S.A.
121 F5 Chester U.S.A.
119 D5 Chester U.S.A.
133 □1 Chester Cas. Jamaica
17 G5 Chesterfield U.K.
95 L2 Chesterfield, Îles is Pac. Oc.
111 L2 Chesterfield Inlet Can.
111 L2 Chesterfield Inlet inlet Can.
121 E5 Chestertown U.S.A.
121 G3 Chestertown U.S.A.
115 H4 Chesterville Can.
120 D4 Chestnut Ridge ridge U.S.A.
121 J1 Chesuncook U.S.A.
121 J1 Chesuncook Lake l. U.S.A.
75 F1 Chetaïbi Algeria
43 A5 Chetamale Andaman and Nicobar Is India
83 D2 Chete Safari Area res. Zimbabwe
113 H4 Chéticamp Can.
50 B2 Cheti La pass China
53 D8 Chetlat i. India
131 H5 Chetumal Mexico
93 E4 Chetwode Is is N.Z.
110 E3 Chetwynd Can.
49 J2 Cheugda Rus. Fed.
45 □ Cheung Chau i. Hong Kong
45 □ Cheung Chau Hong Kong
140 C2 Chevejecure Bolivia
93 D5 Cheviot N.Z.
17 F4 Cheviot Hills h. U.K.
99 E5 Cheviot Ra. h. Aust.
17 F4 Cheviot, The h. U.K.
80 C4 Che'w Bahir salt l. Ethiopia
80 C3 Che'w Bahir Wildlife Reserve res. Ethiopia
126 C1 Chewelah U.S.A.
83 D2 Chewore Safari Area res. Zimbabwe
125 D5 Cheyenne U.S.A.
124 C3 Cheyenne r. U.S.A.
126 F3 Cheyenne U.S.A.
124 C4 Cheyenne Wells U.S.A.
101 B7 Cheyne B. b. Aust.
110 E4 Chezacut Can.
54 D4 Chhabra India
55 F4 Chhapra India
54 D4 Chhata India
55 G4 Chhatak Bangladesh
54 D4 Chhatarpur India
54 B3 Chhatr Pakistan
54 D5 Chhindwara India
43 D4 Chhlong, P. r. Cambodia
56 A1 Chhota Udepur India
55 G4 Chhukha Bhutan
51 H4 Chia-i Taiwan
79 B7 Chiange Angola
42 C3 Chiang Kham Thailand
42 C3 Chiang Khan Thailand
42 B3 Chiang Mai Thailand
131 G5 Chiapas div. Mexico
26 B3 Chiari Italy
26 D4 Chiascio r. Italy
131 F5 Chiautla Mexico
26 B3 Chiavari Italy
26 B2 Chiavenno Italy
47 H6 Chiba Japan
47 H6 Chiba div. Japan
47 □2 Chibana Japan
79 B7 Chibemba Angola
79 B7 Chibia Angola
83 E3 Chiboma Mozambique
115 H2 Chibougamau Can.
115 H2 Chibougamau L. l. Can.
115 J2 Chibougamau, Parc de res. Can.
46 D5 Chibu Japan
46 D6 Chiburi-jima i. Japan
47 F5 Chibu-Sangaku Nat. Park nat. park. Japan
55 G2 Chibuzhang Hu salt l. China
122 D5 Chicago airport U.S.A.
122 D5 Chicago U.S.A.
122 D5 Chicago Heights U.S.A.
122 C5 Chicago Ship Canal canal U.S.A.
79 D6 Chicaluege r. Angola
138 B5 Chicama Peru
138 B5 Chicama r. Peru
83 E2 Chicamba Real, Barragem de dam Mozambique
79 C6 Chicapa r. Angola
72 C4 Chicha well Chad
110 B3 Chichagof U.S.A.
110 B3 Chichagof Island i. U.S.A.
140 C4 Chichas, Cord. de mt. ra. Bolivia
49 E4 Chicheng China
131 H4 Chichén Itza Mexico
17 G6 Chichester U.K.
100 B4 Chichester Ra. Nat. Park nat. park Aust.
100 B4 Chichester Range mt. ra. Aust.
47 G6 Chichibu Japan
47 G6 Chichibu-Tama National Park nat. park. Japan
120 E6 Chickahominy r. U.S.A.
119 C5 Chickamauga L. l. U.S.A.
125 D5 Chickasha U.S.A.
24 C4 Chiclana de la Frontera Spain
138 B5 Chiclayo Peru
147 C5 Chico r. Chubut Arg.
147 B5 Chico r. Chubut/Río Negro Arg.
147 C6 Chico r. Santa Cruz Arg.
147 B7 Chico r. Arg./Chile
128 B2 Chico U.S.A.
83 E2 Chicoa Mozambique
115 F2 Chicobi, Lac l. Can.
79 B6 Chicomba Angola
131 G6 Chicomucelo Mexico
121 G3 Chicopee U.S.A.
41 B2 Chico Sapocoy, Mt mt. Phil.
81 □5 Chicots, Pl. des plain Réunion Indian Ocean
115 K2 Chicoutimi Can.
83 E3 Chicualacuala Mozambique
79 C6 Chicupo Angola
56 B4 Chidambaram India
83 E3 Chidenguele Mozambique
113 H1 Chidley, C. c. Can.
119 D6 Chiefland U.S.A.
18 F5 Chiemsee l. Germany
79 E5 Chiengi Zambia
26 A3 Chieri Italy
27 E4 Chieti Italy
131 F5 Chietla Mexico
49 F4 Chifeng China
65 H4 Chiganak Kazak.
65 H3 Chiganak Kazak.
113 G4 Chignecto B. b. Can.
108 C4 Chignik U.S.A.
138 B2 Chigorodó Colombia
140 C4 Chiguana Bolivia
83 E3 Chigubo Mozambique
55 G3 Chigu Co l. China
130 D2 Chihuahua div. Mexico
130 D2 Chihuahua Mexico
146 C4 Chihuido Medio mt. Arg.
65 G4 Chiili Kazak.
51 E4 Chikan China
56 B3 Chik Ballapur India
54 D5 Chikhali Kalan Parasia India
54 D5 Chikhli India
56 A3 Chikmagalur India
48 C2 Chikoy r. Rus. Fed.
48 C2 Chikoy Rus. Fed.
47 G5 Chikuma-gawa r. Japan
47 G6 Chikura Japan
46 C7 Chikushino Japan
81 B7 Chikwa Zambia
83 E2 Chikwawa Malawi
46 H2 Chikyū-misaki pt Japan
79 B6 Chila Angola
110 E4 Chilanko Forks Can.
131 F5 Chilapa Mexico
54 C2 Chilas Pakistan
65 H5 Chilas Jammu and Kashmir
56 B5 Chilaw Sri Lanka
140 B3 Chilca, Cord. de mt. ra. Peru
128 B2 Chilcoot U.S.A.
110 E4 Chilcotin r. Can.
99 G3 Chilcott I. i. Coral Sea Islands Terr. Pac. Oc.
99 H5 Childers Aust.
125 C5 Childress U.S.A.
136 C7 Chile country S. America
148 D8 Chile Basin Pac. Oc.
147 B6 Chile Chico Chile
146 C2 Chilecito La Rioja Arg.
79 B6 Chilengue, Serra do mts Angola
28 G2 Chilia Veche Romania
122 C5 Chilicothe U.S.A.
65 J4 Chilik Kazak.
55 F6 Chilika Lake l. India
79 E6 Chililabombwe Zambia
110 E4 Chilko r. Can.
110 E4 Chilko L. l. Can.
99 F3 Chillagoe Aust.
146 B4 Chillán Chile
146 E4 Chillar Arg.
124 E4 Chillicothe U.S.A.
120 B5 Chillicothe U.S.A.
140 C3 Chilliculco Peru
54 C1 Chillinji Pakistan
110 E5 Chilliwack Can.
83 E3 Chiloane, Ilha i. Mozambique
147 B5 Chiloé, Isla De i. Chile
147 B5 Chiloé, Parque Nacional nat. park Chile
126 B3 Chiloquin U.S.A.
131 F5 Chilpancingo Mexico
54 C1 Chilpi Pakistan
97 F4 Chiltern Aust.
17 G6 Chiltern Hills h. U.K.
122 C3 Chilton U.S.A.
79 E6 Chilubi Zambia
81 B7 Chilumba Malawi
51 H3 Chi-lung Taiwan
54 D2 Chilung P. pass India
83 F2 Chilwa, Lake l. Malawi
81 B6 Chimala Tanzania
131 H6 Chimaltenango Guatemala
130 L7 Chimán Panama
83 E2 Chimanimani Zimbabwe
83 E2 Chimanimani Mountains mts Mozambique/Zimbabwe
146 C3 Chimbas Arg.
64 E4 Chimbay Uzbekistan
138 B4 Chimborazo mt. Ecuador
140 A1 Chimbote Peru
63 S3 Chimchememel' Rus. Fed.
138 C2 Chimichaguá Colombia
81 □1 Chimney Rocks is Seychelles
83 E2 Chimoio Mozambique
42 A2 Chin div. Myanmar
33 L6 China country Asia
131 F3 China Mexico
138 C2 Chinácota Colombia
131 H5 Chinajá Guatemala
128 D4 China Lake l. U.S.A.
121 J2 China Lake l. U.S.A.
130 J6 Chinandega Nicaragua
128 C5 China Pt pt U.S.A.
140 A2 Chincha Alta Peru
110 F3 Chinchaga r. Can.
140 A2 Chincha, Islas de is Peru
99 G5 Chinchilla Aust.
121 F6 Chincoteague B. b. U.S.A.
83 F2 Chinde Mozambique
49 H6 Chin Do i. S. Korea
50 B1 Chindu China
42 A2 Chindwin r. Myanmar
47 □2 Chinen Japan
54 C2 Chineni India
49 H5 Chinghwa N. Korea
64 D2 Chingirlau Rus. Fed.
65 J3 Chingiz-Tau, Khr. mt. ra. Kazak.
79 E6 Chingola Zambia
79 C6 Chinguar Angola
74 B4 Chinguețți Mauritania
78 C1 Chinguil Chad
49 J6 Chinhae S. Korea
83 E2 Chinhoyi Zimbabwe
54 C3 Chiniot Pakistan
130 C3 Chinipas Mexico
49 J6 Chinju S. Korea
64 E4 Chink Kaplankyr h. Asia
78 D2 Chinko r. C.A.R.
129 H3 Chinle U.S.A.
129 H3 Chinle Valley v. U.S.A.
129 H3 Chinle Wash r. U.S.A.
51 G3 Chinmen Taiwan
80 D2 Chinnile well Djibouti
56 B2 Chinnur India
47 G6 Chino Japan
20 E3 Chinon France
129 F4 Chino Valley U.S.A.
81 B7 Chinsali Zambia
56 B3 Chintamani India
132 D5 Chinú Colombia
46 A6 Chinyang-ho l. S. Korea
64 D4 Chin Zap. escarpment Kazak.
26 D3 Chioggia Italy
29 E5 Chios i. Greece
29 E5 Chios Greece
81 B7 Chipata Zambia
147 C5 Chipchihua, Sa de mt. ra. Arg.
79 E6 Chipili Zambia
79 C6 Chipindo Angola
49 F5 Chiping China
83 E3 Chipinge Zimbabwe
24 C4 Chipiona Spain
56 A2 Chiplun India
114 B2 Chipman Lake l. Can.
79 C6 Chipoia Angola
17 F6 Chippenham U.K.
122 B3 Chippewa r. U.S.A.
122 B3 Chippewa Falls U.S.A.
122 B3 Chippewa, Lake l. U.S.A.
17 G6 Chipping Norton U.K.
28 D3 Chiprovtsi Bulgaria
121 K2 Chiputneticook Lakes lakes U.S.A.
131 H6 Chiquimula Guatemala
138 C2 Chiquinquira Colombia
13 G5 Chir r. Rus. Fed.
56 C3 Chirada India
83 F2 Chiradzulu Malawi
56 A4 Chirakkal India
56 C3 Chirala India
83 E2 Chiramba Mozambique
57 F2 Chiras Afghanistan
65 G4 Chirchik Uzbekistan
83 E3 Chiredzi Zimbabwe
77 G2 Chirfa Niger
48 A2 Chirgalandy Rus. Fed.
129 H5 Chiricahua National Monument res. U.S.A.
129 H6 Chiricahua Peak summit U.S.A.
138 C2 Chiriguaná Colombia
55 H5 Chiringa Bangladesh
130 K7 Chiriquí, Golfo de b. Panama
130 K7 Chiriquí, L. de b. Panama
83 D2 Chirisa Safari Area res. Zimbabwe
83 F2 Chiromo Malawi
28 E3 Chirpan Bulgaria
130 K7 Chirripo mt. Costa Rica
79 E7 Chirundu Zambia
79 E6 Chisamba Zambia
112 E3 Chisasibi Can.
131 H6 Chisec Guatemala
64 E2 Chishmy Rus. Fed.
122 A2 Chisholm U.S.A.
54 C3 Chishtian Mandi Pakistan
50 D2 Chishur China
15 C3 Chişinău Moldova
28 C1 Chişineu-Criş Romania
65 J2 Chistoozernoye Rus. Fed.
12 J4 Chistopol' Rus. Fed.
140 C4 Chita Bolivia
48 E2 Chita Rus. Fed.
49 F1 Chita div. Rus. Fed.
79 B7 Chitado Angola
81 B7 Chitambo Zambia
48 D2 Chitanga Rus. Fed.
79 D5 Chitato Angola
12 J2 Chitayevo Rus. Fed.
111 H4 Chitek Lake Can.
79 C6 Chitembo Angola
81 B6 Chitipa Malawi
83 E3 Chitobe Mozambique
46 H2 Chitose Japan
56 B3 Chitradurga India
54 E4 Chitrakut India
54 B2 Chitral Pakistan
54 B2 Chitral r. Pakistan
130 K8 Chitré Panama
55 G5 Chittagong div. Bangladesh
55 G5 Chittagong Bangladesh
54 C4 Chittaurgarh India
56 B3 Chittoor India
56 B4 Chittur India
81 B7 Chitungulu Zambia
83 E2 Chitungwiza Zimbabwe
131 H5 Chiuchanhá Mexico
81 C7 Chiulezi r. Mozambique
79 D5 Chiumbe r. Angola/Zaire
79 D7 Chiume Angola
81 C7 Chiúre Novo Mozambique
26 C4 Chiusi Italy
83 F1 Chiuta, Lake l. Malawi/Mozambique
25 F3 Chiva Spain
140 C2 Chive Bolivia
83 E2 Chivhu Zimbabwe
83 E3 Chivi Zimbabwe
51 F4 Chixi China
82 D2 Chizarira National Park nat. park Zimbabwe
12 H1 Chizha Rus. Fed.
46 E6 Chizu Japan
15 F3 Chkalove Ukraine
65 H2 Chkalovo Kazak.
14 F1 Chkalovsk Rus. Fed.
19 G3 Chlumec nad Cidlinou Czech Rep.
19 K3 Chmielnik Poland
49 H6 Ch'o i. S. Korea
43 □ Choa Chu Kang Singapore
43 □ Choa Chu Kang h. Singapore
43 D4 Chŏâm Khsant Cambodia
82 C2 Chobe div. Botswana
82 C2 Chobe National Park nat. park Botswana
19 G3 Chocianów Poland
19 G2 Chociwel Poland
129 E5 Chocolate Mts mts U.S.A.
138 C2 Chocontá Colombia
19 H2 Chodzież Poland
147 C4 Choele Choel Arg.
83 E1 Chofombo Mozambique
54 C2 Chogo Lungma Gl. gl. Pakistan
13 H6 Chograyskoye Vdkhr. resr Rus. Fed.
111 J4 Choiceland Can.
90 □1 Choiseul i. Solomon Is.
147 E7 Choiseul Sound chan. Falkland Is.
130 C3 Choix Mexico
19 G2 Chojna Poland
19 H2 Chojnice Poland
19 G3 Chojnów Poland
47 H4 Chōkai-san vol Japan
125 D6 Choke Canyon L. l. U.S.A.
80 C2 Ch'ok'ē Mountains mt. ra. Ethiopia
54 E3 Chokola mt. China
65 H4 Chokpar Kazak.
55 F3 Choksum China
63 Q2 Chokurdakh Rus. Fed.
83 E3 Chókwé Mozambique
50 B1 Chola Shan mt. ra. China
20 D3 Cholet France
147 B5 Cholila Arg.
65 J4 Cholpon-Ata Kyrgyzstan
130 J6 Choluteca Honduras
79 E7 Choma Zambia
55 G4 Chomo Lhari mt. Bhutan
42 B3 Chom Thong Thailand
54 C4 Chomun India
18 F3 Chomutov Czech Rep.
63 M3 Chona r. Rus. Fed.
49 H5 Ch'ŏnan S. Korea
43 C4 Chon Buri Thailand
138 A4 Chone Ecuador
51 G3 Chong'an China
49 H5 Chongchon r. N. Korea
49 J4 Ch'ŏngjin N. Korea
49 H5 Chŏngju N. Korea
49 H5 Ch'ŏngju S. Korea
43 C4 Chŏng Kal Cambodia
50 B2 Chongkü China
51 H2 Chongming Dao i. China
79 B6 Chongoroi Angola
49 H5 Chŏngp'yŏng N. Korea
50 D2 Chongqing China
50 D2 Chongqing China
51 F3 Chongren China
49 H6 Chŏngŭp S. Korea
79 E7 Chongwe Zambia
50 D1 Chongxin China
51 F4 Chongyang China
51 G3 Chongyang Xi r. China
51 F3 Chongyi China
50 D4 Chongzuo China
15 F3 Chonhar Ukraine
15 F3 Chonhar, Pivostriv pen. Ukraine
49 H6 Ch'ŏnju S. Korea
49 E3 Chonogol Mongolia
43 D5 Chơn Thanh Vietnam
55 F3 Cho Oyu mt. China
19 L4 Chop Ukraine
55 E4 Chopan India
43 D5 Chơ Phước Hai Vietnam
143 B6 Chopim r. Brazil
143 B6 Chopimzinho Brazil
15 C1 Chopovychi Ukraine
121 F5 Choptank r. U.S.A.
54 B4 Chor Pakistan
29 C6 Chora Greece
15 E2 Chornobay Ukraine
15 D1 Chornobyl' Ukraine
13 E6 Chornomors'ke Krym Ukraine
15 D3 Chornomors'ke Odesa Ukraine
15 C2 Chornorudka Ukraine
15 E1 Chornukhy Ukraine
15 B2 Chornyy Ostriv Ukraine
146 B2 Choros, Is de los is Chile
19 L2 Choroszcz Poland
142 E2 Chorrochó Brazil
15 A2 Chortkiv Ukraine
49 H5 Ch'ŏrwŏn S. Korea
19 K2 Chorzele Poland
49 J4 Ch'osan N. Korea
45 N4 Chosen-Man b. N. Korea
47 H6 Chōshi Japan
146 B4 Chos Malal Arg.
19 G2 Choszczno Poland
138 B5 Chota Peru
55 E5 Chota Nagpur reg. India
126 D2 Choteau U.S.A.
54 B3 Choti Pakistan
75 D2 Chott ech Chergui salt l. Algeria
75 F2 Chott el Fejaj salt l. Tunisia
75 E1 Chott el Hodna salt l. Algeria
75 F2 Chott el Jerid salt l. Tunisia
75 F2 Chott el Malah salt l. Algeria
75 F2 Chott Melrhir salt l. Algeria
74 B4 Choûm Mauritania
128 B3 Chowchilla U.S.A.
110 F4 Chown, Mt mt. Can.
48 E3 Choybalsan Mongolia
48 D3 Choyr Mongolia
122 D6 Chrisman U.S.A.
93 D5 Christchurch N.Z.
139 F2 Christianburg Guyana
109 M2 Christian, C. pt Can.
114 E4 Christian I. i. Can.
91 □14 Christian, Pt pt Pitcairn I. Pac. Oc.
120 C6 Christiansburg U.S.A.
110 C3 Christian Sound chan. U.S.A.
119 □3 Christiansted Virgin Is Caribbean
111 G3 Christina r. Can.
100 D3 Christmas Cr. r. Aust.
100 D3 Christmas Creek Aust.
149 M4 Christmas Island i. Indian Ocean
19 G4 Chrudim Czech Rep.
29 E7 Chrysi i. Greece
29 E4 Chrysoupoli Greece
65 H4 Chu Kazak.
65 H4 Chu r. Kazak.
65 J4 Chu div. Kyrgyzstan
55 G5 Chuadanga Bangladesh
83 E3 Chuali, L. l. Mozambique
51 H2 Chuansha China
50 B2 Chubalung China
15 G3 Chubarivka Ukraine
126 D3 Chubbuck U.S.A.
147 C5 Chubut div. Arg.
147 C5 Chubut r. Arg.
14 E2 Chuchkovo Rus. Fed.
129 E5 Chuckwalla Mts mts U.S.A.
15 C1 Chudniv Ukraine
12 D3 Chudovo Rus. Fed.
108 D3 Chugach Mountains mt. ra. U.S.A.
46 D6 Chūgoku-sanchi mt. ra. Japan
126 F3 Chugwater U.S.A.
15 G2 Chuhuyiv Ukraine
129 G5 Chuichu U.S.A.
65 H4 Chu-Iliyskiye Gory mt. ra. Kazak.
45 P1 Chukchagirskoye, Ozero l. Rus. Fed.
108 A3 Chukchi Sea sea Rus. Fed./U.S.A.
12 G3 Chukhloma Rus. Fed.
63 T3 Chukotskiy Khrebet mt. ra. Rus. Fed.
108 A3 Chukotskiy, Mys c. Rus. Fed.
108 A3 Chukotskiy Poluostrov pen. Rus. Fed.
15 E3 Chulakivka Ukraine
65 G4 Chulakkurgan Kazak.
12 H1 Chulasa Rus. Fed.
128 D5 Chula Vista U.S.A.
14 F1 Chulkovo Rus. Fed.
138 A5 Chulucanas Peru
48 B2 Chuluut Gol r. Mongolia
65 L2 Chulyshmanskiy Khr. mt. ra. Rus. Fed.
140 C3 Chuma Bolivia
15 F3 Chumaky Ukraine
54 D2 Chumar India
80 C4 Chumba Ethiopia
55 G4 Chumbi China
146 C2 Chumbicha Arg.
65 L3 Chumek Kazak.
63 P4 Chumikan Rus. Fed.
42 C3 Chum Phae Thailand
43 B5 Chumphon Thailand
42 C4 Chum Saeng Thailand
65 K2 Chumysh r. Rus. Fed.
51 G2 Chun'an China
49 H5 Ch'unch'ŏn S. Korea
65 J4 Chundzha Kazak.
79 E7 Chunga Zambia
49 H5 Ch'ungju S. Korea
49 J6 Ch'ungmu S. Korea
81 C7 Chungu Tanzania
131 H5 Chunhuhub Mexico
55 F3 Chunit Tso l. China
63 M3 Chunya r. Rus. Fed.
81 B6 Chunya Tanzania
43 D5 Chuŏr Phnum Dâmrei mt. ra. Cambodia
43 D4 Chuŏr Phnum Dângrêk mt. ra. Cambodia/Thailand
43 C4 Chuŏr Phnum Krâvanh mt. ra. Cambodia
50 C2 Chuosijia China
12 E1 Chupa Rus. Fed.
14 F2 Chupaleyka Rus. Fed.
133 □3 Chupara Pt pt Trinidad Trin. & Tobago
15 D2 Chupyra Ukraine
140 B3 Chuquibamba Peru
140 C4 Chuquicamata Chile
140 D4 Chuquisaca div. Bolivia
21 J3 Chur Switz.
55 H4 Churachandpur India
14 H2 Churachiki Rus. Fed.
63 P3 Churapcha Rus. Fed.
64 E1 Churayevo Rus. Fed.
111 L3 Churchill Can.
111 K3 Churchill r. Can.
113 H3 Churchill r. Can.
111 L3 Churchill, Cape c. Can.
113 H3 Churchill Falls Can.
111 H3 Churchill Lake l. Can.
110 D3 Churchill Peak summit Can.
112 E2 Churchill Sound chan. Can.
124 D1 Churchs Ferry U.S.A.
120 D5 Churchville U.S.A.
55 F4 Churia Ghati Hills mt. ra. Nepal
54 C3 Churu India
138 D1 Churuguara Venezuela
46 J2 Chūrui Japan
54 D2 Chushul India
129 H3 Chuska Mountains mts U.S.A.
62 G4 Chusovoy Rus. Fed.
115 K2 Chute-des-Passes Can.
115 G3 Chute-Rouge Can.
115 H3 Chute-St-Philippe Can.
15 F2 Chutove Ukraine
51 H3 Chu-tung Taiwan
86 G4 Chuuk is Fed. States of Micronesia
14 H2 Chuvashiya div. Rus. Fed.
51 G1 Chu Xian China
50 C3 Chuxiong China
43 E4 Chư Yang Sin mt. Vietnam
15 D3 Chychykliya r. Ukraine
15 E2 Chyhyryn Ukraine
81 C5 Chyulu Range mt. ra. Kenya
15 C3 Ciadâr-Lunga Moldova
40 B3 Ciamis Indon.
40 A3 Cianjur Indon.
144 B5 Cianorte Brazil
40 A3 Cibadak Indon.
40 B3 Cibatu Indon.
40 A3 Cibinong Indon.
127 E6 Cibuta Mexico
26 E3 Čičarija mt. ra. Croatia
29 G5 Çiçekli Turkey
28 C3 Čičevac Yugo.
90 □7 Cicia i. Fiji
60 C1 Cide Turkey
19 K2 Ciechanów Poland
19 L2 Ciechanowiec Poland
19 J2 Ciechocinek Poland
132 C2 Ciego de Avila Cuba
138 C1 Ciénaga Colombia
132 D5 Ciénaga de Oro Colombia
132 D5 Ciénaga Grande l. Colombia
125 C7 Ciénega de Flores Mexico
127 E6 Cieneguita Mexico
132 B2 Cienfuegos Cuba
19 J4 Čierny Balog Slovakia
24 B1 Cíes, Illas is Spain
19 L3 Cieszanów Poland
19 J4 Cieszyn Poland
25 F3 Cieza Spain
29 G4 Çiftlikköy Turkey
25 E2 Cifuentes Spain
25 E2 Cigüela r. Spain
61 C2 Cihanbeyli Turkey
130 D5 Cihuatlán Mexico
24 D3 Cijara, Embalse de resr Spain
28 B3 Cijevna r. Albania
40 B3 Cikalong Indon.
90 □7 Cikobia i. Fiji
26 F4 Čikola r. Croatia
40 B3 Cilacap Indon.
81 □5 Cilaog Réunion Indian Ocean
13 G7 Çıldır Turkey
13 G7 Çıldır Gölü l. Turkey
40 B3 Ciledug Indon.
51 E2 Cili China
61 B1 Cilicia reg. Turkey
61 C1 Cilician Gates pass Turkey
28 E3 Cilieni Romania
64 D4 Çiloy Adasi i. Azerbaijan
129 E4 Cima U.S.A.
40 A3 Cimahi Indon.
127 F4 Cimarron U.S.A.
125 D4 Cimarron r. U.S.A.
15 C3 Cimişlia Moldova
28 D1 Cîmpeni Romania
60 E2 Çınar Turkey
29 G4 Çınarcık Turkey
138 D2 Cinaruco-Capanaparo, Parque Nacional nat. park Venezuela
25 G2 Cinca r. Spain
120 A5 Cincinnati U.S.A.
121 F3 Cincinnatus U.S.A.
147 C5 Cinco Chañares Arg.
60 B2 Çine Turkey
43 A5 Cinque I. i. Andaman and Nicobar Is India
131 G5 Cintalapa Mexico
25 F1 Cintruénigo Spain
144 D5 Cinzas r. Brazil
145 G3 Cipo r. Brazil
147 C4 Cipolletti Arg.
145 G4 Cipotânea Brazil
108 D3 Circle U.S.A.
126 F2 Circle U.S.A.
120 B5 Circleville U.S.A.
129 F2 Circleville U.S.A.
40 B3 Cirebon Indon.
40 B3 Ciremay, G. vol Indon.
17 G6 Cirencester U.K.
25 F2 Ciria Spain
26 A3 Ciriè Italy
15 C2 Ciripcău Moldova
27 F6 Cirò Marina Italy
113 H2 Cirque Mtn mt. Can.
122 C6 Cisco U.S.A.
125 D5 Cisco U.S.A.
129 H2 Cisco U.S.A.
19 L4 Cisna Poland
28 E2 Cisnădie Romania
138 B2 Cisneros Colombia
147 B5 Cisnes r. Chile
24 D1 Cistierna Spain
139 F3 Citaré r. Brazil
131 F5 Citlaltépetl, Vol. vol Mexico
26 F4 Čitluk Bos.-Herz.
139 G3 Citron French Guiana
82 B5 Citrusdal R.S.A.
26 D4 Città della Pieve Italy
26 D4 Città di Castello Italy
28 D1 Ciucea Romania
131 E2 Ciudad Acuña Mexico
131 E5 Ciudad Altamirano Mexico
139 E2 Ciudad Bolívar Venezuela
130 D3 Ciudad Camargo Mexico
131 H6 Ciudad Cuauhtémoc Mexico
131 H5 Ciudad del Carmen Mexico
141 F5 Ciudad del Este Paraguay
130 D2 Ciudad Delicias Mexico
131 F4 Ciudad del Maíz Mexico
138 D2 Ciudad de Nutrias Venezuela
131 F4 Ciudad de Valles Mexico
139 E2 Ciudad Guayana Venezuela
130 D2 Ciudad Guerrero Mexico
130 E5 Ciudad Guzmán Mexico
131 E5 Ciudad Hidalgo Mexico
131 G5 Ciudad Ixtepec Mexico
130 D2 Ciudad Juárez Mexico
130 E3 Ciudad Lerdo Mexico
131 F4 Ciudad Madero Mexico
131 F4 Ciudad Mante Mexico
131 F5 Ciudad Mendoza Mexico
131 F3 Ciudad Mier Mexico
130 C3 Ciudad Obregón Mexico
139 E2 Ciudad Piar Venezuela
24 E3 Ciudad Real Spain
131 F3 Ciudad Río Bravo Mexico
24 C2 Ciudad Rodrigo Spain
131 F4 Ciudad Victoria Mexico
28 E1 Ciumani Romania
25 H2 Ciutadella de Menorca Spain
60 D1 Civa Br. pt Turkey
26 D2 Cividale del Friuli Italy
27 D4 Civita Castellana Italy
26 D4 Civitanova Marche Italy
27 C4 Civitavecchia Italy
27 D5 Civitella Roveto Italy
20 E3 Civray Poitou-Charentes France
60 B2 Çivril Turkey
51 H2 Cixi China
48 E5 Ci Xian China
60 E2 Cizre Turkey
17 H6 Clacton-on-Sea U.K.
111 G3 Claire, Lake l. Can.
126 B3 Clair Engle L. resr U.S.A.
120 D4 Clairton U.S.A.
21 F3 Clamecy France
128 D2 Clan Alpine Mts mts U.S.A.
119 C5 Clanton U.S.A.
82 B5 Clanwilliam R.S.A.
99 E3 Clara r. Aust.
17 D5 Clara Rep. of Ire.
43 B5 Clara I. i. Myanmar
99 E3 Claraville Aust.
97 E3 Clare Aust.
122 E4 Clare U.S.A.
17 B5 Clare Island i. Rep. of Ire.
133 □1 Claremont Jamaica
121 G3 Claremont U.S.A.
125 E4 Claremore U.S.A.
17 C5 Claremorris Rep. of Ire.
97 H2 Clarence r. Aust.
93 D5 Clarence r. N.Z.
93 D5 Clarence N.Z.
82 A4 Clarence Bay b. Ascension Atlantic Ocean
152 B1 Clarence I. i. Ant.
147 B7 Clarence, I. i. Chile
98 B1 Clarence Str. chan. Aust.
110 C3 Clarence Str. chan. U.S.A.
132 D2 Clarence Town The Bahamas
133 □1 Clarendon div. Jamaica
125 C5 Clarendon U.S.A.
133 □1 Clarendon Peak Jamaica
113 K4 Clarenville Can.
110 G5 Claresholm Can.
124 E3 Clarinda U.S.A.
133 F5 Clarines Venezuela
120 C5 Clarington U.S.A.
120 D4 Clarion r. U.S.A.
120 D4 Clarion U.S.A.
151 L4 Clarion Fracture Zone Pac. Oc.
130 □ Clarión, I. i. Mexico
124 D2 Clark U.S.A.
99 F3 Clarke r. Aust.
97 G5 Clarke I. i. Aust.
99 F4 Clarke Ra. mt. ra. Aust.
99 F3 Clarke River Aust.
99 E3 Clarkes Cr. r. Aust.
119 D5 Clark Hill Res. resr U.S.A.
129 E4 Clark Mt mt. U.S.A.
114 E4 Clark, Pt pt Can.
120 C5 Clarksburg U.S.A.
125 F5 Clarksdale U.S.A.
121 F4 Clarks Summit U.S.A.
126 C2 Clarkston U.S.A.
133 □1 Clark's Town Jamaica
125 E5 Clarksville U.S.A.
122 A4 Clarksville U.S.A.
119 C4 Clarksville U.S.A.
144 C3 Claro r. Goiás Brazil
144 C1 Claro r. Goiás Brazil
145 F4 Cláudio Brazil
41 B2 Claveria Phil.
121 G2 Clayburg U.S.A.
124 D4 Clay Center U.S.A.
129 F3 Clayhole Wash r. U.S.A.
119 D5 Clayton U.S.A.
127 G4 Clayton U.S.A.
121 E2 Clayton U.S.A.
121 J1 Clayton Lake U.S.A.
120 C6 Claytor Lake l. U.S.A.
17 C6 Clear, Cape c. Rep. of Ire.
114 E5 Clear Creek Can.
129 G4 Clear Creek r. U.S.A.
108 D4 Cleare, C. c. U.S.A.
120 D4 Clearfield U.S.A.
126 E3 Clearfield U.S.A.
120 B4 Clear Fork Reservoir resr U.S.A.
110 F3 Clear Hills mts Can.
128 A2 Clear Lake l. U.S.A.
124 E3 Clear Lake U.S.A.
129 F2 Clear Lake l. U.S.A.
122 A3 Clear Lake U.S.A.
126 B3 Clear L. Res. resr U.S.A.
111 F4 Clearwater r. Can.
111 H3 Clearwater r. Can.
119 D7 Clearwater U.S.A.
45 □ Clear Water Bay b. Hong Kong
126 D2 Clearwater Mountains mts U.S.A.
111 H3 Clearwater River Provincial Park res. Can.
125 D5 Cleburne U.S.A.
126 B2 Cle Elum U.S.A.
139 G3 Clément French Guiana
43 □ Clementi Singapore
120 C5 Clendenin U.S.A.
120 C4 Clendening Lake l. U.S.A.
41 A4 Cleopatra Needle mt. Phil.
115 F2 Cléricy Can.
100 B3 Clerke Reef reef Aust.
99 F4 Clermont Aust.
119 D6 Clermont U.S.A.
21 F4 Clermont-Ferrand France
26 C2 Cles Italy
96 D3 Cleve Aust.
125 F5 Cleveland U.S.A.
120 C4 Cleveland U.S.A.
119 C5 Cleveland U.S.A.
99 F3 Cleveland, C. hd Aust.
122 D2 Cleveland Cliffs Basin l. U.S.A.
143 B6 Clevelândia Brazil
139 G3 Clevelândia do Norte Brazil
110 G5 Cleveland, Mt mt. U.S.A.
17 C5 Clew Bay b. Rep. of Ire.
119 D7 Clewiston U.S.A.
17 B5 Clifden Rep. of Ire.
129 H5 Cliff U.S.A.
98 D3 Cliffdale r. Aust.
93 E4 Clifford Bay b. N.Z.
99 G5 Clifton Aust.
119 □2 Clifton The Bahamas
129 H5 Clifton U.S.A.
120 D6 Clifton Forge U.S.A.
96 D1 Clifton Hills Aust.
119 □2 Clifton Pt pt The Bahamas
120 B6 Clinch r. U.S.A.
120 B6 Clinch Mountain mt. ra. U.S.A.
110 E4 Clinton Can.
114 E5 Clinton Can.
121 G4 Clinton U.S.A.
122 C5 Clinton U.S.A.
122 B5 Clinton U.S.A.
121 J2 Clinton U.S.A.
121 H3 Clinton U.S.A.
125 F5 Clinton U.S.A.
124 E4 Clinton U.S.A.
119 E5 Clinton U.S.A.
125 D5 Clinton U.S.A.
111 H2 Clinton-Colden Lake l. Can.
122 C5 Clinton Lake l. U.S.A.
122 C3 Clintonville U.S.A.
129 G4 Clints Well U.S.A.
151 K5 Clipperton Fracture Zone Pac. Oc.
151 M5 Clipperton I. i. Pac. Oc.
20 D3 Clisson France
140 C3 Cliza Bolivia
101 A4 Cloates, Pt pt Aust.
17 C6 Clonakilty Rep. of Ire.
98 E4 Cloncurry Aust.
98 E3 Cloncurry r. Aust.
17 D4 Clones Rep. of Ire.
17 D5 Clonmel Rep. of Ire.
18 D2 Cloppenburg Germany
122 A2 Cloquet U.S.A.
146 E2 Clorinda Arg.
126 F2 Cloud Peak summit U.S.A.
93 E4 Cloudy Bay b. N.Z.
45 □ Cloudy Hill h. Hong Kong
115 H2 Clova Can.
128 A2 Cloverdale U.S.A.
127 G5 Clovis U.S.A.
20 E3 Cloyes-sur-le-Loir France
115 G4 Cloyne Can.
111 H3 Cluff Lake Can.
28 D1 Cluj-Napoca Romania
98 D5 Cluny Aust.
21 G3 Cluny France
21 H3 Cluses France
26 B3 Clusone Italy
93 B6 Clutha r. N.Z.
17 F5 Clwydian Range h. U.K.
110 G4 Clyde Can.
93 B6 Clyde N.Z.
16 F4 Clyde r. U.K.
120 E3 Clyde U.S.A.
120 B4 Clyde U.S.A.
16 E4 Clyde, Firth of est. U.K.
109 M2 Clyde River Can.
24 C2 Côa r. Portugal
127 C5 Coachella U.S.A.
131 E5 Coahuayutla de Guerrero Mexico
130 E3 Coahuila div. Mexico
110 D2 Coal r. Can.
122 C5 Coal City U.S.A.
130 E5 Coalcomán Mexico
128 D3 Coaldale U.S.A.
125 D5 Coalgate U.S.A.
93 A7 Coal I. i. N.Z.
128 B3 Coalinga U.S.A.
110 D3 Coal River Can.
119 □3 Coamo Puerto Rico
145 J1 Coaraci Brazil
139 E5 Coari r. Brazil
139 E4 Coari Brazil
139 E4 Coari, Lago l. Brazil
81 C5 Coast div. Kenya
119 C6 Coastal Plain plain U.S.A.
110 D4 Coast Mountains mt. ra. Can.
99 G5 Coast Ra. h. Aust.
126 B2 Coast Range mt. ra. U.S.A.
128 B3 Coast Ranges mts U.S.A.
121 F5 Coatesville U.S.A.
115 K4 Coaticook Can.
109 K3 Coats I. i. Can.
152 C3 Coats Land Ant.
131 G5 Coatzacoalcos Mexico
28 G2 Cobadin Romania
115 F3 Cobalt Can.
131 H6 Cobán Guatemala
97 F2 Cobar Aust.
97 G4 Cobargo Aust.
97 G4 Cobberas, Mt mt. Aust.
115 G4 Cobden Can.
17 C6 Cóbh Rep. of Ire.
111 K4 Cobham r. Can.
90 □6 Cobia reef Fiji
140 C2 Cobija Bolivia
121 F3 Cobleskill U.S.A.
115 F5 Cobourg Can.
98 C1 Cobourg Pen. pen. Aust.
97 F3 Cobram Aust.
81 B7 Cóbuè Mozambique
18 E3 Coburg Germany
24 D2 Coca Spain
140 B3 Cocachacra Peru
143 B2 Cocalinho Brazil
140 C3 Cocapata Bolivia
25 F3 Cocentaina Spain
140 C3 Cochabamba Bolivia
140 C3 Cochabamba div. Bolivia
147 B5 Cochamó Chile
133 G5 Coche, I. i. Venezuela
56 B4 Cochin India
43 D5 Cochin reg. Vietnam
132 B2 Cochinos, B. de b. Cuba
41 B3 Cochinos Pt pt Phil.
129 H5 Cochise U.S.A.
110 G4 Cochrane Can.
114 E2 Cochrane Can.
111 J3 Cochrane r. Can.
147 B6 Cochrane Chile
96 E3 Cockburn Aust.
133 E2 Cockburn Harbour Turks and Caicos Is Caribbean
114 D4 Cockburn I. i. Can.
98 B5 Cockburn, Mt mt. Aust.
100 E2 Cockburn Ra. h. Aust.
133 E2 Cockburn Town Turks and Caicos Is Caribbean
119 F7 Cockburn Town The Bahamas
133 □1 Cockpit h. Jamaica
133 □1 Cockpit Country reg. Jamaica
130 K7 Coclé del Norte Panama
142 C2 Coco r. Brazil
130 J6 Coco r. Honduras/Nicaragua
78 A3 Cocobeach Gabon
43 A4 Coco Channel chan. India
151 O5 Coco, Isla de i. Colombia
129 F4 Coconino Plateau plat. U.S.A.
97 F3 Cocoparra Range h. Aust.
138 B3 Coco, Pta pt Colombia
138 B2 Cocorná Colombia
142 D3 Côcos Brazil
133 □3 Cocos Bay b. Trin. & Tobago
41 □2 Cocos I. i. Guam Pac. Oc.
149 L4 Cocos Is is Indian Ocean
148 D5 Cocos Ridge Pac. Oc.
130 E4 Cocula Mexico
138 C2 Cocuy, Parque Nacional el nat. park Colombia
139 E4 Codajás Brazil
121 H4 Cod, Cape c. U.S.A.
139 D1 Codera, C. c. Venezuela
93 A7 Codfish I. i. N.Z.
26 D3 Codigoro Italy
113 H2 Cod Island i. Can.
28 E2 Codlea Romania
142 D1 Codó Brazil
26 B3 Codogno Italy
26 D3 Codroipo Italy
15 C3 Codru Moldova
17 B6 Cod's Head hd Rep. of Ire.
126 E2 Cody U.S.A.
99 E2 Coen Aust.
99 E2 Coen r. Aust.
139 F3 Coeroeni r. Surinam
149 H4 Coëtivy Island i. Seychelles
126 C2 Coeur d'Alene U.S.A.
126 C2 Coeur d'Alene L. l. U.S.A.
125 E4 Coffeyville U.S.A.
96 C3 Coffin B. b. Aust.
96 C3 Coffin Bay Aust.
97 H2 Coffs Harbour Aust.
15 C3 Cogălniceni Moldova
28 G2 Cogealac Romania
122 B4 Coggon U.S.A.
20 D4 Cognac France
26 A3 Cogne Italy
78 A3 Cogo Equatorial Guinea
146 E1 Cogoi Arg.
120 E3 Cohocton r. U.S.A.
121 G3 Cohoes U.S.A.
97 F3 Cohuna Aust.
132 B6 Coiba, Isla i. Panama
147 B7 Coig r. Arg.
147 B6 Coihaique Chile
146 B4 Coihueco Chile
56 B4 Coimbatore India
24 B2 Coimbra Portugal
24 B2 Coimbra div. Portugal
24 D4 Coín Spain
140 C3 Coipasa, L. de l. Bolivia
133 E5 Cojoro Venezuela
147 C6 Cojudo Blanco, Cerro mt. Arg.
131 H6 Cojutepeque El Salvador
126 E3 Cokeville U.S.A.
97 E4 Colac Aust.
142 C1 Colares Brazil
145 H3 Colatina Brazil
124 C4 Colby U.S.A.
17 H6 Colchester U.K.
122 B5 Colchester U.S.A.
108 B4 Cold Bay b. U.S.A.
75 D2 Col de Jerada Morocco
111 G4 Cold L. l. Can.
111 G4 Cold Lake Can.
16 F4 Coldstream U.K.
20 D5 Col du Somport pass France/Spain
74 C2 Col du Zad Morocco
125 D4 Coldwater U.S.A.
122 E5 Coldwater U.S.A.
114 B2 Coldwell Can.
121 H2 Colebrook U.S.A.
99 E2 Coleman r. Aust.
122 E4 Coleman U.S.A.
125 D6 Coleman U.S.A.
28 E2 Colentina r. Romania
96 E4 Coleraine Aust.
17 D4 Coleraine U.K.
93 C5 Coleridge, L. l. N.Z.
56 B4 Coleroon r. India
97 G5 Coles Bay Aust.
82 D5 Colesberg R.S.A.
140 B3 Coles, Pta de pt Peru
128 B2 Colfax U.S.A.
126 C2 Colfax U.S.A.
147 C6 Colhué Huapi, L. l. Arg.
28 E2 Colibaşi Romania
130 E5 Colima div. Mexico
130 E5 Colima Mexico
144 D4 Colina Brazil
142 D2 Colinas Brazil
16 D3 Coll i. U.K.
24 E2 Collado Villalba Spain
140 C4 Collahuasi Chile
97 G2 Collarenebri Aust.
27 D5 Colleferro Italy
119 C5 College Park U.S.A.
125 D6 College Station U.S.A.
97 F2 Collerina Aust.
27 E5 Colletorto Italy
101 B7 Collie Aust.
100 D3 Collier Bay b. Aust.
101 B5 Collier Range Nat. Park nat. park. Aust.
101 B5 Collier Ranges h. Aust.
114 E4 Collingwood Can.
92 D4 Collingwood N.Z.
114 A1 Collins Can.
125 F6 Collins U.S.A.
95 □1 Collins Hd pt Norfolk I. Pac. Oc.
99 F4 Collinsville Aust.
118 B4 Collinsville U.S.A.
146 B4 Collipulli Chile
17 C4 Collooney Rep. of Ire.
21 H2 Colmar France
24 E2 Colmenar de Oreja Spain
24 E2 Colmenar Viejo Spain
17 H6 Colne r. U.K.
97 G3 Colo r. Aust.
122 C3 Coloma U.S.A.
144 D4 Colômbia Brazil
138 C3 Colombia Colombia
125 D7 Colombia Mexico
136 C2 Colombia country S. America
144 D6 Colombo Brazil
56 B5 Colombo Sri Lanka
115 F2 Colombourg Can.
20 E5 Colomiers France
146 D3 Colón Buenos Aires Arg.
146 E3 Colón Entre Ríos Arg.
132 B2 Colón Cuba
130 L7 Colón Panama
97 E2 Colona Aust.
55 E4 Colonelganj India
132 D2 Colonel Hill The Bahamas
127 C6 Colonet, C. c. Mexico
146 D2 Colonia Arg.
145 J1 Colônia r. Brazil
147 C4 Colonia Choele Choel, Isla i. Arg.
146 E3 Colonia del Sacramento Uruguay
146 D2 Colonia Dora Arg.
146 C4 Colonia Emilio Mitre Arg.
147 C6 Colonia Las Heras Arg.
146 E3 Colonia Lavalleja Uruguay
120 E6 Colonial Heights U.S.A.
129 F6 Colonia Reforma Mexico
27 F6 Colonna, Capo pt Italy
16 D3 Colonsay i. U.K.
146 D4 Colorada Grande, L. l. Arg.
133 G5 Coloradito Venezuela
147 D4 Colorado r. La Pampa/Río Negro Arg.
146 C2 Colorado r. La Rioja Arg.
146 B3 Colorado r. Arg.
144 C5 Colorado Brazil
129 E5 Colorado r. Mexico/U.S.A.
126 E3 Colorado r. U.S.A.
127 F4 Colorado div. U.S.A.
129 F3 Colorado City U.S.A.
125 C5 Colorado City U.S.A.
147 D4 Colorado, Delta del R. delta Arg.
128 D5 Colorado Desert desert U.S.A.
129 H2 Colorado National Monument res. U.S.A.
129 G3 Colorado Plateau plat. U.S.A.
129 E4 Colorado River Aqueduct canal U.S.A.
127 F4 Colorado Springs U.S.A.
130 E4 Colotlán Mexico
140 C3 Colquechaca Bolivia
140 C3 Colquiri Bolivia
128 D4 Colton U.S.A.
121 F2 Colton U.S.A.
129 G2 Colton U.S.A.
126 B2 Columbia r. Can./U.S.A.
120 E5 Columbia U.S.A.
125 F6 Columbia U.S.A.
124 E4 Columbia U.S.A.
120 E4 Columbia U.S.A.
119 D5 Columbia U.S.A.
119 C5 Columbia U.S.A.
109 L1 Columbia, C. c. Can.
122 E5 Columbia City U.S.A.
120 E5 Columbia, District of div. U.S.A.
121 K2 Columbia Falls U.S.A.
126 D1 Columbia Falls U.S.A.
110 F4 Columbia Mountains mt. ra. Can.
110 F4 Columbia, Mt mt. Can.
126 C2 Columbia Plateau plat. U.S.A.
82 B5 Columbine, Cape c. R.S.A.
119 C5 Columbus U.S.A.
118 C4 Columbus U.S.A.
125 F5 Columbus U.S.A.
126 E2 Columbus U.S.A.
124 D3 Columbus U.S.A.
127 F6 Columbus U.S.A.
120 B5 Columbus U.S.A.
125 D6 Columbus U.S.A.
122 C4 Columbus U.S.A.
132 D2 Columbus Bank sand bank The Bahamas
122 B5 Columbus Jct U.S.A.
133 □2 Columbus Point pt Tobago Trin. & Tobago
132 D1 Columbus Pt pt The Bahamas
128 D2 Columbus Salt Marsh salt marsh U.S.A.
128 A2 Colusa U.S.A.
92 E2 Colville N.Z.
108 C3 Colville r. U.S.A.
126 C1 Colville U.S.A.
92 E2 Colville, Cape c. N.Z.
92 E2 Colville Channel chan. N.Z.
108 F3 Colville Lake Can.
17 F5 Colwyn Bay U.K.
26 D3 Comacchio Italy
26 D3 Comacchio, Valli di lag. Italy
55 G3 Comai China
147 B5 Comallo r. Arg.
125 D6 Comanche U.S.A.
152 B1 Comandante Ferraz Brazil Base Ant.
147 C6 Comandante Luis Piedraduena Arg.
146 C3 Comandante Salas Arg.
28 F2 Comandău Romania
28 F1 Comăneşti Romania
140 D3 Comarapa Bolivia
28 E2 Comarnic Romania
130 J6 Comayagua Honduras
146 B3 Combarbalá Chile
115 G4 Combermere Can.
42 A3 Combermere Bay b. Myanmar
97 H2 Comboyne Aust.
115 H1 Comencho, L. l. Can.
144 D3 Comendador Gomes Brazil
17 D5 Comeragh Mountains h. Rep. of Ire.
145 H2 Comercinho Brazil
119 □3 Comerio Puerto Rico
99 G4 Comet Aust.
99 G5 Comet r. Aust.
125 D6 Comfort U.S.A.
133 □1 Comfort Cas. Jamaica
55 G5 Comilla Bangladesh
27 E7 Comino i. Malta
27 B5 Comino, Capo pt Italy
27 E7 Comiso Italy
131 G5 Comitán de Domínguez Mexico
121 G4 Commack U.S.A.
115 F4 Commanda Can.
20 F3 Commentry France
21 G2 Commercy France
119 □1 Commissioner's Pt pt Bermuda
109 K3 Committee Bay b. Can.
152 B6 Commonwealth B. b. Ant.
97 G3 Commonwealth Territory div. Aust.
26 B3 Como Italy
55 G3 Como Chamling l. China
147 C6 Comodoro Rivadavia Arg.
76 D5 Comoé, Parc National de la nat. park Côte d'Ivoire
26 B2 Como, Lago di l. Italy
130 C3 Comondú Mexico
56 B4 Comorin, Cape c. India
69 J7 Comoros country Africa
20 F2 Compiègne France
41 C5 Compostela Phil.
144 E6 Comprida, Ilha i. Brazil
122 C5 Compton U.S.A.
15 C3 Comrat Moldova
125 C6 Comstock U.S.A.
55 H4 Cona China
76 B5 Conakry Guinea
147 C5 Cona Niyeo Arg.
97 F5 Conara Jct. Aust.
20 C3 Concarneau France
145 F2 Conceição r. Brazil
142 E2 Conceição Brazil
145 J3 Conceição da Barra Brazil
144 D3 Conceição das Alagoas Brazil
145 H5 Conceição de Macabu Brazil
142 C2 Conceição do Araguaia Brazil
142 E3 Conceição do Coité Brazil
145 G3 Conceição do Mato Dentro Brazil
146 C2 Concepción Arg.
140 C2 Concepción Beni Bolivia
141 D3 Concepción Santa Cruz Bolivia
146 B4 Concepción Chile
130 K7 Concepción Panama
141 E4 Concepción Paraguay
146 E3 Concepción del Uruguay Arg.
82 A3 Conception Bay b. Namibia
113 K4 Conception Bay South Can.
119 F7 Conception I. i. The Bahamas
128 B4 Conception, Pt pt U.S.A.
83 E2 Concession Zimbabwe
144 D5 Conchas São Paulo Brazil
143 C5 Conchas São Paulo Brazil
127 F5 Conchas L. l. U.S.A.
20 E2 Conches-en-Ouche France
140 C4 Conchi Chile
129 H4 Concho U.S.A.
130 D3 Conchos r. Mexico
128 A3 Concord U.S.A.
119 D5 Concord U.S.A.
121 H3 Concord U.S.A.
146 E3 Concordia Arg.

138 B2 Concordia Antioquia Colombia
138 C3 Concordia Meta Colombia
138 C4 Concordia Peru
124 D4 Concordia Peru
99 G5 Condamine Aust.
99 G5 Condamine r. Aust.
43 D5 Côn Dao Vietnam
142 E3 Conde Brazil
83 E2 Condédézi r. Mozambique
130 J6 Condega Nicaragua
20 D2 Condé-sur-Noireau France
145 H1 Condeúba Brazil
97 F3 Condobolin Aust.
20 E5 Condom France
126 B2 Condon, Cord. del mt. ra. Peru
138 B4 Condon, Cord. del mt. ra. Peru
119 C6 Conecuh r. U.S.A.
26 D3 Conegliano Italy
130 E3 Conejos Mexico
120 D4 Conemaugh r. U.S.A.
114 E5 Conestogo Lake l. Can.
120 E3 Conesus Lake l. U.S.A.
21 F4 Coney France
121 G4 Coney I. i. U.S.A.
90 □1 Conflict Group is P.N.G.
20 E3 Confolens France
129 F2 Confusion Range mts U.S.A.
141 E4 Confuso r. Paraguay
69 □ Congjiang China
78 C4 Congo country Africa
78 C4 Congo r. Congo/Zaïre
145 G4 Congonhas Brazil
144 C5 Congonhinhas Brazil
144 C3 Congress U.S.A.
147 B4 Conguillio, Parque Nacional nat. park Chile
147 B5 Cónico, Co mt. Arg.
24 C4 Conil de la Frontera Spain
114 E3 Coniston Can.
21 F3 Coniston U.K.
111 G3 Conklin Can.
79 B4 Conkouati, Réserve de Faune res. Congo
146 C3 Conlara r. Arg.
114 E2 Connaught Can.
17 C5 Connaught reg. Rep. of Ire.
120 D4 Conneaut U.S.A.
121 G4 Connecticut div. U.S.A.
118 F3 Connecticut r. U.S.A.
120 C4 Connellsville U.S.A.
99 G5 Connemara Aust.
17 C5 Connemara reg. Rep. of Ire.
121 J1 Conners U.S.A.
118 C4 Connersville U.S.A.
17 C4 Conn, Lough l. Rep. of Ire.
43 D4 Côn Sơn i. Vietnam
42 D2 Co Nôi Vietnam
121 E5 Conowingo U.S.A.
144 E3 Conquista Brazil
126 E1 Conrad U.S.A.
125 E6 Conroe U.S.A.
145 H3 Conselheiro Lafaiete Brazil
145 H3 Conselheiro Pena Brazil
43 E6 Côn Sơn i. Vietnam
18 D5 Consort Can.
18 D5 Constance, L. l. Germany/Switz.
139 E5 Constância dos Baetas Brazil
28 E2 Constanţa Romania
24 D4 Constantina Spain
75 F1 Constantine Algeria
122 E5 Constantine U.S.A.
108 C4 Constantine, C. c. Aust.
133 □1 Constant Spring Jamaica
129 E6 Constitución de 1857, Parque Nacional nat. park Mexico
99 G5 Consuelo Aust.
126 D3 Contact U.S.A.
145 E3 Contagem Brazil
138 B5 Contamana Peru
142 D2 Contas r. Brazil
121 G6 Continental U.S.A.
121 H3 Contoocook r. U.S.A.
131 J4 Contoy, I. i. Mexico
115 J4 Contrecoeur Can.
25 C3 Contreras, Embalse de resr Spain
147 B7 Contreras, I. i. Chile
21 E3 Contres France
145 F3 Contria Brazil
138 B5 Contumazá Peru
111 G1 Contwoyto Lake l. Can.
27 F5 Conversano Italy
121 H3 Conway U.S.A.
121 H3 Conway U.S.A.
119 E5 Conway U.S.A.
96 C2 Conway, L. salt flat Aust.
96 C2 Coober Pedy Aust.
96 B2 Coober Aust.
122 A2 Cook U.S.A.
147 B7 Cook, B. de b. Chile
110 D4 Cook, C. c. Can.
101 B7 Cooke, Mt h. Aust.
119 C4 Cookeville U.S.A.
108 C1 Cook Inlet chan. U.S.A.
87 L6 Cook Islands terr. Pac. Oc.
93 C6 Cook, Mt mt. N.Z.
121 F3 Cooksburg U.S.A.
113 J3 Cook's Harbour Can.
115 K4 Cookshire Can.
93 E4 Cook Strait str. N.Z.
69 F5 Cooktown Aust.
97 F2 Coolabah Aust.
101 C6 Cooladdi Aust.
97 G2 Coolah Aust.
97 G4 Coolamon Aust.
101 C6 Coolgardie Aust.
129 G5 Coolidge U.S.A.
129 G5 Coolidge Dam U.S.A.
97 G4 Cooma Aust.
96 E3 Coombah Aust.
97 F4 Coonabarabran Aust.
96 D3 Coonalpyn Aust.
97 G2 Coonamble Aust.
101 C6 Coonana Aust.
99 F5 Coongoola Aust.
96 B2 Coonawarra Aust.
93 C6 Coopers r. w. Aust.
97 H2 Coopernook Aust.
132 C1 Coopers Town The Bahamas
124 D2 Cooperstown U.S.A.
121 F3 Cooperstown U.S.A.
133 □3 Coora Trin. & Tobago
13 C3 Coorabie Aust.
96 B2 Coorabie Aust.
101 B6 Coorow Aust.
99 H5 Cooroy Aust.
126 A3 Coos Bay U.S.A.
17 G4 Cootehill Rep. of Ire.
96 D2 Cootamundra Aust.
146 B4 Copahue, Volcán mt. Chile
131 H5 Copainalá Mexico
125 B2 Copala Mexico
131 H5 Copalillo Mexico
131 H5 Copalis Mexico
125 H6 Cope U.S.A.
26 E3 Copertino Italy
146 B2 Copiapó Chile
146 B2 Copiapó r. Chile
26 C3 Copparo Italy

114 D2 Coppell Can.
79 E6 Copperbelt div. Zambia
114 E3 Copper Cliff Can.
99 F3 Copperfield r. Aust.
122 D2 Copper Harbor U.S.A.
108 G3 Coppermine Can.
108 G3 Coppermine r. Can.
114 C3 Coppername Pt pt Can.
28 E1 Copşa Mică Romania
55 F3 Coqën China
146 B3 Coquimbo div. Chile
146 B2 Coquimbo Chile
28 E3 Corabia Romania
145 F2 Coração de Jesus Brazil
140 B2 Coracora Peru
114 E1 Coral l. Can.
119 D7 Coral Gables U.S.A.
109 K3 Coral Harbour Can.
119 □2 Coral Harbour The Bahamas
150 F7 Coral Sea sea Pac. Oc.
150 E6 Coral Sea Basin Pac. Oc.
86 G6 Coral Sea Islands Territory div. Pac. Oc.
122 B5 Coralville Reservoir resr U.S.A.
97 E4 Corangamite, L. l. Aust.
139 F3 Corantijn r. Surinam
27 F5 Corato Italy
74 A4 Corcovado r. Western Sahara
146 B6 Corcóvio Arg.
146 D4 Corbeil Fr.
111 L2 Corbett Inlet inlet Can.
20 F2 Corbie France
20 A6 Corbin U.S.A.
24 D4 Corbones r. Spain
28 D2 Corbu Romania
128 C3 Corcoran U.S.A.
147 B5 Corcovado Arg.
147 B5 Corcovado, G. de chan. Chile
147 B5 Corcovado, V. vol Chile
142 C2 Corda r. Brazil
119 D6 Cordele U.S.A.
138 C3 Cordillera de los Picachos, Parque Nacional nat. park Colombia
41 B4 Cordilleras Range mt. ra. Phil.
96 E1 Cordillo Downs Aust.
145 F3 Cordisburgo Brazil
146 D3 Córdoba div. Arg.
140 D3 Córdoba Arg.
147 G5 Córdoba Arg.
131 F5 Córdoba Mexico
130 E3 Córdoba Mexico
24 D4 Córdoba Córdoba Spain
146 D3 Córdoba, Sierras de mt. ra. Arg.
140 A2 Cordova Peru
108 D3 Cordova U.S.A.
110 C4 Cordova Bay b. U.S.A.
121 K2 Corea U.S.A.
24 C4 Corella r. Aust.
98 E4 Corella r. Aust.
98 C3 Corella L. salt flat Aust.
99 G4 Corfield Aust.
144 A3 Corguinho Brazil
24 C3 Coria Spain
27 F6 Corigliano Calabro Italy
99 G3 Coringa Is is Coral Sea Islands Terr. Pac. Oc.
97 F5 Corinna Aust.
144 B3 Corinna Brazil
111 J4 Corinne Can.
125 F5 Corinth U.S.A.
121 G3 Corinth U.S.A.
145 F3 Corinto Brazil
141 E3 Corixa Grande r. Bolivia
41 C5 Corkatabo Phil.
17 C6 Cork Rep. of Ire.
27 D7 Corleone Italy
60 A1 Çorlu Turkey
139 G3 Cormontibo French Guiana
111 J4 Cormorant Can.
144 C5 Cornélio Procópio Brazil
139 F2 Corneliskondre Surinam
122 B3 Cornell U.S.A.
113 J4 Corner Brook Can.
97 F4 Corner Inlet b. Aust.
15 C3 Corneşti Moldova
128 A2 Corning U.S.A.
120 E3 Corning U.S.A.
24 C4 Corno, Monte mt. Italy
20 B2 Cornouaille reg. France
115 H4 Cornwall Can.
109 J2 Cornwall I. i. Can.
109 J2 Cornwallis I. i. Can.
55 □1 Corny Pt pt Aust.
138 D1 Coro Venezuela
145 G3 Coroaci Brazil
140 D3 Coroatá Brazil
125 G3 Corocoro Bolivia
133 E6 Coro, Golfete de b. Venezuela
140 C3 Coroico Bolivia
144 B3 Coromandel Brazil
56 C4 Coromandel Coast coastal area India
92 E2 Coromandel Peninsula pen. N.Z.
92 E2 Coromandel Range h. N.Z.
41 B3 Coron Phil.
96 E2 Corona U.S.A.
128 D5 Coronado U.S.A.
130 K7 Coronado, B. de b. Panama
41 B4 Coronados, G. de los inlet Chile
138 C2 Corozal Colombia
108 D3 Coronation Gulf Can.
81 □3 Coronation I. i. S. Orkney Is Atlantic Ocean
100 D2 Coronation I. is U.S.A.
110 C3 Coronation Island i. U.S.A.
146 C3 Coronda Arg.
146 D3 Coronel Dorrego Brazil
145 G3 Coronel Fabriciano Brazil
145 G2 Coronel Murta Brazil
141 E5 Coronel Oviedo Paraguay
146 D4 Coronel Ponce Brazil
146 A4 Coronel Pringles Arg.
146 D5 Coronel Sapucaia Brazil
146 D4 Coronel Suárez Arg.
146 D4 Coronel Vidal Arg.
140 A1 Coropuna Peru
29 C4 Çorovodë Albania
97 F3 Corowa Aust.
132 B3 Corozal Belize
132 D5 Corozal Colombia
133 □3 Corozal Pt pt Trinidad
125 D7 Corpus Christi U.S.A.
125 D7 Corpus Christi, L. l. U.S.A.
140 B3 Corque Bolivia
24 D4 Corral de Almaguer Spain

24 D3 Corral de Cantos mt. Spain
25 □1 Corralejo Canary Is Spain
144 C2 Córrego do Ouro Brazil
145 G3 Córrego Novo Brazil
142 E1 Corrente r. Bahia Brazil
144 C3 Corrente Goiás Brazil
144 C3 Corrente r. Goiás Brazil
145 G3 Corrente Grande r. Brazil
144 A2 Correntes r. Brazil
144 A2 Correntes r. Brazil
146 C3 Correntina Brazil
20 E4 Corrèze r. France
17 C5 Corrib, Lough l. Rep. of Ire.
146 E3 Corrientes r. Arg.
146 E2 Corrientes Arg.
146 E2 Corrientes div. Arg.
146 E2 Corrientes, C. c. Arg.
130 D4 Corrientes, C. c. Mexico
138 B2 Corrientes, Cabo pt Colombia
132 A2 Corrientes, Cabo pt Cuba
125 E6 Corrigan U.S.A.
101 B7 Corrigin Aust.
139 F2 Corriverton Guyana
120 D4 Corry U.S.A.
97 G3 Corryong Aust.
142 D3 Coxá r. Brazil
21 J5 Corse, Cap c. France
21 J5 Corse, Cap c. France
21 J5 Corse France
24 C4 Cortegana Spain
129 H3 Cortez U.S.A.
128 D1 Cortez Mts mts U.S.A.
26 D2 Cortina d'Ampezzo Italy
121 E3 Cortland U.S.A.
24 B3 Cortona Italy
24 B3 Coruche Portugal
60 E1 Çoruh r. Turkey
60 C1 Çorum Turkey
141 D3 Corumbá Brazil
141 E3 Corumbá r. Brazil
144 D1 Corumbá de Goiás Brazil
144 C1 Corumbaíba Brazil
144 C2 Corumbatai r. Brazil
144 C1 Corumbá, Pta pt Brazil
28 E1 Corund Romania
142 E3 Corupe Brazil
126 B2 Corvallis U.S.A.
21 F5 Corwen U.K.
130 D4 Cosalá Mexico
127 D6 Cozón, Co mt. Mexico
131 J4 Cozumel Mexico
131 J4 Cozumel, I. de i. Mexico
27 F6 Cozze del Pellegrino mt. Italy
99 E1 Crab I. i. Aust.
81 □1 Crab I. i. Rodrigues I. Mauritius
97 G3 Craboon Aust.
20 D3 Cossé-le-Vivien France
146 D3 Cosquín Arg.
25 H4 Costa Blanca Spain
25 H2 Costa Brava France/Spain
24 C4 Costa de la Luz reg. Spain
24 C4 Costa del Azahar Spain
24 D4 Costa del Sol reg. Spain
130 K6 Costa de Mosquitos reg. Nicaragua
25 H2 Costa Dorada Spain
140 D2 Costa Marques Brazil
141 E2 Costa Pinheiro, Cap r. Brazil
144 B3 Costa Rica Brazil
104 K8 Costa Rica country Central America
130 D3 Costa Rica Mexico
24 C1 Costa Verde reg. Spain
15 B3 Costeşti Moldova
28 F1 Costeşti Romania
28 F1 Cotaná r. Brazil
142 D3 Cotegipe Brazil
110 C3 Côte, Mt h. Can.
20 D2 Cotentin reg. France
21 G2 Côtes de Meuse ridge France
28 E2 Coteşti Romania
140 E4 Cotia Brazil
139 E3 Cotingo r. Brazil
141 E2 Cravari r. Brazil
138 C2 Cravo Norte Colombia
124 D3 Crawford U.S.A.
122 D5 Crawfordsville U.S.A.
21 G5 Crawley U.K.
126 D2 Crazy Mts mt. ra. U.S.A.
111 H4 Crean L. l. Can.
43 D5 Crédition U.K.
111 H3 Cree r. Can.
79 D7 Creel Mexico
111 H3 Cree Lake l. Can.
20 F2 Creighton Can.
20 F2 Creil France
26 C3 Crema Italy
15 C3 Cres i. Croatia
26 E3 Cres Croatia
128 B2 Crescent City U.S.A.
45 □ Crescent I. i. Hong Kong
129 F6 Crescent Junction U.S.A.
128 C1 Crescent Mills U.S.A.
129 F6 Crescent Peak summit U.S.A.
122 A4 Cresco U.S.A.
98 C2 Cresswell w. Aust.
146 D2 Cresson Arg.
130 E3 Creston U.S.A.
119 C6 Crestview U.S.A.
96 E3 Creswick Aust.
21 H3 Crêt Monniot mt. France
25 H1 Creus, Cap de pt Spain
21 F5 Creuse r. France
24 E1 Crevillente Spain
21 F5 Crewe U.K.
16 E3 Crianlarich U.K.
138 C2 Cricova Moldova
15 C3 Crikvenica Croatia
71 C6 Crisfield U.S.A.
142 D3 Cristalândia Brazil
142 C1 Cristalina Brazil
144 D2 Cristalino r. Brazil
139 E4 Cristal, Monts de mts Eq. Guinea/Gabon
145 H2 Cristiano Dias Brazil
142 D3 Cristino Castro Brazil
130 K7 Cristóbal Colón, Pt pt Colombia
138 □1 Cristóbal, Pta pt Galápagos Is Ecuador
28 E1 Cristuru Secuiesc Romania
15 C3 Criuleni Moldova
142 C3 Crixás Brazil

142 C3 Crixás Brazil
142 B3 Crixás Mirim r. Brazil
28 C3 Crna Gora mts Macedonia/Yugo.
28 B3 Crna Trava Yugo.
26 F3 Çövě Benin
120 E5 Cove Fort U.S.A.
114 C4 Cove I. i. Can.
17 G5 Cove Point U.S.A.
121 E5 Cove Point U.S.A.
24 C2 Covilhã Portugal
125 D5 Covington U.S.A.
120 A5 Covington U.S.A.
119 B5 Covington U.S.A.
120 D6 Covington U.S.A.
114 D3 Cow r. Can.
97 F3 Cowal, L. l. Aust.
101 C6 Cowan, L. salt flat Aust.
115 J4 Cowansville Can.
50 B1 Cowarts Aust.
101 B6 Cowcowing Lakes salt flat Aust.
21 G6 Cowdenbeath U.K.
96 C3 Cowell Aust.
21 G6 Cowes Aust.
99 F5 Cowley Aust.
97 G3 Cowpasture r. U.S.A.
97 G3 Cowra Aust.
142 D3 Coxá r. Brazil
146 E3 Coxilha de Santana h. Brazil/Uruguay
142 E3 Coxilha Grande h. Brazil
143 A4 Coxim Brazil
144 A3 Coxim r. Brazil
57 G5 Cox R. r. Aust.
55 G5 Cox's Bazar Bangladesh
76 B5 Coyah Guinea
147 C2 Coy Aike Arg.
128 C4 Coyote Lake l. Aust.
129 E5 Coyote Peak summit U.S.A.
128 C3 Coyote Peak summit U.S.A.
130 D3 Coyote, Pta pt Mexico
55 F2 Cozhê China

56 B3 Cuddapah India
114 H4 Cudworth Can.
101 B5 Cue Aust.
79 C7 Cuebe r. Angola
79 C6 Cuelei r. Angola
24 D2 Cuéllar Spain
79 C6 Cuemba Angola
25 E2 Cuenca div. Ecuador
130 E3 Cuencamé Mexico
131 F5 Cuernavaca Mexico
125 D6 Cuero U.S.A.
21 H5 Cuers France
21 J4 Cuesta Pass pass France
131 F4 Cuetzalan Mexico
28 D2 Cugir Romania
27 B5 Cuglieri Italy
20 E5 Cugnaux France
79 C5 Cugo r. Angola
138 C1 Cuiabá Brazil
142 A4 Cuiabá de Larga Brazil
131 F5 Cuicatlan Mexico
91 □16 Cuilapa Guatemala
16 D3 Cuillin Hills h. U.K.
16 D3 Cuillin Sound chan. Can./U.S.A.
124 D2 Crookston U.S.A.
79 C5 Cuilo Angola
79 C5 Cuimba Angola
79 B6 Cuio Angola
71 J5 Cross r. Nigeria
119 D6 Cross City U.S.A.
121 K1 Cross Creek Can.
125 E5 Crossett U.S.A.
17 E4 Cross Fell h. U.K.
128 D1 Cross Lake l. U.S.A.
111 K4 Cross Lake l. Can.
120 E3 Cross Lake l. U.S.A.
93 D5 Crossley, Mt mt. N.Z.
128 D2 Crossman Peak summit U.S.A.
77 F5 Cross River div. Nigeria
110 B3 Cross Sound chan. U.S.A.
128 C3 Cross Village U.S.A.
119 C5 Crossville U.S.A.
123 F4 Croswell U.S.A.
27 F6 Crotone Italy
97 F2 Crowal w. Aust.
97 F2 Crowl w. Aust.
128 C3 Crowley, Lake l. U.S.A.
133 □2 Crown Point pt Tobago
99 E1 Crab I. i. Aust.
121 G3 Crown Point U.S.A.
99 E1 Crown Prince Olav Coast Ant.
152 D2 Crown Princess Martha Coast Ant.
99 G5 Crows Nest Aust.
99 G5 Crownest Pass Can.
119 □5 Croydon Aust.
133 □1 Croy, L. de l. Kerguelen Indian Ocean
107 D7 Crozet Basin Indian Ocean
149 H7 Crozet, Îles is Indian Ocean
149 G6 Crozet Plateau Indian Ocean
108 F2 Crozier, Mt h. Can./U.S.A.
81 □4 Crozier, Mth. Kerguelen Indian Ocean
120 B6 Crozon France
146 D3 Cruz del Eje Arg.
144 B5 Cruzeiro do Oeste Brazil
144 B5 Cruzeiro do Sul Acre Brazil
140 B1 Cruzeiro do Sul Paraná Brazil
109 M3 Cruzeiro do Sul Acre Brazil
110 C3 Cruzville U.S.A.
143 F3 Crysdale, Mt mt. Can.
110 E3 Crystal Brook Aust.
142 D2 Crystal City U.S.A.
122 D2 Crystal Falls U.S.A.
18 E3 Csenger Hungary
19 L5 Csongrád Hungary
19 K5 Csongrád Hungary
19 K5 Csongrád Hungary
19 J3 Csorna Hungary
133 □3 Cúa Venezuela
147 C5 Cuadrada, Sierra h. Arg.
138 C2 Cualedro Spain
43 C5 Cua Lon r. Vietnam
54 B5 Cuamba Mozambique
79 D7 Cuanavale r. Angola
79 D7 Cuando Cubango div. Angola
79 C5 Cuangar Angola
79 C5 Cuango Lunda Norte Angola
79 C5 Cuango Uíge Angola
79 C6 Cuanza r. Angola
79 C5 Cuanza Norte div. Angola
79 C5 Cuanza Sul div. Angola
79 C7 Cuarto Arg.
140 D3 Cuatro Ojos Bolivia
131 F5 Cuaútemoc Mexico
130 E3 Cuatro Ciénegas Mexico
138 B2 Cuatro Ojos Colombia
26 D4 Cuaz Maritima Italy
79 C6 Cuba Port.
146 C4 Cuba Port.
146 B3 Cuba Port.
131 □2 Cuba Brazil
145 B2 Cuba Brazil
140 □2 Cubanacan Netherlands Ant.
78 □2 Curaçao Netherlands Ant.
147 B4 Curacautín Chile
146 C4 Cubagua, I. i. Venezuela
119 C6 Cuba country Caribbean
24 D3 Cuba Port.
130 E3 Cuauhtémoc Mexico
132 B5 Cuba Port.
146 C4 Curanilahua Chile
127 F4 Curecanti Nat. Rec. Area res. U.S.A.
81 □4 Curepipe Mauritius
146 B3 Curicó Chile
138 C3 Curiuriari r. Brazil
81 □2 Curieuse i. Seychelles
142 C3 Curimatá Brazil
144 C3 Curitibanos Brazil
145 H2 Curnamona Aust.
142 C5 Curralinho Brazil
142 C1 Currais Novos Brazil
146 C2 Currant U.S.A.
79 □ Cubango r. Angola/Namibia
142 C2 Curuaés r. Brazil
96 E2 Cubal Angola
79 C6 Cubal Angola
79 C6 Cubal r. Angola
79 C5 Cubango r. Angola
142 D2 Curitiba Brazil
142 B5 Curitibanos Brazil
138 D1 Cumana Venezuela
142 C5 Curua, Ilha i. Brazil
139 □3 Coutras France
112 J5 Couture, Lac l. Can.
133 □3 Couva Trin. & Tobago
18 B3 Couvin Belgium
20 E4 Couzeix France
25 E2 Covadela Spain
28 F2 Covasna Romania
71 C6 Covè Benin

99 G4 Curtis I. i. Aust.
92 □4 Curtis I. i. Kermadec Is N.Z.
142 B2 Curuá r. Brazil
142 B1 Curuá do Sul r. Brazil
142 B2 Curuaés r. Brazil
139 G3 Curuá, Ilha i. Brazil
142 B1 Curuá Una r. Brazil
142 C5 Curuçá Brazil
142 B1 Curumu Brazil
139 F5 Cururu r. Brazil
139 F5 Cururu Açu r. Brazil
21 H5 Cuers France
142 B2 Cuesta Pass pass
21 G5 Curuzú Cuatiá Arg.
146 E2 Curuzú Cuatiá Arg.
140 B2 Cusco Peru
125 D4 Cushing U.S.A.
131 D2 Cusihuirachic Mexico
142 C2 Cussata U.S.A.
122 A1 Cusson r. U.S.A.
112 E1 Cusson, Pte pt Can.
126 F2 Custer U.S.A.
124 C3 Custer U.S.A.
79 C6 Cutato r. Angola
126 D1 Cut Bank U.S.A.
138 B5 Cutervo, Parque Nacional nat. park Peru
131 F5 Cuicatlan Mexico
146 A4 Cutral-Có Arg.
55 F5 Cuttack India
129 G5 Cutter U.S.A.
79 C7 Cuvelai Angola
78 C4 Cuvette div. Congo
101 A5 Cuvier, C. hd Aust.
115 G2 Cuvillier, Lac l. Can.
138 B4 Cuyabeno Ecuador
120 C4 Cuyahoga Falls U.S.A.
120 C4 Cuyahoga Valley National Recreation Area res. U.S.A.
41 B4 Cuyapa r. Phil.
41 B4 Cuyo Phil.
41 B4 Cuyo East Pass. chan. Phil.
41 B4 Cuyos is Phil.
41 B4 Cuyo West Pass. chan. Phil.
139 F2 Cuyuni r. Guyana
26 F4 Čvrsnica mts Bos.-Herz.
83 A5 Cyangugu Rwanda
19 H2 Cybinka Poland
120 A5 Cynthiana U.S.A.
111 G5 Cypress Hills mt. ra. U.S.A.
32 G Cyprus country Asia
72 D2 Cyrenaica reg. Libya
19 E1 Czaplinek Poland
19 J2 Czarna Białostocka Poland
19 H2 Czarne Poland
19 H2 Czarnków Poland
4 G4 Czech Republic country Europe
19 L2 Czempiń Poland
19 J2 Czeremcha Poland
19 J2 Czersk Poland
19 H2 Czerwieńsk Poland
19 H2 Częstochowa Poland
19 H2 Człopa Poland
19 H2 Człuchów Poland
11 J3 Czyżew-Osada Poland

D

49 J5 Da'an China
43 J5 Dab'a Jordan
138 C1 Dabajuro Venezuela
76 D5 Dabakala Côte d'Ivoire
48 B5 Daban Shan mt. ra. China
18 J5 Dabas Hungary
50 H1 Daba Shan mt. ra. China
76 B4 Dabatou Guinea
76 B4 Dabeiba Colombia
138 B2 Dabeiba Colombia
54 D1 Dabein Myanmar
55 G4 Dabhoi India
81 D5 Dabl, W. w Saudi Arabia
76 B4 Daboh India
76 B4 Dabola Guinea
76 D5 Dabou Côte d'Ivoire
55 H4 Dabra India
55 J3 Dabra Chuan r. China
55 H1 Dabrsang China
15 G2 Dąbie Poland
19 J3 Dąbrowa Białostocka Poland
19 J3 Dąbrowa Górnicza Poland
19 K3 Dąbrowa Tarnowska Poland
28 D2 Dăbuleni Romania
80 D2 Dabus w. Ethiopia

80 C1 Dahlak Marine National Park nat. park Eritrea
18 C3 Dahlem Germany
54 C3 Dāhod India
54 D2 Dahonglutan China/Jammu and Kashmir
60 E2 Dahūk div. Iraq
142 E1 Dai Hai l. China
55 H3 Daik Indon.
42 B3 Daik-u Myanmar
54 C3 Dailaman Sum China
55 E3 Dailekh Nepal
57 D2 Daim Iran
46 D5 Daimanji-san h. Japan
24 E3 Daimiel Spain
47 F6 Dainichiga-take vol Japan
50 B1 Dainkog China
55 G3 Dainkognubma China
80 D3 Daintree Nat. Park nat. park. Aust.
48 F4 Dairen China
73 F2 Dairût Egypt
122 A2 Dairyland U.S.A.
47 H4 Daisen vol Japan
46 E5 Daishan China
55 F5 Daito-jima is Japan
48 E5 Da Xian China
129 G5 Daiyun Shan mt. ra. China
79 C7 Dajarra Aust.
50 D1 Dajin Chuan r. China
49 J3 Dajing China
55 H1 Da k China
75 D4 Dakar Senegal
150 J6 Danger Islands is Cook Islands Pac. Oc.
76 A4 Dakar el Arâk well Sudan
82 B5 Dakelangsi China
79 B7 Dakingari Nigeria
80 D3 Daketa Shet' w Ethiopia
55 G5 Dakhin Shabazpur I. i. Bangladesh
73 E4 Dakhla Oasis oasis Egypt
74 A4 Dakhlet Nouâdhibou div. Mauritania
76 A4 Dakingari Nigeria
56 F1 Dak Kon r. Vietnam
43 E4 Dak Lak Vietnam
43 E5 Dak Song Vietnam
128 E2 Dakota City U.S.A.
26 G3 Đakovica Yugo.
26 G3 Đakovo Croatia
60 C2 Daktuy Rus. Fed.
83 C6 Dal well Djibouti
79 D6 Dala Angola
54 D1 Dala Nal l. China
70 C4 Dalaba Guinea
54 D2 Dalad Qi China
55 E3 Dalai Nur l. China
19 L2 Dalainhot Mongolia
60 D2 Dalaman Turkey
60 B2 Dalaman r. Turkey
48 C2 Dalandzadgad Mongolia
19 L2 Dalälven r. Sweden
79 □ Dalap-Uliga-Darrit Marshall Is
17 F5 Dalbeattie U.K.
99 H5 Dalby Aust.
11 B3 Dale Hordaland Norway
11 B3 Dale Sogn og Fjordane Norway
42 A3 Dalet Myanmar
54 C1 Daletme Myanmar
11 B3 Dalfors Sweden
101 B6 Dalgaranger, Mt h. Aust.
19 J1 Danzig, Gulf of g. Poland/Rus. Fed.
125 C4 Dalhart U.S.A.
113 G4 Dalhousie Can.
41 B4 Dali Shaanxi China
50 C1 Dali Yunnan China
49 G4 Dalian China
50 C1 Daliang Shan mt. ra. China
49 F4 Dalin China
49 H4 Daling r. China
51 F1 Dalizi China
51 F1 Dalizi China
54 E5 Đakola India
125 E5 Dallas U.S.A.
124 E3 Dallas City U.S.A.
42 A3 Dalet Myanmar
51 E6 Dan Xian China
49 J3 Danyang China
43 E4 Da Lat Vietnam
48 C2 Dalay Mongolia
57 F3 Dalbandin Pakistan
57 D2 Dalbin Iran
60 A1 Dalby Sweden
57 F3 Dalbandin Pakistan
98 B3 Daly r. Aust.
125 G4 Daly City U.S.A.
98 B2 Daly River Abor. Land res. Aust.
98 B2 Daly Waters Aust.
80 E3 Daferur well Ethiopia
54 D4 Dabra India
55 H1 Dafla Hills mt. ra. India
79 C6 Dafeng China
79 C7 Danceng China
54 D1 Daga Medo Ethiopia
76 A3 Dagana Senegal
55 G3 Dagê China
68 D2 Dagestan div. Rus. Fed.
55 H3 Dagg Sd inlet N.Z.
73 F2 Daglet Lagroua Algeria
60 D2 Dağliq Qarabağ reg. Azer.
80 D2 Dagmar C.A.R.
79 B7 Damagaram Takaya Niger
60 D1 Dağmar C.A.R.
55 H3 Dalrymple, L. l. Aust.
99 G4 Dalrymple, Mt mt. Aust.
61 C4 Dar'ā Syria
61 C4 Dar'ā div. Syria
57 C3 Dārāb Iran
60 E1 Darband Iraq
28 E1 Darabani Romania
72 D1 Daraj Libya
57 C2 Dārān Iran
55 F4 Dārasu India
24 D3 Dārestān Iran

E

F

108 A3 Enurmino Rus. Fed.
140 B1 Envira Brazil
78 C3 Enyamba Zaire
78 C2 Enyélli Congo
93 C5 Enys, Mt mt. N.Z.
26 C3 Enza r. Italy
47 G6 Enzan Japan
90 ⁻2 Eo i. Pac. Oc.
21 F2 Epena Congo
23 F2 Epernay France
121 E4 Ephraim U.S.A.
121 E4 Ephrata U.S.A.
120 C2 Ephrata U.S.A.
90 ⁻2 Epi i. Vanuatu
21 H2 Épinal France
139 F2 Epira Guyana
61 B2 Episkopi Cyprus
61 B2 Episkopi B. b. Cyprus
27 D5 Epomeo, Monte h. Italy
17 H6 Epping U.K.
17 G6 Epsom U.K.
146 D4 Epu-pel Arg.
57 G2 Eqlid Iran
78 C3 Équateur div. Zaire
80 B3 Equatorial div. Sudan
69 E5 Equatorial Guinea country Africa
128 E2 Equeipa Venezuela
99 F5 Erac Cr. w. Aust.
71 D4 Erakhsouene well Mali
41 A4 Eran Phil.
54 C5 Erandol India
72 B4 Erba Turkey
73 G3 Erba, Jebel mt. Sudan
18 F4 Erbendorf Germany
18 C4 Erbeskopf h. Germany
60 E2 Erçek Turkey
60 C2 Erciş Turkey
60 C2 Erciyes Daği mt. Turkey
19 J5 Érd Hungary
59 H4 Erdao r. China
49 G4 Erdaogou China
60 A1 Erdek Turkey
61 C1 Erdemli Turkey
48 C2 Erdenet Mongolia
48 A2 Erdenet Mongolia
48 A2 Erdenetsogt Mongolia
72 D4 Erdi reg. Chad
18 E4 Erding Germany
152 B5 Erebus, Mt mt. Ant.
60 F4 Erech Iraq
143 B6 Erechim Brazil
48 D2 Ereentsav Mongolia
60 C2 Ereğli Konya Turkey
60 B1 Ereğli Zonguldak Turkey
29 B5 Ereikoussa i. Greece
27 E1 Eriei, Monti mts Italy
48 E4 Erenhot China
57 D2 Eresk Iran
57 E2 Eresma r. Spain
29 D5 Eretria Greece
74 D2 Erfoud Morocco
18 E3 Erfurt Germany
60 D2 Ergani Turkey
76 C2 Erg Atouila sand dunes Mali
74 C4 'Erg Chech sand dunes Algeria/Mali
72 C4 Erg du Djourab sand dunes Chad
77 G3 Erg du Ténéré sand dunes Niger
60 A1 Ergel Mongolia
60 A1 Ergene r. Turkey
74 D2 Erg er Raoui sand dunes Algeria
74 D3 Erg Iabès sand dunes Algeria
74 C4 Erg Iguidi sand dunes Algeria/Mauritania
75 F3 Erg Issaouane sand dunes Algeria
11 G4 Ergli Latvia
78 C1 Erguig r. Chad
49 G2 Ergun Yougi China
49 G2 Ergun Zuoqi China
50 C3 Er Hai l. China
49 H4 Erhulai China
57 B4 Ericeira Portugal
16 E3 Ericht, Loch l. U.K.
122 B5 Erie U.S.A.
125 E4 Erie U.S.A.
120 C3 Erie U.S.A.
123 F5 Erie, Lake l. Can./U.S.A.
76 C3 'Erîgât sand dunes Mali
46 J2 Erimo Japan
46 J3 Erimo-misaki c. Japan
96 C1 Eringa Aust.
133 ⁻3 Erin Point pt Trinidad Trin. & Tobago
68 H4 Eritrea country Africa
19 F2 Erkner Germany
73 G4 Erkowit Sudan
18 E4 Erlangen Germany
98 C5 Erldunda Aust.
49 J4 Erlong Shan mt. China
49 H4 Erlongshan Sk r. China
48 E2 Ermana, Khr. mt. ra. Rus. Fed.
83 D4 Ermelo R.S.A.
61 B1 Ermenek Turkey
60 C2 Ermenek Turkey
29 E6 Ermoupoli Greece
56 B4 Ernakulam India
101 C5 Ernest Giles Ra. h. Aust.
93 A7 Ernest Is N.Z.
56 B4 Erode India
98 E5 Eromanga Aust.
82 A3 Erongo div. Namibia
82 B3 Erongo mts Namibia
74 D2 Er Rachidia Morocco
73 F5 Er Rahad Sudan
83 F2 Errego Mozambique
82 B4 Er Renk Sudan
17 C4 Errigal h. Rep. of Ire.
17 B4 Erris Head hd Rep. of Ire.
121 H2 Errol U.S.A.
90 ⁻2 Erromango i. Vanuatu
80 B2 Er Roseires Sudan
73 F5 Er Rua'at Sudan
61 D4 Erseké Albania
29 C4 Erseké Albania
124 D2 Erskine U.S.A.
10 F3 Ersmark Sweden
14 E4 Ertil' Rus. Fed.
65 L3 Ertix r. China
96 D2 Erudina Aust.
145 G4 Ervália Brazil
120 D6 Erwin U.S.A.
29 D6 Erymanthos r. Greece
5 H3 Erythres Greece
50 B3 Eryuan China
19 F4 Erzgebirge mt. ra. Czech Rep./Germany
49 H2 Erzhan China
48 C2 Erzin Turkey
60 D1 Erzin Turkey

18 E3 Eschwege Germany
18 C3 Eschweiler Germany
133 E2 Escocesa, Bahía b. Caribbean
140 D3 Escoma Bolivia
128 D5 Escondido U.S.A.
130 D4 Escuinapa Mexico
131 H6 Escuintla Guatemala
133 E5 Escuintla Mexico
145 C2 Escursor. Brazil
138 C2 Escutillas Colombia
58 A6 Esdale Cameroon
57 C1 Esenguly Turkmenistan
18 C2 Esens Germany
57 B2 Esfahan Iran
57 B3 Esfahan div. Iran
57 C3 Esfarjan Iran
57 B3 Esfarjan Iran
64 E5 Eshkanän Iran
61 C4 Esh Sharâ reg. Jordan
57 C3 Eshtehärd Iran
78 E4 Esigodini Zimbabwe
83 E4 Esikhawini R.S.A.
99 H5 Esk Aust.
97 F5 Esk r. U.K.
57 B2 Eskandarï Iran
113 G3 Esker Can.
15 G2 Eskhar Ukraine
10 N2 Eskifjörður Iceland
11 E4 Eskilstuna Sweden
60 D2 Eskipazar Turkey
60 B2 Eskişehir Turkey
24 D1 Esla r. Spain
60 F3 Eslamābād al Gharb Iran
11 D5 Eslöv Sweden
57 B2 Esler Turkey
132 C2 Esmeralda Cuba
147 A6 Esmeralda, Isla i. Chile
138 B3 Esmeraldas Ecuador
11 F3 Esnagami Lake l. Can.
114 C2 Esnagi Lake l. Can.
57 B4 Espakeh Iran
20 F4 Espalion France
114 E3 Espanola Can.
127 F4 Espanola U.S.A.
138 ⁻ Española, i. i. Galapagos Is Ecuador
25 G2 Esparraguera Spain
128 A2 Esparto U.S.A.
101 C7 Esperance Aust.
101 C7 Esperance B. b. Aust.
92 ⁻4 Esperance Rock, L' i. Kermadec Is N.Z.
142 D1 Esperantinópolis Brazil
152 B2 Esperanza Argentina Base Ant.
147 B7 Esperanza Santa Cruz Arg.
146 C3 Esperanza Santa Fé Arg.
130 C3 Esperanza Mexico
140 B1 Esperanza Peru
41 C4 Esperanza Phil.
119 ⁻3 Esperanza Puerto Rico
130 J6 Esperanza, Sa de la mt. ra. Honduras
24 B3 Espichel, Cabo hd Portugal
24 D3 Espiel Spain
24 D1 Espigüete mt. Spain
125 C2 Espinazo Mexico
143 B6 Espinho, Sa do h. Brazil
145 G3 Espinosa Brazil
145 H3 Espírito Santo div. Brazil
81 B2 Espíritu Brazil
90 ⁻2 Espíritu Santo i. Vanuatu
131 J5 Espíritu Santo i. Mexico
130 C3 Espíritu Sto i. Mexico
142 E3 Espiosada Brazil
11 G3 Espoo Finland
83 E3 Espungabera Mozambique
147 B6 Esquel Arg.
110 E5 Esquimalt Can.
146 E3 Esquina Arg.
61 D3 Es Samrā Jordan
41 C5 Essang Indon.
74 C2 Essaouira Morocco
74 B3 Es Semara Western Sahara
18 C3 Essen Germany
101 C5 Essendon, Mt h. Aust.
139 F2 Essequibo r. Guyana
114 D5 Essex Can.
17 H6 Essex div. U.K.
121 G2 Essex Junction U.S.A.
123 F4 Essexville U.S.A.
18 D4 Esslingen am Neckar Germany
11 F4 Essvik Sweden
20 F2 Essonne r. France
91 ⁻12 Eta i. Tokelau Pac. Oc.
10 M2 Etah India
20 F2 Étain France
96 D1 Etamunbanie, L. salt flat Aust.
20 C4 Étampes France
21 E1 Étang de Biscarrosse et de Parentis l. France
21 E1 Étang de Cazaux et de Sanguinet l. France
20 D4 Étang d'Hourtin-Carcans l. France
81 ⁻ Étang Salé Réunion Indian Ocean
20 C4 Étaples France
20 E4 Étawah India

99 E3 Etheridge r. Aust.
69 H5 Ethiopia country Africa
41 C5 Etimesğut Turkey
16 E3 Etive, Loch inlet U.K.
27 E7 Etna, Monte vol Italy
11 B4 Etne Norway
110 C3 Etolin I. i. U.S.A.
99 G4 Eton Aust.
82 B2 Etosha National Park nat. park Namibia
78 B3 Etoumbi Congo
28 E3 Etropole Bulgaria
56 B4 Ettaiyapuram India
18 C2 Ettelbruck Luxembourg
18 B3 Etten-Leur Netherlands
74 A5 Et Tidra i. Mauritania
78 E4 Etumba Zaire
130 D4 Etzatlán Mexico
90 ⁻4 'Eua i. Tonga
90 ⁻4 'Eua Iki i. Tonga
90 ⁻3 Euakafa i. Tonga
101 E6 Eucla Aust.
120 C4 Euclid U.S.A.
142 E3 Euclides da Cunha Brazil
97 C4 Eucumbene, L. l. Aust.
96 D3 Eudunda Aust.
119 C6 Eufaula U.S.A.
125 E5 Eufaula Lake resr U.S.A.
126 B2 Eugene U.S.A.
141 E2 Eugênia r. Brazil
130 A2 Eugenia, Pta c. Mexico
97 G3 Eugowra Aust.
96 B2 Eulo Aust.
97 G2 Eumungerie Aust.
99 G4 Eungella Nat. Park Aust.
125 E6 Eunice U.S.A.
60 F4 Euphrates r. Iraq
11 F3 Eura Finland
20 E2 Eure r. France
126 A3 Eureka U.S.A.
126 D1 Eureka U.S.A.
129 E2 Eureka U.S.A.
125 D4 Eureka U.S.A.
96 E2 Euriowie Aust.
96 E2 Euriowie Aust.
99 G5 Euroa Aust.
99 G5 Eurombah Aust.
99 G5 Eurombah Cr. r. Aust.
149 G5 Europa, Île i. Indian Ocean
24 D1 Europa, Picos de mt. ra. Spain
24 D4 Europa Point hd Gibraltar
97 G3 Euston Aust.
119 C5 Eustak Lake l. Can.
11 C5 Eutin Germany
98 C3 Eva Downs Aust.
119 ⁻1 Evangelista i. Can.
110 F4 Evansburg Can.
99 F2 Evans Head Aust.
152 B3 Evans Ice Stream ice feature Ant.
126 C4 Evans, L. l. Can.
127 F4 Evans, Mt mt. U.S.A.
126 D2 Evans, Mt mt. U.S.A.
109 K3 Evans Strait chan. Can.
114 D4 Evanston U.S.A.
126 C3 Evanston U.S.A.
114 C4 Evansville U.S.A.
122 C4 Evansville U.S.A.
18 E4 Evansville U.S.A.
122 E4 Evart U.S.A.
122 A2 Eveleth U.S.A.
57 C4 Evez Iran
65 K3 Evensk Rus. Fed.
93 ⁻3 Eveque, Cape L' c. Chatham Is N.Z.
96 C2 Everard, L. salt flat Aust.
96 C1 Everard, Mt mt. Aust.
96 C1 Everard Park Aust.
55 F4 Everest, Mt mt. China
121 K1 Everett U.S.A.
126 B1 Everett U.S.A.
119 D7 Everglades Nat. Park nat. park U.S.A.
119 D7 Everglades, The swamp U.S.A.
125 C6 Evergreen U.S.A.
139 F2 Everton Guyana
20 F3 Evesham U.K.
17 G5 Evesham U.K.
11 F3 Evijärvi Finland
78 B3 Evinayong Equatorial Guinea
11 B4 Evje Norway
24 C3 Évora Portugal
57 B2 Evowin Ozero l. Rus. Fed.
20 E2 Évreux France
20 F2 Évron France
29 C6 Evros r. Greece/Turkey
20 F2 Évrotas r. Greece
29 D6 Evvoia i. Greece
91 ⁻12 Ewa Beach U.S.A.
91 ⁻12 Ewasiu Western Samoa
81 D5 Ewaso Ngiro r. Kenya
50 A3 Ewenkizu Zizhiqi China
91 ⁻11 Ewiela Rus. Fed.
92 ⁻1 Ewing I. i. Auckland Is N.Z.
78 B4 Ewo Congo
140 C2 Exaltación Bolivia
24 D3 Excelente r. Spain
128 D2 Excelsior Mtn mt. U.S.A.
128 C2 Excelsior Mts mts U.S.A.
124 E4 Excelsior Springs U.S.A.
152 A2 Executive Committee Range mt. ra. Ant.
17 C6 Exeter U.K.
114 D5 Exeter Can.
121 H3 Exeter U.S.A.
121 G3 Exeter U.S.A.
17 C6 Exmoor reg. U.K.
128 D5 Exmore U.S.A.
17 F7 Exmouth U.K.
101 A4 Exmouth Aust.
101 A5 Exmouth Gulf b. Aust.
149 M5 Exmouth Plateau Indian Ocean
99 G5 Expedition Range mt. ra. Aust.
133 ⁻6 Exploring Is Fiji
24 D3 Extremadura div. Spain
142 E2 Extremo-Nord div. Cameroon
142 E2 Exú Brazil
132 C1 Exuma Cays is The Bahamas
81 C5 Eyasi, Lake salt l. Tanzania
79 B4 Eyemouth U.K.
16 F5 Eyemouth U.K.
20 E4 Eymet France
20 E4 Eymoutiers France
76 B3 Eyn ou Nafti Mali
98 D3 Eyre Cr. w. Aust.
93 B6 Eyre Mountains mt. ra. N.Z.
96 D2 Eyre (North), Lake salt flat Aust.
96 D2 Eyre Peninsula pen. Aust.
96 D2 Eyre (South), L. salt flat Aust.
51 H4 Ezhou China
16 E3 Eyre, L. l. U.K.
10 M2 Eysturoy i. Faeroes
20 E5 Eysus France
78 B2 Eyumojok Cameroon
75 E4 Ezzaki Rus. Fed.
147 C4 Ezequiel Ramos Mexia, resr Arg.
82 C4 Ezibeleni R.S.A.
60 A2 Ezine Turkey

91 ⁻11 Faaa Fr. Poly. Pac. Oc.
53 D9 Faadhippolhu Atoll atoll Maldives
80 D4 Faafxadhuun Somalia
91 ⁻11 Faaite i. Fr. Poly. Pac. Oc.
91 ⁻11 Faaone Fr. Poly. Pac. Oc.
125 B6 Fabens U.S.A.
110 F2 Faber Lake l. Can.
43 ⁻ Faber, Mt h. Singapore
24 C1 Fabero Spain
11 C5 Fåborg Denmark
27 E3 Fabriano Italy
76 A4 Fachi Niger
74 D4 Facture France
145 C2 Fabienne Brazil
41 ⁻2 Facpi Pt pt Guam Pac. Oc.
146 C3 Facundo Arg.
72 D4 Fada Chad
72 E4 Fada-Ngourma Burkina
80 E2 Fadli reg. Yemen
57 F3 Fadnoun, Plateau du plat. Algeria
92 ⁻3 Faenza Italy
16 ⁻5 Faeroes is Atlantic Ocean
78 C2 Fafa r. C.A.R.
53 D10 Fafa i. Tonga
24 B2 Fafe Portugal
80 D3 Fafen Shet' w Ethiopia
91 ⁻12 Fagaloa Bay b. Western Samoa
91 ⁻12 Fagamalo Western Samoa
28 E2 Fǎgǎraş Romania
11 C3 Fagernes Norway
11 D4 Fagersta Sweden
11 D4 Fåget Romania
77 F4 Faggo Nigeria
147 C7 Fagnano, L. l. Arg.
76 D3 Faguibine, Lac l. Mali
80 M3 Fagurhólsmýri Iceland
80 B3 Fagwir Sudan
54 C3 Fahraj Iran
24 ⁻ Faial Madeira Portugal
61 A4 Faïd Saudi Arabia
11 E4 Fair r. Brazil
115 G2 Faillon, Lac l. Can.
108 D3 Fairbanks U.S.A.
124 D3 Fairborn U.S.A.
124 D3 Fairbury U.S.A.
122 B5 Fairfax U.S.A.
128 A2 Fairfield U.S.A.
122 B5 Fairfield U.S.A.
125 D6 Fairfield U.S.A.
121 K1 Fair Haven U.S.A.
41 A4 Fairie Queen sand bank Phil.
16 G2 Fair Isle i. U.K.
99 F2 Fairlight Aust.
120 C5 Fairmont U.S.A.
124 E3 Fairmont U.S.A.
120 C4 Fairmont U.S.A.
142 A1 Fairmount Harbor U.S.A.
99 F2 Fairview Aust.
110 F3 Fairview Can.
123 D3 Fairview U.S.A.
124 C4 Fairview U.S.A.
45 ⁻ Fairview Park Hong Kong
110 B3 Fairweather, Cape c. U.S.A.
110 B3 Fairweather, Mt mt. Can./U.S.A.
39 M5 Fais i. Fed. States of Micronesia
54 C3 Faisalabad Pakistan
116 G1 Faith U.S.A.
119 ⁻3 Fajardo Puerto Rico
57 C3 Fakahina i. Fr. Poly. Pac. Oc.
90 C3 Fakakei i. Tonga
87 K5 Fakaofo i. Tokelau Pac. Oc.
91 ⁻10 Fakarava i. Fr. Poly. Pac. Oc.
17 H5 Fakenham U.K.
10 D3 Fåker Sweden
38 K7 Fakfak Indon.
54 C3 Fakhrabad Iran
49 E4 Faku China
77 B4 Falaba Sierra Leone
77 F4 Falagountou Burkina
20 D2 Falaise France
72 C4 Falaise d'Angamma cliff Chad
76 D4 Falaise de Bandiagara escarpment Mali
76 D4 Falaise de Banfora escarpment Burkina
77 F3 Falaise de Tiguidit escarpment Niger
55 G4 Falakata India
24 D2 Falam Myanmar
57 B2 Falavarjan Iran
54 D3 Falcão Pakistan
143 D4 Fatepuri Sikri India
14 B3 Fateyevka Rus. Fed.
55 G5 Fathabad Iran
119 F4 Fathom Five National Marine Park nat. park Can.
77 A4 Fatick Senegal
143 B6 Fatima do Sul Brazil
90 ⁻3 Fatumanga i. Tonga
79 C4 Fatundu Zaire
114 D2 Fauquier r. Can.
101 A5 Fauro i. Solomon Is
80 C4 Fauresmith R.S.A.
57 D1 Fauske Norway

57 D4 Fannūj Iran
26 D4 Fano Italy
51 H4 Fanshan China
48 E5 Fanshi China
41 A4 Fan Si Pan mt. Vietnam
49 E6 Fan Xian China
64 F5 Farab Turkmenistan
76 B4 Faraba Mali
152 B2 Faraday Ukraine Base Ant.
78 E4 Faradje Zaire
83 H3 Farafangana Madagascar
24 C1 Farafenni The Gambia
73 E2 Farafra Oasis oasis Egypt
57 D4 Farāghēh Iran
57 E2 Farah w Afghanistan
57 F2 Farāh Afghanistan
57 F2 Farāh Afghanistan
39 M2 Farallon de Pajaros i. Northern Mariana Is Pac. Oc.
72 B4 Faranah Guinea
92 B4 Farewell, Cape c. N.Z.
92 B4 Farewell Spit spit N.Z.
124 D2 Färgelanda Sweden
124 D2 Fargo U.S.A.
124 E2 Faribault U.S.A.
113 F2 Faribault, Lac l. Can.
54 C3 Faridkot India
55 G4 Faridpur Bangladesh
54 D3 Faridpur India
57 D2 Farīhy Alaotra l. Madagascar
83 G3 Farīhy Ihotry l. Madagascar
83 H2 Farīhy Kinkony l. Madagascar
83 H2 Farīhy Tsiazompaniry l. Madagascar
83 H2 Farīhy Tsimanampetsotsa l. Madagascar
24 B3 Farilhões i. Portugal
142 C2 Farinha r. Brazil
61 A4 Färiskūr Egypt
11 E4 Färjestaden Sweden
29 C5 Farkadona Greece
65 G5 Farkhor Tajikistan
29 F6 Farmakonisi i. Greece
51 F2 Farm City U.S.A.
112 D2 Farmer Island i. Can.
122 B5 Farmersburg U.S.A.
121 F3 Farmington U.S.A.
122 C5 Farmington U.S.A.
124 E3 Farmington U.S.A.
121 H3 Farmington U.S.A.
121 H3 Farmington U.S.A.
129 H4 Farmington U.S.A.
120 C6 Farmville U.S.A.
17 G6 Farnborough U.K.
17 G6 Farnham U.K.
17 G6 Farnham, Mt mt. Can.
110 F4 Farnham, Mt mt. Can.
46 B4 Faro r. Brazil
24 B4 Faro Portugal
11 F4 Fårö i. Sweden
72 B4 Faro, Serra do mt. ra. Spain
11 E4 Fårösund Sweden
24 C1 Farquhar Group is Seychelles
99 E5 Farrars Cr. w. Aust.
57 C2 Farrashband Iran
120 C4 Farrell U.S.A.
115 H4 Farrokhī Iran
57 C3 Fārs div. Iran
57 C2 Farsala Greece
57 E2 Farsakh i. Iran
126 D3 Farson U.S.A.
11 B4 Farsund Norway
80 C3 Farta, Baía Angola
28 D2 Fârţâneşti Romania
144 C2 Fartura r. Brazil
125 C5 Farwell U.S.A.
27 D5 Fasano Italy
29 D6 Fastiv Ukraine
78 E3 Fastov Ukraine
54 D4 Fatehabad India
54 D4 Fatehgarh India
54 D4 Fatehgarh India
54 C4 Fatehnagar India
54 C4 Fatehpur Rajasthan India
54 E4 Fatehpur Uttar Pradesh India
54 D3 Fatehpur Pakistan

51 G2 Feixi China
51 G1 Fei Xian China
60 C2 Feke Turkey
122 B3 Felch U.S.A.
19 F2 Feldberg Mecklenburg-Vorpommern Germany
18 D5 Feldberg mt. Germany
18 E4 Feldkirch Austria
19 G5 Feldkirchen in Kärten Austria
28 E1 Feldru Romania
145 G4 Feliciano r. Arg.
146 E3 Felicité I. i. Seychelles
53 D10 Felidu Atoll atoll Maldives
145 G4 Felipe C. Puerto Mexico
145 H3 Felixlândia Brazil
122 D3 Felixstowe U.K.
17 J6 Felixstowe U.K.
26 D3 Feltre Italy
11 D4 Femer Bælt str. Denmark/Germany
18 E1 Femer Bælt str. Denmark/Germany
48 D5 Fen r. China
10 D3 Femundsmarka Nasjonalpark nat. park Norway
29 C4 Fener Burnu pt Greece
61 A1 Fenârtepe Turkey
98 C5 Finke w Aust.
98 C5 Finke Gorge Nat. Park nat. park. Aust.
10 E1 Fendow China
50 D3 Fengcheng China
51 H4 Fengcheng China
49 H4 Fengcheng China
48 D5 Fengfeng China
48 F2 Fenggang China
49 H4 Fenghua China
49 H4 Fenghuang China
51 G1 Fengjie China
51 G1 Fengkai China
51 H4 Fengkai China
49 H4 Fengle China
49 F4 Fengnan China
49 G4 Fengning China
50 D2 Fengqing China
51 F1 Fengqiu China
49 F5 Fengrun China
90 ⁻1 Fengshun China
48 D5 Fengtai China
49 G4 Fengxiang China
51 G2 Fengxin China
51 G2 Fengyang China
51 F2 Fengyi China
51 G1 Fengzhen China
51 F1 Fenling China
49 F5 Fengnan China
50 D3 Fengshun China
51 G4 Feni Bangladesh
55 G5 Feni Bangladesh
90 ⁻1 Feni Is P.N.G.
90 ⁻1 Fennimore U.S.A.
122 B4 Fennimore U.S.A.
83 H2 Fenoarivo Atsinanana Madagascar
83 H2 Fenoarivo Be Madagascar
21 J6 Feno, Capo di pt France
21 J6 Feno, The reg. U.K.
37 G3 Fenoun r. China
123 F4 Fenton U.S.A.
151 J7 Fenua Ura is Fr. Poly.
49 F4 Fenxi China
48 D5 Fenyang China
122 C4 Feodosiya Ukraine
15 F5 Feodosiya Ukraine
76 D3 Fer, Cap de c. Algeria
57 D2 Ferdows Iran
29 F4 Ferres Greece
65 H4 Fergana Uzbekistan
65 H4 Fergana Too Tizmegi mt. ra. Kyrgyzstan
114 E5 Fergus Can.
124 E3 Fergus Falls U.S.A.
90 ⁻1 Fergusson I. i. P.N.G.
75 F2 Fériana Tunisia
76 C5 Fèrkessédougou Côte d'Ivoire
76 A4 Ferlo w. Senegal
57 E2 Fèrmo Brazil
26 E3 Fermo Italy
24 C2 Fermoselle Spain
17 C5 Fermoy Rep. of Ire.
119 D6 Fernandina Beach U.S.A.
138 ⁻ Fernandina, I. i. Galapagos Is Ecuador
147 B7 Fernando de Magallanes, Parque Nacional nat. park Chile
148 G6 Fernando de Noronha i. Atlantic Ocean
144 C4 Fernandópolis Brazil
83 B3 Fernão Veloso, Baia de b. Mozambique
110 F5 Fernie Can.
126 C2 Fernley U.S.A.
27 C5 Fernwood U.S.A.
146 C3 Ferreira Arg.
138 B5 Ferreñafe Peru
145 J1 Ferreira Gomes Brazil
144 B4 Ferreiros Brazil
138 B5 Ferrñafe Peru
140 C2 Ferro r. Brazil
145 F3 Ferros Brazil
27 B6 Ferrato, Capo c. Italy
24 B3 Ferreira do Alentejo Portugal
139 G3 Ferreira-Gomes Brazil
144 B4 Ferreiros Brazil
138 B5 Ferrñafe Peru
140 C2 Ferro r. Brazil
145 F3 Ferros Brazil
15 E6 Ferzikovo Rus. Fed.
79 D4 Fès Morocco
79 C4 Feshi Zaire
124 C2 Fessenden U.S.A.
14 D1 Festus U.S.A.
28 D2 Feteşti Romania
60 B2 Fethiye Turkey
60 B2 Fethiye Turkey
16 G1 Fetlar i. U.K.
113 F2 Feuilles, Rivière aux r. Can.
57 F3 Feyzābād Iran
57 G2 Feyzābād Iran
57 B4 Fezzan reg. Libya
76 D4 Fiambalá Arg.
146 B2 Fiambalá Arg.
83 H3 Fianarantsoa Madagascar
83 H3 Fianarantsoa div. Madagascar
72 C4 Fianga Chad
24 C2 Fichê Ethiopia
80 D3 Fichê Ethiopia
83 D4 Ficksburg R.S.A.
26 D3 Fidenza Italy
11 C4 Fiera di Primiero Italy
11 B4 Fiesole Italy
26 D3 Fiesole Italy
28 D2 Fieni Romania
124 C1 Fife div. U.K.
16 F4 Fife Ness pt U.K.
20 F4 Figeac France
24 B2 Figueira da Foz Portugal
25 H1 Figueres Spain
145 H3 Figuig Brazil
74 D2 Figuig Morocco
77 A3 Fiji country Pac. Oc.
133 ⁻6 Fiji country Pac. Oc.
81 reg. Yemen

19 J4 Fifakovo Slovakia
101 A7 Flinders B. b. Aust.
96 D3 Flinders Chase Nat. Park nat. park. Aust.
79 F2 Flinders Grp i. Aust.
99 F2 Flinders I. i. Aust.
99 G3 Flinders Passage chan. Aust.
96 D2 Flinders Ranges mt. ra. Aust.
96 D2 Flinders Ranges Nat. nat. park Aust.
99 G3 Flinders Reefs reef Coral Sea Islands Terr. Pac. Oc.
111 J4 Flin Flon Can.
17 F5 Flint U.K.
123 F4 Flint U.S.A.
123 F4 Flint r. U.S.A.
37 M6 Flint Island i. Kiribati
11 D3 Flisa Norway
21 F4 Florac France
99 E3 Florala U.S.A.
120 B4 Florence U.S.A.
119 C5 Florence U.S.A.
129 G5 Florence U.S.A.
124 D3 Florence U.S.A.
126 A3 Florence U.S.A.
119 D5 Florence U.S.A.
121 E4 Florence Junction U.S.A.
142 E1 Florencia Can.
138 C3 Florencia Colombia
147 C5 Florentino Ameghino, Embalse resr Arg.
146 E2 Flores r. Arg.
142 E2 Flores Pernambuco Brazil
142 E2 Flores Piauí Brazil
142 D1 Flores r. Brazil
131 H5 Flores Guatemala
24 ⁻ Flores i. Azores Portugal
40 D4 Flores i. Indon.
119 ⁻2 Flores, I. i. Solomon Is
128 B2 Florida Uruguay
146 E3 Florida div. Uruguay
119 D6 Florida Bay b. U.S.A.
119 D7 Florida City U.S.A.
119 ⁻2 Florida i. Solomon Is
119 D7 Florida Keys is U.S.A.
90 ⁻1 Florida, Straits of str. The Bahamas/U.S.A.
144 D2 Florida r. Brazil
145 F1 Firmino Alves Brazil
144 C2 Firminópolis Brazil
21 G4 Firminy France
12 E3 Firovo Rus. Fed.
57 D1 Firyuza Turkmenistan
82 B4 Fish w Namibia
82 B4 Fish r. Namibia
122 E2 Fisher Bay b. Ant.
111 J6 Fisherman's I. i. U.S.A.
113 H5 Fishers I. i. U.S.A.
17 C6 Fishguard U.K.
110 E2 Fish Lake l. Can.
110 E2 Fish Lake l. Can.
122 C5 Fish Lake l. U.S.A.
129 G2 Fish Lake l. U.S.A.
76 Fish Ponds lakes Hong Kong
123 B4 Fish Pt pt U.S.A.
77 F4 Fogo Nigeria
111 J6 Fogo i. Cape Verde
122 B3 Fiske, C. c. Ant.
21 B3 Fisme France
111 E4 Fisterra, Cabo c. Spain
113 F3 Fitchburg U.S.A.
140 C2 Fitri, Lac l. Chad
72 C4 Fitri, Lac l. Chad
140 D4 Fitzcarrald Peru
111 G3 Fitzgerald Can.
119 D6 Fitzgerald U.S.A.
101 B7 Fitzgerald River Nat. Park nat. park Aust.
98 B2 Fitzroy r. Aust.
99 G4 Fitzroy r. Aust.
147 B7 Fitzroy, Monte mt. Arg.
100 D4 Fitzroy Crossing Aust.
114 E4 Fitzwilliam I. i. Can.
57 B2 Fivizzano Italy
92 ⁻7 Five Fingers Peninsula pen. N.Z.
94 ⁻3 Flying Fish Cove Christmas I. Indian Ocean
90 ⁻5 Foča Bos.-Herz.
29 F5 Foça Turkey
152 Foch, Î. i. Kerguelen Indian Ocean
28 E2 Focşani Romania
78 B2 Fodé C.A.R.
113 G3 Foelsche r. Aust.
11 B3 Fofoa i. Tonga
11 N2 Fofoa i. Tonga
11 N2 Fofoa i. Tonga
49 E4 Fogang China
75 Foggāret ez Zoûa Algeria
27 E4 Foggia Italy
41 Fogo i. Cape Verde
77 F4 Fogolawa Nigeria
18 D5 Föhr i. Germany
70 F4 Foix France
102 Fokku Nigeria
72 Foggāret ez Zoûa Algeria
141 E2 Folegandros i. Greece
29 E6 Folegandros i. Greece
110 G5 Foley U.S.A.
119 C6 Foley U.S.A.
112 E2 Foleyet Can.
27 E4 Foligno Italy
17 H6 Folkestone U.K.
119 D6 Folkston U.S.A.
11 C4 Folldal Norway
119 C4 Follonica Italy
26 D3 Follonica Italy
21 E4 Folsom U.S.A.
128 B2 Folsom Lake l. U.S.A.
79 D4 Fomboni Comoros
128 E2 Fomenkova Rus. Fed.
65 K2 Fominskaya Rus. Fed.
14 G2 Fominskiy Rus. Fed.
14 J3 Fominskoye Rus. Fed.
83 H3 Fon Going ridge Guinea
76 B4 Fon Going ridge Guinea
79 D4 Fond du Lac Can.
111 H3 Fond-du-Lac r. Can.
122 C4 Fond du Lac U.S.A.
81 ⁻ Fond du Sac Mauritius
27 E4 Fondi Italy
24 D2 Fonelas r. Spain
145 F3 Fonseca, G. de b. Central America
20 E2 Fontainebleau France
114 A1 Fontanges Can.
142 C1 Fontas Can.
110 G2 Fonte Boa Brazil
140 D1 Fonte Boa Brazil
20 D3 Fontenay-le-Comte France
10 N2 Fontur pt Iceland
81 ⁻ Fonuafo'ou i. Tonga
90 ⁻3 Fonuafo'ou i. Tonga
90 ⁻4 Fonua Town Trin. & Tobago
20 F3 Fontvieille France
115 F4 Foot's Bay Can.
97 G5 Foping China
51 F1 Foping China
20 F1 Forbach France
28 D1 Forbesganj India
55 F4 Forbesganj India
97 G3 Forbes Aust.
93 A7 Forbes, Mt mt. N.Z.
110 F4 Forbes, Mt mt. Can.
77 F4 Forçados Nigeria
124 C1 Ford r. U.S.A.
124 E2 Forécariah Guinea
76 B4 Forécariah Guinea
16 ⁻ Foreland Pt pt U.K.
110 E4 Foresight Mtn mt. Can.
119 C6 Forest Can.
114 D5 Forest Can.
124 F2 Forest U.S.A.
125 F5 Forest U.S.A.
99 F2 Forest, C. hd Aust.
121 F3 Forestburg Can.
110 G4 Forest Park U.S.A.
119 C5 Forestier, C. hd Aust.
97 F5 Forestier Pen. pen. Aust.
119 C4 Forest Park U.S.A.
21 F4 Forez, Monts du mt. ra. France
16 F4 Forfar U.K.
20 D2 Forges-les-Eaux France
20 D2 Fougères France

25 G3 Formentera i. Spain
25 H3 Formentor, Cap de pt Spain
26 E3 Formia Italy
145 F4 Formiga Brazil
144 C1 Formosa Arg.
144 E1 Formosa div. Arg.
142 C3 Formosa do R. Prêto Brazil
142 D3 Formosa r. Bahia Brazil
145 E1 Formosa r. Goiás Brazil
144 B4 Formosa r. Mato Grosso do Sul Brazil
142 C3 Formoso r. Tocantins Brazil
142 C3 Formoso Tocantins Brazil
17 F5 Forres U.K.
101 C6 Forrest Aust.
101 E6 Forrest r. Aust.
100 D2 Forrest r. Aust.
125 F5 Forrest City U.S.A.
100 D2 Forrest River Abor. Reserve res. Aust.
99 F3 Forsayth Aust.
11 D3 Forsnäs Sweden
11 F3 Forssa Finland
19 F3 Forst Germany
97 G4 Forster Aust.
120 B4 Forsyth U.S.A.
126 E2 Forsyth U.S.A.
115 F2 Forsyth Can.
98 E3 Forsyth Ra. h. Aust.
54 B3 Fort Abbas Pakistan
124 C3 Fort Albany Can.
142 E1 Fortaleza Bolivia
142 E1 Fortaleza Brazil
129 H5 Fort Apache U.S.A.
142 E1 Fortaleza Brazil
110 E3 Fort Assiniboine Can.
122 C4 Fort Atkinson U.S.A.
16 E3 Fort Augustus U.K.
82 B5 Fort Beaufort R.S.A.
126 E2 Fort Benton U.S.A.
111 F4 Fort Black Can.
111 G4 Fort Bragg U.S.A.
110 F3 Fort Chipewyan Can.
111 E3 Fort Chipewyan Can.
126 F3 Fort Collins U.S.A.
98 A3 Fort Constantine Aust.
121 F2 Fort-Coulonge Can.
125 D6 Fort Davis U.S.A.
133 ⁻4 Fort-de-France Martinique Caribbean
133 ⁻4 Fort de France, Baie de b. Martinique Caribbean
119 C6 Fort Deposit U.S.A.
124 E3 Fort Dodge U.S.A.
101 A5 Fortescue r. Aust.
112 B3 Fort Frances Can.
116 G3 Fort George Can.
119 ⁻ Fort Good Hope Can.
16 E4 Forth r. U.K.
16 F4 Forth, Firth of est. U.K.
126 D2 Fortification Range mts U.S.A.
141 D4 Fortín Ávalos Sánchez Paraguay
141 D4 Fortín Capitán Demattei Paraguay
141 D4 Fortín Carlos Antonio López Paraguay
141 E4 Fortín Coronel Bogado Paraguay
141 D4 Fortín Coronel Eugenio Garay Paraguay
141 E4 Fortín Falcón Paraguay
141 E4 Fortín Galpón Paraguay
141 D4 Fortín General Caballero Paraguay
141 D4 Fortín General Mendoza Paraguay
141 D4 Fortín Hernandarias Paraguay
141 E4 Fortín Infante Rivarola Paraguay
141 E4 Fortín Joe de Zalazar Paraguay
146 D2 Fortín Lavalle Arg.
141 E4 Fortín Linares Paraguay
146 D2 Fortín Madrejón Paraguay
141 D4 Fortín Paredes Bolivia
141 E4 Fortín Pilcomayo Arg.
141 D4 Fortín Presidente Ayala Paraguay
141 D4 Fortín Suárez Arana Bolivia
141 D4 Fortín Tte. Juan E. López Paraguay
119 D7 Fort Lauderdale U.S.A.
110 D2 Fort Liard Can.
133 ⁻ Fort Liberté Haiti
110 F3 Fort Mackay Can.
110 G5 Fort Macleod Can.
122 B5 Fort McCoy U.S.A.
110 G3 Fort McMurray Can.
108 E3 Fort McPherson Can.
122 B5 Fort Madison U.S.A.
126 F2 Fort Morgan U.S.A.
119 D7 Fort Myers U.S.A.
110 E3 Fort Nelson Can.
110 E3 Fort Nelson r. Can.
126 C1 Fort Norman Can.
119 C5 Fort Payne U.S.A.
126 F1 Fort Peck U.S.A.
126 F1 Fort Peck Res. resr U.S.A.
119 D7 Fort Pierce U.S.A.
130 D1 Fort Portal Uganda
110 E2 Fort Providence Can.
111 J4 Fort Qu'Appelle Can.
110 G2 Fort Resolution Can.
83 B1 Fort Rixon Zimbabwe
114 E2 Fortrose Can.
16 E3 Fortrose U.K.
126 A3 Fort Ross U.S.A.
113 G4 Fort Rupert Can.
119 ⁻ Fort St James Can.
110 E3 Fort St John Can.
111 F4 Fort Saskatchewan Can.
111 J4 Fort Severn Can.
112 D2 Fort Severn Can.
57 D1 Fort-Shevchenko Kazak.
110 D2 Fort Simpson Can.
110 G2 Fort Smith Can.
125 E5 Fort Smith U.S.A.
125 C6 Fort Stockton U.S.A.
125 C5 Fort Sumner U.S.A.
129 G4 Fort Thomas U.S.A.
16 F3 Fort Vermilion Can.
110 F3 Fort Vermilion Can.
119 C6 Fort Walton Beach U.S.A.
122 E5 Fort Wayne U.S.A.
16 E4 Fort Wellington Guyana
139 F2 Fort Wellington Guyana
42 A2 Fort White Myanmar
110 E3 Fort William Can.
16 D4 Fort William U.K.
125 D5 Fort Worth U.S.A.
93 Forty Fours, The i. Chatham Is N.Z.
108 D3 Fort Yukon U.S.A.
51 F4 Foshan China
51 F1 Foshan China
10 E3 Fossano Italy
26 B3 Fossano Italy
16 ⁻ Foster Aust.
97 G5 Foster Aust.
120 B4 Foster U.S.A.
110 C3 Fosshiem Pen. pen. Can.
81 B4 Fotadrevo Madagascar
78 B2 Fotokol Cameroon
20 D2 Fougères France
78 B3 Fouesnant France
20 B2 Fougamou Gabon
20 D2 Fougères France

55 G4 Goalpara India
40 D4 Goang Indon.
76 D5 Goaso Ghana
80 D3 Goba Ethiopia
82 B3 Gobabis Namibia
146 C4 Gobernador Duval Arg.
147 B6 Gobernador Gregores Arg.
146 E2 Gobernador Virasoro Arg.
14 B3 Gobi desert Mongolia
14 B3 Gobki Rus. Fed.
18 C3 Gobō Japan
18 C3 Goch Germany
82 B3 Gochas Namibia
36 C3 Go Cong Vietnam
56 C2 Godavari r. India
56 C2 Godavari, Mouths of the India
115 F4 Godbout Can.
54 H3 Godda India
72 D3 Goddard, Mt mt. U.S.A.
139 F3 Goddo Surinam
26 D3 Godech Bulgaria
61 A1 Gödene Turkey
114 E5 Goderich Can.
72 C3 Goderville France
51 D6 Godhra India
80 E3 Godinlabe Somalia
19 J5 Gödöllő Hungary
111 L3 Gods r. Can.
111 L4 Gods l. Can.
111 M2 Gods Mercy, Bay of b. Can.
54 C4 Godwar reg. India
14 H3 Godyaykino Rus. Fed.
115 G2 Goéland, Lac au l. Can.
113 H2 Goélands, Lac aux l. Can.
18 A3 Goes Netherlands
123 F2 Goetzville U.S.A.
129 E4 Goffs U.S.A.
13 G6 Gofitskoye Rus. Fed.
114 E3 Gogama Can.
46 D6 Gō-gawa r. Japan
122 C2 Gogebic, Lake l. U.S.A.
122 C2 Gogebic Range h. U.S.A.
100 D3 Gogo Aust.
76 E2 Gogoue Benin
78 E2 Gogrial Sudan
54 D4 Gohad India
144 D3 Goiana Brazil
144 D3 Goianira Brazil
144 D3 Goianinha Brazil
144 C1 Goianésia Brazil
144 C2 Goiânia Brazil
144 C1 Goiás Brazil
144 C2 Goiás div. Brazil
144 C2 Goiatuba Brazil
41 □ Goikul Palau
50 B2 Goinxab China
144 B6 Goio-Erê Brazil
93 □ Gojeb Wenz r. Ethiopia
47 H4 Gojōme Japan
54 C3 Gojra Pakistan
46 C2 Gokak India
46 C2 Gokase-gawa r. Japan
61 B1 Gök Çay r. Turkey
61 A1 Gökçeada i. Turkey
29 G5 Gökçen Turkey
61 B1 Gökdepe Turkey
55 G3 Gokhar La China
60 C1 Gökirmak r. Turkey
57 E4 Gokprosh Hills mt. ra. Pakistan
61 B1 Göksu r. Turkey
60 D2 Göksun Turkey
83 D2 Gokwe Zimbabwe
11 C3 Gol Norway
55 H4 Golaghat India
19 H2 Gołańcz Poland
57 G2 Golbahār Afghanistan
61 D1 Gölbaşı Turkey
62 K2 Gol'chikha Rus. Fed.
29 G5 Gölcük Balıkesir Turkey
60 B1 Gölcük Kocaeli Turkey
19 L2 Golczewo Poland
19 J1 Gołdap Poland
18 E3 Goldberg Germany
99 H6 Gold Coast Aust.
76 D6 Gold Coast Ghana
10 F4 Golden Can.
92 D4 Golden Bay b. N.Z.
128 E3 Golden Gate National Recreation Area res. U.S.A.
110 D5 Golden Hinde mt. Can.
133 □6 Golden Rock airport St Kitts-Nevis Caribbean
128 D3 Goldfield U.S.A.
128 D3 Gold Point U.S.A.
119 E5 Goldsboro U.S.A.
100 B4 Goldsworthy Aust.
125 D6 Goldthwaite U.S.A.
60 E1 Göle Turkey
19 G2 Goleniów Poland
57 G3 Golestān Afghanistan
57 C3 Golestānak Iran
128 C4 Goleta U.S.A.
48 C1 Golets-Davydov, G. mt. Rus. Fed.
132 K7 Golfito Costa Rica
29 G6 Gölgeli Dağları mt. ra. Turkey
125 D6 Goliad U.S.A.
51 H1 Golija mt. ra. Yugo.
28 D3 Golija Planina mts Yugo.
49 C3 Golin Baixing China
14 C3 Golitsyno Rus. Fed.
14 G3 Golitsyno Rus. Fed.
60 D1 Gölköy Turkey
29 F5 Gölmarmara Turkey
55 H1 Golmud r. China
55 H1 Golmud China
21 J5 Golo r. France
41 B3 Golo i. Phil.
14 D2 Golovanovo Rus. Fed.
14 E2 Golovanovo Rus. Fed.
19 K5 Golovanivs'k Ukr.
14 E2 Golovinshchino Rus. Fed.
46 K2 Golovnino Rus. Fed.
57 C3 Golpāyegān Iran
12 I3 Gol'tsovka Rus. Fed.
19 L4 Golub-Dobrzyń Poland
57 B2 Golubovka Rus. Fed.
14 C3 Golun' Rus. Fed.
79 B5 Golungo Alto Angola
57 E2 Gol Vardeh Iran
81 B4 Golyama Zhelyazna Bulgaria
28 E2 Golyam Persenk mt. Bulgaria
29 G4 Gölyazı Turkey
65 G2 Golyshmanovo Rus. Fed.
78 E4 Goma Zaire
55 C1 Gomang Co l. China
43 □ Gombak, Bukit h. Singapore
39 H6 Gombe r. Indon.
81 B5 Gombe Tanzania
81 C5 Gombi Nigeria
81 □ Gombrani I. i. Rodrigues I. Mauritius
29 F5 Gömeç Turkey
25 □ Gomera, La i. Canary Is Spain
130 D2 Gómez Farias Mexico
130 D2 Gómez Palacio Mexico
131 F3 Gómez, Presa M. R. resr Mexico
57 C1 Gomishān Iran
55 D1 Gomo Co r. China
57 D1 Gonābād Iran
133 E3 Gonaïves Haiti
83 E2 Gonarezhou National Park nat. park Zimbabwe
133 C6 Gonâve, Île de la i. Haiti
54 E3 Gonda India
54 B5 Gondal India
80 D2 Gonda Libah well Ethiopia
80 D2 Gonder Ethiopia

54 E5 Gondia India
60 A1 Gönen Turkey
20 E2 Gonfreville-l'Orcher France
51 F2 Gong'an China
55 H3 Gongbo'gyamda China
51 E3 Gongcheng China
50 C2 Gonggar China
50 C2 Gongga Shan mt. China
48 E4 Gonghui China
65 K4 Gongliu China
72 G4 Gongola r. Nigeria
77 F4 Gongola r. Nigeria
78 A4 Gongoué r. Gabon
50 B3 Gongshan China
50 C3 Gongwang Shan mt. ra. China
51 E4 Gong Xian China
50 D2 Gong Xian China
19 H2 Goniądz Poland
50 B2 Gonjo China
47 H3 Gonohe Japan
46 H3 Gōnoura Japan
131 F4 Gonzáles Mexico
128 B3 Gonzales U.S.A.
125 D6 Gonzales U.S.A.
126 D5 Goochland U.S.A.
101 B6 Goodenough, C. c. Ant.
96 □1 Goodenough I. i. P.N.G.
122 E3 Good Harbor Bay b. U.S.A.
82 B5 Good Hope, Cape of R.S.A.
124 C4 Gooding U.S.A.
81 □4 Goodlands Mauritius
97 F2 Goodooga Aust.
17 G5 Goole U.K.
80 E3 Goolis Mountains mts Somalia
99 F5 Goolgowi Aust.
101 A6 Goomalling Aust.
97 F2 Goondiwindi Aust.
101 C6 Goongarrie, L. salt flat Aust.
115 H2 Goose r. Can.
113 H3 Goose r. U.S.A.
147 E7 Goose Green Falkland Is.
126 B3 Goose L. l. U.S.A.
56 B3 Gooty India
54 F4 Gopālganj India
54 E3 Gopālganj India
3 H7 Gora Bazardyuzi mt. Rus. Fed.
19 K3 Góra Kalwaria Poland
45 O1 Gora Lopatina mt. Rus. Fed.
45 P2 Gora Medvezh'ya mt. China/Rus. Fed.
45 P2 Gora Tardoki-Yani mt. Rus. Fed.
26 G4 Goražde Bos.-Herz.
14 C1 Gorbachevo Rus. Fed.
119 E7 Gorda Cay i. The Bahamas
130 K6 Gorda, Pta mt Nicaragua
130 K7 Gorda, Pta Nicaragua
60 B2 Gördes Turkey
72 F5 Gordil C.A.R.
98 B1 Gordon B. b. Aust.
100 E3 Gordon Downs Aust.
97 F5 Gordon, L. l. Aust.
110 G2 Gordon Lake l. Can.
120 D5 Gordonsville U.S.A.
99 F3 Gordonvale Aust.
78 C4 Goré Chad
80 C3 Gorē Ethiopia
93 B7 Gore N.Z.
114 D4 Gore Bay Can.
14 E3 Gorelki Rus. Fed.
14 B2 Gorelovo Rus. Fed.
17 D5 Gorey Rep. of Ire.
57 D2 Gorg Iran
57 C1 Gorgān Iran
57 C1 Gorgān, B. b. Iran
57 C1 Gorgān, Rūd-e r. Iran
99 F3 Gorge Ra., The mt. ra. Aust.
74 B5 Gorgol div. Mauritania
138 B3 Gorgona, Isla di i. Col.
80 C2 Gorgora Ethiopia
18 B3 Gorinchem Netherlands
57 D2 Goris Armenia
14 C1 Goritsy Rus. Fed.
26 E3 Gorizia Italy
14 E2 Gorka Rus. Fed.
54 F4 Gorkha Nepal
57 B2 Gor'ko-Solenoye, Ozero l. Rus. Fed.
12 G3 Gor'kovskoye Vdkhr. resr Rus. Fed.
19 K4 Gorlice Poland
19 G3 Görlitz Germany
27 E7 Gornalunga r. Italy
28 E3 Gorna Oryakhovitsa Bulgaria
28 E3 Gorni Dūbnik Bulgaria
26 F2 Gornja Radgona Slovenia
28 C3 Gornja Toponica Yugo.
26 G4 Gornji Milanovac Yugo.
26 F4 Gornji Vakuf Bos.-Herz.
65 D2 Gorno-Altaysk Rus. Fed.
28 E2 Gornotrakiyska Nizina lowland Bulgaria
49 K3 Gornyak Rus. Fed.
14 E2 Gornye Klyuchi Rus. Fed.
45 N5 Gornyy Zerentuy Rus. Fed.
38 D2 Goro Indon.
14 D2 Goro r. Rus. Fed.
15 G6 Goro r. C.A.R.
13 G6 Gorodets Rus. Fed.
14 F1 Gorodishche Rus. Fed.
14 H3 Gorodishche Rus. Fed.
15 E6 Gorodovikovsk Rus. Fed.
39 H6 Gorontalo Indon.
77 F4 Goroubi r. Burkina/Niger
97 F2 Gorowai r. Indon.
81 B6 Gorongosa Mozambique
83 E2 Gorongosa Mozambique
83 E2 Gorongosa, Parque Nacional de nat. park Mozambique
39 H6 Goroka P.N.G.
84 E2 Gorom Gorom Burkina

65 G3 Gory Ulutau mt. ra. Kazak.
65 H2 Gory Yerementau h. Kazak.
19 G2 Gorzów Wielkopolski Poland
47 G5 Gosen Japan
99 □ Gosford Aust.
122 E5 Goshen U.S.A.
121 F4 Goshen U.S.A.
46 H3 Goshogawara Japan
18 E3 Goslar Germany
26 E3 Gospić Croatia
17 G6 Gosport U.K.
98 C3 Gosse r. Aust.
76 D3 Gossi Mali
28 C3 Gostivar Macedonia
19 H3 Gostyń Poland
19 J3 Gostynin Poland
80 D3 Gota Ethiopia
11 D4 Göteborg Sweden
11 C4 Göteborg och Bohus div. Sweden
78 B2 Gotel Mountains mt. ra. Cameroon/Nigeria
11 D4 Götene Sweden
18 E3 Gotha Germany
77 F4 Gothèye Niger
11 E4 Gotland i. Sweden
11 E4 Gotland div. Sweden
132 □3 Gotomeer l. Bonaire
46 B7 Gotō-rettō is Japan
29 D4 Gotse Delchev Bulgaria
11 E4 Gotska Sandön i. Sweden
46 D6 Gōtsu Japan
18 D3 Göttingen Germany
110 E4 Gott Peak summit Can.
76 C5 Gouan r. Côte d'Ivoire
48 C5 Gouchengyi China
18 B3 Goudriaan Netherlands
76 B4 Goudiri Senegal
77 D4 Goudoumaria Niger
114 C2 Goudreau Can.
76 C5 Gouéké Guinea
76 B4 Goula i. Atlantic Ocean
148 J8 Gough Island i. Atlantic Ocean
115 H2 Gouin, Réservoir resr Can.
114 D2 Goulais River r. Can.
77 F4 Goulbin Kaba r. Niger
97 G3 Goulburn r. Aust.
97 G3 Goulburn r. Aust.
98 C1 Goulburn Is. is Aust.
122 E2 Gould City U.S.A.
152 B4 Gould Coast Ant.
78 B1 Goulféy Cameroon
76 D3 Goundam Mali
133 □5 Gourbeyre Guadeloupe Caribbean
76 D4 Gourcy Burkina
20 D2 Gourdon France
20 C2 Gourin France
53 G4 Gouripur Bangladesh
81 R.S.A. Gourits r. R.S.A.
76 D3 Gourma-Rharous Mali
20 E2 Gourmeur wadi Chad
20 E2 Gournay-en-Bray France
72 C4 Gouro Chad
97 G4 Gourock Range mt. ra. Aust.
20 F2 Goussainville France
145 G3 Gouvêa Brazil
24 C2 Gouveia Portugal
121 F2 Gouverneur U.S.A.
133 □6 Gouyave Caribbean
63 S4 Govena, Mys hd Rus. Fed.
75 D2 Govenlock U.S.A.
75 F2 Governador Valadares Brazil
41 C5 Governor Generoso Phil.
133 □ Governor's Harbour The Bahamas
112 F3 Govĭaltaу div. Mongolia
48 B3 Govĭaltaу Mongolia
48 B4 Govĭaltaу Nuruu mt. ra. Mongolia
126 D3 Govind Ballash Pant resr India
65 G5 Govind Sāgar resr India
120 D3 Gowanda U.S.A.
57 F3 Gowārān Afghanistan
57 D2 Gowd-e Ahmad Iran
57 D2 Gowd-e Hasht Tekkeh waterhole Iran
57 C3 Gowd-e Mokh salt l. Iran
94 □4 Gower, Mt h. Lord Howe I. Pac. Oc.
17 D5 Gowna, Lough l. Rep. of Ire.
146 E3 Goya Arg.
133 □ Goyave Guadeloupe Caribbean
59 G1 Göyçay Azerbaijan
60 B1 Göynük Turkey
29 G5 Göydünikpelen Turkey
78 B3 Goyoum Cameroon
47 H4 Goyō-zan mt. Japan
72 D2 Gōzareh Afghanistan
72 B4 Goz-Beïda Chad
61 C1 Gözne Turkey
57 D3 Gozo Co salt l. China
73 C4 Gozo i. Malta
82 D5 Graaff-Reinet R.S.A.
76 D4 Grabo Côte d'Ivoire
28 E2 Gračanica Bos.-Herz.
115 G3 Gracefield Can.
64 D2 Gracheva, Pta Mexico
81 C2 Gracias Honduras
25 □ Graciosa i. Canary Is Spain
133 □2 Graciosa i. Canary Is Spain
26 F2 Gradačac Bos.-Herz.
24 C1 Grado Spain
115 K3 Grad Sofiya div. Bulgaria
28 D3 Grad Sofiya div. Bulgaria
126 C2 Gradets Bulgaria
142 D2 Grad Bravo, Sa do h. Brazil

16 E3 Grampian Mts mt. ra. U.K.
97 E4 Grampians mt. ra. Aust.
29 C4 Gramsh Albania
138 C3 Granada Colombia
130 J7 Granada Nicaragua
24 E4 Granada Spain
124 C4 Granada U.S.A.
25 □ Granadilla de Abona Canary Is Spain
147 C6 Gran Altiplanicie Central Seco reg. Arg.
146 C4 Gran Bajo Salitroso salt marsh Arg.
115 J4 Granby Can.
25 □ Gran Canaria i. Canary Is Spain
136 D5 Gran Chaco reg. Arg.
133 □3 Gran Couva Trin. & Tobago
118 C3 Grand r. U.S.A.
124 C2 Grand r. U.S.A.
132 C1 Grand Bahama i. The Bahamas
113 J4 Grand Bank Can.
148 F2 Grand Banks Atlantic Ocean
76 D5 Grand-Bassam Côte d'Ivoire
81 □5 Grand Bassin Réunion Indian Ocean
113 G4 Grand Bay Can.
114 E5 Grand Bend Can.
76 C6 Grand-Béréby Côte d'Ivoire
133 □5 Grand Bourg Guadeloupe Caribbean
81 □5 Grand Brûlé reg. Réunion Indian Ocean
129 F3 Grand Canyon gorge U.S.A.
129 F3 Grand Canyon U.S.A.
129 F3 Grand Canyon Nat. Park nat. park U.S.A.
132 B3 Grand Cayman i. Cayman Is Caribbean
111 G4 Grand Centre Can.
76 C5 Grand Cess Liberia
126 C2 Grand Coulee U.S.A.
133 □5 Grand Cul de Sac Marin b. Guadeloupe Caribbean
146 C4 Grande r. Bolivia
140 D3 Grande r. Bolivia
142 D3 Grande r. Bahia Brazil
144 D4 Grande r. São Paulo Brazil
130 J6 Grande r. Mexico/U.S.A.
140 A7 Grande r. Peru
112 E3 Grande 2, Réservoir de La resr Can.
112 E3 Grande 3, Réservoir de La resr Can.
112 E3 Grande 4, Réservoir de La resr Can.
133 □5 Grande Anse Guadeloupe Caribbean
147 C7 Grande, Bahía b. Arg.
81 □4 Grande Baie Mauritius
110 F4 Grande Cache Can.
142 B1 Grande de Gurupa, Ilha i. Brazil
139 E4 Grande de Jujuy r. Arg.
139 E4 Grande de Manacapuru, Lago l. Brazil
130 D4 Grande de Santiago r. Mexico
140 D4 Grande de Tarija r. Arg./Bolivia
145 G5 Grande, Ilha i. Brazil
141 D3 Grande o'Guapay r. Bolivia
110 F3 Grande Prairie Can.
77 D3 Grand Erg de Bilma sand dunes Niger
75 D2 Grand Erg Occidental desert Algeria
75 F2 Grand Erg Oriental desert Algeria
112 F3 Grande-Rivière Can.
133 □3 Grande Rivière Trinidad Trin. & Tobago
112 F3 Grande Rivière de la Baleine r. Can.
126 D2 Grande Ronde r. U.S.A.
21 H5 Grandes-Pintes Can.
133 □5 Grande Terre i. Guadeloupe Caribbean
133 □5 Grande Vigie, Pointe de la pt Guadeloupe Caribbean
113 H3 Grand Falls Can.
113 J4 Grand Falls Can.
110 F5 Grand Forks Can.
124 D2 Grand Forks U.S.A.
121 K2 Grand Harbour Can.
120 D4 Grand Haven U.S.A.
110 D2 Grandin, Lac l. Can.
124 C3 Grand Island U.S.A.
125 F6 Grand Isle U.S.A.
129 H2 Grand Junction U.S.A.
76 C5 Grand Lahou Côte d'Ivoire
113 G4 Grand Lake l. Can.
113 J4 Grand Lake l. Can.
113 H4 Grand Lake l. Can.
122 E3 Grand Lake l. U.S.A.
125 E6 Grand Lake l. U.S.A.
120 C4 Grand Lake Matagamon l. U.S.A.
122 E3 Grand Lake St Marys l. U.S.A.
121 J1 Grand Lake Seboeis l. U.S.A.
122 E3 Grand Ledge U.S.A.
113 J4 Grand Marais U.S.A.
122 C2 Grand Marais U.S.A.
122 E3 Grand-Mère Can.
24 B2 Grândola Portugal
122 C2 Grand Portage U.S.A.
111 H4 Grand Rapids Can.
122 D4 Grand Rapids U.S.A.
122 A2 Grand Rapids U.S.A.
124 E2 Grand Rapids U.S.A.
90 □7 Grand Récif du Sud reef Pac. Oc.
133 □3 Grand Rivière Martinique Caribbean
81 □5 Grand R.S.E. r. Mauritius
115 K3 Grands-Jardins, Parc des res. Can.
126 E3 Grand Teton mt. U.S.A.
126 E3 Grand Teton Nat. Park nat. park U.S.A.
122 C2 Grand Traverse Bay b. U.S.A.
133 G4 Grand Turk Turks and Caicos Is Caribbean
20 D2 Grand Vallée France
20 C2 Grandvilliers France
129 E4 Grand Wash r. U.S.A.
129 E4 Grand Wash Cliffs U.S.A.
25 F2 Granen Spain
146 E3 Grango Jamaica
11 G4 Grange Hill Jamaica
28 E2 Grängesberg Sweden
26 G4 Grangeville U.S.A.
130 K8 Granisle Can.
113 H4 Granite Falls U.S.A.
142 B1 Granja Brazil
28 B3 Granja Maranhão Brazil
129 F4 Granite Peak summit U.S.A.
126 E2 Granite Peak summit U.S.A.
129 F1 Granite Peak summit U.S.A.

27 D7 Granitola, Capo c. Italy
93 □ Granity N.Z.
142 D1 Granja Brazil
147 C5 Gran Laguna Salada l. Arg.
11 D4 Gränna Sweden
25 H2 Granollers Spain
140 A5 Gran Pajonal plain Peru
26 A3 Gran Paradiso mt. Italy
26 C2 Gran Pilastro mt. Austria/Italy
17 G5 Grantham U.K.
152 A4 Grant I. i. Ant.
98 C1 Grant I. i. Aust.
133 □9 Grantley Adams airport Barbados Caribbean
129 F2 Grant, Mt mt. U.S.A.
24 D2 Gredos, Sa de mt. ra. Spain
16 F3 Grantown-on-Spey U.K.
129 E2 Grant Range mts U.S.A.
126 B3 Grants Pass U.S.A.
20 D3 Granville France
115 G2 Granville Lake l. Can.
145 G3 Grão Mogol Brazil
128 C4 Grapevine U.S.A.
128 C4 Grapevine Mts mts U.S.A.
55 F4 Graphite U.S.A.
112 G2 Gras, Lac de l. Can.
121 F2 Grass r. U.S.A.
20 H5 Grasse France
99 F5 Grasset, Lac l. Can.
99 F5 Grasslands Nat. Park nat. park Can.
126 E2 Grassrange U.S.A.
112 E2 Grass River Prov. Park res. Can.
97 F5 Grassy Cr. r. The Bahamas
11 D4 Grästorp Sweden
122 B4 Gratiot U.S.A.
19 G5 Gratkorn Austria
20 F5 Graulhet France
25 G1 Graus Spain
142 E2 Gravatá Brazil
142 E2 Gravatá Brazil
111 J2 Gravel Hill Lake l. Can.
20 E2 Gravelines France
97 G2 Gravenhurst Can.
20 D3 Grave, Pte de pt France
27 G5 Gravina in Puglia Italy
122 E3 Grawn U.S.A.
121 F3 Gray France
121 H3 Gray U.S.A.
113 H3 Grayling U.S.A.
122 E3 Grays Harbor inlet U.S.A.
126 L3 Grays L. l. U.S.A.
120 C5 Grayson U.S.A.
113 H4 Gray Strait chan. Can.
20 B3 Grayville U.S.A.
15 F1 Grayvoron Rus. Fed.
19 G5 Graz Austria
133 □8 Grazhdanovka Yugo.
132 C1 Great Abaco i. The Bahamas
90 □7 Great Astrolabe Reef reef Fiji
96 B3 Great Australian Bight g. Aust.
133 □4 Great Bacolet Bay b. Grenada Caribbean
132 C1 Great Bahama Bank The Bahamas
92 E2 Great Barrier Island i. N.Z.
99 F3 Great Barrier Reef reef Aust.
99 G4 Great Barrier Reef Marine Park (Cairns Section) nat. park Aust.
99 G4 Great Barrier Reef Marine Park (Capricorn Section) nat. park Aust.
99 G3 Great Barrier Reef Marine Park (Central Section) nat. park Aust.
99 F2 Great Barrier Reef Marine Park (Far North Section) nat. park Aust.
121 C4 Great Barrington U.S.A.
129 E2 Great Basin Nat. Park nat. park U.S.A.
126 A2 Great Bay b. U.S.A.
110 E2 Great Bear r. Can.
110 E2 Great Bear Lake l. Can.
124 D4 Great Bend U.S.A.
17 B5 Great Blasket I. i. Rep. of Ire.
43 A4 Great Coco I. i. Cocos Is Indian Ocean
97 F4 Great Dividing Range mt. ra. Aust.
114 D4 Great Duck I. i. Can.
16 G2 Great Egg Harbor inlet U.S.A.
132 C1 Greater Antilles is Caribbean
92 E2 Great Exhibition Bay b. N.Z.
132 C2 Great Exuma i. The Bahamas
124 E2 Great Falls U.S.A.
82 D5 Great Fish r. R.S.A.
82 D5 Great Fish Pt pt R.S.A.
54 D4 Great Gandak r. India
133 G4 Great Guana Cay i. The Bahamas
132 C1 Great Harbour Cay i. The Bahamas
54 D3 Great Himalaya mt. ra. India
132 C1 Great Inagua i. The Bahamas
82 C5 Great Karoo plat. R.S.A.
82 D5 Great Kei r. R.S.A.
92 D4 Great Mercury I. i. N.Z.
43 A6 Great Nicobar i. Andaman and Nicobar Is India
17 H5 Great North East Channel chan. Aust./P.N.G.
72 E4 Great Oasis, The oasis Egypt
17 H5 Great Ormes Head hd U.K.
17 H5 Great Ouse r. U.K.
99 F3 Great Palm Is. is Aust.
121 G4 Great Peconic Bay b. U.S.A.
81 B6 Great Ruaha r. Tanzania
121 F4 Great Sacandaga l. U.S.A.
20 A3 Great St Bernard Pass pass Italy/Switz.
126 D2 Great Salt Lake l. U.S.A.
126 D3 Great Salt Lake Desert desert U.S.A.
72 E4 Great Sand Sea desert Egypt
100 C4 Great Sandy Desert desert Aust.
76 B4 Great Scarcies r. Guinea/Sierra Leone
90 □7 Great Sea reef reef Fiji
119 D5 Great Smoky Mts mt. ra. U.S.A.
119 D5 Great Smoky Mts Nat. Park nat. park U.S.A.

110 E3 Great Snow Mtn mt. Can.
119 □ Great Sound inlet Bermuda
121 D6 Great South Bay b. U.S.A.
48 D5 Great Wall China
121 K2 Great Wass I. i. U.S.A.
17 H5 Great Yarmouth U.K.
83 D3 Great Zab r. Iraq
83 E3 Great Zimbabwe Zimbabwe
29 F7 Greco, Monte mt. Italy
24 D2 Gredos, Sa de mt. ra. Spain
147 C7 Greece Chile
129 E2 Greece country Europe
55 K5 Greely Fiord inlet Can.
109 K1 Greely Fiord inlet Can.
62 F1 Greem Bell, O. i. Rus. Fed.
48 D5 Green r. U.S.A.
127 F4 Green r. U.S.A.
118 C4 Green r. U.S.A.
122 C4 Green Bay U.S.A.
122 D3 Green Bay b. U.S.A.
97 C7 Green, C. hd Aust.
132 C1 Green Cay i. The Bahamas
119 D6 Green Cove Springs U.S.A.
122 A3 Greene U.S.A.
121 F3 Greene U.S.A.
119 C4 Greeneville U.S.A.
128 B3 Greenfield U.S.A.
122 E6 Greenfield U.S.A.
121 G3 Greenfield U.S.A.
122 C4 Greenfield U.S.A.
101 A6 Green Hd hd Aust.
133 □3 Green Hill Trin. & Tobago
133 □1 Green Island Jamaica
19 G5 Green Island Bay b. Phil.
96 B3 Green Islands is P.N.G.
111 H4 Green Lake l. Can.
129 E2 Green Lake l. U.S.A.
104 O2 Greenland terr. Arctic Ocean
133 □3 Greenland Barbados Caribbean
109 R2 Greenland Sea sea Greenland/Svalbard
121 G2 Green Mountain mts U.S.A.
82 A4 Green Mt h. Ascension Atlantic Ocean
17 D7 Greenock U.K.
17 A6 Greenough r. Aust.
101 A6 Greenough Aust.
82 B3 Greenough Aust.
126 E3 Green River U.S.A.
126 E3 Green River U.S.A.
118 C4 Greensboro U.S.A.
119 E4 Greensboro U.S.A.
118 C4 Greensburg U.S.A.
120 C4 Greensburg U.S.A.
101 A6 Green Valley Aust.
119 C6 Greenvale Aust.
115 G3 Greenview U.S.A.
76 C5 Greenville Liberia
122 C5 Greenville U.S.A.
120 C5 Greenville U.S.A.
125 F5 Greenville U.S.A.
119 E5 Greenville U.S.A.
120 C4 Greenville U.S.A.
122 C4 Greenwater Provincial Park res. Can.
121 C5 Greenwich U.S.A.
120 D5 Greenwich U.S.A.
121 G3 Greenwich U.S.A.
125 F5 Greenwood U.S.A.
147 G5 Greenwood U.S.A.
119 D5 Greers Ferry Lake l. U.S.A.
133 □2 Gregory r. Aust.
146 C2 Gregory, L. salt flat Aust.
144 A5 Gregory Downs Aust.
144 A5 Gregory, L. salt flat Aust.
132 D2 Gregory, L. salt flat Aust.
18 F1 Gregory Nat. Park nat. park Aust.
99 B3 Gregory Range mt. h. Aust.
125 C5 Greifswald Germany
18 F3 Greiz Germany
61 C2 Greko, C. c. Cyprus
14 E2 Gremyachevo Rus. Fed.
48 D1 Gremyach'ye Rus. Fed.
11 C4 Grená Denmark
20 D5 Grenade-sur-l'Adour France
133 G4 Grenadines, The is St Vincent Caribbean
11 C4 Grenaa Denmark
11 D4 Grenchen Switz.
97 G4 Grenfell Aust.
111 J4 Grenfell Can.
20 H4 Grenoble France
24 D3 Grense-Jakobselv Norway
82 C5 Grense-Jakobselv Norway
133 □8 Grenville Grenada Caribbean
119 E4 Grenville, C. hd Aust.
133 □8 Gresham U.S.A.
19 H2 Gresik Indon.
24 D2 Gretna U.K.
29 D4 Grevena Greece
18 E2 Grevesmühlen Germany
93 C5 Grey r. N.Z.
17 E5 Grey Range h. Aust.
83 E4 Greytown R.S.A.
83 E4 Greytown N.Z.
12 H3 Grey, Is i. Can.
93 C5 Greymouth N.Z.
18 C2 Griby Lithuania

16 K2 Grindafjord Norway
10 L3 Grindavík Iceland
11 C4 Grindsted Denmark
28 G2 Grindul Chituc spit Romania
122 A5 Grinnell U.S.A.
28 E3 Grinţieş Romania
19 H2 Grójec Poland
27 C7 Grombalia Tunisia
10 D2 Grong Norway
18 B2 Groningen Netherlands
139 F2 Groningen Surinam
18 E1 Groningen div. Netherlands
139 F2 Groningen Surinam
133 □3 Gros Morne Martinique Caribbean
113 J4 Gros Morne Nat. Pk nat. park Can.
20 G4 Grosne r. France
22 C4 Gros Cap Can.
133 □5 Gros Pointe pt Guadeloupe Caribbean
18 F3 Großenhain Germany
18 E5 Groß-Gerau Germany
19 G5 Großglockner mt. Austria
82 B3 Gross Ums Namibia
82 B3 Gross Ventre Range mt. ra. U.S.A.
19 G2 Grudziądz Poland
82 B4 Grünau Namibia
10 □ Grundarfjörður Iceland
122 A4 Grundy Center U.S.A.
120 C6 Grundy U.S.A.
133 □1 Gryazi Rus. Fed.
12 G3 Gryazovets Rus. Fed.
19 G2 Gryfice Poland
19 G2 Gryfino Poland
19 G3 Gryfów Śląski Poland
10 E1 Gryllefjord Norway
147 G5 Grytviken Atlantic Ocean
133 □1 Guaca Venezuela
146 C2 Guachipas Arg.
112 G2 Guaçu r. Brazil
144 A5 Guaçu Brazil
138 B4 Guacamayo, Cordillera de mt. ra. Col.
132 C2 Guadaje r. Spain
24 D4 Guadajoz r. Spain
130 D4 Guadalajara Mexico
24 E2 Guadalajara Spain
90 □1 Guadalcanal i. Solomon Is
24 D3 Guadalcanal Spain
24 D4 Guadalete r. Spain
24 C4 Guadalquivir r. Spain
130 E3 Guadalupe Nuevo León Mexico
130 A2 Guadalupe Zacatecas Mexico
130 D4 Guadalupe Mexico
138 A2 Guadalupe i. Mexico
133 □2 Guadalupe Bravos Mexico
133 □8 Guadalupe i. Mexico
131 H6 Guadalupe Mts Nat. Park nat. park U.S.A.
130 D3 Guadalupe, Sierra de mt. ra. Spain
130 D3 Guadalupe Victoria Mexico
24 D3 Guadalupe y Calvo Mexico
24 D2 Guadarrama, Sierra de mt. ra. Spain
133 G4 Guadeloupe terr. Caribbean
133 □5 Guadeloupe Passage chan. Guadeloupe Caribbean
133 □5 Guadeloupe Aguilera Mexico
24 D4 Guadiana r. Portugal/Spain
24 E4 Guadix Spain
147 B6 Guafo, I. i. Chile
133 □1 Guáico Trin. & Tobago
146 B3 Guaiçuí Brazil
138 C2 Guaimaca Honduras
146 E3 Guaíra Brazil
144 A5 Guaíra Brazil
132 C2 Guajaba, Cayo i. Cuba
138 C1 Guajará r. Brazil
147 C6 Guaira Venezuela
138 C1 Guajira, Península de la Col.
132 A2 Guanabacoa Cuba
145 G5 Guanabara, Baía de b. Brazil
132 B2 Guanajay Cuba
130 E4 Guanajuato Mexico
130 E3 Guanajuato div. Mexico
131 E4 Guanambi Brazil
142 D3 Guanambi Brazil
132 □ Guanapo r. Trin. & Tobago
146 C2 Guandacol Arg.
145 G4 Guandu r. Brazil
50 D2 Guang'an China
51 F4 Guangchang China
51 E3 Guangdong div. China
50 D3 Guangde China
51 F4 Guangfeng China
51 F2 Guanghe China
51 E2 Guanghua China
50 D3 Guangmao Shan mt. China
50 D3 Guangnan China
51 E4 Guangning China
51 E3 Guangshan China
51 E3 Guangshui China
51 E4 Guangxi div. China
50 D2 Guan Xian China
51 E3 Guangyuan China
51 F3 Guangze China
51 E4 Guangzhou China
51 F2 Guannan China
145 G3 Guanhães Brazil
138 D2 Guánica Puerto Rico
82 C5 Guano Lake l. U.S.A.
82 C5 Guan Xian China
139 E2 Guanipa r. Venezuela
51 F2 Guanjiazhen China
132 B2 Guantánamo Cuba
132 C3 Guantánamo, B. de b. Caribbean
48 E4 Guanting Sk. resr China
51 E4 Guanyang China
51 F2 Guanyun China
139 G5 Guapí Colombia
138 B3 Guapí Colombia
133 □3 Guapo Bay b. Trin. & Tobago
140 C3 Guaporé r. Bolivia/Brazil
146 G2 Guaporé Brazil
142 D3 Guará r. Brazil
140 D3 Guarabira Brazil
144 A6 Guaraciaba Brazil
138 B4 Guarandá Ecuador
144 A6 Guaranhã Brazil
140 D3 Guaraniaçu Brazil
144 B6 Guaranta Brazil
144 B4 Guarapari Brazil
144 B4 Guarapuava Brazil
144 C3 Guararapes Brazil
144 C3 Guaratinga Brazil
145 J2 Guaratinguetá Brazil
143 B4 Guaratuba, B. de b. Brazil
24 C2 Guarda Portugal
24 C2 Guarda div. Portugal
144 E2 Guarda Mor Brazil
26 E3 Guardiagrele Italy
138 C2 Guárico Venezuela
144 E2 Guaribas Brazil
138 D2 Guariba r. Brazil
143 B4 Guaricó r. Venezuela
138 D2 Guárico, Embalse del resr Venezuela
145 G4 Guarujá Brazil
145 H2 Guaruvá Brazil
138 C2 Guasare r. Venezuela
138 B3 Guasave Mexico
132 C1 Guasdualito Venezuela
138 C2 Guasare Venezuela

74 B5 Guérou Mauritania
75 F1 Guerrah Et-Tarf salt pan Algeria
131 E5 Guerrero Mexico
130 B3 Guerrero Negro Mexico
21 G3 Gueugnon France
76 C5 Guéyo Côte d'Ivoire
80 C3 Gugē mt. Ethiopia
57 C2 Gügerd, Küh-e mt. ra. Iran
80 C3 Gugu Mountains mt. ra. Ethiopia
40 A3 Guhakolak, Tg pt Indon.
51 E3 Gui r. China
25 □ Guía de Isora Canary Is Spain
148 F5 Guiana Basin Atlantic Ocean
20 D3 Guichen France
96 A4 Guichi China
51 G2 Guichi China
146 E3 Guichón Uruguay
51 E2 Guidan-Roumji Niger
78 C2 Guidari Chad
48 B6 Guide China
51 E2 Guidel France
78 B4 Guider Cameroon
51 D3 Guidiguis Cameroon
50 D3 Guiding China
51 E3 Guidong China
51 E3 Guidong China
27 D5 Guidonia-Montecelio Italy
50 D3 Guignan China
76 C5 Guiglo Côte d'Ivoire
51 G2 Guignicourt France
51 G3 Guiji Shan mt. ra. China
24 D2 Guijuelo Spain
17 G6 Guildford U.K.
121 J2 Guildford U.S.A.
112 E2 Guillaume-Delisle, Lac l. Can.
21 H4 Guillaumes France
21 H4 Guillestre France
25 □ Güímar Canary Is Spain
142 D3 Guimarães Brazil
24 B2 Guimarães Port.
41 B4 Guimaras Str. chan. Phil.
44 B6 Guimba Phil.
51 F3 Guimarães Brazil
76 A4 Guinea country W. Africa
148 F5 Guinea Basin Atlantic Ocean
76 A4 Guinea-Bissau country W. Africa
76 C5 Guinea, Gulf of g. Africa
76 C5 Guinée-Forestière div. Guinea
76 B4 Guinée-Maritime div. Guinea
132 B2 Güines Cuba
20 C2 Guingamp France
76 B4 Guinguinéo Senegal
20 D3 Guipavas France
51 F3 Guiping China
76 B4 Guir well Mali
51 F2 Guiratinga Brazil
51 F3 Güiria Venezuela
20 F2 Guisanbourg French Guiana
21 F2 Guise France
41 C4 Guiuan Phil.
51 E4 Gui Xian China
51 D3 Guiyang China
50 D3 Guizhou div. China
54 C5 Gujarat div. India
54 C2 Gujar Khan Pakistan
54 C2 Gujranwala Pakistan
54 C2 Gujrat Pakistan
56 B2 Gulbarga India
11 G4 Gulbene Latvia
57 B3 Gulbahar Afghanistan
51 G5 Gülchü Kyrgyzstan
51 G5 Gülek Turkey
60 C1 Gülen Turkey
51 H5 Gulf, The g. Asia
57 E5 Gulran Afghanistan
57 D4 Gul Kach Pakistan
24 E2 Gulpilhi Spain
59 G2 Gulripshi Georgia
65 G4 Gülşehir Turkey
119 C6 Gulf Shores U.S.A.
61 D1 Gülnar Turkey
51 G5 Gulian China
51 F3 Gulin China
65 K3 Gulistan Uzbekistan
48 D1 Guliya China
112 F2 Gull Bay Can.
114 D1 Gull L. l. Can.
133 G4 Gulgong Aust.
54 E2 Gum India
60 C1 Gülnar Turkey
78 E3 Gulu Uganda
28 E3 Gulyantsi Bulgaria
81 C5 Gulyaypole Ukr.
83 B1 Guma China
81 C5 Gumare Botswana
138 A2 Gumbiri, J. mt. Sudan
76 D4 Gumel Nigeria
51 D2 Gumla India
54 E5 Gumma div. Japan
80 C3 Gumma Ethiopia
77 F4 Gumel Nigeria
81 C5 Gumbaxh Turkmenistan
29 F5 Gümüşsuyu Turkey
29 G4 Gümüşova Turkey
60 D1 Gümüşhane Turkey
54 C5 Gunanen India
56 C2 Gundlupet India
109 J3 Gunnbjørn Fjeld mt. Greenland
11 D4 Gunnarn Sweden
57 F2 Gunara, Sierra de mt. - Ethiopia
14 C3 Gunār mt. India
57 F2 Gund r. Tajikistan
29 F5 Güney Denizli Turkey
29 G5 Güney Kütahya Turkey
29 G5 Güngu Turkey
51 G6 Gungu Zaire
84 B4 Gunib Rus. Fed.
60 D2 Gunisao r. Can.
76 C4 The Gambia
77 F4 Gummi Nigeria
97 G3 Gunnedah Aust.
121 J1 Gunnison U.S.A.
60 D2 Gunnison r. U.S.A.
97 H5 Gunning Aust.
109 J3 Gunnbjørn Fjeld mt. Greenland
152 Gunnerus Ridge Antarctic
122 Gunners Quoin i. Mauritius
115 J2 Guérigny France
115 C1 Güeppí, Lac l. Can.
20 D2 Guéret France
76 C4 Guelmim Morocco
75 D2 Guelta d'In Ziza well Algeria
75 E3 Guentaka Mali
130 D3 Guntakal India
119 C5 Guntersville U.S.A.
119 C5 Guntersville L. l. U.S.A.
56 C2 Guntur India
54 C2 Gunugsitoli Indon.
38 B6 Gunungsitoli Indon.
54 E4 Gunupur India
18 E5 Günzburg Germany
65 H5 Gupis Jammu and Kashmir
28 E1 Gura Galbenei Moldova
28 E1 Gura Humorului Romania

47 H4 Himekami-dake mt. Japan
46 C7 Hime-shima i. Japan
47 G4 Hime-zaki pt Japan
47 F5 Himi Japan
18 D2 Himmelpforten Germany
61 D2 Himş div. Syria
61 D2 Himş Syria
46 C7 Hinagu Japan
41 C4 Hinatuan Phil.
133 D1 Hinche Haiti
99 F3 Hinchinbrook I. i. Aust.
42 J2 Hinckley U.S.A.
129 F2 Hinckley U.S.A.
121 F3 Hinckley Reservoir resr U.S.A.
79 B4 Hinda Congo
54 D3 Hindan r. India
54 D4 Hindaun India
120 B6 Hindman U.S.A.
96 E4 Hindmarsh, L. l. Aust.
55 F5 Hindola India
93 C6 Hinds N.Z.
57 G2 Hindu Kush mt. ra. Asia
56 B3 Hindupur India
57 ? Hind, W. al w Saudi Arabia
110 F3 Hines Creek Can.
119 D6 Hinesville U.S.A.
54 D5 Hinganghat India
54 B2 Hinglaj Pakistan
56 B2 Hingoli India
60 E2 Hinis Turkey
128 D4 Hinkley U.S.A.
10 D1 Hinnøya i. Norway
41 B4 Hinobaan Phil.
46 D6 Hino Japan
24 D3 Hinojosa del Duque Spain
46 C7 Hinokage Japan
47 F5 Hino-misaki pt Japan
121 G3 Hinsdale U.S.A.
111 C4 Hinton Can.
120 C6 Hinton U.S.A.
79 C4 Hippopotames de Mangai, Réserve de Faune de res. Zaire
79 E6 Hippopotames de Sakania, Réserve des res. Zaire
79 ? Hippopotames, Réserve de res. Zaire
60 F2 Hirabit Dağ mt. Turkey
46 B7 Hirado Japan
46 B7 Hirado-shima i. Japan
55 E5 Hirakud Reservoir resr India
81 C5 Hiraman w Kenya
54 B4 Hirapur India
46 D6 Hirata Japan
47 G6 Hiratsuka Japan
76 C5 Hiré-Watta Côte d'Ivoire
46 J2 Hiroo Japan
46 H3 Hirosaki Japan
46 D6 Hiroshima div. Japan
46 D6 Hiroshima Japan
18 E4 Hirschaid Germany
18 E3 Hirschberg Germany
15 F3 Hirsivka Ukraine
15 D2 Hirs'ky Tikych r. Ukraine
21 G2 Hirson France
11 C4 Hirtshals Denmark
46 B7 Hisaka-jima i. Japan
60 C1 Hisaronü Turkey
29 F6 Hisarönü Körfezi b. Turkey
65 G5 Hisor Tajikistan
133 F2 Hispaniola i. Caribbean
54 C1 Hispur Gl. gl. Pakistan
54 C3 Hissar India
55 F4 Hisua India
61 D2 Hisyah Syria
60 E3 Hīt Iraq
46 C7 Hita Japan
47 H5 Hitachi Japan
47 H5 Hitachi-ōta Japan
47 ?1 Hitiaa Fr. Poly. Pac. Oc.
46 C7 Hitoyoshi Japan
10 C3 Hitra i. Norway
90 ?2 Hiu i. Vanuatu
47 G5 Hiuchiga-take vol Japan
45 ? Hiva Oa i. Fr. Poly. Pac. Oc.
151 K6 Hiva Oa i. Fr. Poly. Pac. Oc.
110 E4 Hixon Can.
61 C4 Hixon w Israel
60 E2 Hizan Turkey
11 ? Hjälmaren l. Sweden
111 H2 Hjalmar Lake l. Can.
11 C3 Hjerkinn Norway
11 D4 Hjo Sweden
11 C4 Hjørring Denmark
42 B2 Hkok r. Myanmar
42 B1 Hkring Bum mt. Myanmar
42 A1 Hlaing r. Myanmar
55 F3 Hlako Kangri mt. China
83 E4 Hlatikulu Swaziland
14 A3 Hlazove Ukraine
42 B3 Hlegu Myanmar
13 G4 Hlinsko Czech Rep.
15 D1 Hlobyne Ukraine
19 ? Hlohovec Slovakia
82 D4 Hlotse Lesotho
19 E1 Hluchiv Ukraine
13 G5 Hlučín Czech Rep.
19 E1 Hlukhiv Ukraine
42 B2 Hlung-Tan Myanmar
15 B1 Hlushkavichy Belarus
15 E2 Hlyboka Ukraine
15 E2 Hlybokaye Belarus
15 C2 Hlynsk' Ukraine
19 J4 Hnivan' Ukraine
13 J6 Hnúšťa Slovakia
15 G1 Hnylytsya Ukraine
15 D2 Hnylyy Tikych r. Ukraine
77 E5 Ho Ghana
42 D3 Hoa Binh Vietnam
82 B3 Hoachanas Namibia
81 ? Hoanib w Namibia
82 A2 Hoarusib w Namibia
97 F5 Hobart Aust.
125 D5 Hobart U.S.A.
152 A4 Hobbs Coast Ant.
119 D7 Hobe Sound U.S.A.
65 L3 Hoboksar China
11 C4 Hobro Denmark
88 B3 Hobyo Somalia
18 D5 Hochfeld Germany
13 G6 Hô Chi Minh Vietnam
120 B5 Hocking r. U.S.A.
131 H4 Hochschwab mt. Austria
74 C5 Hodh ech Chargui div. Mauritania
74 C5 Hodh el Gharbi div. Mauritania
13 K5 Hódmezővásárhely Hungary
80 E2 Hodmo w Somalia
13 H6 Hodonín Czech Rep.
48 B3 Hoek van Holland Netherlands
92 J4 Hoeryŏng N. Korea
49 F4 Hoeyang N. Korea
18 D4 Hof Bayern Germany
11 H5 Hof Iceland
18 D3 Hofheim in Unterfranken Germany
11 N2 Höfn Iceland
11 D3 Hofors Sweden
11 H5 Hofsjökull ice cap Iceland
10 M2 Hofsós Iceland
46 C6 Hōfu Japan
11 D4 Höganäs Sweden
99 E5 Hogarthulla Cr. r. Aust.
75 F4 Hoggar plat. Algeria
11 E4 Högsby Sweden
18 D3 Hohenloher Ebene plain Germany

19 F5 Hoher Dachstein mt. Austria
43 E4 Hon Lom i. Vietnam
42 D3 Hon Mê i. Vietnam
18 D3 Hohe Rhön mt. ra. Germany
56 A3 Honnali India
18 F5 Hohe Tauern mt. ra. Austria
10 G1 Honningsvåg Norway
48 D4 Hohhot China
127 ?2 Honokaa U.S.A.
77 E5 Hohoe Ghana
127 ?1 Honolulu U.S.A.
46 C6 Hōhoku Japan
42 D5 Hon Rai i. Vietnam
15 E2 Hoholeve Ukraine
24 E2 Honrubia de la Cuesta Spain
15 D1 Hoholiv Ukraine
15 F3 Hoholivka Ukraine
46 D6 Honshū i. Japan
55 G2 Hoh Xil Hu l. China
126 B2 Hood, Mt vol U.S.A.
55 G2 Hoh Xil Shan mt. ra. China
101 B7 Hood pt Aust.
18 C2 Hoogeveen Netherlands
42 A4 Hôi An Vietnam
125 C4 Hooker U.S.A.
81 B4 Hoima Uganda
98 B3 Hooker Creek Abor. Reserve res. Aust.
42 D2 Hôi Xuân Vietnam
17 D5 Hook Head hd Rep. of Ire.
55 H4 Hojai India
99 G4 Hook I. i. Aust.
11 D4 Højer Denmark
99 G3 Hook Rf reef Aust.
54 B4 Höjo Japan
110 B3 Hoonah U.S.A.
92 J1 Hokianga Harbour inlet N.Z.
108 B3 Hooper Bay U.S.A.
47 G5 Hōki-gawa r. Japan
121 E5 Hooper I. i. U.S.A.
93 C5 Hokitika N.Z.
122 C5 Hoopeston U.S.A.
46 J2 Hokkaidō i. Japan
18 B2 Hoorn Netherlands
46 J2 Hokkaidō div. Japan
150 H6 Hoorn, Îles de Wallis & Futuna Pac. Oc.
11 C4 Hokksund Norway
57 D1 Hokmābād Iran
121 G3 Hoosick U.S.A.
93 B6 Hokonui Hills h. N.Z.
129 E3 Hoover Dam dam U.S.A.
60 F1 Hoktemberyan Armenia
120 B4 Hoover Memorial U.S.A.
47 F6 Hokuriku Tunnel tunnel Japan
11 C3 Hol Norway
48 B3 Höövör Mongolia
56 B3 Holalkere India
60 E1 Hopa Turkey
140 D2 Holanda Bolivia
121 F4 Hop Bottom U.S.A.
15 E3 Hola Prystan' Ukraine
110 E5 Hope Can.
99 G3 Holborne I. i. Aust.
93 B6 Hope r. N.Z.
97 F3 Holbrook Aust.
125 C5 Hope U.S.A.
129 G4 Holbrook U.S.A.
133 ?1 Hope Bay Jamaica
122 B3 Holcombe Flowage resr U.S.A.
113 J2 Hopedale Can.
111 G4 Holden U.S.A.
96 D2 Hope, L. salt flat Aust.
129 F2 Holden U.S.A.
101 C7 Hope, L. salt flat Aust.
125 D5 Holdenville U.S.A.
131 H5 Hopelchén Mexico
124 D3 Holdrege U.S.A.
113 H3 Hope Mountains mt. ra. Can.
56 B3 Hole Narsipur India
62 D2 Hopen i. Svalbard Arctic Ocean
132 C2 Holguín Cuba
108 B3 Hope, Point c. U.S.A.
19 H4 Holíč Slovakia
93 D4 Hope Saddle pass N.Z.
11 D3 Höljes Sweden
113 G2 Hopes Advance, Baie b. Can.
18 B4 Hollabrunn Austria
122 D4 Holland U.S.A.
15 F2 Hovtva r. Ukraine
133 ?1 Holland Bay b. Jamaica
15 F2 Hovtva Ukraine
120 C4 Hollidaysburg U.S.A.
48 B4 Höyüün Mongolia
110 C3 Hollis U.S.A.
80 ? Howakil I. i. Eritrea
125 D5 Hollis U.S.A.
99 H5 Howard Aust.
123 F4 Hollister U.S.A.
122 C4 Howard City U.S.A.
128 B3 Hollister U.S.A.
98 C2 Howard I. i. Aust.
125 F5 Holly Springs U.S.A.
93 H4 Howard Lake l. U.S.A.
119 D7 Hollywood U.S.A.
97 G4 Howe, C. hd Aust.
108 G2 Holman Can.
152 ? Howe, I. i. Kerguelen Indian Ocean
99 F3 Holmes Reef reef Coral Sea Islands Terr. Pac. Oc.
123 F4 Howell U.S.A.
10 G1 Holmestrand Finnmark Norway
124 C2 Howes U.S.A.
11 C4 Holmestrand Vestfold Norway
115 H5 Howick Can.
10 N2 Hólmavík Iceland
93 F4 Howick N.Z.
48 A4 Holmøn Ø i. Greenland
96 D2 Howitt, L. salt flat Aust.
15 A1 Holoby Ukraine
97 H4 Howitt, Mt mt. Aust.
61 C3 Holon Israel
121 J2 Howland U.S.A.
90 T2 Holonga Tonga
150 H5 Howland I. i. Pac. Oc.
82 B4 Holoog Namibia
60 D2 Hoy r. Turkey
15 D2 Holovanivs'k Ukraine
57 D2 Howz well Iran
130 D2 Holcatitas Mexico
57 D2 Howz-e Dūmatu Iran
15 E2 Holovkivka Ukraine
57 D2 Howz-e Panj Iran
28 D2 Horezu Romania
16 F2 Hoy i. U.K.
99 E2 Holroyd r. Aust.
19 J3 Hoyanger Norway
11 C4 Holstebro Denmark
19 ? Hoyerswerda Germany
119 D4 Holston r. U.S.A.
19 J3 Hoyle U.S.A.
120 C4 Holston Lake l. U.S.A.
28 D1 Hoym Germany
122 E4 Holt U.S.A.
13 H6 Hozat Slovakia
124 E4 Holton U.S.A.
19 G3 Hradec Králové Czech Rep.
110 C3 Holy Cross U.S.A.
15 C2 Hradz'k Ukraine
16 C4 Holyhead U.K.
15 E2 Hranitne Ukraine
16 C4 Holy Island i. U.K.
19 E2 Hranice Czech Rep.
17 F3 Holy Island i. U.K.
60 E1 Hrazdan Armenia
126 G3 Holyoke U.S.A.
13 H4 Hrebinka Ukraine
121 G3 Holyoke U.S.A.
18 E5 Holzkirchen Germany
15 D1 Hrebinky Ukraine
18 D2 Holzminden Germany
14 G4 Hreyhove Ukraine
81 B5 Homa Bay Kenya
15 F3 Hrebinky Ukraine
42 A1 Homalin Myanmar
15 C2 Hremyach Ukraine
60 F2 Homāyunshahr Iran
15 C1 Hremyach Ukraine
18 D2 Homberg (Efze) Germany
19 G3 Hrodna Belarus
19 E4 Horn Austria
12 B4 Hrodna Belarus
11 C3 Horn r. Iceland
13 G4 Hrubieszów Poland
76 D3 Hombori Mali
15 E1 Hrubieszów Poland
18 D4 Homburg Germany
15 F1 Hrun' r. Ukraine
109 M3 Home Hill Aust.
15 F1 Hrun' r. Ukraine
94 ?1 Home I. i. Cocos Is Indian Ocean
15 E2 Hrushvahivka Ukraine
108 C4 Homer U.S.A.
15 E3 Hryhorivka Chernihiv Ukraine
125 E5 Homer U.S.A.
15 E3 Hryhorivka Kherson Ukraine
119 D6 Homerville U.S.A.
15 B3 Hrymayliv Ukraine
119 D7 Homestead U.S.A.
15 B3 Hrynyava r. Ukraine
119 C5 Homewood U.S.A.
15 D2 Hryshkivtsi Ukraine
56 B2 Homnabad India
15 C2 Hrytsiv Ukraine
18 C1 Homoine Mozambique
42 B3 Hsenwi Myanmar
41 C4 Homonhon pt Phil.
42 B3 Hsi-hkip Myanmar
15 D1 Homyel' Belarus
42 B2 Hsi-hseng Myanmar
14 A1 Homyel' Belarus
43 ? Hsi-hsu-p'ing Hsü i. Taiwan
42 D3 Hon Dah Vietnam
15 A1 Homel Hon Ju China
43 E3 Hsin-chu Taiwan
128 C7 Hondo Japan
42 B3 Hsipaw Myanmar
125 D6 Hondo U.S.A.
43 H3 Hsueh Shan mt. Taiwan
104 N3 Honduras country Central America
82 A3 Huab w Namibia
132 B3 Honduras, Gulf of g. Mexico
140 D3 Huachacalla Bolivia
48 D1 Horqin Shadi reg. China
140 D1 Huachi Bolivia
49 G1 Horqin Youyi Qianqi China
93 H4 Huachi China
49 G3 Horqin Youyi Zhongqi China
140 A1 Huachuca City U.S.A.
49 G2 Horqin Zuoyi Houqi China
48 E4 Huade China
49 G3 Horqin Zuoyi Zhongqi China
49 F4 Huadian China
110 F4 Horqueta Paraguay
49 ? Huai'an China
101 A6 Horrocks Aust.
49 H1 Huai'an China
94 ?1 Horsburgh I. i. Cocos Is Indian Ocean
49 G1 Huaibei China
13 C4 Horse Bend U.S.A.
49 H1 Huaibin China
120 D3 Horseheads U.S.A.
49 G2 Huaide China
113 J3 Horse I. i. Can.
49 H2 Huai'e China
11 C5 Horsens Denmark
49 F5 Huaihua China
133 ?6 Horse Shoe Pt pt St Kitts-Nevis Caribbean
49 G4 Huai Luang r. Thailand
97 C3 Horsham Aust.
49 G3 Huai Nan China
73 B4 Horus, Temple of Egypt
49 H3 Huaining China
114 C4 Horwood Lake l. Can.
48 E4 Huairou China
35 H2 Ho Sai Hu salt l. China
49 F5 Huaiyang China
56 B3 Hosdurga India
49 H1 Huaiyin China
57 A2 Hoseynabad Iran
49 H1 Huaiyuan China
57 B2 Hoseynabad Iran
131 G5 Huajuápan de León Mexico
54 C5 Hoshangabad India
49 G3 Hualahuises Mexico
56 A1 Hoshiarpur India
43 H3 Hua-lien Taiwan
54 D5 Hoshiarpur India
140 A2 Hualgayoc Peru
110 C3 Hoskins P.N.G.
140 C3 Hualhuas Peru
56 B3 Hospet India
49 G4 Hualian China
78 B3 Hossororo Guyana
49 G3 Huallaga r. Peru

147 C7 Hoste, I. i. Chile
51 F2 Huanghaiji China
54 B4 Hyderabad Pakistan
130 D2 Ignacio Zaragoza Mexico
46 D6 Imabari Japan
10 D3 Hotagen r. Sweden
51 G2 Huang Shan mt. China
21 H5 Hyères France
11 G5 Ignalina Lithuania
139 F3 Imabuí r. Brazil
65 K5 Hotan w China
51 G2 Huangshan China
21 H5 Hyères, Îles d' is France
49 G1 Ignashino Rus. Fed.
47 H4 Imaichi Japan
54 E1 Hotan China
51 F2 Huangshi China
60 C1 Hyeça Burnu pt Turkey
63 N2 Igneada Burnu pt Turkey
47 F6 Imajō Japan
82 C4 Hotazel R.S.A.
48 B5 Huang Shui r. China
102 O2 Hyland r. Can.
43 A5 Ignoitijala Andaman and Nicobar Is India
83 H1 Imala Mozambique
18 C5 Hotienka U.S.A.
48 C5 Huangtu Gaoyuan plat. ra. China
11 B3 Hyllestad Norway
47 H3 Imandra, Ozero l. Rus. Fed.
101 B7 Hotham r. Aust.
49 G5 Huang Xian China
10 F4 Hyltebruk Sweden
81 B6 Igoma Tanzania
93 H3 Imanombo Madagascar
98 B2 Hotham, C. c. Aust.
19 K4 Humenné Slovakia
47 H6 Hyōgo div. Japan
81 B5 Igombe r. Tanzania
146 E2 Iman, Sa del h. Arg.
97 F4 Hotham, Mt mt. Aust.
93 C6 Humnock h. N.Z.
46 E6 Hyōnosen mt. Japan
81 B5 Igombe Tanzania
143 C6 Imaruí Brazil
10 E2 Hoting Sweden
140 C3 Humanta Peru
10 H2 Hyrynsalmi Finland
62 H3 Igoumenitsa Greece
143 D6 Imaruí Brazil
125 E5 Hot Springs U.S.A.
140 D2 Humanuni Bolivia
110 F3 Hythe Can.
80 E3 Igoumenitsa Greece
11 H3 Imatra Finland
124 C3 Hot Springs U.S.A.
48 C5 Huan Xian China
46 D7 Hyūga Japan
145 H1 Iguaí Brazil
143 E6 Imazu Brazil
11 E3 Hotte, Massif de la mt. Haiti
82 B4 Huanza, Cord. de mt. ra. Peru
10 G3 Hyvinkää Finland
131 F5 Iguala Mexico
143 C6 Imbituba Brazil
82 A4 Hottentots Bay b. Namibia
50 C3 Huaping China
25 G2 Igualada Spain
143 C6 Imbituva Brazil
90 ?2 Houaïlu Pac. Oc.
49 J4 Hua r. China
145 H4 Iguatemi r. Brazil
64 F1 im. Chapayeva Turkmenistan
122 D4 Houdan France
72 C2 Hūn Libya
144 A5 Iguatemi Brazil
29 L2 Igly r. Rus. Fed.
72 G3 Imeni Babushkina Rus. Fed.
18 B3 Houffalize Belgium
10 L2 Húnaflói b. Iceland
144 D4 Iacanga Brazil
144 A5 Iguatu Brazil
29 L2 Imeni Karla Libknekhta Rus. Fed.
43 ? Hougang Singapore
80 D2 Hunayshiyah Yemen
28 E1 Iacobeni Romania
146 E2 Iguazú, Cataratas del waterfall Arg./Brazil
12 H5 Imeni M.I. Kalinina Rus. Fed.
122 C2 Houghton U.S.A.
49 H4 Hunchun r. China
144 C4 Iaçu Brazil
78 A4 Iguéla Gabon
60 E2 Imeni Stepana Razina Rus. Fed.
122 C3 Houghton Lake l. U.S.A.
11 C4 Hundested Denmark
28 E2 Iacoveni Romania
78 A4 Iguéla, Lagune lag. Gabon
14 E2 Imeni Vorovskogo Rus. Fed.
122 K1 Houghton r. Aust.
18 D3 Hünfeld Germany
15 C3 Ialoveni Moldova
81 B6 Igunga Tanzania
15 F2 Imeni Lenina, Ozero l. Ukraine
140 A2 Huari Peru
54 E1 Hunga r. China
28 F2 Ianca Romania
81 B5 Ihanda Madagascar
80 D3 Ìmì Ethiopia
140 C3 Huarina Bolivia
4 G4 Hungary country Europe
15 C3 Iargara Moldova
83 H1 Iharaña Madagascar
74 C2 Imi-n-Tanoute Morocco
146 E2 Huarmey Peru
90 T1 Hunga Ha'apai i. Tonga
28 F1 Iaşi Romania
73 F3 Iherir Algeria
74 C2 Imirikliy Labyad reg. Western Sahara
51 E4 Hua Shan mt. China
99 F6 Hungerford Aust.
41 A3 Iba Phil.
48 B3 Ihhayrhan Mongolia
60 G2 Imişli Azerbaijan
51 E1 Huashixia China
61 D1 Hûngnam N. Korea
77 E5 Ibadan Nigeria
46 D7 Iizuka Japan
74 A4 Inânâsa el Madîna Egypt
126 D1 Hungry Horse Res. resr U.S.A.
138 B3 Ibalpô Colombia
47 G5 Iida Japan
59 J5 Imîdja Di- S. Korea
81 A6 Ihiala Nigeria
45 ? Hung Shui Kiu Hong Kong
81 A5 Ibaiti Brazil
46 D6 Iinan Japan
74 A4 Imlili Western Sahara
42 D4 Hung Yên Vietnam
61 A5 Inhâsa el Madîna Egypt
77 E5 Imo Nigeria
49 H4 Hunjiang China
77 F5 Ibara Japan
10 H3 Iisalmi Finland
77 F5 Imo r. Nigeria
17 H5 Hunstanton U.K.
47 H5 Ibaraki div. Japan
49 G4 Ih Tal China
26 C3 Imola Croatia
129 H4 Hunsur India
138 B3 Ibarra Ecuador
47 G5 Iiyama Japan
26 ? Imotski Croatia
60 F2 Hunter r. Germany
77 E5 Ibarreta Arg.
46 D7 Iizuka Japan
140 A2 Imperatriz Brazil
97 G2 Hunter r. N.Z.
144 E4 Ibaté Brazil
80 B3 Ijara Kenya
84 ? Imperia Italy
93 B6 Hunter r. N.Z.
80 D2 Ibb Yemen
15 H2 Ijevan Armenia
140 A2 Imperial Peru
121 J1 Hunter U.S.A.
77 E5 Ibbenbüren Germany
10 G3 Ijoki r. Finland
128 D5 Imperial Beach U.S.A.
97 G5 Hunter I. i. Aust.
18 C2 IJsselmeer l. Netherlands
128 D5 Imperial Valley v. U.S.A.
110 B3 Hunter I. i. Can.
51 C6 Ibia Brazil
18 B2 IJmuiden Netherlands
100 B3 Imperieuse Reef Aust.
150 G7 Hunter I. i. Pac. Oc.
145 H3 Ibiá Brazil
74 B5 Ijsselstein Netherlands
15 F4 Imphal India
115 H4 Huntingdon Can.
145 J1 Ibicaraí Brazil
77 F4 Iberito Nigeria
55 H4 Imphal India
120 C3 Huntingdon U.S.A.
143 B6 Ibicuí r. Brazil
81 B6 Iberá, L. l. Arg.
29 J4 Imrali Adasi i. Turkey
122 E5 Huntington U.S.A.
144 E2 Ibicuí r. Brazil
138 C5 Iberá Peru
29 G4 Imroz Turkey
120 B5 Huntington U.S.A.
144 E4 Ibiporã Brazil
77 F4 Iberto Nigeria
60 D3 Imtân Syria
128 D5 Huntington Beach U.S.A.
145 K3 Ibiracu Brazil
144 D2 Iберá Brazil
130 C2 Imuris Mexico
92 B7 Huntly N.Z.
145 H3 Ibirá Brazil
81 B6 Ikanda-Nord Zaire
41 B4 Imuruan Bay b. Phil.
16 F3 Huntly U.K.
143 H4 Ibirama Brazil
77 F5 Ikare Nigeria
47 G6 Ina Japan
115 H4 Huntsville Can.
143 H6 Ibirapuitã r. Brazil
29 F6 Ikaria i. Greece
47 F6 Ina r. Japan
125 F5 Huntsville U.S.A.
145 G4 Ibitinga Brazil
11 G3 Ikast Denmark
76 E3 I-n-Àbâlene well Mali
119 C5 Huntsville U.S.A.
144 D4 Ibitirama Brazil
46 J2 Ikeda Japan
82 A1 Inaccessible I. i. Tristan da Cunha Atlantic Ocean
115 E6 Huntsville U.S.A.
25 F3 Ibiza i. Spain
46 J2 Ikeda Japan
144 E2 Inácio Martins Brazil
48 E5 Hunyuan China
25 F3 Ibiza Spain
47 H5 Ikeda Japan
74 C4 I-n-Afaleleh well Algeria
54 C1 Hunza Pakistan
70 D2 Iboundji, Mont mt. Gabon
77 F5 Ikeja Nigeria
47 G5 Ina-gawa r. Japan
65 H3 Hunza reg. Jammu and Kashmir
77 F5 Ikeja Nigeria
77 F4 Inaja Brazil
75 K4 Huochang r. China
59 J5 Ibrā' Oman
81 B6 Ikela Zaire
44 ? Inaja Brazil
51 F1 Huojia China
59 J5 Ibrī Rus. Fed.
77 F4 Ikerre Nigeria
142 D3 Inajá Brazil
43 G1 Huolin r. China
47 ? Ibuki Japan
77 E3 Ikhtiman Bulgaria
140 A3 Inambari Peru
49 H3 Huolongmen China
41 B3 Ibusuki Japan
62 H3 Ikhtiman Bulgaria
76 E2 In Aménas Algeria
90 ?2 Huon i. Pac. Oc.
42 D3 Ikibusu Japan
46 D7 Ikhtsang R.S.A.
75 E3 In Amguel Algeria
42 D3 Huong Khê Vietnam
90 ?1 Ibusuki Japan
46 J1 Iki i. Japan
140 A3 Inambari Peru
42 D3 Huong Thuy Vietnam
42 D3 Ica r. Brazil
46 J1 Iki-Burul Rus. Fed.
77 F4 Inanga Peru
90 ?1 Huon Peninsula pen. P.N.G.
140 A2 Ica Peru
46 C7 Iki-suidō chan. Japan
93 K2 Inangahua Junction N.Z.
28 D1 Huntata Romania
140 A3 Içá r. Brazil
81 B6 Ikoma Tanzania
41 B5 Inanwatan Indon.
130 D2 Huehuento, Co mt. Mexico
138 D4 Içana r. Brazil
81 B6 Ikongo Madagascar
29 K2 Iñapari Peru
131 F5 Huejotzingo Mexico
133 ?3 Icacos Pt pt Trinidad Trin. & Tobago
77 F4 Ikorodu Nigeria
140 A3 Iñapari Peru
131 E5 Huejutla Mexico
133 ?3 Icana Brazil
81 B6 Ikorodu Nigeria
41 A4 Inarajan Guam Pac. Oc.
24 C4 Huelma Spain
138 D4 Içana Brazil
77 E4 Ikosi Zaire
10 G1 Inari Finland
24 C4 Huelva div. Spain
28 D2 Icaraíma Brazil
77 E3 Ikot Ekpene Nigeria
10 G1 Inarijärvi l. Finland
24 C4 Huelva Spain
144 B5 Icaraíma Brazil
77 E3 Ikoyi Rus. Fed.
10 G2 Inarijoki r. Finland
147 B5 Huemul Arg.
129 E3 Iceberg Canyon U.S.A.
77 E3 Ikpiarjuk Can.
76 E3 I-n-Atankarer well Mali
25 F1 Huesca Spain
60 B1 Içel div. Turkey
12 D4 Ikshinskoye Rus. Fed.
11 D5 Inawashiro-ko l. Japan
25 F2 Huesca Spain
60 B1 Içel Turkey
81 B5 Ikungu Tanzania
75 E2 In-Azaoua well Niger
131 G5 Huescar Spain
11 B3 Iceland country Europe
15 A1 Ikva r. Ukraine
75 E2 In Azer well Libya
25 F2 Huete Spain
45 ? Ice Pt pt Macquarie I.
77 E3 Ila Nigeria
73 F4 Inazawa Japan
131 H4 Hueycan Aust.
29 E2 Ichalkaranji India
81 B6 Ilagan Phil.
75 E4 I-n-Azerraf well Mali
111 H4 Hugenden Aust.
14 G2 Ichalki Rus. Fed.
57 A2 Ilam Nepal
75 E3 I-n-Belbel Algeria
21 G3 Hugh r. Aust.
83 H2 Ichchapuram India
55 F3 Ilam Nepal
146 C2 Inca Peru
98 C5 Hughenden Aust.
46 C7 Ichifusa-yama mt. Japan
56 A1 Ilanz Switz.
146 B2 Inca, Paso del pass Arg./Chile
98 B2 Hughes Aust.
20 D3 Ichihara France
19 H4 Ilanz Switz.
24 F2 Inca Spain
101 D6 Hughes Aust.
47 H6 Ichinomiya Japan
47 ? Ilanz Switz.
16 E3 Inch'ang U.K.
108 C3 Hughes U.S.A.
47 H3 Ichinoseki Japan
14 C4 Ilanskiy Rus. Fed.
49 H3 Ince Burun hd Turkey
113 K2 Hughes, L. salt flat Aust.
15 E1 Ichnya Ukraine
111 H4 Île-à-la-Crosse Can.
29 F4 Ince Burun hd Turkey
79 E4 Hughenden Aust.
49 ? Ich'ôn S. Korea
111 H4 Île-à-la-Crosse, Lac l. Can.
80 C4 Inch'ôn S. Korea
122 D4 Hugo U.S.A.
25 ? Icod de los Vinos Canary Is Spain
79 C4 Île-à-la-Crosse, Lac l. Can.
92 ?4 Inch'ôn Tg pt Turkey
122 E4 Hugoton U.S.A.
43 A5 Ila U.K.
49 E2 Ile Nepal
49 ? Inch'ôn Terara mt. Ethiopia
55 E6 Huhudi R.S.A.
57 A5 Ilek r. Rus. Fed.
79 B7 Inda Iceland
55 G1 Hui'an China
49 J5 Ida, Mt mt. N.Z.
57 A5 Ilek r. Rus. Fed.
20 F2 Île-de-France div. France
74 A5 Inchiri div. Mauritania
82 A2 Huiarau Range mt. ra. N.Z.
18 D4 Idar-Oberstein Germany
80 A4 Ilek Rus. Fed.
80 C4 Inch'ôn S. Korea
82 B4 Huib-Hoch Plateau plat. Namibia
73 F4 Idaho-a-Nova Germany
77 F5 Ilesha Nigeria
76 E3 I-n-Dagouber well Mali
51 E5 Huichang China
85 C2 Iday well Niger
110 C3 Iliama Lake l. U.S.A.
145 H1 Indaiá r. Brazil
51 H4 Huichon N. Korea
77 F4 Ide Japan
41 B4 Ilagan Bay b. Phil.
143 B5 Indaial Brazil
51 H4 Huidong China
57 B2 Idehan Marzûq desert Libya
41 B4 Iligan Phil.
144 A3 Indaiatuba Brazil
129 G6 Huifia r. China
73 E4 Idel' Rus. Fed.
14 G2 Ilin'skoye Rus. Fed.
55 G4 Indaw Myanmar
51 H4 Huihe China
48 E1 Ideriyn Gol r. Mongolia
47 F6 Iliodromia i. Greece
54 A2 Indian, L. l. Myanmar
50 C3 Huili China
48 B4 Idfu Egypt
62 D1 Iliç Turkey
55 H4 Indaw Myanmar
131 H5 Huimanguillo Mexico
73 F4 Idhan Awbârî desert Libya
47 G4 Iligan Phil.
111 J4 Indbir Ethiopia
51 F2 Huimin China
72 C2 Idhan Awbârî desert Libya
14 G1 Ilino-Zaborskoye Rus. Fed.
142 D2 Independência Brazil
48 D5 Huinan China
80 D1 Idlib div. Syria
62 ? Iliysk Kazak.
146 C1 Independencia Bolivia
146 C3 Huinca Renancó Arg.
60 D2 Idlib Syria
47 D2 Ilirska Bistrica Slovenia
146 B4 Independencia, B. de b. Peru
51 G2 Huishui China
49 F4 Idol Myanmar
26 ? Ilkal India
28 D1 Independenţa Călăraşi Romania
50 C3 Huitong China
11 D3 Idre Sweden
56 B3 Ilkal India
28 D1 Independenţa Galaţi Romania
10 F3 Huittinen Finland
14 F3 Idrica Rus. Fed.
17 F4 Ilkeston U.K.
28 F2 Independenţa Galaţi Romania
51 G2 Huiten Nur l. China
57 A2 Idrija Slovenia
141 E5 Ilha Grande Brazil
80 D3 Inderacha Ethiopia
131 F5 Huixtla Mexico
62 E2 Ifakara Tanzania
145 G5 Ilha Grande Brazil
65 F1 Inder, Oz. salt l. Kazak.
50 C3 Huize China
26 E2 Iferta Italy
146 A3 Ilhausi Chile
65 F1 Inderborskiy Kazak.
51 F3 Huizhou China
62 H3 Iferouâne Niger
145 H5 Ilha Grande, Baía da b. Brazil
53 E7 India country Asia
48 C4 Hujirt Mongolia
77 F4 Iferouâne Niger
145 J1 Ilhéus Brazil
56 B2 Indian r. India
48 D3 Hukawng Valley v. Myanmar
59 J2 Ifif r. Algeria
24 ? Ilhéus Secos ou do Rombo i. Cape Verde
122 B4 Indiana div. U.S.A.
42 B1 Hukawng Valley v. Myanmar
77 F5 Ife Nigeria
51 E2 Ilha Branca i. Fr. Poly. Pac. Oc.
120 C4 Indiana U.S.A.
82 C2 Hukuntsi Botswana
62 H3 Ifferten Algeria
76 D2 Ilíman r. Rus. Fed.
122 C6 Indianapolis U.S.A.
49 E2 Hulan r. China
73 E3 Iflafrene mt. Algeria
59 J2 Ilig r. Somalia
122 C5 Indianapolis airport U.S.A.
49 H3 Hulan China
122 B5 Iga r. Japan
57 C5 Iliysk Kazak.
113 J3 Indian Harbour Can.
49 H2 Hulayfah Saudi Arabia
75 F2 Igalula Tanzania
51 E3 Iljima Japan
75 C4 Indian Lake l. U.S.A.
26 F4 Hulin China
81 B6 Igarapava Brazil
25 F3 Illana Bay b. Phil.
121 F3 Indian Lake l. U.S.A.
26 F4 Hvar i. Croatia
81 B6 Iganga Uganda
41 B4 Illapel Chile
75 F4 Indiana Dunes National Lakeshore res. U.S.A.
27 A2 Hulilán Iran
145 F3 Igapó Brazil
46 C6 Illela Niger
149 O7 Indian-Antarctic Ridge Pac. Oc.
55 H4 Hulin Peru
145 F3 Igarapé Grande Brazil
77 F3 Illapel Chile
149 Indian-Antarctic Ridge
49 J2 Hulun Nur salt l. China
141 E4 Igarapé Açu Brazil
146 A3 Illapel Chile
75 F4 Indian Dunes Nat. U.S.A.
10 F3 Hultsfred Sweden
142 B1 Igarapé-Açu Brazil
146 A3 Illapel Chile
122 B5 Indian r. U.S.A.
49 E4 Hulun Nur salt l. China
81 B6 Igawa Tanzania
47 E1 Iller r. Germany
57 E4 Indian and Mississippi Canal canal U.S.A.
82 A4 Hum mt. Croatia
62 H3 Igdir Turkey
18 E5 Iller r. Germany
130 D2 Indé Mexico
50 E1 Huma China
81 C6 Igembe Tanzania
25 F3 Illescas Spain
131 F5 Indianola U.S.A.
50 E1 Huma r. China
62 H3 Igerem Morocco
29 G4 Illescas Spain
122 B6 Indianola U.S.A.
140 B1 Humaitá Brazil
10 D3 Iggesund Sweden
24 E2 Illescas Spain
125 F6 Indianola U.S.A.
143 B6 Humaitá Brazil
143 B6 Iglesias Brazil
28 H3 Illichivs'k Ukraine
145 H2 Indianópolis Brazil
141 E4 Humaitá Paraguay
26 B5 Iglesias Italy
29 H2 Illinois div. U.S.A.
129 F2 Indian Peak summit U.S.A.
146 E2 Humaitá Paraguay
73 E2 Igli Algeria
122 B5 Illinois div. U.S.A.
48 ? Indian River U.S.A.
97 H4 Humber, Mouth of the riv. mouth U.K.
50 ? Igli Algeria
122 B5 Illinois r. U.S.A.
13 B5 Indiga Rus. Fed.
17 G4 Humber, Mouth of the U.K.
61 B3 Iglinskiy Rus. Fed.
143 C6 Illkirch France
14 E3 Indigirka r. Rus. Fed.
79 B6 Humbe, Serra do mts Angola
75 Ig'o-Zi- Rus. Fed.
18 C3 Illkirch France
54 E4 Indi Lake l. Can.
44 ? Humbedt, Mt mt. Aust.
10 G2 Igloolik Can.
42 A1 Ilménau r. Germany
55 G4 Indin Lake l. Can.
72 C2 Humboldt r. U.S.A.
111 J4 Ignace Can.
18 E3 Ilmenau Germany
33 N10 Indonesia country Asia
111 J4 Humboldt Can.
14 F1 Il'ino Rus. Fed.
62 C3 Ilmen, Oz. l. Rus. Fed.
40 B3 Indonesia country Asia
126 C2 Humboldt r. U.S.A.
14 E3 Il'inskiy Rus. Fed.
140 C4 Ilo Peru
54 C5 Indore India
126 C2 Humboldt Range mts U.S.A.
57 C5 Il'inskiy Rus. Fed.
41 B3 Iloilo Phil.
42 A2 Indramayu, Tg pt Indon.
128 C1 Humboldt Salt Marsh marsh U.S.A.
73 E1 Il'inskiy Rus. Fed.
77 E4 Ilorin Nigeria
138 A4 Indús, Mouths of the riv. mouth Pakistan
99 F5 Huoburn Aust.
62 ? Il'inskoye Rus. Fed.
77 F3 Ilti Nigeria
26 B1 Inebolu Turkey
11 D4 Hümedän Iran
65 ? Il'pyrskiy Rus. Fed.
77 F3 Ilti Nigeria
29 K4 Iñeedum well Mali
94 ?1 Hu Men chan. China
48 B3 Ilt Mongolia
65 F1 Il'yaly Turkmenistan
60 C1 İnebolu Turkey
19 K4 Humenné Slovakia
12 H5 Il'ya-Vysokovo Rus. Fed.
112 B4 Ignace Can.
14 F1 İ-n-Échaï well Mali

10 M2 Jökulsá á Fjöllum r. Iceland
10 N2 Jökulsá í Fljótsdal r. Iceland
60 F2 Jolfa Iran
122 C5 Joliet U.S.A.
115 J3 Joliette Can.
41 B5 Jolo Phil.
41 B5 Jolo i. Phil.
41 B3 Jomalig i. Phil.
40 C3 Jombang Indon.
11 G5 Jonava Lithuania
50 C1 Jonê China
125 F5 Jonesboro U.S.A.
121 K2 Jonesboro U.S.A.
152 A3 Jones Mts mts Ant.
121 K2 Jonesport U.S.A.
94 □2 Jones Pt pt Christmas I. Indian Ocean
109 K2 Jones Sound chan. Can.
120 B6 Jonesville U.S.A.
80 B3 Jonglei Sudan
80 B3 Jonglei Canal canal Sudan
55 E5 Jonk r. India
11 D4 Jönköping Sweden
11 D4 Jönköping div. Sweden
115 K2 Jonquière Can.
131 G5 Jonuta Mexico
20 D4 Jonzac France
125 E4 Joplin U.S.A.
121 E5 Joppatowne U.S.A.
54 D4 Jora India
61 C3 Jordan r. Asia
32 E6 Jordan country Asia
126 F2 Jordan U.S.A.
126 E3 Jordan r. U.S.A.
99 F4 Jordan Cr. w Aust.
145 H1 Jordânia Brazil
126 C3 Jordan Valley U.S.A.
143 B6 Jordão r. Brazil
11 D3 Jordet Norway
55 H4 Jorhat India
65 J5 Jor Hu l. China
57 G1 Jorm Afghanistan
10 F2 Jörn Sweden
11 G3 Joroinen Finland
11 B4 Jørpeland Norway
77 F5 Jos Nigeria
41 C5 Jose Abad Santos Phil.
140 C2 José A de Palacios Bolivia
142 B2 José Bispo r. Brazil
141 D2 José Bonifácio Rondônia Brazil
144 D4 José Bonifácio São Paulo Brazil
131 F5 José Cardel Mexico
147 B5 José de San Martin Arg.
143 A4 Joselândia Brazil
146 F3 José Pedro Varela Uruguay
100 E2 Joseph Bonaparte Gulf g. Aust.
129 G4 Joseph City U.S.A.
113 G3 Joseph, Lac l. Can.
54 D3 Joshimath India
47 G5 Jōshinetsu-kōgen National Park nat. park. Japan
129 E5 Joshua Tree National Monument res. U.S.A.
77 F5 Jos Plateau plat. Nigeria
20 C3 Josselin France
119 □3 Jost Van Dyke I. i. Virgin Is Caribbean
82 D4 Jouberton R.S.A.
61 C3 Joûnié Lebanon
115 F2 Joutel Can.
11 G3 Joutsa Finland
11 H3 Joutseno Finland
55 H4 Jowai India
19 L3 Józefów Zamosć Poland
74 A5 Jreïda Mauritania
130 E3 Juan Aldama Mexico
49 E6 Juancheng China
126 A1 Juan de Fuca, Str. of chan. U.S.A.
83 G2 Juan de Nova i. Indian Ocean
151 O8 Juan Fernández, Islas is Chile
133 G5 Juangriego Venezuela
138 B5 Juanjuí Peru
10 H3 Juankoski Finland
130 J7 Juan Santamaria airport Costa Rica
131 E3 Juaréz Mexico
130 A1 Juárez, Sierra de mt. ra. Mexico
142 D2 Juàzeiro Brazil
142 E2 Juàzeiro do Norte Brazil
76 C5 Juazohn Liberia
55 E5 Juba India
80 B4 Juba Sudan
80 D4 Jubba r. Somalia
81 D4 Jubbada Dhexe div. Somalia
81 D4 Jubbada Hoose div. Somalia
101 D6 Jubilee L. salt flat Aust.
128 D4 Jubilee Pass pass U.S.A.
74 B3 Juby, Cap pt Morocco
25 F3 Júcar r. Spain
132 C2 Jucaro Cuba
131 F5 Juchatengo Mexico
130 E4 Juchipila Mexico
131 G5 Juchitán Mexico
130 D4 Juchitlán Mexico
144 C1 Juçura Brazil
145 J2 Jucurucu Brazil
145 J2 Jucururu r. Brazil
60 E4 Judaidat al Hamir Iraq
60 E4 Judayyidat 'Ar'ar well Iraq
19 G5 Judenburg Austria
11 C5 Juelsminde Denmark
145 J2 Juerana Brazil
48 D5 Juh China
73 G2 Juhaynah reg. Saudi Arabia
49 G4 Juhua Dao i. China
130 J6 Juigalpa Nicaragua
141 E2 Juina r. Brazil
141 E2 Juinamirim r. Brazil
18 C2 Juist i. Germany
145 G4 Juiz de Fora Brazil
146 C1 Jujuy div. Arg.
140 C4 Julaca Bolivia
126 G3 Julesburg U.S.A.
140 C3 Juli Peru
140 B3 Juliaca Peru
99 E4 Julia Cr. r. Aust.
99 E4 Julia Cr. Aust.
139 F3 Juliana Top summit Surinam
26 D2 Julijske Alpe mts Slovenia
146 D4 Julio, 9 de Arg.
98 D4 Julius, Lake l. Aust.
20 D2 Jullouville France
50 B1 Jumanggoin China
138 B5 Jumbilla Peru
25 F3 Jumilla Spain
55 E3 Jumla Nepal
61 C4 Jum Suwwāna mt. Jordan
54 B5 Junagadh India
56 C2 Junagarh India
51 G1 Junan China
49 F3 Jun Bulen China
146 B3 Juncal mt. Chile
147 D5 Juncal, L. l. Arg.
119 □3 Juncos Puerto Rico
125 D6 Junction U.S.A.
127 D4 Junction U.S.A.
98 C1 Junction B. b. Aust.
124 D4 Junction City U.S.A.
99 E5 Jundah Aust.
145 E5 Jundiaí Brazil
110 C3 Juneau U.S.A.
61 C3 Jūn el Khudr b. Lebanon
65 L3 Junggar Pendi basin China
54 A4 Jungshahi Pakistan
80 B2 Junguls Sudan
120 E4 Juniata r. U.S.A.
146 D3 Junín Arg.
140 A2 Junín Peru
147 B4 Junín de los Andes Arg.
121 K1 Juniper Can.
128 B3 Junipero Serro Peak summit U.S.A.
47 H3 Jūnisho reg. Japan
50 D2 Junlian China
56 A2 Junnar India
10 E3 Junsele Sweden
51 G2 Junshan Hu l. China
126 C3 Juntura U.S.A.
51 E1 Jun Xian China
50 B1 Ju'nyunggoin China
11 G4 Juodupe Lithuania
145 H3 Juparanã, Lagoa l. Brazil
144 C4 Jupiá Brazil
144 E6 Juquiá r. Brazil
144 E6 Juquiá Brazil
78 E2 Jur r. Sudan
16 E4 Jura i. U.K.
142 D3 Jurací Brazil
138 B2 Juradó Colombia
145 G2 Juramento Brazil
16 E4 Jura, Sound of chan. U.K.
11 F5 Jurbarkas Lithuania
11 F5 Jurbarkas Lithuania
60 C4 Jurf ed Darāwīsh Jordan
49 G3 Jurh China
49 G3 Jurhe China
55 G2 Jurhen Ul Shan mt. ra. China
28 G2 Jurilovca Romania
142 A1 Juriti Velho Brazil
11 F4 Jūrmala Latvia
10 G2 Jurmu Finland
51 G2 Jurong China
43 □ Jurong Singapore
139 D4 Juruá Brazil
138 D5 Juruá r. Brazil
138 C5 Juruá Mirim r. Brazil
141 E1 Juruena r. Brazil
142 B3 Juruna r. Brazil
142 A1 Juruti Brazil
11 F3 Jurva Finland
46 H3 Jūsan-ko l. Japan
133 G5 Jusepín Venezuela
61 D2 Jūsīyah Syria
146 C3 Justo Daract Arg.
138 D5 Jutaí Brazil
138 D5 Jutaí r. Brazil
142 B1 Jutai, Sa do h. Brazil
18 F3 Jüterbog Germany
144 A5 Juti Brazil
131 H6 Jutiapa Guatemala
130 J6 Juticalpa Honduras
10 E2 Jutis Sweden
10 H3 Juuka Finland
11 G3 Juva Finland
132 B2 Juventud, Isla de la i. Cuba
57 E3 Juwain Afghanistan
40 B3 Juwana Indon.
49 F6 Ju Xian China
48 B4 Juyan China
51 G1 Juye China
57 D2 Jūymand Iran
57 C3 Jūyom Iran
82 C3 Jwaneng Botswana
11 G3 Jyväskylä Finland
11 G3 Jyväskylän mlk Finland

K

54 D2 K2 mt. China/Jammu and Kashmir
77 E4 Ka r. Nigeria
49 H5 Ka i. N. Korea
64 E5 Kaakhka Turkmenistan
127 □1 Kaala mt. U.S.A.
90 □2 Kaala-Gomen Pac. Oc.
81 D5 Kaambooni Kenya
11 F3 Kaarina Finland
76 C4 Kaarta reg. Mali
10 H3 Kaavi Finland
39 H8 Kabaena i. Indon.
64 F5 Kabakly Turkmenistan
76 B5 Kabala Sierra Leone
81 A5 Kabale Uganda
79 E5 Kabalo Zaire
79 E5 Kabamba, Lac l. Zaire
79 E4 Kabambare Zaire
79 D6 Kabangu Zaire
48 C2 Kabansk Rus. Fed.
90 □7 Kabara i. Fiji
13 G7 Kabardino-Balkariya div. Rus. Fed.
78 E4 Kabare Zaire
46 B7 Kaba-shima i. Japan
10 F2 Kâbdalis Sweden
46 D6 Kabe Japan
114 C2 Kabenung Lake l. Can.
75 E3 Kabertene Algeria
114 C2 Kabinakagami r. Can.
114 C2 Kabinakagami Lake l. Can.
79 D5 Kabinda Zaire
78 C2 Kabo C.A.R.
79 D6 Kabompo r. Zambia
79 D6 Kabompo Zambia
40 B1 Kabong Malaysia
79 E5 Kabongo Zaire
77 E5 Kabou Togo
57 E2 Kabūdeh Iran
57 D1 Kabūd Gonbad Iran
57 B2 Kabūd Rāhang Iran
41 B2 Kabugao Phil.
57 G2 Kabul r. Afghanistan
57 G2 Kābul Afghanistan
79 E6 Kabunda Zaire
40 D4 Kabunduk Indon.
41 C6 Kaburuang i. Indon.
73 F4 Kabushiya Sudan
79 E6 Kabwe Zambia
79 E5 Kabwe, Lac l. Zaire
64 F2 Kabyrga r. Kazak.
28 C3 Kačanik Yugo.
57 E3 Kacha Kuh mt. ra. Iran/Pakistan
13 H5 Kachalinskaya Rus. Fed.
54 B5 Kachchh, Gulf of g. India
54 A3 Kachh Pakistan
77 F5 Kachia Nigeria
42 B1 Kachin State div. Myanmar
81 B5 Kachira, Lake l. Uganda
65 J2 Kachiry Kazak.
44 J1 Kachug Rus. Fed.
60 E1 Kackar Daği mt. Turkey
14 H3 Kadada r. Rus. Fed.
42 B3 Kadaingti Myanmar
56 B4 Kadaiyanallur India
80 B4 Kadam mt. Uganda
57 F3 Kadanai r. Afghanistan/Pakistan
43 B4 Kadan Kyun i. Myanmar
40 C3 Kadapongan i. Indon.
54 D4 Kadaura India
90 □7 Kadavu i. Fiji
90 □8 Kadavu Passage chan. Fiji
49 F2 Kadaya Rus. Fed.
78 C3 Kadéï r. C.A.R.
47 □2 Kadena Japan
60 F3 Kādhimain Iraq
54 C5 Kadi India
60 B1 Kadıköy Turkey
96 D3 Kadina Aust.
60 C2 Kadınhanı Turkey
76 C4 Kadiolo Mali
76 B4 Kadiondola, Mt mt. Guinea
56 B3 Kadiri India
60 D2 Kadirli Turkey
77 E5 Kadjebi Ghana
53 D8 Kadmat i. India
12 G3 Kadnikov Rus. Fed.
124 C3 Kadoka U.S.A.
14 F2 Kadom Rus. Fed.
83 D2 Kadoma Zimbabwe
42 A4 Kadonkani Myanmar
14 G2 Kadoshkino Rus. Fed.
42 B1 Kadu Myanmar
78 E1 Kadugli Sudan
77 F4 Kaduna div. Nigeria
77 F4 Kaduna Nigeria
77 F5 Kaduna r. Nigeria
50 B2 Kadusam mt. China
12 F3 Kaduy Rus. Fed.
56 A2 Kadwa r. India
14 H2 Kadyshevo Rus. Fed.
12 G3 Kadyy Rus. Fed.
49 H5 Kaechon N. Korea
74 B5 Kaédi Mauritania
78 B1 Kaélé Cameroon
127 □1 Kaena Pt pt U.S.A.
92 D1 Kaeo N.Z.
49 H5 Kaesŏng N. Korea
73 G1 Kāf Saudi Arabia
79 D5 Kafakumba Zaire
77 F5 Kafanchan Nigeria
77 G4 Kaffin-Hausa Nigeria
76 A4 Kaffrine Senegal
78 D2 Kafia Kingi Sudan
61 D2 Kafr Buhum Syria
73 F1 Kafr el Sheik Egypt
61 A4 Kafr Sa'd Egypt
80 B4 Kafu r. Uganda
79 E7 Kafue r. Zambia
79 E7 Kafue Zambia
79 E6 Kafue National Park nat. park Zambia
47 F5 Kaga Japan
78 C2 Kaga Bandoro C.A.R.
54 C2 Kagan Pakistan
64 F5 Kagan Uzbekistan
50 C1 Kagang China
77 F5 Kagarko Nigeria
46 E6 Kagawa div. Japan
114 D4 Kagawong Can.
10 F2 Kåge Sweden
81 B5 Kagera div. Tanzania
114 B2 Kagiano Lake l. Can.
60 E1 Kağızman Turkey
73 F5 Kagmar Sudan
77 F5 Kagoro Nigeria
46 C8 Kagoshima Japan
46 C8 Kagoshima div. Japan
46 C8 Kagoshima-wan b. Japan
48 A2 Kagzhirba Rus. Fed.
57 B2 Kahak Iran
61 C6 Kahala, W. al w Saudi Arabia
127 □1 Kahaluu U.S.A.
81 B5 Kahama Tanzania
54 B3 Kahan Pakistan
127 □1 Kahana U.S.A.
15 D2 Kaharlyk Ukraine
82 A3 Kahawero waterhole Namibia
40 C2 Kahayan r. Indon.
79 C5 Kahemba Zaire
93 A6 Kaherekoau Mts mts N.Z.
57 D4 Kahnūj Iran
122 B5 Kahoka U.S.A.
127 □2 Kahoolawe i. U.S.A.
60 D2 Kahraman Maraş Turkey
54 B3 Kahror Pakistan
60 D2 Kahta Turkey
93 □1 Kahuitara Pt pt Chatham Is N.Z.
127 □1 Kahuku U.S.A.
127 □1 Kahuku Pt pt U.S.A.
127 □2 Kahului U.S.A.
57 D3 Kahurak Iran
92 D4 Kahurangi Point pt N.Z.
78 E4 Kahuzi-Biega, Parc National du nat. park Zaire
77 E5 Kaiama Nigeria
90 □1 Kaiapit P.N.G.
93 D5 Kaiapoi N.Z.
129 F3 Kaibab U.S.A.
127 D4 Kaibab Plat. plat. U.S.A.
46 E6 Kaibara Japan
39 K8 Kai Besar i. Indon.
129 G3 Kaibito U.S.A.
129 G3 Kaibito Plateau plat. U.S.A.
65 K4 Kaidu r. China
51 F1 Kaifeng China
51 F1 Kaifeng China
92 D1 Kaihu N.Z.
51 G2 Kaihua China
82 C4 Kaiingbulte reg. R.S.A.
50 D2 Kaijiang China
39 K8 Kai Kecil i. Indon.
39 K8 Kai, Kepulauan is Indon.
92 D1 Kaikohe N.Z.
93 D5 Kaikoura N.Z.
93 D5 Kaikoura Peninsula pen. N.Z.
45 □ Kai Kung Leng h. Hong Kong
76 B5 Kailahun Sierra Leone
55 G4 Kailāshahar India
50 D3 Kaili China
80 C4 Kailongong waterhole Kenya
49 G4 Kailu China
127 □1 Kailua U.S.A.
127 □2 Kailua Kona U.S.A.
92 E2 Kaimai Range h. N.Z.
39 K7 Kaimana Indon.
92 E3 Kaimanawa Mountains mt. ra. N.Z.
50 A1 Kaimar China
54 D4 Kaimganj India
55 E4 Kaimur Range h. India
11 F4 Käina Estonia
46 E7 Kainan Japan
47 E6 Kainan Japan
42 A2 Kaing Myanmar
77 E4 Kaingiwa Nigeria
77 F5 Kainji Lake National Park nat. park Nigeria
77 E4 Kainji Lake National Park nat. park Nigeria
77 E4 Kainji Reservoir resr Nigeria
56 D1 Kaintarāgarh India
92 E2 Kaipara Harbour inlet N.Z.
129 G3 Kaiparowits Plateau plat. U.S.A.
51 F4 Kaiping China
113 J3 Kaipokok Bay inlet Can.
54 D3 Kairana India
75 G1 Kairouan Tunisia
18 C4 Kaiserslautern Germany
49 J4 Kaishantun China
92 D1 Kaitaia N.Z.
93 B7 Kaitangata N.Z.
92 F3 Kaitawa N.Z.
54 D3 Kaithal India
40 A2 Kait, Tg pt Indon.
10 F2 Kaitum Sweden
39 J8 Kaiwatu Indon.
127 □2 Kaiwi Channel chan. U.S.A.
50 E2 Kai Xian China
50 D3 Kaiyang China
50 C4 Kaiyuan China
49 H4 Kaiyuan China
10 G2 Kajaani Finland
98 E4 Kajabbi Aust.
57 F2 Kajaki Afghanistan
40 E3 Kajang Indon.
43 C7 Kajang Malaysia
54 B3 Kajanpur Pakistan
57 F2 Kajrān Afghanistan
77 F4 Kajuru Nigeria
65 J4 Kajy-Say Kyrgyzstan
80 B2 Kaka Sudan
112 C4 Kakabeka Falls Can.
98 C2 Kakadu Nat. Park nat. park Aust.
82 C4 Kakamas R.S.A.
81 B4 Kakamega Kenya
47 F6 Kakamigahara Japan
43 A5 Kakana Andaman and Nicobar Is India
26 G3 Kakanj Bos.-Herz.
93 C6 Kakanui Mts mts N.Z.
77 G4 Kakarahil well Niger
92 E3 Kakaramea N.Z.
76 B5 Kakata Liberia
92 E3 Kakatahi N.Z.
55 H4 Kakching India
46 D6 Kake Japan
110 C3 Kake U.S.A.
47 G6 Kakegawa Japan
79 D4 Kakenge Zaire
15 E3 Kakhovka Ukraine
15 E3 Kakhovs'ke Vodoskhovyshche resr Ukraine
57 B3 Kākī Iran
56 C2 Kākināda India
110 F2 Kakisa Can.
110 F2 Kakisa r. Can.
110 F2 Kakisa Lake l. Can.
46 E6 Kakogawa Japan
19 L3 Kąkolewnica Wschodnia Poland
54 E4 Kakori India
79 E4 Kakoswa Zaire
76 D5 Kakpin Côte d'Ivoire
54 D4 Kakrala India
76 B4 Kakrima r. Guinea
108 D2 Kaktovik U.S.A.
47 H5 Kakuda Japan
110 F4 Kakwa r. Can.
54 B3 Kala Pakistan
81 B6 Kala Tanzania
54 B2 Kalabagh Pakistan
39 H8 Kalabahi Indon.
41 A5 Kalabakan Malaysia
80 E3 Kalabaydh Nugaal Somalia
80 D3 Kalabaydh Woqooyi Galbeed Somalia
96 E2 Kalabity Aust.
79 D6 Kalabo Zambia
13 G5 Kalach Rus. Fed.
57 F2 Kalacha Afghanistan
80 C4 Kalacha Dida Kenya
65 H2 Kalachinsk Rus. Fed.
13 G5 Kalach-na-Donu Rus. Fed.
42 A2 Kaladan r. India/Myanmar
115 G4 Kaladar Can.
127 □2 Ka Lae c. U.S.A.
40 E2 Kalaena r. Indon.
42 B2 Kalagwe Myanmar
82 C3 Kalahari Desert desert Botswana
82 C4 Kalahari Gemsbok National Park nat. park R.S.A.
64 F5 Kala-I-Mor Turkmenistan
10 G2 Kalajoki r. Finland
10 F2 Kalajoki Finland
77 E4 Kalalé Benin
54 C2 Kalam Pakistan
29 D4 Kalamaria Greece
29 D6 Kalamata Greece
122 E4 Kalamazoo U.S.A.
122 D4 Kalamazoo r. U.S.A.
40 C3 Kalambau i. Indon.
29 C5 Kalampaka Greece
29 E4 Kalampaki Greece
76 C4 Kalana Mali
54 C3 Kalanaur India
15 E3 Kalanchak Ukraine
57 E3 Kalandi Pakistan
81 B5 Kalangala Uganda
49 F2 Kalanguy Rus. Fed.
101 B6 Kalannie Aust.
54 C3 Kalanwali India
40 E3 Kalao i. Indon.
41 C5 Kalaong Phil.
56 C4 Kala Oya r. Sri Lanka
40 A2 Kalapa Indon.
57 E4 Kalar w Iran
60 F3 Kalār Iraq
14 B1 Kalashnikovo Rus. Fed.
54 A3 Kalat Pakistan
90 □4 Kalau i. Tonga
127 □2 Kalaupapa U.S.A.
13 G6 Kalaus r. Rus. Fed.
29 D5 Kalavryta Greece
42 B2 Kalaw Myanmar
101 A5 Kalbarri Aust.
101 A5 Kalbarri Nat. Park nat. park Aust.
57 D2 Kalbū Iran
15 G3 Kal'chyk r. Ukraine
29 G6 Kale Denizli Turkey
61 A1 Kale Turkey
61 A1 Kaleardı Br. pt Turkey
60 C1 Kalecik Turkey
78 E4 Kalehe Zaire
42 A3 Kaleindaung inlet Myanmar
79 D4 Kalema Zaire
79 E5 Kalémié Zaire
42 A2 Kalemyo Myanmar
122 D3 Kaleva U.S.A.
10 H2 Kalevala Rus. Fed.
42 A2 Kalewa Myanmar
60 F2 Kaleybar Iran
49 F2 Kalga Rus. Fed.
101 B7 Kalgan r. Aust.
101 C6 Kalgoorlie Aust.
77 G4 Kalguéri Niger
26 E3 Kali Croatia
54 E3 Kali r. India
40 A3 Kalianda Indon.
41 B4 Kalibo Phil.
55 E4 Kali Gadaki r. Nepal
14 D3 Kalikino Rus. Fed.
79 E4 Kalima Zaire
40 C2 Kalimantan reg. Indon.
40 B2 Kalimantan Barat div. Indon.
40 C2 Kalimantan Selatan div. Indon.
40 C2 Kalimantan Tengah div. Indon.
40 D1 Kalimantan Timur div. Indon.
55 G4 Kālimpang India
56 A3 Kalinadi r. India
54 D3 Kali Nadi r. India
64 E4 Kalinin Turkmenistan
11 F5 Kaliningrad Rus. Fed.
14 H2 Kalinino Rus. Fed.
13 H5 Kalininsk Rus. Fed.
13 F6 Kalininskaya Rus. Fed.
15 E3 Kalinins'ke Ukraine
13 D4 Kalinkavichy Belarus
64 E3 Kalinovka Kazak.
14 B4 Kalinovka Rus. Fed.
80 E3 Kalis Somalia
54 D5 Kali Sindh r. India
126 D1 Kalispell U.S.A.
19 J3 Kalisz Poland
19 G2 Kalisz Pomorski Poland
13 F5 Kalitva r. Rus. Fed.
81 B6 Kaliua Tanzania
10 F2 Kalix Sweden
10 F2 Kalixälven r. Sweden
54 D3 Kalka India
15 G3 Kalka r. Ukraine
60 B2 Kalkan Turkey
98 B3 Kalkaringi Aust.
122 E3 Kalkaska U.S.A.
82 B3 Kalkfeld Namibia
96 D1 Kallakoopah Cr. w Aust.
43 □ Kallang Singapore
11 G4 Kallaste Estonia
10 G3 Kallavesi l. Finland
29 C5 Kallifoni Greece
10 D3 Kallsedet Sweden
10 D3 Kallsjön l. Sweden
65 K2 Kalmanka Rus. Fed.
11 E4 Kalmar Sweden
11 D4 Kalmar div. Sweden
13 F6 Kal'mius r. Ukraine
57 D1 Kalmūkh Qaléh Iran
56 C5 Kalmunai Sri Lanka
13 H6 Kalmykiya div. Rus. Fed.
64 D3 Kalmykovo Kazak.
55 G4 Kalni r. Bangladesh
19 J5 Kalocsa Hungary
54 C5 Kalol India
41 C6 Kaloma i. Indon.
81 B6 Kaloma Tanzania
79 E7 Kalomo Zambia
110 D4 Kalone Pk summit Can.
61 B2 Kalopanagiotis Cyprus
54 D3 Kalpa India
56 A4 Kalpeni i. India
65 J4 Kalpin China
108 C3 Kaltag U.S.A.
65 L2 Kaltan Rus. Fed.
18 D2 Kaltenkirchen Germany
77 G5 Kaltungo Nigeria
54 C3 Kalu India
14 C2 Kaluga Rus. Fed.
14 B2 Kaluga div. Rus. Fed.
14 F3 Kalugino Rus. Fed.
15 E3 Kaluha Ukraine
40 D3 Kalukalukuang i. Indon.
40 D2 Kaluku Indon.
79 E6 Kalulushi Zambia
100 D2 Kalumburu Aust.
100 D2 Kalumburu Abor. Land Reserve res. Aust.
11 C5 Kalundborg Denmark
79 E5 Kalungwishi r. Zambia
54 B2 Kalur Kot Pakistan
15 A2 Kalush Ukraine
19 K2 Kałuszyn Poland
56 B5 Kalutara Sri Lanka
19 L1 Kalvarija Lithuania
10 F3 Kälviä Finland
56 A2 Kalyan India
14 C1 Kalyazin Rus. Fed.
29 F6 Kalymnos i. Greece
29 F6 Kalymnos Greece
15 D1 Kalynivka Kyyiv Ukraine
15 C2 Kalynivka Vinnytsya Ukraine
15 D1 Kalyta Ukraine
77 G5 Kam Nigeria
42 A3 Kama Myanmar
12 K3 Kama r. Rus. Fed.
79 E4 Kama Zaire
47 H4 Kamaishi Japan
47 □1 Kama-iwa i. Japan
47 G6 Kamakura Japan
76 B5 Kamakwie Sierra Leone
72 C3 Kamal Chad
54 C3 Kamalia Pakistan
42 B3 Kamamaung Myanmar
54 D4 Kaman India
60 C2 Kaman Turkey
78 E4 Kamande Zaire
82 A2 Kamanjab Namibia
79 E4 Kamanyola Zaire
80 D1 Kamaran Yemen
80 D1 Kamarān I. i. Yemen
57 F2 Kamard reg. Afghanistan
56 B2 Kamareddi India
29 C5 Kamares Dytiki Ellas Greece
57 E4 Kamarod Pakistan
76 B5 Kamaron Sierra Leone
15 D1 Kamaryn Belarus
65 G5 Kamashi Uzbekistan
82 D2 Kamativi Zimbabwe
42 B1 Kambaiti Myanmar
101 C6 Kambalda Aust.
56 B4 Kambam India
40 B4 Kambangan i. Indon.
64 D1 Kambarka Rus. Fed.
65 K4 Kamberdi China
76 B5 Kambia Sierra Leone
94 □1 Kambling I. i. Cocos Is Indian Ocean
49 J4 Kambo Ho mt. N. Korea
79 E6 Kambove Zaire
40 E2 Kambuno, Bukit mt. Indon.
63 R4 Kamchatka r. Rus. Fed.
63 S4 Kamchatka pen. Rus. Fed.
57 G2 Kamdesh Afghanistan
13 J5 Kamelik r. Rus. Fed.
28 E3 Kamen Bulgaria
79 D5 Kamende Zaire
19 G4 Kamenice nad Lipou Czech Rep.
64 D2 Kamenka Kazak.
12 H1 Kamenka Rus. Fed.
14 G3 Kamenka Rus. Fed.
13 F5 Kamenka Rus. Fed.
14 A2 Kamenka Rus. Fed.
14 G1 Kamenka Rus. Fed.
14 E3 Kamenka Rus. Fed.
14 B2 Kamenka Rus. Fed.
65 K2 Kamen'-na-Obi Rus. Fed.
14 D1 Kamenniki Rus. Fed.
11 H3 Kamennogorsk Rus. Fed.
28 F3 Kameno Bulgaria
13 G6 Kamenolomni Rus. Fed.
49 K3 Kamen'-Rybolov Rus. Fed.
63 S3 Kamenskoye Rus. Fed.
14 D3 Kamenskoye Rus. Fed.
13 G5 Kamensk-Shakhtinskiy Rus. Fed.
64 F1 Kamensk-Ural'skiy Rus. Fed.
19 G3 Kamenz Germany
14 E1 Kameshkovo Rus. Fed.
54 D3 Kamet mt. China
29 B4 Kamëz Albania
46 B6 Kamiagata Japan
19 H3 Kamienna Gora Poland
19 G2 Kamień Pomorski Poland
46 J2 Kamikawa Japan
46 B8 Kami-Koshiki-jima i. Japan
98 E3 Kamileroi Aust.
111 J2 Kamilukuak Lake l. Can.
79 D5 Kamina Zaire
79 E5 Kamina Base Zaire
111 L2 Kaminak Lake l. Can.
15 A1 Kamin'-Kashyrs'kyy Ukraine
46 H3 Kaminokuni Japan
47 H4 Kaminoyama Japan
26 E2 Kaminške in Savinjske Alpe mt. ra. Slovenia
14 E1 Kaminskiy Rus. Fed.
47 F5 Kamioka Japan
29 F6 Kamiros Greece
46 J2 Kamishihoro Japan
46 B6 Kamitsushima Japan
79 E4 Kamituga Zaire
47 □2 Kamiyama-jima i. Japan
55 H4 Kamjong India
55 F4 Kamla r. India
65 L2 Kamlak Rus. Fed.
110 E4 Kamloops Can.
47 G5 Kamo Japan
92 E1 Kamo N.Z.
139 F3 Kamoa Mts mts Guyana
46 H2 Kamoenai Japan
47 H6 Kamogawa Japan
54 C3 Kamoke Pakistan
79 D5 Kamonia Zaire
19 G4 Kamp r. Austria
81 B4 Kampala Uganda
43 C6 Kampar Malaysia
18 B2 Kampen Netherlands
79 E4 Kampene Zaire
42 B3 Kamphaeng Phet Thailand
56 B3 Kampli India
79 E6 Kampolombo, Lake l. Zambia
43 D5 Kâmpóng Cham Cambodia
43 D4 Kâmpóng Chhnăng Cambodia
43 D4 Kâmpóng Khleăng Cambodia
43 D5 Kâmpóng Spoe Cambodia
43 D4 Kâmpóng Thum Cambodia
43 D5 Kâmpong Tranch Cambodia
43 D5 Kâmpôt Cambodia
76 D4 Kampti Burkina
39 K7 Kamrau, Teluk b. Indon.
111 J4 Kamsack Can.
76 B4 Kamsar Guinea
12 J4 Kamskoye Ust'ye Rus. Fed.
62 G4 Kamskoye Vdkhr. resr Rus. Fed.
81 D4 Kamsuuma Somalia
111 J3 Kamuchawie Lake l. Can.
81 B4 Kamuli Uganda
15 B1 Kam"yane Rivne Ukraine
15 F1 Kam"yane Sumy Ukraine
15 B2 Kam"yanets'-Podil's'kyy Ukraine
15 E2 Kam"yanka Cherkasy Ukraine
15 G2 Kam"yanka Kharkiv Ukraine
15 D3 Kam"yanka Odesa Ukraine
15 A1 Kam"yanka-Buz'ka Ukraine
15 F3 Kam"yanka-Dniprovs'ka Ukraine
28 G2 Kam"yans'ke Ukraine
13 B4 Kamyanyets Belarus
15 B1 Kam"yanyy Brid Ukraine
15 D3 Kam"yanyy Mist Ukraine
60 F3 Kāmyārān Iran
13 F6 Kamyshevatskaya Rus. Fed.
13 H5 Kamyshin Rus. Fed.
64 F3 Kamyshlybash Kazak.
64 F3 Kamyslybas, Oz. l. Kazak.
13 J6 Kamyzyak Rus. Fed.
57 D4 Kamzar Oman
80 B3 Kan Sudan
78 F3 Kana Zaire
83 D2 Kana r. Zimbabwe
112 F3 Kanaaupscow r. Can.
129 F3 Kanab U.S.A.
129 F3 Kanab Creek r. U.S.A.
90 □6 Kanacea i. Fiji
47 G6 Kanagawa div. Japan
54 A3 Kanak Pakistan
29 C5 Kanallaki Greece
79 D5 Kananga Zaire
97 G3 Kanangra Nat. Park nat. park Aust.
129 F3 Kanarraville U.S.A.
14 H2 Kanash Rus. Fed.
120 C5 Kanawha r. U.S.A.
47 F6 Kanayama Japan
47 F5 Kanazawa Japan
47 F5 Kanazu Japan
42 A2 Kanbalu Myanmar
43 B4 Kanchanaburi Thailand
56 B3 Kanchipuram India
19 L4 Kańczuga Poland
54 A3 Kand mt. Pakistan
57 F3 Kandahār Afghanistan
10 J2 Kandalaksha Rus. Fed.
12 E1 Kandalakshskiy Zaliv g. Rus. Fed.
40 C2 Kandangan Indon.
77 E5 Kandé Togo
54 B3 Kandhkot Pakistan
54 B2 Kandhura Pakistan
77 E4 Kandi Benin
54 A3 Kandi Pakistan
54 B4 Kandiaro Pakistan
29 C5 Kandila Sterea Ellas Greece
77 G3 Kandil Bouzou well Niger
60 B1 Kandıra Turkey
54 B5 Kandla India
97 G3 Kandos Aust.
83 H2 Kandreho Madagascar
90 □1 Kandrian P.N.G.
56 B3 Kandukur India
56 C5 Kandy Sri Lanka
120 D4 Kane U.S.A.
109 M2 Kane Basin b. Greenland
57 C4 Kaneh w Iran
72 C5 Kanem div. Chad
127 □1 Kaneohe U.S.A.
127 □1 Kaneohe Bay b. U.S.A.
12 F1 Kanevka Rus. Fed.
13 F6 Kanevskaya Rus. Fed.
47 H4 Kaneyama Japan
82 C3 Kang Botswana
55 G5 Kanga r. Bangladesh
78 F3 Kanga Zaire
109 N3 Kangaatsiaq Greenland
76 C4 Kangaba Mali
60 D2 Kangal Turkey
57 D4 Kangān Iran
57 C4 Kangan Iran
43 C6 Kangar Malaysia
96 D3 Kangaroo I. i. Aust.
139 F2 Kangaruma Guyana
11 H3 Kangaslampi Finland
11 G3 Kangasniemi Finland
57 A2 Kangāvar Iran
49 E4 Kangbao China
55 G4 Kangchenjunga mt. Nepal
50 C2 Kangding China
49 H5 Kangdong N. Korea
40 C3 Kangean i. Indon.
40 C3 Kangean, Kep. is Indon.
80 B3 Kangen r. Sudan
109 O3 Kangeq hd Greenland
109 N3 Kangerluarsoruseq Greenland
109 N3 Kangerlussuaq Greenland
109 P3 Kangerlussuaq inlet Greenland
109 N2 Kangersuatsiaq Greenland
109 P3 Kangertittivatsiaq inlet Greenland
80 C4 Kangetet Kenya
49 H4 Kanggye N. Korea
109 Q2 Kangikajik c. Greenland
49 F1 Kangil Rus. Fed.
113 G2 Kangiqsualujjuaq Can.
109 L3 Kangiqsujuaq Can.
113 G1 Kangirsuk Can.
46 A6 Kangjon S. Korea
50 C1 Kangle China
55 F3 Kangmar China
55 G3 Kangmar China
49 J5 Kangnŭng S. Korea
78 B3 Kango Gabon
47 □1 Kangoku-iwa i. Japan
49 G4 Kangping China
54 D2 Kangra India
55 H3 Kangri Karpo Pass India
55 E3 Kangrinboqê Feng mt. China
55 H4 Kangto mt. China
55 F2 Kangtog China
50 D1 Kang Xian China
54 D1 Kangxiwar China
42 A3 Kangyidaung Myanmar
56 B1 Kanhan r. India
55 E4 Kanhar r. India
76 C5 Kani Côte d'Ivoire
42 A2 Kani Myanmar
79 D5 Kaniama Zaire
93 C5 Kaniere N.Z.
93 C5 Kaniere, L. l. N.Z.
76 A4 Kanifing The Gambia
56 B3 Kanigiri India
54 B2 Kaniguram Pakistan
62 F3 Kanin Nos Rus. Fed.
62 F3 Kanin Nos, Mys c. Rus. Fed.
62 F3 Kanin, P-ov pen. Rus. Fed.
46 H3 Kanita Japan
15 D2 Kaniv Ukraine
96 E4 Kaniva Aust.
28 C1 Kanjiža Yugo.
11 F3 Kankaanpää Finland
122 D5 Kankakee U.S.A.
122 C5 Kankakee r. U.S.A.
76 C4 Kankan Guinea
76 C5 Kankan, Réserve Naturelle de res. Guinea
55 E5 Kanker India
56 C4 Kankesanturai Sri Lanka
54 C1 Kankhun P. pass Afghanistan/Pakistan
43 B5 Kanmaw Kyun i. Myanmar
54 D4 Kannanj India
119 D5 Kannapolis U.S.A.
56 B4 Kanniyakumari India
54 D5 Kannod India
10 G3 Kannonkoski Finland
10 F3 Kannus Finland
46 C6 Kano Japan
77 F4 Kano div. Nigeria
77 F4 Kano Nigeria
46 D6 Kan-onji Japan
40 C1 Kanowit Malaysia
46 C8 Kanoya Japan
54 E4 Kanpur India
54 B3 Kanpur Pakistan
54 A4 Kanrach reg. Pakistan
124 D4 Kansas r. U.S.A.
124 D4 Kansas div. U.S.A.
124 E4 Kansas City U.S.A.
124 E4 Kansas City U.S.A.
63 L4 Kansk Rus. Fed.
65 J5 Kansu China
65 H4 Kant Kyrgyzstan
80 C3 Kanta mt. Ethiopia
43 D4 Kantaralak Thailand
77 E4 Kantchari Burkina
13 F5 Kantemirovka Rus. Fed.
55 F5 Kānthi India
55 F4 Kanti India
150 H6 Kanton Island i. Kiribati
47 G6 Kanto-sanchi mt. ra. Japan
17 C5 Kanturk Rep. of Ire.
139 F3 Kanuku Mts mts Guyana
47 G5 Kanuma Japan
82 B4 Kanus Namibia
90 □1 Kanuwe r. P.N.G.
83 E4 KaNyamazane R.S.A.
82 D3 Kanye Botswana
14 A2 Kanyutino Rus. Fed.
90 □5 Kao i. Tonga
43 C5 Kaôh Kŏng i. Cambodia
43 C5 Kaôh Rŭng i. Cambodia
51 H4 Kao-hsiung Taiwan
43 C5 Kaôh Smăch i. Cambodia
82 A2 Kaokoveld plat. Namibia
76 A4 Kaolack Senegal
79 D6 Kaoma Zambia
72 C4 Kaortchi well Chad
78 D2 Kaouadja C.A.R.
127 □2 Kapaa U.S.A.
127 □2 Kapaau U.S.A.
65 J3 Kapal Kazak.
79 D5 Kapanga Zaire
81 B6 Kapatu Zambia
65 J4 Kapchagay Kazak.
65 J4 Kapchagayskoye Vdkhr. resr Kazak.
80 B4 Kapchorwa Uganda
19 G5 Kapfenberg Austria
55 H4 Kapili r. India
150 F5 Kapingamarangi Rise Pac. Oc.
54 B3 Kapip Pakistan
79 E6 Kapiri Mposhi Zambia
109 N3 Kapisigdlit Greenland
112 D3 Kapiskau Can.
112 D3 Kapiskau r. Can.
114 E3 Kapiskong Lake l. Can.
40 C1 Kapit Malaysia
15 D2 Kapitanivka Ukraine
92 E4 Kapiti I. i. N.Z.
139 F3 Kapiting Brazil
72 D5 Kapka, Massif du mts Chad
19 G4 Kaplice Czech Rep.
43 B5 Kapoe Thailand
80 B4 Kapoeta Sudan
92 E3 Kaponga N.Z.
19 H5 Kaposvár Hungary
57 E4 Kappar Pakistan
18 D1 Kappeln Germany
18 E5 Kappl Austria
81 C4 Kapsabet Kenya
49 J4 Kapsan N. Korea
49 F2 Kaptsegaytuy Rus. Fed.
40 B1 Kapuas r. Kalimantan Barat Indon.
40 C2 Kapuas r. Kalimantan Tengah Indon.
96 D3 Kapunda Aust.
54 C4 Kapūriya India
54 C3 Kapurthala India
114 D2 Kapuskasing Can.
114 D2 Kapuskasing r. Can.
13 H5 Kapustin Yar Rus. Fed.
15 D1 Kapustyntsi Ukraine
97 G2 Kaputar mt. Aust.
80 C4 Kaputir Kenya
19 H5 Kapuvár Hungary
12 C4 Kapyl' Belarus
14 A2 Kapyrevshchina Rus. Fed.
77 E5 Kara Togo
60 E2 Kara r. Turkey
29 F6 Kara Ada i. Turkey
29 F5 Kara Ada i. Turkey
65 H4 Kara-Balta Kyrgyzstan
14 D1 Karabanovo Rus. Fed.
64 F5 Karabekaul Turkmenistan
60 A1 Karabiga Turkey
64 D4 Kara-Bogaz-Gol Turkmenistan
64 D4 Kara-Bogaz Gol, Zaliv b. Turkmenistan
60 C1 Karabük Turkey
14 E2 Karabukhino Rus. Fed.
65 J4 Karabulak Kazak.
65 K3 Karabulak Kazak.
65 J3 Karabulakskaya Kazak.
29 F5 Karaburun Turkey
64 F3 Karabutak Kazak.
29 G4 Karacabey Turkey
60 B1 Karacaköy Turkey
60 D2 Karacalı Dağ mt. Turkey
61 B1 Karaçal T. mt. Turkey
29 G6 Karacasu Turkey
13 G7 Karachayevo-Cherkesiya div. Rus. Fed.
13 G7 Karachayevsk Rus. Fed.
14 B3 Karachev Rus. Fed.
54 A4 Karachi Pakistan
56 A2 Karad India
60 C2 Kara Dağ mt. Turkey
65 H4 Kara-Darya r. Kyrgyzstan
76 D5 Karaga Ghana
65 H3 Karaganda Kazak.
65 J3 Karagayly Kazak.
63 S4 Karaginskiy, O. i. Rus. Fed.
63 S4 Karaginskiy Zaliv b. Rus. Fed.
81 B5 Karagwe Tanzania
28 F4 Karahalil Turkey
29 G6 Karahisar Turkey
56 B4 Kāraikāl India
56 B4 Karaikkudi India
65 K3 Kara Irtysh r. Kazak.
60 C2 Karaisalı Turkey
57 B2 Karaj Iran
60 C4 Karak Jordan
64 E5 Kara Kala Turkmenistan
64 E4 Karakalpakiya Uzbekistan
65 J5 Karakax r. China
41 C5 Karakelong i. Indon.
41 C6 Karakitang i. Indon.
60 E2 Karakoçan Turkey
65 G3 Karakoin, Oz. salt l. Kazak.
64 D3 Karakol' Kazak.
65 H4 Kara-Köl Kyrgyzstan
65 J4 Karakol Kyrgyzstan
54 D2 Karakoram Pass pass China/Jammu and Kashmir
54 C1 Karakoram Range mt. ra. Asia
80 C2 Kara K'orē Ethiopia
49 E2 Karaksar Rus. Fed.
64 F5 Karakul' Uzbekistan
65 H5 Karakul', Ozero l. Tajikistan
78 B1 Karal Chad
11 F4 Karala Estonia
40 D2 Karama r. Indon.
61 B1 Karaman div. Turkey
60 C2 Karaman Turkey
65 K3 Karamay China
65 H5 Karambar Pass pass Afghanistan/Pakistan
40 D2 Karambu Indon.
93 D4 Karamea N.Z.
93 C4 Karamea Bight b. N.Z.
93 D4 Karamea River r. N.Z.
57 F1 Karamet-Niyaz Turkmenistan
40 C3 Karamian i. Indon.
55 F1 Karamiran China
55 F1 Karamiran Shankou pass China
12 D3 Karamyshevo Rus. Fed.
57 G1 Karan r. Afghanistan
57 B4 Karān i. Saudi Arabia
60 F3 Karand Iran
40 A2 Karangagung Indon.
40 A3 Karangan Indon.
40 C4 Karangasem Indon.
40 B4 Karangbolong, Tg pt Indon.
40 D2 Karang, Tg pt Indon.
54 D5 Karanja India
56 B2 Karanja r. India
55 F5 Karanjia India
65 J2 Karaoba Kazak.
29 F6 Karaova Turkey
65 H3 Karaoy Kazak.
28 F3 Karapelit Bulgaria
60 C2 Karapınar Turkey
29 G5 Karapürçek Turkey
82 B4 Karas div. Namibia
55 E1 Karasay China
65 J4 Kara-Say Kyrgyzstan
82 B4 Karasburg Namibia
14 D1 Karash Rus. Fed.
10 G1 Karasjok Norway
65 G2 Karasu Kazak.
64 F2 Karasu Kazak.
65 H2 Karasu r. Kazak.
61 D1 Karasu r. Turkey
13 D7 Karasu Turkey
65 K2 Karasuk r. Rus. Fed.
65 J2 Karasuk Rus. Fed.
65 H4 Kara-Suu Kyrgyzstan
15 A1 Karasyn Ukraine
57 E2 Karāt Iran
65 L3 Karatan Kazak.
60 C2 Karataş Turkey
61 C1 Karataş Burun c. Turkey
65 H4 Karatau Kazak.
65 G4 Karatau, Khr. mt. ra. Kazak.
54 E2 Karatax Shan mt. ra. China
43 B5 Karathuri Myanmar
56 B4 Karativu i. Sri Lanka
64 D3 Karatobe Kazak.
64 F4 Karatobe, Mys pt Kazak.
65 J3 Karatol r. Kazak.
64 D3 Karaton Kazak.
55 G4 Karatoya r. Bangladesh
46 B7 Karatsu Japan
41 C5 Karatung i. Indon.
65 G2 Karaturgay r. Kazak.
65 J3 Karaul Kazak.
54 D4 Karauli India
64 E4 Karauzyak Uzbekistan
65 H4 Karavan Kyrgyzstan
29 D6 Karavi i. Greece
29 F7 Karavonisia i. Greece
61 B2 Karavostasi Cyprus
40 A3 Karawang Indon.
14 F4 Karay r. Rus. Fed.
65 K4 Karayulgan China
65 H3 Karazhal Kazak.
64 E4 Karazhar Uzbekistan
65 H3 Karazhingil Kazak.
60 E3 Karbalā' div. Iraq
60 F3 Karbalā' Iraq
65 J3 Karbushevka Kazak.
19 K5 Karcag Hungary
28 G3 Kardam Bulgaria
29 C5 Karditsa Greece
11 F4 Kärdla Estonia
14 A2 Kardymovo Rus. Fed.
73 F4 Kareima Sudan
54 D5 Kareli India
12 D1 Kareliya div. Rus. Fed.
12 E1 Karel'skiy Bereg Rus. Fed.
81 B6 Karema Tanzania
54 D4 Karera India
10 F1 Karesuando Sweden
57 E4 Kārevāndar Iran
13 H7 Kargalinskaya Rus. Fed.
64 E2 Kargalinskoye Kazak.
61 D1 Kargamiş Turkey
64 F1 Kargapol'ye Rus. Fed.
65 K1 Kargat r. Rus. Fed.
65 K1 Kargat Rus. Fed.
13 E7 Kargı Turkey
54 D2 Kargil Jammu and Kashmir
14 H3 Kargino Rus. Fed.
12 F2 Kargopol' Rus. Fed.
19 G2 Kargowa Poland
11 E3 Karholmsbruk Sweden
77 G4 Kari Nigeria
14 E3 Karian Rus. Fed.
83 D2 Kariba Zimbabwe
83 D2 Kariba, Lake resr Zambia/Zimbabwe
46 G2 Kariba-yama vol Japan
82 B3 Karibib Namibia
82 C5 Kariega w R.S.A.
10 G1 Karigasniemi Finland
11 F3 Karijoki Finland
46 J2 Karikachi Pass pass Japan
92 D1 Karikari, Cape c. N.Z.
57 C2 Karīmābād Iran
40 B2 Karimata i. Indon.
40 B2 Karimata, P.P. is Indon.
57 B2 Karim Khanch Iran
56 B2 Karimnagar India
40 B3 Karimunjawa i. Indon.
40 B3 Karimunjawa, P.P. is Indon.
80 E2 Karin Somalia
57 D2 Karit Iran
47 F6 Kariya Japan
56 A2 Karjat India
55 F5 Karkai r. India
56 A3 Karkal India
65 J3 Karkaralinsk Kazak.
41 C5 Karkaralong, Kepulauan is Indon.
90 □1 Karkar I. i. P.N.G.
57 B3 Karkheh r. Iran
57 D4 Kārkīn Dar Iran
13 E6 Karkinits'ka Zatoka g. Ukraine
11 G3 Kärkölä Finland
19 G1 Karlino Poland
60 E2 Karlıova Turkey
15 F2 Karlivka Ukraine
65 H5 Karl Marks mt. Tajikistan
26 E3 Karlovac Croatia
28 E3 Karlovo Bulgaria
18 F3 Karlovy Vary Czech Rep.
11 D4 Karlsborg Sweden
11 D4 Karlshamn Sweden
11 D4 Karlskoga Sweden
11 D4 Karlskrona Sweden
18 D4 Karlsruhe Germany
11 D4 Karlstad Sweden
124 D1 Karlstad U.S.A.
18 D4 Karlstadt Germany
13 D4 Karma Belarus
78 C1 Karma r. Chad
77 E4 Karma Niger
56 A2 Karmala India
14 B2 Karmanovo Rus. Fed.
11 B4 Karmøy i. Norway
55 H5 Karnafuli Reservoir resr Bangladesh
54 D3 Karnal India
55 E3 Karnali r. Nepal
54 D3 Karnaprayag India
56 A3 Karnataka div. India
28 F3 Karnobat Bulgaria
72 D4 Karnoi Sudan
19 F5 Kärnten div. Austria
54 A4 Karodi Pakistan
83 D2 Karoi Zimbabwe
90 □6 Karoko Fiji
42 B4 Karokpi Myanmar
55 G3 Karo La China
55 H4 Karong India
81 B6 Karonga Malawi
81 A5 Karonje mt. Rwanda
96 D3 Karoonda Aust.
54 B3 Karor Pakistan
80 C1 Karora Eritrea
40 D2 Karossa Indon.
40 D4 Karossa, Tg pt Indon.
29 F7 Karpathos Greece
29 F7 Karpathos i. Greece
29 C5 Karpenisi Greece
12 H1 Karpogory Rus. Fed.
61 A1 Karpuz r. Turkey
29 F6 Karpuzlu Aydın Turkey
29 F4 Karpuzlu Edirne Turkey
15 B1 Karpylivka Ukraine
100 B4 Karratha Aust.
57 E2 Karrukh Afghanistan
57 E1 Karrychirla Turkmenistan
60 E1 Kars Turkey
10 G3 Kärsämäki Finland
11 G4 Kārsava Latvia
64 D4 Karshi Turkmenistan
65 G5 Karshi Uzbekistan
29 F5 Karşıyaka Turkey
62 G3 Karskiye Vorota, Proliv chan. Rus. Fed.
62 J2 Karskoye More sea Rus. Fed.
18 E2 Karstädt Germany
10 G3 Karstula Finland
14 H2 Karsun Rus. Fed.
60 B1 Kartal Turkey
81 D7 Kartala crater Comoros
64 F2 Kartaly Rus. Fed.
12 K1 Kartayel' Rus. Fed.
10 G3 Karttula Finland
19 J1 Kartuzy Poland
99 E3 Karumba Aust.
57 B3 Kārūn r. Iran
81 B5 Karungu Bay b. Kenya
40 D4 Karuni Indon.
56 B4 Karur India
11 F3 Karvia Finland
11 F3 Karvianjoki r. Finland
19 J4 Karviná Czech Rep.
56 A3 Karwar India
29 C5 Karya Greece
48 E2 Karymskoye Rus. Fed.
29 E5 Karystos Greece
14 G3 Karzhimant Rus. Fed.
112 C3 Kasabonika Can.
112 C3 Kasabonika Lake l. Can.
46 E6 Kasai Japan
79 C4 Kasai r. Zaire
79 D5 Kasai Occidental div. Zaire
79 D5 Kasai Oriental div. Zaire
79 D6 Kasaji Zaire
47 H5 Kasama Japan
81 B7 Kasama Zambia
65 G5 Kasan Uzbekistan
82 D2 Kasane Botswana
79 C4 Kasangulu Zaire
65 H4 Kasansay Uzbekistan
56 A3 Kasaragod India
111 J2 Kasba Lake l. Can.
74 C2 Kasba Tadla Morocco
46 C8 Kaseda Japan
79 E6 Kasempa Zambia
79 E6 Kasenga Zaire
79 E5 Kasengu Zaire
78 F3 Kasenye Zaire
81 B4 Kasese Uganda
78 E4 Kasese Zaire
54 D4 Kasganj India
57 B2 Kāshān Iran
13 G5 Kashary Rus. Fed.
112 D3 Kashechewan Can.
65 J5 Kashi China
47 E6 Kashihara Japan
46 C7 Kashima Japan
47 H5 Kashima-nada b. Japan
14 C1 Kashin Rus. Fed.
14 C1 Kashinka r. Rus. Fed.
54 D3 Kashipur India
14 D2 Kashira Rus. Fed.
13 F5 Kashirskoye Rus. Fed.
47 G5 Kashiwazaki Japan
65 H3 Kashkanteniz Kazak.
12 F1 Kashkarantsy Rus. Fed.
15 G3 Kashlahach r. Ukraine
14 F3 Kashma r. Rus. Fed.
57 D2 Kāshmar Iran
54 B3 Kashmor Pakistan
57 G2 Kashmund reg. Afghanistan
79 E5 Kashyukulu Zaire
55 E4 Kasia India
14 A3 Kasilovo Rus. Fed.
40 D2 Kasimbar Indon.
14 E2 Kasimov Rus. Fed.
118 B4 Kaskaskia r. U.S.A.
111 L3 Kaskattama r. Can.
65 J4 Kaskelen Kazak.
11 F3 Kaskinen Finland
64 F1 Kasli Rus. Fed.
40 C2 Kasongan Indon.
79 E4 Kasongo Zaire
79 C5 Kasongo-Lunda Zaire
29 F7 Kasos i. Greece
13 H7 Kaspi Georgia
13 H7 Kaspiysk Rus. Fed.
73 G4 Kassala Sudan
29 D4 Kassandra pen. Greece
29 D4 Kassandreia Greece
18 D3 Kassel Germany
75 F1 Kasserine Tunisia
73 F4 Kassinger Sudan
122 A3 Kasson U.S.A.
60 C1 Kastamonu Turkey
29 E7 Kastelli Kriti Greece
29 D7 Kastelli Kriti Greece
29 C4 Kastoria Greece
14 D4 Kastornoye Rus. Fed.
29 C5 Kastos i. Greece
46 C7 Kasuga Japan
47 F6 Kasugai Japan
78 E4 Kasuku Zaire
81 B5 Kasulu Tanzania
79 E6 Kasumbalesa Zaire
46 E6 Kasumi Japan
47 H5 Kasumiga-ura l. Japan
13 J7 Kasumkent Rus. Fed.
81 B7 Kasungu Malawi
81 B7 Kasungu National Park nat. park Malawi
54 C3 Kasur Pakistan
121 J2 Katahdin, Mt mt. U.S.A.
54 D2 Kataklik Jammu and Kashmir
79 D4 Katako-Kombe Zaire
80 B4 Katakwi Uganda
54 D5 Katangi India
101 B7 Katanning Aust.
78 E4 Katanti Zaire
29 C6 Katastari Greece
81 B6 Katavi National Park nat. park Tanzania
64 E2 Katav Ivanovsk Rus. Fed.
57 G2 Katawaz Afghanistan
64 F1 Kataysk Rus. Fed.
43 A6 Katchall i. Andaman and Nicobar Is India
79 E5 Katea Zaire
79 D5 Katenge Zaire
29 D4 Katerini Greece
15 D2 Katerynopil' Ukraine
81 C5 Katesh Tanzania
110 C3 Kate's Needle mt. Can./U.S.A.
81 B7 Katete Zambia
55 E5 Katghora India
42 B1 Katha Myanmar
61 B5 Katherîna, G. mt. Egypt
98 C2 Katherine r. Aust.
98 C2 Katherine Aust.
99 E4 Katherine Cr. w Aust.
98 C2 Katherine Gorge Nat. Park nat. park Aust.
54 B5 Kathiawar India
61 B4 Kathîb el Henu h. Egypt
61 B4 Kathîb el Makhâzin sand dunes Egypt
56 C4 Kathiraveli Sri Lanka
55 F4 Kathmandu Nepal
82 C4 Kathu R.S.A.
54 C2 Kathua India
81 C5 Kathua w Kenya
76 C4 Kati Mali
55 F4 Katihar India
92 E2 Katikati N.Z.

108 C1	Kocheriv Ukraine
14 G4	Kochetovka Rus. Fed.
14 E3	Kochevo Rus. Fed.
46 D7	Kōchi div. Japan
46 D7	Kōchi Japan
47 □2	Kochinada Japan
65 K2	Kochki Rus. Fed.
65 J4	Kochkor Kyrgyzstan
15 G1	Kochubey Rus. Fed.
13 G6	Kochubeyevskoye Rus. Fed.
19 L3	Kock Poland
56 B4	Kodaikanal India
15 D1	Kodaky Ukraine
55 F4	Kodala India
54 D3	Kodari Nepal
19 L3	Kodeń Poland
108 C4	Kodiak U.S.A.
108 C4	Kodiak Island i. U.S.A.
12 F2	Kodoma Rus. Fed.
80 B3	Kodok Sudan
46 H3	Kodomari-misaki pt Japan
13 G7	Kodori r. Georgia
15 C1	Kodra Ukraine
15 C2	Kodyma r. Ukraine
29 E4	Kodzhaele mt. Bulgaria/Greece
55 E4	Koel r. India
56 C4	Koel, S. r. India
55 F5	Koës Namibia
82 B4	Koës Namibia
129 F5	Kofa Mts mts U.S.A.
15 F2	Kofçaz Turkey
82 C4	Koffiefontein R.S.A.
19 G5	Köflach Austria
76 D5	Koforidua Ghana
47 G6	Kōfu Japan
112 E2	Kogaluc r. Can.
112 E2	Kogaluc, Baie de b. Can.
11 H2	Kogaluk r. Can.
11 D5	Kage Denmark
77 F5	Kogi div. Nigeria
76 B4	Kogon r. Guinea
46 A6	Kogūm do i. S. Korea
54 C6	Kogushi Japan
54 A4	Kohan Pakistan
54 B2	Kohat Pakistan
57 F2	Koh-i-Hisar mt. ra. Afghanistan
11 G4	Kohila Estonia
55 H4	Kohima India
57 F2	Koh-i-Mazar mt. Afghanistan
54 A4	Koh-i-Patandar mt. Pakistan
57 F2	Koh-i-Sangan mt. Afghanistan
57 G2	Kohistan reg. Afghanistan
54 C2	Kohistan reg. Pakistan
57 E3	Koh-i-Sultan mt. Pakistan
57 H2	Kohklüyeh va Büyer Ahmadī div. Iran
152 A1	Kohler Ra. mt. ra. Ant.
54 B3	Kohlu Pakistan
57 E2	Kohsan Afghanistan
11 G4	Kohtla-Järve Estonia
92 E2	Kohukohunui h. N.Z.
49 H6	Kohŭng S. Korea
15 D2	Kohursu mt. Rus. Fed.
45 C5	Koide Japan
110 A2	Koidern Can.
43 A5	Koihoa Andaman and Nicobar Is India
56 B3	Koilkuntla India
60 F2	Koi Sanjaq Iraq
46 B6	Koje-do i. S. Korea
47 G7	Ko-jima i. Japan
46 E5	Ko-jima i. Japan
101 B7	Kojonup Aust.
43 B6	Ko r. Thailand
121 J2	Kokadjo U.S.A.
65 H4	Kokalaat Kazak.
65 J4	Kokand Uzbekistan
11 F4	Kökar Finland
51 H2	Kokcha r. Afghanistan
11 F4	Kökemäenjoki r. Finland
80 C3	K'ok' Hāyk' i. Ethiopia
54 B3	Kokhma Rus. Fed.
76 A3	Koki Senegal
56 C4	Kokkilai Sri Lanka
10 F3	Kokkola Finland
65 L3	Ko Kuduk well China
77 E4	Koko Nigeria
76 B5	Kokofata Mali
108 D3	Koko Hd hd U.S.A.
122 D5	Kokomo U.S.A.
65 K4	Kokorevka Rus. Fed.
14 B3	Kokorevka Rus. Fed.
77 E5	Kokoro Benin
76 B4	Kokou mt. Guinea
65 A4	Kokpekty Kazak.
65 J4	Koksaray Kazak.
65 L4	Kokshaal-Tau mt. ra. China/Kyrgyzstan
65 G2	Kokshetau div. Kazak.
65 G2	Kokshetau Kazak.
113 G2	Koksoak r. Can.
83 D5	Kokstad R.S.A.
10 F2	Kokstrandia Norway
65 J4	Koktal Kazak.
65 L3	Kokterek Kazak.
43 C6	Ko Kut i. Thailand
49 F1	Kokuy Rus. Fed.
10 J1	Kola r. Rus. Fed.
54 C3	Kolachi r. Pakistan
52 C2	Kolahoi mt. India
39 H7	Kolaka Indon.
43 B6	Ko Lanta Thailand
43 B6	Ko Lanta i. Thailand
56 C2	Kolar India
56 B3	Kolar India
56 B3	Kolar Gold Fields India
10 F2	Kolari Finland
28 E3	Kolašin Yugo.
19 K3	Kolbuszowa Poland
14 B3	Kol'chugino Rus. Fed.
11 C5	Kolding Denmark
80 E3	Kole Haute-Zaire Zaire
79 C4	Kole Kasai-Oriental Zaire
10 F2	Koler Sweden
15 F2	Kolguyev, O. i. Rus. Fed.
55 E5	Kolhan India
56 A2	Kolhapur India
43 B6	Ko Libong i. Thailand
76 B3	Kolimbiné w Mali/Mauritania
19 G3	Kolín Czech Rep.
80 B3	K'olíto Ethiopia
11 G4	Kolkasrags pt Latvia
55 E4	Kolkhozobod Tajikistan
31 H1	Kolky Ukraine
56 B3	Kollegal India
19 G3	Kollerud L. I. Norway
17 E4	Kollo Niger
19 G2	Kolo Poland
19 J2	Kolo Rus. Fed.
79 B5	Kolo Rus. Fed.
90 □2	Koloa i. Tonga
76 □	Kolobeng w Botswana
19 G2	Kolobrzeg Poland
76 C4	Koloko Côte d'Ivoire
14 G4	Kolokani Mali
14 B3	Koloksha r. Rus. Fed.
14 B4	Kolomak Ukraine
90 □1	Kolombangara i. Solomon Is.
14 B3	Kolomna Rus. Fed.
29 B4	Kolonjë Albania

15 F2	Kolontayiv Ukraine
65 H1	Kolosovka Rus. Fed.
90 □4	Kolovai Tonga
64 D2	Kolovertnoye Kazak.
14 E2	Kolp' Rus. Fed.
62 K4	Kolpashevo Rus. Fed.
14 C3	Kolpny Rus. Fed.
29 D4	Kolpos Agiou Orous b. Greece
29 D7	Kolpos Chanion b. Greece
14 D1	Kolpos Ierissou b. Greece
29 E7	Kolpos Irakleiou b. Greece
42 B2	Kolpos Kassandras b. Greece
29 E4	Kolpos Kavalas b. Greece
29 D7	Kolpos Kissamou b. Greece
29 D6	Kolpos Orfanou b. Greece
62 E3	Kolpos Ydras chan. Greece
14 G3	Kol'skiy Poluostrov pen. Rus. Fed.
80 D2	Koltovskoye Rus. Fed.
53 D10	Koluli Eritrea
	Kolumadulu Atoll atoll Maldives
65 G2	Koluton Kazak.
56 A2	Kolvan India
10 C2	Kolvereid Norway
10 G1	Kolvik Norway
12 E1	Kolvitskoye, Ozero I. Rus. Fed.
57 F4	Kolwa reg. Pakistan
79 E6	Kolwezi Zaire
14 D3	Kolybel'skoye Rus. Fed.
63 R3	Kolyma r. Rus. Fed.
63 R3	Kolymskaya Nizmennost lowland Rus. Fed.
63 S3	Kolymskiy, Khrebet mt. ra. Rus. Fed.
15 D2	Kolyshley Rus. Fed.
14 G3	Kolyshley r. Rus. Fed.
65 K1	Kolyvan' Rus. Fed.
77 G4	Komadugu-gana w Nigeria
47 F6	Komagane Japan
46 H2	Komaga-take vol Japan
82 B4	Komaggas Mts mts R.S.A.
19 L4	Komańcza Poland
63 S4	Komandorskiye Ostrova is Rus. Fed.
14 B3	Komarichi Rus. Fed.
15 B2	Komarne Ukraine
19 J5	Komárno Slovakia
47 F5	Komatsu Japan
47 E6	Komatsushima Japan
79 E4	Kombe Zaire
76 D4	Kombissiri Burkina
77 E4	Kombongou Burkina
55 H3	Komdi mt. India
41 □1	Komebail Lagoon lag. Palau
29 G5	Köm Channel chan. Greece
15 A2	Kopychyntsi Ukraine
57 B3	Kor w Iran
28 C4	Korab mt. ra. Albania/Macedonia
14 E3	Korablino Rus. Fed.
80 E3	Koraf well Ethiopia
80 D3	K'orahē Ethiopia
25 E4	Kominternivs'ke Ukraine
26 F4	Komiza Croatia
19 J5	Komló Hungary
14 B2	Kommunar Rus. Fed.
65 L2	Kommunar Rus. Fed.
40 D4	Komodo i. Indon.
76 C5	Komodou Guinea
76 D5	Komoé r. Côte d'Ivoire
76 D5	Komoé r. Côte d'Ivoire
73 F3	Kôm Ombo Egypt
76 D5	Komono Congo
47 G5	Komoro Japan
29 E4	Komotini Greece
82 C5	Kompanyevka Ukraine
82 C5	Komsberg mts R.S.A.
63 M1	Komsomolets, O. i. Rus. Fed.
64 D3	Komsomolets, Zaliv b. Rus. Fed.
14 E1	Komsomol'sk Rus. Fed.
64 F5	Komsomol'sk Turkmenistan
15 E2	Komsomol's'k Ukraine
15 G2	Komsomol's'k Ukraine
13 H6	Komsomol'skiy Rus. Fed.
64 F5	Komsomol'skiy Rus. Fed.
45 P1	Komsomol'sk-na-Amure Rus. Fed.
64 F4	Komsomol'sk-na-Ustyurte Uzbekistan
48 D1	Komsomol'skoye Kazak.
14 H2	Komsomol'skoye Rus. Fed.
29 B4	Kolonjë Albania
14 G3	Kômürlü Turkey
129 F6	Kom Vo U.S.A.
28 B3	Kom Vojnik mts Yugo.
15 E1	Komyshnya Ukraine
15 F2	Komyshuvakha Ukraine
14 C1	Konakovo Rus. Fed.
76 C5	Konar r. Côte d'Ivoire
57 B3	Konār Takhteh Dālakī Iran
54 C2	Konda India
76 B5	Kondebela Sierra Leone
115 G3	Kondiaronk, Lac I. Can.
81 C5	Kondoa Tanzania
14 C1	Kondol' Rus. Fed.
12 E2	Kondopoga Rus. Fed.
14 E1	Kondrovo Rus. Fed.
19 H5	Körmend Hungary
61 B2	Kormakitis, C. c. Cyprus
19 H5	Kormilovka Rus. Fed.
55 G2	Körmend Hungary
13 J5	Korneyevka Rus. Fed.
15 C1	Kornyn Ukraine
90 □8	Koro i. Fiji
90 □4	Koro Mali
90 □4	Koro i. Fiji
55 C1	Koro r. India
19 M3	Koröğlu Tepesi mt. Turkey
81 C6	Korogwe Tanzania
97 E4	Koroit Aust.
15 D1	Korop Ukraine
29 C6	Koroni Greece
15 F2	Koronowo Poland
90 □6	Koro Sea sea Fiji
19 K5	Körösladány Hungary
15 C1	Korosten' Ukraine
15 C1	Korostyshiv Ukraine
90 □	Korotaere Fiji
77 H4	Koro Toro Chad
90 □1	Korovou Solomon Is.
90 □8	Korovou Fiji
11 G4	Korpilahti Finland
10 F3	Korpilombolo Sweden
11 F3	Korppoo Finland
49 E3	Korsakov Rus. Fed.
11 C5	Korsnäs Finland
15 D2	Korsun'-Shevchenkivs'kyy Ukraine

15 E1	Konotop Ukraine
43 E4	Kon Plong Vietnam
41 □1	Konrei Palau
19 K3	Końskie Poland
80 C3	Konso Ethiopia
49 H2	Konstantinovka Rus. Fed.
13 G6	Konstantinovsk Rus. Fed.
14 D1	Konstantinovskiy Rus. Fed.
18 D5	Konstanz Germany
77 F4	Kontagora Nigeria
42 B2	Kontha Myanmar
10 H3	Kontiolahti Finland
10 G2	Konttila Finland
43 D4	Kon Tum Vietnam
43 E4	Kon Tum, Plateau du plat. Vietnam
12 G1	Konushin, Mys pt Rus. Fed.
61 B1	Konya div. Turkey
60 C2	Konya Turkey
76 C4	Konyshevka Rus. Fed.
101 C6	Kookynie Aust.
127 □1	Koolau Range mt. ra. U.S.A.
98 D5	Koolivoo, L. salt flat Aust.
101 B6	Koolyanobbing Aust.
97 F3	Koondrook Aust.
96 C2	Koonibba Aust.
120 D5	Koon Lake I. U.S.A.
97 G3	Koorawatha Aust.
101 B6	Koorda Aust.
82 A3	Koosa waterhole Namibia
126 C2	Kooskia U.S.A.
110 F5	Kootenay r. Can./U.S.A.
110 F5	Kootenay L. I. Can.
110 F4	Kootenay Nat. Park nat. park Can.
28 C3	Kopaonik mt. ra. Yugo.
56 A2	Kopargaon India
77 E5	Kopargo Benin
10 M2	Köpasker Iceland
15 B2	Kopayhorod Ukraine
65 J3	Kopbirlik Kazak.
26 D3	Koper Slovenia
11 C4	Kopervik Norway
64 E5	Kopet Dag, Khrebet mt. ra. Turkmenistan
64 T1	Kopeysk Rus. Fed.
43 C5	Ko Phangan i. Thailand
43 B5	Ko Phra Thong i. Thailand
43 B6	Ko Phuket i. Thailand
11 E4	Köping Sweden
28 B3	Koplik Albania
10 E3	Köpmanholmen Sweden
14 B2	Koporka h. Rus. Fed.
56 B3	Koppal India
11 D4	Koppang Norway
11 D3	Kopparberg Sweden
11 D3	Kopparberg div. Sweden
26 F2	Koprivnica Croatia
60 B2	Köprü r. Turkey
57 G2	Korang r. Pakistan
54 A4	Korangi India
57 G1	Korān va Monjan Afghanistan
56 C2	Koraput India
76 D3	Korarou, Lac I. Mali
55 E5	Korba India
75 G1	Korba Tunisia
18 D3	Korbach Germany
78 C2	Korbol Chad
43 C6	Korbu, Gunung mt. Malaysia
29 B4	Korçë Albania
26 F4	Korčula i. Croatia
26 F4	Korčulanski Kanal chan. Croatia
57 A2	Kördestān div. Iran
57 C1	Kord Küy Iran
73 E4	Kordofan div. Sudan
57 E4	Kords reg. Iran
57 E4	Kord Sheykh Iran
49 G5	Korea Bay g. China/North Korea
46 B6	Korea Strait str. Japan/South Korea
76 D3	Koréba Burkina
76 D5	Koregaon India
14 E1	Korenevo Ethiopia
15 G1	Korenev Rus. Fed.
15 F1	Korenovsk Rus. Fed.
15 G1	Korets' Ukraine
72 B5	Korhogo Côte d'Ivoire
55 F1	Kori Creek r. India
29 D6	Korinthiakos Kolpos chan. Greece
29 D6	Korinthos Greece
19 H5	Köris-hegy mt. Hungary
54 E4	Köriyama Japan
10 E1	Korksdal Norway
80 B4	Korla China
44 □	Korlyaki mt. Rus. Fed.
61 B2	Kormakitis, C. c. Cyprus
19 H5	Körmend Hungary
13 J5	Korneyevka Rus. Fed.
15 C1	Kornyn Ukraine

19 K1	Korsze Poland
10 F3	Kortesjärvi Finland
73 F4	Korti Sudan
12 J2	Kortkeros Rus. Fed.
18 A3	Kortrijk Belgium
78 B4	Korup, Parc National de nat. park Cameroon
10 G2	Korvala Finland
54 D4	Korwai India
63 R4	Koryakskaya Sopka vol Rus. Fed.
63 S3	Koryakskiy Khrebet mt. ra. Rus. Fed.
29 F6	Korycin Poland
15 E1	Korynkivka Ukraine
62 H4	Korzhevka Rus. Fed.
29 E6	Kos i. Greece
29 F6	Kos i. Greece
13 E6	Kosa Arabats'ka Strilka spit Ukraine
15 D1	Kosachivka Ukraine
43 C5	Ko Samui i. Thailand
29 B3	Kosanica Gora Yugo.
28 E2	Koschagyl Kazak.
19 H2	Kościan Poland
19 H1	Kościerzyna Poland
125 F5	Kosciusko U.S.A.
110 C3	Kosciusko i. U.S.A.
97 G4	Kosciusko, Mt mt. Aust.
97 G4	Kosciusko National Park nat. park Aust.
60 D1	Köse Daği mt. Turkey
56 B2	Kosgi India
44 E2	Kosh-Agach Rus. Fed.
15 C2	Koshary Ukraine
46 B8	Koshikijima-retto is Japan
15 A1	Kovel' Ukraine
14 F1	Kovernino Rus. Fed.
56 B4	Kovilpatti India
28 C2	Kovin Yugo.
14 E1	Kovrov Rus. Fed.
15 F2	Kov"yahy Ukraine
14 E1	Kovylkino Rus. Fed.
12 F2	Kovzhskoye, Ozero I. Rus. Fed.
99 E2	Kowanyama Aust.
82 A2	Kowares waterhole Namibia
93 C5	Kowhitirangi N.Z.
114 B1	Kowkash r. Can.
45 □	Kowloon Hong Kong
45 □	Kowloon Pk h. Hong Kong
65 K5	Koxlax China
65 M2	Koxtag China
46 C5	Kōyama-misaki pt Japan
43 B5	Ko Yao Yai i. Thailand
60 B2	Köyceğiz Turkey
60 B2	Köyceğiz Gölü I. Turkey
14 D3	Koynare Bulgaria
56 A2	Koyna Res. resr India
14 E1	Koyoshi-gawa r. Japan
15 A2	Kozacha Lopan' Ukraine
46 B6	Kōzan-dō i. Japan
46 D6	Kōzan Japan
15 A2	Kozani Greece
29 B4	Kozara mt. ra. Bos.-Herz.
26 F2	Kozarac Bos.-Herz.
15 D1	Kozats'ke Ukraine
15 D1	Kozelets' Ukraine
14 E2	Kozel'shchyna Ukraine
14 D4	Kozel'sk Rus. Fed.
15 D4	Kozen well Chad
64 F3	Kozhabakhy Kazak.
65 G2	Kozhanka Ukraine
15 D2	Kozhevnikov Rus. Fed.
15 G1	Kozienice Poland
28 D3	Kozloduy Bulgaria
14 D2	Kozlovo Rus. Fed.
15 F2	Kozlovo Rus. Fed.
60 D1	Kozlu Turkey
19 H3	Koźmin Poland
19 J3	Koźmin Poland
12 G3	Kostroma Rus. Fed.
12 G3	Kostroma div. Rus. Fed.
29 G4	Kožuchów Poland
28 B4	Kožuf mts Greece/Macedonia
47 G6	Kōzu-shima i. Japan
15 F3	Koz"yatyn Ukraine
15 D2	Kozyryök Turkey
29 F4	Kozyörük Turkey
77 E5	Kpalimé Togo
77 E5	Kpandae Ghana
77 E5	Kpandu Ghana
43 B5	Krabi Thailand
43 C6	Kra Buri Thailand
19 H3	Krâchéh Cambodia
10 E2	Kradelse Sweden
15 E1	Kraftov Macedonia
11 C4	Kragerø Norway
28 C3	Kragujevac Yugo.
43 E5	Kra, Isthmus of isth. Thailand
19 K2	Krajenka Poland
43 A2	Krakatau i. Indon.
43 □	Krakôr Cambodia
15 F2	Kraków Poland
19 F4	Krakovets' Ukraine
19 J3	Krâlânh Cambodia
132 □1	Kralendijk Bonaire Netherlands Ant.
26 E3	Kraljevica Croatia
28 C3	Kraljevo Yugo.
19 G3	Kral'ova hol'a mt. Slovakia
19 G4	Kralovice Czech Rep.
19 F4	Královský Chlmec Slovakia
19 H4	Kralupy nad Vltavou Czech Rep.
15 E1	Kramators'k Ukraine
10 E3	Kramfors Sweden
29 G4	Kranidi Greece
26 E2	Kranj Slovenia
43 □	Kranji Reservoir resr Singapore
28 B3	Kranjska Gora Slovenia
28 B3	Kranjska Gora Slovenia
29 C5	Krikellos Greece
83 D3	Kril'on, Mys c. Rus. Fed.
45 D2	Krim-Krim Chad
26 E4	Krk Croatia
26 E4	Krk i. Croatia
26 E3	Krka r. Slovenia
26 F4	Krka r. Croatia
26 E4	Krško Slovenia
14 B3	Kruchi Rus. Fed.
15 E3	Krupanj Yugo.

78 B2	Koum Cameroon
78 C2	Kouma r. C.A.R.
90 □2	Koumac Pac. Oc.
99 B4	Koumala Aust.
78 B4	Koumbia Guinea
78 C2	Koumogo Chad
10 G2	Korvala Finland
76 B4	Koundâra Guinea
76 B4	Koundougou Burkina
29 F6	Koungheul r. Greece
76 B4	Koungheul Senegal
76 B4	Koupéla Burkina
76 B4	Kourak Burkina
76 B4	Kourak Burkina
76 C5	Kouradou mt. Guinea
76 C5	Kourayadjé Chad
76 B4	Kourémalé Mali
47 □2	Kouri-jima i. Japan
139 G2	Kourou French Guiana
76 B4	Kouroussa Guinea
72 C4	Kourtdi well Chad
76 B4	Koussanar Senegal
51 G1	Kousseri Cameroon
76 C4	Koutiala Mali
76 B4	Koutoumo i. Pac. Oc.
29 F5	Koutsomyti i. Greece
11 G3	Kouvola Finland
13 E6	Kouyou r. Congo
10 H2	Kovdozero, Oz. I. Rus. Fed.
15 A1	Kovel' Ukraine
14 F1	Kovernino Rus. Fed.
56 B4	Kovilpatti India
28 C2	Kovin Yugo.
14 E1	Kovrov Rus. Fed.
15 F2	Kov"yahy Ukraine
14 E1	Kovylkino Rus. Fed.
12 F2	Kovzhskoye, Ozero I. Rus. Fed.
99 E2	Kowanyama Aust.
82 A2	Kowares waterhole Namibia
93 C5	Kowhitirangi N.Z.
114 B1	Kowkash r. Can.
45 □	Kowloon Hong Kong
45 □	Kowloon Pk h. Hong Kong
65 K5	Koxlax China
65 M2	Koxtag China
46 C5	Kōyama-misaki pt Japan
43 B5	Ko Yao Yai i. Thailand

14 H2	Krasnoarmeyskoye Rus. Fed.
15 G2	Krasnoarmiys'k Ukraine
12 H2	Krasnoborsk Rus. Fed.
13 G6	Krasnobrodskiy Rus. Fed.
13 F6	Krasnodar div. Rus. Fed.
13 F6	Krasnodar Rus. Fed.
12 D3	Krasnogorodskoye Rus. Fed.
14 C2	Krasnogorsk Rus. Fed.
49 P1	Krasnogorskiy Rus. Fed.
64 F2	Krasnogorskiy Rus. Fed.
14 E1	Krasnogvardeyskiy Rus. Fed.
13 G6	Krasnogvardeyskoye Rus. Fed.
15 F2	Krasnohrad Ukraine
13 E6	Krasnohvardiys'ke Ukraine
49 F2	Krasnokamensk Rus. Fed.
15 A2	Krasnooktyabr'skiy Rus. Fed.
14 H1	Krasnooktyabr'skiy Rus. Fed.
15 G2	Krasnopavlivka Ukraine
13 E6	Krasnoperekops'k Ukraine
15 F1	Krasnopillya Ukraine
12 F1	Krasnoshchel'ye Rus. Fed.
15 B2	Krasnosilka Ukraine
64 B2	Krasnoslobodsk Rus. Fed.
14 G3	Krasnoslobodsk Rus. Fed.
18 F3	Krušné Hory mt. ra. Czech Rep.
62 H4	Krasnotur'insk Rus. Fed.
64 E1	Krasnousol'skiy Rus. Fed.
62 G3	Krasnovishersk Rus. Fed.
64 D4	Krasnovodsk Turkmenistan
64 D5	Krasnovodskiy Zaliv b. Turkmenistan
64 D5	Krasnovodsk, Mys pt Turkmenistan
64 D5	Krasnovodskoye Plato plat. Turkmenistan
64 E2	Krasnoyar Kazak.
62 L4	Krasnoyarsk Rus. Fed.
65 J2	Krasnoyarskoye Vdkhr. resr Rus. Fed.
14 D3	Krasnoye Rus. Fed.
15 E1	Krasnoye Ozero I. Ukraine
14 E1	Krasnoye Ekho Rus. Fed.
15 D2	Krasnoye-na-Volge Rus. Fed.
14 B1	Krasnoye Znamya Rus. Fed.
14 G1	Krasnoye Znamya Rus. Fed.
15 A2	Krasnoyil's'k Ukraine
12 J2	Krasnozatonskiy Rus. Fed.
15 D1	Krasnozavodsk Rus. Fed.
65 J2	Krasnozerskoye Rus. Fed.
14 C2	Kshen' r. Rus. Fed.
15 F2	Kzyl-Ordinskaya div. Kazak.
15 E2	Kozel'shchyna Ukraine
14 D3	Krasnyy Rus. Fed.
14 E1	Krasnyy Bogatyr' Rus. Fed.
15 G2	Krasnyy Chikoy Rus. Fed.
13 H6	Krasnyye Baki Rus. Fed.
14 H2	Krasnyye Barrikady Rus. Fed.
14 H2	Krasnyye Chetai Rus. Fed.
14 F1	Krasnyy Kholm Rus. Fed.
15 F1	Krasnyy Kolyadyn Ukraine
13 H5	Krasnyy Luch Rus. Fed.
15 F2	Krasnyy Lyman Ukraine
14 F1	Krasnyy Most Rus. Fed.
15 D1	Krasnyy Okyabr' Rus. Fed.
14 G4	Krasnyy Oktyabr' Rus. Fed.
14 D1	Krasnyy Profintern Rus. Fed.
14 H3	Krasnyy Rog Rus. Fed.
13 J5	Krasnyy Yar Rus. Fed.
15 F2	Krasnyy Yar Rus. Fed.
14 H3	Krasnyy Yar Rus. Fed.
15 F2	Krasyliv Ukraine
43 C6	Kratovo Macedonia
28 D4	Kratovo Macedonia
18 D4	Kraynovka r. Rus. Fed.
18 C4	Krefeld Germany
15 D1	Kremaston, Techniti Limni resr Greece
15 E2	Kremenchuk Ukraine
15 D2	Kremenchuts'ka Vodoskhovshche resr Ukraine
15 A2	Kremenets' Ukraine
15 D1	Kremennaya Ukraine
15 E3	Kremenki Rus. Fed.
14 E1	Kremnki Rus. Fed.
14 E1	Kremenki Rus. Fed.
15 F2	Kremsti r. Rus. Fed.
19 H2	Kretinga Lithuania
18 D4	Kreuth Germany
18 C4	Kreuzlingen Switz.
78 A3	Kribi Cameroon
28 E4	Krichim Bulgaria
12 G3	Krichim Bulgaria
126 F3	Kremmling U.S.A.
19 H4	Krems an der Donau Austria
19 H4	Kremsmünster Austria
117 Q3	Krenitzin Islands is U.S.A.
65 J1	Kreshchenka Rus. Fed.
11 B4	Kretinga Lithuania
11 C5	Kristiansand Norway
11 C5	Kristianstad Sweden
11 C4	Kristianstad div. Sweden
10 C3	Kristiansund Norway
10 E3	Kristinestad Sweden
11 C5	Kristinehamn Sweden
11 E3	Kristinestad Finland
29 E7	Kriti div. Greece
29 E7	Kriti i. Greece
49 H5	Krivoy Porog Rus. Fed.
29 B4	Kriva Palanka Macedonia
14 B3	Kriva r. Bos.-Herz.
62 K4	Kriva Palanka Macedonia
29 C5	Krivaja r. Bos.-Herz.
29 E4	Krivaja r. Yugo.

14 B3	Kroma r. Rus. Fed.
64 E2	Kromy Rus. Fed.
18 E3	Kronach Germany
43 C5	Krŏng Kaôh Kŏng Cambodia
10 E2	Kronoberg div. Sweden
10 F3	Kronoby Finland
109 Q1	Kronprins Christian Ld reg. Greenland
109 P3	Kronprins Frederik Bjerge nunatak Greenland
18 E1	Kronshagen Germany
42 B4	Kronwa Myanmar
82 D4	Kroonstad R.S.A.
13 G6	Kropotkin Rus. Fed.
19 K4	Krosno Poland
19 G2	Krosno Odrzańskie Poland
19 J3	Krotoszyn Poland
26 E3	Krško Slovenia
28 D3	Kruševac Yugo.
29 C4	Kruševo Macedonia
18 F3	Krušné Hory mt. ra. Czech Rep.
110 B3	Kruzof I. i. U.S.A.
14 E1	Krylov Ukraine
15 B1	Krylov Ukraine
13 F6	Krymsk Rus. Fed.
13 E6	Krym pen. Ukraine
15 E6	Kryms'ki Hori mt. ra. Ukraine
15 E2	Kryva Ruda Ukraine
14 D3	Kryvchunka Ukraine
15 E3	Kryve Ozero I. Ukraine
15 E3	Kryvyy Rih Ukraine
15 D2	Kryzhopil' Ukraine
19 J2	Krzyż Wielkopolski Poland
19 F2	Krzyż Wielkopolski Poland
75 E1	Ksabi Algeria
75 E1	Ksar Chellala Algeria
75 E1	Ksar el Boukhari Algeria
74 C1	Ksar el Kebir Morocco
24 D5	Ksar Sghir Morocco
62 G2	Ksenofontova Rus. Fed.
14 C2	Kshen' r. Rus. Fed.
75 D2	Ksour Essaf Tunisia
75 D2	Ksour, Monts des mts Algeria
15 D2	Kstovo Rus. Fed.
43 B6	Kuah Malaysia
43 C6	Kuala Kangsar Malaysia
43 C6	Kualakapuas Indon.
43 C6	Kuala Kerai Malaysia
43 C6	Kuala Kubu Baharu Malaysia
43 C6	Kuala Lipis Malaysia
43 C6	Kuala Lumpur Malaysia
43 C6	Kuala Nerang Malaysia
43 A6	Kualapembuang Indon.
43 C6	Kuala Pilah Malaysia
43 C6	Kuala Rompin Malaysia
43 A6	Kualasimpang Indon.
43 C6	Kuala Terengganu Malaysia
40 A2	Kualatungal Indon.
41 A5	Kuamut Malaysia
49 G5	Kuancheng China
43 C6	Kuantan Malaysia
13 H6	Kuban' r. Rus. Fed.
61 C2	Kubaybāt Syria
14 F1	Kubenskoye, Ozero I. Rus. Fed.
14 F1	Kubenskoye, Ozero I. Rus. Fed.
65 J2	Kubovo Rus. Fed.
29 F4	Kubrat Bulgaria
29 B4	Kučevo Yugo.
54 D5	Kuchaman India
14 F1	Kuchema Rus. Fed.
10 H2	Kuchevka Rus. Fed.
43 C6	Kuching Malaysia
14 C2	Kuchinskoye, salt I. Rus. Fed.
15 E2	Kuchurhan r. Ukraine
29 B4	Kuçurhan Albania
15 D2	Kudara-Somon Rus. Fed.
46 □2	Kudaka-jima i. Japan
56 B3	Kudal India
46 □2	Kudamatsu Japan
56 A3	Kudara India
40 D2	Kudat Malaysia
132 □1	Kudarebi Aruba Caribbean
62 K3	Kudrinskiy Rus. Fed.
13 J5	Kudymkar Rus. Fed.
43 A4	Kudus Indon.
62 H3	Kudymkar Rus. Fed.
19 G5	Kufstein Austria
55 E1	Kugaly Kazak.
111 H3	Kugmallit Bay b. Can.
43 C6	Kūhak Iran
57 D4	Kūhbonān Iran
57 C2	Kūh-e Sahand mt. Iran
57 B3	Kūh-e Sabalan mt. ra. Iran
57 B3	Kūhdasht Iran
57 C2	Kūh, Ra's pt Iran
10 J2	Kuhmo Finland
11 G3	Kuhmoinen Finland
92 □1	Kuian Island i. U.S.A.
92 □1	Kuivaniemi Finland
57 C2	Kuiseb Pass pass Namibia

65 J4	Kulanak Kyrgyzstan
64 E3	Kulandy Kazak.
57 E4	Kulaneh reg. Pakistan
57 F3	Kular r. Pakistan
65 J2	Kular Rus. Fed.
35 E1	Kulassein i. Phil.
43 C6	Kulai, G. mt. Indon.
11 H4	Kulaura Bangladesh
40 D2	Kulawi Indon.
11 F4	Kuldīga Latvia
11 F4	Kuldīga Latvia
14 F2	Kulebaki Rus. Fed.
54 D4	Kuleri Cambodia
13 G6	Kuleshi Rus. Fed.
15 C1	Kulevatovo Rus. Fed.
98 C4	Kulgera r. Aust.
14 H2	Kulikovo Rus. Fed.
43 C6	Kulim Malaysia
14 F1	Kulmyzh Rus. Fed.
101 B7	Kulin Aust.
65 H5	Kuli Sarez I. Tajikistan
11 D6	Kulja i. Aust.
57 F4	Kulduduk Uzbekistan
101 B6	Kulja Aust.
65 J1	Kulunda r. Rus. Fed.
54 D3	Kullu India
18 E3	Kulmbach Germany
12 D1	Kulovatovo Rus. Fed.
60 C2	Kulu Turkey
121 H4	Kulpsville U.S.A.
64 D3	Kul'sary Kazak.
48 D1	Kul'skiy Rus. Fed.
14 F1	Kulstvatk Rus. Fed.
29 C4	Kruševo Macedonia
18 F3	Krušné Hory mt. ra. Czech Rep.
64 E2	Kulunda r. Rus. Fed.
65 H1	Kulunda Rus. Fed.
65 J1	Krutoye Rus. Fed.
49 E2	Kuluntay Kazak.
15 E1	Krutoye Rus. Fed.
15 E1	Krutoye Ukraine
65 K2	Kulundinskaya Step' plain Kazak./Rus. Fed.
65 J2	Kulundinskoye, Oz. salt I. Rus. Fed.
64 B3	Kulusutay Rus. Fed.
57 B3	Kūlvand Iran
14 B3	Kulwin Aust.
97 F3	Kulwin Aust.
15 D1	Kulykivka Ukraine
49 H5	Kūm r. S. Korea
47 F7	Kumano Japan
46 D6	Kumamoto div. Japan
46 D6	Kumamoto Japan
93 C5	Kumara N.Z.
65 J2	Kumamovo Rus. Fed.
28 B4	Kumanovo Macedonia
93 C5	Kumara N.Z.
19 H2	Kumasi Ghana
76 D5	Kumasi Ghana
78 B4	Kumba Cameroon
56 B4	Kumbakonam India
57 C2	Kumel well Iran
12 J3	Kumeny Rus. Fed.
19 J5	Kumertau Rus. Fed.
75 D2	Kumguri India
49 J5	Kumi S. Korea
29 F5	Kumkale Turkey
64 F3	Kumkuduk well China
62 J3	Kummerower See I. Germany
77 G4	Kumo Nigeria
55 H3	Kumon Range mt. ra. Myanmar
42 A2	Kümphrawapi Thailand
43 C6	Kumta India
64 C4	Kumub Israel
14 H1	Kum'ya r. Rus. Fed.
98 C3	Kumyk w Aust.
29 F5	Kumzari Oman
65 J4	Kunashir, Ostrov i. Rus. Fed.
15 F1	Kumzari Oman
42 B3	Kunchaung Myanmar
55 H3	Kunchha Nepal
54 E5	Kunchuk Tso salt I. China
11 G4	Kunda Estonia
98 B2	Kunda-dia-Baze Angola
56 A3	Kundapura India
55 G4	Kundelungu, Monts mts Zaire
79 E6	Kundelungu, Parc National de nat. park Zaire
54 C1	Kundian Pakistan
54 D3	Kundla India
55 G4	Kunene div. Namibia
82 A2	Kunene r. Angola
24 G2	Kungälv Sweden
11 C4	Kungälv Sweden
65 K4	Kungei Alatau mt. ra. Kazak./Kyrgyzstan
79 C5	Kungu Zaire
12 J3	Kungur Rus. Fed.
42 B2	Kunhing Myanmar
55 H4	Kunhit Nepal
55 G1	Kunlun Shan mt. ra. China
13 G7	Kura r. Azerbaijan/Georgia

101 B4	Kurabuka r. Aust.
46 D6	Kurahashi-jima i. Japan
60 F1	Kurakh Rus. Fed.
15 G3	Kurakhove Ukraine
14 G3	Kurakino Rus. Fed.
49 J2	Kura Kurk chan. Estonia/Latvia
55 E5	Kurasia India
55 E5	Kurasia India
46 C6	Kurashiki Japan
65 L2	Kurayskiy Khr. mt. ra. Rus. Fed.
14 G3	Kurchatov Rus. Fed.
65 K3	Kurchum Kazak.
60 D1	Kürdämir Azerbaijan
57 F2	Kūr Dili pen. Azerbaijan
54 D3	Kurduvadi India
14 F1	Kurdyum Rus. Fed.
29 E4	Kŭrdzhali Bulgaria
46 D7	Kure Japan
60 C1	Küre Turkey
87 K3	Kure Atoll atoll U.S.A.
11 G4	Kuressaare Estonia
14 G3	Kurgan Rus. Fed.
13 G6	Kurgannaya Rus. Fed.
65 G3	Kurgasyn Kazak.
47 E5	Kuri Japan
64 F5	Kuri Afghanistan
29 E4	Kuri Japan
11 F3	Kurikka Finland
47 H4	Kurikoma-yama vol Japan
13 J5	Kurilovka Rus. Fed.
65 K2	Kuril'sk Rus. Fed.
63 C5	Kuril'skiye Ostrova is Rus. Fed.
14 B3	Kurkino Rus. Fed.
49 F1	Kurkeya Rus. Fed.
73 F4	Kurmuk Sudan
56 B3	Kurnool India
80 B2	Kuroki Rus. Fed.
47 G5	Kurobe Japan
46 E7	Kurogi Japan
46 H2	Kuroishi Japan
46 H2	Kuroiso Japan
46 H2	Kuromatsunai Japan
73 F3	Kuror, Jebel mt. Sudan
47 G4	Kurort-Darasun Rus. Fed.
49 F2	Kurort-Darasun Rus. Fed.
15 F2	Kurovskoy Rus. Fed.
14 D2	Kurovskoye Rus. Fed.
93 C6	Kurow N.Z.
54 B2	Kurram r. Afghanistan/Pakistan
97 G3	Kurri Kurri Aust.
97 G3	Kursavka Rus. Fed.
11 F5	Kursēla India
	Kuršių Marios b. Lithuania
14 C3	Kursk Rus. Fed.
14 C3	Kurskoye Vdkhr. resr Rus. Fed.
28 D3	Kuršumlija Yugo.
64 F3	Kurşunlu Turkey
60 C1	Kurtalan Turkey
29 F5	Kurtamysh Rus. Fed.
64 B3	Kurtoğlu Burnu pt Turkey
65 J4	Kuruçay r. Turkey
55 G4	Kuru w Sudan
15 C3	Kuruçay Turkey
44 □	Kurukshetra India
82 C3	Kuruman r. R.S.A.
82 C3	Kuruman R.S.A.
46 C7	Kurume Japan
45 H4	Kurun' r. Aust.
98 B3	Kurundi w Aust.
56 C5	Kurunegala Sri Lanka
58 C3	Kurush, Jebel h. Sudan
65 J5	Kur"ya Rus. Fed.
60 E3	Kuşadası Turkey
60 B2	Kuşadası Körfezi b. Turkey
14 C2	Kusawa Lake I. Can.
110 B2	Kusawa Lake I. Can.
14 H2	Kushalino Rus. Fed.
57 D3	Kūshānk Iran
47 H3	Kushida-gawa r. Japan
46 J2	Kushiro Japan
46 J2	Kushiro-Shitsugen National Park nat. park Japan
64 F5	Kushka r. Turkmenistan
64 F5	Kushka Turkmenistan
64 B3	Kushtia Bangladesh
55 G4	Kushtia Bangladesh
46 J2	Kushtih Rus. Fed.
57 E3	Kūshkī Iran
57 C3	Kūshk r. China
55 H4	Kushum r. Afghanistan
108 B4	Kuskokwim r. U.S.A.
108 B4	Kuskokwim Bay b. U.S.A.
108 B3	Kuskokwim Mountains mt. ra. U.S.A.
49 H5	Kusŏng N. Korea
15 D3	Kussharo-ko I. Japan
55 C3	Kustanay div. Kazak.
64 F2	Kustanay Kazak.
15 F2	Kustrovtsi Ukraine
92 E2	Kutaraaghe N.Z.
57 G1	Kutchan Japan
77 G5	Kutigi Nigeria
77 G5	Kutina Croatia
19 H3	Kutná Hora Czech Rep.
19 J3	Kutno Poland
79 B4	Kutu Zaire
72 B5	Kutubdia I. i. Bangladesh
72 D5	Kutum Sudan
15 E2	Kuty Ukraine
10 H2	Kuusamo Finland
11 G3	Kuusankoski Finland
14 H2	Kuvatka Finland
113 G4	Kuujjuaq Can.
113 F3	Kuujjuarapik Can.
64 F5	Kuʻurdzheyli Turkmenistan
13 H6	Kuvandyk Rus. Fed.
10 H2	Kuusamo Finland
11 G3	Kuusankoski Finland
79 B6	Kuvango Angola
14 E2	Kuvshinovo Rus. Fed.
51 F4	Kuwait country Asia
57 B4	Kuwait Kuwait
57 B4	Kuwana Japan
47 H4	Kuwana Japan
13 H5	Kuybyshev Rus. Fed.
65 J1	Kuybyshev Rus. Fed.
15 F3	Kuybysheve Zaporizhzhya Ukraine
15 E1	Kuybysheve Zaporizhzhya Ukraine
65 K4	Kuytun China
139 F3	Kuyuwini r. Guyana
60 E1	Kuzey Anadolu Daglari mt. ra. Turkey
14 F1	Kuzomen' Rus. Fed.
15 F1	Kuzemyn Ukraine

57 E2 Mandal Afghanistan
54 C4 Mandal India
48 C2 Mandal Mongolia
11 B4 Mandal Norway
39 M7 Mandala, Pk mt. Indon.
42 A2 Mandalay div. Myanmar
42 B2 Mandalay Myanmar
48 C3 Mandalgovĭ Mongolia
60 F3 Mandalī Iraq
48 E3 Mandalt Sum China
124 C2 Mandan U.S.A.
41 B3 Mandaon Phil.
78 C2 Manda, Parc National de nat. park Chad
78 B1 Mandara Mountains mts Cameroon/Nigeria
40 D2 Mandar, Teluk b. Indon.
27 B6 Mandas Italy
26 B3 Mandello del Lario Italy
80 D4 Mandera Kenya
129 F2 Manderfield U.S.A.
133 □1 Mandeville Jamaica
93 B6 Mandeville N.Z.
54 B4 Mandha India
80 D3 Mandheera Somalia
54 D3 Mandi India
76 D4 Mandiakui Mali
76 C4 Mandiana Guinea
54 C3 Mandi Burewala Pakistan
83 E2 Mandié Mozambique
83 F1 Mandimba Mozambique
76 C4 Manding, Mts mts Mali
141 E3 Mandioré, Lagoa l. Bolivia
55 F5 Mandira Dam India
78 B4 Mandji Gabon
54 E5 Mandla India
40 B1 Mandor Indon.
83 H2 Mandoro Madagascar
77 E4 Mandouri Togo
83 H3 Mandrare r. Madagascar
83 H2 Mandritsara Madagascar
54 C4 Mandsaur India
101 A7 Mandurah Aust.
27 F5 Manduria Italy
54 C5 Mandvi India
54 B5 Mandvi India
56 B3 Mandya India
41 □2 Manell Pt pt Guam Pac. Oc.
56 B2 Maner r. India
26 C3 Manerbio Italy
15 A1 Manevychi Ukraine
73 F2 Manfalūt Egypt
27 E5 Manfredonia Italy
27 F5 Manfredonia, Golfo di g. Italy
145 G1 Manga Brazil
76 D4 Manga Burkina
79 C4 Mangai Zaire
151 J7 Mangaia i. Cook Islands Pac. Oc.
92 E3 Mangakino N.Z.
56 C2 Mangalagiri India
55 H4 Mangaldai India
28 G3 Mangalia Romania
72 C5 Mangalmé Chad
56 A3 Mangalore India
56 A2 Mangalvedha India
55 G4 Mangan India
56 C2 Mangapet India
41 C6 Mangarang Indon.
82 D4 Mangaung R.S.A.
92 F3 Mangaweka mt. N.Z.
92 E3 Mangaweka N.Z.
55 G4 Mangde r. Bhutan
79 E4 Mangembe Zaire
16 K1 Manger Norway
93 □1 Mangere I. i. Chatham Is N.Z.
40 B2 Manggar Indon.
41 □2 Mangilao Guam Pac. Oc.
64 D4 Mangistauz Kazak.
64 F4 Mangit Uzbekistan
40 D1 Mangkalihat, Tg pt Indon.
40 C2 Mangkutup r. Indon.
42 B1 Mangkyi Myanmar
44 F4 Mangnai China
83 F1 Mangochi Malawi
76 D5 Mangodara Burkina
83 G3 Mangoky r. Toliara Madagascar
83 H3 Mangoky r. Toliara Madagascar
39 J7 Mangole i. Indon.
92 D1 Mangonui N.Z.
83 H2 Mangoro r. Madagascar
54 B5 Māngral India
54 D4 Mangrol India
132 C1 Mangrove Cay The Bahamas
24 C2 Mangualde Portugal
54 A3 Manguchar Pakistan
78 D1 Mangueigne Chad
146 F3 Mangueira, L. l. Brazil
143 B6 Mangueirinha Brazil
77 G2 Manguéni, Plateau du plat. Niger
142 C3 Mangues r. Brazil
49 G1 Mangui China
142 E3 Manguinha, Pontal do pt Brazil
41 C5 Mangupung i. Indon.
48 E2 Mangut Rus. Fed.
64 D4 Mangyshlak Kazak.
64 D4 Mangyshlak, Pov. pen. Kazak.
64 D4 Mangyshlakskiy Zal. b. Kazak.
48 A2 Manhan Mongolia
124 D4 Manhattan U.S.A.
128 D2 Manhattan U.S.A.
83 E4 Manhiça Mozambique
145 H3 Manhuaçu r. Brazil
145 G4 Manhuaçu Brazil
145 H4 Manhumirim Brazil
138 C3 Mani Colombia
83 H3 Mania r. Madagascar
26 D2 Maniago Italy
81 B7 Maniamba Mozambique
83 E2 Manica div. Mozambique
83 E2 Manicaland div. Zimbabwe
139 E5 Manicoré Brazil
113 G3 Manicouagan Can.
113 G3 Manicouagan r. Can.
113 G3 Manicougan, Réservoir resr Can.
57 B4 Manīfah Saudi Arabia
99 G4 Manifold, C. pt Aust.
50 B2 Maniganggo China
55 F4 Manihari India
91 □10 Manihi i. Fr. Poly. Pac. Oc.
150 J6 Manihiki atoll Cook Islands Pac. Oc.
109 N3 Maniitsoq Greenland
79 E6 Manika, Plateau de la plat. Zaire
55 G5 Manikganj Bangladesh
54 E4 Manikpur India
41 B3 Manila Phil.
126 E3 Manila U.S.A.
41 B3 Manila Bay b. Phil.
97 G3 Manildra Aust.
97 G2 Manilla Aust.
40 D2 Manimbaya, Tg pt Indon.
98 C2 Maningrida Aust.
90 □3 Maninita i. Tonga
55 H4 Manipur India
55 H4 Manipur r. India/Myanmar
29 F5 Manisa div. Turkey
60 A2 Manisa Turkey
25 F3 Manises Spain
17 E4 Man, Isle of terr. Europe
40 B2 Manismata Indon.
142 B3 Manissauá Missu r. Brazil
122 D3 Manistee U.S.A.
122 E3 Manistee r. U.S.A.
122 D3 Manistique U.S.A.
122 E2 Manistique Lake l. U.S.A.
112 B2 Manitoba div. Can.
108 J4 Manitoba, Lake l. Can.
111 H4 Manito L. l. Can.
111 K5 Manitou Can.
120 E3 Manitou Beach U.S.A.
112 B3 Manitou Falls Can.
122 D2 Manitou Island i. U.S.A.
118 C2 Manitou Islands is U.S.A.
114 E4 Manitou, Lake l. Can.
114 E4 Manitoulin I. i. Can.
114 C2 Manitouwadge Can.
114 E4 Manitowaning Can.
114 C2 Manitowik Lake l. Can.
122 D3 Manitowoc U.S.A.
115 H3 Maniwaki Can.
138 B2 Manizales Colombia
83 G3 Manja Madagascar
83 H2 Manjak Madagascar
73 F3 Manjam Umm Qurayyāt waterhole Egypt
56 B4 Manjeri India
57 G4 Manjhand Pakistan
101 B7 Manjimup Aust.
78 A3 Manjo Cameroon
56 B2 Manjra r. India
42 B1 Man Kabat Myanmar
55 G4 Mankachar India
124 E2 Mankato U.S.A.
54 B3 Mankera Pakistan
78 B2 Mankim Cameroon
15 D2 Man'kivka Ukraine
76 C5 Mankono Côte d'Ivoire
56 C4 Mankulam Sri Lanka
42 B1 Manlc Myanmar
25 H2 Manlleu Spain
54 C5 Manmad India
98 C2 Mann r. Aust.
42 B2 Man Na Myanmar
96 D3 Mannahill Aust.
56 B4 Mannar Sri Lanka
56 B4 Mannar, Gulf of g. India/Sri Lanka
56 B3 Manneru r. India
18 D4 Mannheim Germany
97 G2 Manning r. Aust.
110 F3 Manning Can.
119 D5 Manning U.S.A.
96 B1 Mann Ranges mt. ra. Aust.
27 B6 Mannu r. Italy
27 B5 Mannu, Capo pt Italy
96 D3 Mannum Aust.
76 B5 Mano r. Liberia/Sierra Leone
76 B5 Mano Sierra Leone
140 C1 Manoa Bolivia
133 □2 Man of War B. b. Tobago Trin. and Tobago
54 D4 Manohar Thana India
39 K7 Manokwari Indon.
28 E1 Manoleasa Romania
83 G3 Manombo Atsimo Madagascar
83 H2 Manompana Madagascar
79 E5 Manono Zaire
76 B5 Mano River Liberia
43 B5 Manoron Myanmar
21 G5 Manosque France
115 H3 Manouane Can.
115 H3 Manouane, Lac l. Can.
42 B2 Man Pan Myanmar
49 H4 Manp'o N. Korea
150 H6 Manra i. Kiribati
25 G2 Manresa Spain
54 C3 Mānsa India
79 E6 Mansa Zambia
76 A4 Mansabá Guinea-Bissau
76 A4 Mansa Konko The Gambia
54 C2 Mansehra Pakistan
109 K3 Mansel I. i. Can.
97 F4 Mansfield Aust.
17 G5 Mansfield U.K.
125 E5 Mansfield U.S.A.
120 B4 Mansfield U.S.A.
120 E4 Mansfield U.S.A.
42 A1 Mansi Myanmar
76 A4 Mansôa Guinea-Bissau
110 E3 Manson Creek Can.
138 A4 Manta Ecuador
138 A4 Manta, B. de b. Ecuador
41 A4 Mantalingajan, Mount mt. Phil.
49 J4 Mantapsan mt. N. Korea
128 B3 Manteca U.S.A.
138 D2 Mantecal Venezuela
145 H3 Mantena Brazil
119 F5 Manteo U.S.A.
20 E2 Mantes-la-Jolie France
56 B2 Manthani India
129 G2 Manti U.S.A.
122 E3 Manton U.S.A.
29 D5 Mantoudi Greece
26 C3 Mantova Italy
11 G3 Mäntsälä Finland
11 G3 Mänttä Finland
26 C3 Mantua Italy
99 F5 Mantuan Downs Aust.
12 H3 Manturovo Rus. Fed.
15 G1 Manturovo Rus. Fed.
11 G3 Mäntyharju Finland
10 G2 Mäntyjärvi Finland
140 B2 Manú Peru
91 □13 Manua Is is American Samoa Pac. Oc.
142 C3 Manuel Alves r. Brazil
142 C2 Manuel Alves Grande r. Brazil
142 C2 Manuel Alves Pequeno r. Brazil
129 H4 Manuelito U.S.A.
144 C6 Manuel Ribas Brazil
147 B7 Manuel Rodriguez, I. i. Chile
140 C1 Manuel Urbano Brazil
142 B2 Manuelzinho Brazil
91 □10 Manuhangi i. Fr. Poly. Pac. Oc.
39 H7 Manui i. Indon.
57 D4 Manūjān Iran
41 B4 Manukan Phil.
92 E2 Manukau N.Z.
92 E2 Manukau Harbour inlet N.Z.
41 A5 Manuk Manka i. Phil.
96 D3 Manunda w Aust.
140 B2 Manu, Parque Nacional nat. park Peru
90 □1 Manus I. i. P.N.G.
56 B3 Manvi India
83 E2 Manyame r. Mozambique/Zimbabwe
83 E2 Manyame, Lake l. Zimbabwe
81 C5 Manyara, Lake salt l. Tanzania
29 F4 Manyas Turkey
13 G6 Manych-Gudilo, Ozero l. Rus. Fed.
129 H3 Many Farms U.S.A.
15 B2 Manykivtsi Ukraine
81 B6 Manyoni Tanzania
83 E3 Manyuchi Dam dam Zimbabwe
54 B2 Manzai Pakistan
24 E3 Manzanares Spain
133 □3 Manzanilla Bay b. Trinidad Trin. and Tobago
133 □3 Manzanilla Pt pt Trinidad Trin. and Tobago
132 C2 Manzanillo Cuba
130 D5 Manzanillo Mexico
130 L7 Manzanillo, Pta pt Panama
79 E5 Manzanza Zaire
57 B2 Manẓariyeh Iran
49 F2 Manzhouli China
61 D4 Manzil Jordan
83 E4 Manzini Swaziland
72 C5 Mao Chad
25 J3 Maó Spain
48 C5 Maojiachuan China
82 D4 Maokeng R.S.A.
48 B5 Maomao Shan mt. China
51 E4 Maoming China
45 □ Ma On Shan h. Hong Kong
50 C3 Maotou Shan mt. China
83 E3 Mapai Mozambique
55 E3 Mapam Yumco l. China
40 E2 Mapane Indon.
130 E3 Mapimí Mexico
41 A5 Mapin i. Phil.
83 F3 Mapinhane Mozambique
139 E2 Mapire Venezuela
140 C3 Mapiri Bolivia
122 E4 Maple r. U.S.A.
111 H5 Maple Creek Can.
99 E1 Mapoon Aust.
99 E2 Mapoon Abor. Reserve res. Aust.
40 A1 Mapor i. Indon.
90 □1 Maprik P.N.G.
139 F4 Mapuera r. Brazil
83 E3 Mapulanguene Mozambique
83 E4 Maputo div. Mozambique
83 E4 Maputo Mozambique
83 E4 Maputo r. Mozambique/R.S.A.
60 D4 Maqar an Na'am well Iraq
50 C1 Maqên China
50 B1 Maqên Gangri mt. China
65 L4 Maqiao China
61 C5 Maqla, J. al mt. Saudi Arabia
61 C5 Maqnā Saudi Arabia
74 B4 Maqṭeïr reg. Mauritania
50 C1 Maqu China
55 E3 Maquan r. China
41 C3 Maqueda Channel chan. Phil.
79 C5 Maquela do Zombo Angola
147 C5 Maquinchao r. Arg.
147 C5 Maquinchao Arg.
122 B4 Maquoketa r. U.S.A.
122 B4 Maquoketa U.S.A.
54 A4 Mar r. Pakistan
111 H1 Mara r. Can.
139 F2 Mara Guyana
55 E5 Māra India
83 D3 Mara R.S.A.
81 B5 Mara div. Tanzania
138 C1 Mara Venezuela
139 D4 Maraã Brazil
91 □11 Maraa Fr. Poly. Pac. Oc.
142 C2 Maraba Brazil
144 C5 Marabá Paulista Brazil
40 C3 Marabatua is Indon.
99 F4 Maraboon, L. resr Aust.
139 G3 Maracá r. Brazil
142 C1 Maracaçumé r. Brazil
144 C5 Maracaí Brazil
138 C1 Maracaibo Venezuela
138 C2 Maracaibo, Lago de l. Venezuela
139 D4 Maracaí, Lago de l. Brazil
139 G3 Maracá, Ilha de i. Brazil
144 A4 Maracaju Brazil
141 E4 Maracaju, Sa de h. Paraguay
142 C1 Maracanã Brazil
133 □3 Maracas B. b. Trinidad Trin. and Tobago
138 D1 Maracay Venezuela
72 C2 Marādah Libya
77 F4 Maradi Niger
77 F4 Maradi div. Niger
60 F2 Marāgheh Iran
142 E3 Maragogipe Brazil
41 B3 Maragondon Phil.
139 D3 Marahuaca, Co mt. Venezuela
142 C1 Marajó, Baía de est. Brazil
142 B1 Marajó, Ilha de i. Brazil
56 B3 Marakkanam India
81 C4 Maralal Kenya
78 C2 Marali C.A.R.
96 B2 Maralinga Aust.
90 □1 Maramasike i. Solomon Is.
41 C5 Marampit i. Indon.
28 E1 Maramuresului, Munții mt. ra. Romania
43 C7 Maran Malaysia
129 G5 Marana U.S.A.
60 F2 Marand Iran
43 C6 Marang Malaysia
43 B5 Marang Myanmar
142 E1 Maranguape Brazil
142 C1 Maranhão div. Brazil
142 C3 Maranhão r. Brazil
99 G5 Maranoa r. Aust.
138 B4 Marañón r. Peru
20 D3 Marans France
76 C5 Maraoué r. Côte d'Ivoire
76 C5 Maraoué, Parc National de la nat. park Côte d'Ivoire
142 C1 Marapanim Brazil
138 D5 Marari Brazil
93 A6 Mararoa r. N.Z.
40 D3 Marasende i. Indon.
28 F2 Mărășești Romania
114 B2 Marathon Can.
119 D7 Marathon U.S.A.
125 C6 Marathon U.S.A.
29 D5 Marathonas Greece
142 E3 Maraú Brazil
40 B2 Marau Indon.
133 □3 Maraval Trin. and Tobago
41 C4 Marawi Phil.
24 D4 Marbella Spain
100 B4 Marble Bar Aust.
129 G3 Marble Canyon gorge U.S.A.
129 G3 Marble Canyon U.S.A.
83 D3 Marble Hall R.S.A.
121 H3 Marblehead U.S.A.
111 L2 Marble I. i. Can.
21 G3 Marboz France
54 C2 Marbul Pass pass India
18 D3 Marburg Germany
83 E5 Marburg R.S.A.
120 E5 Marburg, Lake l. U.S.A.
19 H5 Marcali Hungary
79 B7 Marca, Pta do pt Angola
17 H5 March U.K.
54 E3 Marcha India
20 E3 Marche reg. France
26 D4 Marche div. Italy
18 B3 Marche-en-Famenne Belgium
24 D4 Marchena Spain
138 □ Marchena, I. i. Galapagos Is Ecuador
20 E3 Marche, Plateaux de la plat. France
133 □9 Marchfield Barbados Caribbean
146 D3 Mar Chiquita, L. l. Arg.
19 G4 Marchtrenk Austria
119 D7 Marco U.S.A.
141 E2 Marcolino r. Brazil
140 A3 Marcona Peru
112 E2 Marcopeet Islands is Can.
146 D3 Marcos Juárez Arg.
121 G2 Marcy, Mt mt. U.S.A.
54 C2 Mardan Pakistan
146 E4 Mar del Plata Arg.
100 A4 Mardie Aust.
60 E2 Mardin Turkey
48 B3 Mardzad Mongolia
90 □2 Maré i. Pac. Oc.
26 D4 Marecchia r. Italy
144 A6 Marechal Cândido Rondon Brazil
25 J3 Mare de Déu del Toro h. Spain
99 F3 Mareeba Aust.
16 E3 Maree, Loch l. U.K.
26 C4 Maremma reg. Italy
122 C4 Marengo U.S.A.
122 A5 Marengo U.S.A.
20 D4 Marennes France
27 D7 Marettimo, Isola i. Italy
20 D3 Mareuil-sur-Lay-Dissais France
14 A1 Marevo Rus. Fed.
125 B6 Marfa U.S.A.
55 F2 Margai Caka salt l. China
96 D2 Margaret w Aust.
100 D3 Margaret r. Aust.
101 A7 Margaret River Aust.
139 E1 Margarita, I. de i. Venezuela
17 H6 Margate U.K.
21 F4 Margeride, Monts de la mts France
55 H4 Margherita India
28 D1 Marghita Romania
65 H4 Margilan Uzbekistan
28 E1 Marginea Romania
41 B5 Margosatubig Phil.
122 E3 Margrethe, Lake l. U.S.A.
110 E4 Marguerite Can.
152 B2 Marguerite Bay b. Ant.
55 G3 Margyang China
15 F3 Marhanets' Ukraine
75 D2 Marhoum Algeria
42 B1 Mari Myanmar
144 A4 Maria r. Brazil
130 D4 María Cleofas, I. i. Mexico
140 C4 María Elena Chile
98 C2 Maria I. i. Aust.
97 G5 Maria I. i. Aust.
151 J7 Maria, Îles is Fr. Poly. Pac. Oc.
130 D4 María Madre, I. i. Mexico
130 D4 María Magdalena, I. i. Mexico
99 G4 Marian Aust.
145 G4 Mariana Brazil
132 B2 Marianao Cuba
150 E4 Marianas Ridge Pac. Oc.
150 E5 Marianas Tr. Pac. Oc.
55 H4 Mariani India
110 F2 Marian Lake l. Can.
125 F5 Marianna U.S.A.
119 C6 Marianna U.S.A.
146 E2 Mariano Loza Arg.
18 F4 Mariánské Lázně Czech Rep.
130 D4 Marías, Islas is Mexico
130 K8 Mariato, Pta pt Panama
92 D1 Maria van Diemen, Cape c. N.Z.
19 G5 Mariazell Austria
80 E1 Ma'rib Yemen
26 E2 Maribor Slovenia
129 F5 Maricopa U.S.A.
128 C4 Maricopa U.S.A.
129 F5 Maricopa Mts mts U.S.A.
78 E3 Maridi Sudan
78 E2 Maridi w Sudan
81 □1 Marie-Anne I. i. Seychelles
152 A4 Marie Byrd Land reg. Ant.
133 □5 Marie Galante i. Guadeloupe Caribbean
11 E3 Mariehamn Finland
14 H1 Mari-El div. Rus. Fed.
142 B3 Mariembero r. Brazil
82 B3 Mariental Namibia
11 D4 Mariestad Sweden
119 C5 Marietta U.S.A.
120 C5 Marietta U.S.A.
21 G5 Marignane France
152 □ Marigny, C. c. Kerguelen Indian Ocean
133 G3 Marigot Guadeloupe Caribbean
133 □4 Marigot Martinique Caribbean
11 F5 Marijampolė Lithuania
144 D5 Marília Brazil
100 B4 Marillana Aust.
144 B6 Mariluz Brazil
139 F4 Marimari r. Brazil
79 C5 Marimba Angola
40 C2 Marimun Indon.
125 C7 Marin Mexico
24 B1 Marín Spain
27 F6 Marina di Gioiosa Ionica Italy
12 D4 Mar"ina Horka Belarus
41 B3 Marinduque i. Phil.
122 D3 Marinette U.S.A.
144 C5 Maringá Brazil
78 D3 Maringa r. Zaire
83 E2 Maringué Mozambique
24 B3 Marinha Grande Portugal
118 B4 Marion U.S.A.
122 E5 Marion U.S.A.
121 K2 Marion U.S.A.
120 B4 Marion U.S.A.
119 E5 Marion U.S.A.
120 C6 Marion U.S.A.
98 D4 Marion Downs Aust.
119 D5 Marion, L. l. U.S.A.
99 H3 Marion Reef reef Coral Sea Islands Terr. Pac. Oc.
139 D2 Maripa Venezuela
139 G3 Maripasoula French Guiana
128 C3 Mariposa U.S.A.
141 D4 Mariscal Estigarribia Paraguay
28 E1 Mărișelu Romania
28 E3 Maritsa r. Bulgaria
15 G3 Mariupol' Ukraine
60 F3 Marīvān Iran
61 C3 Marjayoûn Lebanon
80 D4 Marka Somalia
65 L3 Markakol', Oz. l. Kazak.
76 C4 Markala Mali
50 B2 Markam China
56 B3 Markapur India
11 D4 Markaryd Sweden
57 B2 Markazī div. Iran
114 E4 Markdale Can.
17 F5 Market Drayton U.K.
17 G5 Market Harborough U.K.
17 G5 Market Weighton U.K.
63 O3 Markha r. Rus. Fed.
115 F5 Markham Can.
152 B4 Markham, Mt mt. Ant.
65 J5 Markit China
29 D6 Markopoulo Greece
78 C2 Markounda C.A.R.
14 E1 Markovo Rus. Fed.
63 T3 Markovo Rus. Fed.
15 F1 Markovo Rus. Fed.
77 E4 Markoye Burkina
14 H4 Marks Rus. Fed.
18 D4 Marktheidenfeld Germany
18 E5 Marktoberdorf Germany
18 F3 Marktredwitz Germany
122 B6 Mark Twain Lake l. U.S.A.
18 C3 Marl Germany
96 C1 Marla Aust.
99 G4 Marlborough Aust.
93 D4 Marlborough div. N.Z.
121 H3 Marlborough U.S.A.
21 F2 Marle France
125 D6 Marlin U.S.A.
120 C5 Marlinton U.S.A.
97 G4 Marlo Aust.
20 E4 Marmande France
29 F4 Marmara Turkey
29 F5 Marmara Adası i. Turkey
60 B1 Marmara Denizi sea Turkey
29 F4 Marmaraereğlisi Turkey
60 B2 Marmaris Turkey
124 C2 Marmarth U.S.A.
25 F4 Mar Menor lag. Spain
120 C5 Marmet U.S.A.
112 B4 Marmion L. l. Can.
101 C6 Marmion, Lake salt pan Aust.
26 C2 Marmolada mt. Italy
24 D3 Marmolejo Spain
131 G5 Mar Muerto l. Mexico
21 G2 Marne r. France
18 D2 Marne Germany
20 F2 Marne-la-Vallée France
78 C2 Maro Chad
83 H2 Maroantsetra Madagascar
145 J2 Maroba r. Brazil
91 □10 Marokau i. Fr. Poly. Pac. Oc.
54 D2 Marol Pakistan
65 J6 Marol Jammu and Kashmir
83 H3 Marolambo Madagascar
83 H1 Maromokotro mt. Madagascar
83 H1 Maromony, Lohatanjona hd Madagascar
83 E2 Marondera Zimbabwe
139 G3 Maroni r. French Guiana
20 F4 Maronne r. France
99 H5 Maroochydore Aust.
133 □1 Maroon Town Jamaica
40 D3 Maros Indon.
83 H2 Maroseranana Madagascar
19 K5 Maros-Körös Köze plain Hungary
87 N7 Marotiri is Fr. Poly. Pac. Oc.
83 H1 Marotolana Madagascar
78 B1 Maroua Cameroon
139 G3 Marouini r. French Guiana
83 H2 Marovoay Madagascar
139 G2 Marowijne r. Surinam
60 E3 Marqādah Syria
50 C1 Mar Qu r. China
119 D7 Marquesas Keys is U.S.A.
122 D2 Marquette U.S.A.
20 E1 Marquise France
151 K6 Marquises, Îles is Fr. Poly. Pac. Oc.
97 F2 Marra r. Aust.
83 E4 Marracuene Mozambique
74 C2 Marrakech Morocco
83 E3 Marrangua, L. l. Mozambique
72 D5 Marra Plateau plat. Sudan
97 F5 Marrawah Aust.
142 D2 Marrecas, Sa das h. Brazil
96 D2 Marree Aust.
125 F6 Marrero U.S.A.
83 F2 Marromeu Mozambique
83 F2 Marromeu, Reserva de res. Mozambique
81 C7 Marrupa Mozambique
73 F2 Marsa Alam Egypt
72 C1 Marsa al Burayqah Libya
80 C4 Marsabit Kenya
80 C4 Marsabit National Reserve res. Kenya
61 C5 Marsa Dahab b. Egypt
27 D7 Marsala Italy
72 E1 Marsa Matrûh Egypt
76 A4 Marsassoum Senegal
82 A4 Mars Bay b. Ascension Atlantic Ocean
18 D3 Marsberg Germany
26 D4 Marsciano Italy
97 F3 Marsden Aust.
21 G5 Marseille France
122 C5 Marseilles U.S.A.
10 D2 Marsfjället mt. Sweden
98 D4 Marshall w Aust.
111 H4 Marshall Can.
76 B5 Marshall Liberia
125 E5 Marshall U.S.A.
118 C4 Marshall U.S.A.
122 E4 Marshall U.S.A.
124 E2 Marshall U.S.A.
124 E4 Marshall U.S.A.
125 E5 Marshall U.S.A.
97 F4 Marshall B. b. Aust.
86 H3 Marshall Islands country Pac. Oc.
114 B1 Marshall Lake l. Can.
124 E3 Marshalltown U.S.A.
122 B3 Marshfield U.S.A.
132 C1 Marsh Harbour The Bahamas
121 K1 Mars Hill U.S.A.
125 F6 Marsh Island i. U.S.A.
110 C2 Marsh Lake l. Can.
126 C3 Marsing U.S.A.
11 E4 Märsta Sweden
55 F3 Marsyangdi r. Nepal
42 B3 Martaban Myanmar
42 B3 Martaban, Gulf of g. Myanmar
40 A3 Martapura Indon.
40 C2 Martapura Indon.
115 F3 Marten River Can.
111 H4 Martensville Can.
121 H4 Martha's Vineyard i. U.S.A.
21 H3 Martigny Switz.
19 J4 Martin Slovakia
25 F2 Martín r. Spain
124 C3 Martin U.S.A.
119 B4 Martin U.S.A.
27 F5 Martina Franca Italy
25 G1 Martinet Spain
131 F4 Martínez Mexico
130 D3 Martínez, E. Mexico
129 E5 Martinez Lake U.S.A.
145 F3 Martinho Campos Brazil
104 M8 Martinique terr. Caribbean
133 G4 Martinique Passage chan. Dominica/Martinique
119 C5 Martin, L. l. U.S.A.
29 D5 Martino Greece
142 D1 Martinópole Brazil
144 C5 Martinópolis Brazil
152 A3 Martin Pen. pen. Ant.
93 A6 Martins Bay b. N.Z.
120 D4 Martinsburg U.S.A.
120 E5 Martinsburg U.S.A.
120 C4 Martins Ferry U.S.A.
120 D6 Martinsville U.S.A.
148 H7 Martin Vas, Ilhas is Atlantic Ocean
92 E4 Marton N.Z.
25 G2 Martorell Spain
24 E4 Martos Spain
110 F2 Martre, Lac la l. Can.
64 E2 Martuk Kazak.
15 C1 Martynovychi Ukraine
57 E2 Maruchak Afghanistan
41 A5 Marudu, Tk b. Malaysia
46 D6 Marugame Japan
93 D5 Maruia r. N.Z.
142 E3 Maruim Brazil
90 □2 Marum, Mt mt. Vanuatu
54 B4 Marusthali reg. India
91 □10 Marutéa i. Fr. Poly. Pac. Oc.
57 C3 Marvast Iran
21 F4 Marvejols France
129 G2 Marvine, Mt mt. U.S.A.
54 C4 Marwar Jct India
111 G4 Marwayne Can.
98 B2 Mary r. Aust.
64 F5 Mary div. Turkmenistan
64 F5 Mary Turkmenistan
15 G3 Mar"yanivka Zaporizhzhya Ukraine
15 B1 Mar"yanivka Zhytomyr Ukraine
65 H2 Mar'yanovka Rus. Fed.
99 H5 Maryborough Aust.
97 E4 Maryborough Aust.
82 C4 Marydale R.S.A.
14 H3 Mar'yevka Rus. Fed.
111 H2 Mary Frances Lake l. Can.
15 G3 Mar"yinka Ukraine
121 E5 Maryland div. U.S.A.
28 E1 Marynychi Ukraine
17 F4 Maryport U.K.
113 J3 Mary's Harbour Can.
113 K4 Marystown Can.
129 F2 Marysvale U.S.A.
113 G4 Marysville Can.
128 B2 Marysville U.S.A.
124 D4 Marysville U.S.A.
120 B4 Marysville U.S.A.
99 F3 Maryvale Aust.
124 E3 Maryville U.S.A.
144 D2 Marzagão Brazil
61 A4 Masabb Dumyât river mouth Egypt
61 A4 Masabb Rashîd river mouth Egypt
130 J7 Masachapa Nicaragua
60 D3 Maṣāf Syria
81 B5 Masai Mara National Reserve res. Kenya
81 C5 Masai Steppe plain Tanzania
81 B5 Masaka Uganda
82 C3 Masalanyane Pan salt pan Botswana
40 C3 Masalembu Besar i. Indon.
40 C3 Masalembu Kecil i. Indon.
60 G2 Masallı Azerbaijan
40 E2 Masamba Indon.
40 E2 Masamba mt. Indon.
49 J6 Masan S. Korea
121 J1 Masardis U.S.A.
81 C7 Masasi Tanzania
141 D3 Masavi Bolivia
130 J7 Masaya Nicaragua
41 B3 Masbate Phil.
41 B3 Masbate i. Phil.
75 E1 Mascara Algeria
149 H5 Mascarene Basin Indian Ocean
149 J4 Mascarene Ridge Indian Ocean
145 J1 Mascote Brazil
115 J4 Mascouche Can.
81 B4 Maseno Kenya
115 G2 Masères, Lac l. Can.
82 D4 Maseru Lesotho
16 K1 Masfjorden Norway
50 E4 Mashan China
83 E3 Mashava Zimbabwe
54 D2 Masherbrum mt. Pakistan
57 D1 Mashhad Iran
54 C4 Mashi r. India
46 H2 Mashike Japan
15 F2 Mashivka Ukraine
57 D3 Mashīz Iran
57 E4 Mashket r. Pakistan
57 E3 Mashki Chah Pakistan
57 E4 Māshkīd r. Iran
83 E2 Mashonaland Central div. Zimbabwe
83 E2 Mashonaland East div. Zimbabwe
83 D2 Mashonaland West div. Zimbabwe
46 K2 Mashū-ko l. Japan
10 F1 Masi Norway
130 C3 Masiáca Mexico
82 D5 Masibambane R.S.A.
82 D4 Masilo R.S.A.
79 C4 Masi-Manimba Zaire
40 D2 Masimbu Indon.
80 B4 Masindi Uganda
81 C5 Masinga Res. resr Kenya
41 A3 Masinloc Phil.
59 J5 Maṣīrah Oman
59 J6 Maṣīrah, Gulf of b. Oman
140 B1 Masisea Peru
78 E4 Masisi Zaire
57 B3 Masjed Soleymān Iran
60 D2 Maskanah Syria
115 J3 Maskinongé Can.
17 C5 Mask, Lough l. Rep. of Ire.
57 D4 Maskūtān Iran
15 G1 Maslova Pristan' Rus. Fed.
57 F3 Maslti Pakistan
65 K2 Maslyanino Rus. Fed.
83 J2 Masoala, Tanjona c. Madagascar
83 G2 Masoarivo Madagascar
122 E4 Mason U.S.A.
128 C2 Mason U.S.A.
125 D6 Mason U.S.A.
93 A7 Mason Bay b. N.Z.
122 C5 Mason City U.S.A.
124 E3 Mason City U.S.A.
120 D5 Masontown U.S.A.
59 J5 Masqaṭ Oman
26 C3 Massa Italy
121 G3 Massachusetts div. U.S.A.
121 H3 Massachusetts Bay b. U.S.A.
129 H1 Massadona U.S.A.
27 F5 Massafra Italy
78 C1 Massaguet Chad
78 C1 Massakory Chad
26 C4 Massa Marittimo Italy
78 B4 Massana Gabon
83 E3 Massangena Mozambique
79 C5 Massango Angola
81 C7 Massangulo Mozambique
142 D1 Massapê Brazil
79 B4 Massassa-Lewémé Congo
80 C1 Massawa Eritrea
80 C1 Massawa Channel chan. Eritrea
115 K4 Massawippi, Lac l. Can.
121 F2 Massena U.S.A.
78 C1 Massenya Chad
110 C4 Masset Can.
20 E5 Masseube France
114 D3 Massey Can.
21 F4 Massiac France
21 F4 Massif Central mts France
76 C4 Massigui Mali
120 C4 Massillon U.S.A.
76 C4 Massina Mali
83 F3 Massinga Mozambique
83 E3 Massingir Mozambique
83 E3 Massingir, Barragem de resr Mozambique
83 E3 Massintonto r. Mozambique/R.S.A.
152 D3 Massivet mts Ant.
115 H4 Masson Can.
152 D5 Masson I. i. Ant.
73 G3 Mastābah Saudi Arabia
60 G1 Maştağa Azerbaijan
65 G5 Mastchoh Tajikistan
64 D3 Masteksay Kazak.
93 E4 Masterton N.Z.
119 E7 Mastic Point The Bahamas
115 J3 Mastigouche, Réserve faunique de res. Can.
16 K1 Mastrevik Norway
54 C1 Mastuj Pakistan
54 A3 Mastung Pakistan
73 G3 Mastūrah Saudi Arabia
12 C4 Masty Belarus
46 C6 Masuda Japan
83 E3 Masvingo Zimbabwe
83 E3 Masvingo div. Zimbabwe
81 B5 Maswe Tanzania
81 B5 Maswe Game Reserve res. Tanzania
42 B1 Mata Myanmar
92 G2 Mata r. N.Z.
80 E3 Matabaan Somalia
82 D2 Matabeleland North div. Zimbabwe
83 D3 Matabeleland South div. Zimbabwe
55 G4 Matabhanga India
114 E3 Matachewan Can.
127 F6 Matachic Mexico
79 B5 Matadi Zaire
130 J6 Matagalpa Nicaragua
115 G2 Matagami Can.
115 F2 Matagami, Lac l. Can.
125 D6 Matagorda I. i. U.S.A.
132 B2 Matahambre Cuba
61 A5 Matâi Egypt
91 □11 Mataiea Fr. Poly. Pac. Oc.
91 □10 Mataiva i. Fr. Poly. Pac. Oc.
43 D7 Matak i. Indon.
92 F2 Matakana Island i. N.Z.
79 C6 Matala Angola
56 C5 Matale Sri Lanka
76 B3 Matam Senegal
92 E2 Matamata N.Z.
77 F4 Matamey Niger
130 E3 Matamoros Coahuila Mexico
131 F3 Matamoros Tamaulipas Mexico
41 B5 Matanal Point pt Phil.
72 D3 Ma'tan as Sārah well Libya
72 D3 Ma'ṭan Bishrah well Libya
81 C6 Matandu r. Tanzania
113 G4 Matane Can.
132 B2 Matanzas Cuba
144 D4 Matão Brazil
130 K7 Matapalo, C. c. Costa Rica
113 G4 Matapédia r. Can.
24 D1 Mataporquera Spain
146 B4 Mataquito r. Chile
56 C5 Matara Sri Lanka
29 C5 Mataragka Dytiki Ellas Greece
40 D4 Mataram Indon.
98 C2 Mataranka Aust.
25 H2 Mataró Spain
40 C3 Matasiri i. Indon.
73 E4 Matassi well Sudan
91 □13 Matatula, C. c. American Samoa Pac. Oc.
93 B7 Mataura r. N.Z.
93 B7 Mataura N.Z.
91 □12 Matautu Western Samoa
90 □3 Mata'utuliki i. Tonga
91 □12 Matavanu Crater crater Western Samoa
91 □16 Mataveri Easter I. Chile
92 F3 Matawai N.Z.
115 J3 Matawin r. Can.
141 D2 Mategua Bolivia
131 E4 Matehuala Mexico
144 B6 Matelândia Brazil
133 □3 Matelot Trin. and Tobago
81 C7 Matemanga Tanzania
81 D7 Matemo, Ilha i. Mozambique
27 F5 Matera Italy
19 L5 Mátészalka Hungary
82 D2 Matetsi r. Zimbabwe
27 B7 Mateur Tunisia
145 F3 Mateus Leme Brazil
80 B4 Matheniko Game Reserve res. Uganda
114 E2 Matheson Can.
125 D6 Mathis U.S.A.
29 B5 Mathraki i. Greece
54 D4 Mathura India
41 C5 Mati Phil.
77 E4 Matiacoali Burkina
55 G4 Matiali India
51 F3 Matianxu China
54 B4 Matiari Pakistan
145 G4 Matias Barbosa Brazil
145 G1 Matias Cardoso Brazil
131 G5 Matías Romero Mexico
113 G3 Matimekosh Can.
114 D3 Matinenda Lake l. Can.
142 C1 Matinha Brazil
121 J3 Matinicus I. i. U.S.A.
91 □11 Matiti Fr. Poly. Pac. Oc.
55 G5 Matla r. India
82 D3 Matlabas r. R.S.A.
17 G5 Matlock U.K.
83 D3 Matobo Hills mts Zimbabwe
62 G2 Matochkin Shar, Proliv chan. Rus. Fed.
141 E3 Mato Grosso Brazil
142 A3 Mato Grosso div. Brazil
144 A3 Mato Grosso do Sul div. Brazil
83 E4 Matola Mozambique
78 B3 Matomb Cameroon
24 B2 Matosinhos Portugal
145 G1 Mato Verde Brazil
145 F3 Matozinhos Brazil
19 J5 Mátra mts Hungary
59 J5 Maṭraḩ Oman
18 F5 Matrei in Osttirol Austria
76 B5 Matru Sierra Leone
77 G4 Matsena Nigeria
13 F7 Matsesta Rus. Fed.
83 H3 Matsiatra r. Madagascar
46 D6 Matsue Japan
46 H3 Matsumae Japan
47 F5 Matsumoto Japan
47 F6 Matsusaka Japan
51 G3 Matsu Tao i. Taiwan
46 B7 Matsuura Japan
46 D7 Matsuyama Japan
114 E2 Mattagami r. Can.
115 F3 Mattawa Can.
121 J2 Mattawamkeag U.S.A.
126 D3 Matterhorn mt. U.S.A.
19 H5 Mattersburg Austria
139 E2 Matthews Ridge Guyana
132 D2 Matthew Town The Bahamas
114 D2 Mattice Can.
47 F5 Mattō Japan
118 B4 Mattoon U.S.A.
140 A2 Matucana Peru
56 C5 Matugama Sri Lanka
90 □7 Matuku i. Fiji
79 C6 Matumbo Angola
73 F5 Ma'tuq Sudan
133 □3 Matura Trin. and Tobago
133 □3 Matura Bay b. Trinidad Trin. and Tobago
139 E2 Maturín Venezuela
83 D2 Matusadona National Park nat. park Zimbabwe
145 F3 Matutina Brazil
41 C5 Matutuang i. Indon.
14 H1 Matvinur Rus. Fed.
15 D3 Matviyivka Mykolayiv Ukraine
15 F3 Matviyivka Zaporizhzhya Ukraine
14 E3 Matyra r. Rus. Fed.
14 D3 Matyrskiy Rus. Fed.
14 D3 Matyrskoye Vdkhr. resr Rus. Fed.
55 E4 Mau India
54 D4 Mau India
81 C5 Mau mt. Kenya
81 C7 Maúa Mozambique
55 E4 Mau Aimma India
21 F1 Maubeuge France
42 B1 Ma-ubin Myanmar
20 E5 Maubourguet France
54 E4 Maudaha India
97 F3 Maude Aust.
152 C3 Maudheimvidda mt. ra. Ant.
101 A4 Maud, Pt pt Aust.
152 D2 Maud Seamount Ant.
139 F4 Maués r. Brazil
139 F4 Maués Brazil
55 E4 Mauganj India
39 M2 Maug Islands is Northern Mariana Is Pac. Oc.
127 □2 Maui i. U.S.A.
151 J7 Mauke i. Cook Islands Pac. Oc.
42 A2 Maukkadaw Myanmar
146 B4 Maule r. Chile
146 B4 Maule div. Chile
20 D3 Mauléon France
20 D5 Mauléon-Licharre France
147 B5 Maullín Chile
55 G4 Maulvi-Bazar Bangladesh
120 B4 Maumee U.S.A.
120 B4 Maumee r. U.S.A.
123 F5 Maumee Bay b. U.S.A.
39 H8 Maumere Indon.
82 C2 Maun Botswana
127 □2 Mauna Kea vol U.S.A.
127 □2 Mauna Loa vol U.S.A.
127 □1 Maunalua B. b. U.S.A.
92 F3 Maungahaumi mt. N.Z.
92 F3 Maungapohatu mt. N.Z.
92 F3 Maungataniwha mt. N.Z.
92 E1 Maungatapere N.Z.
92 E2 Maungaturoto N.Z.
42 A2 Maungdaw Myanmar
43 B4 Maungmagan Is is Myanmar
43 B4 Maungmagon Myanmar
108 F3 Maunoir, Lac l. Can.
54 D4 Mau Rampur India
21 H5 Maures, Massif des reg. France
140 C3 Mauri r. Bolivia
20 F4 Mauriac France
96 B2 Maurice, L. salt flat Aust.
115 J3 Mauricie, Parc National de la nat. park Can.
68 C4 Mauritania country Africa
69 K7 Mauritius country Indian Ocean
20 C2 Mauron France
20 F4 Maurs France
122 B4 Mauston U.S.A.
20 D3 Mauzé-sur-le-Mignon France
78 E3 Mava Zaire
81 C7 Mavago Mozambique
79 C7 Mavengue Angola
79 D7 Mavinga Angola
54 D3 Mawana India
79 C5 Mawanga Zaire
51 F2 Ma Wang Dui China
43 B5 Mawdaung Pass pass Myanmar/Thailand
92 G3 Mawhal Pt pt N.Z.
42 B1 Mawhun Myanmar
80 D2 Māwiyah Yemen
42 B2 Mawkmai Myanmar
42 A2 Mawlaik Myanmar
55 G4 Mawphlang India
73 H2 Mawqaq Saudi Arabia
80 D2 Mawshij Yemen
152 D4 Mawson Australia Base Ant.
152 D5 Mawson Coast Ant.
152 D4 Mawson Escarpment escarpment Ant.
152 B6 Mawson Pen. pen. Ant.
43 B5 Maw Taung mt. Myanmar
124 C2 Max U.S.A.
80 E4 Maxaas Somalia
146 C2 Maxán Arg.
131 H4 Maxcanú Mexico
27 B6 Maxia, Punta mt. Italy
122 D5 Maxinkuckee, Lake l. U.S.A.
10 F3 Maxmo Finland
123 F2 Maxton U.S.A.
128 A2 Maxwell U.S.A.
99 E4 Maxwelton Aust.
40 B2 Maya Indon.
63 P4 Maya r. Rus. Fed.
15 F2 Mayachka Ukraine
60 E3 Mayādīn Syria
133 D2 Mayaguana i. The Bahamas
132 D2 Mayaguana Passage chan. The Bahamas
119 □3 Mayagüez Puerto Rico
77 F4 Mayahi Niger
79 B4 Mayama Congo
57 C1 Mayamey Iran
131 H5 Maya Mountains mt. ra. Belize
50 D1 Mayan China
51 E3 Mayang China
133 □3 Mayaro div. Trinidad Trin. and Tobago
47 G4 Maya-san mt. Japan
17 E4 Maybole U.K.
80 C2 Maych'ew Ethiopia
14 E1 Maydakovo Rus. Fed.
61 D1 Maydān Ikbis Turkey
80 C2 May Darashet' r. Ethiopia
57 G2 Maydā Shahr Afghanistan
133 □1 May Day Mts mts Jamaica
80 E2 Maydh Somalia
18 C3 Mayen Germany
20 D3 Mayenne r. France
20 D2 Mayenne France
129 F4 Mayer U.S.A.
110 F4 Mayerthorpe Can.
93 C5 Mayfield N.Z.
118 B4 Mayfield U.S.A.
48 B3 Mayhan Mongolia
127 F5 Mayhill U.S.A.
49 J3 Mayi r. China
16 F3 May, Isle of i. U.K.
65 J2 Maykain Kazak.
65 J3 Maykamys Kazak.
13 G6 Maykop Rus. Fed.
64 F3 Maylibash Kazak.
65 H4 Mayly-Say Kyrgyzstan
65 L2 Mayma Rus. Fed.
42 B2 Maymyo Myanmar
12 H4 Mayna Rus. Fed.
99 E4 Mayne w Aust.
56 A2 Mayni India
115 G4 Maynooth Can.
147 B6 Mayo r. Arg.
110 B2 Mayo Can.
146 D4 Mayo, 25 de Buenos Aires Arg.
146 C4 Mayo, 25 de La Pampa Arg.
78 B2 Mayo Alim Cameroon
41 C5 Mayo Bay b. Phil.
77 G5 Mayo-Belwa Nigeria
78 B2 Mayo Darlé Cameroon
78 B2 Mayo-Kébbi div. Chad
78 B4 Mayoko Congo
110 B2 Mayo Lake l. Can.
140 C2 Mayo Mayo Bolivia
41 B3 Mayon vol Phil.
147 D4 Mayor Buratovich Arg.
92 F2 Mayor I. i. N.Z.
133 □3 Mayoro Bay b. Trinidad Trin. and Tobago
141 D3 Mayor Pablo Lagerenza Paraguay
69 J7 Mayotte i. Africa
133 □1 May Pen Jamaica
41 B2 Mayraira Point pt Phil.
18 E5 Mayrhofen Austria
60 F4 Maysān div. Iraq
15 G1 Mayskiy Rus. Fed.
14 H1 Mayskiy Rus. Fed.
45 N1 Mayskiy Rus. Fed.
120 B5 Maysville U.S.A.
79 B4 Mayumba Gabon
55 E3 Mayum La pass China
56 B4 Mayuram India
123 F4 Mayville U.S.A.
124 D2 Mayville U.S.A.
120 D3 Mayville U.S.A.
122 C4 Mayville U.S.A.
124 C3 Maywood U.S.A.
63 P3 Mayya Rus. Fed.
146 D4 Maza Arg.
79 E7 Mazabuka Zambia
142 B1 Mazagão Brazil
20 F5 Mazamet France
57 B1 Māzandarān div. Iran
54 D1 Mazar China
61 C4 Mazār Jordan
27 D7 Mazara del Vallo Italy
27 D7 Mazara, Val di v. Italy
57 F1 Mazār-e Sharīf Afghanistan
25 E2 Mazarete Spain
147 C6 Mazarredo Arg.
25 F4 Mazarrón Spain
25 F4 Mazarrón, Golfo de b. Spain
65 K5 Mazartagh mt. China
139 F2 Mazaruni r. Guyana
130 C2 Mazatán Mexico
131 H6 Mazatenango Guatemala
130 D4 Mazatlán Mexico
129 G4 Mazatzal Peak summit U.S.A.
11 F4 Mažeikiai Lithuania
77 F3 Mazelet well Niger
64 D3 Mazhambet Kazak.
29 F6 Mazı Turkey
11 F4 Mazirbe Latvia
130 C2 Mazocahui Mexico
140 C3 Mazocruz Peru
81 C6 Mazomora Tanzania
83 E2 Mazowe r. Zimbabwe
61 C4 Mazra Jordan
73 E5 Mazrub well Sudan
83 D3 Mazunga Zimbabwe
13 D4 Mazyr Belarus
27 E7 Mazzarino Italy
83 E4 Mbabane Swaziland
76 A4 Mbacké Senegal
76 D5 Mbahiakro Côte d'Ivoire
78 C3 Mbaïki C.A.R.
78 B2 Mbakaou, Lac de l. Cameroon
81 B6 Mbala Zambia
83 D3 Mbalabala Zimbabwe
78 B3 Mbalam Cameroon
81 B4 Mbale Uganda
78 B3 Mbalmayo Cameroon
78 B2 Mbam r. Cameroon
81 B7 Mbamba Bay Tanzania
78 C4 Mbandaka Zaire
78 B3 Mbang Cameroon
78 A3 Mbanga Cameroon
79 B5 M'banza Congo Angola
79 B5 Mbanza-Ngungu Zaire
81 B5 Mbarara Uganda
78 D3 Mbari r. C.A.R.
81 C6 Mbarika Mountains mts Tanzania
78 C3 Mbata C.A.R.
81 B7 Mbati Zambia
76 D5 Mbatto Côte d'Ivoire
78 B2 Mbé Cameroon
81 C6 Mbemkuru r. Tanzania
78 B2 Mbengwi Cameroon
76 C4 Mbenqué Côte d'Ivoire
83 D3 Mberengwa Zimbabwe
81 B6 Mbeya Tanzania
81 B6 Mbeya div. Tanzania
78 C3 Mbi r. C.A.R.
78 B4 Mbigou Gabon
78 A4 Mbilapé Gabon
78 B4 Mbinda Congo
81 C7 Mbinga Tanzania
78 A3 Mbini Equatorial Guinea
83 E3 Mbizi Zimbabwe
81 B6 Mbizi Mts mts Tanzania
78 E2 Mboki C.A.R.
78 B3 Mbomo Congo
78 D3 Mbomou r. C.A.R.
78 D2 Mbomou div. C.A.R.
76 A3 Mboro Senegal
78 B2 Mbouda Cameroon
76 A4 Mbour Senegal
74 B5 Mbout Mauritania
78 C2 Mbrès C.A.R.
79 D5 Mbuji-Mayi Zaire
81 C5 Mbulu Tanzania
81 C6 Mbuyuni Tanzania
108 H2 McClintock Channel chan. Can.
74 D3 Mcherrah reg. Algeria
81 C6 Mchinga Tanzania
81 B7 Mchinji Malawi
108 C3 McKinley, Mount mt. U.S.A.
81 B6 Mdandu Tanzania
82 D5 Mdantsane R.S.A.
75 F1 M'Daourouch Algeria
74 C4 Mdennah reg. Mali/Mauritania
24 D5 Mdiq Morocco
114 D2 Mead Can.
125 C4 Meade U.S.A.
129 E3 Mead, Lake l. U.S.A.
111 H4 Meadow Lake Can.
111 H4 Meadow Lake Provincial Park res. Can.
129 E3 Meadow Valley Wash r. U.S.A.
120 C4 Meadville U.S.A.
114 E4 Meaford Can.
46 K2 Meaken-dake vol Japan
24 B2 Mealhada Portugal
113 J3 Mealy Mountains mt. ra. Can.
57 E1 Meana Turkmenistan
99 G5 Meandarra Aust.
110 F3 Meander River Can.
41 C5 Meares i. Indon.
142 D1 Mearim r. Brazil
79 B5 Mebridege r. Angola
121 H2 Mechanic Falls U.S.A.
120 B4 Mechanicsburg U.S.A.
122 B5 Mechanicsville U.S.A.
18 B3 Mechelen Belgium
75 D2 Mecheria Algeria
72 C5 Mechiméré Chad
29 F4 Mecidiye Turkey
60 C1 Mecitözü Turkey
18 C3 Meckenheim Germany
18 E1 Mecklenburger Bucht b. Germany
18 F2 Mecklenburg-Vorpommern div. Germany
83 F1 Meconta Mozambique
83 F1 Mecubúri Mozambique
83 F1 Mecubúri r. Mozambique
81 C7 Mecula Mozambique
100 D3 Meda r. Aust.
24 C2 Meda Portugal
56 B2 Medak India
38 C6 Medan Indon.
40 D4 Medang i. Indon.
146 C3 Medano Arg.
147 D4 Médanos Buenos Aires Arg.
147 C6 Medanosa, Pta pt Arg.
138 D1 Médanos de Coro, Parque Nacional nat. park Venezuela
56 C4 Medawachchiya Sri Lanka
56 B2 Medchal India
121 K2 Meddybemps L. l. U.S.A.
75 E1 Médéa Algeria
145 H2 Medeiros Neto Brazil
138 B2 Medellín Colombia
75 G2 Medenine Tunisia
74 A5 Mederdra Mauritania
61 C1 Medetsiz T. mt. Turkey
126 B3 Medford U.S.A.
122 B3 Medford U.S.A.
121 F5 Medford Farms U.S.A.
28 G2 Medgidia Romania
122 B5 Media U.S.A.
146 C3 Media Luna Arg.
130 K6 Media Luna, Arrecife de la is Honduras
144 A6 Medianeira Brazil
28 E1 Mediaș Romania
126 C2 Medical Lake U.S.A.
126 F3 Medicine Bow U.S.A.
126 F3 Medicine Bow Mts mt. ra. U.S.A.
126 F3 Medicine Bow Peak summit U.S.A.
111 G4 Medicine Hat Can.
125 D4 Medicine Lodge U.S.A.
145 H2 Medina Brazil
120 D3 Medina U.S.A.
120 C4 Medina U.S.A.
24 D2 Medina del Campo Spain
24 E1 Medina de Pomar Spain
24 D2 Medina de Rioseco Spain
76 B4 Medina Gounas Senegal
76 A4 Médina Sabakh Senegal
24 D4 Medina-Sidonia Spain

33 L5 Mongolia country Asia
78 B3 Mongomo Equatorial Guinea
77 G4 Mongonu Nigeria
54 C2 Mongora Pakistan
72 D5 Mongororo Chad
78 C3 Mongoumba C.A.R.
42 B2 Mong Pan Myanmar
42 B2 Mong Pat Myanmar
42 B2 Mong Ping Myanmar
42 B2 Mong Pu-awn Myanmar
42 B2 Mong Ton Myanmar
79 D7 Mongu Zambia
42 C2 Mong Un Myanmar
42 B2 Mong Yai Myanmar
42 B2 Mong Yawng Myanmar
42 B2 Mong Yu Myanmar
121 J3 Monhegan I. i. U.S.A.
21 G4 Monistrol-sur-Loire France
128 D2 Monitor Mt mt. U.S.A.
128 D2 Monitor Range mts U.S.A.
145 F3 Monjolos Brazil
83 F1 Monkey Bay Malawi
19 L2 Mońki Poland
98 E5 Monkira Aust.
78 D4 Monkoto Zaire
114 E5 Monkton Can.
122 B5 Monmouth U.S.A.
121 H2 Monmouth U.S.A.
110 E4 Monmouth Mt. mt. Can.
77 E5 Mono r. Benin/Togo
128 C3 Mono Lake l. U.S.A.
121 H4 Monomoy Pt pt U.S.A.
120 B4 Monon U.S.A.
122 B4 Monona U.S.A.
27 F5 Monopoli Italy
19 J5 Monor Hungary
120 C5 Monongahela r. U.S.A.
133 □3 Monos I. i. Trinidad Trin. and Tobago
72 D4 Monou Chad
25 F3 Monóvar Spain
25 F2 Monreal del Campo Spain
27 D6 Monreale Italy
125 E5 Monroe U.S.A.
123 F5 Monroe U.S.A.
119 D5 Monroe U.S.A.
121 F4 Monroe U.S.A.
129 F2 Monroe U.S.A.
122 C4 Monroe U.S.A.
122 B6 Monroe City U.S.A.
120 C5 Monroeville U.S.A.
76 B5 Monrovia Liberia
18 A3 Mons Belgium
26 C3 Monselice Italy
18 C3 Montabaur Germany
83 H1 Montagne d'Ambre, Parc National de la nat. park Madagascar
122 D4 Montague U.S.A.
101 B5 Montague Ra. h. Aust.
100 D2 Montague Sd b. Aust.
152 C1 Montagu I. i. S. Sandwich Is Atlantic Ocean
25 E3 Montalbo Spain
21 G4 Montalieu-Verceu France
27 E6 Montalto mt. Italy
27 F6 Montalto Uffugo Italy
138 B4 Montalvo Ecuador
28 D3 Montana div. Bulgaria
126 E2 Montana div. U.S.A.
24 C3 Montánchez, Sierra de mt. ra. Spain
145 H3 Montanha Brazil
20 F3 Montargis France
20 E4 Montauban Midi-Pyrénées France
121 G4 Montauk U.S.A.
121 H4 Montauk Pt pt U.S.A.
21 G3 Montbard France
21 H3 Montbéliard France
25 G2 Montblanc Spain
81 □4 Mont Blanche Mauritius
21 G3 Montbrison France
21 G3 Montceau-les-Mines France
20 E4 Mont-de-Marsan France
20 D5 Mont-de-Marsan France
20 F2 Montdidier France
140 D3 Monteagudo Bolivia
80 A1 Monte Alegre Brazil
142 C3 Monte Alegre de Goiás Brazil
144 D3 Monte Alegre de Minas Brazil
144 D4 Monte Aprazível Brazil
145 G1 Monte Azul Brazil
144 D4 Monte Azul Paulista Brazil
115 H4 Montebello Can.
100 A4 Monte Bello Is is Aust.
21 H5 Montebelluna Italy
146 F2 Montecarlo Arg.
21 H5 Monte Carlo Monaco
144 E3 Montecarlo Brazil
146 E3 Monte Caseros Arg.
26 C4 Montecatini Terme Italy
146 C5 Monte Comán Arg.
133 E3 Monte Cristi Dominican Rep.
138 A4 Montecristi Ecuador
27 C4 Montecristo, Isola di i. Italy
147 D2 Monte Dinero Arg.
26 D4 Montefiascone Italy
133 □1 Montego Bay b. Jamaica
24 C2 Montehermoso Spain
98 B3 Montejinnie Aust.
21 G4 Montélimar France
146 E2 Monte Lindo r. Arg.
26 D3 Montella Italy
24 D3 Montellano Spain
122 C4 Montello U.S.A.
131 F3 Montemorelos Mexico
24 B3 Montemor-o-Novo Portugal
20 D4 Montendre France
143 B6 Montenegro Brazil
146 E2 Montepuez Mozambique
81 D7 Montepuez r. Mozambique
26 C4 Montepulciano Italy
146 D2 Monte Quemado Arg.
20 F2 Montereau-faut-Yonne France
128 B3 Monterey U.S.A.
120 D5 Monterey U.S.A.
128 B3 Monterey Bay b. U.S.A.
138 B2 Montería Colombia
140 C3 Montero Bolivia
146 C2 Monteros Arg.
27 D4 Monterotondo Italy
26 E4 Monterrey Mexico
26 D4 Monterubbiano Italy
142 C2 Montes Claros Brazil
27 E5 Monte Sant'Angelo Italy
26 E4 Monte Santo Brazil
145 E4 Monte Santo de Minas Brazil
27 B5 Monte Santu, Capo di pt Italy
145 G2 Montes Claros Brazil
24 D3 Toledo, Montes de mt. ra. Spain
26 E4 Montesilvano Italy
26 D4 Montesquieu-Volvestre France
26 C4 Montevarchi Italy
146 E3 Montevideo Uruguay
122 E4 Montevideo U.S.A.
127 F4 Monte Vista U.S.A.
123 C4 Montezuma U.S.A.
146 C2 Montezuma Arg.
129 H3 Montezuma Castle National Monument U.S.A.
128 D3 Montezuma Creek U.S.A.
129 H3 Montezuma Peak summit U.S.A.
20 E2 Montfort-le-Gesnois France

17 F5 Montgomery U.K.
119 C5 Montgomery U.S.A.
21 H3 Monthey Switz.
27 B5 Monti Italy
125 F5 Monticello U.S.A.
119 D6 Monticello U.S.A.
122 D5 Monticello U.S.A.
122 B4 Monticello U.S.A.
122 B5 Monticello U.S.A.
121 K1 Monticello U.S.A.
129 H3 Monticello U.S.A.
122 C4 Monticello U.S.A.
20 E4 Montignac France
24 □3 Montijo Spain
130 K8 Montijo, G. de b. Panama
24 D4 Montilla Spain
144 C2 Montividiu Brazil
20 E2 Montivilliers France
113 G4 Mont Joli Can.
115 H3 Mont-Laurier Can.
115 H3 Mont Louis Can.
21 F2 Montmagny Can.
21 F2 Montmirail Champagne-Ardenne France
122 D5 Montmorenci U.S.A.
115 H3 Montmorency r. Can.
20 E3 Montmorillon France
99 G5 Monto Aust.
24 D3 Montoro Spain
76 C5 Mont Peko, Parc National du nat. park Côte d'Ivoire
133 □1 Montpelier Jamaica
126 E3 Montpelier U.S.A.
122 E5 Montpelier U.S.A.
120 A4 Montpelier U.S.A.
121 G2 Montpelier U.S.A.
21 F5 Montpellier Hérault France
20 E4 Montpon-Ménestérol France
114 E3 Montreal r. Can.
114 D3 Montreal r. Can.
115 J4 Montréal Can.
114 C3 Montreal I. i. Can.
114 H4 Montreal L. l. Can.
114 H4 Montreal Lake l. Can.
121 F2 Montréal-Mirabel Can.
114 C3 Montreal River Can.
20 E1 Montreuil France
20 D3 Montreuil-Bellay France
21 H3 Montreux Switz.
21 H3 Montrichard France
82 C4 Montrose well R.S.A.
16 F3 Montrose U.K.
77 F4 Montrose U.S.A.
127 F4 Montrose U.S.A.
123 F4 Montrose U.S.A.
21 G5 Monts France
20 E3 Montsalvy France
76 C5 Mont Sangbé, Parc National du nat. park Côte d'Ivoire
104 M8 Montserrat terr. Caribbean
139 G3 Montsinéry French Guiana
21 G3 Mont-sous-Vaudrey France
113 G4 Monts, Pte des pt Can.
20 E2 Mont-St-Aignan France
133 □3 Mont-Tremblant, Parc du res. Can.
92 □2 Monument Harb. inlet Campbell I. N.Z.
129 G3 Monument Valley reg. U.S.A.
78 B4 Monveda Zaire
42 A2 Monywa Myanmar
26 B3 Monza Italy
79 E7 Monze Zambia
140 A1 Monzón Peru
25 G2 Monzón Spain
85 □ Mooi r. R.S.A.
68 D2 Mookane Botswana
82 C4 Mookwatana Aust.
114 D2 Moonbeam Can.
97 G2 Moonbi Ra. mt. ra. Aust.
98 E5 Moonda L. salt flat Aust.
99 G5 Moonie Aust.
97 G2 Moonie r. Aust.
96 D3 Moora Aust.
98 E5 Moorarie Aust.
126 F2 Moorcroft U.S.A.
101 A6 Moore r. Aust.
91 □11 Moorea i. Fr. Poly. Pac. Oc.
120 D5 Moorefield U.S.A.
101 B6 Moore, Lake salt flat Aust.
119 E7 Moores I. is The Bahamas
121 K2 Moores Mills Can.
16 F4 Moorfoot Hills h. U.K.
102 F4 Mooroopna Aust.
13 G5 Moorosyvsk Rus. Fed.
112 D3 Moose Factory Can.
121 J2 Moosehead Lake l. U.S.A.
111 H4 Moose Jaw Can.
111 J4 Moose Lake U.S.A.
122 A2 Moose Lake U.S.A.
121 H2 Mooselookmeguntic Lake l. U.S.A.
112 D3 Moose River Can.
111 J4 Moosomin Can.
112 D3 Moosonee Can.
81 C6 Mopeia Mozambique
76 D4 Mopti Mali
76 D4 Mopti div. Mali
57 F2 Moqor Afghanistan
140 B3 Moquegua Peru
19 J5 Mór Hungary
77 E4 Mora Cameroon
24 B3 Mora Portugal
24 E3 Mora Spain
11 D3 Mora Sweden
124 □2 Morada U.S.A.
28 B3 Morača r. Yugo.
146 B4 Mora Campanario, Cerro summit Chile
54 A3 Morad r. Pakistan
142 E2 Morada Nova Brazil
145 H3 Morada Nova de Minas Brazil
83 G2 Morafenobe Madagascar
19 K2 Morąg Poland
19 J5 Mórahalom Hungary
101 A6 Morawa Aust.
139 F2 Morawhanna Guyana
16 F3 Moray Firth est. U.K.
143 E4 Moray Downs Aust.
18 C3 Morbach Germany
54 B5 Morbi India
20 B3 Morbihan, Golfe de b. France
20 D4 Morcenx France
26 C2 Mordano Italy
49 O2 Mordaga China
11 K5 Mordoğan Turkey

14 F2 Mordoviya div. Rus. Fed.
14 E3 Mordovo Rus. Fed.
14 D2 Mordves Rus. Fed.
19 L2 Mordy Poland
124 C2 Moreau r. U.S.A.
17 F4 Morecambe U.K.
17 F4 Morecambe Bay b. U.K.
97 G2 Moree Aust.
90 □1 Morehead P.N.G.
120 B5 Morehead U.S.A.
125 E5 Morehead City U.S.A.
54 D4 Morel r. India
131 E5 Morelia Mexico
99 E4 Morella Aust.
25 F2 Morella Spain
131 H5 Morelos div. Mexico
131 H5 Morelos Mexico
82 C2 Moremi Wildlife Reserve res. Botswana
54 D4 Morena India
24 D3 Morena, Sierra mt. ra. Spain
129 H5 Morenci U.S.A.
123 C6 Morenci U.S.A.
28 E2 Moreni Romania
131 F2 Moreno Mexico
128 D5 Moreno Valley U.S.A.
10 B3 Møre og Romsdal div. Norway
141 E2 Mererú r. Brazil
110 C4 Moresby Island i. Can.
82 C3 Mereswe Pan salt pan Botswana
99 H5 Moreton B. b. Aust.
99 H5 Moreton I. i. Aust.
20 F2 Moreuil France
14 C1 Morez France
61 B2 Morfou Cyprus
61 B2 Morfou B. b. Cyprus
96 D3 Morgan Aust.
125 F6 Morgan City U.S.A.
128 B3 Morgan Hill U.S.A.
128 D3 Morgan, Mt mt. U.S.A.
120 D5 Morgantown U.S.A.
120 D5 Morgantown U.S.A.
84 B4 Morgenzon R.S.A.
21 H3 Morges Switz.
55 F4 Morhar r. India
44 F3 Mori China
46 H2 Mori Japan
133 K7 Mosquitos, Golfo de los b. Panama
111 J2 Moriah Tobago Trin. and Tobago
92 □2 Moriah, Mt mt. U.S.A.
127 F5 Moriarty U.S.A.
76 C5 Moriarty's Ra. h. Aust.
76 C5 Moribaya Guinea
82 C5 Morich Pakistan
79 B4 Morichal Colombia
77 F4 Moriki Nigeria
49 M3 Morin Dawa China
47 H4 Morioka Japan
97 G3 Morisset Aust.
83 G1 Mossuril Mozambique
49 H4 Moriyama Japan
47 H6 Moriyoshi-zan vol Japan
11 D3 Morjärv Sweden
54 C5 Morjen r. Pakistan
12 J3 Morki Rus. Fed.
20 C2 Morlaix France
129 G4 Mormon Lake l. U.S.A.
133 □3 Morne-à-l'Eau Guadeloupe Caribbean
133 □3 Morne Constant, h. Guadeloupe Caribbean
133 G4 Morne Diablotin vol Dominica
152 Morne, Pte pt Kerguelen Indian Ocean
81 □2 Morne Seychellois h. Seychelles
99 E5 Morney w. Aust.
83 F1 Mornington Aust.
147 A6 Mornington, I. i. Chile
54 A4 Moro Pakistan
90 □1 Morobe P.N.G.
68 D2 Morocco country Africa
92 D5 Morocco U.S.A.
140 A2 Morococha Peru
47 □1 Moro-yama h. Japan
83 C5 Morogoro Tanzania
79 B6 Morogoro div. Tanzania
28 D2 Morogoro r. Romania
138 B4 Morona Ecuador
83 H4 Morondava Madagascar
24 D4 Morón de la Frontera Spain
83 G4 Morondo Côte d'Ivoire
81 □7 Moroni Comoros
39 H6 Morotai i. Indon.
80 B3 Moroto Uganda
13 G5 Morozovsk Rus. Fed.
13 G5 Morozovo-Borki Rus. Fed.
142 B2 Morpara Brazil
17 F4 Morpeth U.K.
17 H5 Morpeth Can.
142 D6 Morretes Brazil
11 F3 Mörrum Sweden
92 E2 Morrinsville N.Z.
111 K5 Morris Can.
124 C2 Morris U.S.A.
115 H4 Morrisburg Can.
99 E7 Morris, Mt mt. Aust.
129 F5 Morristown U.S.A.
121 F3 Morristown U.S.A.
119 D4 Morristown U.S.A.
121 F4 Morrisville U.S.A.
121 G2 Morrisville U.S.A.
142 D7 Morro Brazil
144 C3 Morro Agudo Brazil
138 A4 Morro Bay U.S.A.
131 F5 Moro, Can. de chan. Ecuador
120 C5 Moundsville U.S.A.
144 C4 Morrocoy, Parque Nacional nat. park Venezuela
145 J3 Morro d'Anta Brazil
146 B4 Morro de Petatlán hd Mexico
142 D3 Morro do Chapéu Brazil
144 C3 Morro do Coco Brazil
142 C2 Morro Grande h. Brazil
138 B2 Morrosquillo, G. de b. Colombia
83 D7 Morrumbala Mozambique
83 D7 Morrumbene Mozambique
14 E3 Morse Reservoir resr U.S.A.
14 C3 Morshansk Rus. Fed.
12 E2 Morskaya Masel'ga Rus. Fed.
13 H6 Morskiy Biryuchek, O. i. Rus. Fed.
52 C4 Mortes r. Brazil
99 E5 Mortes r. Aust.
83 F1 Mortlock Is is Micronesia
24 C2 Mortagne-au-Perche France
20 E2 Mortagne-sur-Sèvre France
20 D3 Mortara Italy
21 H2 Morteau France
146 E3 Moray Downs Aust.
142 D6 Mortes, Brazil
145 F4 Mortes, Rio das r. Brazil
122 C5 Morton U.S.A.
123 E4 Morton U.S.A.
133 □3 Moruga Trin. and Tobago
133 □3 Moruga Pt pt Trinidad Trin. and Tobago

97 F3 Morundah Aust.
80 B4 Morungole mt. Uganda
97 G3 Moruya Aust.
21 G3 Morvan reg. France
98 D4 Morven Aust.
93 C6 Morven N.Z.
97 F4 Morwell Aust.
12 G1 Morzhovets, O. i. Rus. Fed.
14 E2 Mosal'sk Rus. Fed.
14 B2 Mosana Moldova
18 D4 Mosbach Germany
126 C2 Moscow U.S.A.
152 C6 Moscow Univ. Ice Shelf ice feature Ant.
152 B4 Mose, C. c. Ant.
21 H2 Moselle r. France
21 H2 Moselle r. France
128 D1 Moses, Mt mt. U.S.A.
84 B3 Moses Lake U.S.A.
12 H1 Moseyevo Rus. Fed.
93 C6 Mosgiel N.Z.
114 C2 Mosher U.S.A.
80 B3 Moshi Tanzania
123 E5 Mosinee U.S.A.
122 D3 Mosinee U.S.A.
19 H2 Mosina Poland
10 D2 Mosjøen Norway
65 H2 Moskalenki r. Norway
14 D2 Moskva r. Rus. Fed.
14 D2 Moskva div. Rus. Fed.
14 C1 Moskvy, Kanal imeni canal Rus. Fed.
90 □2 Moso i. Vanuatu
14 □3 Mosolovo Rus. Fed.
19 H5 Mosonmagyaróvár Hungary
26 F4 Mosor mts Croatia
142 C1 Mosqueiro Brazil
142 E2 Mosquero Brazil
138 B3 Mosquera Colombia
127 F5 Mosquero U.S.A.
130 K6 Mosquitia reg. Honduras
145 H1 Mosquito r. Brazil
120 C4 Mosquito Creek Lake l. U.S.A.
130 K7 Mosquitos, Golfo de los b. Panama
111 J2 Mosquito Lake l. Can.
14 C4 Moss Norway
79 B4 Mossaka Congo
144 C2 Mossâmedes Brazil
93 B6 Mossburn N.Z.
82 C5 Mossel Bay R.S.A.
82 C5 Mossel Bay R.S.A.
79 B4 Mossendjo Congo
99 F3 Mossgiel Aust.
142 E2 Mossoró Brazil
83 G1 Mossuril Mozambique
97 F3 Moss Vale Aust.
19 F3 Most Czech Rep.
57 D4 Moçtafaabad Iran
75 F1 Mostaganem Algeria
26 F4 Mostar Bos.-Herz.
143 B7 Mostardas Brazil
25 F3 Mosteiro Spain
113 J3 Mostos Hills In. Can.
15 D3 Mostove Ukraine
13 G6 Mostovskoy Rus. Fed.
19 L4 Mostyn Malaysia
15 D1 Mostys'ka Ukraine
11 B4 Mesvatnet l. Norway
80 C2 Mot'a Ethiopia
21 H4 Mota i. Vanuatu
90 □1 Mota Lava i. Vanuatu
28 F1 Motaia Aust.
83 D4 Motetehai Botswana
95 □1 Moth India
92 F2 Motiti I. i. N.Z.
78 B4 Motloutse w. Botswana
82 D5 Motokwe Botswana
47 □1 Moto-yama h. Japan
24 E3 Motril Spain
28 D2 Motru Romania
46 E2 Motsuta-misaki pt Japan
91 □10 Motu Iti i. Easter I. Chile
91 □10 Motu Nui i. Easter I. Chile
91 □10 Motu One i. Fr. Poly. Pac. Oc.
87 M6 Motu, Pte i. Fr. Poly. Pac. Oc.
90 □ Mota, Pte pt Kerguelen Indian Ocean
42 B3 Motai Myanmar
82 D2 Motokwe Botswana
92 B6 Moturiki i. Fiji
91 □10 Motutapu I. i. Fiji
91 □10 Motu Tautara i. Easter I. Chile
79 C6 Mouka r. Angola
142 E2 Moxotó r. Brazil
61 C4 Mouanko Congo
139 G3 Mouchoir Bank sand bank Turks and Caicos Is Caribbean
133 E2 Mouchoir Passage chan. Turks and Caicos Is Caribbean
50 C2 Mouding China
74 B5 Moudjéria Mauritania
21 H3 Moudon Switz.
11 F3 Mouhijärvi Finland
78 A4 Mouhoun r. Africa
79 B5 Mouila Gabon
78 B4 Mouilah well Algeria
79 □ Moul well Niger
79 □ Moulamein Aust.
97 F3 Moulamein r. Aust.
133 □5 Moule Guadeloupe Caribbean
79 B5 Moulèngui Binza Gabon
55 H4 Moulmein Myanmar
42 A3 Moulmein Myanmar
42 A3 Moulmeingyun Myanmar
17 D6 Moulouya r. Africa
118 B4 Mound City U.S.A.
124 C2 Mound City U.S.A.
120 C5 Moundsville U.S.A.
54 C4 Mount Abu India
119 D5 Mountain Brook U.S.A.
125 C6 Mountain City U.S.A.
124 E2 Mountain Grove U.S.A.
124 E2 Mountain Home U.S.A.
126 C3 Mountain Home U.S.A.
120 C5 Mount Airy U.S.A.
93 B6 Mount Aspiring National Park nat. park N.Z.
124 E2 Mount Ayr U.S.A.
96 D3 Mount Barker Aust.
17 C5 Mount Bellew Rep. of Ire.
97 F4 Mount Buffalo Nat. Nat. park Aust.
114 C3 Mount Carleton Provincial Park res. Can.
129 H4 Mount Carmel Junction U.S.A.
93 C4 Mount Carroll U.S.A.
93 C6 Mount Cook N.Z.
93 C6 Mount Cook National Park nat. park N.Z.
125 C6 Mount Coulon U.S.A.
98 C3 Mount Darwin Zimbabwe
121 J2 Mount Desert Island i. U.S.A.
96 D4 Mount Eba Aust.
80 B4 Mount Elgon National Park nat. park Uganda
97 F3 Mount Field Nat. Park nat. park Aust.
114 C3 Mount Forest Can.
96 E4 Mount Gambier Aust.
90 □1 Mount Garnet Aust.
120 C4 Mount Gilead U.S.A.
90 □1 Mount Hagen P.N.G.
108 D3 Mount Hayes mt. U.S.A.

97 F3 Mount Hope Aust.
96 C3 Mount Hope Aust.
99 E5 Mount Howitt Aust.
98 D4 Mount Isa Aust.
121 G4 Mount Kisco U.S.A.
114 E3 Mount MacDonald Can.
101 B6 Mount Magnet Aust.
97 F3 Mount Manara Aust.
128 B1 Mount Meadows Reservoir resr U.S.A.
99 G4 Mount Molloy Aust.
99 G4 Mount Morgan Aust.
96 D3 Mount Perry Aust.
99 □2 Mount Pleasant Aust.
122 B5 Mount Pleasant The Bahamas
122 E4 Mount Pleasant U.S.A.
118 C4 Mount Pleasant U.S.A.
119 E5 Mount Pleasant U.S.A.
129 G2 Mount Pleasant U.S.A.
122 D3 Mount Pleasant U.S.A.
126 B2 Mount Rainier Nat. Park nat. park. U.S.A.
110 F4 Mount Robson Prov. Park res. Can.
120 C6 Mount Rogers National Recreation Area res. U.S.A.
17 E6 Mount's Bay b. U.K.
93 C6 Mount Somers N.Z.
120 D5 Mount Sterling U.S.A.
120 D5 Mount Sterling U.S.A.
99 F3 Mount Surprise Aust.
98 C4 Mount Swan Aust.
101 B5 Mount Union U.S.A.
120 D5 Mount Vernon U.S.A.
118 B4 Mount Vernon U.S.A.
122 B5 Mount Vernon U.S.A.
120 D5 Mount Vernon U.S.A.
126 B2 Mount Vernon U.S.A.
99 G5 Mount William Nat. Park nat. park. Aust.
96 D3 Mount Wedge Aust.
42 B3 Mouydir, Monts du plat. Algeria
79 □4 Mouyondzi Congo
72 C5 Mouzaki Greece
72 C5 Mouzarak r. Chad
72 C4 Mourdiah Mali
72 C5 Mourdi, Depression du depression Chad
20 D5 Mourenx France
99 F3 Mourilyan Harbour Aust.
17 D4 Mourne Mountains h. U.K.
18 A3 Mouscron Belgium
78 C2 Mousgougou Chad
72 C4 Moussa well Chad
72 C5 Moutamba Congo
40 C2 Moutong Indon.
44 E3 Mouding China
79 B4 Mouyanga Aust.
61 C5 Movas Mexico
142 C2 Moxotó r. Brazil
79 C6 Mova Angola
142 D2 Moyobamba Peru
64 C3 Moyale Ethiopia
76 B4 Moyamba Sierra Leone
56 A4 Moyar r. India
74 C2 Moyen Atlas mt. ra. Morocco
14 F4 Moyenkapskiy Rus. Fed.
12 J1 Moyenmes Rus. Fed.
72 C5 Moyen-Chari div. Chad
20 H2 Moyenmoutier France
21 H2 Moyenmoutier France
78 B4 Moyen-Ogooué div. Gabon
14 B3 Moylovo Rus. Fed.
48 B2 Moynalyk Rus. Fed.
113 G2 Moyne, Lac Le l. Can.
40 D4 Moyo i. Indon.
99 G5 Moyowamba Peru
72 C5 Moyto Chad
65 J5 Moyu China
80 B4 Moyum waterhole Kenya
99 □ Moynty Kazak.
68 G2 Mozambique country Africa
83 G2 Mozambique Channel str. Africa
120 C5 Mozambique Ridge Indian Ocean
144 G1 Mozarlândia Brazil
13 H7 Mozdok Rus. Fed.
57 E1 Mozdūran Iran
14 C2 Mozharov Maydan Rus. Fed.
57 D4 Mūd-e-Dahanāb Iran
61 D4 Modesisat, J. h. Jordan
64 C4 Mozhgga Rus. Fed.
65 A2 Mozhnābād Iran
80 A3 Mpala r. India
12 F2 Mpala Tanzania
79 D6 Mpanda Tanzania
83 C5 Mpanda Tanzania
77 H3 Mpigi Uganda
79 B5 Mpoko r. C.A.R.
79 B5 Mpokro r. C.A.R.
79 C6 Mpouya Congo
79 □6 Mpulungu Zambia
55 H4 Mpwapwa Tanzania
81 B2 Mpigi Uganda
81 B6 Mporokoso Zambia
51 F2 Mufu Shan mt. ra. China
79 B5 Mpé Congo
55 H4 Mpessoba Mali
83 B7 Mpigi Uganda
81 C5 Mpika Zambia
79 □6 Mpokro C.A.R.
83 C6 Mpwapwa Tanzania
81 B7 Mporokoso Zambia
83 G2 Mpumalanga div. R.S.A.
120 C5 Mpwapwa Tanzania
79 B6 Mpwapwa Tanzania
83 C7 Mputa Zambia
83 C6 Msaken Tunisia
81 C7 Msambweni Kenya
81 C6 Msata Tanzania
12 D2 Mshinskaya Rus. Fed.
75 F1 M'Sila Algeria
75 G1 M'Saken Tunisia
93 □6 Mstera Rus. Fed.
14 F1 Mstera Rus. Fed.
14 E1 Mstislav Belarus
60 B4 Muğla div. Turkey
61 A2 Muğla Turkey

57 E4 Mubārak, J. mt. Jordan/Saudi Arabia
42 D3 Muang Lamphun Thailand
42 D3 Muang Loei Thailand
42 C3 Muang Lom Sak Thailand
42 C4 Muang Long r. Thailand
42 D4 Muang Luang r. Thailand
42 D4 Muang Mai Thailand
42 C2 Muang Mok Thailand
42 C3 Muang Nakhon Phanom Thailand
42 C3 Muang Nakhon Sawan Thailand
42 D3 Muang Nan Thailand
42 C3 Muang Ngoy Laos
42 C2 Muang Nong Laos
42 D3 Muang Ou Nua Laos
42 C3 Muang Pakbeng Laos
42 C2 Muang Paklay Laos
42 C3 Muang Phalan Laos
42 C3 Muang Phan Thailand
42 D3 Muang Phayao Thailand
42 C3 Muang Phetchabun Thailand
42 D3 Muang Phiang Laos
42 C3 Muang Phichai Thailand
42 C3 Muang Phichit Thailand
42 D3 Muang Phin Laos
42 C3 Muang Phitsanulok Thailand
42 C3 Muang Phôn-Hông Laos
42 D3 Muang Phrae Thailand
42 D3 Muang Renu Nakhon Thailand
42 C3 Muang Roi Et Thailand
42 D3 Muang Sakon Nakhon Thailand
42 C4 Muang Samut Prakan Thailand
42 C3 Muang Sing Laos
42 C2 Muang Souy Laos
42 C3 Muang Thoen Thailand
42 C3 Muang Uthai Thani Thailand
42 C2 Muang Va Laos
42 C3 Muang Vangviang Laos
42 C3 Muang Xaignabouri Laos
42 C2 Muang Xay Laos
42 C4 Muang Xon Laos
42 D4 Muang Yasothon Thailand
43 C7 Muar r. Malaysia
43 C7 Muar Malaysia
40 A2 Muaraatap Indon.
40 A2 Muarabulian Indon.
40 A3 Muaraburo Indon.
40 A3 Muaradua Indon.
40 A3 Muaraenim Indon.
40 D2 Muarajawa Indon.
40 A2 Muarakaman Indon.
40 D2 Muaralakitan Indon.
40 D1 Muaramayang Indon.
40 A2 Muaranawai Indon.
38 C7 Muarasiberut Indon.
40 C2 Muarateweh Indon.
40 A2 Muaratua Malaysia
40 A2 Muarawahau Indon.
55 E4 Mubarakpur India
81 B4 Mubende Uganda
77 G4 Mubi Nigeria
61 C4 Mubrak, J. mt. Jordan
139 E4 Mucajaí r. Brazil
81 B7 Muchinga Escarpment escarpment Zambia
12 J1 Muchkas. Rus. Fed.
16 D3 Muck i. U.K.
99 G5 Muckadilla Aust.
81 C6 Mucojo Mozambique
79 B6 Mucope Angola
79 B7 Mucope Angola
145 H5 Mucuri Brazil
145 J2 Mucuri r. Brazil
79 C6 Mucuchies Venezuela
100 C1 Mucusso Angola
81 C6 Muda r. Malaysia
65 G5 Mudanjiang China
61 C4 Mudanya Turkey
56 A3 Muddebihal India
55 H2 Muddus National Park nat. park Sweden
120 C5 Muddy Creek r. U.S.A.
129 G2 Muddy Peak summit U.S.A.
97 G2 Mudgee Aust.
64 D4 Mudon Myanmar
80 D2 Mudug div. Somalia
42 A3 Mudon Myanmar
81 B6 Mueda Mozambique
79 B6 Mufindi Tanzania
51 F2 Mufu Shan mt. ra. China
48 B2 Mugalzhar, G. mt. Mongolia
99 □1 Munning Pt pt Chatham Is N.Z.
147 B7 Nuñoz Gamero, Pen. de pen. Chile
21 H3 Münsingen Switz.
18 C4 Münster Germany
18 D3 Münster Germany
17 B5 Munster reg. Rep. of Ire.
95 □1 Muntok Indon.
65 J3 Muodoslompolo Sweden
126 C3 Muofors Norway
11 F3 Muonio Finland
11 F2 Muonionjoki r. Finland/Sweden
80 C2 Muqaddam w. Sudan
80 E5 Muqdisho Somalia
65 H5 Muqi China
64 F2 Muğla div. Turkey
61 A2 Muğla Turkey
18 E3 Mühlhausen (Thüringen) Germany
11 H3 Muhos Finland
80 C4 Muhulu Zaire
145 H4 Mui Brazil
79 B5 Mui Ca Mau c. Vietnam
39 J8 Mui Chiang Rai Thailand
90 □4 Mui Hopohoponga pt ...
14 B3 Muir India
42 A3 Muang Hiam Laos
42 D3 Muang Hôngsa Laos
42 C3 Muang Kalasin Thailand
42 C3 Muang Khammouan Laos
42 C4 Muang Khongxédôn Laos
42 C3 Muang Khong Laos
42 C3 Muang Khoua Laos
42 C3 Muang Khon Kaen Thailand
42 C3 Muang Khuan Thailand
42 C3 Muang Lampang Thailand

94 □4 Mutton Bird I. i. Lord Howe I. Pac. Oc.
93 B7 Mutton I. is N.Z.
93 A7 Muttonbird Islands is N.Z.
83 F1 Mutuali Mozambique
139 E5 Mutum Amazonas Brazil
145 H3 Mutum Minas Gerais Brazil
142 E2 Mutunópolis Brazil
10 G1 Mutusjärvi I. Finland
15 F1 Mutyn Ukraine
10 G2 Muurola Finland
48 D5 Mu Us Shamo desert China
79 B6 Muxaluando Angola
79 B5 Muxima Angola
12 E2 Muyezerskiy Rus. Fed.
64 F4 Muyinga Burundi
79 B5 Muymanak Uzbekistan
81 B7 Muyumbwe Zaire
54 C2 Muzaffarabad Pakistan
54 B3 Muzaffargarh Pakistan
55 F4 Muzaffarnagar India
54 D4 Muzaffarnagar India
65 K4 Muzat r. China
57 E4 Mūzīn Iran
110 C4 Muzon, C. c. U.S.A.
131 E3 Múzquiz Mexico
65 J3 Muztag mt. China
65 J5 Muztagata mt. China
78 B3 Mvadi Gabon
78 B3 Mvangan Cameroon
78 D4 Mvolo Sudan
81 C6 Mvomero Tanzania
83 F2 Mvoma Zimbabwe
81 B5 Mwanza div. Tanzania
81 B5 Mwanza Tanzania
79 D4 Mweka Zaire
79 D5 Mwenda Zambia
83 F3 Mwene-Ditu Zaire
83 E3 Mwenezi r. Zimbabwe
83 E3 Mwenezi Zimbabwe
79 C6 Mwenga Zaire
79 E5 Mweru, Lake l. Zambia
79 E5 Mweru Wantipa, Lake l. Zambia
79 E5 Mweru Wantipa Nat. Park nat. park Zambia
79 D6 Mwinilunga Zambia
42 A3 Myaing Myanmar
54 B4 Myājlar India
42 A3 Myanaung Myanmar
42 A2 Myanmar country Asia
14 C2 Myatlevo Rus. Fed.
42 B3 Myayamgmya Myanmar
42 B3 Myawadi Thailand
42 A2 Myebon Myanmar
42 A2 Myedu Myanmar
42 A3 Myingyan Myanmar
42 A3 Myinkyado Myanmar
43 B4 Myinmoletkat mt. Myanmar
42 A3 Myitta Myanmar
42 B2 Myitkyina Myanmar
42 A3 Myittson Myanmar
42 A2 Myittha r. Myanmar
42 A3 Myittha Myanmar
42 A2 Myitnge r. Myanmar
28 A2 Myjava Slovakia
42 B3 Myaungmya Myanmar
14 D5 Myakka City U.S.A.
14 C2 Myatlevo Rus. Fed.
14 E2 Myebon Myanmar
11 F3 Mynämäki Finland
17 E5 Mynydd Epynt h. U.K.
17 D5 Mynydd Preseli h. U.K.
47 □2 Myōkō Japan
47 G5 Myōkō-san vol Japan
42 A2 Myothit Myanmar
10 M2 Mýrdalsjökull ice cap Iceland
10 J1 Myre Norway
10 F2 Myrhorod Ukraine
15 E2 Myrhorod Ukraine
15 D1 Myrne Kyiv Ukraine
15 E3 Myrne Donets'k Ukraine
15 D3 Myrne Kherson Ukraine
15 E3 Myrne Odesa Ukraine
15 D2 Myronivka Novorosiys'ka Ukraine
29 E6 Myrtos Greece
55 G4 Myrtle Beach U.S.A.
126 B3 Myrtle Creek U.S.A.
119 E6 Myrtle Point U.S.A.
29 E6 Mysia reg. Turkey
19 H2 Myślenice Poland
19 L5 Myślibórz Poland
19 H3 Myszków Poland
63 T3 Mys Shmidta Rus. Fed.
19 J3 Myszków Poland
29 F6 Mytilíni Greece
29 F5 Mytilini Strait chan. Greece/Turkey
14 C2 Mytishchi Rus. Fed.
81 B7 Mzimba Malawi
81 B7 Mzuzu Malawi

N

78 C1 Naala Chad
127 □2 Naalehu U.S.A.
80 □ Na'am w. Sudan
75 H1 Naama Algeria
11 F3 Naantali Finland
17 C5 Naas Rep. of Ire.
42 D5 Naba Myanmar
82 B4 Nababeep R.S.A.
63 R3 Nabari Japan
54 C2 Nabha India
81 C5 Nabire Indon.
90 □2 Nabavatu Fiji
61 C3 Nabatiyet et Tahta Lebanon
90 □3 Nabouwalu Fiji
47 □1 Nabari Japan
75 H1 Naberezhnyye Chelny Rus. Fed.
75 G1 Nabeul Tunisia

P

Q

R

142 A3 Rosário Oeste Brazil
130 B2 Rosarito Mexico
130 A1 Rosarito Mexico
130 C3 Rosarito Sur Mexico
27 F6 Rosarno Italy
138 B3 Rosa Zárate Ecuador
11 H3 Roschino Rus. Fed.
121 F4 Roscoe U.S.A.
20 C2 Roscoff France
17 C5 Roscommon Rep. of Ire.
122 E3 Roscommon U.S.A.
17 D5 Roscrea Rep. of Ire.
98 C2 Rose r.
133 G4 Roseau Dominica
111 K5 Roseau U.S.A.
81 □4 Rose Belle Mauritius
97 H5 Rosebery Aust.
81 J4 Rose Blanche Can.
126 B3 Roseburg U.S.A.
123 E3 Rose City U.S.A.
99 G5 Rosedale Aust.
133 □1 Rose Hall Jamaica
81 □4 Rosehearty U.K.
80 B2 Roseires Reservoir resr Sudan
87 L6 Rose Island i. American Samoa Pac. Oc.
122 A3 Rosemount U.S.A.
128 C2 Rosenberg U.S.A.
125 E6 Rosenberg U.S.A.
11 B4 Rosendal Norway
95 H2 Rosenheim Germany
110 C4 Rose Pt pt Can.
25 H1 Roses Spain
119 F7 Roses The Bahamas
25 H1 Roses, Golf de b. Spain
26 E4 Roseto degli Abruzzi Italy
111 H4 Rosetown Can.
20 G2 Rosetti, C. A. Romania
114 C2 Rose Valley Can.
128 B2 Roseville U.S.A.
122 B5 Roseville U.S.A.
14 D2 Roshal' Rus. Fed.
57 D2 Roshkhvār Iran
82 B4 Rosh Pinah Namibia
26 C4 Rosignano Marittimo Italy
139 F2 Rosignol Guyana
28 E2 Rosiorii de Vede Romania
28 E3 Rositsa Bulgaria
11 D5 Roskilde Denmark
24 E5 Roslavl' Rus. Fed.
10 J1 Roslyakovo Rus. Fed.
142 H3 Roslyn Lake l. Can.
14 B2 Roslyn Lake l. Can.
27 E7 Rosolini Italy
20 C3 Rosporden France
97 F5 Ross r. Can.
93 C6 Ross r. N.Z.
17 C4 Rossan Point pt Rep. of Ire.
125 F5 Ross Barnett Res. l. U.S.A.
113 G3 Ross Bay Junction Can.
152 A5 Ross Dependency reg. Ant.
114 C2 Rosseau Lake l. Can.
90 □1 Rossel i. P.N.G.
113 Rush Hill h. Christmas I. Indian Ocean
152 B4 Ross Ice Shelf ice feature Ant.
113 H5 Rossignol, L. l. Can.
17 D5 Ross Island i. Ant.
17 D5 Rosslare Rep. of Ire.
115 G4 Rossmore Can.
152 □ Ross, Mt mt. Kerguelen Indian Ocean
93 A6 Ross, Mt mt. N.Z.
74 A5 Rosso Mauritania
21 J5 Rosso, Capo pt France
17 F6 Ross-on-Wye U.K.
99 G5 Rossosh' Rus. Fed.
114 B2 Rossport Can.
110 C2 Ross River Can.
152 A5 Ross Sea sea Ant.
10 D2 Rossvatnet l. Norway
122 D5 Rossville U.S.A.
110 D3 Rosswood Can.
57 G3 Rostaq Afghanistan
27 C5 Rostaq Iran
14 H4 Rostashi Rus. Fed.
15 F5 Rostavytsya r. Ukraine
111 H4 Rosthern Can.
18 F1 Rostock Germany
13 G6 Rostov Rus. Fed.
14 D1 Rostov Rus. Fed.
13 F6 Rostov-na-Donu Rus. Fed.
20 C2 Rostrenen France
10 D2 Rosvik Sweden
115 F5 Roswell U.S.A.
127 F5 Roswell U.S.A.
35 M4 Rota i. Northern Mariana Is Pac. Oc.
24 C4 Rota Spain
39 H8 Rote i. Indon.
95 F5 Rotenburg (Wümme) Germany
18 D5 Rote Wand mt. Austria
18 D3 Roth Germany
18 D3 Rothaargebirge h. Germany
18 E4 Rothenburg ob der Tauber Germany
19 G3 Rothenburg (Oberlausitz) Germany
152 B2 Rothera U.K. Base Ant.
93 D5 Rotherham U.K.
16 E4 Rothes U.K.
16 E4 Rothesay U.K.
123 G2 Rothschild U.S.A.
152 B2 Rothschild I. i. Ant.
76 B5 Rotifunk Sierra Leone
97 H3 Roto Aust.
91 □10 Rotoaira Fr. Poly. Pac. Oc.
93 C5 Rotoiti, L. l. N.Z.
92 G3 Rotomanu N.Z.
93 D4 Rotorua N.Z.
93 D4 Rotorua, L. N. Z.
93 D4 Rotorua, L. l. N.Z.
18 D3 Rott r. Germany
18 E5 Rottenmann Austria
101 A7 Rottnest I. i. Aust.
18 D2 Rottumeroog i. Netherlands
150 D6 Rotuma i. Fiji
10 D3 Rötviken Sweden
21 F1 Roubaix France
12 □ Roudnice nad Labem Czech Rep.
20 E2 Rouen France
133 □1 Rouge, Point pt Trinidad Trin. & Tobago
93 B6 Rough Ridge ridge N.Z.
18 A3 Roulers Belgium
81 □1 Roundeyed, Lac l. Can.
81 □1 Round I. i. Rodrigues I. Mauritius
128 D2 Round Mountain U.S.A.
97 H2 Round Mt mt. Aust.
129 G3 Round Rock U.S.A.
111 D Roundup U.S.A.
49 J2 Roura French Guiana
16 E3 Rousay i. U.K.
21 G4 Roussillon France
16 D5 Rouyn Can.
13 F6 Roven'ki Rus. Fed.
13 F5 Rovereto Italy
21 F1 Rôviëng Tbong Cambodia
26 D2 Rovigo Italy
13 □1 Rovinj Croatia
C7 Rovuma r. Mozambique

90 □2 Rowa is Vanuatu
57 B2 Row'ān Iran
97 G2 Rowena Aust.
100 B3 Rowley Shoals sand bank Aust.
41 B4 Roxas Phil.
41 B3 Roxas Phil.
41 B2 Roxas Phil.
41 B6 Roxas Phil.
41 A4 Roxas Phil.
119 E4 Roxboro U.S.A.
133 □2 Roxborough Tobago Trin. & Tobago
98 B4 Roxborough Downs Aust.
93 B6 Roxburgh N.Z.
96 D2 Roxby Downs Aust.
99 E2 Roxby Nat. Park nat. park Aust.
76 A4 Roxo, Cabo pt Senegal
115 J4 Roxton-Sud Can.
127 F4 Roy U.S.A.
17 D5 Royal Canal canal Rep. of Ire.
122 C1 Royale, Isle i. U.S.A.
114 A2 Royal, Mount h. Can.
123 F4 Royal Oak U.S.A.
20 D4 Royan France
20 F2 Roye France
17 G5 Royston U.K.
28 C3 Rožaj Yugo.
19 K2 Rożan Poland
15 D3 Rozdol'ne Ukraine
15 E1 Rozdol'ne Ukraine
15 E1 Rozdol'ne Ukraine
122 B5 Rushville U.S.A.
55 H3 Rushon Tajik.
122 B5 Rushville U.S.A.
132 H2 Rushville U.S.A.
28 F3 Rusokastro Bulgaria
142 E1 Russas Brazil
111 J4 Russell Man.
92 E1 Russell N.Z.
124 D4 Russell U.S.A.
110 F2 Russel Lake l. Can.
109 J2 Russell Is i. Solomon Is
101 C7 Russell Ra. h. Aust.
125 D5 Russellville U.S.A.
125 E6 Russellville U.S.A.
119 C6 Russellville U.S.A.
18 D3 Rüsselsheim Germany
62 G3 Russian Federation country Asia
63 Q2 Russkoye Ust'ye Rus. Fed.
13 H7 Rust'avi Georgia
14 G1 Rustay Rus. Fed.
82 C4 Rustenburg R.S.A.
125 E5 Ruston U.S.A.
81 A5 Rutana Burundi
24 D4 Rute Spain
40 E4 Ruteng Indon.
129 E2 Ruth U.S.A.
115 F3 Rutherglen Can.
14 H1 Rutka r. Rus. Fed.
121 G3 Rutland U.S.A.
43 A5 Rutland I. i. Andaman and Nicobar Is
110 G2 Rutland Water resr U.K.
54 D2 Rutog China
114 E3 Rutter Can.
13 H7 Rutul Rus. Fed.
10 G2 Ruukki Finland
57 D4 Rū'us al Jibāl mts Oman
81 C7 Ruvuma div. Tanzania
81 C7 Ruvuma r. Tanzania
61 A5 Ruwaydah Aust.
100 C4 Ruwayshid, Wādī w Jordan
61 C5 Ruweijil pt Saudi Arabia
81 A5 Ruweis U.A.E.
61 C5 Ruweita, W. w Jordan
81 A5 Ruwenzori Range mt. ra. Uganda/Zaire
81 A5 Ruyuan China
14 C2 Ruza r. Rus. Fed.
14 C2 Ruzayevka Kazak.
14 F2 Ruzayevka Rus. Fed.
15 C2 Ruzhyn Ukraine
19 J4 Ružomberok Slovakia
79 C5 Rwanda country Africa
81 A5 Rweru, Lake l. Burundi
12 F3 Ryadovo Rus. Fed.
14 F2 Ryas'ke Ukraine
12 H2 Ryasnopil' Ukraine
12 F4 Ryazan' div. Rus. Fed.
13 F5 Ryazan' Rus. Fed.
14 G2 Ryazanka Rus. Fed.
14 G2 Ryazanovskiy Rus. Fed.
14 D1 Ryazantsevo Rus. Fed.
62 E2 Rybachiy, Poluostrov pen. Rus. Fed.
14 D1 Rybinsk Rus. Fed.
24 F1 Rybinsk Rus. Fed.
12 E3 Rybinskoye Vdkhr. resr Rus. Fed.
19 H3 Rybnik Poland
19 H3 Rybnoye Rus. Fed.
19 H3 Rychnov nad Kněžnou Czech Rep.
110 7 Rycroft Can.
11 D4 Ryd Sweden
152 B3 Rydberg Pen. pen. Ant.
15 A2 Rydomyl' Ukraine
17 H6 Rye U.K.
15 A1 Rykhal's'ke Ukraine
126 C2 Rygaca China
11 D4 Ryl'sk U.K.
97 G3 Rylstone Aust.
19 K4 Rymanów Poland
19 H4 Ryn Peski desert Kazak.
46 E4 Ryōri-zaki pt Japan
47 J6 Ryōtsu Japan
19 J2 Rypin Poland
16 K1 Ryshkovo Rus. Fed.
14 B3 Ryukyu Is is Japan
14 B3 Ryukyu Trench Japan
15 D2 Rzhaksa Rus. Fed.
54 C4 Rzeszów Poland
15 D2 Rzhyshchiv Ukraine

S

83 E3 Runde r. Zimbabwe
82 B2 Rundu Namibia
10 E3 Rundvik Sweden
40 C2 Rungan r. Indon.
78 E3 Rungu r. Zaire
81 B6 Rungwa Rukwa Tanzania
81 B6 Rungwa Singida Tanzania
81 B6 Rungwa r. Tanzania
81 B6 Rungwa Game Reserve res. Tanzania
51 L1 Runheji China
101 C4 Runton Ra. h. Aust.
50 C1 Ru'nying China
11 H3 Ruokolahti Finland
44 E4 Ruoqiang China
48 A4 Ruo Shui r. China
91 E4 Rupa India
97 E4 Rupanyup Aust.
28 E1 Rupea Romania
112 F3 Rupert r. Can.
126 D3 Rupert U.S.A.
112 E3 Rupert r. Can.
112 F3 Rupert Bay b. Can.
126 D3 Ruppert Coast Ant.
139 F3 Rupununi r. Guyana
87 N7 Rurutu i. Fr. Poly. Pac. Oc.
83 E2 Rusape Zimbabwe
82 B2 Rushinga Zimbabwe
122 C4 Rush Lake l. U.S.A.
55 H3 Rushon Tajik.
122 B5 Rushville U.S.A.
119 D7 Ruskin U.S.A.
28 F3 Rusokastro Bulgaria
142 E1 Russas Brazil
111 J4 Russell Man.
92 E1 Russell N.Z.
124 D4 Russell U.S.A.
110 F2 Russel Lake l. Can.
109 J2 Russell Is i. Solomon Is
101 C7 Russell Ra. h. Aust.
125 D5 Russellville U.S.A.
125 E6 Russellville U.S.A.
119 C6 Russellville U.S.A.
18 D3 Rüsselsheim Germany
62 G3 Russian Federation country Asia
63 Q2 Russkiy Brod Rus. Fed.
14 H3 Russkiy Kameshkir Rus. Fed.
63 Q2 Russkoye Ust'ye Rus. Fed.
13 H7 Rust'avi Georgia
14 G1 Rustay Rus. Fed.
82 C4 Rustenburg R.S.A.
125 E5 Ruston U.S.A.
81 A5 Rutana Burundi
24 D4 Rute Spain
40 E4 Ruteng Indon.
129 E2 Ruth U.S.A.
115 F3 Rutherglen Can.
14 H1 Rutka r. Rus. Fed.
121 G3 Rutland U.S.A.
43 A5 Rutland I. i. Andaman and Nicobar Is
110 G2 Rutland Water resr U.K.
54 D2 Rutog China
114 E3 Rutter Can.
13 H7 Rutul Rus. Fed.
10 G2 Ruukki Finland
57 D4 Rū'us al Jibāl mts Oman
81 C7 Ruvuma div. Tanzania
81 C7 Ruvuma r. Tanzania

133 G3 Saba i. Netherlands Ant.
61 B4 Saba'a Egypt
133 G3 Saba Bank Caribbean
13 □ Sab' Ābār Syria
32 B2 Sabac Yugo.
25 H2 Sabadell Spain
43 F5 Sabah Malaysia
41 A5 Sabah div. Malaysia
43 C7 Sabak Malaysia
40 D3 Sabalana i. Indon.
40 D3 Sabalana, Kep. is Indon.
54 D4 Sabalgarh India
139 F2 Sabana Surinam
132 B2 Sabana, Arch. de is Cuba
130 J6 Sabana Gde Honduras
138 C1 Sabanalarga Colombia
138 C1 Sabaneta Venezuela
40 C2 Sabang Indon.
40 D1 Sabang Indon.
28 F1 Săbăoani Romania
145 G3 Sabará Brazil
56 C2 Sābāri r. India
61 C2 Sabastiya Israel
57 D1 Sabaru i. Indon.
140 D3 Sabaya Bolivia
57 D2 Sabeh Iran
72 B2 Sabhā Libya
57 □ Şabḩā' Saudi Arabia
54 D4 Sabi r. India
83 E4 Sabie r. Mozambique/R.S.A.
130 D2 Sabinal Mexico
131 B5 Sabinas Mexico
131 B5 Sabinas Hidalgo Mexico
125 E6 Sabine l. U.S.A.
27 D4 Sabini, Monti mts Italy
145 G3 Sabinópolis Brazil
19 K4 Sabinov Slovakia
14 C2 Sabirabad Azerbaijan
74 B4 Sabkhat Aghzoumal salt flat Western Sahara
72 C1 Sabkhat al Hayshah salt pan Libya
61 D2 Sabkhat al Jabbūl salt flat Syria
74 B3 Sabkhat al Marāghah salt flat Syria
74 B3 Sabkhat Aridal salt pan Western Sahara
74 B3 Sabkhat Oum Dba salt pan Western Sahara
74 B3 Sabkhat Tah salt pan Morocco
61 B4 Sabkhet el Bardawil lag. Egypt
41 B3 Sablayan Phil.
119 D7 Sable, Cape c. U.S.A.
90 □2 Sable, Î. de i. Pac. Oc.
113 J5 Sable Island i. Can.
114 D3 Sables, River aux r. Can.
20 D3 Sablé-sur-Sarthe France
142 E2 Saboeiro Brazil
77 F4 Sabon Kafi Niger
76 D4 Sabou Burkina
20 D4 Sabres France
130 C2 Sabrina Coast Ant.
57 G3 Sabugal Portugal
122 B4 Sabula U.S.A.
40 E2 Sabulu Indon.
59 □ Şabyā Saudi Arabia
57 D1 Sabzevār Iran
57 D4 Sabzvārān Iran
140 D3 Sacaca Bolivia
28 E2 Sacalinul Mare, Insula i. Romania
131 H5 Sacbe Mexico
27 D5 Sacco r. Italy
28 E2 Săcel Romania
28 E2 Săcele Romania
79 C6 Sachanga Angola
112 B3 Sachigo r. Can.
112 B3 Sachigo L. l. Can.
55 M3 Sach'on S. Korea
46 F3 Sach'ŏn S. Korea
18 F3 Sachsen div. Germany
18 E2 Sachsen-Anhalt div. Germany
108 F2 Sachs Harbour Can.
121 E3 Sackets Harbor U.S.A.
114 C2 Sackville Can.
121 H3 Saco U.S.A.
126 F1 Saco U.S.A.
41 B5 Sacol i. Phil.
144 E3 Sacramento Brazil
128 B2 Sacramento U.S.A.
128 B2 Sacramento airport U.S.A.
127 F5 Sacramento Mts mt. ra. U.S.A.
128 B1 Sacramento Valley v. U.S.A.
141 E2 Sacri r. Brazil
28 E1 Săcueni Romania
82 D5 Sacuriuiná r. Brazil
32 B5 Sada R.S.A.
25 H1 Sádaba Spain
57 B3 Sa'dabad Iran
60 D3 Sadad Syria
73 H4 Sada'h Yemen
54 C4 Sadiqabad Pakistan
132 □ Sada, W. w. Saudi Arabia
54 B3 Sadda Pakistan
18 E4 Saddle Peak summit Andaman and Nicobar Is
43 A5 Sa Đec Vietnam
55 H4 Sadēng China
54 B3 Sadhaura India
57 E4 Sadij r. Iran
53 E3 Sadiqabad Pakistan
54 C4 Sadiya India
60 D3 Sa'dīyah, Hawr as l. Iraq
24 B2 Sado r. Portugal
47 G5 Sado i. Japan
46 E2 Sadon r. Malaysia
55 H4 Sadon Myanmar
47 G5 Sado-shima i. Japan
55 G4 Sadri India
54 C4 Sadri India
47 E6 Sadowara Japan
11 C4 Sæby Denmark
61 C3 Safa lava Syria
61 □ Safafal Maqūf well Iraq
60 H5 Safed Khirs mts Afghanistan
11 F4 Säffle Sweden
129 H5 Safford U.S.A.
17 H6 Saffron Walden U.K.
74 C2 Safi Morocco
57 C3 Safidabeh Iran
57 C3 Safīd Dasht Iran
57 E4 Safīd Sagak Iran
61 D2 Şāfītā Syria
79 B4 Safonovo Rus. Fed.
14 A1 Safonovo Rus. Fed.
14 J1 Safonovo Rus. Fed.
29 H5 Safranbolu Turkey
60 E2 Safwān Iraq
55 G3 Saga China

46 C7 Saga div. Japan
64 H4 Saga Kazak.
47 H4 Sagae Japan
42 A2 Sagaing div. Myanmar
42 A2 Sagaing Myanmar
47 G6 Sagamihara Japan
47 G6 Sagami-nada g. Japan
47 G6 Sagami-wan b. Japan
138 C2 Sagamoso r. Colombia
55 E4 Saganthit Kyun i. Myanmar
56 A2 Sagar India
56 B2 Sagar India
13 H7 Sagarejo Georgia
55 G5 Sagar I. i. India
57 E2 Saghand Iran
57 E2 Saghar Afghanistan
123 H4 Saginaw U.S.A.
123 F4 Saginaw Bay b. U.S.A.
29 J5 Sağlar Turkey
64 D3 Sagiz r. Kazak.
64 D3 Sagiz Kazak.
76 C4 Sagleipie Liberia
113 H2 Saglek Bay b. Can.
21 J5 Sagone, Golfe de b. France
24 B4 Sagres Portugal
24 B4 Sagres, Pta de pt Portugal
49 F2 Sagsay r. Mongolia
42 A2 Sagu Myanmar
127 F4 Saguache U.S.A.
132 D2 Sagua de Tánamo Cuba
132 C2 Sagua la Grande Cuba
129 G5 Saguaro National Monument res. U.S.A.
113 G3 Saguenay r. Can.
25 F3 Sagunto Spain
55 G4 Sagwara India
64 D4 Sagyndyk, Mys pt Kazak.
60 C4 Sahāb Jordan
138 D2 Sahagún Colombia
24 D1 Sahagún Spain
73 H4 Sahara desert Africa
54 D3 Saharanpur India
54 E4 Saharsa India
54 D4 Sahaswan India
60 C2 Sahbuz Azerbaijan
55 H4 Sahibganj India
43 B6 Sai Buri Thailand
43 B6 Sai Buri r. Thailand
75 G2 Saïda Algeria
61 C3 Saïda Lebanon
57 C3 Sa'īdābād Iran
57 E3 Sa'īdābād Iran
54 C3 Saidpur Bangladesh
54 E4 Saidpur India
47 H5 Saigō Japan
55 H5 Saiha India
48 E4 Saihan Toroi China
47 F5 Saijō Japan
47 D6 Saiki Japan
41 □ Sai Kung Hong Kong China
10 H3 Saimaa l. Finland
130 D4 Sain Alto Mexico
29 H5 Sainbeyli Turkey
60 D2 Sa'īn Iran
57 D4 Sa'indezh Iran
76 A4 Sainsoboug Senegal
16 F4 St Abb's Head hd U.K.
81 □5 St-Affrique France
115 J4 St-Agapit Can.
20 F4 St-Aignan France
17 D3 St Alban's Can.
113 J4 St Alban's Can.
120 C5 St Albans U.S.A.
17 F6 St Albans U.K.
17 E7 St Alban's Head hd U.K.
110 G4 St Albert Can.
20 D3 Saint-Alexis-des-Monts France
20 F2 St-Amand-Montrond France
115 F2 St-Ambroise Can.
21 F3 St-Amour France
19 G5 St André Austria
133 □7 St Andrew div. Trinidad Trin. & Tobago
133 □1 St Andrew div. Jamaica
16 F3 St Andrews U.K.
113 H4 St Andrews Can.
16 F4 St Andrew's U.K.
133 G4 St Andrews U.S.A.
133 □1 St Ann div. Jamaica
132 C3 St Anna-'baai b. Curaçao Netherlands Ant.
115 H4 St Ann I. i. Seychelles
133 □1 St Ann's Bay Jamaica
133 □5 St Anne Guadeloupe Caribbean
121 G2 St Ansgar U.S.A.
133 G4 St Anthony Mon. of Egypt
99 C4 St George Bermuda
115 J4 St George Can.
133 G3 St George's Grenada Caribbean
115 H4 St George Bermuda
113 H4 St George's b. Can.
16 F3 St George's Channel chan. Rep. of Ire./U.K.
119 C4 St George I. i. U.S.A.

122 E3 St Helen U.S.A.
148 J7 St Helena i. Atlantic Ocean
128 A2 St Helena U.S.A.
82 B5 St Helena Bay b. R.S.A.
148 J6 St Helena Fracture Atlantic Ocean
97 G5 St Helens Aust.
126 B2 St Helens U.S.A.
122 A4 St Helens U.K.
124 F4 St Helens U.S.A.
97 G5 St Helens Pt pt Aust.
17 F7 St Helier Jersey Channel Is
20 D3 St-Hilaire-du-Harcouët France
115 K2 St-Honoré Can.
18 B3 St-Hubert Belgium
122 E3 St-Hyacinthe Can.
114 D5 St Clair, Lake l. Can.
114 D5 St Clair Shores U.S.A.
133 □5 St Claude Guadeloupe Caribbean
20 F2 St-Claude France
124 E2 St Cloud U.S.A.
115 K2 St-Coeur-de-Marie Can.
113 H4 St Croix r. Can.
133 F3 St Croix i. Virgin Is Caribbean
133 □5 St Croix Falls U.S.A.
133 F3 St Croix I. i. Virgin Is Caribbean
133 □7 St David div. Trinidad Trin. & Tobago
133 □1 St David div. Jamaica
119 □1 St David's Head hd U.K.
113 □4 St David's Island i. Bermuda
81 □5 St-Denis Réunion Indian Ocean
81 □5 St-Dié France
21 H2 St-Dizier France
115 H4 St-Donat Can.
115 H4 St-Adèle Can.
111 K5 St-Agathe-des-Monts Can.
115 K3 St Anne Can.
115 K3 St Anne Can.
76 C5 St Anne r. Liberia
129 F1 St Anne i. U.S.A.
133 G4 St Anne Martinique Caribbean
115 K3 Ste-Anne-de-Beaupré Can.
121 J1 Ste-Anne-de-Madawaska Can.
115 H3 Ste-Anne-du-Lac Can.
119 D6 St Anne, L. L. Can.
122 E4 Ste-Camille-de-Lellis Can.
121 H1 Ste-Camille-de-Lellis Can.
115 J4 Ste-Croix Can.
115 K3 Ste-Émélie-de-l'Energie Can.
121 H1 Ste-Foy Can.
21 G4 Ste-Foy-la-Grande France
132 B4 Ste-Julie Trin. & Tobago
20 E4 Ste-Julienne Can.
121 H1 Sainte-Justine Can.
114 D3 St Elias, C. c. U.S.A.
110 B2 St Elias Mountains mt. ra. Can.
132 C3 St Jozefsdal Curaçao Netherlands Ant.
139 G3 St Elie French Guiana
133 □1 St Elizabeth div. Jamaica
20 F3 St-Éloy-les-Mines France
20 F2 St-Just-en-Chaussée France
133 □6 Ste Luce Martinique Caribbean
113 H5 St Kilda i. N.Z.
76 C5 St Kilda i. U.K.
133 G3 St Kitts i. St Kitts-Nevis Caribbean
133 G3 St Kitts-Nevis country Caribbean
132 C3 St Kruis Curaçao Netherlands Ant.
152 □ St Lanne Gramont, I. i. Kerguelen Indian Ocean
113 H4 St Laurent Can.
21 G5 Stes-Maries-de-la-Mer France
139 G2 St-Laurent-du-Maroni French Guiana
133 G4 St Lawrence Aust.
113 K4 St Lawrence r. Can./U.S.A.
113 H4 St Lawrence inlet Can.
113 H4 St Lawrence, Gulf of g. Can.
108 B3 St Lawrence I. i. U.S.A.
115 J3 St Lawrence Islands National Park nat. park Can./U.S.A.
113 J4 St Lawrence Seaway chan. Can./U.S.A.
115 J3 St-Léonard Can.
20 E4 St-Léonard-de-Noblat France
81 □5 St-Leu Réunion Indian Ocean
133 G3 St Lewis r. Can.
20 D2 St-Lô France
76 A3 St Louis Senegal
123 F4 St Louis U.S.A.
124 F4 St Louis U.S.A.
21 H3 St-Louis France
133 □5 St Louis Guadeloupe Caribbean
104 M8 St Lucia country Caribbean
133 G4 St Lucia Channel chan. Martinique/St Lucia
81 J3 St Lucia, Lake l. R.S.A.
133 G4 St Lucia Passage chan. St Lucia/St Vincent
21 H4 St-Lyé France
133 □5 St-Maixent-l'Ecole France
115 □5 St Maarten i. Caribbean
21 H5 St Gallen Switz.
20 C2 St Gaudens France
20 C2 St-Gaultier France
20 C2 St-Gédéon Can.
99 G3 St George Aust.
113 □4 St George Bermuda
81 □5 Saint-Marc-Marin France
81 □5 St-Marcellin France

20 C4 St-Médard-en-Jalles France
19 F5 St Michael im Langau Austria
113 J3 St Michaels Bay b. Can.
133 D3 St Michel de l'Atalaye Haiti
21 H4 St-Michel-de-Maurienne France
115 J3 Saint-Michel-des-Saints Can.
132 □2 St Michiel Curaçao Netherlands Ant.
21 G2 St Moritz France
21 H5 St Moritz Switz.
20 C3 St-Nazaire France
115 J4 St-Nicéphore Can.
133 E4 St Nicolaas Aruba
20 C3 St-Nicolas-de-Port France
21 H2 St Niklaus Belgium
21 H3 St Niklaus Switz.
21 H2 St-Omer France
20 D4 Saintonge reg. France
121 J1 St-Pamphile Can.
113 G4 St Pascal Can.
133 □3 St Patrick div. Trinidad Trin. & Tobago
81 □5 St-Paul Réunion Indian Ocean
76 B5 St Paul r. Liberia
124 D3 St Paul U.S.A.
120 B6 St Paul U.S.A.
81 □5 St-Paul, B. de b. Réunion Indian Ocean
77 F5 St Paul, Cape c. Ghana
149 K6 St Paul, Île i. Indian Ocean
108 B4 St Paul Island U.S.A.
113 G4 St-Paul-de-Joliette Can.
113 G3 St-Paul, Mon. of Egypt
20 □14 St Paul's Point pt Pitcairn I. Pac. Oc.
18 D1 St Peter-Ording Germany
17 F7 St Peter Port Guernsey Channel Is
13 D4 St Petersburg Rus. Fed.
119 D7 St Petersburg U.S.A.
40 B1 St Petrus i. Indon.
21 H4 St-Philbert-de-Grand-Lieu France
81 □5 St-Philippe Réunion Indian Ocean
133 □7 St-Pie Martinique Caribbean
133 □4 St-Pierre Martinique Caribbean
81 □5 St-Pierre Réunion Indian Ocean
113 H4 St-Pierre St Pierre and Miquelon N. America
113 □3 St Pierre i. St Pierre and Miquelon N. America
104 N5 St Pierre and Miquelon terr. N. America
20 D4 St-Pierre-d'Oléron France
115 J3 St-Pierre, Lac l. Can.
20 D2 St-Pierre-le-Moûtier France
20 D2 St-Pierre-sur-Dives France
20 F1 St-Pol-de-Léon France
20 F1 St-Pol-sur-Ternoise France
19 F5 St Pölten Austria
20 F3 St-Pourçain-sur-Sioule France
21 F3 St-Pourçain-sur-Sioule France
121 H1 St-Prosper Can.
21 H3 St-Quentin Can.
21 H3 St-Raphaël France
132 □2 St Regis r. U.S.A.
115 H3 St Regis Falls U.S.A.
115 J3 St-Rémi Can.
20 C2 St-Renan France
20 B2 St-Rigaud, Mont mt. France
113 H4 St-Sauveur-des-Monts Can.
20 F1 St-Sébastien Can.
21 F3 St-Siméon Can.
21 F3 St Stephen Can.
20 C2 St Stephen U.S.A.
21 F3 St-Symphorien France
21 F3 St-Théophile Can.
111 H4 St Theresa Point Can.
115 J3 St Thomas Can.
133 F3 St Thomas i. Virgin Is Caribbean
133 □1 St Thomas I. i. Virgin Is Caribbean
20 F1 St-Tite Can.
21 H5 St-Tropez France
20 D3 St-Vaast-la-Hougue France
20 E1 St-Valery-en-Caux France
20 E1 St-Valéry-sur-Somme France
21 G3 St-Vallier Bourgogne France
21 G4 St-Vallier Rhône-Alpes France
20 E3 St-Vaury France
19 F5 St Veit an der Glan Austria
21 H4 St-Véran France
133 G4 St-Vincent France
81 □5 St-Vincent and the Grenadines country Caribbean
96 D3 St Vincent, Gulf b. Aust.
133 G4 St Vincent Passage chan. St Lucia/St Vincent
18 B3 St-Vith Belgium
18 E4 St Wendel Germany
132 C3 St Willebrordus Curaçao Netherlands Ant.
114 E5 St Williams Can.
27 F4 St-Xdt U.S.A.
20 E4 St-Yrieix-la-Perche France
55 M3 Sajama mt. Nepal
144 E3 Saitama div. Japan
42 A2 Saitlai Myanmar
20 E4 St-Vincent, Cap c. France
39 J6 Sa Wan Hong Kong China
61 B2 Saïd Saudi Arabia
19 G3 Sakai Ethiopia
27 E6 Sakai Japan
46 D5 Sakaide Japan
46 D5 Sakaiminato Japan
59 F4 Saka Kalat Pakistan
57 F4 Sakala i. Indon.
54 C3 Sakami r. Can.
112 F3 Sakami Can.
112 F3 Sakami, L. l. Can.
28 D4 Sakar mts Bulgaria
83 □1 Sakaraha Madagascar
57 F1 Sakar-Chaga Turkm.
29 K5 Sakarya r. Turkey
29 J5 Sakarya Turkey
46 C7 Sakata Japan
29 J4 Sakçagöze Turkey

49 H4 Sachkuu N. Korea
54 C2 Sa Keo r. Thailand
77 E5 Sakété Benin
63 Q4 Sakhalin, O. i. Rus. Fed.
83 D4 Sakhalin Rus. Fed.
63 Q4 Sakhalinskiy Zaliv b. Rus. Fed.
15 F2 Sakharovo Rus. Fed.
54 C3 Sakhi India
83 D4 Sakhile R.S.A.
15 F2 Saknovshchyna Ukraine
13 H7 Sakht-Sar Iran
60 F1 Şǎki Azerbaijan
11 F5 Šakiai Lithuania
13 F5 Sakir mt. Pakistan
45 M7 Sakishima-guntō is Japan
42 A2 Sa-koi Myanmar
14 F2 Sakony Rus. Fed.
40 A2 Sakpiegu Ghana
54 B3 Sakrand Pakistan
43 Sakra, P. i. Singapore
82 B5 Sakrivier R.S.A.
15 F2 Saksaul'skiy Kazak.
46 J2 Saku Japan
47 G6 Sakuma Japan
47 H6 Sakura Japan
47 H6 Sakura-jima vol Japan
11 F3 Säkylä Finland
76 □ Sal i. Cape Verde
46 K1 Sal r. Rus. Fed.
19 H4 Sal r. Rus. Fed.
115 J4 Salaberry-de-Valleyfield Can.
11 D4 Salacgrīva Latvia
27 D5 Sala Consilina Italy
146 B3 Salada, Bahía b. Chile
130 B1 Salada, L. salt l. Mexico
129 E5 Salada, Laguna salt l. Mexico
108 B4 Saladas Arg.
61 C3 Saladih, W. w Jordan
146 C3 Saladillo Buenos Aires Arg.
146 D2 Saladillo r. Córdoba Arg.
146 C2 Saladillo r. Santa Fé Arg.
146 C2 Saladillo r. Santiago del Estero Arg.
18 D1 Saladillo r. Buenos Aires Arg.
146 C4 Salado r. Formosa Arg.
146 C3 Salado r. La Rioja Arg.
146 C2 Salado r. Mendoza/San Luis Arg.
147 C5 Salado r. Río Negro Arg.
146 D3 Salado r. Santa Fé Arg.
146 D2 Salado r. Andalucía Spain
146 C4 Salado, Quebrada de r. Chile
76 B5 Saladou Guinea
76 D5 Salaga Ghana
61 G3 Şalāḩ ad Dīn div. Iraq
82 C4 Salajwe Botswana
40 A3 Salak, G. vol. Indon.
72 C5 Salal Chad
73 G3 Salālah Sudan
131 H6 Salamá Guatemala
130 J6 Salamá Honduras
146 B3 Salamanca Chile
131 E4 Salamanca Mexico
24 D2 Salamanca Spain
120 D3 Salamanca U.S.A.
72 C5 Salamat r. Chad
57 D2 Salamatabad Iran
138 B2 Salamina Colombia
29 E6 Salamina i. Greece
61 B1 Salamis Cyprus
61 B1 Salamís i. Greece
121 H1 Salamonie r. U.S.A.
122 E5 Salamonie Lake l. U.S.A.
55 G4 Salandi r. India
91 □12 Salani Western Samoa
146 C2 Salar de Arizaro salt flat Arg.
140 C4 Salar de Atacama salt flat Chile
140 C4 Salar de Coipasa salt flat Bolivia
140 C4 Salar de Uyuni salt flat Bolivia
15 D2 Salaspils Latvia
64 E3 Salavat Rus. Fed.
40 E3 Salawati i. Indon.
40 E3 Salaya i. Indon.
147 D5 Sala y Gómez, Isla i. Chile
27 E6 Salazar Arg.
81 □5 Salazie Réunion Indian Ocean
20 F3 Salbris France
11 E5 Šalčininkai Lithuania
15 D1 Šal'čininkai Lithuania
138 C2 Saldaña Colombia
82 B5 Saldanha R.S.A.
82 B5 Saldanha Bay b. R.S.A.
146 D3 Saldungaray Arg.
11 E4 Saldus Latvia
97 G4 Sale Aust.
74 D2 Salé Morocco
16 F4 Sale U.K.
133 □5 Salée r. Guadeloupe Caribbean
81 □5 Salazie Réunion Indian Ocean
138 B2 Sálchar India
55 G5 Salem India
55 G4 Salem India
124 E4 Salem U.S.A.
121 H3 Salem U.S.A.
121 G4 Salem U.S.A.
122 B6 Salem U.S.A.
126 B2 Salem U.S.A.
120 C5 Salem U.S.A.
16 C4 Salen U.K.
27 E5 Salerno Italy
27 E5 Salerno, Golfo di g. Italy
142 C3 Salesópolis Brazil
16 F4 Salford U.K.
142 E2 Salgado r. Brazil
19 J4 Salgótarján Hungary
142 E2 Salgueiro Brazil
127 F4 Salida U.S.A.
21 H5 Salies-de-Béarn France
29 L5 Salihli Turkey
11 G5 Salihorsk Belarus
79 D5 Salima Malawi
79 D5 Salima Mozambique
42 A2 Salin Myanmar
127 F4 Salina U.S.A.
124 D4 Salina U.S.A.
27 E5 Salina, Isola i. Italy
131 F5 Salina Cruz Mexico
142 C1 Salina La Antigua salt flat Arg.
146 D2 Salinas Llancanelo salt flat Arg.
132 □1 Salina Pt pt The Bahamas
145 G2 Salinas Brazil
130 C4 Salinas Mexico
128 B3 Salinas r. U.S.A.
128 B3 Salinas U.S.A.
140 C3 Salinas de Garci Mendoza Bolivia

143 C5 São Bernardo do Campo Brazil
143 A6 São Borja Brazil
143 B6 São Carlos *Santa Catarina* Brazil
144 E5 São Carlos *São Paulo* Brazil
142 D3 São Desidério Brazil
142 D3 São Desidério r. Brazil
144 C3 São Domingos r. *Goiás* Brazil
144 B3 São Domingos r. *Mato Grosso do Sul* Brazil
145 E1 São Domingos r. *Minas Gerais* Brazil
142 C3 São Domingos Brazil
142 B3 São Félix *Mato Grosso* Brazil
142 B2 São Félix *Pará* Brazil
145 H4 São Fidélis Brazil
76 □ São Filipe Cape Verde
144 A6 São Francisco r. *Paraná* Brazil
142 E2 São Francisco r. Brazil
145 F1 São Francisco Brazil
143 A6 São Francisco de Assis Brazil
144 D1 São Francisco de Goiás Brazil
144 D3 São Francisco de Sales Brazil
143 C6 São Francisco do Sul Brazil
143 C6 São Francisco, I. de i. Brazil
146 F3 São Gabriel Brazil
145 H3 São Gabriel da Palha Brazil
144 E1 São Gabriel de Goiás Brazil
145 G5 São Gonçalo Brazil
145 F3 São Gonçalo do Abaeté Brazil
142 E1 São Gonçalo do Amirante Brazil
145 F4 São Gonçalo do Sapucaí Brazil
145 E3 São Gotardo Brazil
142 B3 São João r. *Mato Grosso* Brazil
143 B5 São João r. *Paraná* Brazil
144 E1 São João da Aliança Brazil
145 H4 São João da Barra Brazil
145 E4 São João da Boa Vista Brazil
24 B2 São João da Madeira Portugal
145 F1 São João da Ponte Brazil
144 C4 São João das Duas Pontas Brazil
145 F4 São João del Rei Brazil
142 C2 São João do Araguaia Brazil
142 E2 São João do Cariri Brazil
145 G1 São João do Paraíso Brazil
142 D2 São João do Piauí Brazil
142 D2 São João dos Patos Brazil
145 G3 São João Evangelista Brazil
145 G4 São João Nepomuceno Brazil
142 C1 São Joaquim *Pará* Brazil
143 C6 São Joaquim *Santa Catarina* Brazil
144 E4 São Joaquim da Barra Brazil
144 B5 São Jorge do Ivaí Brazil
138 D4 São José *Amazonas* Brazil
143 C6 São José *Santa Catarina* Brazil
142 C3 São José r. Brazil
142 D1 São José, Baia de b. Brazil
142 E2 São José de Mipibu Brazil
143 D5 São José do Calçado Brazil
145 H3 São José do Divino Brazil
145 G3 São José do Jacurí Brazil
146 F3 São José do Norte Brazil
145 E4 São José do Rio Pardo Brazil
144 D4 São José do Rio Prêto Brazil
145 F5 São José dos Campos Brazil
144 C4 São José dos Dourados r. Brazil
144 D6 São José dos Pinhais Brazil
143 B6 São Leopoldo Brazil
145 F5 São Lourenço Brazil
141 F3 São Lourenço r. Brazil
144 A2 São Lourenço Brazil
146 F3 São Lourenço do Sul Brazil
142 D1 São Luís Brazil
144 C2 São Luis de Montes Belos Brazil
145 F5 São Luís do Paraitinga Brazil
143 B6 São Luís Gonzaga Brazil
142 D1 São Luís, Ilha de i. Brazil
144 D5 São Manuel Brazil
144 E2 São Marcos r. Brazil
142 D1 São Marcos, Baia de b. Brazil
145 H3 São Mateus r. Brazil
145 J3 São Mateus Brazil
145 E1 São Miguel r. Brazil
144 E5 São Miguel Arcanjo Brazil
144 A6 São Miguel do Iguaçu Brazil
142 E2 São Miguel dos Campos Brazil
142 D2 São Miguel do Tapuio Brazil
21 G3 Saône r. France
140 A3 Sã Nicolás, Bahía b. Peru
142 D2 São Nicolau r. Brazil
143 A6 São Nicolãu Brazil
76 □ São Nicolau i. Cape Verde
145 E5 São Paulo Brazil
144 D4 São Paulo div. Brazil
138 D4 São Paulo de Olivença Brazil
139 F4 São Pedro *Amazonas* Brazil
144 C3 São Pedro *Mato Grosso do Sul* Brazil
141 D1 São Pedro *Rondônia* Brazil
144 E5 São Pedro *São Paulo* Brazil
142 D2 São Pedro r. Brazil
145 G5 São Pedro da Aldeia Brazil
144 C5 São Pedro do Ivaí Brazil
24 B2 São Pedro do Sul Portugal
148 H5 São Pedro e São Paulo is Atlantic Ocean
142 C2 São Raimundo das Mangabeiras Brazil
142 D2 São Raimundo Nonato Brazil
145 F2 São Romão Brazil
144 E5 São Roque Brazil
142 E2 São Roque, C. de c. Brazil
145 E4 São Roque de Minas Brazil
142 B2 São Sebastião *Pará* Brazil
141 D1 São Sebastião *Rondônia* Brazil
145 F5 São Sebastião *São Paulo* Brazil
142 C1 São Sebastião da Boa Vista Brazil
145 E4 São Sebastião do Paraíso Brazil
145 F5 São Sebastião, Ilha do i. Brazil
143 B7 São Sepé Brazil
144 E4 São Simão Brazil
144 C3 São Simão Brazil
144 C3 São Simão, Barragem de resr Brazil
39 J6 Sao-Siu Indon.
145 F4 São Tiago Brazil
76 □ São Tiago i. Cape Verde
79 □ São Tomé i. Sao Tome and Principe
79 □ São Tomé Sao Tome and Principe
69 E5 Sao Tome and Principe country Africa
145 H4 São Tomé, Cabo de c. Brazil
143 C5 São Vicente Brazil
76 □ São Vicente i. Cape Verde
24 B4 São Vicente, Cabo de c. Portugal
60 B1 Sapanca Turkey
142 C3 Sapão r. Brazil
39 J7 Saparua Indon.
77 F5 Sapele Nigeria
29 E4 Sapes Greece
147 C5 Sa Pire Mahuida mt. ra. Arg.
25 H3 Sa Pobla Spain
76 C5 Sapo National Park nat. park Liberia
144 C5 Sapopema Brazil
19 L2 Sapotskina Belarus
14 E3 Sapozhok Rus. Fed.
46 H2 Sapporo Japan
27 E5 Sapri Italy
145 F4 Sapucai r. *Minas Gerais* Brazil
144 E4 Sapucai r. *São Paulo* Brazil
40 C3 Sapudi i. Indon.
125 D4 Sapulpa U.S.A.
40 C3 Sapulu Indon.
57 D2 Sāqī Iran
109 N2 Saqqaq Greenland
60 F2 Saqqez Iran
138 B4 Saquisilí Ecuador
60 F2 Sarāb Iran
61 B5 Sarabît el Khâdim Egypt
43 C4 Sara Buri Thailand
25 F2 Saragossa *Zaragoza* Spain
138 B4 Saraguro Ecuador
14 E3 Sarai Rus. Fed.
54 C3 Sarai Sidhu Pakistan
26 G4 Sarajevo Bos.-Herz.
57 E1 Sarakhs Iran
29 E5 Sarakino i. Greece
64 E2 Saraktash Rus. Fed.
65 L2 Sarala Rus. Fed.
55 H4 Saramati mt. India
65 H3 Saran' Kazak.
121 G2 Saranac r. U.S.A.
121 F2 Saranac Lake U.S.A.
112 E5 Saranac Lakes lakes U.S.A.
29 C5 Sarandë Albania
143 B6 Sarandi Brazil
146 E3 Sarandí del Yí Uruguay
146 E3 Sarandí Grande Uruguay
40 B2 Saran, G. mt. Indon.
41 C5 Sarangani i. Phil.
41 C5 Sarangani Bay b. Phil.
41 C5 Sarangani Islands is Phil.
41 C5 Sarangani Str. chan. Phil.
55 E5 Sarangarh India
54 D5 Sarangpur India
14 G2 Saransk Rus. Fed.
64 D1 Sarapul Rus. Fed.
119 D7 Sarasota U.S.A.
54 B5 Saraswati r. India
15 C3 Sarata Ukraine
15 C3 Sărătenii Vechi Moldova
126 F3 Saratoga U.S.A.
121 G3 Saratoga Springs U.S.A.
40 B1 Saratok Malaysia
14 G4 Saratov Rus. Fed.
14 H4 Saratov div. Rus. Fed.
64 C2 Saratovskoye Vdkhr. resr Rus. Fed.
57 E4 Saravan Iran
42 D4 Saravan Laos
43 B4 Sarawa r. Myanmar
40 B1 Sarawak div. Malaysia
60 A1 Saray Turkey
76 B4 Saraya Senegal
61 C2 Sarāyā Syria
60 B2 Sarayköy Turkey
60 C2 Sarayönü Turkey
57 E4 Sarbāz Iran
57 E4 Sarbāz r. Iran
55 G4 Sarbhang Bhutan
57 D2 Sarbīsheh Iran
19 J5 Sárbogárd Hungary
26 C3 Sarca r. Italy
146 B2 Sarco Chile
54 E3 Sarda r. India/Nepal
54 C5 Sardarpur India
54 C3 Sardarshahr India
60 F2 Sar Dasht Iran
27 C5 Sardegna i. Italy
27 B5 Sardegna div. Italy
138 C2 Sardinata Colombia
80 C4 Sardindida Plain plain Kenya
57 B4 Sareb, Rās-as pt U.A.E.
40 D3 Sarege i. Indon.
10 E2 Sareks National Park nat. park Sweden
10 E2 Sarektjåkkå mt. Sweden
40 C2 Sarempaka, G. mt. Indon.
57 F1 Sar-e Pol Afghanistan
57 C3 Sare Yazd Iran
148 E4 Sargasso Sea sea Atlantic Ocean
65 H1 Sargatskoye Rus. Fed.
54 C2 Sargodha Pakistan
78 C2 Sarh Chad
57 E3 Sarhad reg. Iran
74 C2 Sarhro, Jbel mts Morocco
57 C1 Sārī Iran
29 F7 Saria i. Greece
57 F2 Sar-i-Bum Afghanistan
28 G2 Sarichioi Romania
39 M3 Sarigan i. *Northern Mariana Is* Pac. Oc.
60 B2 Sarıgöl Turkey
60 E1 Sarıkamış Turkey
60 C2 Sarıkaya Turkey
29 F6 Sarıkemer Turkey
29 F4 Sarıköy Turkey
43 □ Sarimbun Res. resr Singapore
99 G4 Sarina Aust.
25 F2 Sariñena Spain
57 F2 Sar-i-Pul Afghanistan
57 C1 Sāri Qamīsh Iran
72 C3 Sarīr Tibesti desert Libya
72 D2 Sarir Water Wells' Field well Libya
49 H5 Sariwŏn N. Korea
60 B1 Sarıyer Turkey
55 E4 Sarju r. India
17 F7 Sark i. Channel Islands
65 K3 Sarkand Kazak.
54 B4 Sarkāri Tala India
60 B2 Şarkikaraağaç Turkey
60 D2 Şarkişla Turkey
60 A1 Şarköy Turkey
57 F3 Sarlath Ra. mt. ra. Afghanistan/Pakistan
20 E4 Sarlat-la-Canéda France
14 F2 Sarma r. Rus. Fed.
28 E1 Sărmaşu Romania
39 L7 Sarmi Indon.
147 C6 Sarmiento Arg.
11 D3 Särna Sweden
21 J3 Sarnen Switz.
114 D5 Sarnia Can.
27 E5 Sarno Italy
15 B1 Sarny Ukraine
38 D7 Sarolangun Indon.
46 J1 Saroma-ko l. Japan
29 D6 Saronikos Kolpos g. Greece
29 F4 Saros Körfezi b. Turkey
19 K4 Sárospatak Hungary
54 C4 Sarotra India
14 F2 Sarova Rus. Fed.
57 G2 Sarowbī Afghanistan
13 H6 Sarpa, Oz. l. *Kalmykiya* Rus. Fed.
13 H5 Sarpa, Ozero l. *Volgograd* Rus. Fed.
41 □1 Sar Passage chan. Palau
28 C4 Šar Planina mt. ra. Macedonia/Yugo.
11 C4 Sarpsborg Norway
21 H2 Sarrebourg France
21 H2 Sarreguemines France
24 C1 Sarria Spain
21 G2 Sarry France
21 J6 Sartène France
20 D3 Sarthe r. France
57 B2 Sarud r. Iran
46 J2 Saru-gawa r. Japan
29 F5 Saruhanlı Turkey
46 D6 Sarumasa-yama mt. Japan
54 A4 Saruna Pakistan
60 F2 Şärur Azerbaijan
61 D2 Sarūt r. Syria
19 H5 Sárvár Hungary
57 C3 Sarvestān Iran
54 C4 Sarwar India
65 G4 Saryagach Kazak.
64 F3 Sarybasat Kazak.
65 J3 Sary-Ishikotrau, Peski desert Kazak.
64 D3 Sarykamys Kazak.
64 E4 Sarykamyshkoye Ozero salt l. Turkmenistan
65 H2 Sarykiyak Kazak.
65 H5 Sarykol Range mt. ra. China/Tajikistan
65 H3 Sarykomey Kazak.
65 J4 Saryozek Kazak.
65 H3 Saryshagan Kazak.
65 G3 Sarysu r. Kazak.
65 H5 Sary Tash Kyrgyzstan
57 E1 Sary Yazikskoye Vdkhr. resr Turkmenistan
26 B3 Sarzana Italy
20 C3 Sarzeau France
129 G6 Sasabe U.S.A.
55 F4 Sasaram India
40 E4 Sasar, Tg pt Indon.
15 E1 Saschnivka Ukraine
46 B7 Sasebo Japan
15 E2 Sasivka Ukraine
111 J4 Saskatchewan r. Can.
108 H4 Saskatchewan div. Can.
111 H4 Saskatoon Can.
63 N2 Saskylakh Rus. Fed.
130 J6 Saslaya mt. Nicaragua
14 E2 Sasovo Rus. Fed.
121 F5 Sassafras U.S.A.
76 C6 Sassandra Côte d'Ivoire
76 C5 Sassandra r. Côte d'Ivoire
27 B5 Sassari Italy
19 F1 Sassnitz Germany
26 D4 Sassocorvaro Italy
26 D4 Sassoferrato Italy
76 C6 Sass Town Liberia
26 C3 Sassuolo Italy
65 K3 Sasykkol', Oz. l. Kazak.
13 H6 Sasykoli Rus. Fed.
76 B4 Satadougou Mali
46 C8 Sata-misaki c. Japan
54 C5 Satana India
15 B2 Sataniv Ukraine
91 □12 Satapuala Western Samoa
56 A2 Satara India
91 □12 Sataua Western Samoa
40 D3 Satengar i. Indon.
14 E3 Satinka Rus. Fed.
140 B2 Satipo Peru
14 F2 Satis r. Rus. Fed.
14 F2 Satis Rus. Fed.
64 E1 Satka Rus. Fed.
55 G5 Satkhira Bangladesh
56 B2 Satmala Range h. India
54 E4 Satna India
19 K4 Sátoraljaújhely Hungary
65 G3 Satpayev Kazak.
54 C5 Satpura Range mt. ra. India
46 C8 Satsuma-hantō pen. Japan
46 J2 Satsunai-gawa r. Japan
47 G5 Satte Japan
54 D2 Satti *Jammu and Kashmir*
28 D1 Satu Mare Romania
43 C6 Satun Thailand
91 □12 Satupaitea Western Samoa
146 E3 Sauce Arg.
138 B5 Sauce Peru
125 C7 Sauceda Mexico
129 F5 Sauceda Mts mts U.S.A.
130 D2 Saucillo Mexico
11 B4 Sauda Norway
10 M2 Sauðárkrókur Iceland
32 F7 Saudi Arabia country Asia
141 E2 Sauêruiná r. Brazil
122 D4 Saugatuck U.S.A.
121 G3 Saugerties U.S.A.
21 F4 Saugues France
146 C2 Saujil Arg.
20 D4 Saujon France
124 E2 Sauk Center U.S.A.
122 C4 Sauk City U.S.A.
139 G3 Saul French Guiana
18 D4 Saulgau Germany
21 G3 Saulieu France
114 C3 Sault Ste Marie Can.
122 E2 Sault Ste Marie U.S.A.
99 H4 Saumarez Reef reef *Coral Sea Islands Terr.* Pac. Oc.
39 K8 Saumlakki Indon.
20 D3 Saumur France
93 C6 Saunders, Cape c. N.Z.
152 A4 Saunders Coast Ant.
152 C1 Saunders I. i. *S. Sandwich Is* Atlantic Ocean
98 B2 Saunders, Mt h. Aust.
43 B5 Saung Thailand
42 B1 Saungka Myanmar
64 D4 Saura Rus. Fed.
79 D5 Saurimo Angola
40 E2 Sausu Indon.
79 C6 Sautar Angola
133 □8 Sauters *Grenada* Caribbean
26 G3 Sava r. Europe
130 J6 Sava Honduras
91 □12 Savaii i. Western Samoa
14 E4 Savala r. Rus. Fed.
77 E5 Savalou Benin
122 B4 Savanna U.S.A.
119 D6 Savannah U.S.A.
119 D5 Savannah r. U.S.A.
119 B5 Savannah U.S.A.
119 E7 Savannah Sound The Bahamas
42 D3 Savannakhét Laos
133 □1 Savanna la Mar Jamaica
112 B3 Savant Lake Can.
56 A3 Savanur India
10 F3 Sävar Sweden
60 A2 Savaştepe Turkey
77 E5 Savè Benin
83 E3 Save r. Mozambique
57 B2 Sāveh Iran
76 D5 Savelugu Ghana
20 D3 Savenay France
28 F1 Săveni Romania
21 H2 Saverne France
10 H3 Saviaho Finland
28 F1 Săvineşti Romania
14 E1 Savino Rus. Fed.
12 G2 Savinskiy Rus. Fed.
28 B3 Šavnik Yugo.
26 B3 Savona Italy
11 H3 Savonranta Finland
15 D2 Savran' Ukraine
15 C2 Savranka r. Ukraine
11 D4 Sävsjö Sweden
39 H8 Savu i. Indon.
10 H2 Savukoski Finland
60 E2 Savur Turkey
90 □6 Savusavu Fiji
90 □6 Savusavu B. b. Fiji
82 C2 Savuti Botswana
49 F2 Savvo-Borzya Rus. Fed.
15 E1 Savynky Ukraine
15 G2 Savyntsi Ukraine
42 A2 Saw Myanmar
54 D4 Sawai Madhopur India
90 □8 Sawaleke Fiji
40 C2 Sawan Indon.
42 B3 Sawankhalok Thailand
47 G5 Sawasaki-bana pt Japan
47 G5 Sawata Japan
127 F4 Sawatch Mts mt. ra. U.S.A.
72 B2 Sawdā', Jabal as h. Libya
19 L3 Sawin Poland
122 B2 Sawtooth Mountains h. U.S.A.
39 H8 Sawu Sea g. Indon.
115 K4 Sawyerville Can.
99 E3 Saxby r. Aust.
10 D2 Saxnäs Sweden
18 F3 Saxony div. Germany
77 E4 Say Niger
65 J3 Sayak Kazak.
77 G4 Sayam well Niger
140 A2 Sayán Peru
65 M2 Sayanogorsk Rus. Fed.
64 F5 Sayat Turkmenistan
131 H5 Sayaxché Guatemala
73 H4 Şayh well Yemen
58 H6 Sayḩūt Yemen
13 H5 Saykhin Kazak.
80 D2 Sāylac Somalia
48 D3 Saynshand Mongolia
65 K4 Sayram Hu salt l. China
125 D5 Sayre U.S.A.
120 E4 Sayre U.S.A.
130 E5 Sayula *Jalisco* Mexico
131 G5 Sayula *Veracruz* Mexico
64 D4 Say-Utes Kazak.
29 B4 Sazan i. Albania
15 G1 Sazhnoye Rus. Fed.
54 C2 Sazin Pakistan
12 E3 Sazonovo Rus. Fed.
75 D3 Sbaa Algeria
75 F1 Sbeitla Tunisia
101 C7 Scaddan Aust.
17 F4 Scafell Pike mt. U.K.
27 E6 Scalea Italy
16 G1 Scalloway U.K.
26 C4 Scansano Italy
28 F2 Scânteia Romania
16 F2 Scapa Flow inlet U.K.
115 F5 Scarborough Can.
133 □2 Scarborough *Tobago* Trin. & Tobago
17 G4 Scarborough U.K.
41 A3 Scarborough Shoal sand bank Phil.
93 D5 Scargill N.Z.
43 D6 Scawfell Shoal sand bank S. China Sea
26 F4 Šćedro i. Croatia
21 J3 Schaffhausen Switz.
18 B2 Schagen Netherlands
57 E3 Schao w Afghanistan
18 E1 Scharbeutz Germany
18 F4 Schärding Austria
18 D2 Scharhörn sand bank Germany
113 G3 Schefferville Can.
19 G4 Scheibbs Austria
18 B3 Schelde r. Belgium
129 E2 Schell Creek Range mt. ra. U.S.A.
121 G3 Schenectady U.S.A.
18 D2 Schenefeld *Niedersachsen* Germany
18 D5 Schesaplana mt. Austria/Swit.
18 F4 Schierling Germany
18 C2 Schiermonnikoog i. Netherlands
29 D5 Schimatari Greece
26 C3 Schio Italy
28 F1 Schitu Duca Romania
18 C3 Schleiden Germany
18 D1 Schleswig Germany
18 D1 Schleswig-Holstein div. Germany
18 D3 Schlüchtern Germany
18 D2 Schneverdingen Germany
121 G3 Schodack Center U.S.A.
133 □4 Schoelcher *Martinique* Caribbean
122 C3 Schofield U.S.A.
127 □1 Schofield Barracks U.S.A.
18 E2 Schönebeck *Sachsen-Anhalt* Germany
18 E2 Schöningen Germany
121 J2 Schoodic Lake l. U.S.A.
122 E4 Schoolcraft U.S.A.
97 G5 Schouten I. i. Aust.
90 □1 Schouten Islands is P.N.G.
114 B2 Schreiber Can.
19 G4 Schrems Austria
18 E4 Schrobenhausen Germany
121 G3 Schroon Lake l. U.S.A.
129 F5 Schuchuli U.S.A.
17 C6 Schull Rep. of Ire.
111 K2 Schultz Lake l. Can.
128 C2 Schurz U.S.A.
121 G3 Schuylerville U.S.A.
18 E4 Schwabach Germany
18 D4 Schwäbische Alb mts Germany
18 D4 Schwäbisch Gmünd Germany
18 D4 Schwäbisch Hall Germany
18 E4 Schwabmünchen Germany
21 J3 Schwanden Switz.
18 F4 Schwandorf Germany
18 E5 Schwangau Germany
18 E2 Schwarzenbek Germany
18 F3 Schwarzenberg Germany
82 B4 Schwarzrand mts Namibia
18 D4 Schwarzwald mts Germany
18 E5 Schwaz Austria
19 G2 Schwedt Germany
18 E3 Schweinfurt Germany
18 D4 Schwenningen Germany
18 E2 Schwerin Germany
18 E2 Schweriner See l. Germany
21 J3 Schwyz Switz.
27 D7 Sciacca Italy
27 E7 Scicli Italy
17 D7 Scilly, Isles of is. U.K.
120 B5 Scioto r. U.S.A.
129 F2 Scipio U.S.A.
126 F1 Scobey U.S.A.
97 G3 Scone Aust.
109 Q2 Scoresby Land reg. Greenland
109 Q2 Scoresby Sund chan. Greenland
28 E2 Scorniceşti Romania
152 B1 Scotia Ridge Atlantic Ocean
148 G9 Scotia Sea sea Atlantic Ocean
114 E5 Scotland Can.
16 E3 Scotland div. U.K.
115 K4 Scotstown Can.
115 K3 Scott Can.
152 B5 Scott Base N.Z. Base Ant.
83 E5 Scottburgh R.S.A.
98 B2 Scott, C. c. Aust.
110 D4 Scott, C. c. Can.
124 C4 Scott City U.S.A.
152 B5 Scott Coast Ant.
120 D4 Scottdale U.S.A.
152 B4 Scott Gl. gl. Ant.
109 L2 Scott Inlet inlet Can.
152 A5 Scott Island i. Ant.
111 H3 Scott Lake l. Can.
152 D4 Scott Mts mt. ra. Ant.
92 D1 Scott Pt pt N.Z.
100 C2 Scott Reef reef Aust.
124 C3 Scottsbluff U.S.A.
119 C5 Scottsboro U.S.A.
118 C4 Scottsburg U.S.A.
97 F5 Scottsdale Aust.
127 E5 Scottsdale U.S.A.
128 A3 Scotts Valley U.S.A.
122 D4 Scottville U.S.A.
128 D3 Scotty's Junction U.S.A.
16 E2 Scourie U.K.
121 F4 Scranton U.S.A.
17 G5 Scunthorpe U.K.
21 K3 Scuol Switz.
101 B6 Seabrook, L. salt flat Aust.
121 F5 Seaford U.S.A.
99 G4 Seaforth Aust.
114 E5 Seaforth Can.
133 □1 Seaforth Jamaica
41 A4 Seahorse Bank sand bank Phil.
111 K3 Seal r. Can.
97 E3 Sea Lake Aust.
82 A5 Seal Bay b. *Tristan da Cunha* Atlantic Ocean
82 C5 Seal, Cape c. R.S.A.
133 E2 Seal Cays is *Turks and Caicos Is* Caribbean
121 J3 Seal I. i. U.S.A.
113 H3 Seal Lake l. Can.
129 E3 Seaman Range mts U.S.A.
129 E4 Searchlight U.S.A.
125 F5 Searcy U.S.A.
128 D4 Searles Lake l. U.S.A.
122 E4 Sears U.S.A.
121 J2 Searsport U.S.A.
128 B3 Seaside U.S.A.
126 B2 Seaside U.S.A.
126 B2 Seattle U.S.A.
99 F3 Seaview Ra. mt. ra. Aust.
121 F5 Seaville U.S.A.
93 D5 Seaward Kaikoura Ra. mt. ra. N.Z.
121 H3 Sebago Lake l. U.S.A.
40 D2 Sebakung Indon.
40 C2 Sebangan, Tk b. Indon.
40 A1 Sebangka i. Indon.
130 B2 Sebastián Vizcaíno, B b. Mexico
121 J2 Sebasticook r. U.S.A.
41 A5 Sebatik i. Indon.
77 E4 Sebba Burkina
75 D2 Sebdou Algeria
76 C4 Sébékoro Mali
28 D2 Sebeş Romania
40 A3 Sebesi i. Indon.
123 F4 Sebewaing U.S.A.
12 D3 Sebezh Rus. Fed.
82 D3 Sebina Botswana
60 D1 Şebin Karahisar Turkey
28 D1 Sebiş Romania
75 E3 Sebkha Azzel Matti salt pan Algeria
74 B4 Sebkhet Chemchâm salt l. Mauritania
75 G1 Sebkhet de Sidi El Hani salt pan Tunisia
74 B3 Sebkhet Oum ed Droûs Telli salt flat Mauritania
74 B4 Sebkhet Oum ed Droûs Guebli salt l. Mauritania
74 A5 Sebkhet Te-n-Dghâmcha salt marsh Mauritania
121 J2 Seboeis Lake l. U.S.A.
121 J2 Seboomook U.S.A.
121 J2 Seboomook Lake l. U.S.A.
119 D7 Sebring U.S.A.
40 D2 Sebuku i. Indon.
40 B1 Sebuyau Malaysia
80 C3 Seccia Mts mts Ethiopia
14 G2 Sechenovo Rus. Fed.
138 A5 Sechura Peru
138 A5 Sechura, Bahía de b. Peru
73 F3 2nd Cataract rapids Sudan
121 H2 Second Lake l. U.S.A.
99 E2 2nd Three Mile Opening chan. Aust.
114 C5 Secord Lake l. U.S.A.
93 A6 Secretary Island i. N.Z.
56 B2 Secunderabad India
140 C3 Sécure r. Bolivia
124 E4 Sedalia U.S.A.
56 B2 Sedam India
96 D3 Sedan Aust.
21 G2 Sedan France
93 E4 Seddon N.Z.
93 C4 Seddonville N.Z.
60 A1 Seddülbahir Turkey
61 C4 Sede Boqer Israel
57 D2 Sedeh Iran
61 C4 Sederot Israel
121 J2 Sedgwick U.S.A.
76 A4 Sédhiou Senegal
19 G4 Sedlčany Czech Rep.
15 A1 Sedlyshche Ukraine
15 D1 Sedniv Ukraine
61 C4 Sedom Israel
129 G4 Sedona U.S.A.
27 A7 Sédrata Algeria
40 D1 Sedulang Indon.
11 F5 Šeduva Lithuania
19 G2 Seebad Heringsdorf Germany
18 E2 Seehausen Germany
82 B4 Seeheim Namibia
18 D4 Seeheim-Jugenheim Germany
129 E5 Seeley U.S.A.
152 B3 Seelig, Mt mt. Ant.
19 G2 Seelow Germany
20 E2 Sées France
18 E3 Seesen Germany
18 E2 Seevetal Germany
76 B5 Sefadu Sierra Leone
29 F5 Seferihisar Turkey
57 B2 Sēfīd Dasht Iran
83 D3 Sefophe Botswana
74 D2 Sefrou Morocco
76 B4 Ségala Mali
11 C3 Segalstad Norway
41 A5 Segama r. Malaysia
43 C7 Segamat Malaysia
24 E5 Segangane Morocco
28 D2 Şegarcea Romania
77 E4 Ségbana Benin
40 D3 Segeri Indon.
12 E2 Segezha Rus. Fed.
57 G1 Seghnān Afghanistan
25 F3 Segorbe Spain
76 C4 Ségou Mali
76 C4 Ségou div. Mali
138 C2 Segovia Colombia
24 D2 Segovia Spain
12 E2 Segozerskoye, Oz. l. Rus. Fed.
20 D3 Segré France
77 G2 Séguédine Niger
76 C5 Séguéla Côte d'Ivoire
76 C5 Séguélon Côte d'Ivoire
125 D6 Seguin U.S.A.
146 D3 Segundo r. Arg.
25 E3 Segura r. Spain
25 E4 Segura, Sierra de mt. ra. Spain
82 C3 Sehithwa Botswana
54 D5 Sehore India
54 A4 Sehwan Pakistan
42 A2 Seikpyu Myanmar
10 F1 Seiland i. Norway
125 D4 Seiling U.S.A.
10 F3 Seinäjoki Finland
112 B4 Seine r. Can.
21 G3 Seine r. France
20 D2 Seine, Baie de b. France
20 F2 Seine, Val de v. France
28 D1 Seini Romania
40 C2 Seipinang Indon.
19 L1 Sejny Poland
40 B1 Sekadau Indon.
40 A2 Sekanak, Tk b. Indon.
41 A6 Sekatak Bengara Indon.
40 A2 Sekayu Indon.
47 F6 Seki Japan
76 D6 Sekondi Ghana
14 G3 Sekretarka Rus. Fed.
57 E3 Seküneh Iran
40 B1 Sekura Indon.
80 C3 Sela Dingay Ethiopia
126 B2 Selah U.S.A.
40 B1 Selakau Indon.
43 C7 Selangor div. Malaysia
39 K8 Selaru i. Indon.
40 D4 Selat Alas chan. Indon.
40 C3 Selatan, Tg pt Indon.
40 C4 Selat Bali chan. Indon.
40 A2 Selat Bangka chan. Indon.
40 A2 Selat Berhala chan. Indon.
39 K7 Selat Dampir chan. Indon.
40 A2 Selat Gaspar chan. Indon.
43 □ Selat Johor chan. Malaysia/Singapore
43 □ Selat Jurong chan. Singapore
40 B2 Selat Karimata str. Indon.
40 C2 Selat Laut chan. Indon.
40 C4 Selat Lombok chan. Indon.
40 C3 Selat Madura chan. Indon.
43 □ Selat Pandan chan. Singapore
40 E3 Selat Salayar chan. Indon.
40 D4 Selat Sape chan. Indon.
40 D4 Selat Sumba chan. Indon.
40 A3 Selat Sunda chan. Indon.
39 L7 Selat Yapen chan. Indon.
108 B3 Selawik U.S.A.
10 C3 Selbekken Norway
10 C3 Selbu Norway
17 G5 Selby U.K.
124 C2 Selby U.S.A.
29 F6 Selçuk Turkey
27 E5 Sele r. Italy
82 D3 Selebi-Phikwe Botswana
29 C4 Selečka Planina mt. ra. Macedonia
29 G5 Selendi Turkey
48 C2 Selenduma Rus. Fed.
48 C1 Seleng r. Rus. Fed.
48 B2 Selenge Mongolia
48 C2 Selenge div. Mongolia
78 C4 Selenge Zaire
48 C2 Selenge Mörön r. Mongolia
48 C2 Selenginsk Rus. Fed.
29 B4 Selenicë Albania
21 H2 Sélestat France
43 □ Seletar Singapore
43 □ Seletar, P. i. Singapore
43 □ Seletar Res. resr Singapore
65 H2 Seletinskoye Kazak.
65 H2 Selety r. Kazak.
65 H2 Seletyteniz, Oz. salt l. Kazak.
124 C2 Selfridge U.S.A.
12 J2 Selib Rus. Fed.
74 B5 Sélibabi Mauritania
14 B3 Selichnya Rus. Fed.
14 A1 Seliger, Oz. l. Rus. Fed.
129 F4 Seligman U.S.A.
73 E3 Selīma Oasis oasis Sudan
40 C1 Selimbau Indon.
61 A1 Selimiye *Antalya* Turkey
29 F6 Selimiye *Muğla* Turkey
76 C4 Sélingué, Lac de l. Mali
123 J5 Selinsgrove U.S.A.
14 A1 Selishche Rus. Fed.
14 F2 Selishchi Rus. Fed.
13 H6 Selitrennoye Rus. Fed.
14 A1 Selizharovo Rus. Fed.
11 C4 Seljord Norway
111 K4 Selkirk Can.
110 F4 Selkirk Mountains mt. ra. Can.
129 G6 Sells U.S.A.
119 C5 Selma U.S.A.
128 C3 Selma U.S.A.
119 B5 Selmer U.S.A.
40 D4 Selong Indon.
21 G3 Selongey France
76 B4 Sélouma Guinea
81 C6 Selous Game Reserve res. Tanzania
57 E3 Selseleh-ye Pīr Shūrān mt. ra. Iran
17 G6 Selsey Bill hd U.K.
14 B3 Sel'tso *Bryansk* Rus. Fed.
14 B3 Sel'tso *Bryansk* Rus. Fed.
144 C4 Selviria Brazil
111 J3 Selwyn Lake l. Can.
110 C2 Selwyn Mountains mt. ra. Can.
98 D4 Selwyn Range h. Aust.
15 A3 Selyatyn Ukraine
15 G2 Selydove Ukraine
29 B4 Seman r. Albania
40 A3 Semangka, Tk b. Indon.
40 B3 Semarang Indon.
40 B1 Sematan Malaysia
40 C2 Semayang, D. l. Indon.
41 A6 Sembakung r. Indon.
43 □ Sembawang Singapore
78 B3 Sembé Congo
40 C4 Semenanjung Blambangan pen. Indon.
79 C4 Semendua Zaire
14 D1 Semendyayevo Rus. Fed.
13 E4 Semenivka *Chernihiv* Ukraine
15 E2 Semenivka *Poltava* Ukraine
14 G1 Semenov Rus. Fed.
14 D1 Semibratovo Rus. Fed.
12 G3 Semigorodnyaya Rus. Fed.
14 G3 Semiley Rus. Fed.
14 F2 Semilovo Rus. Fed.
14 D4 Semiluki Rus. Fed.
126 F3 Seminoe Res. resr U.S.A.
125 C5 Seminole U.S.A.
119 C6 Seminole, L. l. U.S.A.
65 L2 Seminskiy Khrebet mt. ra. Rus. Fed.
14 E2 Semion Rus. Fed.
64 F2 Semiozernoye Kazak.
48 D2 Semiozer'ye Rus. Fed.
65 K2 Semipalatinsk Kazak.
65 J3 Semipalatinsk div. Kazak.
41 B3 Semirara i. Phil.
41 B4 Semirara Islands is Phil.
57 B3 Semīrom Iran
40 B1 Semitau Indon.
65 J2 Semiyarka Kazak.
65 H2 Semiz-Bugu Kazak.
57 C2 Semnān div. Iran
57 C2 Semnān Iran
48 B5 Sêmnyi China
18 B4 Semois r. Belgium
41 A5 Semporna Malaysia
40 C4 Sempu i. Indon.
142 B1 Sem Tripa Brazil
14 A3 Semtsy Rus. Fed.
21 G3 Semur-en-Auxois France
12 H1 Semzha Rus. Fed.
140 C2 Sena Bolivia
144 D2 Senador Canedo Brazil
142 E2 Senador Pompeu Brazil
41 A5 Senaja Malaysia
140 C1 Sena Madureira Brazil
56 C5 Senanayake Samudra l. Sri Lanka
79 D7 Senanga Zambia
40 B1 Senaning Indon.
21 G5 Sénas France
15 E1 Sencha Ukraine
47 H4 Sendai Japan
46 C8 Sendai Japan
46 C8 Sendai-gawa r. Japan
18 E4 Senden Germany
50 A2 Sêndo China
43 C7 Senebui, Tanjung pt Indon.
129 G5 Seneca U.S.A.
122 C5 Seneca U.S.A.
126 C2 Seneca U.S.A.
120 E3 Seneca Falls U.S.A
120 E3 Seneca Lake l. U.S.A.
120 D5 Seneca Rocks U.S.A.
120 C5 Senecaville Lake l. U.S.A.
68 C4 Senegal country Africa
76 B3 Sénégal r. Mauritania/Senegal
122 E2 Seney U.S.A.
19 G3 Senftenberg Germany
81 B6 Senga Hill Zambia
54 D4 Sengar r. India
40 D1 Sengata Indon.
81 B5 Sengerema Tanzania
12 J4 Sengiley Rus. Fed.
64 D4 Sengiri, Mys pt Kazak.
147 B6 Senguerr r. Arg.
83 D2 Sengwa r. Zimbabwe
142 D3 Senhor do Bonfim Brazil
19 H4 Senica Slovakia
26 D4 Senigallia Italy
26 E3 Senj Croatia
10 E1 Senja i. Norway
76 C5 Senko Guinea
15 G2 Sen'kove Ukraine
54 D2 Senku India
20 F2 Senlis France
43 D4 Senmonorom Cambodia
47 E6 Sennan Japan
73 F5 Sennar Sudan
73 F5 Sennar Dam dam Sudan
115 G2 Senneterre Can.
14 H3 Sennoy Rus. Fed.
147 B7 Seno Otway b. Chile
83 D5 Senqu r. Lesotho
21 F2 Sens France
130 H6 Sensuntepeque El Salvador
28 C2 Senta Yugo.
129 F5 Sentinel U.S.A.
110 E3 Sentinel Pk summit Can.
152 B3 Sentinel Ra. mt. ra. Ant.
43 □ Sentosa i. Singapore
40 D1 Senyiur Indon.
60 E2 Şenyurt Turkey
46 C6 Senzaki Japan
46 D7 Sen-zaki pt Japan
54 D5 Seoni India
55 E5 Seorinarayan India
40 C3 Sepanjang i. Indon.
92 D4 Separation Pt pt N.Z.
40 D1 Sepasu Indon.
40 B1 Sepauk Indon.
143 D5 Sepetiba, Baía de b. Brazil
57 B3 Sepidān Iran
90 □1 Sepik r. P.N.G.
40 D1 Sepinang Indon.
27 E5 Sepino Italy
19 H2 Sępólno Krajeńskie Poland
141 E3 Sepotuba r. Brazil
113 G3 Sept-Îles Can.
20 C2 Sept-Îles, Les is France
40 A3 Seputih r. Indon.
128 C3 Sequoia National Park nat. park U.S.A.
13 G5 Serafimovich Rus. Fed.
57 E1 Serakhs Turkmenistan
39 J7 Seram i. Indon.
39 J7 Seram Sea g. Indon.
40 A3 Serang Indon.
43 □ Serangoon Harbour chan. Singapore
43 □ Serangoon, P. i. Singapore
43 E7 Serasan i. Indon.
43 E7 Seraya i. Indon.
43 □ Seraya, P. i. Singapore
61 B5 Serbâl, G. mt. Egypt
130 D2 Serdán Mexico
80 D2 Serdo Ethiopia
14 G3 Serdoba r. Rus. Fed.
14 G3 Serdobsk Rus. Fed.
65 K3 Serebryansk Kazak.
14 D2 Serebryanyye Prudy Rus. Fed.
19 H4 Sered' Slovakia
14 E1 Sereda Rus. Fed.
14 B2 Seredeyskiy Rus. Fed.
11 H4 Seredka Rus. Fed.
14 D2 Serednikovo Rus. Fed.
19 L4 Serednye Ukraine
14 B3 Seredyna-Buda Ukraine
60 C2 Şereflikoçhisar Turkey
21 F3 Serein r. France
43 C7 Seremban Malaysia
24 D3 Serena, Embalse de la resr Spain
81 B5 Serengeti National Park nat. park Tanzania
81 C5 Serengeti Plains plain Kenya
81 B7 Serenje Zambia
142 C2 Sereno r. Brazil
80 B4 Serere Uganda
15 A2 Seret r. Ukraine
14 F2 Serezha r. Rus. Fed.
14 G2 Sergach Rus. Fed.
48 D3 Sergelen Mongolia
48 E2 Sergelen Mongolia
65 G2 Sergeyevka Kazak.
142 E3 Sergipe div. Brazil
14 D1 Sergiyev Posad Rus. Fed.
64 D2 Sergiyevsk Rus. Fed.
14 C3 Sergiyevskoye Rus. Fed.
14 D3 Sergiyevskoye Rus. Fed.
15 E1 Serhiyivka *Chernihiv* Ukraine
15 D3 Serhiyivka *Odesa* Ukraine
15 D3 Serhiyivka *Odesa* Ukraine
38 F6 Seria Brunei
40 B1 Serian Malaysia
29 E6 Serifos i. Greece
113 G2 Sérigny, Lac l. Can.
60 B2 Serik Turkey
65 J5 Serikbuya China
100 C2 Seringapatam Reef reef Aust.
96 D2 Serle, Mt h. Aust.
39 J8 Sermata, Kepulauan is Indon.
12 J3 Sernur Rus. Fed.
64 E5 Sernyy Zavod Turkmenistan
132 □1 Seroe Colorado *Aruba* Caribbean
13 H6 Seroglazovka Rus. Fed.
25 E4 Serón Spain
82 C2 Seronga Botswana
75 F4 Serouenout well Algeria
62 H4 Serov Rus. Fed.
82 D3 Serowe Botswana
24 C4 Serpa Portugal
96 B2 Serpentine Lakes salt flat Aust.
139 E2 Serpent's Mouth chan. Trinidad/Venezuela
14 B2 Serpeysk Rus. Fed.
25 F3 Serpis r. Spain
15 C3 Serpneve Ukraine
14 E3 Serpovoye Rus. Fed.
14 C2 Serpukhov Rus. Fed.
145 H4 Serra Brazil
139 F3 Serra Acari h. Brazil/Guyana
144 A1 Serra Azul h. Brazil
145 E1 Serra Bonita Brazil
139 E3 Serra Curupira mt. ra. Brazil
143 B5 Serra da Apucarana h. Brazil
145 F5 Serra da Bocaina, Parque Nacional da nat. park Brazil
143 A5 Serra da Bodoquena h. Brazil
145 H2 Serra da Cana Brava h. Brazil
144 C1 Serra da Canastra mts *Goiás* Brazil
145 E3 Serra da Canastra mt. ra. *Minas Gerais* Brazil
145 E4 Serra da Canastra, Parque Nacional da nat. park Brazil
143 D4 Serra da Espinhaco mt. ra. Brazil
142 D1 Serra da Ibiapaba h. Brazil
145 F5 Serra da Mantiqueira mt. ra. Brazil
144 B3 Serra da Mombuca h. Brazil
144 B6 Serra das Araras mt. ra. Brazil
145 F1 Serra das Araras Brazil
144 B3 Serra das Araras h. Brazil
144 C2 Serra das Divisões ou de Santa Marta mt. ra. Brazil
142 D3 Serra da Tabatinga h. Brazil
141 E4 Serra de Amambaí h. Brazil/Paraguay
144 C6 Serra de Esperanca mt. ra. Brazil
142 C2 Serra de Itapicuru h. Brazil
144 A4 Serra de Maracaju h. Brazil
24 B1 Serra de Outes Spain
144 B4 Serra de Santa Bárbara h. Brazil
145 E1 Serra de Santa Maria h. Brazil
145 F1 Serra de São Felipe h. Brazil
144 A2 Serra de São Jerônimo h. Brazil
27 E7 Serra di Burgio h. Italy
142 B1 Serra do Almeirim h. Brazil
145 F2 Serra do Cabral mts Brazil
142 A2 Serra do Cachimbo h. Brazil
144 B2 Serra do Caiapó mts Brazil
145 H2 Serra do Chifre mt. ra. Brazil
140 B1 Serra do Divisor, Parque Nacional de nat. park Brazil
142 D2 Serra do Dois Irmãos h. Brazil
143 B6 Serra do Espigao mts Brazil
145 G2 Serra do Espinhaco mt. ra. Brazil
142 C1 Serra do Gurupi h. Brazil
144 B5 Serra do Lagarto h. Brazil
145 G5 Serra do Mar mt. ra. *Rio de Janeiro* Brazil
143 B6 Serra do Mar mt. ra. *Rio Grande do Sul/Santa Catarina* Brazil
145 F5 Serra do Mar mt. ra. *São Paulo* Brazil
139 E3 Serra do Mucajaí mt. ra. Brazil
139 G3 Serra do Navio Brazil
141 E2 Serra do Norte h. Brazil
142 D3 Serra do Ramalho h. Brazil
145 E2 Serra do Rio Prêto h. Brazil
142 B3 Serra do Roncador h. Brazil
145 H2 Serra dos Aimorés Brazil
142 A3 Serra dos Apiacas h. Brazil
142 A3 Serra dos Caiabis h. Brazil
142 B2 Serra dos Carajás h. Brazil
144 E2 Serra dos Cristais mts Brazil
144 B5 Serra dos Dourados h. Brazil
142 B2 Serra dos Gradaús h. Brazil
140 D2 Serra dos Pacaás h. Brazil
141 D2 Serra dos Parecis h. Brazil
144 E2 Serra dos Pilões mt. ra. Brazil
145 F1 Serra dos Tropeiros h. Brazil
142 B1 Serra do Tapara h. Brazil
144 B1 Serra do Taquaral h. Brazil
144 B3 Serra do Taquari h. Brazil
142 C1 Serra do Tiracambu h. Brazil
141 E2 Serra do Tombador h. Brazil
142 C3 Serra Dourada mt. ra. Brazil
144 C2 Serra Dourada h. Brazil
142 C2 Serra do Uruçuí h. Brazil
142 C2 Serra Estrondo h. Brazil
142 A3 Serra Formosa h. Brazil
144 C6 Serra Geral mt. ra. *Paraná* Brazil
143 B6 Serra Geral mt. ra. *Santa Catarina* Brazil
142 C3 Serra Geral de Goiás h. Brazil
144 E1 Serra Geral do Paraná h. Brazil
139 F3 Serra Iricoumé h. Brazil
139 G3 Serra Lombarda h. Brazil
132 B4 Serrana Bank Colombia
145 G3 Serra Negra mts Brazil
138 B2 Serranía de Abibe mt. ra. Colombia
138 B2 Serranía de Baudo mt. ra. Colombia
25 E2 Serranía de Cuenca mt. ra. Spain
139 E2 Serranía de Imataca mt. ra. Venezuela
138 D3 Serranía de la Neblina, Parque Nacional nat. park Venezuela
130 L7 Serranía del Darién mt. ra. Panama
132 C6 Serranía del Sapo mt. ra. Panama
24 D4 Serranía de Ronda mt. ra. Spain
131 E2 Serranías del Burro mt. ra. Mexico
139 E2 Serranía Turagua mt. Venezuela
147 B6 Serrano i. Chile
144 B3 Serranópolis Brazil
139 E3 Serra Pacaraima mt. ra. Brazil
144 D6 Serra Paranapiacaba mt. ra. Brazil
139 E3 Serra Parima mt. ra. Brazil
144 D1 Serra Pouso Alegre mts Brazil
142 E2 Serra Talhada Brazil
139 E3 Serra Tepequem mt. ra. Brazil
139 F3 Serra Tumucumaque h. Brazil
29 D4 Serres Greece
146 C3 Serrezuela Arg.
142 E3 Serrinha Brazil
145 G3 Sêrro Brazil
147 B5 Serrucho mt. Arg.
27 B7 Sers Tunisia
142 E2 Sertânia Brazil
144 C5 Sertanópolis Brazil
144 B3 Sertão de Camapuã reg. Brazil
144 E4 Sertãozinho Brazil
50 C1 Sêrtar China
11 H3 Sertolovo Rus. Fed.
40 A3 Sertung i. Indon.
39 L7 Serui Indon.
82 D3 Serule Botswana
40 C2 Seruyan r. Indon.
29 D4 Servia Greece
50 B1 Sêrxu China
41 A6 Sesayap r. Indon.
41 A6 Sesayap Indon.
112 B3 Seseganaga L. l. Can.
81 B5 Sese Is i. Uganda
114 E2 Sesekinika Can.
90 □6 Seseleka h. Fiji
82 A2 Sesfontein Namibia
14 A3 Seshcha Rus. Fed.
79 D7 Sesheke Zambia
29 F6 Sesklio i. Greece
47 □2 Sesoko Japan
47 □2 Sesoko-jima i. Japan
25 G3 S'Espalmador i. Spain
79 D6 Sessa Angola
27 D5 Sessa Aurunca Italy
26 B3 Sestri Levante Italy
11 H3 Sestroretsk Rus. Fed.
46 G2 Setana Japan
21 F5 Sète France
144 E6 Sete Barras Brazil
145 F3 Sete Lagoas Brazil
10 E1 Setermoen Norway
11 B4 Setesdal v. Norway
55 F3 Seti r. *Gandakhi* Nepal
54 E3 Seti r. *Seti* Nepal
75 F1 Sétif Algeria
73 G5 Setit r. Africa
47 F6 Seto Japan
46 D7 Seto-naikai sea Japan
42 A4 Setsan Myanmar
74 C2 Settat Morocco
79 A4 Setté Cama Gabon
26 B3 Settepani, Monte mt. Italy
26 A3 Settimo Torinese Italy
17 F4 Settle U.K.
98 D3 Settlement Cr. r. Aust.
145 G2 Setubal r. Brazil
24 B3 Setúbal Portugal
24 B3 Setúbal div. Portugal
24 B3 Setúbal, Baía de b. Portugal
122 E3 Seul Choix Pt pt U.S.A.
112 B3 Seul, Lac l. Can.
21 G3 Seurre France
14 B3 Sev r. Rus. Fed.
60 F1 Sevan Armenia
60 F1 Sevana Lich l. Armenia
13 E6 Sevastopol' Ukraine
113 H2 Seven Islands Bay b. Can.
21 F4 Sévérac-le-Château France
14 D2 Severka r. Rus. Fed.
97 G2 Severn r. Aust.
112 B3 Severn r. Can.
93 D5 Severn mt. N.Z.
17 F5 Severn r. U.K.
12 G2 Severnaya Dvina r. Rus. Fed.
13 G7 Severnaya Osetiya div. Rus. Fed.
63 M2 Severnaya Zemlya is Rus. Fed.
112 B3 Severn L. l. Can.
64 D2 Severnoye Rus. Fed.
65 J1 Severnoye Rus. Fed.
62 H3 Severnyy Rus. Fed.
14 G1 Severnyy Rus. Fed.
15 G1 Severnyy Rus. Fed.
64 E3 Severnyy Chink Ustyurta escarpment Kazak.
19 G3 Severočeský div. Czech Rep.
65 L2 Severo-Chuyskiy Khrebet mt. ra. Rus. Fed.
12 F1 Severodvinsk Rus. Fed.
65 G2 Severo-Kazakhstan div. Kazak.
63 R4 Severo-Kuril'sk Rus. Fed.
19 H4 Severomoravský div. Czech Rep.
10 J1 Severomorsk Rus. Fed.
12 F2 Severoonezhsk Rus. Fed.
63 L3 Severo-Yeniseyskiy Rus. Fed.
15 G1 Severskiy Donets r. Rus. Fed.
127 D4 Sevier r. U.S.A.
129 G2 Sevier Bridge Reservoir resr U.S.A.
129 F2 Sevier Desert desert U.S.A.
129 F2 Sevier Lake salt l. U.S.A.
138 B3 Sevilla Colombia
24 D4 Sevilla Spain
28 E3 Sevlievo Bulgaria
14 B3 Sevsk Rus. Fed.
76 B5 Sewa r. Sierra Leone
54 C3 Sewāni India
108 D3 Seward U.S.A.
124 D3 Seward U.S.A.
108 B3 Seward Peninsula pen. U.S.A.
110 F3 Sexsmith Can.
57 E2 Seyah Band Koh mt. ra. Afghanistan
62 J2 Seyakha Rus. Fed.
131 H5 Seybaplaya Mexico
81 □1 Seychelles country Indian Ocean
64 F5 Seydi Turkmenistan
60 B2 Seydişehir Turkey
10 N2 Seyðisfjörður Iceland
60 C2 Seyhan r. Turkey
61 C1 Seyhan Barajı resr Turkey
60 B2 Seyitgazi Turkey
14 B4 Seym r. Rus. Fed.
15 G1 Seym Rus. Fed.
15 E1 Seym r. Ukraine
63 R3 Seymchan Rus. Fed.
97 F4 Seymour Aust.
118 C4 Seymour U.S.A.
125 D5 Seymour U.S.A.
57 G2 Seyyedābād Afghanistan
21 F2 Sézanne France
14 B2 Sezha r. Rus. Fed.
27 D5 Sezze Italy
29 E7 Sfakia Greece
28 E2 Sfântu Gheorghe Romania
28 G2 Sfântu Gheorghe Romania
75 G2 Sfax Tunisia
18 B2 's-Gravenhage Netherlands
48 E5 Sha r. China
48 D6 Shaanxi div. China
79 E5 Shaba div. Zaire
80 E4 Shabeellaha Dhexe div. Somalia
80 D4 Shabeellaha Hoose div. Somalia
60 F2 Shabestar Iran
61 C5 Shabibī, J. esh mt. Jordan
28 G3 Shabla Bulgaria
14 B3 Shablykino Rus. Fed.
113 G3 Shabogamo Lake l. Can.
79 E4 Shabunda Zaire
65 J5 Shache China
152 B4 Shackleton Coast Ant.
152 B4 Shackleton Gl. gl. Ant.
152 D6 Shackleton Ice Shelf ice feature Ant.
152 C3 Shackleton Ra. mt. ra. Ant.
54 A4 Shadadkot Pakistan
57 F3 Shadikhak P. pass Afghanistan
57 C3 Shādkām w Iran
64 F1 Shadrinsk Rus. Fed.

110 F2 Tathlina Lake l. Can.
73 H4 Tathlīth Saudi Arabia
73 H3 Tathlīth, W. w Saudi Arabia
74 B3 Tâtilt well Mauritania
111 K2 Tatinnai Lake l. Can.
14 G4 Tatishchevo Rus. Fed.
42 B2 Tatkon Myanmar
126 A1 Tatla Lake l. Can.
19 J4 Tatry mts Poland/Slovakia
110 B3 Tatshenshini r. Can.
13 G5 Tatsinskiy Rus. Fed.
46 E6 Tattapani India
54 A4 Tatta Pakistan
55 H4 Tatty Kazak.
144 E5 Tatui Brazil
110 E4 Tatuk Mtn mt. Can.
124 C5 Tatum U.S.A.
60 E2 Tatvan Turkey
11 B4 Tau Norway
91 ☐13 Tau i. American Samoa Pac. Oc.
91 ☐13 Tau i. Tonga
142 D2 Taua Brazil
139 E5 Tauariá Brazil
145 F5 Taubaté Brazil
18 D4 Tauberbischofsheim Germany
64 D4 Tauchik Kazak.
91 ☐10 Tauére i. Fr. Poly. Pac. Oc.
18 F4 Taufkirchen (Vils) Germany
90 ☐3 Taula i. Tonga
55 E4 Taulihawa Nepal
92 E3 Taumarunui N.Z.
42 A2 Taungdwingyi Myanmar
42 B2 Taung-gyi Myanmar
42 A2 Taungnyo Range mt. ra. Myanmar
42 A2 Taungup Myanmar
91 ☐11 Taunoa Fr. Poly. Pac. Oc.
54 B3 Taunsa Pakistan
17 F6 Taunton U.K.
121 H4 Taunton U.S.A.
93 ☐1 Taupeka Pt pt Chatham Is N.Z.
92 E3 Taupo N.Z.
92 E3 Taupo, Lake l. N.Z.
11 F5 Taurage Lithuania
92 F3 Tauranga N.Z.
115 J3 Taureau, Réservoir resr Can.
27 F6 Taurianova Italy
92 D1 Tauroa Pt pt N.Z.
25 ☐1 Tauste Spain
91 ☐14 Tautama pt Pitcairn I. Pac. Oc.
91 ☐11 Tautira Fr. Poly. Pac. Oc.
90 ☐1 Tauu or Mortlock Is is P.N.G.
60 E2 Tavas Turkey
21 G3 Tavaux France
25 ☐1 Tavernes de la Valldigna Spain
90 ☐6 Taveuni i. Fiji
21 J5 Tavignano r. France
24 C4 Tavira Portugal
17 E6 Tavistock U.K.
43 B4 Tavoy Myanmar
43 H2 Tavricheskoye Rus. Fed.
15 E3 Tavur'y Ukraine
60 B2 Tavşanlı Turkey
90 ☐8 Tavua i. Fiji
90 ☐8 Tavua Fiji
93 C4 Tawa r. N.Z.
123 F3 Tawas Bay b. U.S.A.
123 F3 Tawas City U.S.A.
41 A5 Tawau Malaysia
41 A5 Tawau, Telukan b. Malaysia
41 A5 Tawitawi i. Phil.
42 B1 Tawmaw Myanmar
51 H4 T'a-wu Taiwan
131 F5 Taxco Mexico
65 J3 Taxkorgan China
110 C2 Tay r. Can.
16 F3 Tay r. U.K.
41 A4 Tayabas Bay b. Phil.
40 B1 Tayan Indon.
10 J1 Taybola Rus. Fed.
80 D4 Tayeeglow Somalia
48 A3 Tayega Mongolia
15 D3 Tayirove Ukraine
101 C7 Tay, L. salt flat Aust.
16 F3 Tay, Loch l. U.K.
110 E3 Taylor Can.
129 F4 Taylor U.S.A.
123 F6 Taylor r. U.S.A.
123 C5 Taylor, Mt mt. N.Z.
121 E5 Taylors Island U.S.A.
118 B4 Taylorville U.S.A.
73 G2 Taymā' Saudi Arabia
63 L3 Taymura r. Rus. Fed.
63 M2 Taymyr, Poluostrov pen. Rus. Fed.
43 D5 Tây Ninh Vietnam
16 F3 Tayport U.K.
41 A4 Taytay Phil.
41 B3 Taytay Phil.
41 A4 Taytay Bay b. Phil.
40 B3 Tayu Indon.
49 H2 Tayuan China
57 E2 Tayyebād Iran
61 C5 Ṭayyib al Ism Saudi Arabia
62 K3 Taz r. Rus. Fed.
74 D1 Taza Morocco
60 F3 Taza Khurmātū Iraq
47 H4 Tazawa-ko l. Japan
42 A2 Taze Myanmar
60 F2 Tazeh Kand Azerbaijan
120 B6 Tazewell U.S.A.
120 C6 Tazewell U.S.A.
111 H3 Tazin Lake l. Can.
72 D2 Tāzirbū Libya
72 D2 Tāzirbū Water Wells' Field well Libya
62 J3 Tazovskaya G. chan. Rus. Fed.
75 F4 Tazrouk Algeria
13 H7 T'bilisi Georgia
13 G6 Tbilisskaya Rus. Fed.
78 B2 Tchabal Mbabo mt. Cameroon
77 F5 Tchamba Togo
77 E5 Tchaourou Benin
79 B4 Tchibanga Gabon
77 F3 Tchié well Niger
77 G2 Tchigaï, Plateau du plat. Niger
79 B6 Tchindjenje Angola
77 F2 Tcholliré Cameroon
19 J1 Tczew Poland
100 C5 Teague, L. salt flat Aust.
91 ☐11 Teahupoo Fr. Poly. Pac. Oc.
51 A6 Te Anau N.Z.
93 A6 Te Anau, L. l. N.Z.
92 G2 Te Araroa N.Z.
92 E3 Te Aroha N.Z.
91 ☐11 Teavaro Fr. Poly. Pac. Oc.
40 B1 Tebakang Malaysia
40 D3 Tebas Indon.
115 H3 Tebedu Malaysia
141 E3 Tebicuary r. Paraguay
40 B2 Tebingtinggi Indon.
40 A1 Tebingtinggi Indon.
75 F1 Tébessa Algeria
27 B7 Téboursouk Tunisia

130 A1 Tecate Mexico
64 F1 Techa r. Rus. Fed.
76 D5 Techiman Ghana
28 D2 Techirghiol Romania
147 B5 Tecka r. Arg.
147 B5 Tecka Arg.
131 F4 Tecolutla Mexico
130 E5 Tecomán Mexico
128 D4 Tecopa U.S.A.
130 C2 Tecoripa Mexico
131 E5 Tecpan Mexico
28 F2 Tecuci Romania
123 F5 Tecumseh U.S.A.
80 D4 Ted Somalia
79 B4 Tédogora w Chad
72 C3 Tédjéré well Niger
64 F5 Tedzhen r. Turkmenistan
57 E1 Tedzhenstroy Turkmenistan
129 H3 Teec Nos Pos U.S.A.
65 M2 Teeli Rus. Fed.
17 G4 Tees r. U.K.
139 D4 Tefé r. Brazil
75 F4 Tefedest mts Algeria
139 E4 Tefé, Lago l. Brazil
60 B2 Tefenni Turkey
40 B3 Tegal Indon.
77 F4 Tegina Nigeria
40 A3 Tegineneng Indon.
90 ☐2 Tégua i. Vanuatu
130 J6 Tegucigalpa Honduras
77 F3 Teguidda-n-Tessoumt Niger
25 ☐ Teguise Canary Is Spain
128 C4 Tehachapi U.S.A.
127 C5 Tehachapi Mts mt. ra. U.S.A.
128 C4 Tehachapi Pass pass U.S.A.
111 K2 Tehek Lake l. Can.
76 D5 Téhini Côte d'Ivoire
57 B2 Tehrān div. Iran
57 B2 Tehrān Iran
54 D3 Tehri India
131 F5 Tehuacán Mexico
131 G6 Tehuantepec, Golfo de g. Mexico
131 G5 Tehuantepec, Istmo de isth. Mexico
131 G5 Tehuantepec Ridge Mexico
131 F5 Tehuitzingo Mexico
25 ☐ Teide, Pico del mt. Canary Is Spain
17 E5 Teifi r. U.K.
17 F6 Teign r. U.K.
47 ☐2 Teima Japan
28 D1 Teiuş Romania
142 E2 Teixeira Brazil
145 J2 Teixeira de Freitas Brazil
145 H2 Teixeiras Brazil
40 C4 Tejakula Indon.
25 ☐ Tejeda Canary Is Spain
77 F4 Tejira well Niger
24 B3 Tejo r. Portugal
129 C4 Tejon Pass pass U.S.A.
92 D1 Te Kao N.Z.
93 C6 Tekapo r. N.Z.
93 C5 Tekapo, L. l. N.Z.
55 F4 Tekari India
92 E2 Te Kauwhata N.Z.
131 H4 Tekax Mexico
55 G4 Tekeli India
55 H2 Teke, Oz. salt l. Kazak.
65 K4 Tekes r. China
80 C2 Tekezē Wenz r. Africa
54 E1 Tekiliktag mt. China
49 K2 Tekin Rus. Fed.
29 F4 Tekirdağ div. Turkey
60 A1 Tekirdağ Turkey
54 D2 Tekkali India
55 H5 Teknaf Bangladesh
122 E4 Tekonsha U.S.A.
92 E2 Te Kopuru N.Z.
92 E3 Te Kuiti N.Z.
55 E5 Tel r. India
13 G6 Tela Honduras
75 D2 Télagh Algeria
77 E3 Télataï Mali
13 H7 T'elavi Georgia
61 C3 Tel Aviv-Yafo Israel
19 G4 Telč Czech Rep.
131 H4 Telchac Puerto Mexico
14 C3 Tel'ch'ye Rus. Fed.
28 E1 Telciu Romania
78 D3 Tele r. Zaire
40 C2 Telegapulang Indon.
110 C3 Telegraph Creek Can.
144 C6 Telêmaco Borba Brazil
11 B4 Telemark div. Norway
146 C4 Telén r. Arg.
40 D1 Telen r. Indon.
15 C2 Teleneşti Moldova
131 H5 Telépi Ch Mexico
28 E2 Teleorman r. Romania
131 H5 Teleorman, Monte m. Mexico
128 C3 Telescope Pk pt summit U.S.A.
133 ☐8 Telescope Pt pt Grenada Caribbean
141 E1 Teles Pires r. Brazil
65 L2 Teletskoye, Ozero l. Rus. Fed.
17 F5 Telford U.K.
11 F5 Telfs Austria
130 J6 Telica Nicaragua
77 E4 Télig well Mali
76 B4 Télimélé Guinea
131 G4 Teljo, Jebel mt. Sudan
60 E2 Tel Kotchek Syria
110 A2 Telkwa Can.
108 B3 Teller U.S.A.
61 C4 Tel es Suwar Syria
77 F4 Tellicherry India
11 F5 Tellodar Ukraine
48 A4 Tel'mansk salt l. Mongolia
40 A2 Telok Blangah Singapore
40 A2 Telokbahan Indon.
40 A3 Telokbetung Indon.
42 B2 Telukbakela Indon.
14 C3 Telyazh'ye Rus. Fed.
76 B5 Tema Ghana
115 G2 Temagami Lake l. Can.
40 B3 Temanggung Indon.
92 E2 Te Mapou h. N.Z.
40 A2 Temau Indon.
131 H4 Temax Mexico
63 L3 Tembenchi r. Rus. Fed.
64 F3 Tembenchuan Kazak.
79 B6 Tembo Aluma Angola
138 D2 Teme r. U.K.
128 C4 Temecula, G. mt. Rus. Fed.
76 D3 Témera Mali
19 J4 Temerloh Malaysia
64 D2 Temir Kazak.
65 G2 Temirlanovka Kazak.
64 E2 Temirtau Kazak.
115 G3 Temiscaming Can.
114 F2 Témiscamingue, Lac l. Can.
12 G4 Temnikov Rus. Fed.
13 F5 Temora Aust.
130 D4 Temósachic Mexico
131 H5 Tempe, D. l. Indon.
40 D4 Temoe i. Indon.
40 A2 Tempino Indon.

27 B5 Tempio Pausania Italy
122 B3 Temple U.S.A.
125 D6 Temple U.S.A.
99 E2 Temple B. b. Aust.
17 D5 Templemore Rep. of Ire.
41 A4 Templer Bank sand bank Phil.
98 D4 Templeton r. Aust.
131 H4 Tempoal Mexico
13 F6 Temryuk Rus. Fed.
13 F6 Temryukskiy Zaliv b. Rus. Fed.
147 B4 Temuco Chile
93 C6 Temuka N.Z.
138 B4 Tena Ecuador
55 F4 Tenabo, Mt mt. U.S.A.
76 D4 Ténado Burkina
56 C2 Tenali India
131 F5 Tenancingo Mexico
43 B4 Tenasserim Myanmar
43 B4 Tenasserim div. Myanmar
43 B4 Tenasserim r. Myanmar
17 E6 Tenby U.K.
114 D3 Tenby Bay Can.
21 G4 Tence France
80 D2 Tendaho Ethiopia
21 H4 Tende France
24 A5 Ten Degree Channel chan. Andaman and Nicobar Is India
73 F5 Tendelti Sudan
47 H4 Tendō Japan
74 B1 Tendrara Morocco
15 D3 Tendriv'ka Kosa, Ostriv spit Ukraine
15 D3 Tendriv'ka Zatoka b. Ukraine
60 E2 Tendürük Dağı mt. Turkey
76 D4 Ténenkou Mali
141 E2 Tenente Marques r. Brazil
111 K2 Tenes Lake l. Can.
76 D5 Téhini Côte d'Ivoire
57 B2 Ténéré reg. Niger
57 B2 Ténéré du Tafassâsset desert Niger
25 ☐ Tenerife i. Canary Is Spain
75 E1 Ténès Algeria
40 D3 Tengah, Kep. is Indon.
50 B3 Tengchong China
43 ☐ Tengah Res. resr Singapore
40 D2 Tenggarong Indon.
48 C5 Tengger Shamo desert China
43 C6 Tenggul i. Malaysia
65 G2 Tengiz, Oz. salt l. Kazak.
76 C4 Tengréla Côte d'Ivoire
51 G1 Teng Xian China
51 F2 Teng Xian China
141 D4 Teniente Enciso, Parque Nacional nat. park Paraguay
152 B2 Teniente Jubany Argentina Base Ant.
152 B2 Teniente Rodolfo Marsh Chile Base Ant.
79 B6 Tenke Zaire
63 Q3 Tenkeli Rus. Fed.
76 D4 Tenkodogo Burkina
26 D4 Tenna r. Italy
98 C3 Tennant Creek Aust.
118 B4 Tennessee r. U.S.A.
119 B6 Tennessee div. U.S.A.
127 F4 Tennessee Pass pass U.S.A.
10 E1 Tennevoll Norway
146 B4 Teno r. Chile
10 G1 Tenojoki r. Finland
131 H5 Tenosique Mexico
47 F6 Tenryū Japan
47 F6 Tenryū r. Japan
121 F4 Ten Sleep U.S.A.
126 F2 Tenterfield Aust.
119 D7 Ten Thousand Islands is U.S.A.
24 J3 Tentudia mt. Spain
144 B5 Teodoro Sampaio Brazil
145 G2 Teófilo Otôni Brazil
74 C1 Tétouan Morocco
41 B5 Teomabal i. Phil.
93 ☐1 Te One Chatham Is N.Z.
55 E4 Teonthar India
131 G5 Teopisca Mexico
131 F5 Teotihuacan Mexico
131 F5 Teôuta Pac. Oc.
92 E1 Te Paki N.Z.
131 F5 Tepalcatepec Mexico
91 ☐11 Tepati Fr. Poly. Pac. Oc.
130 D3 Tepatitlán Mexico
130 D3 Tepehuanes Mexico
131 F5 Tepeji Mexico
131 F5 Tepelmemec Mexico
28 C4 Tepelenë Albania
130 D4 Tepic Mexico
19 F3 Teplice Czech Rep.
12 F4 Teplaya r. Rus. Fed.
14 H3 Teploozersk Rus. Fed.
14 C2 Teplovka Rus. Fed.
14 D3 Teploye Rus. Fed.
15 C2 Teplyk Ukraine
130 D4 Tepoca, Cabo pt Mexico
91 ☐1 Tepoto i. Fr. Poly. Pac. Oc.
92 F3 Te Puke N.Z.
131 F5 Tequisistlán Mexico
131 F5 Tequisquiapan Mexico
25 H1 Ter r. Spain
77 F4 Téra Niger
24 D2 Tera r. Spain
55 J4 Teraina i. Kiribati
87 B4 Teram Kangri mt. China/Jammu and Kashmir
111 K2 Tha-anne r. Can.
26 D4 Teramo Italy
97 F4 Terang Aust.
54 C4 Teratani r. Pakistan
93 E4 Terawhiti, Cape c. N.Z.
17 F4 Terbuny Rus. Fed.
26 D4 Tercan Turkey
60 E2 Terebeni' r. Rus. Fed.
28 D2 Terebovlya Ukraine
13 H7 Terek r. Rus. Fed.
65 L2 Terektinskiy Khr. mt. ra. Rus. Fed.
12 G4 Teren'ga r. Rus. Fed.
64 D2 Terenos Brazil
64 F3 Terenozek Kazak.
138 D2 Terepaima, Parque Nacional nat. park Venezuela

19 H5 Ternitz Austria
15 G2 Ternivka Dnipropetrovs'k Ukraine
15 E3 Ternivka Mykolayiv Ukraine
15 C2 Ternivka Vinnytsya Ukraine
15 A2 Ternopil' div. Ukraine
15 A2 Ternopil' Ukraine
14 E4 Ternovka Rus. Fed.
15 G3 Ternuvate Ukraine
15 E1 Terny Ukraine
96 D3 Terowie Aust.
45 Q2 Terpeniya, Mys Rus. Fed.
45 Q2 Terpeniya, Zaliv g. Rus. Fed.
144 B5 Terra Boa Brazil
145 G2 Terra Branca Brazil
110 D4 Terrace Can.
114 B2 Terrace Bay Can.
101 C6 Terraces, The h. Aust.
27 D5 Terranova di Pollino Italy
82 C4 Terra Firma R.S.A.
10 D2 Terråk Norway
113 K4 Terra Nova Nat. Pk nat. park Can.
27 D6 Terrasini Italy
20 E4 Terrasson-la-Villedieu France
152 B6 Terre Adélie reg. Ant.
125 F6 Terre Bonne Bay b. U.S.A.
133 ☐5 Terre de Bas i. Guadeloupe Caribbean
133 ☐5 Terre de Haut i. Guadeloupe Caribbean
118 C4 Terre Haute U.S.A.
113 K4 Terrenceville Can.
21 G3 Terre Plaine plain France
126 F2 Tersa r. Rus. Fed.
65 G2 Terskaan r. Kazak.
21 J6 Terschelling i. Netherlands
65 J4 Terskey Ala-Too mt. ra. Kyrgyzstan
12 F1 Terskiy Bereg Rus. Fed.
15 E3 Tersyanka Ukraine
27 B6 Tertenia Italy
26 E4 Teruel Spain
43 B6 Terutao i. Thailand
28 D3 Tervel Bulgaria
10 G2 Tervola Finland
26 F3 Tešanj Bos.-Herz.
80 C1 Tesenay Eritrea
47 G3 Tes-gushevo Rus. Fed.
51 G1 Tesha r. Rus. Fed.
46 H1 Teshikaga Japan
46 J2 Teshio-gawa r. Japan
46 H1 Teshio Japan
46 H1 Teshio-sanchi mt. ra. Japan
48 A2 Tesiyn Gol r. Mongolia
26 J2 Teslic Bos.-Herz.
110 C2 Teslin r. Can.
110 C2 Teslin Can.
110 C2 Teslin Lake l. Can.
142 D2 Tesouras r. Brazil
144 B2 Tesouro Brazil
12 D3 Tesovo-Netyl'skiy Rus. Fed.
77 D3 Tessalit Mali
77 F3 Tessaoua Niger
77 F3 Tesséroukane well Niger
77 F3 Tessoünfat well Mali
27 B7 Testour Tunisia
73 F2 Tetas, Pta pt Chile
78 D2 Tété r. C.A.R.
113 J3 Tête-à-la-Baleine Can.
72 B3 Tête Nord de l' plat. Western Sahara
90 ☐1 Tetepare i. Solomon Is.
15 E2 Teteriv r. Ukraine
19 F2 Teterow Germany
28 D3 Teteven Bulgaria
63 R3 Tetiaroa i. Fr. Poly. Pac. Oc.
91 ☐10 Tetiaroa i. Fr. Poly. Pac. Oc.
15 C2 Tetiyiv Ukraine
15 F1 Tetkino Rus. Fed.
120 D4 Teton r. U.S.A.
121 F3 Tetonia U.S.A.
101 B5 Tetoora r. Aust.
74 C1 Tétouan Morocco
28 C3 Tetovo Macedonia
54 B5 Tetpur India
12 J4 Tetyushi Rus. Fed.
147 C7 Teulada Italy
24 C2 Teuco r. Arg.
27 B6 Teulada, Capo pt Italy
27 C7 Teuladu Malaysia
111 J4 Teulon Can.
46 H1 Teuri-tô i. Japan
26 D3 Tevere r. Italy
61 C3 Teverya Israel
17 F4 Teviot r. U.K.
93 A7 Te Waewae Bay b. N.Z.
40 C2 Tewah Indon.
92 F3 Te Whaiti N.Z.
92 E1 Te Whanga Lagoon lag. Chatham Is N.Z.
93 C4 Te Wharau N.Z.
50 C2 Tewo China
110 D4 Texada I. i. Can.
99 E5 Texas Aust.
125 E5 Texarkana U.S.A.
125 E6 Texas div. U.S.A.
125 E6 Texas City U.S.A.
18 B2 Texel i. Netherlands
125 D5 Texhoma U.S.A.
125 C5 Texola U.S.A.
131 F4 Texistepec Mexico
14 E1 Teykovo Rus. Fed.
14 C2 Teza r. Rus. Fed.
54 C3 Tezpur India
87 J6 Tezu India
111 K2 Thabana-Ntlenyana mt. Lesotho
83 F4 Thaba Putsoa mt. Lesotho
83 F4 Thaba-Tseka Lesotho
42 A3 Thabeikkyin Myanmar
110 B4 Thabazimbi R.S.A.
42 A2 Tha Bo Laos
42 B3 Thabong R.S.A.
42 B2 Thabyu Myanmar
33 L8 Thailand country Asia
33 L8 Thailand, Gulf of g. Asia
42 A2 Thai Nguyen Vietnam
43 C5 Thai, Mui pt Vietnam
54 A3 Thakhek Laos
43 C6 Thalang Thailand
42 B3 Thale Luang lag. Thailand
43 B4 Tha Li Thailand
18 D3 Thalang Austria
42 B4 Thallon Aust.
72 C2 Thamad Bū Hashīshah well Libya
82 D1 Thamaga Botswana
60 B2 Thamar, J. mt. Yemen
17 G6 Thames r. U.K.

100 C3 Thangoo Aust.
99 G5 Thangool Aust.
42 D3 Thanh Hoa Vietnam
11 C4 Thanjavur India
99 E5 Thylungra Aust.
82 C2 Thaoge r. Botswana
42 A3 Tha Pla Thailand
43 B5 Thap Sakae Thailand
50 D4 Tharad India
50 D4 Tharaud India
99 E5 Thargomindah Aust.
50 D3 Thar (or Indian) Desert desert India
42 A3 Tharrawaddy Myanmar
42 A3 Tharrawaw Myanmar
29 E4 Thasos i. Greece
29 F5 Thasos Greece
28 E4 Thasos Greece
42 A3 Thật Khê Vietnam
42 A3 Thaton Myanmar
21 F5 Thau, Bassin de lag. France
42 A1 Thaungdut Myanmar
42 B3 Thaungyin r. Myanmar/Thailand
42 A3 Thayetchaung Myanmar
42 A3 Thayetmyo Myanmar
42 B2 Thazi Myanmar
42 B2 Thazi Myanmar
129 F5 Theba U.S.A.
73 F5 Thebes Egypt
42 A3 Theinkun Myanmar
42 B2 Theinkeik Myanmar
111 H2 Thekulthili Lake l. Can.
75 E1 Theniet el Had Algeria
91 ☐12 Thenia France
111 J2 Thelon Game Sanctuary res. Can.
18 E3 Themar Germany
114 A2 Theodore Can.
99 G4 Theodore Aust.
129 G5 Theodore Roosevelt Lake l. U.S.A.
120 D2 Theodore Roosevelt Nat. Park nat. park U.S.A.
61 C4 Theresa U.S.A.
29 C5 Thermon Greece
29 C5 Thermopolis U.S.A.
108 F2 Thesiger Bay b. Can.
29 C4 Thessalia div. Greece
29 D4 Thessaloniki Greece
115 F3 Thetford U.K.
42 D3 Tharn r. Can.
28 D2 Thetford Mines Can.
131 H4 Ticul Mexico
29 C6 Thira i. Greece
29 E6 Thirasia i. Greece
17 G4 Thirsk U.K.
101 C7 Thirsty, Mt h. Aust.
11 C4 Thisted Denmark
10 N2 Distilfjörður b. Iceland
20 D5 Thiva Greece
111 K2 Thlewiaza r. Can.
73 D2 Thoa r. Can.
42 C3 Thoeng Thailand
83 D3 Thohoyandou R.S.A.
101 B5 Thomas r. Aust.
100 B5 Thomas r. Aust.
119 C5 Thomaston U.S.A.
17 D5 Thomastown Rep. of Ire.
119 D6 Thomasville U.S.A.
122 B4 Thompson r. Can.
111 K3 Thompson Can.
118 B3 Thompson r. U.S.A.
114 A2 Thompson Falls U.S.A.
93 A6 Thompson Sound inlet N.Z.
110 E4 Thompson w Aust.
119 E5 Thomson U.S.A.
99 E4 Thomson w Aust.
43 D4 Thôn Cư Lai Vietnam
42 B3 Thông Myanmar
43 C4 Thôn Sơn Hai Vietnam
43 D4 Thôn Ta Ma Vietnam
74 B2 Thornaby-on-Tees U.K.
17 G4 Thornbury U.K.
121 F4 Thorne U.K.
128 B3 Thorne Bay U.S.A.
17 G5 Thornton U.K.
119 D6 Thorntown U.S.A.
92 E3 Thorpdale Aust.
20 D3 Thouars France
55 G4 Thoubal India
119 G3 Thousand Islands is Can.
121 J2 Thousand Lake Mt mt. U.S.A.
128 C4 Thousand Oaks U.S.A.
29 F4 Thrakiko Pelagos sea Greece
82 D4 Three Hills Can.
92 D1 Three Kings Is is N.Z.
122 C5 Three Lakes U.S.A.
119 D5 Three Oaks U.S.A.
42 B3 Three Pagodas Pass pass Myanmar/Thailand
76 D6 Three Points, Cape c. Ghana
122 D5 Three Rivers U.S.A.
125 D6 Three Rivers U.S.A.
128 C3 Three Sisters mt. U.S.A.
101 C5 Throssell, L. salt flat Aust.
101 B5 Throssell Ra. h. Aust.
42 A5 Thub un Lakes l. Can.
43 D6 Thu Dâu Môt Vietnam
21 E2 Thuin Belgium
83 E2 Thuli Zimbabwe
18 F3 Thum Germany
54 B1 Thun Switz.
122 C2 Thunder Bay b. Can.
123 F3 Thunder Bay b. U.S.A.
123 F3 Thunder Bay U.S.A.
43 C4 Thung Song Thailand
43 B5 Thung Wa Thailand
18 E3 Thüringen div. Germany
18 E3 Thüringer Becken reg. Germany
18 E3 Thüringer Wald mts Germany
17 C4 Thurles Rep. of Ire.
42 D5 Thurman U.S.A.
17 F5 Thurmont U.S.A.
120 D5 Thurso r. U.K.
16 F2 Thurso r. U.K.
16 F2 Thurso U.K.

16 F2 Thurso r. U.K.
83 F2 Timbué, Pta pt Mozambique
77 D3 Timétrine well Mali
77 D3 Timétrine reg. Mali
11 J3 Timmia N.Greece
11 J3 Timmia Norway
75 G4 Tiaret Algeria
119 C5 Timur India
45 Q2 Tinaca Pt pt Phil.
91 ☐10 To Awai well Fr. Poly. Pac. Oc.
73 G3 To Awai well Fr. Poly. Pac. Oc.
75 D2 Toba China
11 E3 Toba Japan
47 F6 Toba Japan
54 C3 Toba & Kakar Ranges mt. ra. Pakistan
133 ☐7 Tobago i. Trin. & Tobago
25 J3 Tobarra Spain
39 J6 Tobelo Indon.
110 D4 Tobermory U.K.
114 E4 Tobermory U.K.
16 C3 Tobermory U.K.
47 H5 Tobishi-hana c. Japan
109 J2 Tobin, Kap c. Greenland
121 K1 Tobique r. Can.
40 A3 Toboali Indon.
64 E2 Tobol r. Kazak.
62 G4 Tobol Kazak./Rus. Fed.
62 G4 Tobol'sk Rus. Fed.
10 D3 Toboso Aust.
97 G2 Tocantins Brazil
47 D5 Tochio Japan
47 G5 Tochigi Japan
47 G5 Tochigi div. Japan
11 C3 Töcksfors Sweden
133 ☐3 Tobago i. Trin. & Tobago
138 D1 Tocoa Honduras
146 B2 Toconao Chile
80 B2 Tocopilla Chile
138 C3 Tocuyo r. Venezuela
55 E4 Toda Bhim India
54 D3 Todela India
39 H7 Todeli Indon.
47 G4 Todogda-saki pt Japan
113 G4 Todohokke Japan
145 H4 Todos os Santos r. Brazil
143 D6 Todos Santos Bolivia
17 D5 Todos Santos Mexico
130 B3 Todos Santos, Bahía de b. Mexico
122 B5 Tofield Can.
110 E4 Tofino Can.
90 ☐5 Tofua i. Tonga
90 ☐5 Tofua i. Tonga
122 B2 Tofte U.S.A.
40 D2 Togian, Kepulauan is Indon.
69 E5 Togo country Africa
65 H3 Toguchin Rus. Fed.
122 A1 Togtoh China
110 A2 Tohoka mt. Pakistan
91 ☐4 Tohiea mt. Fr. Poly. Pac. Oc.
10 G3 Toholampi Finland
49 E1 Tohom China
45 P3 Toi Japan
47 G6 Toi Japan
10 H3 Toijala Finland
47 G3 Toi-misaki pt Japan
122 D3 Toiyabe Range mts U.S.A.
128 D2 Tôjô Japan
46 B7 Toju Japan
65 K4 Tokachi-gawa r. Japan
46 J2 Tokamachi Japan
47 G5 Tōkamachi Japan
93 B7 Tokanui N.Z.
73 G4 Tokar Sudan
51 M5 Tokara-rettô is Japan
60 D1 Tokat Turkey
49 H5 Tŏkchŏk-do i. S. Korea
49 H5 Tŏkch'ŏn N. Korea
49 E3 Tokelau terr. Pac. Oc.
91 ☐5 Tokelau terr. Pac. Oc.
47 G5 Tōkke well Africa
15 C1 Tokmak Kyrgyzstan
15 G3 Tokmak Ukraine
92 F3 Tokomaru Bay N.Z.
51 F5 Tokoroa N.Z.
65 K4 Tokoro-gawa r. Japan
80 D3 Toksun China
65 G4 Toktogul Kyrgyzstan
65 G4 Toktogul Suu Saktagychy resr Kyrgyzstan
14 C2 Tokur Rus. Fed.
49 H4 Tokushima Japan
47 D6 Tokushima div. Japan
46 D6 Tokuyama Japan
47 G6 Tōkyō Japan
47 G6 Tōkyō div. Japan
92 F3 Tolaga Bay N.Z.
83 J3 Tôlañaro Madagascar
60 D1 Tolbazy Rus. Fed.

40 E1 Tolitoli, Tk b. Indon.
62 K3 Tol'ka Rus. Fed.
19 J1 Tolkmicko Poland
18 F2 Tollense r. Germany
19 J5 Tolmachevo Rus. Fed.
26 D2 Tolmezzo Italy
19 J5 Tolna Hungary
19 J5 Tolna Hungary
45 ☐ Tolo Channel chan. Hong Kong
45 ☐ Tolo Harbour b. Hong Kong
24 D1 Tolosa Spain
114 D4 Tolsmaville Can.
138 B2 Tolú Colombia
131 F5 Toluca Mexico
12 J4 Tol'yatti Rus. Fed.
64 E2 Tolybay Kazak.
118 B5 Tom' r. Rus. Fed.
122 A4 Tomah U.S.A.
122 C3 Tomahawk U.S.A.
46 H2 Tomakomai Japan
46 H1 Tomanivi mt. Fiji
24 B3 Tomar Portugal
24 B3 Tomar Portugal
15 C1 Tomarovka Rus. Fed.
144 C3 Tomás Barron Bolivia
146 E3 Tomás Gomensoro Uruguay
15 B1 Tomashhorod Ukraine
19 L5 Tomashpil' Ukraine
19 K3 Tomaszów Lubelski Poland
19 K3 Tomaszów Mazowiecki Poland
130 D5 Tomatlán Mexico
144 C3 Tomazina Brazil
142 D2 Tombador, Serra do h. Brazil
76 B5 Tombigbee r. U.S.A.
79 B5 Tombôco Angola
79 B6 Tombos Brazil
76 D3 Tombouctou Mali
76 D3 Tombouctou div. Mali
129 H6 Tombstone U.S.A.
79 B6 Tombua Angola
83 D3 Tom Burke R.S.A.
146 B4 Tomé Chile
11 C4 Tomelilla Sweden
24 E3 Tomelloso Spain
41 B4 Tomiko Can.
97 G3 Tomingley Aust.
76 B4 Tominian Mali
40 D2 Tomini, Teluk g. Indon.
47 F5 Tomioka Japan
96 B2 Tomislavgrad Bos.-Herz.
100 C2 Tomkinson Ranges mt. ra. Aust.
10 D2 Tømmerneset Norway
10 E2 Tomo r. Rus. Fed.
138 C3 Tomo r. Colombia
14 J2 Tomorit Albania
122 D1 Tompa Indon.
40 D2 Tompo Indon.
100 B4 Tom Price Aust.
49 J2 Tomtor Rus. Fed.
47 H5 Tomtor Rus. Fed.
61 C1 Tömük Turkey
46 G3 Tomuraushi-yama mt. Japan
131 H5 Tonalá Mexico
131 H5 Tonalá Mexico
144 A6 Tonami Japan
139 E4 Tonantins Brazil
138 B4 Tonasket U.S.A.
139 G3 Tonate French Guiana
138 B4 Tonawanda U.S.A.
17 H6 Tonbridge U.K.
49 J3 Tondano Indon.
11 B5 Tønder Denmark
87 K7 Tone-gawa r. Japan
91 ☐5 Tonga country Pac. Oc.
122 F2 Tongaat R.S.A.
90 ☐5 Tofua i. Tonga
92 E3 Tongariro, Mt vol N.Z.
92 E3 Tongariro National Park nat. park N.Z.
90 ☐4 Tongatapu i. Tonga
90 ☐4 Tongatapu Group is Tonga
92 E3 Tonga Tr. Pac. Oc.
49 E5 Tongbai China
50 E2 Tongbai Shan mt. ra. China
51 F3 Tongcheng China
51 E3 Tongchuan China
50 E3 Tongchuan China
49 F4 Tongde China
49 G5 Tongeren Belgium
51 G2 Tonggu China
50 C4 Tonghai China
49 H3 Tonghe China
49 H4 Tonghua China
49 H4 Tongjiang China
50 D3 Tongjiang China
43 D4 Tongking, Gulf of g. China/Vietnam
49 J2 Tongliao China
51 F3 Tongling China
51 F4 Tonglu China
51 G2 Tongren China
50 D3 Tongren China
55 H4 Tongsa Bhutan
49 E4 Tongshan China
50 E1 Tongshi China
126 A3 Tong U.K.
131 G5 Tonga r. U.S.A.
49 J1 Tongyu China
51 F3 Tongzi China
57 B1 Tonkābon Iran
130 C3 Tónichi Mexico
51 D4 Tonkin reg. Vietnam
43 D5 Tônlé Sab l. Cambodia
21 G3 Tonnerre France
47 G6 Tonoshō Japan
130 K7 Tonosi Panama
11 B4 Tønsberg Norway
11 B4 Tonstad Norway
129 F2 Tooele U.S.A.
96 D4 Tooleybuc Aust.
97 G2 Toompine Aust.
100 B4 Toora-Khem Aust.
97 G2 Toowoomba Aust.

14 C1 Ul'yanikha Rus. Fed.
12 H4 Ul'yankovo Rus. Fed.
15 D2 Ul'yanovka Ukraine
14 B3 Ul'yanovo Rus. Fed.
12 J4 Ul'yanovsk Rus. Fed.
14 H3 Ul'yanovsk div. Rus. Fed.
65 H2 Ul'yanovskiy Kazak.
49 F2 Ulyatuy Rus. Fed.
125 C4 Ulysses U.S.A.
65 G3 Ulytau Kazak.
65 G3 Ulyzhilanshik r. Kazak.
49 G1 Uma Rus. Fed.
131 H4 Umán Mexico
15 D2 Uman' Ukraine
146 C2 Umango, Co mt. Arg.
54 A3 Umarao Pakistan
54 E5 Umaria India
56 B2 Umarkhed India
56 C2 Umarkot India
54 B4 Umarkot Pakistan
41 □2 Umatac *Guam* Pac. Oc.
126 C2 Umatilla U.S.A.
12 E1 Umba Rus. Fed.
121 H2 Umbagog Lake l. U.S.A.
78 D2 Umbelasha w Sudan
26 D4 Umbertide Italy
90 □1 Umboi i. P.N.G.
93 B6 Umbrella Mts mts N.Z.
133 □1 Umbrella Pt pt Jamaica
26 D4 Umbria div. Italy
83 D2 Ume r. Zimbabwe
10 F3 Umeå Sweden
10 D2 Umeälven r. Sweden
61 C3 Um ed Daraj, J. mt. Jordan
14 F3 Umet Rus. Fed.
14 F2 Umet Rus. Fed.
108 H3 Umingmaktok Can.
112 E2 Umiujaq Can.
83 E4 Umlazi R.S.A.
73 G3 Umm al Birak Saudi Arabia
57 C4 Umm al Qaywayn U.A.E.
73 H2 Umm at Qalbān Saudi Arabia
57 B4 Umm Bāb Qatar
73 E5 Umm Bel Sudan
61 B5 Umm Bugma Egypt
72 C2 Umm Farud Libya
73 F3 Umm Gerifat waterhole Sudan
73 E5 Umm Keddada Sudan
73 G2 Umm Lajj Saudi Arabia
61 C5 Umm Mafrûd, G. mt. Egypt
61 C5 Umm Nukhaylah well Saudi Arabia
60 F4 Umm Qasr Iraq
73 E4 Umm Qurein well Sudan
73 F5 Umm Rimtha well Sudan
73 F5 Umm Ruwaba Sudan
72 E1 Umm Sa'ad Libya
73 F5 Umm Saiyala Sudan
61 D5 Umm Shajtiya waterhole Saudi Arabia
61 B5 Umm Shomar, G. mt. Egypt
73 E4 Umm Sunaita well Sudan
61 B5 Umm Tināṣṣib, G. mt. Egypt
73 G2 Umm Urūmah i. Saudi Arabia
61 B5 Umm Zanatir mt. Egypt
104 B4 Umnak I. i. U.S.A.
83 F1 Umpilua Mozambique
126 A3 Umpqua r. U.S.A.
79 C6 Umpulo Angola
54 D5 Umred India
56 A1 Umreth India
83 D5 Umtata R.S.A.
77 F5 Umuahia Nigeria
144 B5 Umuarama Brazil
90 □3 Umuna i. Tonga
29 F4 Umurbey Turkey
83 E5 Umzinto R.S.A.
26 F3 Una r. Bos.-Herz./Croatia
145 J1 Una Brazil
61 D4 'Unāb, W. al w Jordan
145 E2 Unaí Brazil
57 G2 Unai P. pass Afghanistan
108 B3 Unalakleet U.S.A.
108 B4 Unalaska U.S.A.
108 B4 Unalaska I. i. U.S.A.
81 C7 Unango Mozambique
60 C4 'Unayzah Jordan
73 H2 'Unayzah Saudi Arabia
54 E4 Unchahra India
140 C3 Uncia Bolivia
127 E4 Uncompahgre Plateau plat. U.S.A.
49 F2 Unda r. Rus. Fed.
49 F2 Unda Rus. Fed.
96 E3 Underbool Aust.
124 C2 Underwood U.S.A.
40 E4 Undu, Tg pt Indon.
13 D4 Unecha Rus. Fed.
14 H2 Unga r. Rus. Fed.
108 B4 Unga I. i. U.S.A.
97 F3 Ungarie Aust.
113 G2 Ungava Bay b. Can.
112 F1 Ungava, Péninsule d' pen. Can.
49 J4 Unggi N. Korea
15 B3 Ungheni Moldova
28 E1 Ungurași Romania
81 D5 Ungwana Bay b. Kenya
12 J3 Uni Rus. Fed.
142 D1 União Brazil
143 B6 União da Vitória Brazil
142 E2 União dos Palmares Brazil
54 D4 Uniara India
19 J3 Uniejów Poland
108 B4 Unimak I. i. U.S.A.
139 E4 Unini r. Brazil
140 B2 Unini Peru
141 E4 Unión Paraguay
133 G4 Union i. St Vincent
121 J2 Union U.S.A.
119 D5 Union U.S.A.
120 C6 Union U.S.A.
120 A4 Union City U.S.A.
120 D4 Union City U.S.A.
119 B4 Union City U.S.A.
129 F4 Union, Mt mt. U.S.A.
119 C5 Union Springs U.S.A.
120 D5 Uniontown U.S.A.
81 □4 Union Vale Mauritius
123 F4 Unionville U.S.A.
126 E3 Unita Mts. mts U.S.A.
32 G7 United Arab Emirates country Asia
4 E3 United Kingdom country Europe
104 H6 United States of America country N. America
111 H4 Unity Can.
121 J2 Unity U.S.A.
126 C2 Unity U.S.A.
82 A3 Unjab w Namibia
54 C5 Unjha India
54 E4 Unnão India
49 H5 Ŭnp'a N. Korea
49 H5 Ŭnsan N. Korea
16 G1 Unst i. U.K.
47 □2 Unten Japan
55 G2 Unuli Horog China
46 C7 Unzen-dake vol Japan
47 F5 Uozu Japan
14 C2 Upa r. Rus. Fed.
55 F5 Upar Ghat India
139 E2 Upata Venezuela
79 E5 Upemba, Lac l. Zaire
79 E5 Upemba, Parc National de l' nat. park Zaire
109 N2 Upernavik Greenland
109 N2 Upernavik Kujalleq Greenland
41 C5 Upi Phil.
138 C3 Upía r. Colombia
82 C4 Upington R.S.A.
54 B5 Upleta India
10 H2 Upoloksha Rus. Fed.
91 □12 Upolu i. Western Samoa
120 B4 Upper Arlington U.S.A.
110 F4 Upper Arrow L. l. Can.
76 D4 Upper East div. Ghana
93 E4 Upper Hutt N.Z.
122 B4 Upper Iowa r. U.S.A.
121 K1 Upper Kent Can.
126 B3 Upper Klamath L. l. U.S.A.
126 B3 Upper L. l. U.S.A.
128 A2 Upper Lake U.S.A.
110 D2 Upper Liard Can.
17 D4 Upper Lough Erne l. U.K.
133 □3 Upper Manzanilla Trin. & Tobago
120 E5 Upper Marlboro U.S.A.
80 B3 Upper Nile div. Sudan
43 □ Upper Peirce Res. resr Singapore
113 J4 Upper Salmon Reservoir resr Can.
120 B4 Upper Sandusky U.S.A.
121 F2 Upper Saranac Lake l. U.S.A.
93 D4 Upper Takaka N.Z.
76 D4 Upper West div. Ghana
11 E4 Uppsala div. Sweden
11 E4 Uppsala Sweden
112 B4 Upsala Can.
54 D2 Upshi India
99 F3 Upstart B. b. Aust.
99 F3 Upstart, C. hd Aust.
121 H2 Upton U.S.A.
92 E1 Upua N.Z.
61 D2 'Uqayribāt Syria
61 C4 'Uqeiqa, W. w Jordan
60 F4 Uqlat al 'Udhaybah well Iraq
73 H2 'Uqlat aş Şuqūr Saudi Arabia
138 B2 Urabá, Golfo de b. Colombia
48 D4 Urad Qianqi China
48 D4 Urad Zhonghou Lianheqi China
57 D3 Ūrāf Iran
47 G6 Uraga-suid ō chan. Japan
47 G5 Uragawara Japan
46 J2 Urahoro Japan
144 C5 Uraí Brazil
46 J2 Urakawa Japan
97 F3 Ural h. Aust.
64 D2 Ural r. Kazak./Rus. Fed.
97 G2 Uralla Aust.
64 D2 Ural'sk Kazak.
62 G4 Ural'skiy Khrebet mt. ra. Rus. Fed.
81 B6 Urambo Tanzania
97 F3 Urana Aust.
97 F3 Urana, L. l. Aust.
98 D4 Urandangi Aust.
145 G1 Urandi Brazil
111 H3 Uranium City Can.
139 E3 Uraricoera Brazil
139 E3 Uraricuera r. Brazil
47 □2 Urasoe Japan
129 H2 Uravan U.S.A.
14 G2 Urazovka Rus. Fed.
122 C5 Urbana U.S.A.
120 B4 Urbana U.S.A.
142 D1 Urbano Santos Brazil
26 D4 Urbino Italy
140 B2 Urcos Peru
13 H5 Urda Kazak.
24 E3 Urda Spain
12 J2 Urdoma Rus. Fed.
65 K3 Urdzhar Kazak.
17 G4 Ure r. U.K.
12 H3 Uren' Rus. Fed.
62 J3 Urengoy Rus. Fed.
14 H2 Ureno-Karlinskoye Rus. Fed.
92 E3 Urenui N.Z.
90 □2 Uréparapara i. Vanuatu
92 F3 Urewera National Park nat. park N.Z.
61 B6 'Urf, G. el mt. Egypt
14 G2 Urga r. Rus. Fed.
49 K2 Urgal r. Rus. Fed.
64 F4 Urgench Uzbekistan
60 C2 Ürgüp Turkey
65 L3 Urho China
10 G1 Urho Kekkosen kansallispuisto nat. park Finland
54 C2 Uri India
93 C5 Uriah, Mt mt. N.Z.
138 C1 Uribia Colombia
97 E2 Urisino Aust.
65 G2 Uritskiy Kazak.
14 D4 Uritskoye Rus. Fed.
80 C2 Urī Wenz r. Ethiopia
11 F3 Urjala Finland
60 A2 Urla Turkey
28 F2 Urlați Romania
48 C2 Urluk Rus. Fed.
49 K2 Urmi r. Rus. Fed.
45 □ Urmston Road chan. Hong Kong
77 F5 Uromi Nigeria
28 C3 Uroševac Yugo.
65 G5 Ŭroteppa Tajikistan
55 F3 Urru Co salt l. China
14 E2 Urshel'skiy Rus. Fed.
19 L3 Urszulin Poland
48 B4 Urt Mongolia
144 D1 Uru r. Brazil
130 C3 Uruáchic Mexico
142 C3 Uruaçu Brazil
144 D1 Uruana Brazil
130 E5 Uruapan Mexico
140 B2 Urubamba r. Peru
139 F4 Urubu r. Brazil
144 C4 Urubupungá, Salto do waterfall Brazil
139 F4 Urucara Brazil
14 A3 Uruch'ye Rus. Fed.
139 F5 Urucu r. Brazil
145 J1 Uruçuca Brazil
142 D2 Uruçuí Brazil
145 F2 Urucuia r. Brazil
145 F2 Urucuia Brazil
142 C2 Uruçuí Prêto r. Brazil
139 F4 Urucurituba Brazil
143 B6 Uruguai r. Brazil
146 E2 Uruguaiana Brazil
139 F5 Uruguatos r. Brazil
146 E3 Uruguay r. Arg./Uruguay
136 E6 Uruguay country S. America
49 H2 Uruhe China
41 □1 Urukthapel i. Palau
61 D1 Urūmaş Şughrá Syria
44 E3 Ürümqi China
97 H2 Urunga Aust.
13 G6 Urup r. Rus. Fed.
63 R5 Urup, O. i. Rus. Fed.
13 H7 Urus-Martan Rus. Fed.
14 F3 Urusovo Rus. Fed.
64 D2 Urussu Rus. Fed.
144 D2 Urutaí Brazil
92 E3 Uruti N.Z.
65 L3 Uryl' Kazak.
46 H2 Uryūgawa r. Japan
49 G1 Uryupino Rus. Fed.
13 G5 Uryupinsk Rus. Fed.
12 J3 Urzhum Rus. Fed.
28 F2 Urziceni Romania
46 C7 Usa Japan
12 J4 Usa r. Rus. Fed.
29 G5 Uşak div. Turkey
60 B2 Uşak Turkey
82 B3 Usakos Namibia
152 B5 Usarp Mts mts Ant.
147 E7 Usborne, Mt h. Falkland Is.
28 C3 Ušće Yugo.
19 F2 Usedom Germany
19 G2 Usedom i. Germany
101 A5 Useless Loop Aust.
73 G3 Usfān Saudi Arabia
62 J1 Ushakova, O. i. Rus. Fed.
73 H3 'Ushayrah Saudi Arabia
48 A2 Ush-Bel'dyr Rus. Fed.
46 C7 Ushibuka Japan
14 F3 Ushinka Rus. Fed.
14 E2 Ushna Rus. Fed.
14 E2 Ushna r. Rus. Fed.
65 J3 Ushtobe Kazak.
147 C7 Ushuaia Arg.
49 H1 Ushumun Rus. Fed.
55 E4 Uska India
14 D3 Usman' r. Rus. Fed.
14 D3 Usman' Rus. Fed.
11 F4 Usmas Ezers l. Latvia
24 D3 Uso r. Spain
12 J2 Usogorsk Rus. Fed.
44 H1 Usol'ye-Sibirskoye Rus. Fed.
14 B3 Usozha r. Rus. Fed.
15 G3 Uspenivka Ukraine
65 J2 Uspenka Kazak.
15 E1 Uspenka Ukraine
65 H3 Uspenskiy Kazak.
13 G6 Uspenskoye Rus. Fed.
20 F4 Ussel *Limousin* France
49 J4 Ussuriysk Rus. Fed.
12 H3 Usta r. Rus. Fed.
65 M2 Ust'-Abakan Rus. Fed.
12 H2 Ust'- Alekseyevo Rus. Fed.
54 B3 Usta Muhammad Pakistan
64 F1 Ust'-Bagaryak Rus. Fed.
45 J1 Ust'-Barguzin Rus. Fed.
12 K2 Ust'-Chernaya Rus. Fed.
49 F1 Ust'-Chernaya Rus. Fed.
13 G6 Ust'-Donetskiy Rus. Fed.
27 D6 Ustica, Isola di i. Italy
63 M4 Ust'Ilimsk Rus. Fed.
48 E2 Ust'-Ilya Rus. Fed.
62 G3 Ust'-Ilych Rus. Fed.
19 G3 Ústí nad Labem Czech Rep.
19 H4 Ústí nad Orlicí Czech Rep.
19 H1 Ustka Poland
63 S4 Ust'-Kamchatsk Rus. Fed.
65 K3 Ust'-Kamenogorsk Kazak.
65 K2 Ust'-Kan Rus. Fed.
49 F1 Ust'-Karsk Rus. Fed.
64 E2 Ust'-Katav Rus. Fed.
65 L2 Ust'-Koksa Rus. Fed.
12 K2 Ust'-Kulom Rus. Fed.
63 M4 Ust'-Kut Rus. Fed.
63 P2 Ust'-Kuyga Rus. Fed.
13 F6 Ust'-Labinsk Rus. Fed.
49 G1 Ust'-Lubiya Rus. Fed.
11 H4 Ust'-Luga Rus. Fed.
63 P3 Ust'-Maya Rus. Fed.
62 K3 Ust-Mukduyka Rus. Fed.
49 F1 Ust'-Nachin Rus. Fed.
63 Q3 Ust'-Nera Rus. Fed.
49 K2 Ust'-Niman Rus. Fed.
63 N2 Ust'-Olenek Rus. Fed.
63 Q3 Ust'omchug Rus. Fed.
48 C1 Ust'-Ordynskiy Buryatskiy Avt. Okrug div. Rus. Fed.
63 S3 Ust' Penzhino Rus. Fed.
28 F3 Ustrem Bulgaria
19 L4 Ustrzyki Dolne Poland
14 F4 Ust'-Shcherbedino Rus. Fed.
65 J1 Ust'-Tarka Rus. Fed.
49 J2 Ust'-Tyrma Rus. Fed.
49 K2 Ust'-Umalta Rus. Fed.
12 H2 Ust'-Ura Rus. Fed.
49 K2 Ust'-Urgal Rus. Fed.
64 F2 Ust'-Uyskoye Kazak.
12 G2 Ust'-Vayen'ga Rus. Fed.
12 H2 Ust'-Vyyskaya Rus. Fed.
12 H2 Ust'ya r. Rus. Fed.
14 D1 Ust'ye r. Rus. Fed.
14 E3 Ust'ye Rus. Fed.
12 F3 Ust'ye Rus. Fed.
19 L3 Ustyluh Ukraine
15 A1 Ustyluh Ukraine
15 E3 Ustynivka Ukraine
64 D4 Ustyurta escarpment Kazak.
64 E4 Ustyurt, Plato plat. Uzbekistan
12 F3 Ustyuzhna Rus. Fed.
65 K4 Usu China
47 G5 Usuda Japan
46 C7 Usuki Japan
130 H6 Usulután El Salvador
131 H5 Usumacinta r. Mexico
12 D4 Usvyaty Rus. Fed.
129 G2 Utah div. U.S.A.
129 G1 Utah Lake l. U.S.A.
10 G2 Utajärvi Finland
46 J2 Utashinai Japan
46 K1 Utashinai Rus. Fed.
90 □3 'Uta Vava'u i. Tonga
73 H3 'Utaybah reg. Saudi Arabia
57 B4 Utayyiq Saudi Arabia
25 F2 Utebo Spain
79 D7 Utembo r. Angola
11 G5 Utena Lithuania
81 C6 Utete Tanzania
54 A4 Uthal Pakistan
61 D2 'Uthmānīyah Syria
43 B4 U Thong Thailand
141 E2 Utiariti Brazil
121 F3 Utica U.S.A.
25 F3 Utiel Spain
110 F3 Utikuma Lake l. Can.
142 D3 Utinga r. Brazil
15 F3 Utlyuks'kyy Lyman est. Ukraine
46 C7 Uto Japan
55 E4 Utraula India
18 B2 Utrecht Netherlands
18 B2 Utrecht div. Netherlands
24 D4 Utrera Spain
16 K2 Utsira Norway
10 G1 Utsjoki Finland
47 G5 Utsunomiya Japan
13 H6 Utta Rus. Fed.
42 C3 Uttaradit Thailand
54 D3 Uttarkashi India
54 D4 Uttar Pradesh India
119 □3 Utuado Puerto Rico
65 L3 Utubulak China
91 □11 Utuofai *Fr. Poly.* Pac. Oc.
91 □10 Uturoa *Fr. Poly.* Pac. Oc.
64 D2 Utva r. Kazak.
109 M2 Uummannaq Greenland
109 N2 Uummannaq Fj. inlet Greenland
109 O4 Uummannarsuaq c. Greenland
11 G3 Uurainen Finland
48 B2 Üür Gol r. Mongolia
11 F3 Uusikaupunki Finland
11 G3 Uusimaa div. Finland
82 A2 Uutapi Namibia
125 D6 Uvalde U.S.A.
14 B2 Uvarovka Rus. Fed.
14 F4 Uvarovo Rus. Fed.
14 G3 Uvarovo Rus. Fed.
81 B6 Uvinza Tanzania
79 E4 Uvira Zaire
14 E1 Uvod' r. Rus. Fed.
83 E5 Uvongo R.S.A.
44 F1 Uvs Nuur salt l. China
46 D7 Uwa Japan
46 D7 Uwajima Japan
72 B2 'Uwaynāt Wannīn Libya
72 E3 Uweinat, Jebel mt. Sudan
40 A1 Uwi i. Indon.
48 D5 Uxin Ju China
48 D5 Uxin Qi China
142 A1 Uxituba Brazil
131 H4 Uxmal Mexico
64 F2 Uy r. Rus. Fed.
64 F4 Uyaly Kazak.
48 C3 Üydzin Mongolia
63 Q3 Uyega Rus. Fed.
77 F5 Uyo Nigeria
42 A1 Uyu Chaung r. Myanmar
65 H4 Uyuk Kazak.
61 B5 'Uyûn Mûsa spring Egypt
13 H4 Uza r. Rus. Fed.
32 H5 Uzbekistan country Asia
64 D4 Uzen' Kazak.
20 E4 Uzerche France
21 G4 Uzès France
15 C1 Uzh r. Ukraine
13 B5 Uzhhorod Ukraine
14 G2 Uzhovka Rus. Fed.
14 D3 Uzlovaya Rus. Fed.
14 F1 Uzola r. Rus. Fed.
60 B2 Üzümlü Turkey
65 J4 Uzunagach Kazak.
60 A1 Uzunköprü Turkey
15 D2 Uzyn Ukraine
64 F4 Uzynkair Kazak.

V

78 D2 Va r. C.A.R.
82 C4 Vaal r. R.S.A.
10 G2 Vaala Finland
83 D4 Vaal Dam dam R.S.A.
10 F3 Vaasa Finland
10 F3 Vaasa div. Finland
64 F4 Vabkent Uzbekistan
14 A3 Vablya r. Rus. Fed.
19 J5 Vác Hungary
145 F4 Vacaré r. Brazil
145 G2 Vacaria r. Brazil
143 B6 Vacaria Brazil
144 A4 Vacaria r. Brazil
143 B5 Vacaria, Serra h. Brazil
128 B2 Vacaville U.S.A.
14 F2 Vacha Rus. Fed.
81 □4 Vacoas Mauritius
14 F2 Vad r. Rus. Fed.
14 G2 Vad Rus. Fed.
56 A2 Vada India
28 F2 Vădeni Romania
14 F3 Vadinsk Rus. Fed.
11 B4 Vadla Norway
54 C5 Vadodara India
10 H1 Vadsø Norway
18 D5 Vaduz Liechtenstein
10 D2 Værøy i. Norway
12 G2 Vaga r. Rus. Fed.
11 C3 Vågåmo Norway
26 E3 Vaganski Vrh mt. Croatia
16 D1 Vágar i. Faeroes
24 B2 Vagos Portugal
10 E2 Vägsele Sweden
19 H4 Váh r. Slovakia
10 F3 Vähäkyrö Finland
91 □11 Vaiau, Pte pt *Fr. Poly.* Pac. Oc.
11 G4 Vaida Estonia
56 B4 Vaigai r. India
91 □16 Vaihu *Easter I.* Chile
129 G5 Vail U.S.A.
91 □12 Vailoa Western Samoa
90 □4 Vaina Tonga
91 □11 Vairao *Fr. Poly.* Pac. Oc.
21 G4 Vaison-la-Romaine France
91 □13 Vaitogi *American Samoa* Pac. Oc.
150 G6 Vaitupu i. Tuvalu
91 □12 Vaiusu Western Samoa
90 □3 Vaka'eitu i. Tonga
78 D2 Vakaga div. C.A.R.
62 K3 Vakh r. Rus. Fed.
54 C1 Vakhan Tajikistan
65 G5 Vakhsh Tajikistan
57 D3 Vakīlābād Iran
56 C5 Valachchenai Sri Lanka
12 K3 Valamaz Rus. Fed.
29 D4 Valandovo Macedonia
19 J4 Valašské Klobouky Czech Rep.
19 H4 Valašské Meziříčí Czech Rep.
29 E5 Valaxa i. Greece
115 H3 Val-Barrette Can.
147 C5 Valcheta Arg.
114 D2 Val-Côté Can.
26 C3 Valdagno Italy
21 H3 Valdahon France
24 D1 Valdavia r. Spain
12 E3 Valday Rus. Fed.
14 A1 Valdayskaya Vozvyshennost' h. Rus. Fed.
24 D3 Valdecañas, Embalse de resr Spain
11 F4 Valdemārpils Latvia
11 E4 Valdemarsvik Sweden
21 G2 Val-de-Meuse France
24 E2 Valdemoro Spain
24 E3 Valdepeñas Spain
24 D1 Valderaduey r. Spain
24 D1 Valderas Spain
20 E2 Val-de-Reuil France
115 H4 Val-des-Bois Can.
147 D5 Valdés, Península pen. Arg.
138 B3 Valdez Ecuador
108 D3 Valdez U.S.A.
21 H4 Val-d'Isère France
147 B4 Valdivia Chile
26 C3 Valdobbiadene Italy
115 G2 Val-d'Or Can.
119 D6 Valdosta U.S.A.
11 C3 Valdres v. Norway
13 G7 Vale Georgia
126 C2 Vale U.S.A.
28 D1 Valea lui Mihai Romania
110 F4 Valemount Can.
145 G5 Valença Brazil
142 E3 Valença Brazil
142 D2 Valença do Piauí Brazil
20 E3 Valençay France
21 G4 Valence *Rhône-Alpes* France
25 F3 Valencia Spain
25 F3 Valencia div. Spain
133 □3 Valencia Trin. & Tobago
138 D1 Valencia Venezuela
24 C3 Valencia de Alcántara Spain
24 D1 Valencia de Don Juan Spain
25 G3 Valencia, Golfo de g. Spain
17 B6 Valencia Island i. Rep. of Ire.
133 F5 Valencia, L. de l. Venezuela
21 F1 Valenciennes France
28 F2 Vălenii de Munte Romania
21 H5 Valensole, Plateau de plat. France
129 F4 Valentine U.S.A.
124 C3 Valentine U.S.A.
125 B6 Valentine U.S.A.
26 B3 Valenza Italy
41 B3 Valenzuela Phil.
11 C3 Våler Norway
138 C2 Valera Venezuela
145 J2 Vale Verde Brazil
20 E5 Valier, Mont mt. France
90 □6 Valili Pk h. Fiji
21 J6 Valinco, Golfe de b. France
115 J2 Val-Jalbert Can.
28 B2 Valjevo Yugo.
11 G4 Valka Estonia
11 G4 Valka Latvia
11 G3 Valkeakoski Finland
18 B3 Valkenswaard Netherlands
15 F2 Valky Ukraine
152 C4 Valkyrjedomen ice feature Ant.
131 H4 Valladolid Mexico
24 D2 Valladolid Spain
130 D4 Vallarta, Pto Mexico
21 H5 Vallauris France
25 F3 Vall de Uxó Spain
11 B4 Valle Norway
24 D1 Valle Spain
26 A3 Valle d'Aosta div. Italy
139 D2 Valle de la Pascua Venezuela
138 C1 Valledupar Colombia
115 K3 Vallée-Jonction Can.
146 C3 Valle Fértil, Sa de mt. ra. Arg.
140 D3 Valle Grande Bolivia
147 C6 Valle Hermosa Arg.
131 F3 Valle Hermoso Mexico
25 □ Vallehermoso *Canary Is* Spain
128 A2 Vallejo U.S.A.
27 D7 Vallelunga Pratameno Italy
131 F5 Valle Nacional Mexico
146 B2 Vallenar Chile
27 E7 Valletta Malta
124 D2 Valley City U.S.A.
126 B3 Valley Falls U.S.A.
41 B2 Valley Head pt Phil.
120 C5 Valley Head U.S.A.
73 F2 Valley of The Kings Egypt
133 G3 Valley, The *Anguilla* Caribbean
110 F3 Valleyview Can.
25 G2 Valls Spain
111 H5 Val Marie Can.
11 G4 Valmiera Latvia
20 D2 Valognes France
24 C2 Valpacos Portugal
115 F2 Val-Paradis Can.
144 C4 Valparaíso Brazil
146 B3 Valparaíso div. Chile
146 B3 Valparaíso Chile
130 E4 Valparaíso Mexico
122 D5 Valparaiso U.S.A.
26 G3 Valpovo Croatia
21 G4 Valréas France
54 C5 Valsād India
28 C2 Valška Yugo.
82 C4 Valspan R.S.A.
39 L8 Vals, Tg c. Indon.
12 H1 Val'tevo Rus. Fed.
10 H3 Valtimo Finland
81 □4 Valton Mauritius
29 C5 Valtou mt. ra. Greece
26 A3 Valtournenche Italy
90 □8 Valukoula Fiji
14 A3 Valuyets Rus. Fed.
13 F5 Valuyki Rus. Fed.
25 □ Valverde *Canary Is* Spain
24 C4 Valverde del Camino Spain
19 H3 Vamberk Czech Rep.
43 D5 Vam Co Tay r. Vietnam
81 D7 Vamizi, Ilha i. Mozambique
11 F3 Vammala Finland
56 C2 Vamsadhara r. India
60 E2 Van Turkey
60 F1 Vanadzor Armenia
63 M3 Vanavara Rus. Fed.
115 J3 Van Bruyssel Can.
125 E5 Van Buren U.S.A.
121 K1 Van Buren U.S.A.
43 E4 Vân Canh Vietnam
121 K2 Vanceboro U.S.A.
120 B5 Vanceburg U.S.A.
110 E5 Vancouver Can.
126 B2 Vancouver U.S.A.
101 B7 Vancouver, C. c. Aust.
110 D5 Vancouver Island i. Can.
110 B2 Vancouver, Mt mt. Can./U.S.A.
92 □3 Vancouver Rock i. *Snares Is* N.Z.
118 B4 Vandalia U.S.A.
120 A5 Vandalia U.S.A.
25 G2 Vandellós Spain
82 D4 Vanderbijlpark R.S.A.
122 E3 Vanderbilt U.S.A.
120 D4 Vandergrift U.S.A.
110 E4 Vanderhoof Can.
98 D2 Vanderlin I. i. Aust.
129 H4 Vanderwagen U.S.A.
98 B1 Van Diemen, C. c. Aust.
98 D3 Van Diemen, C. c. Aust.
98 C1 Van Diemen Gulf b. Aust.
11 G4 Vändra Estonia
115 J3 Vandry Can.
11 D4 Vänern b. Sweden
11 D4 Vänersborg Sweden
120 E3 Van Etten U.S.A.
83 H3 Vangaindrano Madagascar
60 E2 Van Gölü salt l. Turkey
90 □1 Vangunu i. Solomon Is.
125 B6 Van Horn U.S.A.
115 H4 Vanier Can.
90 □1 Vanimo P.N.G.
45 Q2 Vanino Rus. Fed.
56 B3 Vanivilasa Sagara resr India
56 B3 Vaniyambadi India
28 D2 Vânju Mare Romania
108 A3 Vankarem Rus. Fed.
115 H4 Vankleek Hill Can.
10 E1 Vanna i. Norway
10 E3 Vännäs Sweden
20 C3 Vannes France
65 H4 Vannovka Kazak.
21 H4 Vanoise, Massif de la mts France
82 B5 Vanrhynsdorp R.S.A.
99 E3 Vanrook Aust.
99 E3 Vanrook Cr. r. Aust.
11 D3 Vansbro Sweden
100 D2 Vansittart B. b. Aust.
109 K3 Vansittart I. i. Can.
11 G3 Vantaa Finland
90 □7 Vanua Bailavu i. Fiji
90 □2 Vanua Lava i. Vanuatu
90 □6 Vanua Levu i. Fiji
90 □8 Vanua Levu Barrier Reef reef Fiji
86 H6 Vanuatu country Pac. Oc.
120 A4 Van Wert U.S.A.
82 C5 Vanwyksvlei l. R.S.A.
82 C5 Vanwyksvlei R.S.A.
42 D2 Văn Yên Vietnam
90 □2 Vao Pac. Oc.
15 C2 Vapnyarka Ukraine
21 H5 Var r. France
56 A3 Varada r. India
11 G4 Varakļāni Latvia
76 D5 Varalé Côte d'Ivoire
26 B3 Varallo Italy
57 B2 Varāmīn Iran
55 E4 Varanasi India
10 H1 Varangerfjorden chan. Norway
10 H1 Varangerhalvøya pen. Norway
26 F2 Varaždin Croatia
26 B3 Varazze Italy
11 D4 Varberg Sweden
57 B2 Varcheh Iran
29 C5 Varda Greece
56 B2 Vardannapet India
28 C4 Vardar r. Macedonia
11 C5 Varde Denmark
60 F1 Vardenis Armenia
10 H1 Vardø Norway
14 D1 Varegovo Rus. Fed.
18 D2 Varel Germany
11 G5 Varėna Lithuania
115 J4 Varennes Can.
26 G3 Vareš Bos.-Herz.
26 B3 Varese Italy
28 D1 Vârful Bihor mt. Romania
28 E1 Vârful Bivolu mt. Romania
28 E2 Vârful Cozia mt. Romania
15 A3 Vârful Harghita-Mădăra mt. Romania
28 C2 Vârful Leordișu mt. Romania
28 E2 Vârful Moldoveanu mt. Romania
28 D2 Vârful Padeșu mt. Romania
15 B3 Vârful Şandru Mare mt. Romania
28 D1 Vârful Vlădeasa mt. Romania
11 D4 Vårgårda Sweden
142 E2 Vargem r. Brazil
145 E4 Vargem Grande do Sul Brazil
145 F4 Varginha Brazil
140 B4 Varillas Chile
62 D3 Varkaus Finland
11 D4 Värmland div. Sweden
28 F3 Varna div. Bulgaria
28 F3 Varna Bulgaria
64 F2 Varna Rus. Fed.
11 D4 Värnamo Sweden
11 D3 Värnäs Sweden
14 G1 Varnavino Rus. Fed.
61 B2 Varosia Cyprus
26 F3 Varoška Rijeka Bos.-Herz.
10 G3 Varpaisjärvi Finland
19 J5 Várpalota Hungary
57 G1 Varsaj Afghanistan
60 E2 Varto Turkey
28 D2 Vârtop Romania
55 E4 Varuna r. India
15 E1 Varva Ukraine
28 C3 Varvarin Yugo.
15 G1 Varvarivka *Kharkiv* Ukraine
15 B1 Varvarivka *Khmel'nyts'kyy* Ukraine
120 D3 Varysburg U.S.A.
57 C2 Varzaneh Iran
60 F2 Varzaqān Iran
143 C6 Varzea r. *Paraná* Brazil
143 B6 Varzea r. *Rio Grande do Sul* Brazil
145 F2 Várzea da Palma Brazil
145 F1 Varzelândia Brazil
26 B2 Varzo Italy
12 F1 Varzuga Rus. Fed.
142 E3 Vasa Barris r. Brazil
19 L4 Vásárosnamény Hungary
28 D1 Vaşcău Romania
12 H1 Vashka r. Rus. Fed.
15 A2 Vashkivtsi Ukraine
12 H2 Vasilevo Rus. Fed.
14 H1 Vasil'sursk Rus. Fed.
14 B1 Vasil'yevskiy Mokh Rus. Fed.
14 G1 Vasil'yevskoye Rus. Fed.
14 E1 Vasil'yevskoye Rus. Fed.
11 G4 Vasknarva Estonia
15 C1 Vas'kovychi Ukraine
28 F1 Vaslui Romania
123 F4 Vassar U.S.A.
145 G5 Vassouras Brazil
11 E4 Västerås Sweden
10 E2 Västerbotten div. Sweden
11 D3 Västerdalälven r. Sweden
10 E2 Västerfjäll Sweden
11 E4 Vasterhaninge Sweden
10 E3 Västernorrland div. Sweden
11 E4 Västervik Sweden
11 D4 Västmanland div. Sweden
27 E4 Vasto Italy
19 H5 Vasvár Hungary
15 E2 Vasylivka *Kirovohrad* Ukraine
15 F1 Vasylivka *Sumy* Ukraine
15 F3 Vasylivka *Zaporizhzhya* Ukraine
15 D1 Vasyl'kiv Ukraine
15 G2 Vasyl'kivka Ukraine
15 B2 Vasyutyntsi Ukraine
20 E3 Vatan France
56 A2 Vathar India
90 □8 Vatia Pt pt Fiji
27 D5 Vatican City country Europe
10 M2 Vatnajökull ice cap Iceland
90 □7 Vatoa i. Fiji
83 H2 Vato Loha mt. Madagascar
83 H2 Vatomandry Madagascar
28 E1 Vatra Dornei Romania
28 E1 Vatra Moldoviței Romania
11 D4 Vättern l. Sweden
90 □8 Vatu-i-Ra Channel chan. Fiji
90 □8 Vatu-i-Thake i. Fiji
90 □8 Vatulele i. Fiji
15 D2 Vatutine Ukraine
90 □6 Vatu Vara i. Fiji
21 G5 Vaucluse, Monts de mts France
21 G2 Vaucouleurs France
127 F5 Vaughn U.S.A.
138 C3 Vaupés r. Colombia
21 G5 Vauvert France
83 H2 Vavatenina Madagascar
90 □3 Vava'u Group is Tonga
76 C5 Vavoua Côte d'Ivoire
56 C4 Vavuniya Sri Lanka
12 C4 Vawkavysk Belarus
11 D4 Växjö Sweden
56 B3 Vāyalpād India
62 G2 Vaygach, O. i. Rus. Fed.
145 E2 Vazante Brazil
12 H1 Vazhgort Rus. Fed.
14 B2 Vazuza r. Rus. Fed.
14 B2 Vazuzskoye Vdkhr. resr Rus. Fed.
65 K1 Vdovino Rus. Fed.
43 C4 Veal Vêng Cambodia
18 D2 Vechta Germany
18 C2 Vechte r. Germany
56 B4 Vedaranniyam India
11 D4 Veddige Sweden
28 E2 Vedea r. Romania
28 E3 Vedea Romania
60 F2 Vedi Armenia
146 D3 Vedia Arg.
12 E2 Vedlozero Rus. Fed.
122 D5 Veedersburg U.S.A.
18 C2 Veendam Netherlands
18 B2 Veenendaal Netherlands
10 C2 Vega i. Norway
125 C5 Vega U.S.A.
119 □3 Vega Baja Puerto Rico
24 C1 Vegadeo Spain
111 G4 Vegreville Can.
11 G3 Vehkalahti Finland
54 B3 Vehoa r. Pakistan
142 B1 Veiros Brazil
57 G4 Veirwaro Pakistan
19 L1 Veisiejis Lithuania
11 C5 Vejle Denmark
57 E1 Vekīl'-Bazar Turkmenistan
138 C1 Vela, Cabo de la pt Colombia
26 F4 Vela Luka Croatia
56 B4 Velanai I. i. Sri Lanka
138 □ Velasco Ibarra *Galapagos Is* Ecuador
146 C2 Velasco, Sa de mt. ra. Arg.
26 E3 Velebit mt. ra. Croatia
26 E3 Velebitski Kanal chan. Croatia
18 C3 Velen Germany
26 E2 Velenje Slovenia
28 C4 Veles Macedonia
14 F2 Velet'ma Rus. Fed.
26 F4 Velež mts Bos.-Herz.
138 C2 Vélez Colombia
24 D4 Vélez-Málaga Spain
25 E4 Vélez-Rubio Spain
145 E3 Velhas r. *Minas Gerais* Brazil
145 F2 Velhas r. *Minas Gerais* Brazil
13 H6 Velichayevskoye Rus. Fed.
15 A2 Velika Berezovytsya Ukraine
26 F3 Velika Gorica Croatia
15 A1 Velika Hlusha Ukraine
26 E3 Velika Kapela mt. ra. Croatia
28 C3 Velika Kruša Yugo.
15 B1 Velika Ozera Ukraine
28 C2 Velika Plana Yugo.
12 J3 Velikaya r. *Kirov* Rus. Fed.
12 D3 Velikaya r. *Pskov* Rus. Fed.
12 E2 Velikaya Guba Rus. Fed.
15 A2 Veliki Birky Ukraine
28 C3 Veliki Jastrebac mts Yugo.
12 D3 Velikiye Luki Rus. Fed.
15 A2 Velikiy Hlybochok Ukraine
15 D1 Velikiy Lystven Ukraine
12 H2 Velikiy Ustyug Rus. Fed.
15 B2 Velikiy Zhvanchyk Ukraine
14 E2 Velikodvorskiy Rus. Fed.
28 C2 Veliko Gradište Yugo.
56 B3 Velikonda Ra. h. India
14 A1 Velikooktyabr'skiy Rus. Fed.
28 E3 Veliko Tŭrnovo Bulgaria
14 D1 Velikoye Rus. Fed.
14 C1 Velikoye, Oz. l. Rus. Fed.
14 E2 Velikoye, Oz. l. Rus. Fed.
26 E3 Veli Lošinj Croatia
76 B4 Vélingara *Kolda* Senegal
76 B3 Vélingara *Louga* Senegal
28 D3 Velingrad Bulgaria
27 D4 Velino, Monte mt. Italy
12 D4 Velizh Rus. Fed.
19 J4 Veľká Fatra mts Slovakia
19 L4 Veľké Kapušany Slovakia
19 H4 Velké Meziříčí Czech Rep.
19 J4 Veľký Krtíš Slovakia
19 H5 Veľký Meder Slovakia
90 □1 Vella Lavella i. Solomon Is.
56 B4 Vellar r. India
56 B3 Vellore India
29 D6 Velopoula i. Greece
12 G2 Vel'sk Rus. Fed.
18 F2 Velten Germany
111 J5 Velva U.S.A.
14 C2 Vel'yaminovo Rus. Fed.
15 E2 Velyka Bahachka Ukraine
15 F3 Velyka Bilozerka r. Ukraine
15 E2 Velyka Burimka Ukraine
15 D3 Velyka Korenykha Ukraine
15 E3 Velyka Lepetykha Ukraine
15 C3 Velyka Mykhaylivka Ukraine
15 G3 Velyka Novosilka Ukraine
15 E3 Velyka Oleksandrivka Ukraine
15 F1 Velyka Pysarivka Ukraine
15 F2 Velyka Rublivka Ukraine
15 B1 Velyka Tsvilya Ukraine
15 D2 Velyka Vys' r. Ukraine
15 D2 Velyka Vyska Ukraine
15 C2 Velyki Korovyntsi Ukraine
15 E2 Velyki Krynky Ukraine
15 A1 Velyki Mosty Ukraine
15 E1 Velyki Sorochyntsi Ukraine
15 E2 Velykiy Khutir Ukraine
15 D3 Velykodolyns'ke Ukraine
15 G3 Velykomykhaylivka Ukraine
15 G1 Velykyy Burluk Ukraine
28 E1 Velykyy Bychkiv Ukraine
148 G5 Vema Fracture Atlantic Ocean
149 J4 Vema Trough Indian Ocean
56 B4 Vembanād L. l. India
146 D3 Venado Tuerto Arg.
27 E5 Venafro Italy
26 A3 Venaria Italy
144 D5 Venceslau Brás Brazil
145 H4 Venda Nova Brazil
12 H2 Vendinga Rus. Fed.
20 E3 Vendôme France
15 B2 Vendychany Ukraine
26 D3 Veneta, Laguna lag. Italy
26 C3 Veneto div. Italy
12 F4 Venev Rus. Fed.
26 D3 Venezia Italy
26 D3 Venezia, Golfo di g. Italy
136 D2 Venezuela country S. America
138 C1 Venezuela, Golfo de g. Venezuela
56 A3 Vengurla India
119 D7 Venice U.S.A.
21 G4 Vénissieux France
56 B3 Venkatagiri India
56 C2 Venkatapuram India
11 B4 Vennesla Norway
26 C2 Venosta, Val v. Italy
18 B3 Venray Netherlands
11 F4 Venta r. Lithuania
11 F4 Venta Lithuania
24 D2 Venta de Baños Spain
146 D4 Ventan, Serra de la h. Arg.
91 □10 Vent, Îles du is *Fr. Poly.* Pac. Oc.
91 □10 Vent, Îles sous le is *Fr. Poly.* Pac. Oc.
147 B5 Ventisquero mt. Arg.
17 G6 Ventnor U.K.
27 D5 Ventotene, Isola i. Italy
21 G4 Ventoux, Mont mt. France
49 J3 Ventselevo Rus. Fed.
11 F4 Ventspils Latvia
139 D3 Ventuari r. Venezuela
128 C4 Ventucopa U.S.A.
128 C4 Ventura U.S.A.
97 F4 Venus B. b. Aust.
91 □11 Vénus, Pte pt *Fr. Poly.* Pac. Oc.
26 D2 Venzone Italy
146 D2 Vera Arg.
25 F4 Vera Spain
140 C1 Vera Cruz Brazil
131 F4 Veracruz div. Mexico
131 F5 Veracruz Mexico
141 E5 Verá, L. l. Paraguay
54 B5 Veraval India
15 A1 Verba *Rivne* Ukraine
26 B3 Verbania Italy
14 C1 Verbilki Rus. Fed.
15 F3 Verbove Ukraine
15 A2 Verbovets' Ukraine
14 E2 Verbovskiy Rus. Fed.
15 F3 Verby Ukraine
26 B3 Vercelli Italy
115 J4 Verchères Can.
21 G4 Vercors reg. France
14 E3 Verda r. Rus. Fed.
10 C3 Verdalsøra Norway
147 C5 Verde r. Arg.
142 D3 Verde r. *Bahia* Brazil
144 C2 Verde r. *Goiás* Brazil
144 D1 Verde r. *Goiás* Brazil
144 C3 Verde r. *Goiás* Brazil
144 E2 Verde r. *Goiás/Minas Gerais* Brazil
141 E2 Verde r. *Mato Grosso* Brazil
141 E2 Verde r. *Mato Grosso* Brazil
144 B4 Verde r. *Mato Grosso do Sul* Brazil
144 D3 Verde r. *Minas Gerais* Brazil
145 F4 Verde r. *Minas Gerais* Brazil
146 E1 Verde r. Paraguay
129 G4 Verde r. U.S.A.
145 G2 Verde Grande r. Brazil
133 F3 Verde, Isla airport Puerto Rico
41 B3 Verde Island Pass. chan. Phil.
18 D2 Verden (Aller) Germany
147 D4 Verde, Pen. pen. Arg.
145 G1 Verde Pequeno r. Brazil
125 E4 Verdigris r. U.S.A.
144 C2 Verdinho r. Brazil
21 G2 Verdun France
20 E5 Verdun-sur-Garonne France
83 D4 Vereeniging R.S.A.
15 E2 Veremiyivka Ukraine
115 G3 Vérendrye, Réserve faunique La res. Can.
14 C2 Vereya Rus. Fed.
76 B4 Verga, Cap pt Guinea
146 F3 Vergara Uruguay
99 E4 Vergemont Cr. w Aust.
121 G2 Vergennes U.S.A.
14 D1 Verigino Rus. Fed.
24 C2 Verín Spain
144 D3 Veríssimo Brazil
15 F2 Verkhivtseve Ukraine
64 E2 Verkhne-Avzyan Rus. Fed.
14 A2 Verkhnedneprovskiy Rus. Fed.
62 K3 Verkhneimbatskoye Rus. Fed.
12 H3 Verkhnespasskoye Rus. Fed.
10 H1 Verkhnetulomskiy Rus. Fed.
14 D4 Verkhneturovo Rus. Fed.
64 E2 Verkhneural'sk Rus. Fed.
63 O3 Verkhnevilyuysk Rus. Fed.
14 A1 Verkhnevolzhskoye Vdkhr. resr Rus. Fed.
14 G2 Verkhneye Talyzino Rus. Fed.
13 H5 Verkhniy Baskunchak Rus. Fed.
15 G2 Verkhniy Byshkyn Ukraine
13 J5 Verkhniy Kushum Rus. Fed.
14 F1 Verkhniy Landekh Rus. Fed.
14 F3 Verkhniy Lomov Rus. Fed.
15 F3 Verkhniy Rohachyk Ukraine
48 D2 Verkhniy Shergol'dzhin Rus. Fed.
64 F1 Verkhniy Ufaley Rus. Fed.
48 E2 Verkhniy Ul'khun Rus. Fed.
12 E1 Verkhniy Vyalozerskiy Rus. Fed.
15 F2 Verkhn'odniprovs'k Ukraine
15 D2 Verkhnyachka Ukraine
14 C4 Verkhnyaya Grayvoronka Rus. Fed.
65 K2 Verkhnyaya Irmen' Rus. Fed.
14 D4 Verkhnyaya Khava Rus. Fed.
49 E2 Verkhnyaya Khila Rus. Fed.
10 J2 Verkhnyaya Pirenga, Oz. l. Rus. Fed.
12 H2 Verkhnyaya Toyma Rus. Fed.
14 C1 Verkhnyaya Troitsa Rus. Fed.
12 J3 Verkhoshizhem'ye Rus. Fed.
12 G2 Verkhovazh'ye Rus. Fed.
14 C3 Verkhov'ye Rus. Fed.
15 A2 Verkhovyna Ukraine
63 P3 Verkhoyansk Rus. Fed.
63 O2 Verkhoyanskiy Khrebet mt. ra. Rus. Fed.
14 H3 Verkhozim Rus. Fed.
49 E1 Verkh-Usugli Rus. Fed.
10 H2 Verkneye Kuyto, Oz. l. Rus. Fed.
12 H2 Verkola Rus. Fed.
142 C2 Vermelho r. Brazil
144 C1 Vermelho r. Brazil
142 C2 Vermelho r. Brazil
111 G4 Vermilion Can.
122 C5 Vermilion r. U.S.A.
129 F3 Vermilion Cliffs cliff U.S.A.
122 A2 Vermilion Lake l. U.S.A.
122 A2 Vermilion Range h. U.S.A.
124 D3 Vermillion U.S.A.
112 B4 Vermillion Bay Can.
121 G3 Vermont div. U.S.A.
14 F3 Vernadovka Rus. Fed.
126 E3 Vernal U.S.A.
114 E3 Verner Can.
20 E2 Verneuil-sur-Avre France
110 F4 Vernon Can.
20 E2 Vernon France
129 H4 Vernon U.S.A.
121 G4 Vernon U.S.A.
125 D5 Vernon U.S.A.
129 F1 Vernon U.S.A.
119 D7 Vero Beach U.S.A.
29 D4 Veroia Greece
26 C3 Verona Italy
146 E4 Verónica Arg.
26 A3 Verres Italy
22 D2 Versailles France
49 E1 Vershino-Darasunskiy Rus. Fed.
76 A4 Vert, Cap c. Senegal
142 B3 Vertentes r. Brazil
132 C2 Vertientes Cuba
15 D1 Vertiyivka Ukraine
20 D3 Vertou France
18 B3 Verviers Belgium
21 F2 Vervins France
21 J5 Vescovato France
64 E2 Veselaya, G. mt. Rus. Fed.
15 F3 Vesele Ukraine
14 C2 Veselevo Rus. Fed.
19 G4 Veselí nad Lužnicí Czech Rep.
19 H4 Veselí nad Moravou Czech Rep.
15 C1 Veselivka Ukraine
13 G6 Veselovskoye Vdkhr. resr Rus. Fed.
15 D3 Veselynove Ukraine
13 G6 Veselyy Rus. Fed.
13 G5 Veshenskaya Rus. Fed.
14 H2 Veshkayma Rus. Fed.
12 G1 Veshkoma Rus. Fed.
21 G2 Vesle r. France
21 H3 Vesoul France
11 B4 Vest-Agder div. Norway
10 D1 Vesterålen is Norway
10 D1 Vesterålsfjorden chan. Norway
10 G1 Vestertana Norway
10 L2 Vestfirðir div. Iceland
152 C3 Vestfjella mts Ant.
10 D2 Vestfjorden chan. Norway
11 C4 Vestfold div. Norway
16 D1 Vestmanna Faeroes
10 L3 Vestmannaeyjar Iceland
10 L3 Vestmannaeyjar is Iceland
10 N2 Vesturhorn c. Iceland
10 L2 Vesturland div. Iceland
27 E5 Vesuvio vol Italy
12 F3 Ves'yegonsk Rus. Fed.
19 H5 Veszprém Hungary
90 □6 Vetauua i. Fiji
10 F3 Veteli Finland
11 D4 Vetlanda Sweden
14 H1 Vetluga r. Rus. Fed.
12 H3 Vetluga Rus. Fed.
14 G1 Vetluzhskiy Rus. Fed.
28 F3 Vetovo Bulgaria
26 D4 Vettore, Monte mt. Italy
18 A3 Veurne Belgium
21 H3 Vevey Switz.
21 G4 Veynes France
129 F3 Veyo U.S.A.
20 E4 Vézère r. France
60 C1 Vezirköprü Turkey
11 E3 Vi Sweden
140 C3 Viacha Bolivia
140 A2 Viajas, I. de las i. Peru
79 B5 Viana Angola
145 H4 Viana *Espírito Santo* Brazil
142 D1 Viana *Maranhão* Brazil
24 C3 Viana do Alentejo Portugal
24 C1 Viana do Bolo Spain
24 B2 Viana do Castelo Portugal
24 B2 Viana do Castelo div. Portugal
42 C3 Viangchan Laos
42 C2 Viangphoukha Laos
144 D2 Vianópolis Brazil
24 D4 Viar r. Spain
26 C4 Viareggio Italy
20 F4 Viaur r. France
11 C4 Viborg Denmark
27 F6 Vibo Valentia Italy
25 H2 Vic Spain
152 B2 Vicecomodoro Marambio Argentina Base Ant.
20 E5 Vic-en-Bigorre France
130 A2 Vicente Guerrero Mexico
128 C5 Vicente, Pt pt U.S.A.
26 C3 Vicenza Italy
20 E5 Vic-Fezensac France
138 D3 Vichada r. Colombia
146 C2 Vichina r. Arg.
14 E1 Vichuga Rus. Fed.
146 B3 Vichuquén Chile
21 F3 Vichy France
129 F5 Vicksburg U.S.A.
125 F5 Vicksburg U.S.A.
21 F4 Vic-le-Comte France
145 G4 Viçosa Brazil
20 F4 Vic-sur-Cère France
122 A5 Victor U.S.A.
96 D3 Victor Harbour Aust.
146 D3 Victoria Arg.
98 B2 Victoria r. Aust.
97 F4 Victoria div. Aust.
110 E5 Victoria Can.
133 □8 Victoria *Grenada* Caribbean
146 B4 Victoria Chile
130 J6 Victoria Honduras
27 E7 Victoria Malta
28 F2 Victoria *Brăila* Romania
28 E2 Victoria *Braşov* Romania
81 □2 Victoria Seychelles
133 □3 Victoria div. *Trinidad* Trin. & Tobago
125 D6 Victoria U.S.A.
132 C2 Victoria de las Tunas Cuba
79 E7 Victoria Falls waterfall Zambia/Zimbabwe
82 D2 Victoria Falls Zimbabwe
109 O1 Victoria Fjord inlet Greenland
45 □ Victoria Harbour chan. Hong Kong
132 D1 Victoria Hill The Bahamas
147 B6 Victoria, Isla i. Chile
108 H2 Victoria Island i. Can.
81 B5 Victoria, Lake l. Africa
96 E3 Victoria, Lake l. Aust.
113 J4 Victoria Lake l. Can.
152 B5 Victoria Land reg. Ant.
42 A2 Victoria, Mt mt. Myanmar
93 D5 Victoria, Mt mt. N.Z.
90 □1 Victoria, Mt mt. P.N.G.
81 B4 Victoria Nile r. Sudan/Uganda
94 □3 Victoria Pt pt *Macquarie I.* Pac. Oc.
93 D5 Victoria Range mt. ra. N.Z.
98 B2 Victoria River Aust.
98 B3 Victoria River Downs Aust.
146 F2 Victoria, Sa de la h. Arg.
115 K3 Victoriaville Can.
82 C5 Victoria West R.S.A.
146 C4 Victorica Arg.
152 D3 Victor, Mt mt. Ant.
128 D4 Victorville U.S.A.
146 D3 Vicuña Mackenna Arg.
129 E4 Vidal Junction U.S.A.
28 E2 Videle Romania
28 D3 Vidin Bulgaria
54 D5 Vidisha India
12 E2 Vidlitsa Rus. Fed.
14 C2 Vidnoye Rus. Fed.
26 G4 Viduša mts Bos.-Herz.
12 J2 Vidz'yuyar Rus. Fed.
18 F4 Viechtach Germany
147 D5 Viedma Arg.
147 B6 Viedma, L. l. Arg.
24 B3 Vieira de Leiria Portugal
130 B2 Viejo, Co mt. Mexico
25 G1 Vielha Spain
18 B3 Vielsalm Belgium
18 E3 Vienenburg Germany
118 B4 Vienna U.S.A.
121 F5 Vienna U.S.A.
120 C5 Vienna U.S.A.
20 E3 Vienne r. France
21 G4 Vienne France
146 B4 Viento, C. del mt. ra. Arg.
146 B4 Viento, Cordillera del mt. ra. Arg.
133 F3 Vieques i. Puerto Rico
119 □3 Vieques, Isla de i. Puerto Rico
10 G3 Vieremä Finland
21 J3 Vierwaldstätter See l. Switz.
20 F3 Vierzon France
125 C7 Viesca Mexico
11 G4 Viesīte Latvia
27 F5 Vieste Italy
10 E2 Vietas Sweden
33 M8 Vietnam country Asia
42 D2 Viêt Tri Vietnam
133 □5 Vieux Bourg *Guadeloupe* Caribbean
133 □5 Vieux Fort *Guadeloupe* Caribbean
133 G4 Vieux Fort St Lucia
133 □5 Vieux Fort, Pte du pt *Guadeloupe* Caribbean
133 □5 Vieux Habitants *Guadeloupe* Caribbean
41 B2 Vigan Phil.
26 B3 Vigevano Italy
142 C1 Vigia Brazil
131 J5 Vigía Chico Mexico
20 F1 Vignacourt France
26 C3 Vignola Italy
24 B1 Vigo Spain
10 G2 Vihanti Finland
54 C3 Vihari Pakistan
19 L4 Vihorlat mt. Slovakia
11 G3 Vihti Finland
10 G3 Viitasaari Finland
54 C3 Vijainagar India
56 A2 Vijayadurg India
56 C2 Vijayawada India
10 M3 Vík Iceland
10 G2 Vikajärvi Finland
111 G4 Viking Can.
10 C2 Vikna i. Norway
11 B3 Vikøyri Norway
15 D3 Viktorivka Ukraine
65 H1 Vikulovo Rus. Fed.
138 D4 Vila Bittencourt Brazil
140 C3 Vilacaya Bolivia
76 □ Vila da Ribeira Brava Cape Verde
76 □ Vila de Sal Rei Cape Verde
83 F2 Vila de Sena Mozambique
24 B2 Vila do Conde Portugal
76 □ Vila do Tarrafal Cape Verde
24 C2 Vila Flor Portugal
25 G2 Vilafranca del Penedès Spain

W

ɔergwaun see Fishguard
ɔertawe see Swansea
ɔkhazskaya Respublika see Abkhazia
ɔqaiq see Buqayq
ɔu Dhabi see Abū Ẓabī
cre see 'Akko
.C.T. div. see Australian Capital Territory
dalia see Antalya
den see 'Adan
dzharia see Ajaria
dzharskaya Respublika see Ajaria
fal w see 'Ifāl, W.
gdash see Agdaş
gdzhabedi see Ağcabädi
guapei r. see Feio ou Aguapei
hwāz see Ahvāz
anta Range h. see Sahyadriparvat
-Jiddét gravel area see Jiddat al Ḥarāsīs
khsu see Ağsu
kyab see Sittwe
agez mt. see Aragats Lerr
appuzha see Alleppey
ataw Shankou pass see Dzungarian Gate
eppo see Ḥalab
evisik see Samandağı
exandretta see İskenderun
giers see Alger
ma-Ata see Almaty
mazon r. see Amazonas
mboina see Ambon
mherst see Kyaikkami
mirabad see Fūlād Maïalleh
nne Machin Range mt. ra. see A'nyêmaqên Shan
moy see Xiamen
nadyrskiy Khrebet mt. ra. see Chukotskiy Khrebet
naypazari see Gülnar
n Cóbh see Cóbh
nda see Daqing
ngmagssalik see Tasiilaq
nhwei see Anhui
njouan i. see Nzwani
n Muileann gCearr see Mullingar
n Nás see Naas
n Tairbeart see Tarbert
ntakya see Hatay
n tAonach see Nenagh
nti-Lebanon mt. ra. see Sharqi, Jebel esh
n tInbhear Mór see Arklow
ntioch see Hatay
ntwerp see Antwerpen
n Uaimh see Navan
nvers see Antwerpen
oraki, Mt mt. see Cook, Mt
aks r. see Araz
aks r. see Aras
al'skoye More salt l. see Aral Sea
arat, Mt mt. see Büyük Ağri
changel see Arkhangel'sk
mageddon see Megiddo
mavir see Hoktemberyan
hkhabad see Ashgabat
h Shurayf see Khaybar
talu I. i. see Astola I.
terabad see Gorgān
tin Tagh mt. ra. see Altun Shan
tipalaia i. see Astypalaia
trakhan' Bazar see Cäilabad
as I. i. see South Island
hens see Athina
talea see Antalya
bine mts see Aïr, Massif de l'
daojiang see Hunjiang
go see Pegu
grax Hu l. see Bosten Hu
hāmabād see Rafsanjān
ikal, Lake l. see Baykal, Ozero
ile Átha Cliath see Dublin
ile Átha Luain see Athlone
ku see Bakı
ky see Bakı
learic Islands see Baleares, Islas
lkan Mts mts see Stara Planina
lmer see Barmer
lykchy see Ysyk-Köl
ndar see Machilipatnam
ndar-e Pahlavi see Bandar-e Anzalī
ndar-e Shāhpūr see Bandar Khomeynī
n Don see Surat Thani
now see Andarāb
n Pla Soi see Chon Buri
'oan see Shenzhen
rak see Kargamiş
rcoo Creek w see Cooper Cr.
roda see Vadodara
sle see Basel
sra see Al Başrah
suo see Dongfang
tum see Bat'umi
y see Baicheng
al an Átha see Ballina
al Átha na Sluaighe see Ballinasloe
ersheba see Be'ér Sheva'
inn na Faoghla i. see Benbecula
lgrade see Beograd
llin see Kangirsuk
yrouth see Beirut
zwada see Vijayawada

Bhādrachalam Road Sta. see Kottagudem
Bhatnair see Hanumangarh
Biblos see Jbail
Bideford Bay b. see Barnstaple Bay
Billabong r. see Moulamein
Bi'r Ibn Hirmās see Al Bi'r
Bishbek see Bishkek
Black Pagoda see Konārka
Black River r. see Sông Đa
Black Rock h. see El 'Ināb
Black Volta r. see Mouhoun
Blue Nile r. see Bahr el Azraq
Bokombayevskoye see Bökönbaev
Bol'shoy Kavkaz mt. ra. see Caucasus
Bonin Is is see Ogasawara-shotō
Bortala see Bole
Borzhomi see Borjomi
Bosporus str. see İstanbul Boğazı
Bowo see Bomi
Bozyaka see Beskonak
Bré see Bray
Brewster, Kap c. see Kangikajik
Brezhnev see Naberezhnyye Chelny
Brittany div. see Bretagne
Brothers, The is see Al Ikhwān
Bruges see Brugge
Brussel see Bruxelles
Brussels see Bruxelles
Bucharest see București
Buckner Bay b. see Nakagusuku-wan
Bügür see Luntai
Burgundy div. see Bourgogne
Burma see Myanmar
Bûr Sa'îd see Port Said
Būr Sudan see Port Sudan
Burultokay see Fuhai
Bushire see Būshehr
Cabora Bassa Dam dam see Cahora Bassa, Barragem de
Caerdydd see Cardiff
Caerfyrddin see Carmarthen
Caergybi see Holyhead
Caisléan an Bharraigh see Castlebar
Çamalan see Gülek
Cambay see Khambhat
Cambay, Gulf of b. see Khambhat, Gulf of
Canary Islands is see Canarias, Islas
Cantabrian Mountains mt. ra. see Cantábrica, Cordillera
Canton see Guangzhou
Carraig na Siuire see Carrick-on-Suir
Casnewydd see Newport
Castell-y-Nedd see Neath
Ceanannus Mór see Kells
Ceatharlach see Carlow
Celebes i. see Sulawesi
Cephalonia i. see Kefallonia
Chanda see Chandrapur
Charleville see Rathluirc
Charlotte Town see Gouyave
Chayek see Chaek
Chechenia div. see Chechnya
Chefoo see Yantai
Chekiang see Zhejiang
Chengchow see Zhengzhou
Chengtu see Chengdu
Chernobyl see Chornobyl'
Chicacole see Srikakulam
Chihli, Gulf of g. see Bo Hai
Chonggye see Qonggyai
Christianshåb see Qasigiannguit
Christmas Island i. see Kiritimati
Chudskoye Ozero l. see Peipus, Lake
Chungking see Chongqing
Churubay Nura see Abay
Cill Airne see Killarney
Cill Chainnigh see Kilkenny
Cill Mhantáin see Wicklow
Cluain Meala see Clonmel
Cocanada see Kākināda
Colair L. l. see Kolleru L.
Cologne see Köln
Coney I. i. see Serangoon, P.
Coondapoor see Kundāpura
Copenhagen see København
Coracesium see Alanya
Corcaigh see Cork
Cordova see Córdoba
Corfu i. see Kerkyra
Corn Is i. see Maíz, Is del
Correntina r. see Éguas
Corsica i. see Corse
Cort Adelaer, Kap hd see Kangeq
Crete i. see Kriti
Crete div. see Kriti
Crimea pen. see Krym'
Cristalino r. see Mariembero
Cumberland, Cape c. see Nahoï, Cap
Cuzco see Cusco
Cyclades is see Kyklades
Dabba see Daocheng
Dagxoi see Yidun
Dairen see Dalian
Dalmatia reg. see Dalmacija
Damascus see Dimashq
Damietta see Dumyât
Dammam see Ad Dammām
Damqoq Kanbab r. see Maquan
Dangla mt. ra. see Tanggula Shan
Dannebrogsø i. see Qillak

Dantu see Zhenjiang
Danube r. see Donau
Danube r. see Dunav
Danube r. see Dunaj
Dardanelles str. see Çanakkale Boğazı
Dardo see Kangding
Dashkesan see Daşkäsän
Daulatabad see Malāyer
Dawei see Tavoy
Dawukou see Shizuishan
Deh Barez see Rudan
Deir-ez-Zor see Dayr az Zawr
Den Haag see 's-Gravenhage
Derry see Londonderry
Dhahran see Aẓ Ẓahrān
Dilizhan see Dilijan
Disappointment Is is see Désappointement, Îles de
Disko i. see Qeqertarsuatsiaq
Disko Bugt b. see Qeqertarsuup Tunua
Divichi see Däväci
Dizak see Dāvar Panāh
Dnieper r. see Dnyapro
Dnieper r. see Dnepr
Dnieper r. see Dnipro
Dniester r. see Dnister
Dodecanese is see Dodekanisos
Doha see Ad Dawḥah
Dohad see Dāhod
Dolonnur see Duolon
Domel I. i. see Letsok-aw Kyun
Dorbiljin see Emin
Dorbod Qi see Siziwang Qi
Droichead Átha see Drogheda
Dubai see Dubayy
Duke of Gloucester Is is see Duc de Gloucester, Îles
Dundas see Uummannaq
Dún Dealgan see Dundalk
Dún Garbhán see Dungarvan
Dunkirk see Dunkerque
Dura Europos see Qal'at as Sālihīyah
Durlas see Thurles
Duzdab see Zāhedān
Dzhalalabad see Cäilabad
Dzhalal-Abad see Jalal-Abad
Dzhul'fa see Culfa
Dzungarian Basin basin see Junggar Pendi
East Cape c. see Dezhneva, Mys
Eastern Group is see Lau Group
East Retford see Retford
East Siberian Sea sea see Vostochno-Sibirskoye More
Echmiadzin see Ejmiadzin
Edwardesabad see Banmi
Eilat see Elat
Eilean Barraigh i. see Barra
Eilean Leodhais i. see Lewis
Eksere see Gündoğmuş
El Iskandarîya see Alexandria
El Khartum see Khartoum
El Qâhira see Cairo
El Suweis see Suez
El Uqşur see Luxor
Elvanlı see Tömük
Engaños, R. de los r. see Yari
Eochaill see Youghal
Epirus div. see Ipeiros
Erevan see Yerevan
Ergun r. see Argun'
Erronan i. see Futuna
Euboea i. see Evvoia
Eynihal see Kale
Færingehavn see Kangerluarsoruseq
Falcon i. see Fonuafo'ou
Famagusta see Ammochostos
Farrukhabad see Fatehgarh
Farvel, Kap c. see Uummannarsuaq
Fener Burun c. see Karataş Burun
Fergana Range mt. ra. see Fergana Too Tizmegi
Fez see Fès
Finisterre, Cape c. see Fisterra, Cabo
Firuzabad see Rāsk
Fiskenæsset see Qeqertarsuatsiaat
Florence see Firenze
Foochow see Fuzhou
Formosa see Taiwan
Føroyar is see Faeroes
Fort-Chimo see Kuujjuaq
Fort Hertz see Putao
Fort Sandeman see Zhob
Franz Josef Land is see Zemlya Frantsa-Iosifa
Frederikshåb see Paamiut
Frunze see Bishkek
Fujairah see Al Fujayrah
Fukien see Fujian
Fuxian see Wafangdian
Gaillimh see Galway
Galilee, Sea of l. see Tiberias, L.
Gand see Gent
Gandzha see Gäncä
Ganges r. see Ganga
Gaoxiong see Kao-hsiung
Gargunsa see Gar
Gartar see Qianning
Gartok see Garyarsa
Gascuña, Golfo de g. see Gascogne, Golfe de
Geneva see Genève
Geneva, Lake l. see Léman, Lac
Genoa see Genova
Gey see Nikshahr

Ghent see Gent
Gılındire see Aydıncık
Godthåb see Nuuk
Godwin-Austen, Mt mt. see K2
Gogra r. see Ghaghara
Gomel' see Homyel'
Gonabad see Jüymand
Goradiz see Horadiz
Gor'kiy see Nizhniy Novgorod
Graham Bell I. i. see Greem Bell,O.
Grande Comore i. see Njazidja
Grodno see Hrodna
Guanghua see Laohekou
Guanyinqiao see Chuosijia
Gulja see Yining
Gūma see Pishan
Gurdzhaani see Gurjaani
Gyaisi see Jiulong
Gyandzha see Gäncä
Gyangtse see Gyangzê
Hague, The see 's-Gravenhage
Haifa see Ḥefa
Hainan Strait see Qiongzhou Haixia
Hakha see Haka
Hangchow see Hangzhou
Hanjiang see Yangzhou
Hanoi see Ha Nôi
Hardy, Mt mt. see Rangipoua
Havana see Habana
Heihe see Aihui
Hengnan see Hengyang
Herlen Gol r. see Kerulen
Hermon, Mt mt. see Shaykh, Jabal esh
High Atlas mt. ra. see Haut Atlas
Hingol r. see Girdar Dhor
Hobot Xar Qi see Xianghuang Qi
Hodeida see Al Hudaydah
Hofuf see Al Hufuf
Hokang see Hegang
Holsteinsborg see Sisimiut
Homs see Ḥimş
Horn, C. c. see Hornos, Cabo de
Hpa-an see Pa-an
Huang Hai sea see Yellow Sea
Huhehot see Hohhot
Huiyang see Huizhou
Hulun see Hailar
Hupeh div. see Hubei
Hwlffordd see Haverfordwest
Ibiza i. see Eivissa
Ibiza see Eivissa
Iguaçu Falls rapids see Iguazú, Cataratas del
Il'ichevsk see Şärur
imeni 26 Bakinskikh Komissarov see Bakı Komissarı, 26
Imishli see İmişli
Indur see Nizamabad
Inguri r. see Enguri
Inis see Ennis
Inis Córthaidh see Enniscorthy
Inland Sea see Seto-naikai
Inner Mongolian Aut. Region div. see Nei Monggol Zizhiqu
Ionian Islands div. see Ionioi Nisoi
Iraklion see Irakleio
Iranshahr see Fahraj
Isfahan see Eşfahan
Isfandaqeh see Gāv Koshī
Ismailly see İsmayıllı
Issyk-Kul', Ozero salt l. see Ysyk-Köl
Istria pen. see Istra
Ithaca see Ithaki
Iwo Jima i. see Iō-Jima
Jacobshavn see Ilulissat
Jaffa see Tel Aviv-Yafo
Jagok Tso salt l. see Urru Co
Japan Alps Nat. Park see Chibu-Sangaku Nat. Park
Java i. see Jawa
Javaés r. see Formoso
Jedda see Jiddah
Jethro see Maghā'ir Shu'ayb
Jiaji see Qionghai
Jiayi see Chia-i
Jilong see Chi-lung
Jing see Jinghe
Jogjakarta see Yogyakarta
Kaba see Habahe
Kadzhi-Say see Kajy-Say
Kahnu see Kahnūj
Kailas mt. see Kangrinboqê Feng
Kailas Range mt. ra. see Gangdisê Shan
Kakhi see Qax
Kalaallit Nunaat terr. see Greenland
Kalāt see Kabūd Gonbad
Kalgan see Zhangjiakou
Kalinino see Tashir
Kâmpóng Saôm see Sihanoukville
Kampuchea country see Cambodia
Kang-ma see Kangmar
Kanniya Kumari c. see Comorin, Cape
Kannur see Cannanore
Kansu div. see Gansu
Kara Deniz sea see Black Sea
Karaklis see Vanadzor
Kara Sea sea see Karskoye More
Karaxahar r. see Kaidu
Karghalik see Yecheng
Karl-Marx-Stadt see Chemnitz
Karpaty mt. ra. see Carpathian Mts
Kashgar see Kashi
Kashmir terr. see Jammu and Kashmir

Kaspiyskoye More sea see Caspian Sea
Kazakh see Qazax
Kazi Magomed see Qazımämmäd
Kéamu i. see Anatom
Keferdiz see Sakçagöze
Keriya see Yutian
Kerulen r. see Herlen
Khabis see Shahdāb
Khachmas see Xaçmaz
Khankendi see Xankändi
Khan Tengri mt. see Hantengri Feng
Kharari see Abu Road
Khar'kov see Kharkiv
Khudat see Xudat
Kiangsu see Jiangsu
Kiev see Kyyiv
Kilyazi see Gilazi
King I. i. see Kadan Kyun
Kingisseppa see Kuressaare
Kirgizskiy Khrebet mt. ra. see Kirghiz Range
Kirobasi see Mağara
Kirovabad see Gäncä
Kirovakan see Vanadzor
Kishinev see Chișinău
Kisseraing I. i. see Kanmaw Kyun
Kistna r. see Krishna
Koartac see Quaqtaq
Kochi see Cochin
Koktokay see Fuyun
Kolab r. see Sābari
Kola Peninsula pen. see Kol'skiy Poluostrov
Kollam see Quilon
Korat see Nakhon Ratchasima
Kozhikode see Calicut
Krivoy Rog see Kryvyy Rih
Krungkao see Ayutthaya
Krung Thep see Bangkok
Kuba see Quba
Kumayri see Gyumri
Künes see Xinyuan
Kura r. see Kür
Kuril Is is see Kuril'skiye Ostrova
Kurinskaya Kosa pen. see Kür Dili
Kurskiy Zaliv lag. see Courland Lagoon
Kusary see Qusar
Kut-al-Imara see Al Kūt
Kuujjuarapik see Poste-de-la-Baleine
Kuwaé i. see Tongoa
Kuwait see Al Kuwayt
Kuybyshev see Samara
Kvareli see Qvareli
Kwangsi div. see Guangxi
Kwangtung div. see Guangdong
Kweichow see Guizhou
Kweiyang see Guiyang
Kyurdamir see Kürdämir
Ladoga, Lake l. see Ladozhskoye Ozero
Lanchow see Lanzhou
Langmusi see Dagcanglhamo
Languiaru r. see Iquê
Laowohi see Khardung La
Laptev Sea sea see Laptevykh, More
Laranda see Karaman
Latakia see Al Lādhiqīyah
Leghorn see Livorno
Leizhou see Haikang
Leninakan see Gyumri
Leningrad see Sankt-Peterburg
Lesbos i. see Lesvos
Lesser Caucasus mt. ra. see Malyy Kavkaz
Lianzhou see Hepu
Lima Is is see Wanshan Qundao
Limassol see Lemesos
Lindisfarne i. see Holy Island
Lisbon see Lisboa
Loch Garman see Wexford
Lohil r. see Zavü Qu
Lower California pen. see Baja California
Loyalty Is is see Loyauté, Îs
Loyang see Luoyang
Luar I. i. see Horsburgh I.
Lucerne see Luzern
Lüda see Dalian
Luik see Liège
Luimneach see Limerick
Lyallpur see Faisalabad
Macar see Gebiz
Macintyre r. see Barwon
Mackillop, L. salt flat see Yamma Yamma, L.
Magas see Zābolī
Magway see Magwe
Mahabalipuram see Māmallapuram
Makharadze see Ozurget'i
Makran Coast Range mt. ra. see Talar-i-Band
Mala see Mallow
Malawi, Lake l. see Nyasa, Lake
Malvinas, Islas is see Falkland Islands
Mamisonskiy Pereval pass see Mamisonis Ugheltekhili
Manche, La str. see English Channel
Mangshi see Luxi
Manikgarh see Rajura
Manipur see Imphal
Mar Cantábrico see Biscay, Bay of
Marjan see Wazi Khwa

Marmara, Sea of sea see Marmara Denizi
Marquesas Islands is see Marquises, Îles
Marrakesh see Marrakech
Mashtagi see Maştağa
Masulipatam see Machilipatnam
Matapan, Cape pt see Akra Tainaro
Matturai see Matara
Matun see Khowst
Mawlamyine see Moulmein
Mecca see Makkah
Medina see Al Madīnah
Medu Kongkar see Maizhokunggar
Meilü see Wuchuan
Mei Xian see Meizhou
Mekong r. see Mènam Khong
Mersin see İçel
Merv see Mary
Meshed see Mashhad
Midway see Thamarīt
Milan see Milano
Mindzhivan see Mincivan
Mingechaur see Mingäçevir
Mingechaurskoye Vdkhr. l. see Mingäçevir Su Anbarı
Min-Kush see Ming-Kush
Minya Konka mt. see Gongga Shan
Mobutu, Lake l. see Albert, Lake
Mocha see Al Mukhā
Mogadishu see Muqdisho
Moḥammadābād see Darreh Gaz
Moheli i. see Mwali
Moluccas is see Maluku
Môn i. see Anglesey
Monggolküre see Zhaosu
Monze, C. c. see Mauri, Ras
Mortes r. see Rio Manso
Morvi see Morbi
Mosul see Al Mawşil
Mughalbhin see Jati
Muineachán see Monaghan
Mukden see Shenyang
Mumbai see Bombay
Munich see München
Muscat see Masqaţ
Nada see Dan Xian
Nagorno-Karabakh div. see Qarabağ
Nagornyy Karabakh div. see Qarabağ
Nai-tung see Nêdong
Nakhichevan' see Naxçıvan
Nam Mao r. see Shweli
Nandi see Nadi
Nanking see Nanjing
Naples see Napoli
Narbada r. see Narmada
Nasirabad see Mymensingh
Nasosnyy see Hacı Zeynalabdin
Nasratabad see Zābol
Neftechala see Neftçala
New Siberia Islands is see Novosibirskiye Ostrova
Ngawa see Aba
Niassa, L. l. see Nyasa, Lake
Nicosia see Lefkosia
Nimbhera see Nimbahera
Ningsia div. see Ningxia
Nippon Hai sea see Japan, Sea of
Nīshāpūr see Neyshābūr
Niya see Minfeng
Nonni r. see Nen
Normandes, Îles is see Channel Islands
Northern Sporades is see Voreioi Sporades
Nouveau-Comptoir see Wemindji
Nouvelle Calédonie terr. see New Caledonia
Nowgong see Nagaon
Nyagquka see Yajiang
Nyagrong see Xinlong
Nyenchen Tanglha Range mt. ra. see Nyainqêntanglha Shan
Oder r. see Odra
Odessa see Odesa
Okhotsk, Sea of sea see Okhotskoye More
Oktemberyan see Hoktemberyan
Omba i. see Aoba
Onega, Lake l. see Onezhskoye Ozero
Oporto see Porto
Oranje r. see Orange
Ordu see Yayladaği
Ordzhonikidze see Vladikavkaz
Orontes r. see Asi
Ostend see Oostende
Padua see Padova
Paknampho see Muang Nakhon Sawan
Palakkat see Palghat
Palmyra see Tadmur
Panama City see Panamá
Panjang I. i. see West I.
Panjim see Panaji
Papagaio r. see Sauêruiná
Paphos see Pafos
Pascua, Isla de i. see Easter I.
Pas de Calais str. see Dover, Strait of
Patan see Somnath
Pathein see Bassein
Patteson Pass. chan. see Lolvavana, Pass.
Pechora Sea sea see Pechorskoye More

Peipsi Järve l. see Peipus, Lake
Peking see Beijing
Pelusium, B. of b. see Khalîg el Tîna
Pentecôte, Î. i. see Pentecost I.
Pereval Bedel pass see Bedel Pass
Pereval Torugart pass see Turugart Pass
Persia see Iran
Persian Gulf g. see Gulf, The
Pescadores is see P'eng-hu Lieh-tao
Phnom Penh see Phnum Penh
Pindu Pass pass see Pedo La
Pindus Mountains mt. ra. see Pindos
Pingdong see P'ing-tun
Piraeus see Peiraias
Pishpek see Bishkek
Pomo Tso l. see Puma Yumco
Poona see Pune
Port Arthur see Lüshun
Port Harrison see Inukjuak
Port Klang see Pelabuhan Kelang
Port Láirgé see Waterford
Port-Nouveau-Québec see Kangiqsualujjuaq
Porto Novo see Parangipettai
Port Taufiq see Bûr Taufiq
Prague see Praha
Pripet r. see Prypyats'
Pripet r. see Pryp"yat'
Prome see Pyè
Prøven see Kangersuatsiaq
Przheval'sk see Karakol
Pudai w see Dor
Puduchcheri see Pondicherry
Pushkino see Biläsuvar
Qagchêng see Xiangcheng
Qarkilik see Ruoqiang
Qarqan see Qiemo
Qogir Feng mt. see K2
Qomolangma Feng mt. see Everest, Mt
Qoqek see Tacheng
Queen Maud Land reg. see Dronning Maud Land
Quelpart I. i. see Cheju Do
Quemoy see Chinmen
Quqên see Jinchuan
Qurlurtuuq see Coppermine
Qu Xian see Quzhou
Qyteti Stalin see Kuçovë
Rabkob see Dharmjaygarh
Rahaeng see Tak
Raibu i. see Air
Ramnad see Ramanathapuram
Rampur Boalia see Rajshahi
Rangoon see Yangon
Razdan see Hrazdan
Rebiana Sand Sea desert see Ramlat Rabyānah
Red River r. see Hồng, S.
Red Volta r. see Nazinon
Reef Islands is see Rowa
Renland reg. see Tuttut Nunaat
Rhine r. see Rhein
Rhodes i. see Rodos
Rhum i. see Rum
Rīgas Jūras Līcis b. see Riga, Gulf of
Riia Laht g. see Riga, Gulf of
Riyadh see Ar Riyāḍ
Rome see Roma
Rongzhag see Danba
Rosetta see Rashîd
Ross Island i. see Daung Kyun
Roti i. see Rote
Routh Bank sand bank see Seahorse Bank
Rubha Robhanais hd see Butt of Lewis
Rybach'ye see Ysyk-Köl
Saatly see Saatlı
Sabzawar see Shindand
Sabzvārān see Jīroft
Saddle I. i. see Mota Lava
Safad see Ẓefat
Sagaredzho see Sagarejo
Saharan Atlas mt. ra. see Atlas Saharien
Sahyadri mt. ra. see Western Ghats
Saigon see Hô Chi Minh
Saīn Qal'eh see Sa'īndezh
St Christopher i. see St Kitts
St Christopher see Fig Tree
St Luke's i. see Zadetkale Kyun
St Matthew's I. i. see Zadetkyi Kyun
St Petersburg see Sankt-Peterburg
St Vincent, Cape c. see São Vicente, Cabo de
Sal'yany see Salyan
Samirum see Yazd-e Khvāst
Sangachaly see Sanqaçal
Santorini i. see Thira
Sardinia i. see Sardegna
Sar Eskandar see Āzarān
Sarıoğlan see Belören
Sāūjbolāgh see Mahābād
Savanat see Eşţahbānāt
Sawu i. see Savu
Scarpanto i. see Karpathos
Scheldt r. see Schelde
Scoresbysund see Ittoqqortoormiit
Seleucia see Silifke
Seleucia Pieria see Samandağı
Sellore I. i. see Saganthit Kyun

Seoul see Sŏul
Serbia div. see Srbija
Sevan, Ozero l. see Sevana Lich
Seven Pagodas see Māmallapuram
Seville see Sevilla
Seyhan see Adana
Shāhpūr see Salmās
Shahrezā see Qomishēh
Shakhagach see Şahağac
Shakhbuz see Şahbuz
Shamkhor see Şämkir
Shangxian see Shangzhou
Shantung div. see Shandong
Shan Xian see Sanmenxia
Sharjah see Ash Shāriqah
Sharur see Şärur
Sheikh Othman see Ash Shaykh 'Uthman
Sheki see Şäki
Shemakha see Şamaxı
Shensi div. see Shaanxi
Shiliu see Changjiang
Shiquanhe see Ali
Shohi Pass pass see Tal Pass
Shuicheng see Liupanshui
Shusha see Şuşa
Sian see Xi'an
Siazan' see Siyäzän
Sicily i. see Sicilia
Side see Selimiye
Sidon see Saïda
Silistat see Bozkır
Simbirsk see Ul'yanovsk
Simbor i. see Pānikoita
Sinai, Mount mt. see Katherîna,G.
Sind see Thul
Singora see Songkhla
Sinkiang Uighur Aut. Region div. see Xinjiang Uygur Zizhiqu
Sinneh see Sanandaj
Sirjan see Sa'īdābād
Sirte see Surt
Sirte, Gulf of g. see Khalīj Surt
Sis see Kozan
Sligeach see Sligo
Society Islands is see Société, Archipel de la
Socotra i. see Suquṭrā
Sofia see Sofiya
Soochow see Suzhou
South Cape c. see Ka Lae
Stalingrad see Volgograd
Stampalia i. see Astypalaia
Stepanakert see Xankändi
Sui Xian see Suizhou
Sukhumi see Sokhumi
Sukkertoppen see Maniitsoq
Sulaymaniyah see As Sulaymānīyah
Sullivan I. i. see Lanbi Kyun
Sultanabad see Arāk
Sumatra i. see Sumatera
Sumgait see Sumqayıt
Sungari r. see Songhua
Sungqu see Songpan
Su Xian see Suzhou
Sverdlovsk see Yekaterinburg
Syracuse see Siracusa
Syrian Desert desert see Bādiyat ash Shām
Szechwan div. see Sichuan
Taganrogskiy Zaliv g. see Taganrog, Gulf of
Tagus r. see Tejo
Taibei see T'ai-pei
Taiwan Haixia str. see Taiwan Strait
Taizhong see T'ai-chung
Taklimakan Desert desert see Taklimakan Shamo
Talas Range mt. ra. see Talas Ala-Too
Taldysu see Taldy-Suu
Talyshskiye Gory mts see Talış Dağları
Tangdan see Dongchuan
Tangier see Tanger
Tanintharyi see Tenasserim
Tanjore see Thanjavur
Taranaki, Mt vol see Egmont, Mt
Tarim Basin basin see Tarim Pendi
Tashi Chho see Thimphu
Tāshqurghān see Kholm
Tauriuiná r. see Verde
Tauz see Tovuz
Tavoy I. i. see Mali Kyun
Teheran see Tehrān
Tehri see Tikamgarh
Terter r. see Tärtär
Tetuán see Tétouan
Tha Hin see Lop Buri
Thalassery see Tellicherry
Thanlwin r. see Salween
Thiruvananthapuram see Trivandrum
Thrissur see Trichur
Thule see Qaanaaq
Tian Shan mt. ra. see Tien Shan
Tiber r. see Tevere
Tiberias see Teverya
Tibet Aut. Region see Xizang Zizhiqu
Tibet, Plateau of plat. see Xizang Gaoyuan
Tientsin see Tianjin
Tiflis see T'bilisi
Tirana see Tiranë
Tkibuli see Tqibuli
Tkvarcheli see Tqvarch'eli
Tokkuztara see Gongliu

Toksu see Xinhe
Toling see Zanda
Tomur Feng mt. see Pobedy, Pik
Tongshan see Xuzhou
Trá Lí see Tralee
Trá Mhór see Tramore
Transylvanian Alps mts see Carpații Meridionali
Trefaldwyn see Montgomery
Tripoli see Ṭarābulus
Truk is see Chuuk
Tsinan see Jinan
Tsinghai div. see Qinghai
Tsingtao see Qingdao
Tsiteli Tskaro see Dedoplis Tsqaro
Tsitsihar see Qiqihar
Tskhaltubo see Tsqaltubo
Tsona see Cona
Tsushima-kaikyō str. see Korea Strait
Tulach Mhór see Tullamore
Tunxi see Huangshan
Tupai i. see Motu Iti
Turfan see Turpan
Turin see Torino
Tuva div. see Tyva
Tuz, L. salt l. see Tuz Gölü
Tyre see Soûr
Tyuratam see Leninsk
Udzhary see Ucar
Uibhist a' Deas i. see South Uist
Uibhist a' Tuath i. see North Uist
Ulan Bator see Ulaanbaatar
Ulanhad see Chifeng
Ulanhot see Horqin Youyi Qianqi
Uluru h. see Ayers Rock
Ulvéah i. see Lopévi
Upper Chindwin see Mawlaik
Uqturpan see Wushi
Uracas i. see Farallon de Pajaros
Ural Mountains mt. ra. see Ural'skiy Khrebet
Urmia see Orūmīyeh
Urmia, L. salt l. see Daryācheh-ye Orūmīyeh
Uruk see Erech
Urumchi see Ürümqi
Ussuri r. see Wusuli
Ustinov see Izhevsk
Utu see Miao'ergou
Van, L. salt l. see Van Gölü
Vartashen see Oğuz
Vasht see Khāsh
Vaté i. see Éfaté
Venice see Venezia
Vesuvius vol see Vesuvio
Victoria, Mt mt. see Tomanivi
Vienna see Wien
Vientiane see Viangchan
Vistula r. see Wisła
Vizagapatam see Vishakhapatnam
Volcano Bay b. see Uchiura-wan
Volcano Is. is see Kazan-rettō
Volta Blanche w see Nakambé
Volta Rouge r. see Nazinon
Voroshilovgrad see Luhans'k
Wakeham see Kangiqsujuaq
Wang Mai Khon see Sawankhalok
Warsaw see Warszawa
Western Dvina r. see Zapadnaya Dvina
White Sea g. see Beloye More
White Volta w see Nakambé
Wrangel I. i. see Vrangelya, O.
Wrecsam see Wrexham
Wujin see Changzhou
Wuxing see Huzhou
Xangdoring see Xungba
Xianguan see Dali
Xiangyang see Xiangfan
Xiaoshi see Benxi
Xinzhu see Hsin-chu
Xulun Hobot Qagan Qi see Zhengxiangbai Qi
Xulun Hoh Qi see Zhenglan Qi
Yacha see Baisha
Yangtse, Mouth of the river mouth see Changjiang Kou
Yangtze r. see Jinsha
Yangtze r. see Chang
Yardymly see Yardımlı
Yarkant see Shache
Yaxian see Sanya
Yekhegnadzor see Yeghegnadzor
Yeotmal see Yavatmāl
Yeo Yeo r. see Bland
Yerushalayim see Jerusalem
Yevlakh see Yevlax
Y-Fenni see Abergavenny
Yin Xian see Ningbo
Yr Wyddfa mt. see Snowdon
Yugo-Osetinskaya Avtonomnaya Oblast' see South Ossetia
Yushuwan see Huaihua
Zainlha see Xiaojin
Zakataly see Zaqatala
Zante i. see Zakynthos
Zestafoni see Zestap'oni
Zhaggo see Luhuo
Zhangde see Anyang
Zhanghua see Chang-hua
Zhi Qu r. see Tongtian
Zhiziluo see Bijiang
Zhuji see Shangqiu
Zogainrawar see Huashixia
Zongga see Gyirong